I0729483

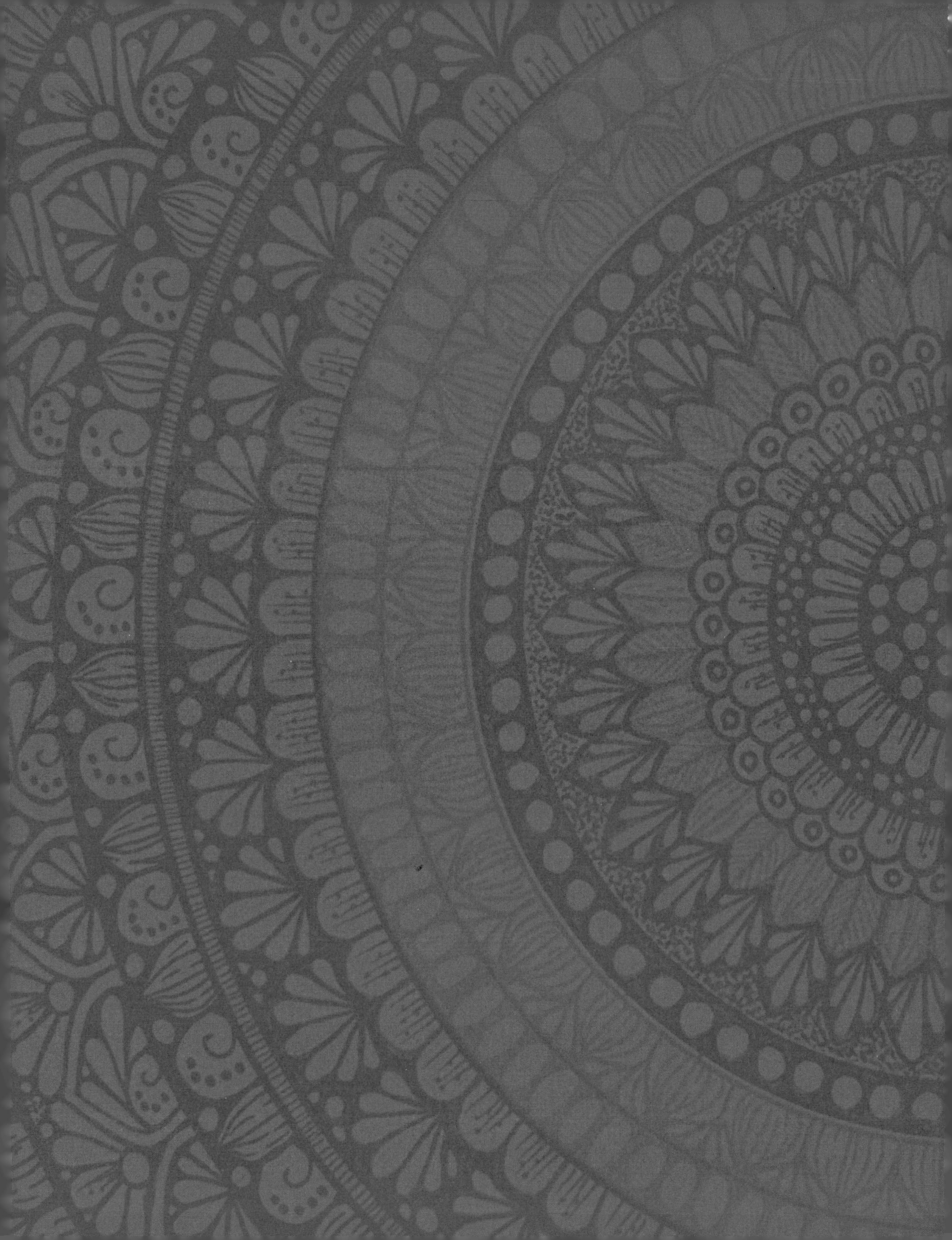

A BRIGHT & BEAUTIFUL GUIDE TO DRAWING
MANDALAS

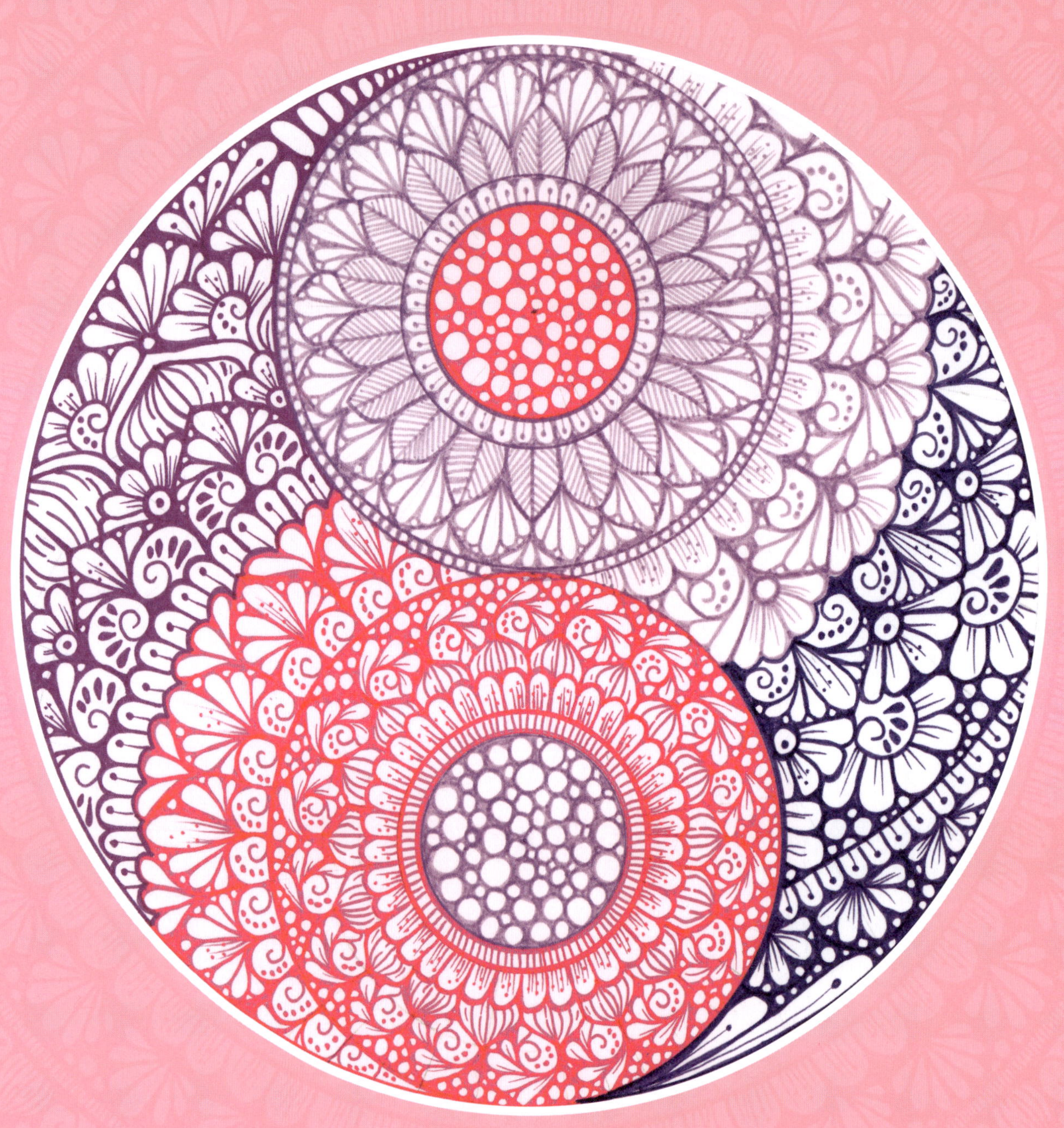

A BRIGHT & BEAUTIFUL GUIDE TO DRAWING

MANDALAS

30 Step-by-Step Tutorials to Unlock the Meditative Magic of Drawing Repeat Patterns

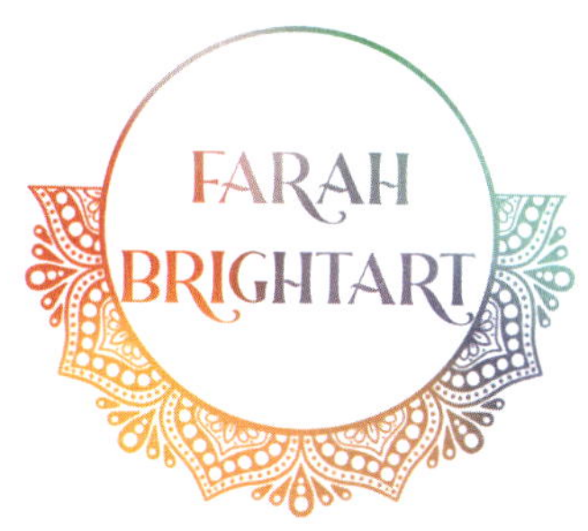

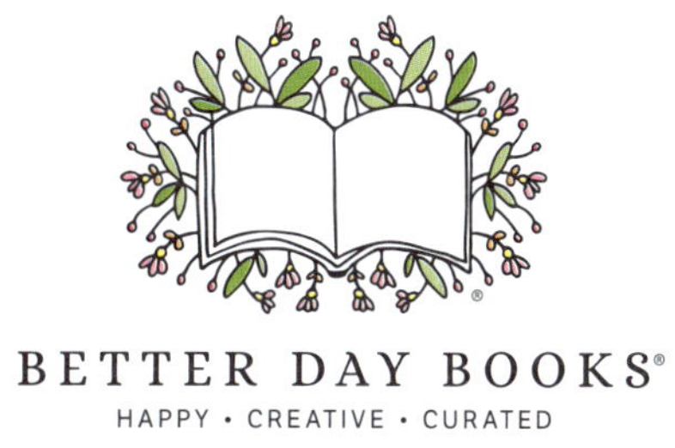

BETTER DAY BOOKS®

HAPPY · CREATIVE · CURATED

DEDICATION

I would like to dedicate this book to all the young artists who carry big dreams in their hearts. Remember, every step you take toward your dreams is a step toward making them reality, so don't give up. I'd also like to dedicate it to my younger self, for never giving up on chasing my dreams, even when the path was really tough.

A Bright & Beautiful Guide to Drawing Mandalas
© 2025 by Farah Alhamawi and Better Day Books,
an imprint of Schiffer Publishing, Ltd

Publisher: Peg Couch
Book Designer: Michael Douglas
Cover Designer: Llara Pazdan
Editor: Colleen Dorsey

All rights reserved. No part of this work may be reproduced or used in any form or by any means — graphic, electronic, or mechanical, including photocopying or information storage and retrieval systems — without written permission from the publisher.

The scanning, uploading, and distribution of this book or any part thereof via the internet or any other means without the permission of the publisher is illegal and punishable by law. Please purchase only authorized editions and do not participate in or encourage the electronic piracy of copyrighted materials.

"Better Day Books," the floral book logo, and "It's a Good Day to Have a Better Day" are registered trademarks of Schiffer Publishing, Ltd.

"Schiffer," "Schiffer Publishing, Ltd.," and the pen and inkwell logo are registered trademarks of Schiffer Publishing, Ltd.

Library of Congress Control Number: 2024948525

ISBN: 978-0-7643-6946-9
Printed in India
10 9 8 7 6 5 4 3 2 1

Published by Better Day Books, an imprint of Schiffer Publishing, Ltd.

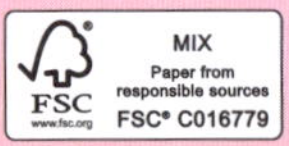

Better Day Books
Email: hello@betterdaybooks.com
Web: www.betterdaybooks.com
Visit us on Instagram!
@better_day_books

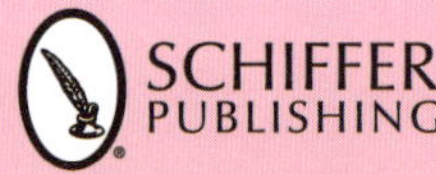

Schiffer Publishing
4880 Lower Valley Road
Atglen, PA 19310
Phone: 610-593-1777
Fax: 610-593-2002
Email: info@schifferbooks.com
Web: www.schifferbooks.com

For our complete selection of fine books on this and related subjects, please visit our website at www.betterdaybooks.com. You may also write for a free catalog.

Better Day Books titles are available at special discounts for bulk purchases for sales promotions or premiums. Special editions, including personalized covers, corporate imprints, and excerpts, can be created in large quantities for special needs. For more information, contact the publisher.

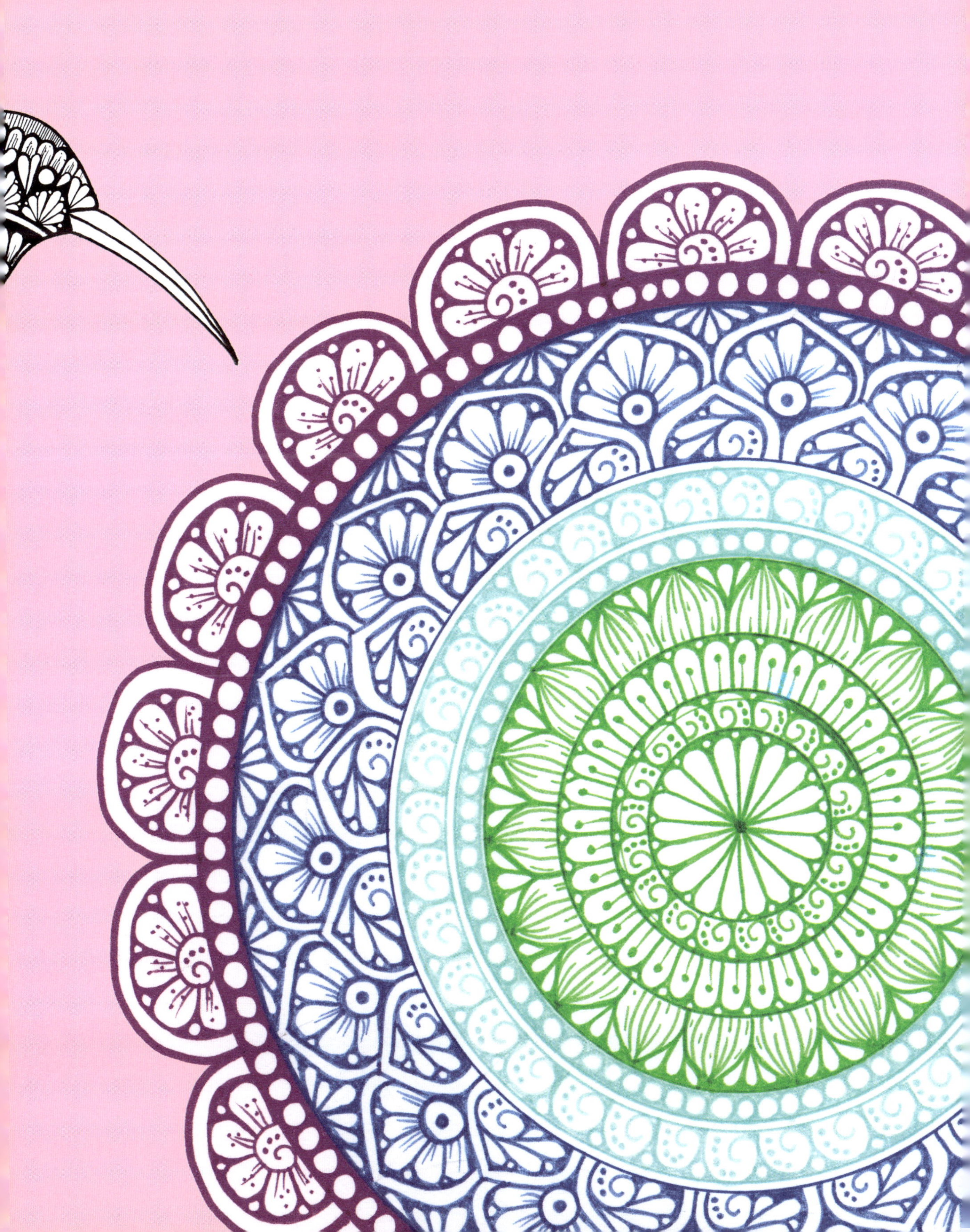

Contents

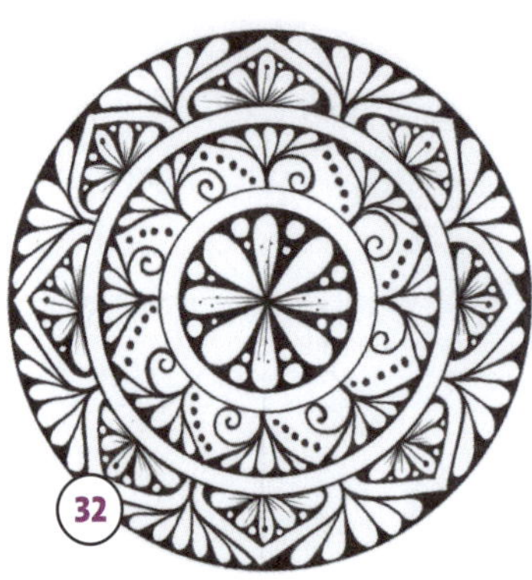
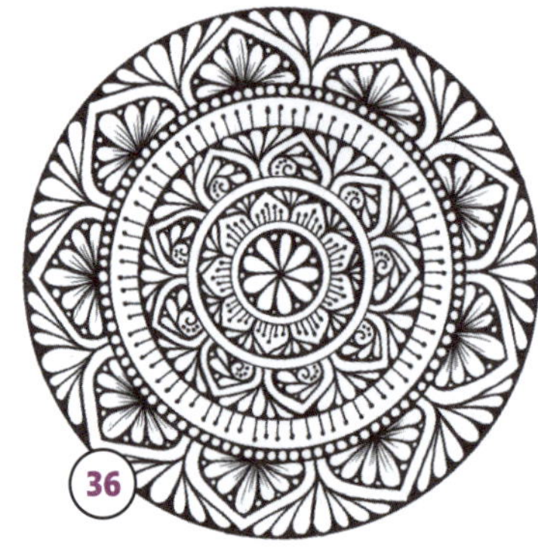
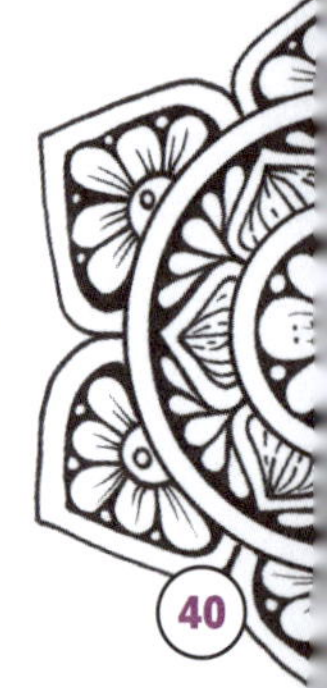

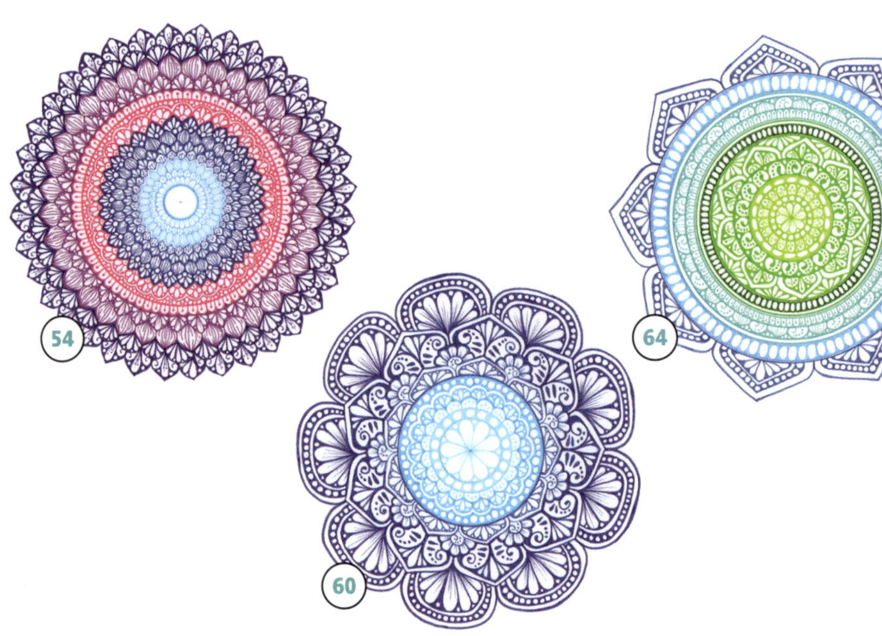

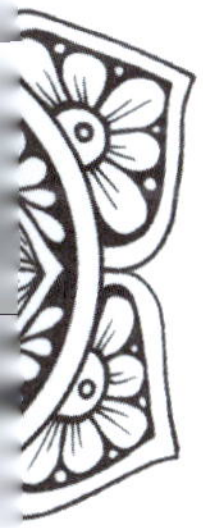

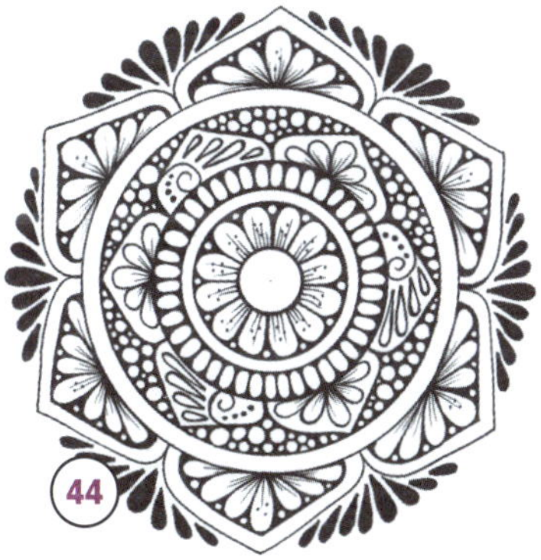

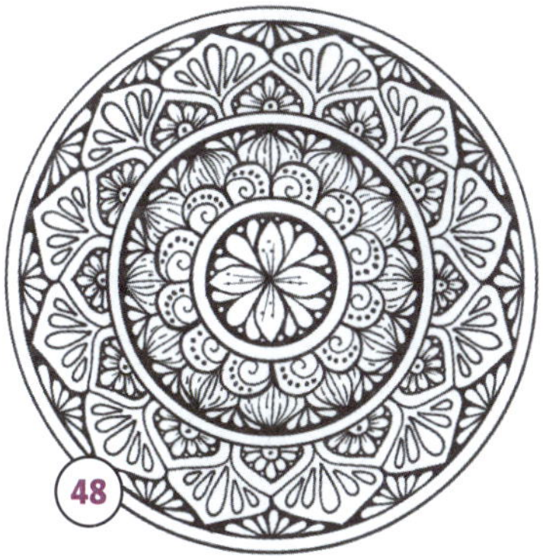

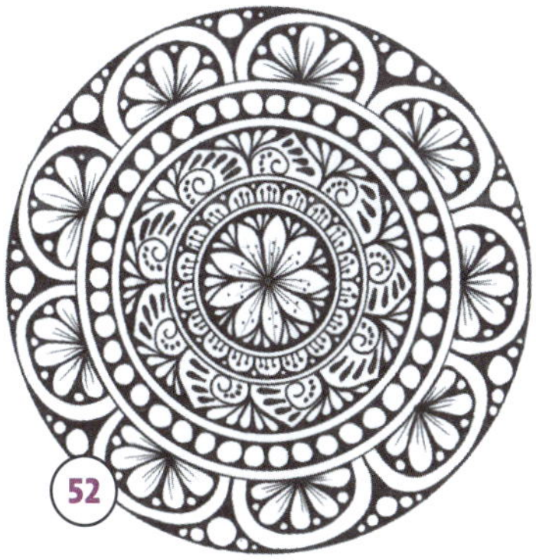

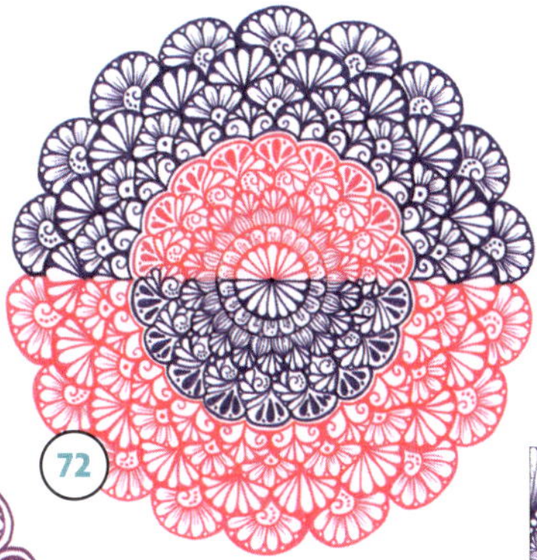

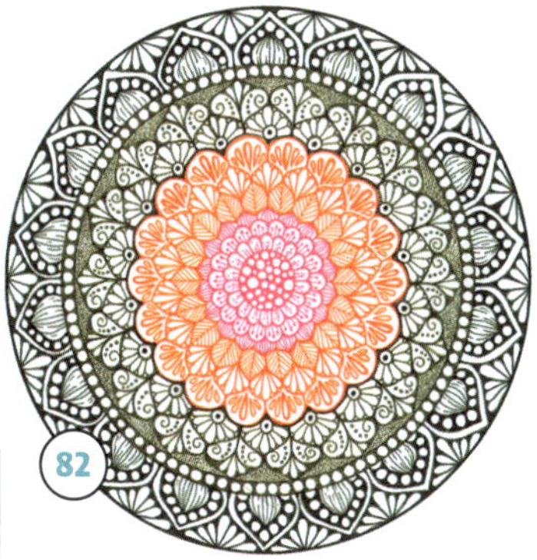

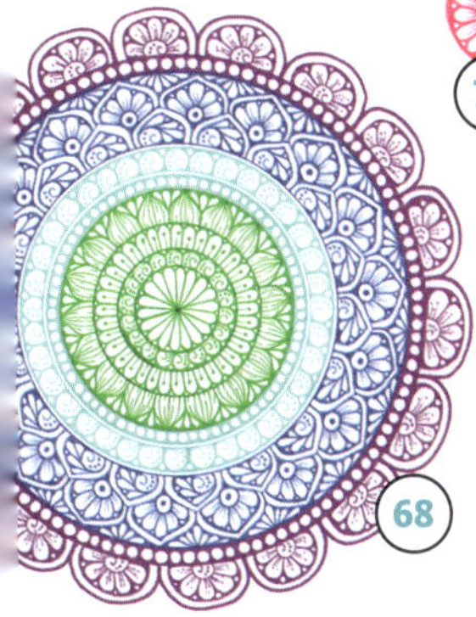

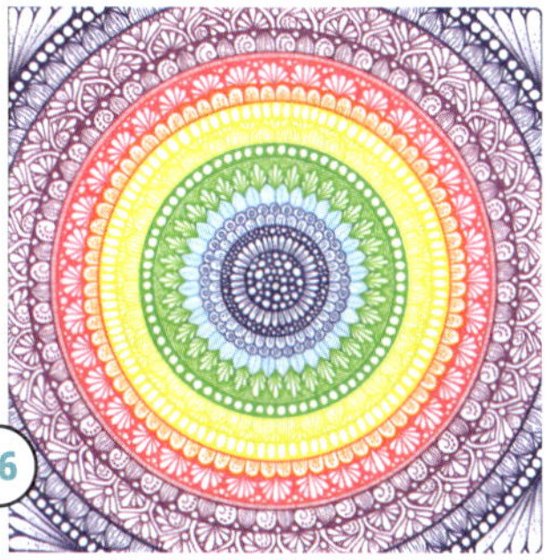

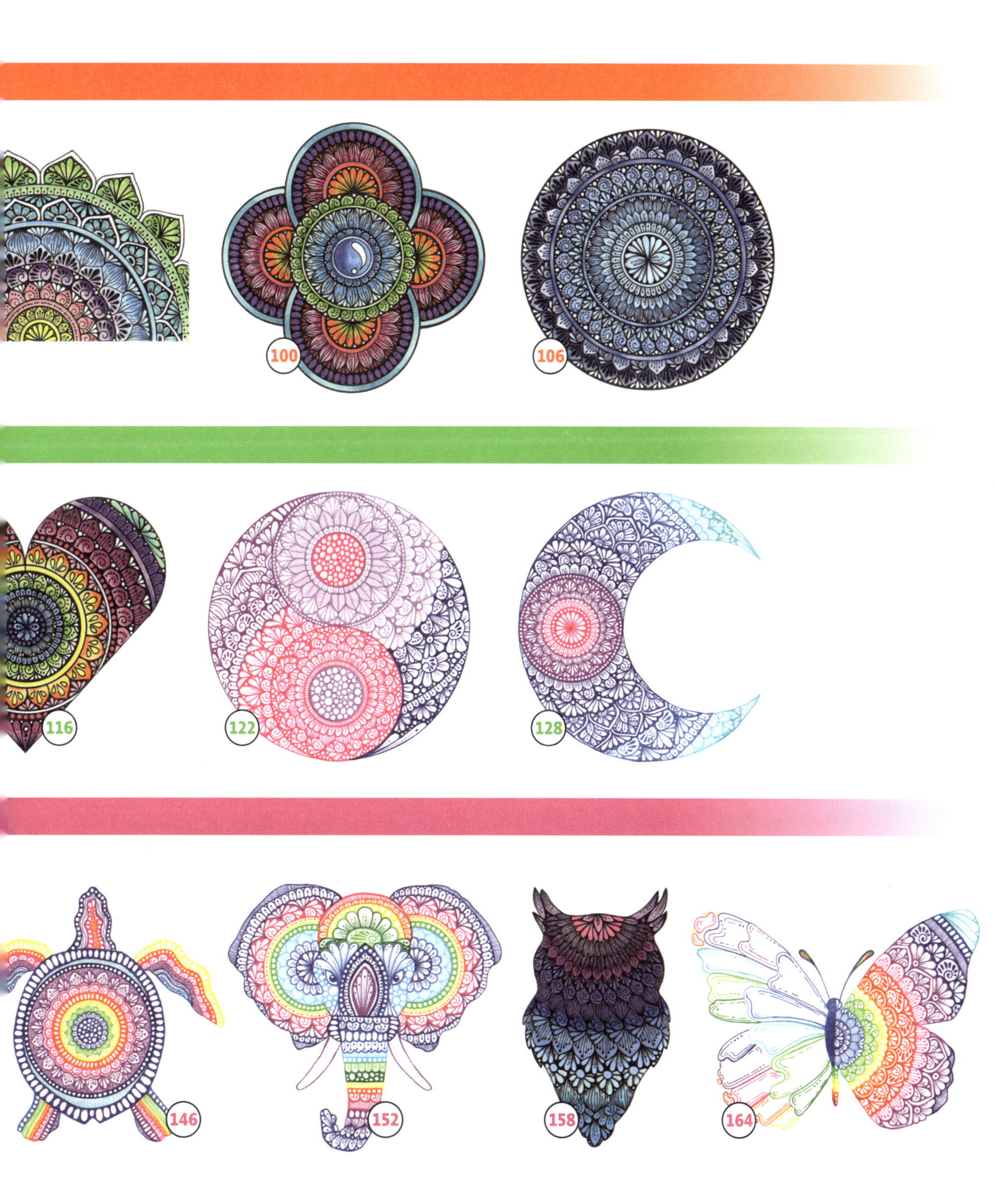

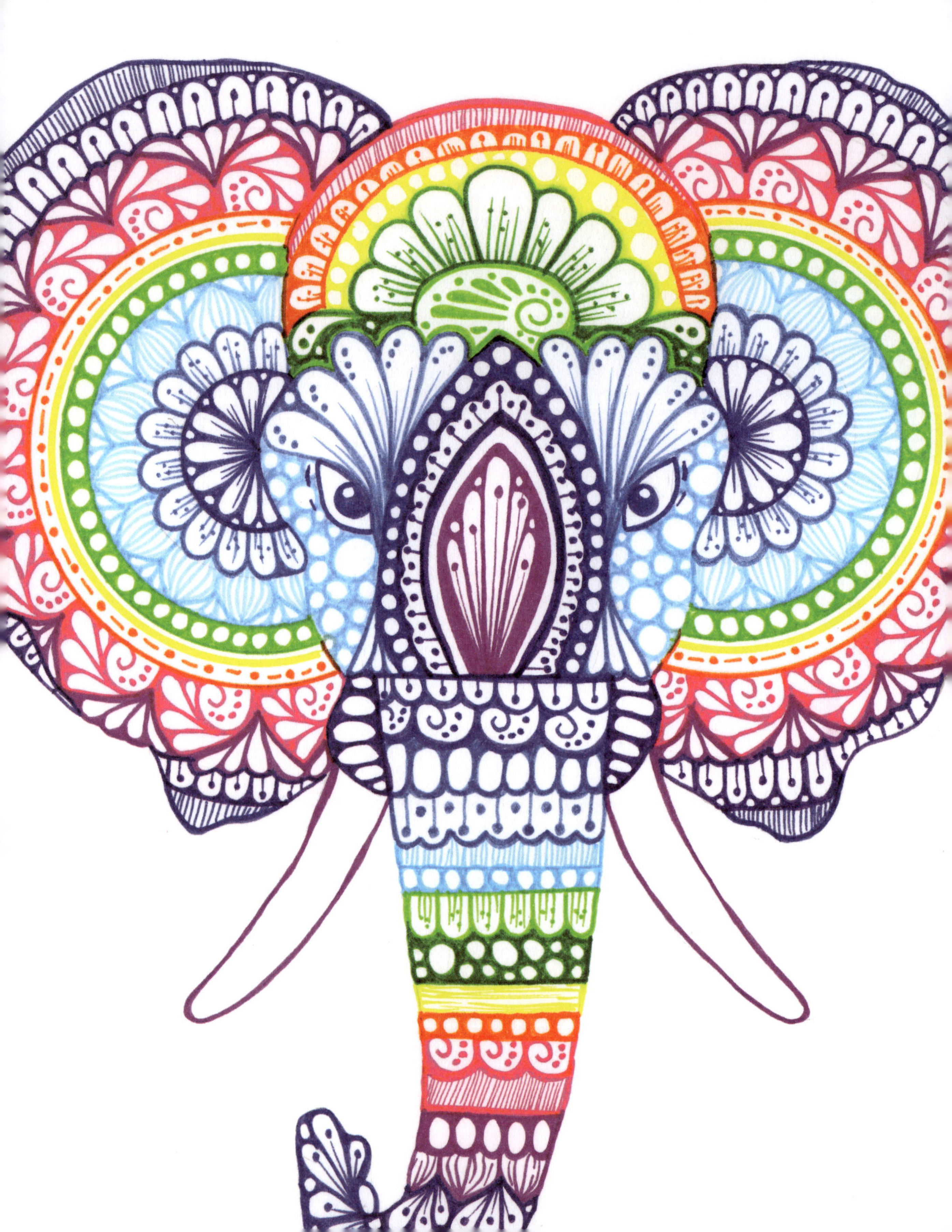

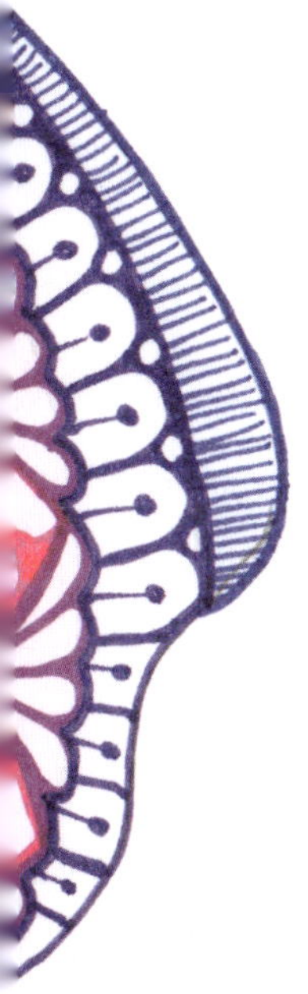

Welcome

Hello! I'm so happy to have you with me on this creative new journey.

This book will not only teach you how to draw mandalas step by step but will also lead you to explore and enjoy the meditative process of drawing without rush or stress. Each mandala includes an intention to focus on while you draw, and there are also journaling questions mixed in here and there to prompt you to reflect on your own artistic process.

Throughout these pages, we will explore classic black-and-white mandalas, color mandalas, and unique mandala shapes—all in a progressive-learning approach that will get you comfortable with more and more complexity as you work through the book.

But I don't want you to simply draw the designs one by one and then close the book as soon as you're done. Rather, I want this book to serve as a resource for your creative practice and to guide you along the way as you branch out into creating your own mandalas. I hope that my colorful designs and lessons give you inspiration, and I would love for you to try challenging yourself to come up with your own unique designs!

The more you create, the more practice you'll get, and the more interesting and special your mandalas will be. Combine different colors, patterns, and themes to make your mandalas truly your own! And, of course, remember to be patient with yourself—don't get so caught up in trying to make your work look "perfect" that you lose the joyful and calming effects that are the core of mandala drawing.

I can't wait to see what you create!

Farah

Meet the Author

We sat down with Farah to learn a little more about her and her artistic journey. Join us!

Tell us a bit about yourself. Where are you from, and where do you call home?

Hi, I'm Farah! I'm originally from Jordan, but I was raised in China and then moved to Turkey, where I currently live. China is the country that I grew up in, and I learned a lot of life lessons there, so that's why I still call China my home.

How did you get started in art?

I've been drawing since I was very young—so young that I can't actually remember when I started! I always enjoyed art in general, and I picked up drawing as soon as I could learn how to hold a pencil. I used to draw everything—plants, characters, or anything I saw around me.

How did you become a mandala artist? What made you fall in love with mandalas specifically?

Back in 2016, a friend drew a mandala on my hand. I didn't even know at the time that this type of art was called a mandala, but I enjoyed watching her draw it so much that I felt I really wanted to learn how to do it myself. So I went back home and started doing tons of research on this type of art, and then I started learning how to draw them. I truly enjoy the process of drawing mandalas because it makes me feel so relaxed and calm, and that has been true ever since the very first mandala I drew.

How long did it take you to develop your mandala drawing and coloring skills?

I would say it took me about two years to master mandala drawing completely, as well as finding my own style and my favorite colors to work with.

What do you find relaxing about mandalas?

Drawing mandalas sometimes requires a lot of focus, but its particular kind of focus brings calmness to your mind and lets you stop thinking about anything except what you're creating. Even though it takes a good deal of concentration, the repetition becomes meditative. Also, repeating the patterns and working with different colors, I find, is simply a joy.

You are truly a social media sensation! How did you get started?

I started my accounts because of my younger sister, Hala, who is actually my assistant now! She was the one who encouraged me to share my drawings with the world via social media. Once I started posting, I found that I really enjoyed it, so I began sharing consistently on multiple different platforms, including Instagram and TikTok.

Your book is unique in that it does not just teach how to draw mandalas but also includes a strong focus on mindfulness. What do you hope readers will get from your book?

I hope readers will enjoy every single creation in the book! I hope that they will not only learn how to draw the mandalas I've designed, but also benefit from many relaxing hours while drawing and coloring each one. The intentions and journal questions included will hopefully make the reader's experience even more soothing and self-reflective.

What advice can you give readers who want to spend more time on creative pursuits?

Set a regular time for it and keep on practicing. All the magic will happen when you practice consistently and put your mind and heart into it.

What else do you do besides your art and social media?

I run my own art and stationery business, which is a lot of fun! You can find my creations in my shop, farahbrightart.etsy.com.

What does a perfect day look like for you?

A perfect day for me is a sunny day when I finish my daily workout, start getting creative, and film new videos for my social media.

What is your favorite music to enjoy while creating art?

I love listening to music that hypes me up and gets me energized, but I also really enjoy Adele's songs; she is one of my favorite artists.

What other passions do you have in life, outside of your art?

I love teaching; I actually used to be an art and language teacher at a kindergarten in China. When I was a kid, I used to collect all my classmates after our classes and reteach them the lessons we had just learned. Now, through this book, I feel like I am getting a fresh opportunity to teach readers.

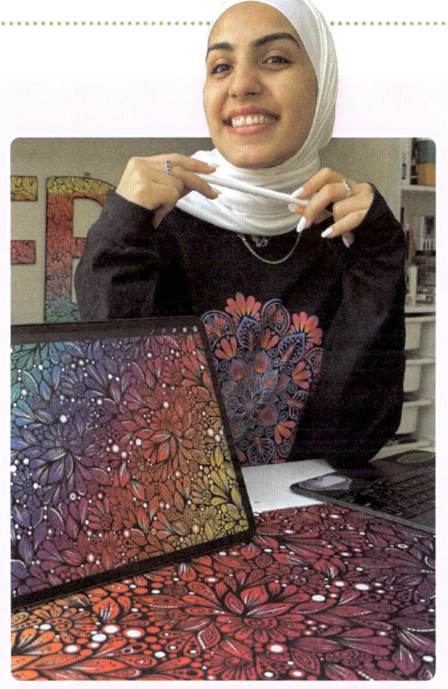

Farah Brightart *(Farah Alhamawi)* is a lifelong artist and viral content creator with over 2 million followers and is the founder and creative mind behind Farah Brightart. Originally from Jordan, Farah was raised in China and is currently living in Turkey, where she is a mandala and Zentangle artist and watercolor illustrator. During her creative journey, Farah has collaborated with many international brands such as Disney+, Marvel, Staedtler, Ravensburger, Jiggy, Daughters for Earth, and many others. Her first book, *Coloring Zentangle Style,* was published in Germany (Frech). This is her debut drawing book! Learn more @farah.brightart (Instagram) and @farahbrightart (TikTok).

How to Use This Book

Before you dive straight into the book, I'd love to explain how I've set it up so that you can learn frustration-free and truly embrace the magic of mandala drawing!

In the Getting Started part of the book, you'll learn all the basics you need, including the essential tools and how to draw nice, neat circles and rays as guidelines. These basics will set you up for success, so don't skip them, but don't worry—they're really easy! In this section, you'll also get a chance to practice drawing basic mandala shapes as well as more-complicated patterns, right inside the book. This will get your hands familiar with the kinds of shapes and lines you'll be including in your mandalas.

Once you've collected all your tools and done a little practice, you can dive into the mandalas themselves! In the Mandalas section of the book, you'll find 30 step-by-step mandalas. The mandalas are divided into five thematic sections (see facing page!), and they increase in complexity and difficulty within each section, allowing you to learn as you progress through the book. They also increase in complexity and difficulty from section to section—you'll start off simple with black-and-white mandalas, progress to color, and then progress to shapes. At the end of each of the five sections, you'll get a chance to take the training wheels off and tackle a "challenge yourself" mandala where you have less step-by-step guidance and can apply what you've been learning.

The 30 mandalas aren't just instructional, though. Each one includes an intention for you to focus on while drawing. These intentions will get you thinking and leaning into a peaceful, focused meditative state. Many of the mandalas also include reflection prompts at the end for you to answer after you've completed the mandala. These journaling questions will help you better understand your relationship to mandala drawing and enrich your artistic journey.

For a preview of the five mandala themes, see the facing page!

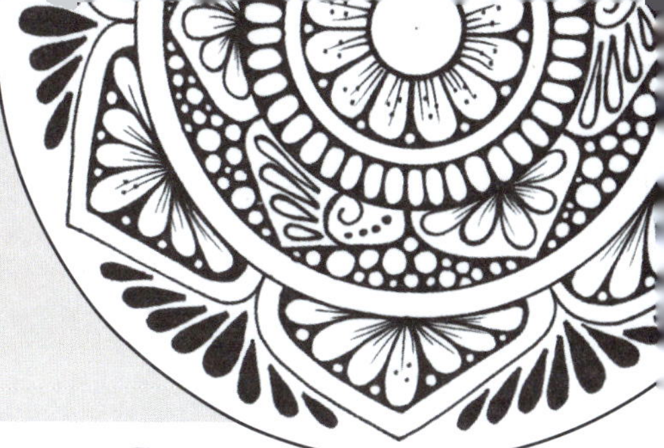

BLACK & WHITE

The first mandala theme is dedicated to classic black-and-white mandalas. In this section, you'll learn how to draw consistent, clean lines and patterns, and you'll get familiar with terminology that will pop up throughout the book.

COLORED LINES

This section is dedicated to using colored pens instead of black pens to draw your mandalas. You'll learn how to plan ahead with colored circles as well as how to improvise with color as you go. You'll also get a chance to go "off the page"!

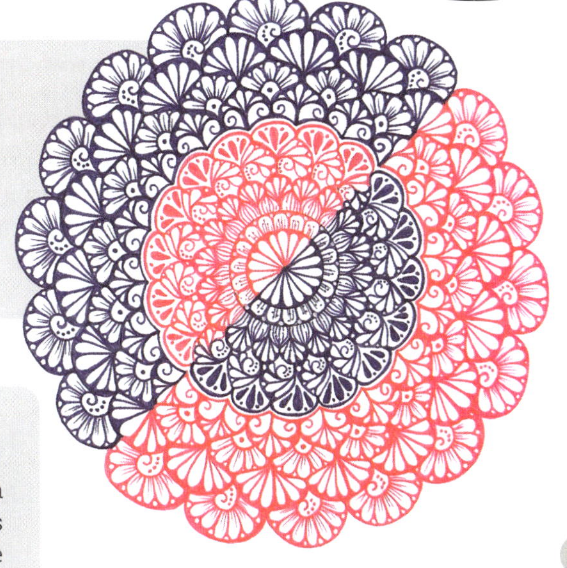

COLORED IN

In this section, you will first draw the mandala in black and white, then color it using markers or colored pencils. You will learn how to create pretty gradients and smooth blends, and your mandalas will come to life!

SPECIAL SHAPES

It's time to break away from simple circles! This theme is dedicated to drawing mandalas that are in shapes such as a heart, a crescent moon, or a yin-yang. You'll use a mix of black and white, colored lines, and coloring in from what you learned in the previous sections.

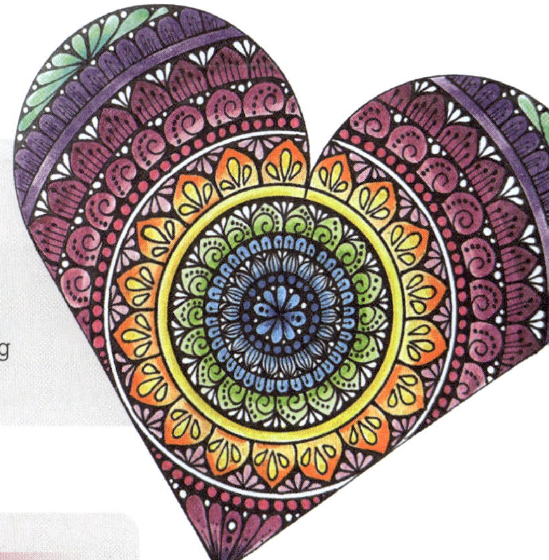

ANIMALS

In this final section, the mandalas take on the shapes of wild creatures. You'll apply everything you've learned so far in order to create stunning designs that will seem to fly (or swim or walk) off the page.

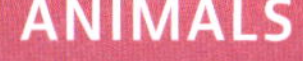

GETTING STARTED

In this section, you'll learn what essential tools you'll need and how to draw nice, neat circles and ray guidelines using a compass and a ruler. These basics will set you up for success, so don't skip them, but don't worry—they're really easy! You'll also practice drawing basic mandala shapes and patterns right inside the book. This will get your hands familiar with the kinds of shapes and lines you'll be including in your mandalas.

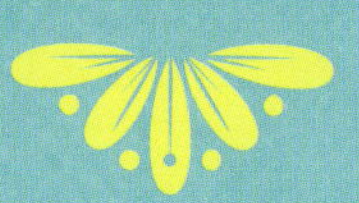

All the Materials You'll Need

It doesn't take much to draw and color a gorgeously detailed and precise mandala!
Collect the items in this basic toolkit.

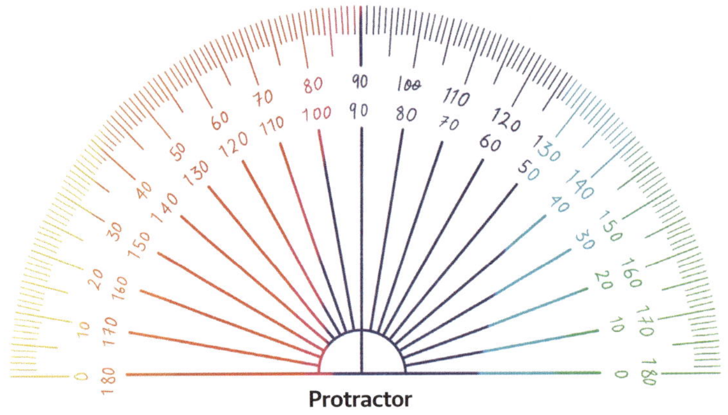

Protractor

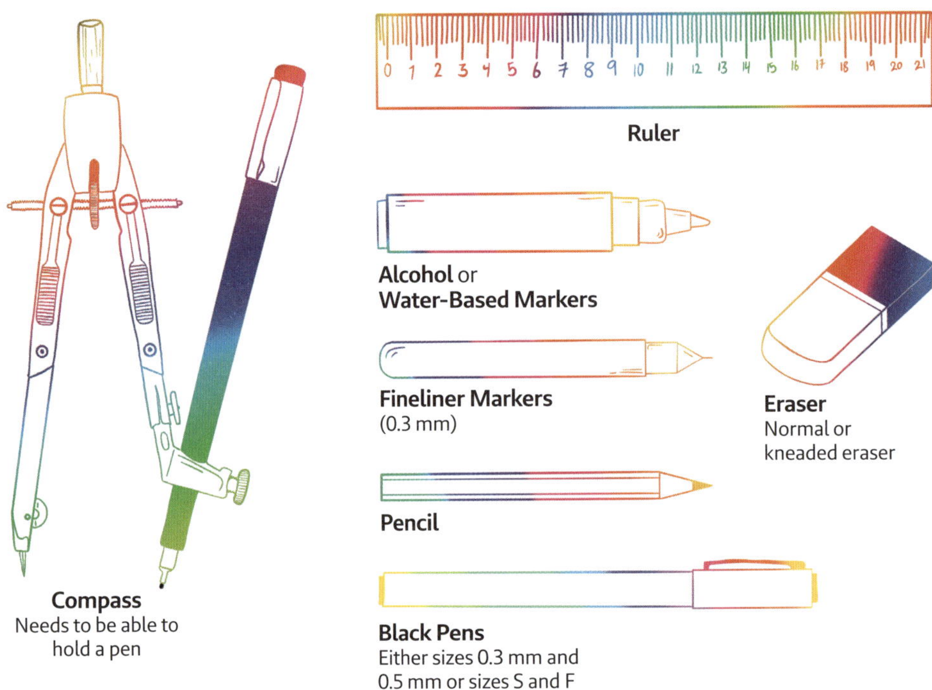

Ruler

Compass
Needs to be able to
hold a pen

Alcohol or
Water-Based Markers

Fineliner Markers
(0.3 mm)

Pencil

Black Pens
Either sizes 0.3 mm and
0.5 mm or sizes S and F

Eraser
Normal or
kneaded eraser

You can also choose to color your mandalas with colored pencils instead of markers!

Basic Mandala Shapes

Practice these simple repeating rows to get familiar with different easy shapes and to train your hand at creating consistent designs! This page includes basic domes and pointed leaves, which will be used in almost every mandala.

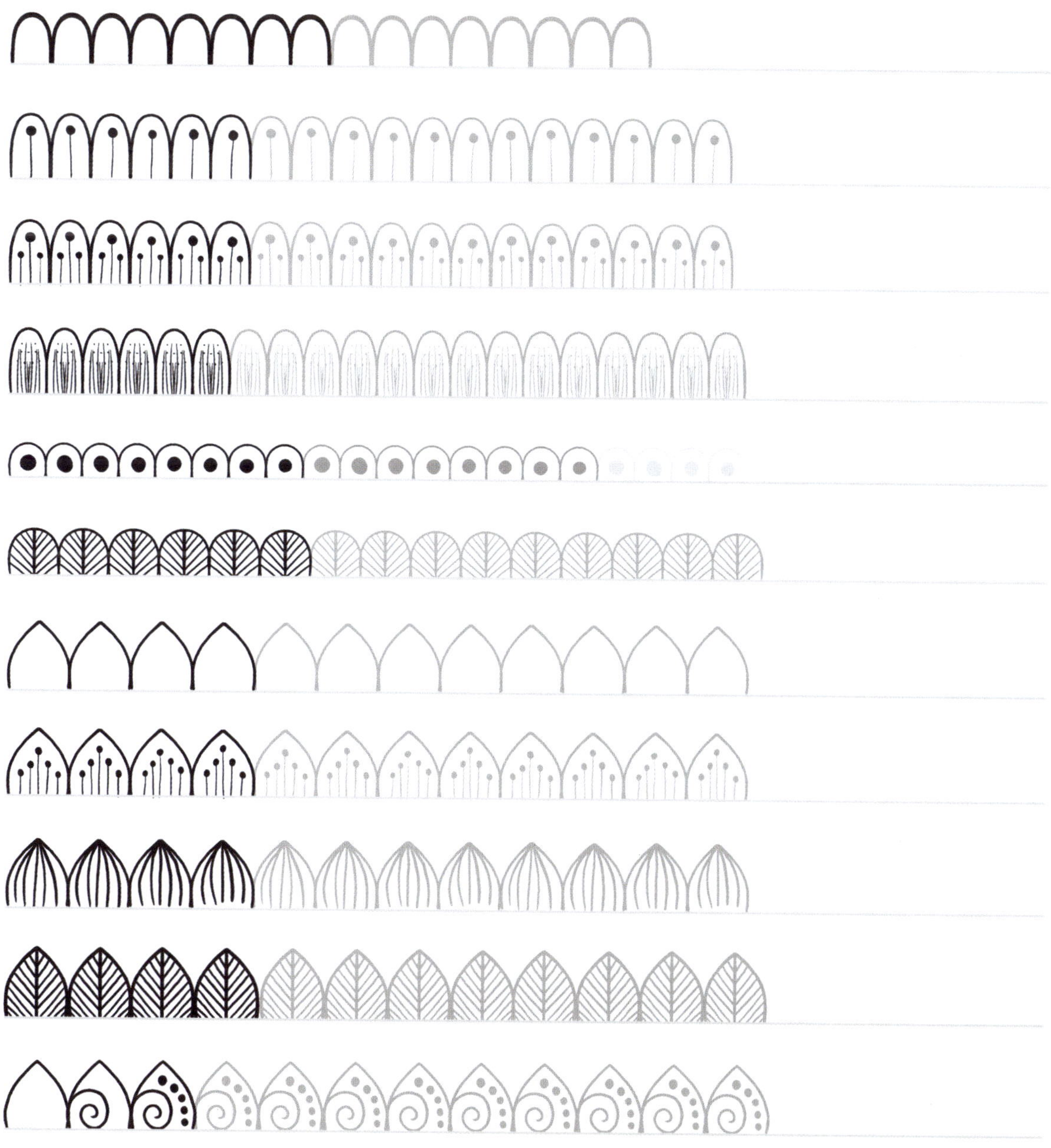

Dome Mandala Patterns

Time to up the ante a bit! Try practicing these slightly more complicated dome patterns.
Each design is built up through small individual steps.

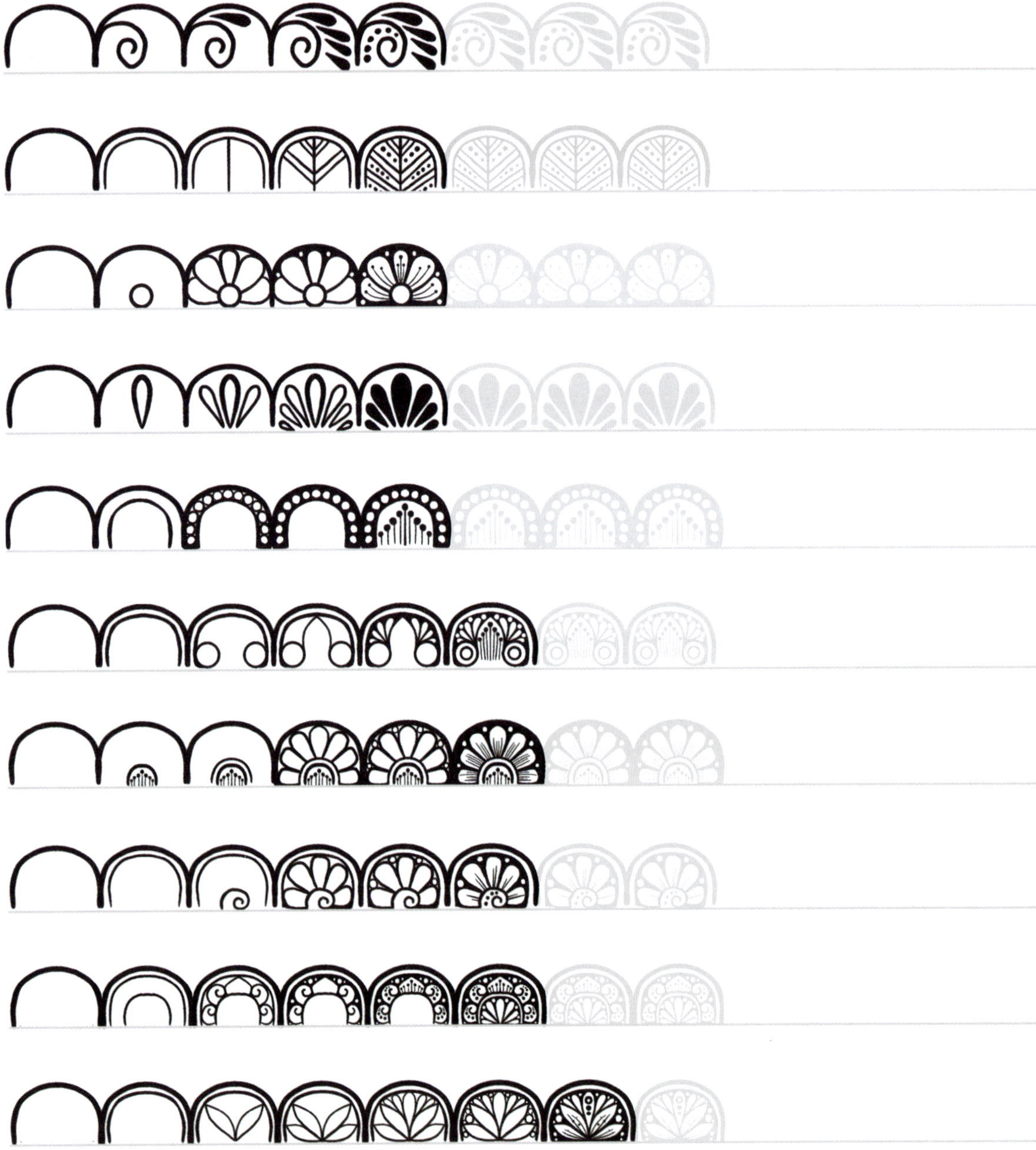

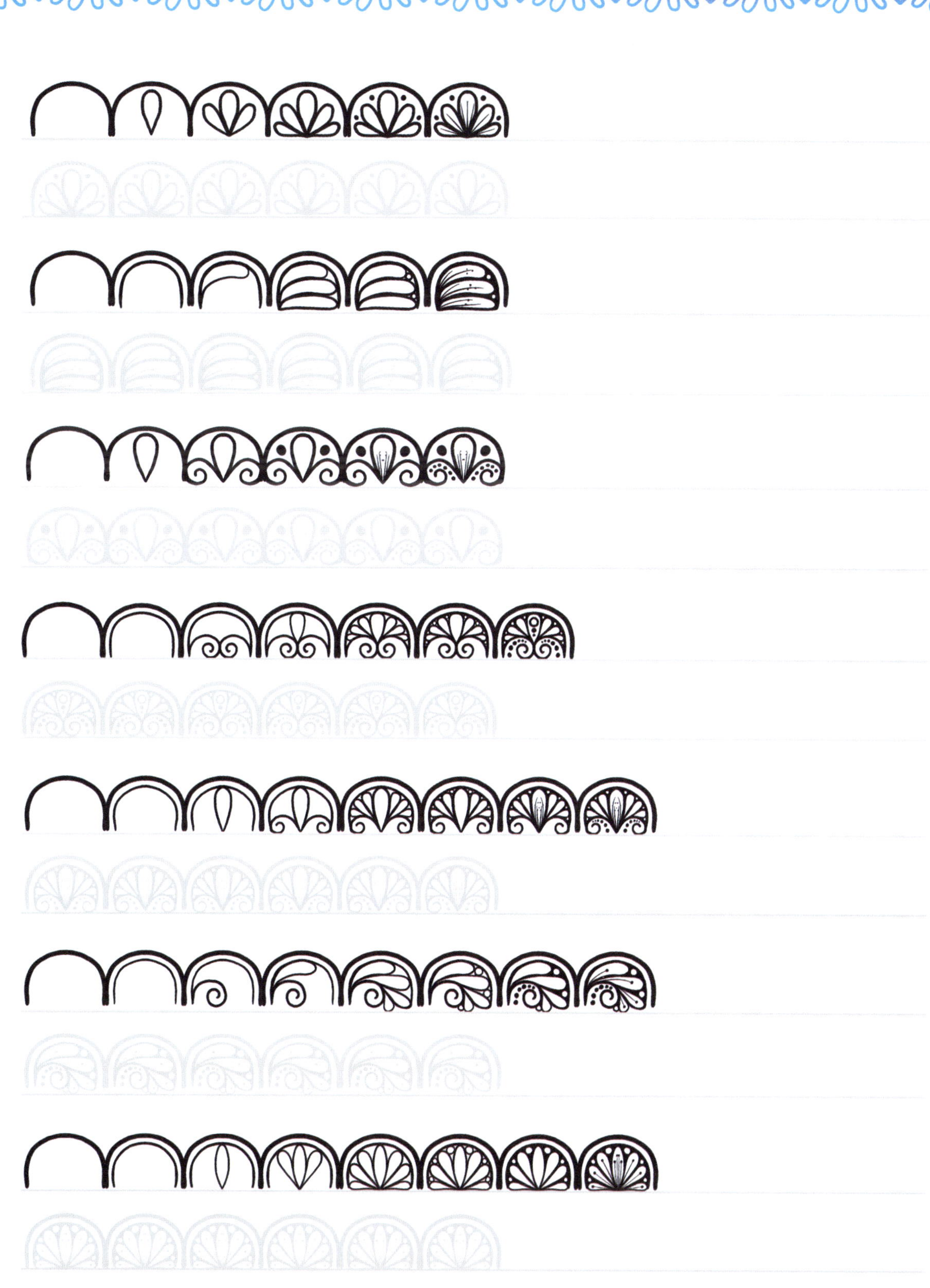

Pointed-Leaf Mandala Patterns

Now let's get really elaborate! Try practicing these more challenging pointed-leaf patterns. Each design is still built up through small individual steps, making even the most complicated-looking leaf pattern achievable.

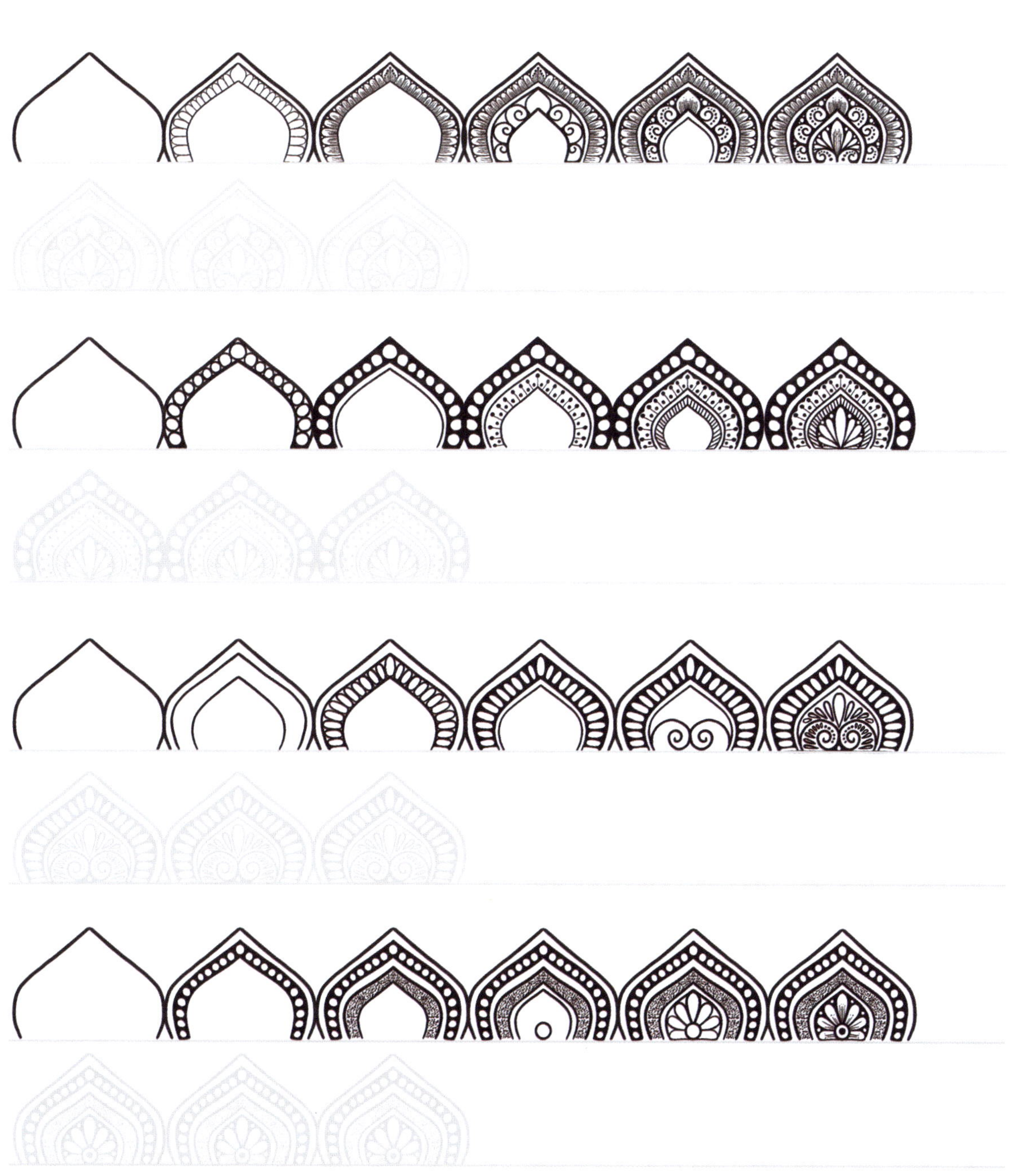

23

How to Draw Mandala Guidelines:
THE CIRCLES

To start any mandala, you will need a pencil and pen, a compass, and a ruler.

1. Find the center of your page and mark it with a pencil dot.

2. Load your compass with your pencil. (You can start with pen if you choose, but starting with pencil will allow you to fix any mistakes.)

3. Use your ruler to measure the size circle you want (the radius of your desired circle) from the center dot, making another pencil dot where you want the circle to go.

4. Then place your compass point on the center dot, open the compass so the pencil precisely hits your circle dot, and draw the circle!

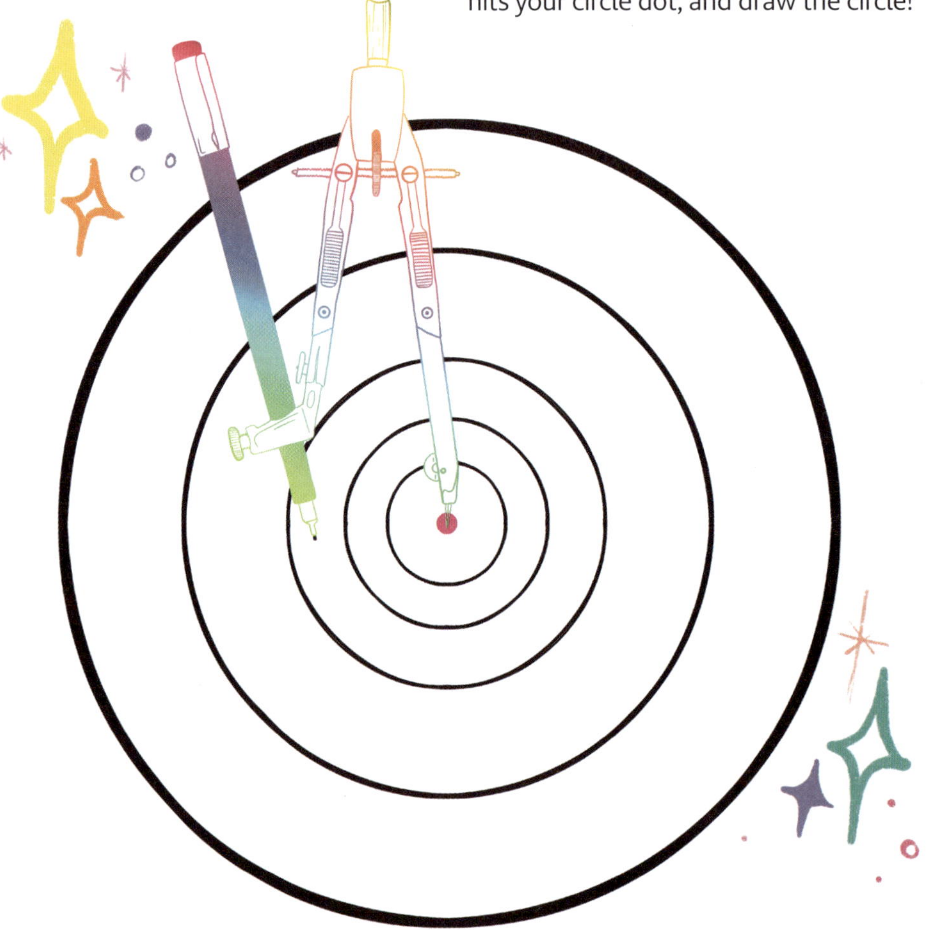

Sometimes you will draw the circles first; sometimes you will draw the rays first (see next page). In most cases, it doesn't matter which you draw first!

How to Draw Mandala Guidelines:
THE RAYS

If you are adding radial rays to your mandala, you will need
to get out your protractor, ruler, and pencil!

1. Align the center bottom of the protractor
with the center dot of the mandala. In this
image, two protractors have been laid down:
one on the top half and one on the bottom half.

2. Use a pencil to mark the correct angles
where you want to draw rays, according to the
mandala instructions. For example, you might
mark every 20°, 10°, or 5°. Be careful not to
move the protractor as you make these marks!

3. Remember that the more marks you draw,
the more densely detailed your mandala will be.

Continued on next page

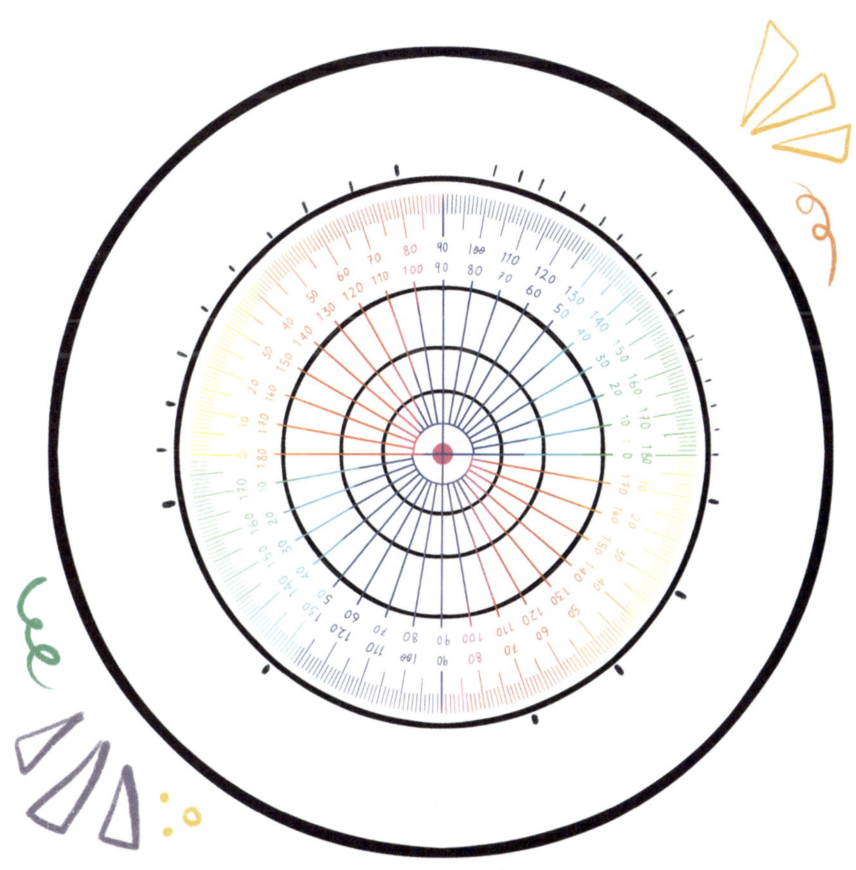

The more rays you draw, the more densely detailed your mandala will be.

How to Draw Mandala Guidelines:
THE RAYS
(continued)

4. Put away the protractor and get out your ruler. Place the very tip of the ruler on the center dot of the mandala.

5. Use a pencil to connect each angle mark with the center dot, drawing neat, straight lines from the center dot out through each mark. Make these lines stretch farther than your desired final mandala size; you can always erase later, but it's harder to lengthen at an accurate angle later.

6. Make sure to keep your hand and ruler steady! Continue until you've drawn all the rays you need.

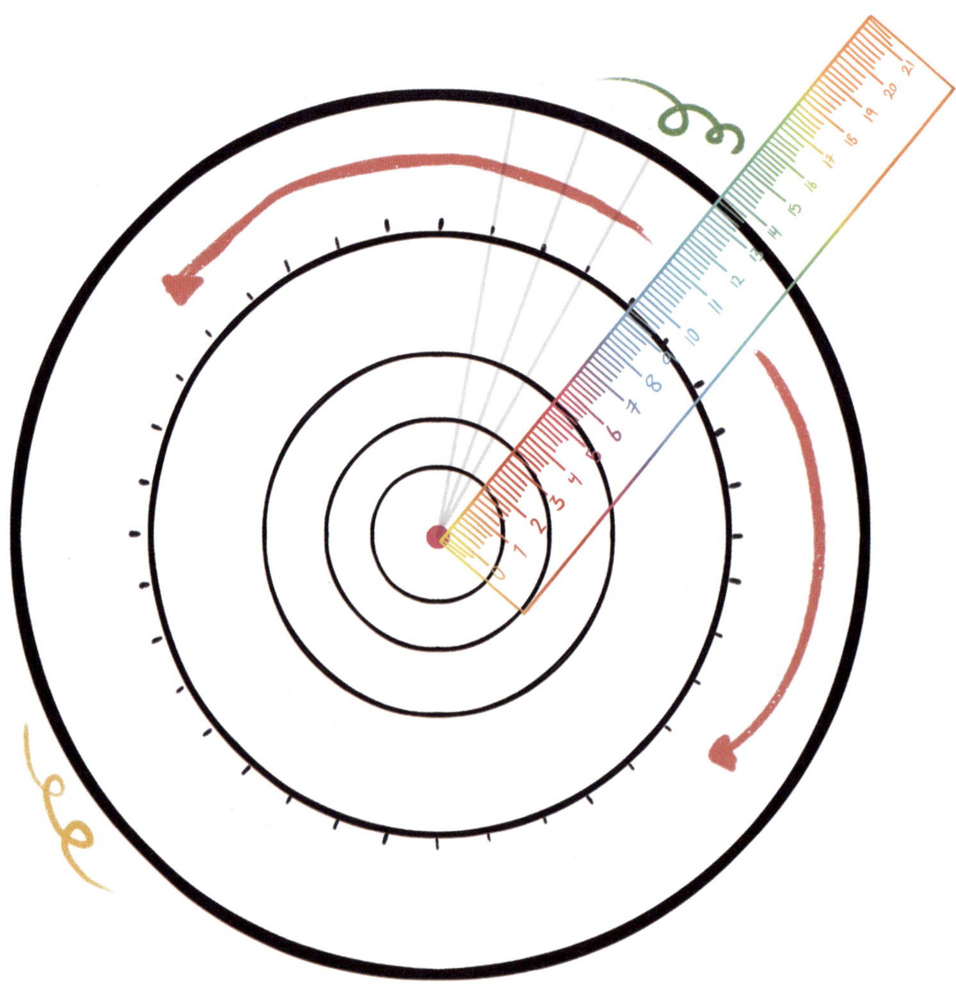

Mandala Center Ideas

Here is a small treasure trove of options for filling the central circle when starting any mandala. Mix and match these designs within your own custom mandalas! Each option is broken down step by step here; try tracing each one in the faded version provided and re-creating each one in the blank circle provided.

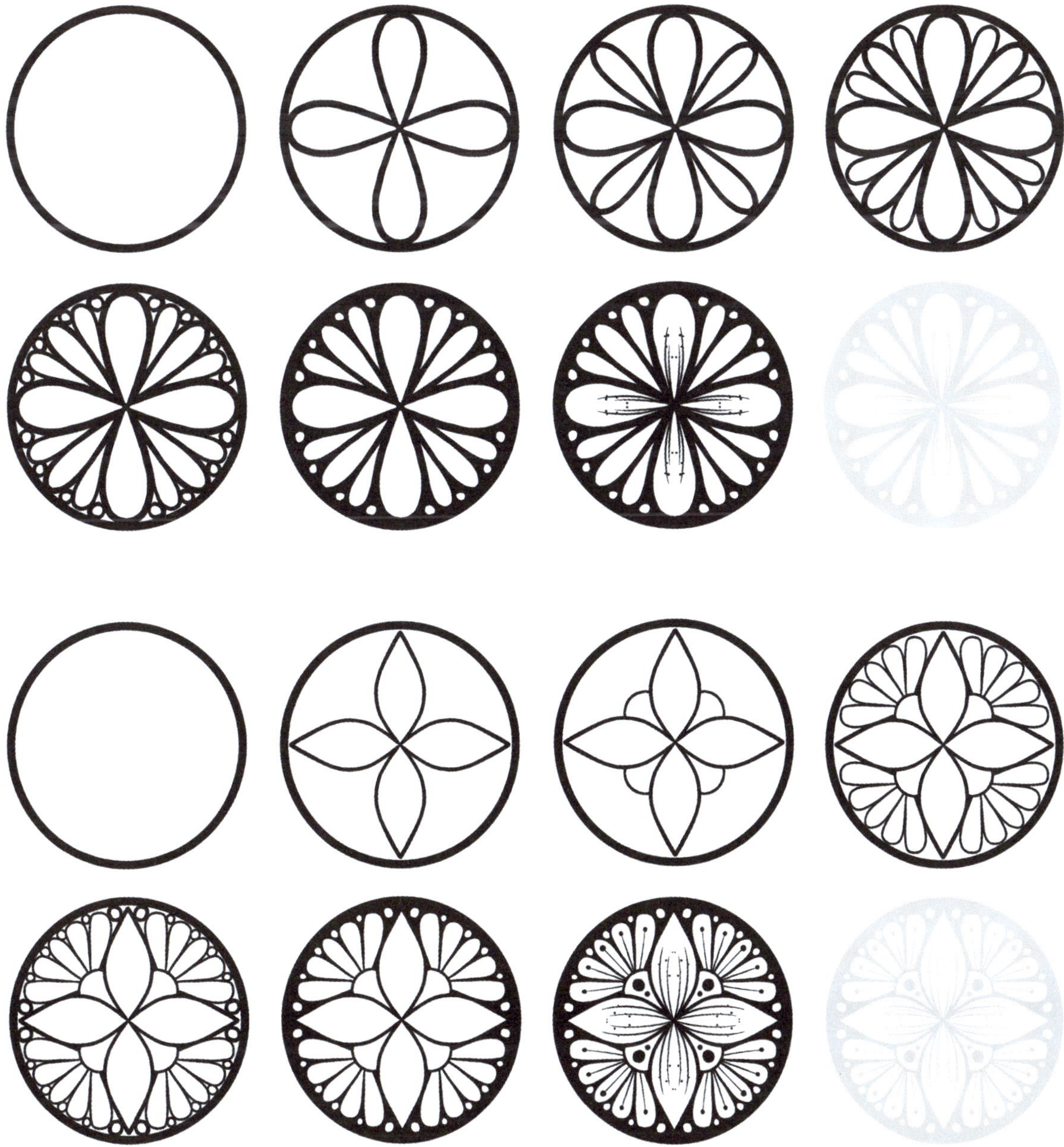

Mandala Center Ideas
(continued)

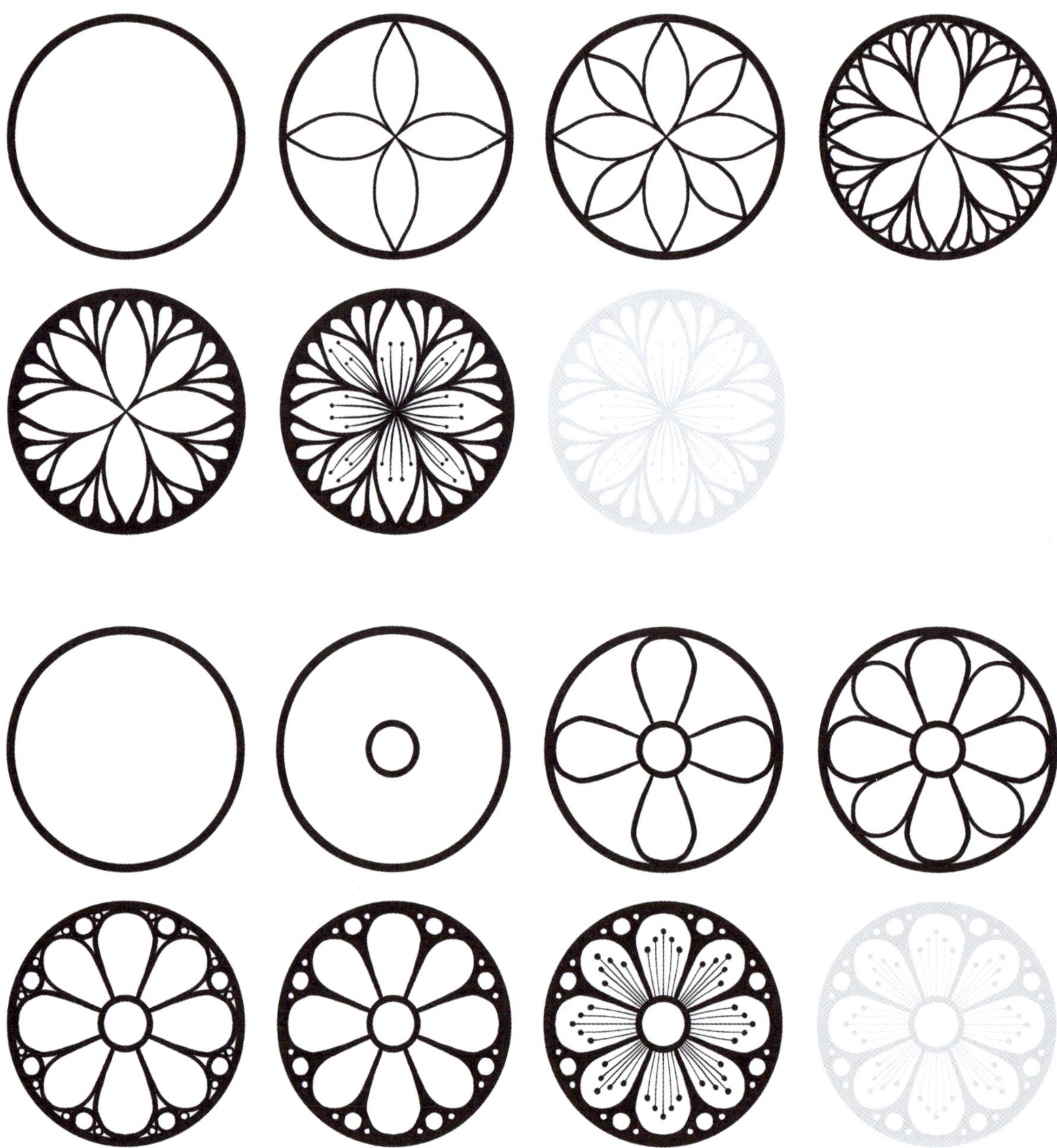

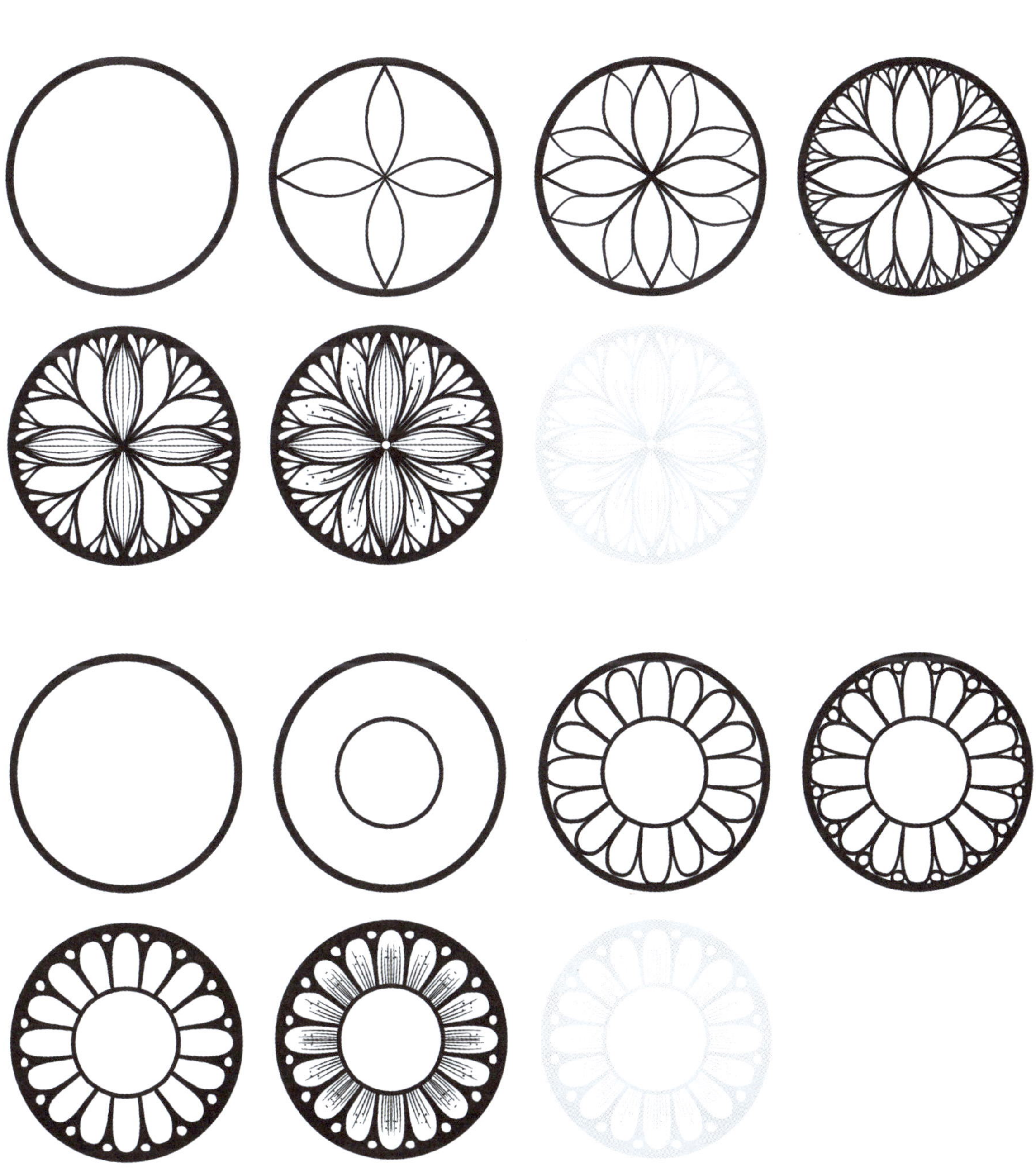

Mandala Center Ideas

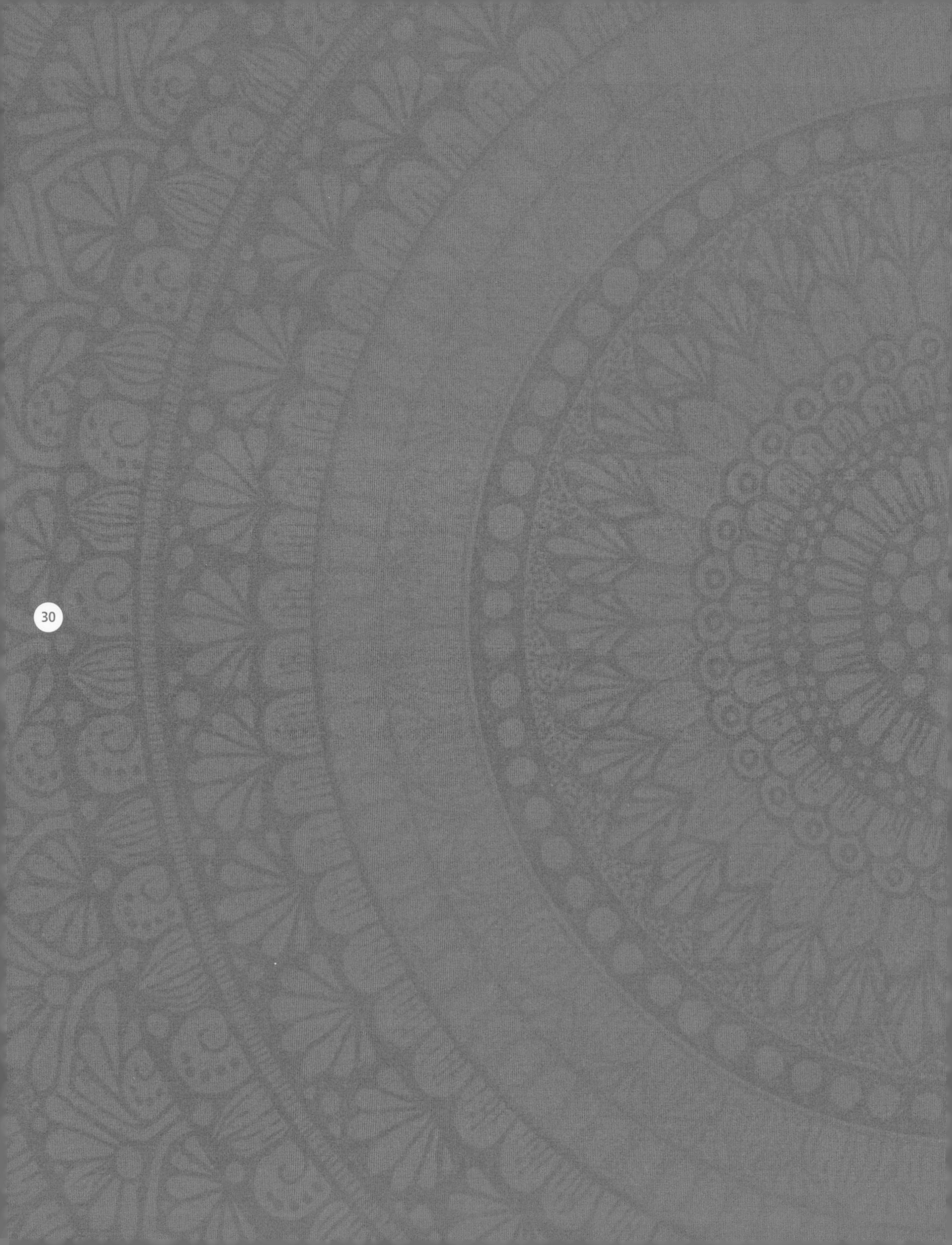

30

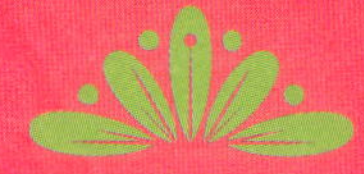

MANDALAS

I know you're ready to start drawing! This section of the book includes 30 step-by-step mandalas divided into five themes. They increase in complexity and difficulty within each theme and from theme to theme, allowing you to learn as you progress through the book. When you feel ready, you can tackle the "challenge yourself" mandala at the end of each theme. It's time to let your creativity flow!

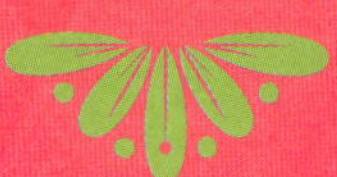

Simple Starter

Welcome to your first mandala! It may look complex at first glance, but with just five circles and only adorning the center and two rings, you'll be surprised at how quickly it comes together. Use this mandala to practice drawing consistent, clean lines and patterns.

As you draw this mandala, try to relax into the process without stressing about the result. If you'd like, think about what you hope to get out of learning to draw mandalas.

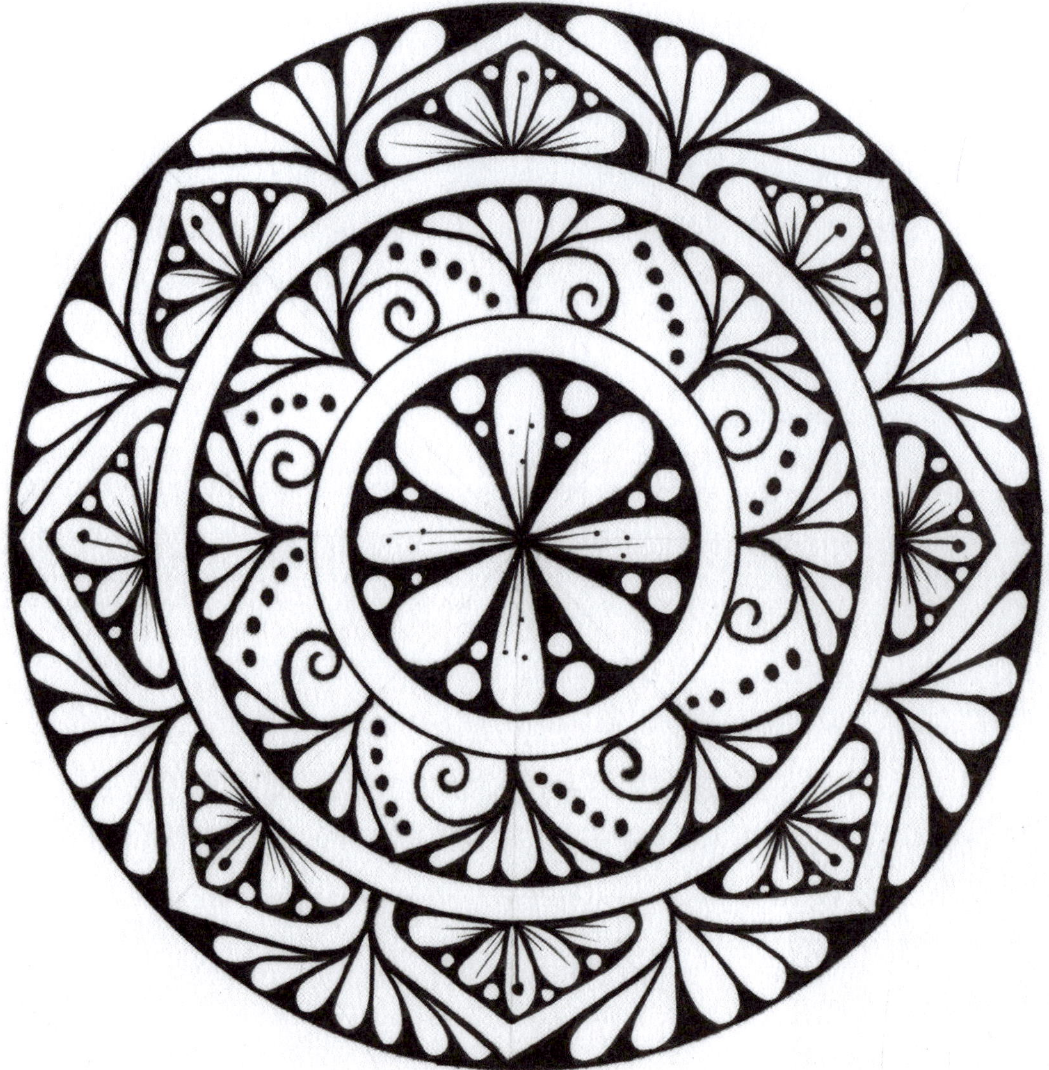

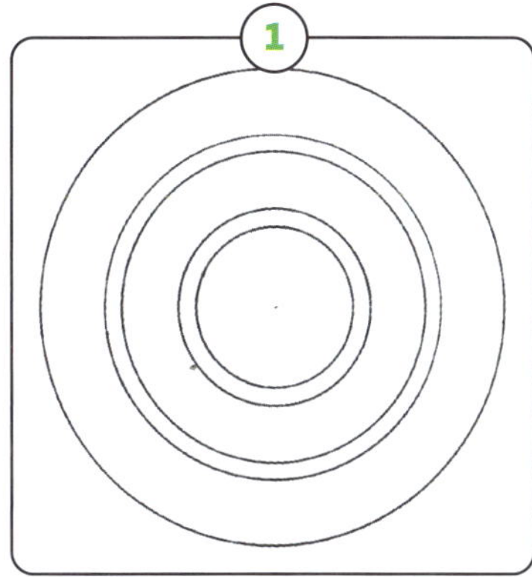

Draw circles. Draw 5 circles as shown. For reference, the outermost circle radius is 2⅜" (6 cm); the innermost circle radius is ⅞" (2 cm).

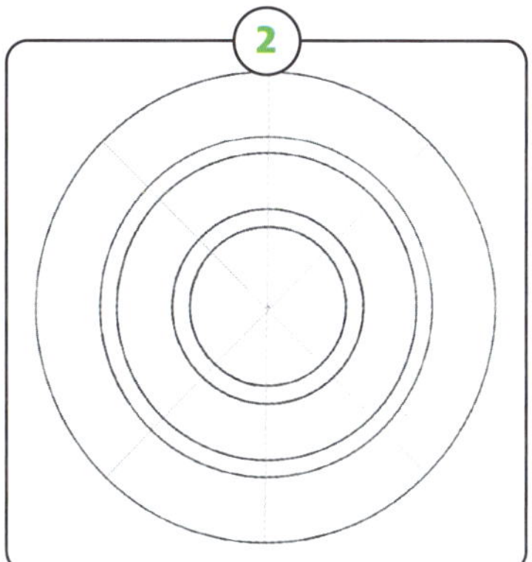

Draw rays. Using pencil, draw an X and a + at perfect right angles. These ray guidelines will be erased at the end.

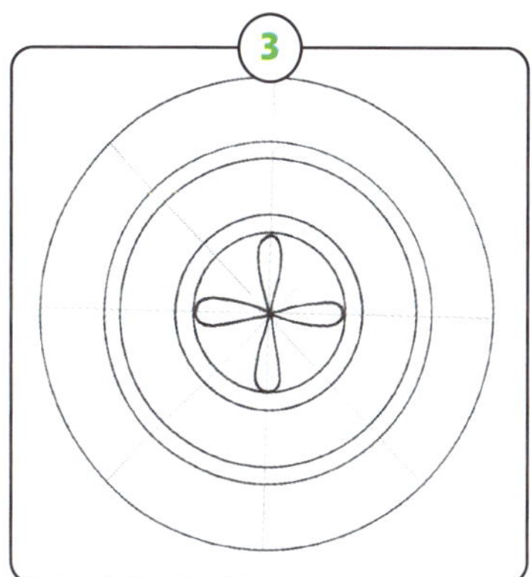

Start the central flower. Draw four teardrops centered on the + rays.

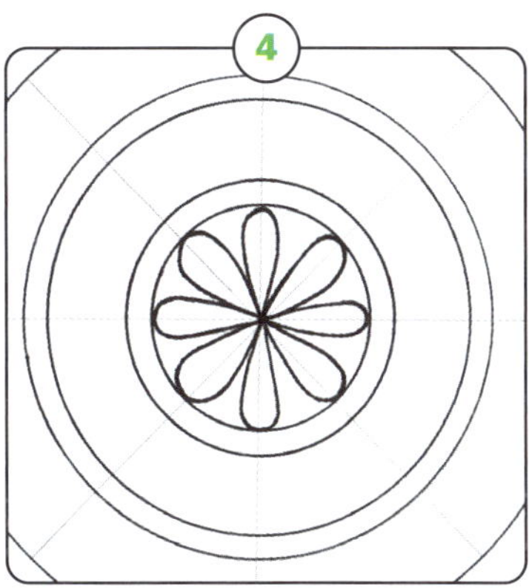

Finish the flower. Draw four more teardrops centered on the X rays.

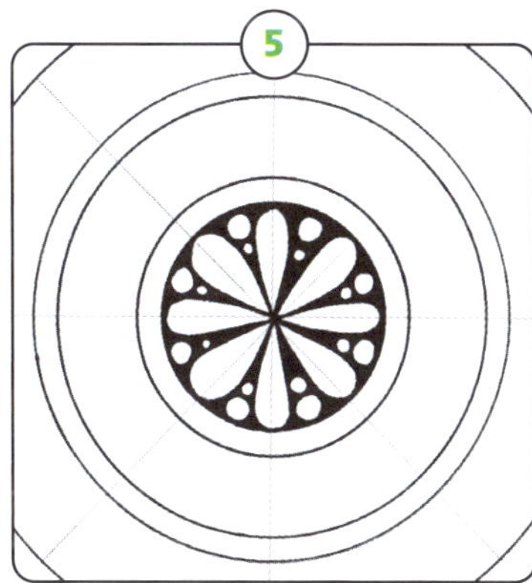

Fill in the center. Draw two freehand circles between each teardrop, then fill in around them.

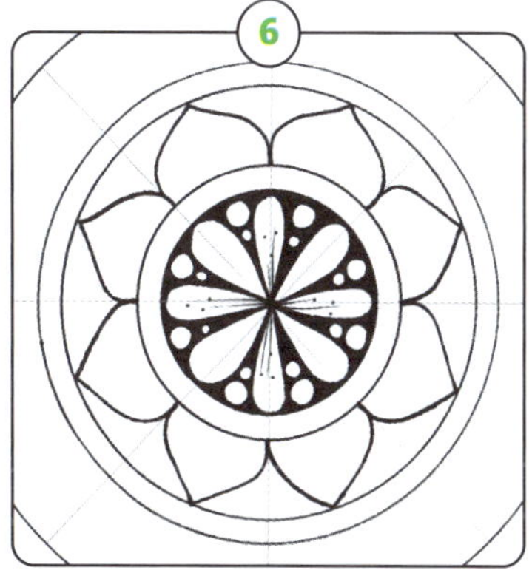

Start the middle ring. Add some delicate lines and dots within the first four teardrops. Then, in the middle ring, draw a pointed leaf between each ray.

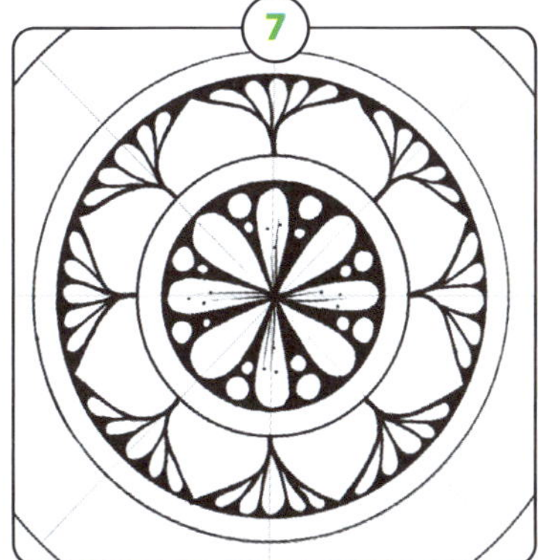

Add filler. Draw five fanning-out teardrops between each pointed leaf, then fill in around them.

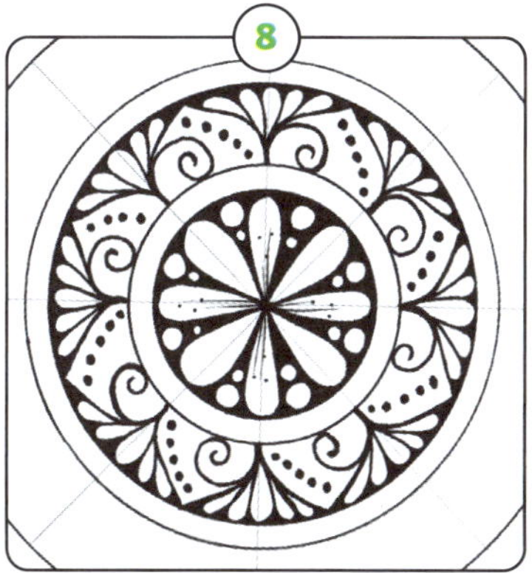

Detail the leaves. Add a curling line and five dots to each pointed leaf.

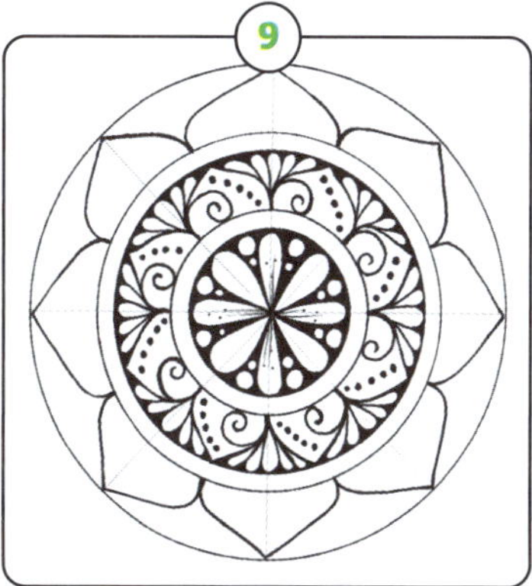

Start the outer ring. In the outer ring, draw a pointed leaf centered on each ray.

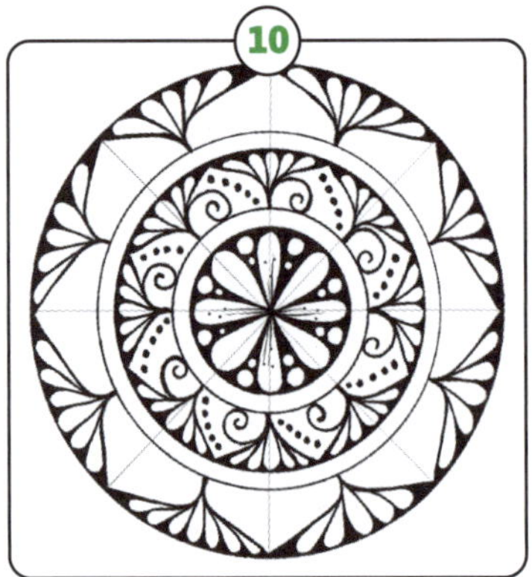

10

Add filler. Draw five fanning-out teardrops between each pointed leaf, then fill in around them.

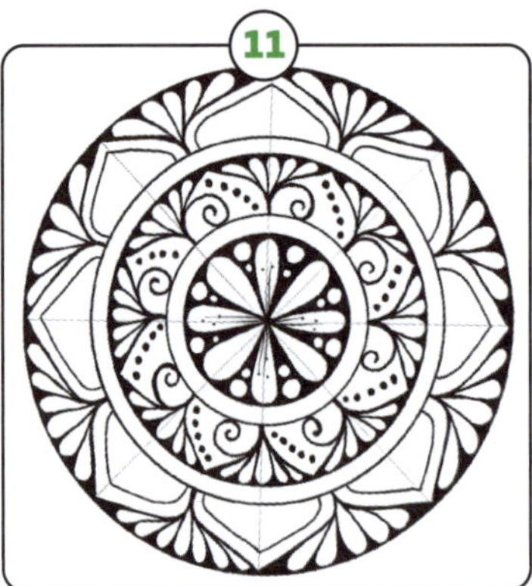

11

Add an inset leaf. Inside each pointed leaf, draw a smaller, inset pointed leaf that follows the same contour.

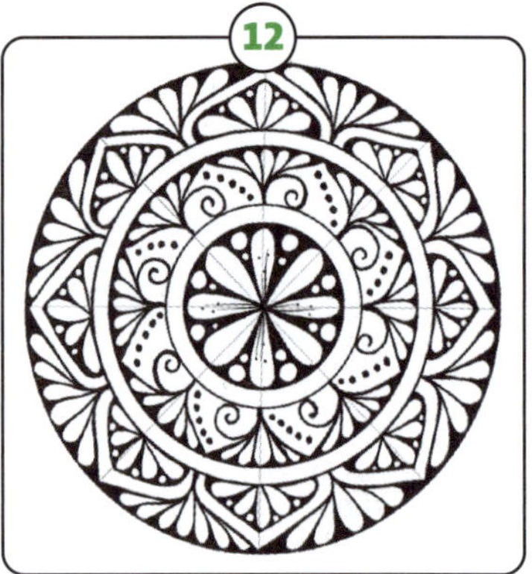

12

Add filler. Draw five fanning-out teardrops inside each small pointed leaf, draw a circle between each teardrop, then fill in around them.

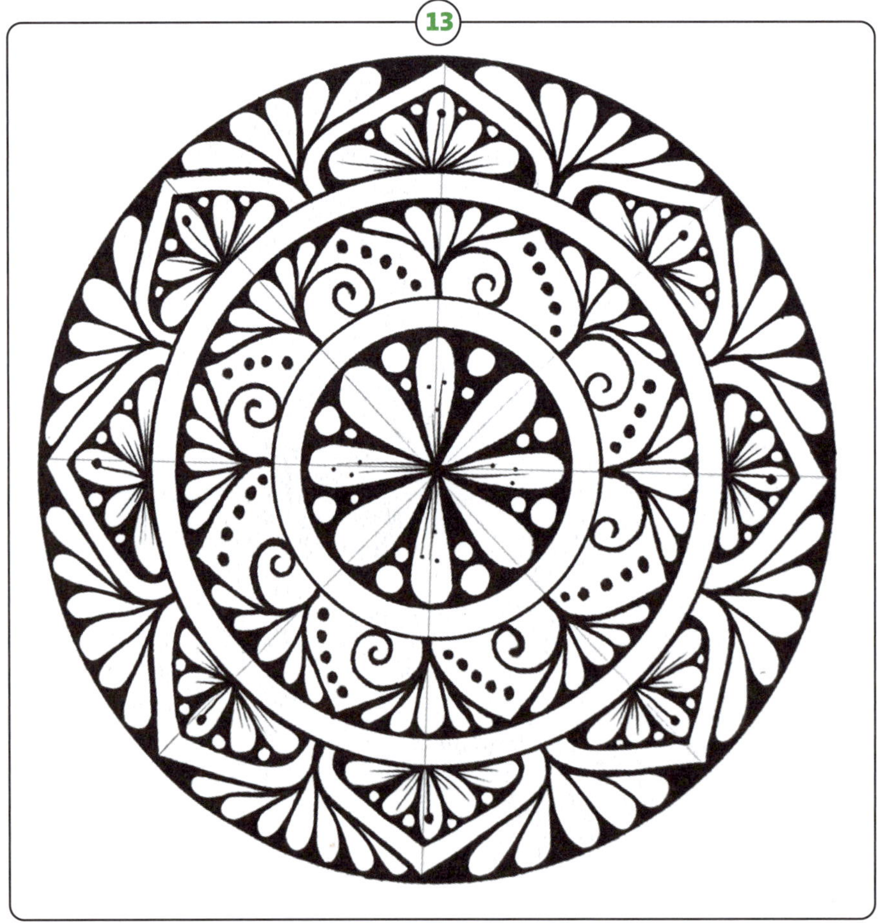

13

Finish detailing. Add some delicate lines and a dot within the teardrops of the pointed leaves.

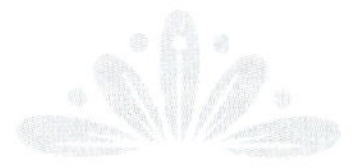

LET'S CHECK IN

How did you feel while drawing the base circles and rays? Did it require a lot of concentration? Did you feel pressure to do them perfectly?

How did you feel while drawing the details?

How did it feel to relax into the drawing process? Were you able to tell stray thoughts to go away peacefully?

The beautiful thing about learning is nobody can take it away from you.
–B.B. King

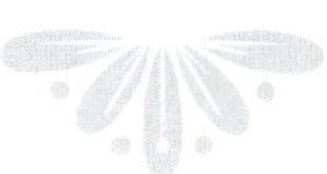

Dense Designs

For your next mandala, we're increasing the number of circles and rings and the density of lines and details. Remember, even something that looks this complex is actually totally achievable when it's broken down step by step!

As you draw this mandala, focus on only paying attention to one step at a time. Don't read ahead and don't compare your unfinished work to the pictured design.

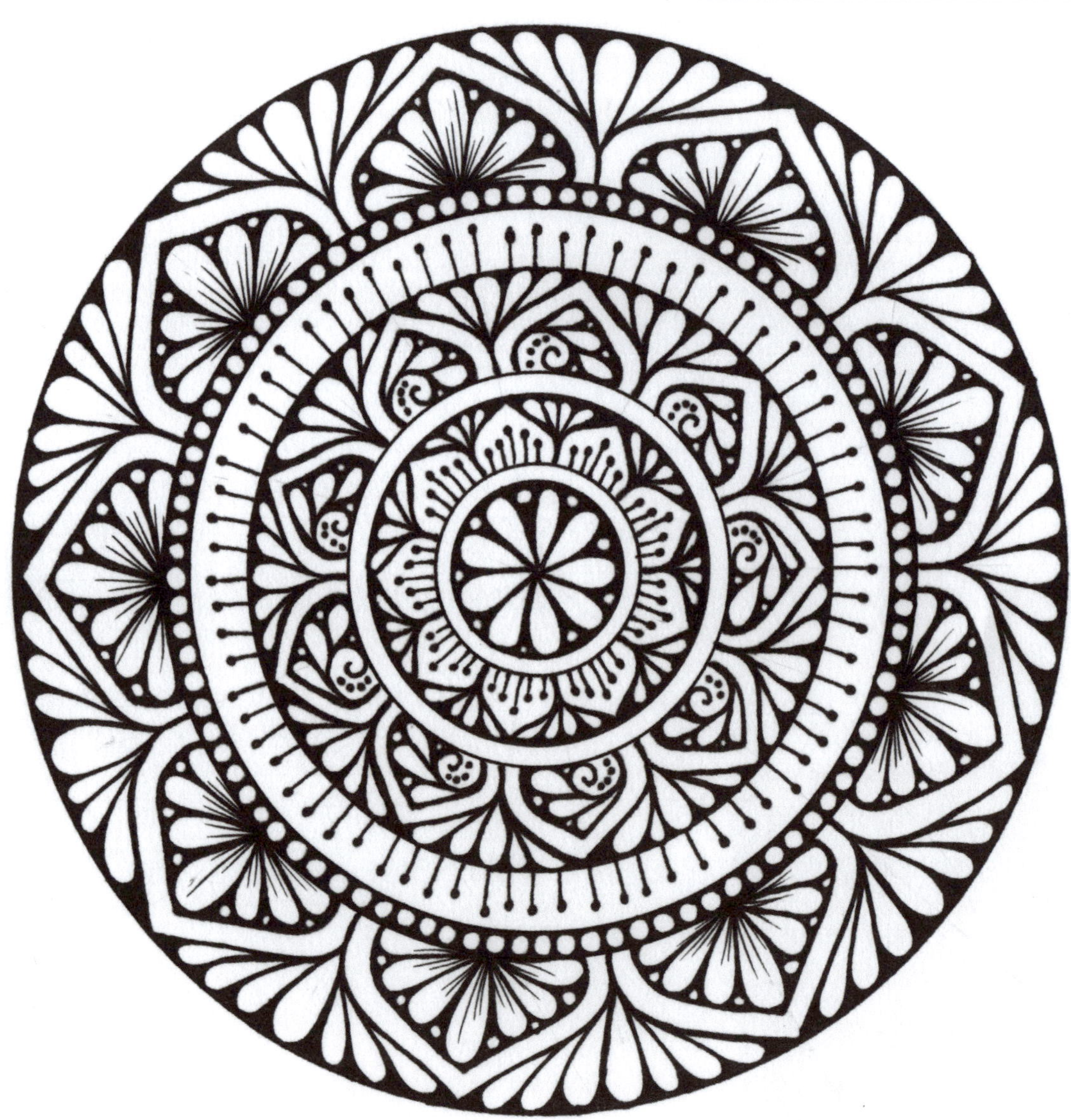

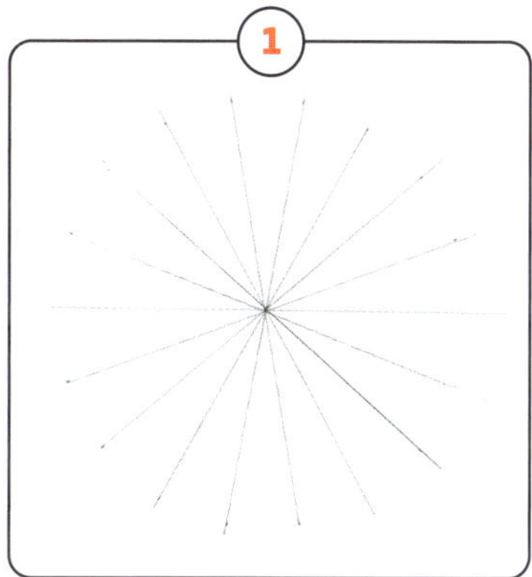

Draw rays. Using pencil, draw a straight horizontal line, then draw a ray every 20° on the top half and bottom half (eight rays total on each half).

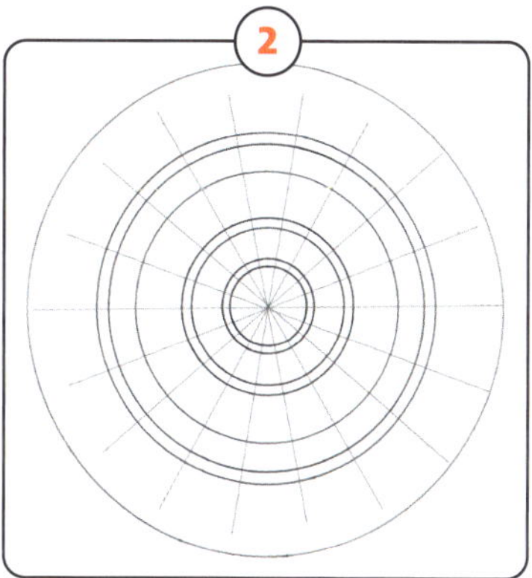

Draw circles. In pen, draw eight circles as shown. For reference, the outermost circle radius is 3½" (9 cm); the innermost circle radius is ⅝" (1.5 cm).

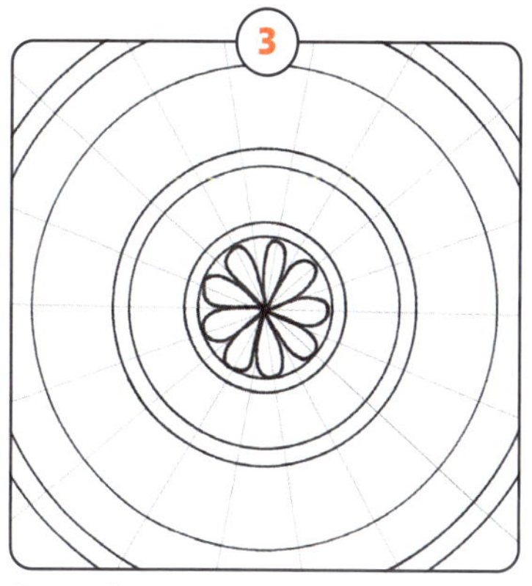

Start the center. Draw nine teardrops centered on alternating rays.

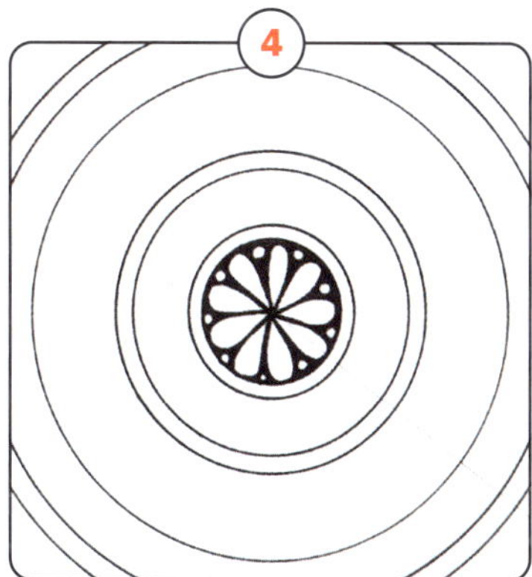

Finish the center. Draw a circle between each teardrop, then fill in around them.

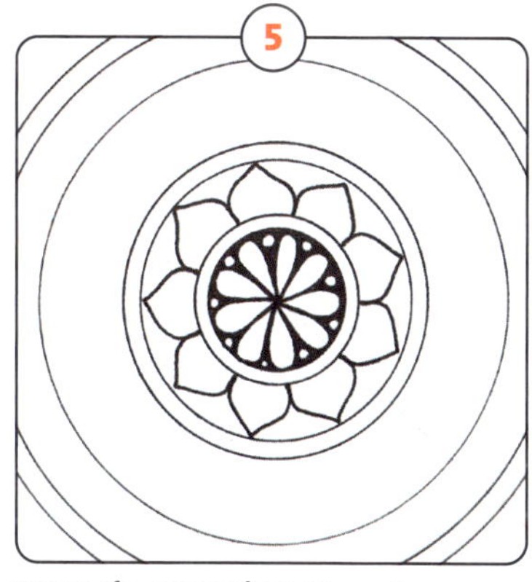

Start the next ring. Draw nine pointed leaves centered on alternating rays—not the same rays as the centers of the initial teardrops.

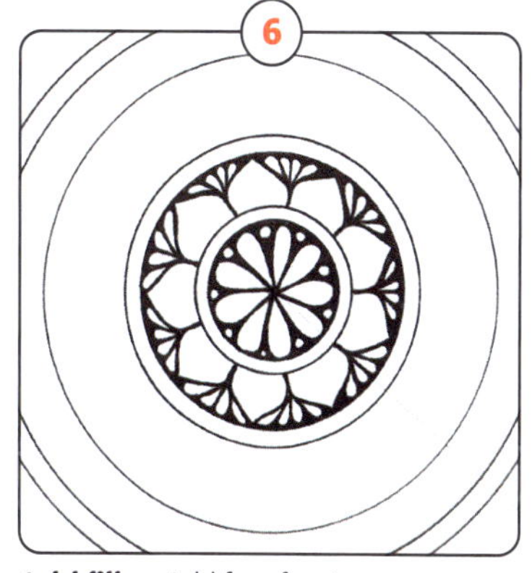

Add filler. Add four fanning-out teardrops between each pointed leaf, then fill in around them.

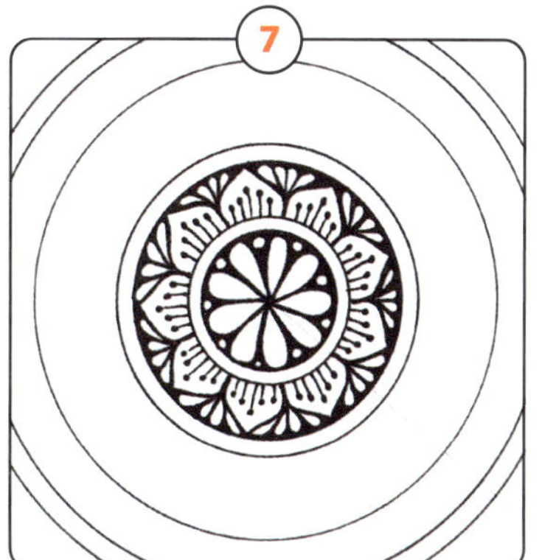

Add details. Add five lines capped with dots to each pointed leaf.

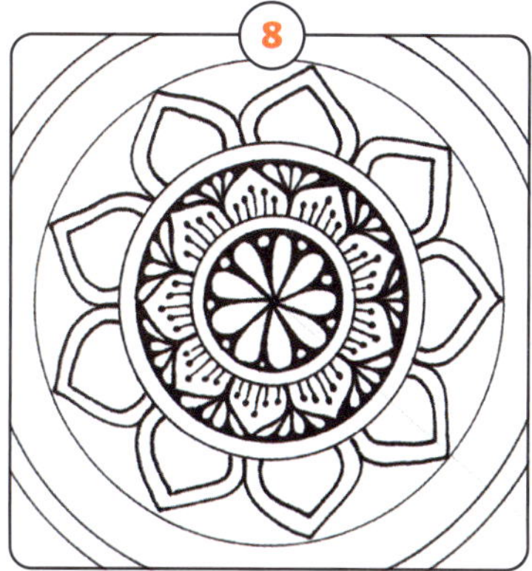

Start the next ring. Draw nine pointed leaves with inset pointed leaves centered on alternating rays—the same rays as the centers of the initial teardrops.

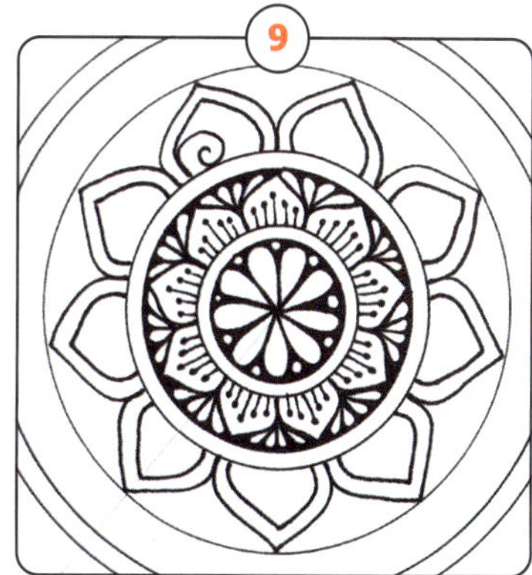

Draw a curl. Inside one inset pointed leaf, draw a curling line.

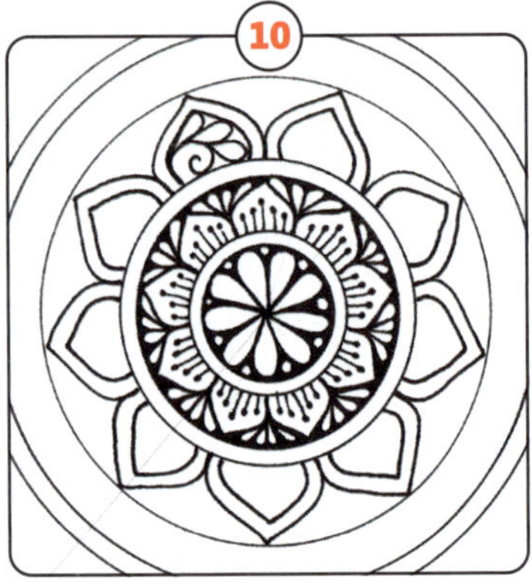

Add teardrops. Add three teardrops along the outside of the curling line.

Add dots and fill in. Add four dots inside the curling line. Freehand three tiny circles between the teardrops, then fill in around them.

Repeat this pattern. Repeat the established design inside all inset pointed leaves in this ring.

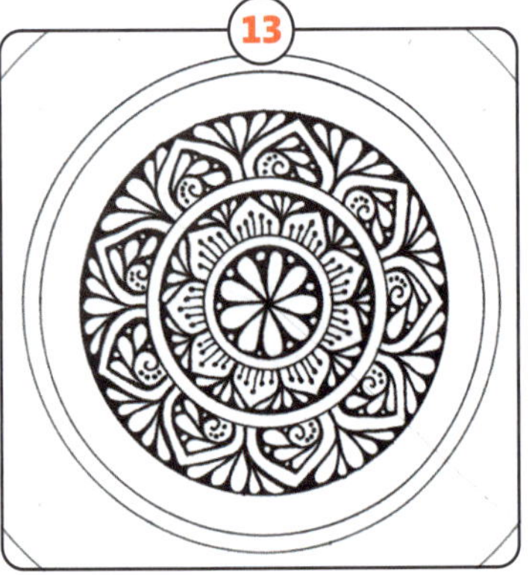

Finish the ring. Add five fanning-out teardrops between each pointed leaf, then fill in around them.

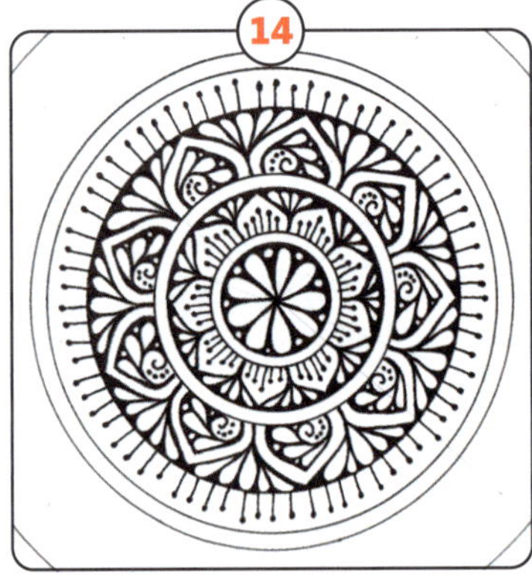

Complete the next small ring. Around the entire next ring, draw lines capped with dots.

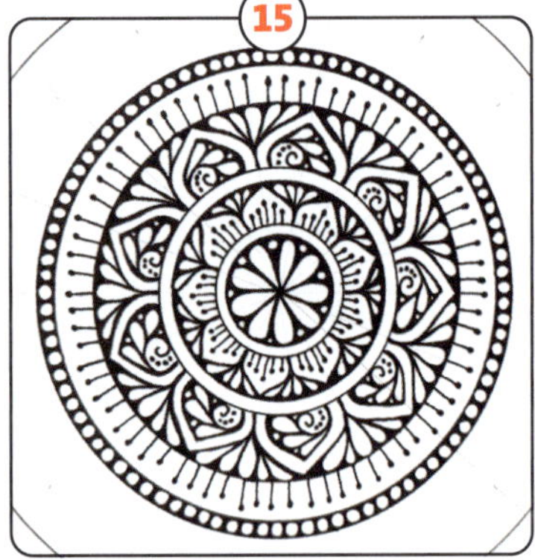

Complete the next very small ring. Around the entire next ring, draw freehand circles, then fill in around them.

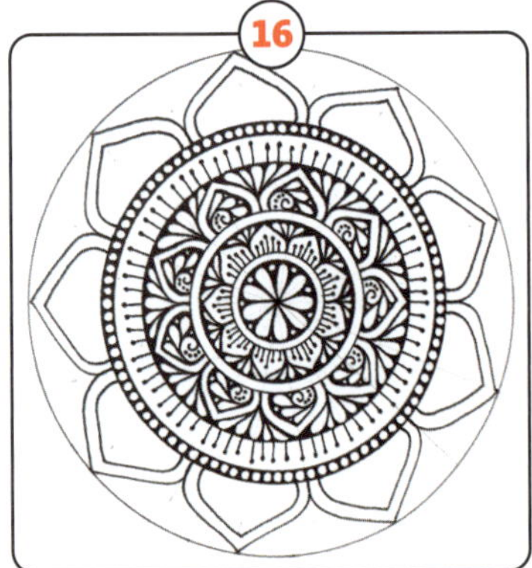

Start the final ring. Draw nine pointed leaves with inset pointed leaves centered on alternating rays—not the same rays as the centers of the initial teardrops.

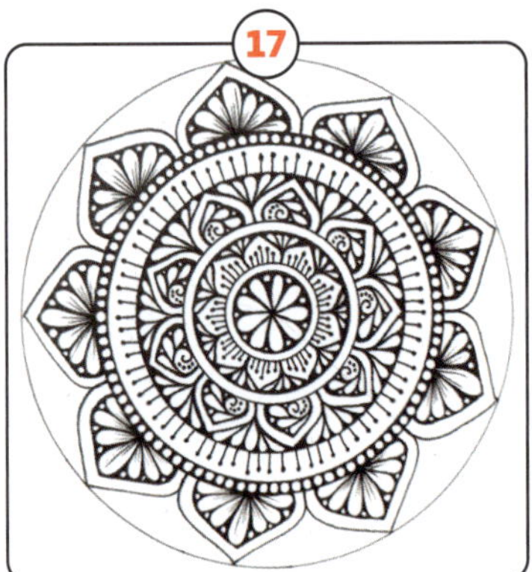

Add a pattern. Inside each inset leaf, draw seven fanning-out teardrops, draw a circle between each teardrop and fill in around them, and add delicate line details.

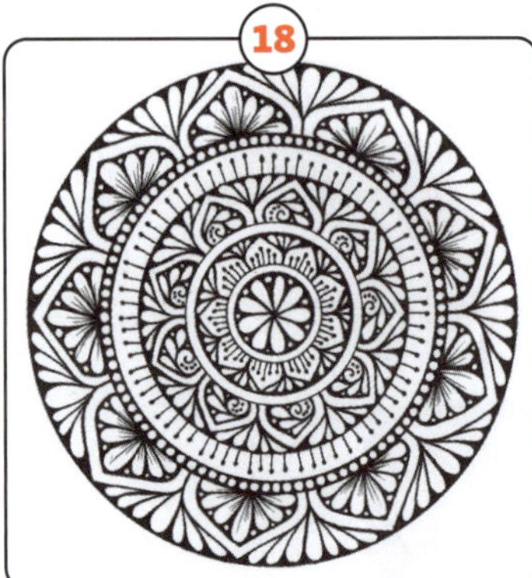

Finish the final ring. Add seven fanning-out teardrops between each pointed leaf, then fill in around them.

LET'S CHECK IN

How did you feel while tackling this more complicated mandala?

Did you trip up anywhere or make any mistakes while drawing? How did you react? How did you move on?

Were you able to follow the set intention? How happy are you with your finished mandala? How much does the finished mandala matter to you, versus the experience of drawing it?

If you aren't making any mistakes,
it's a sure sign you're playing it too safe.
–John Maxwell

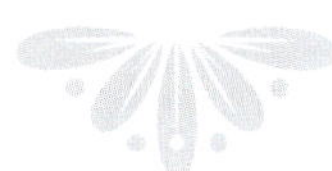

Simple Flower

Let's break away from the classic circle and learn how to add "petals"! The basic pointed-leaf shape can easily be turned into large petals that seem to sprout from the mandala circle, turning it into a flower. For this design, we'll lean into the floral theme through the details.

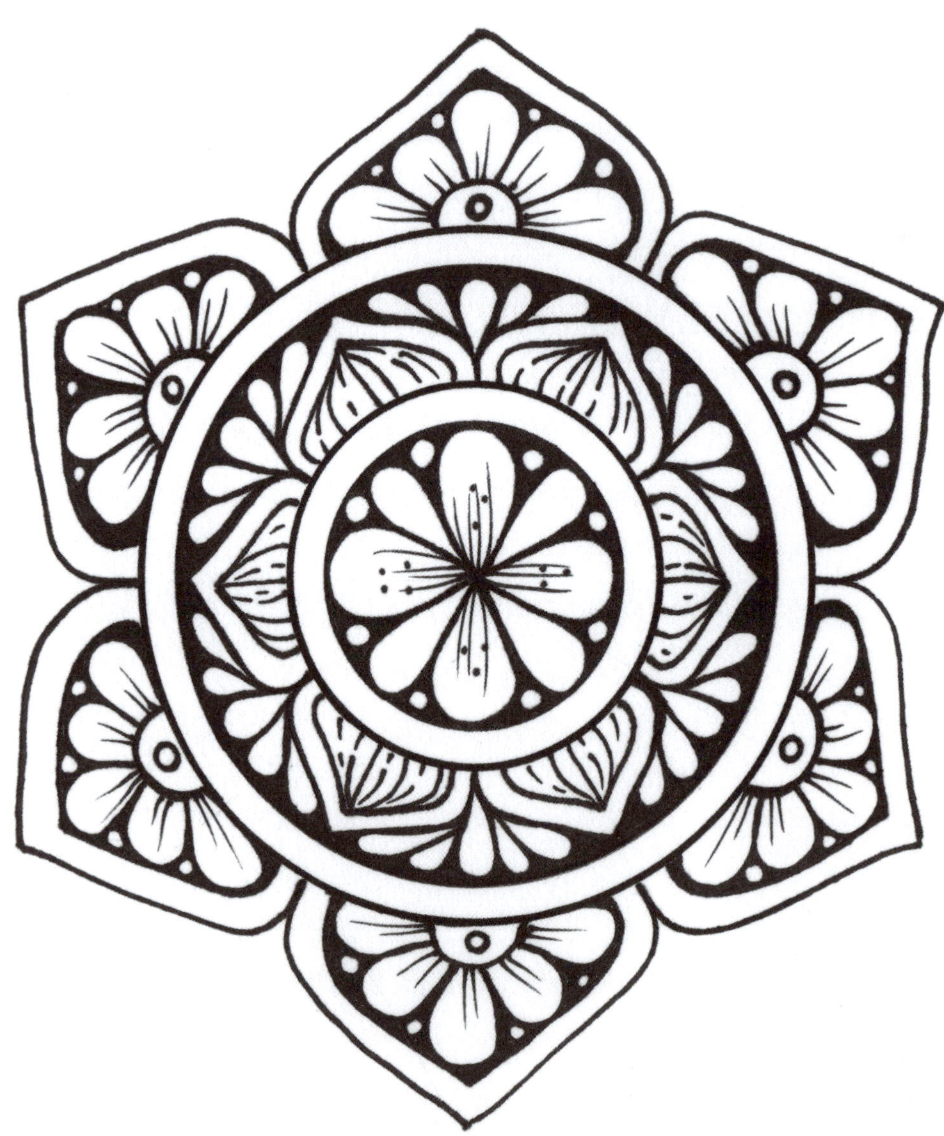

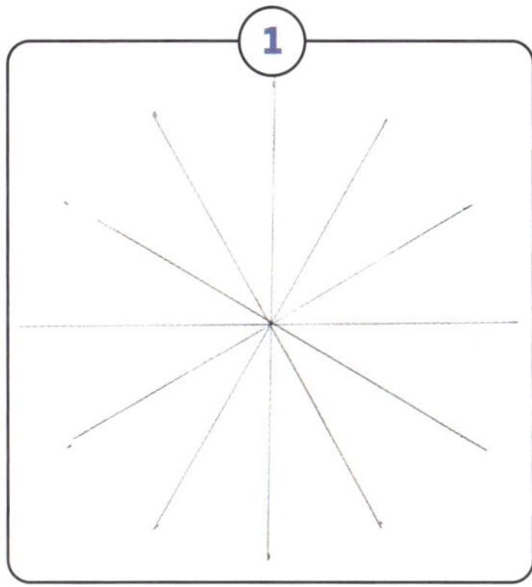

Draw rays. Using pencil, draw a straight horizontal line, then draw a ray every 30° on the top half and bottom half (five rays total on each half).

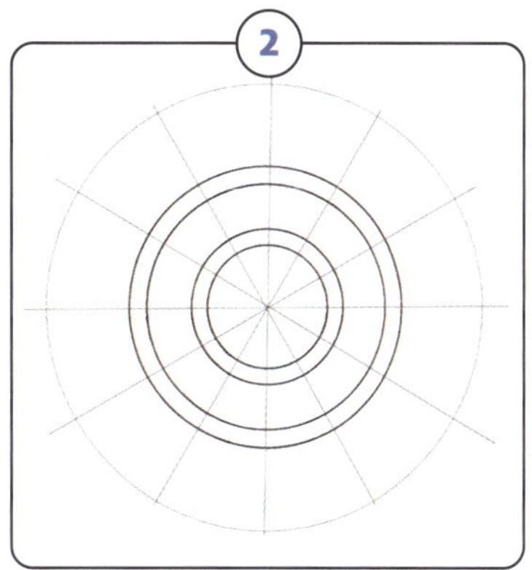

Draw circles. Draw five circles as shown, the last only in pencil. For reference, the outermost circle radius is 2¾" (7 cm); the innermost circle radius is ¾" (2 cm).

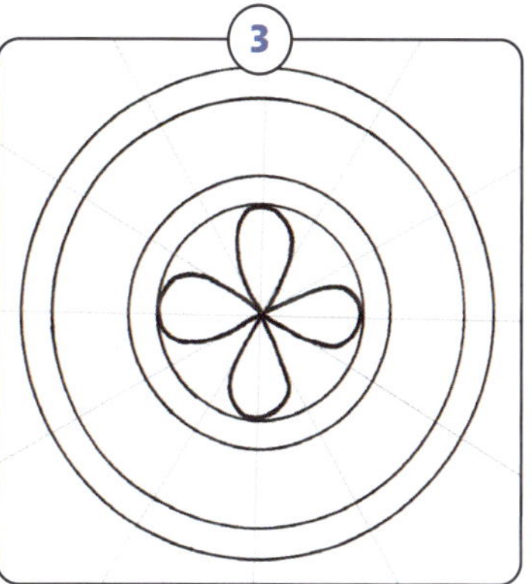

Draw teardrops. Draw four teardrops centered on the vertical and horizontal rays.

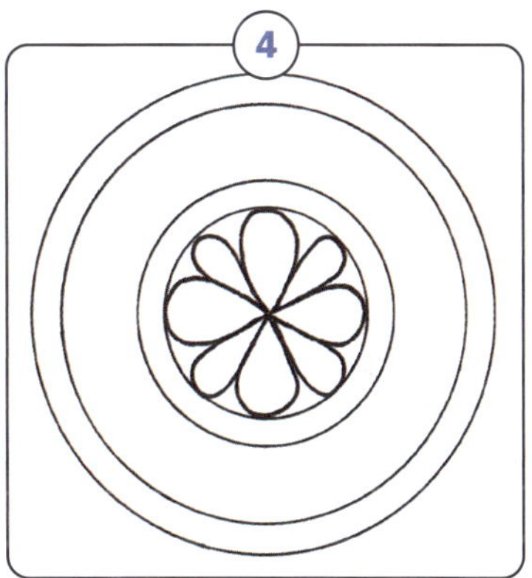

Add more teardrops. Draw four more teardrops, one between each existing teardrop.

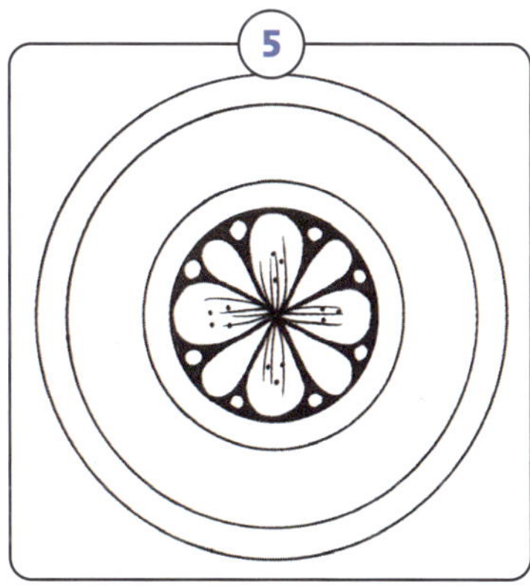

Add filler and details. Draw a freehand circle between each teardrop, then fill in around them. Add some delicate lines and dots within the first four teardrops.

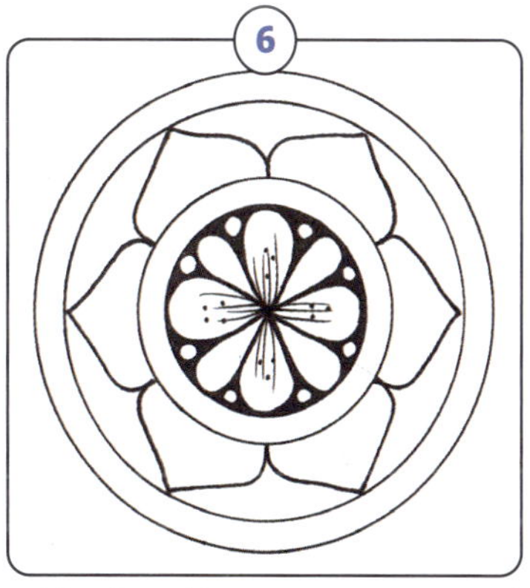

Add pointed leaves. Draw six pointed leaves centered on alternating rays, starting with the horizontal ray.

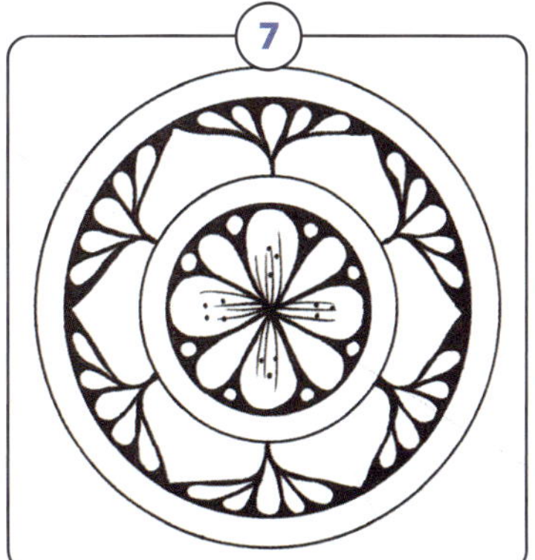

Draw teardrops. Draw five teardrops between each pointed leaf, then fill in around them.

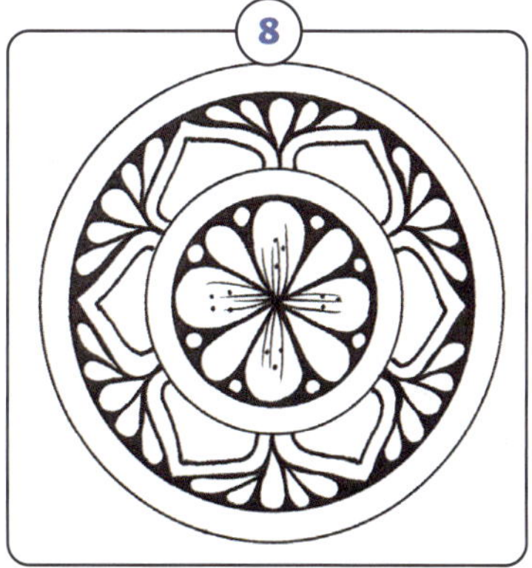

Add insets. Add an inset pointed leaf to each existing pointed leaf.

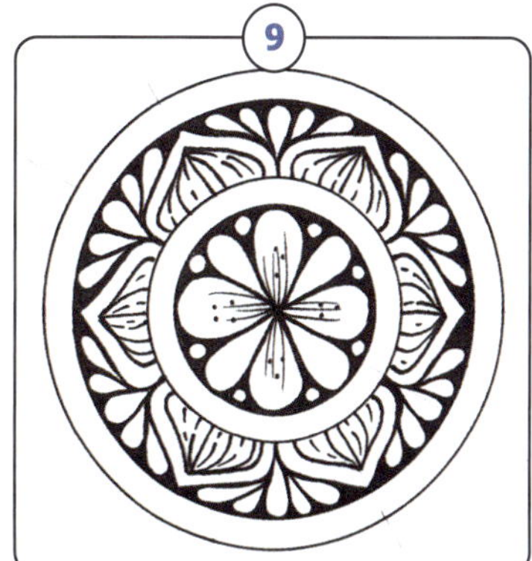

Detail the insets. Add solid and broken lines to the inset pointed leaves to give them a textured, rounded effect—imagine an onion.

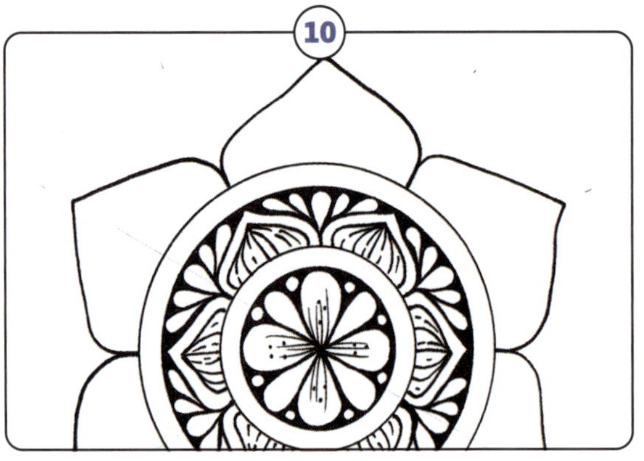

Add pointed leaves. Draw six pointed leaves centered on alternating rays, starting with the vertical ray.

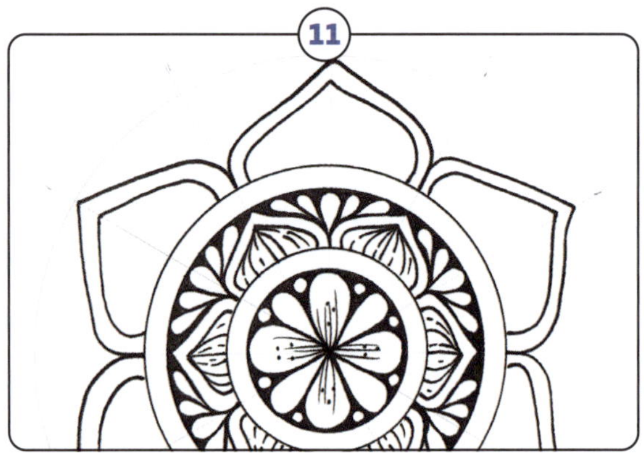

Add insets. Add an inset pointed leaf to each of these new pointed leaves.

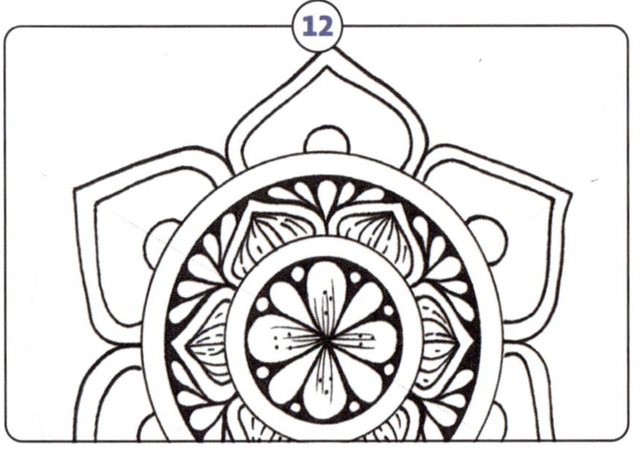

Add domes. Add a dome (a semicircle) at the bottom of each of the pointed leaves.

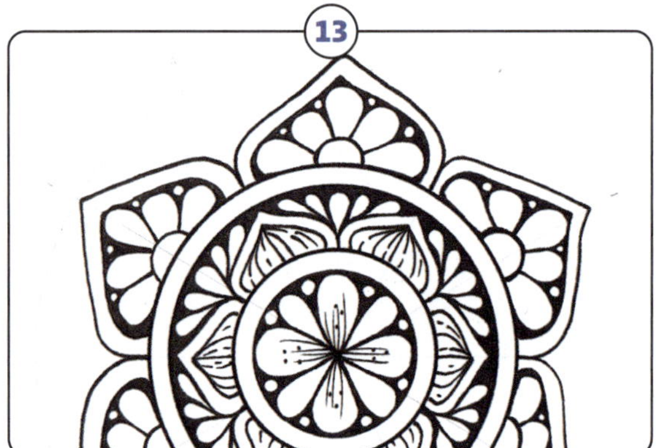

Add petals and filler. Draw five petals emanating from each dome. Draw a freehand circle between each petal, then fill in around them.

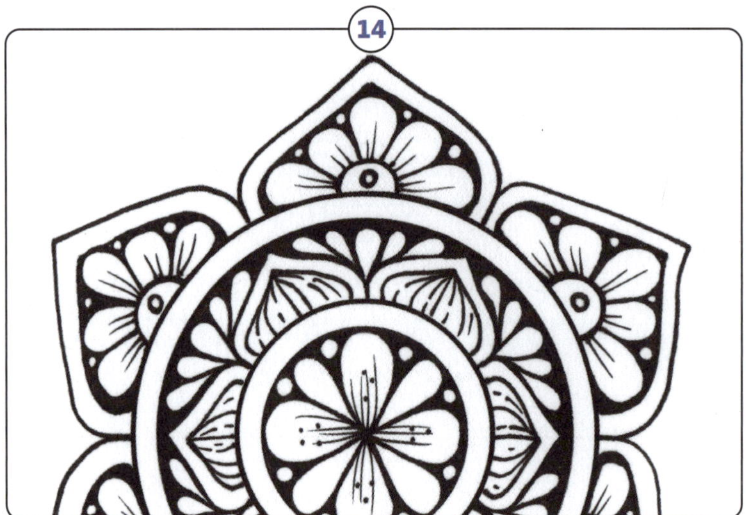

Finish with final details. Add some delicate lines within each of the five petals. Draw one freehand circle inside each dome. And don't forget to erase!

LET'S CHECK IN

How did it feel to break away from the classic circle mandala shape?
Do you prefer one shape over the other?

Did you enjoy having something concrete—a flower—in mind as you
drew this mandala, or did you find it distracting?

Can you feel your own mandala drawing skills blooming and growing
like a flower? Describe the feeling.

A flower blossoms for its own joy.
–Oscar Wilde

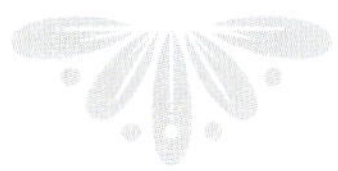

Elaborate Flower

It's time to build on what you learned in the previous mandala to make an even bigger, more complex flower-style design. This time, you'll practice adding lots of freehand circles as well as aura details—that is, details that fall outside of the established circles or core shape of the mandala.

As you draw this mandala, imagine the mandala is a growing flower and all the dots and circles and teardrops you are adding are droplets of rain, nourishing the flower and your creativity.

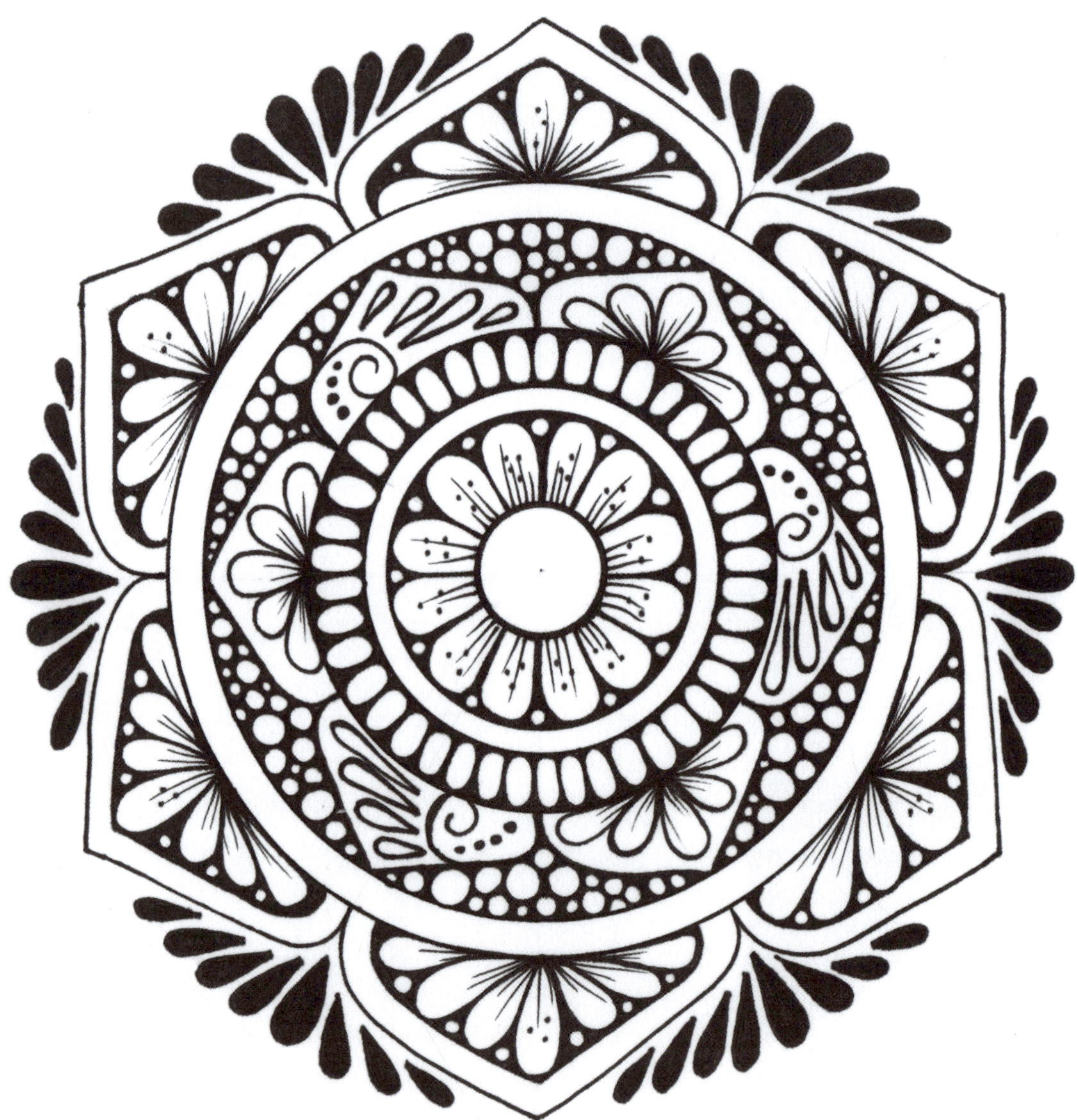

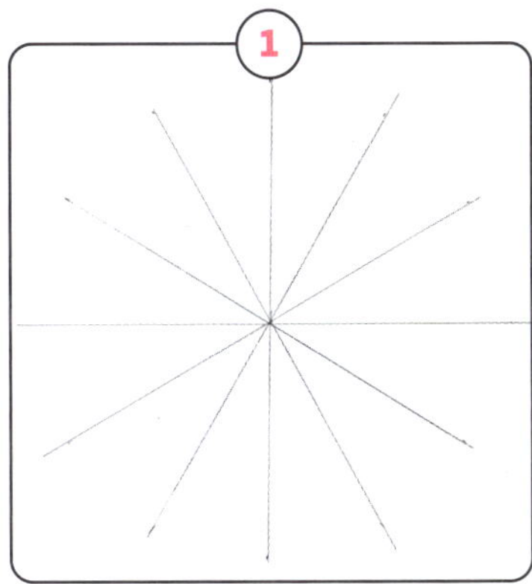

Draw rays. Using pencil, draw a straight horizontal line, then draw a ray every 30° on the top half and bottom half (five rays total on each half).

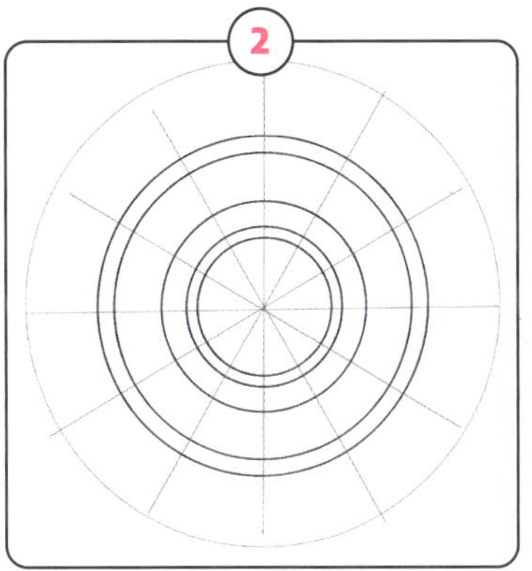

Draw circles. Draw six circles as shown, the last only in pencil. For reference, the outermost circle radius is 3⅜" (8.5 cm); the innermost circle radius is ⅜" (1 cm).

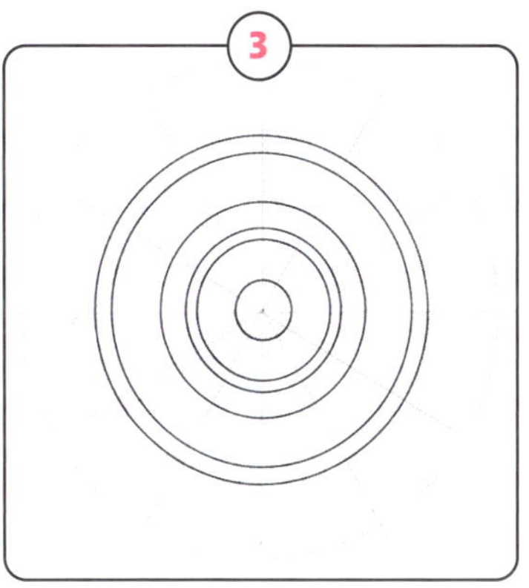

Add one more circle. Add one more circle to the very center. This is an opportunity for you to learn that you can always adjust a mandala after you start!

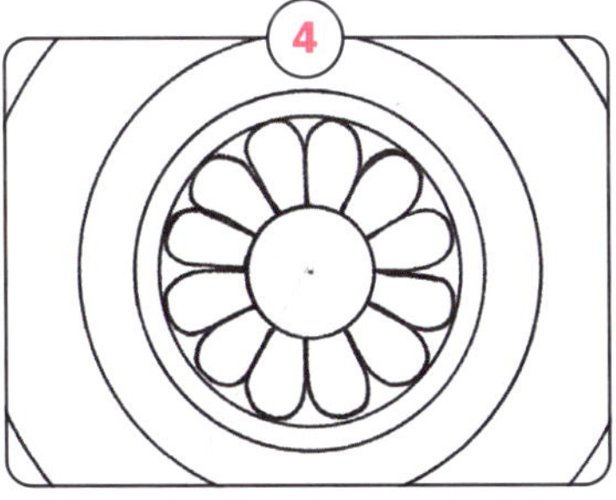

Add petals. Along the outside of the innermost circle, add a petal between each ray.

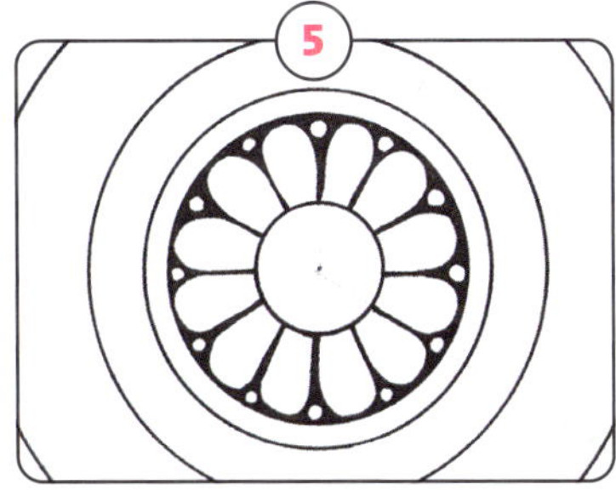

Add circles and filler. Draw a freehand circle between each petal, then fill in around them.

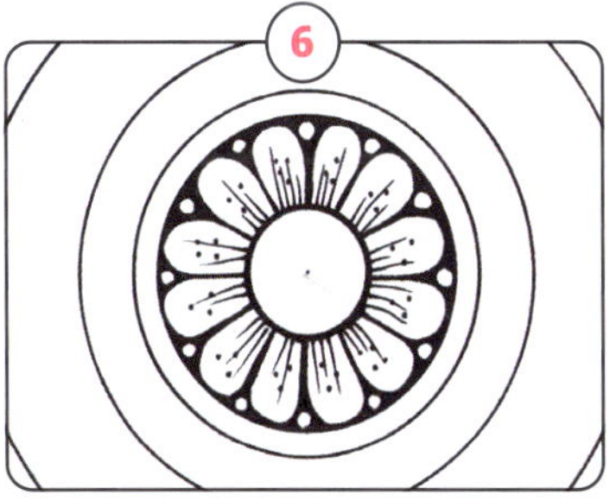

Add details. Draw delicate lines and dots inside each petal.

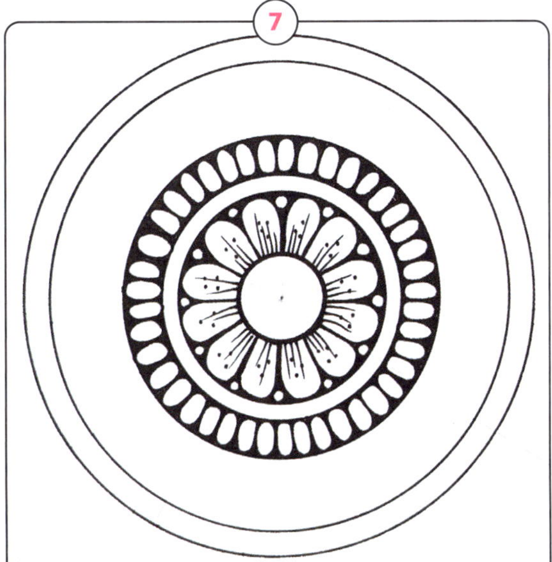

Fill the next ring. In the next medium ring, draw tightly packed ovals, then fill in around them.

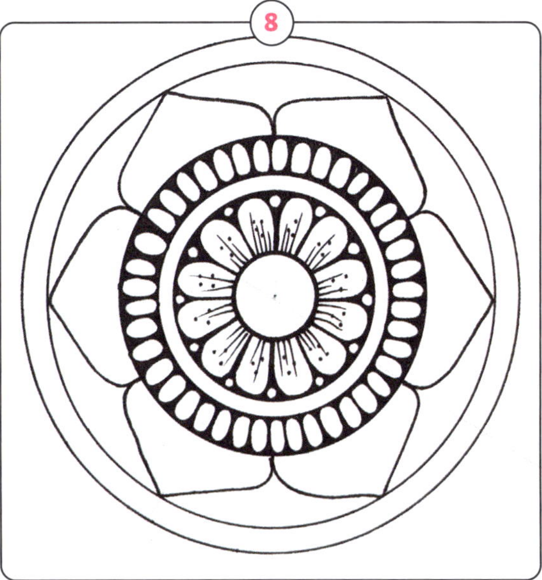

Add pointed leaves. In the next ring, draw six pointed leaves centered on alternating rays, starting with the horizontal ray.

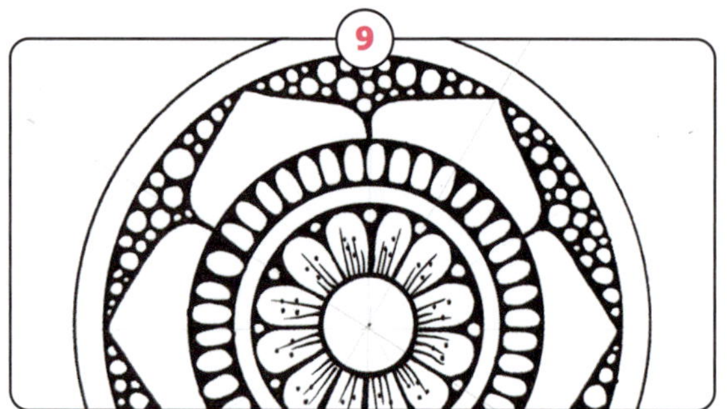

Add lots of circles. Draw lots of freehand circles of varying sizes between each pointed leaf, then fill in around them.

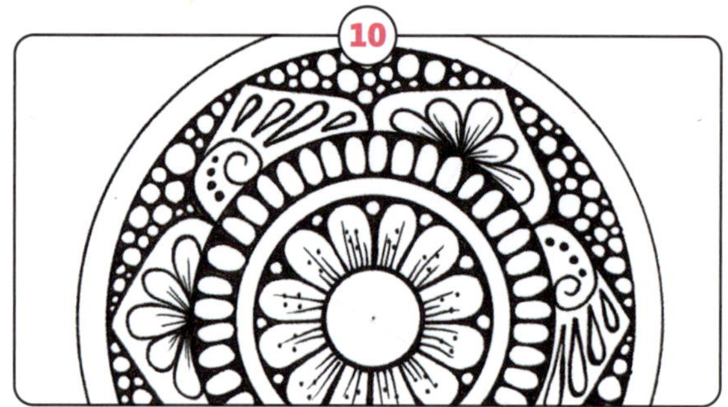

Get creative with patterns. Taking inspiration from previous mandalas in this book, fill the six pointed leaves with two different alternating patterns as shown.

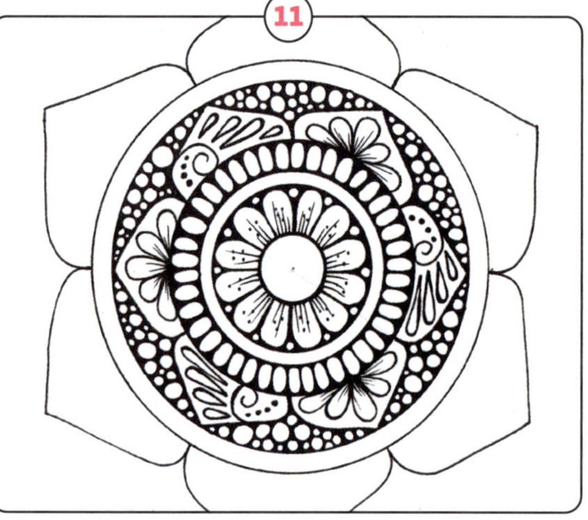

Add more pointed leaves. In a new ring, draw six pointed leaves centered on alternating rays, starting with the vertical ray.

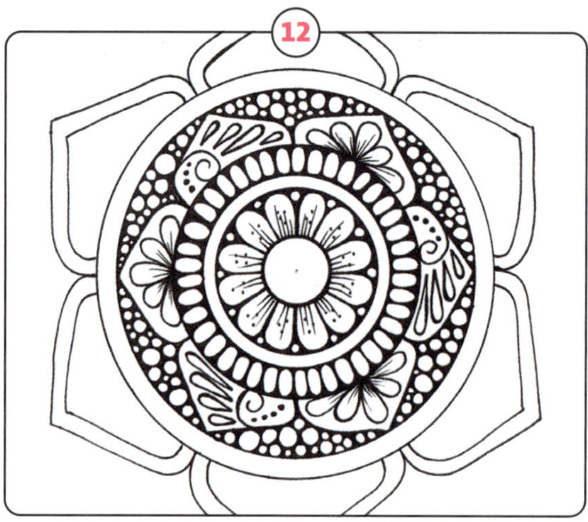

Add insets. Add an inset pointed leaf to each of these new pointed leaves.

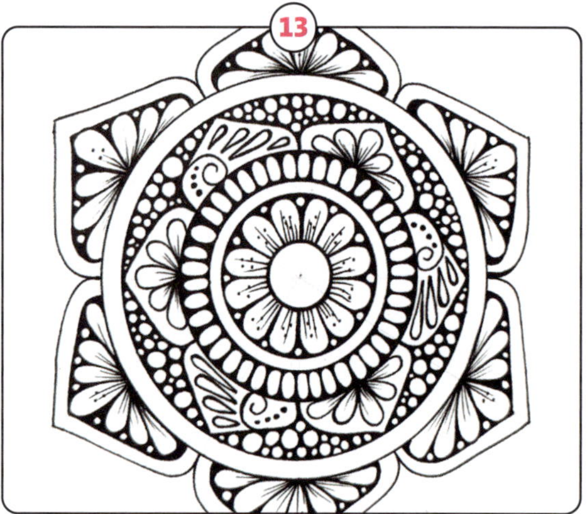

Fill the leaves. In each leaf, draw seven teardrops with a freehand circle between each one, then fill in around them. Add delicate lines and dots inside the teardrops.

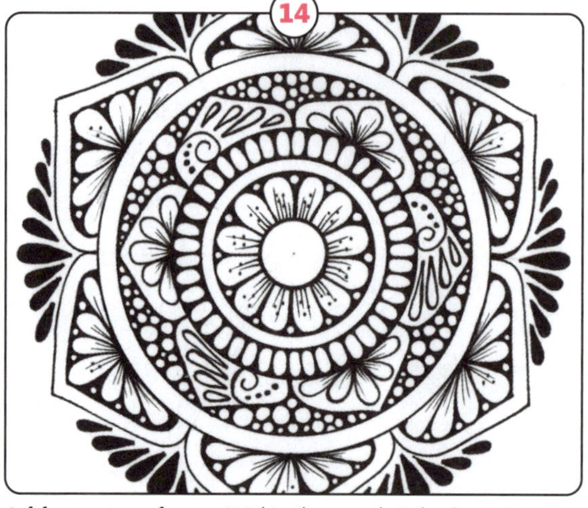

Add aura teardrops. Within the pencil circle, draw nine filled-in teardrops emanating or spraying out from the mandala, but not touching it, between each leaf.

LET'S CHECK IN

At one point in these mandala steps, you examined the mandala to understand the pattern to draw. Was it easy, hard, fun, or frustrating?

How did you feel while freehanding the final teardrops? Did you notice that the final mandala doesn't have exactly nine teardrops per section?

Do you feel nourished and refreshed after completing this mandala, or do you feel tired or strained? If the latter, what could you change about your drawing process?

*If you tend to a flower, it will bloom,
no matter how many weeds surround it.*
–Matshona Dhliwayo

Lovely Layers

For the last step-by-step mandala of this section before you tackle the final challenge, come back to the classic circular mandala design, but take it to the next level by incorporating more-dense designs within single rings, working with even more rays, and adding in some new shapes, such as domes.

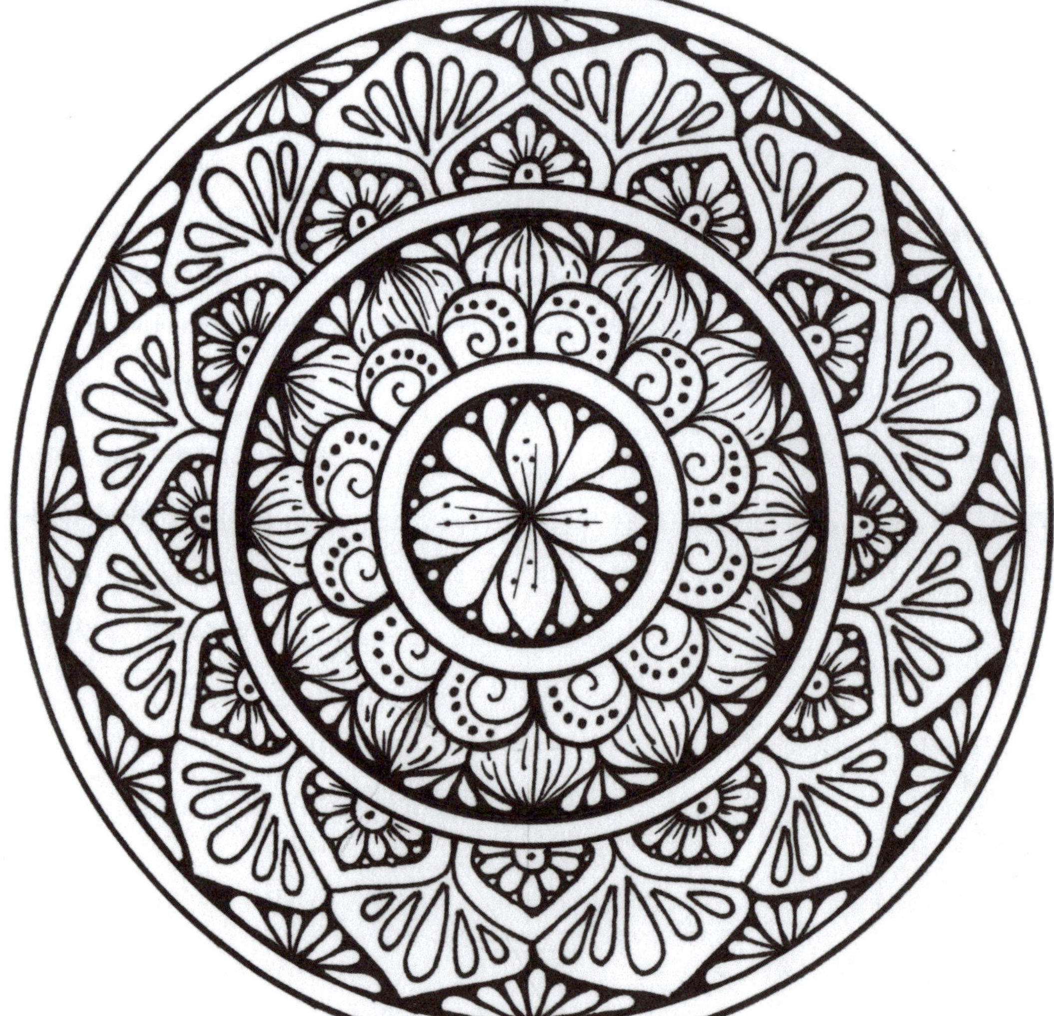

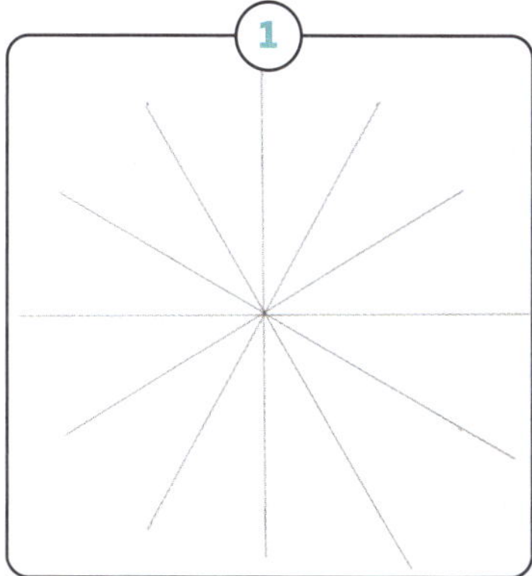

Draw rays. Using pencil, draw a straight horizontal line, then draw a ray every 30° on the top half and bottom half (five rays total on each half).

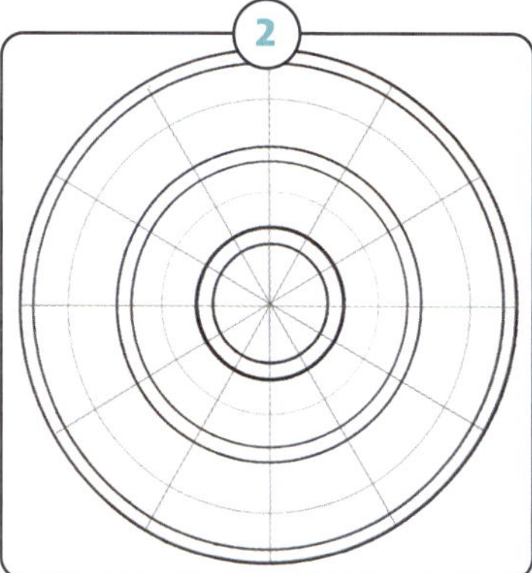

Draw circles. Draw eight circles as shown, in a mix of pencil and pen. For reference, the outermost circle radius is 3⅛" (8 cm); the innermost circle radius is ¾" (2 cm).

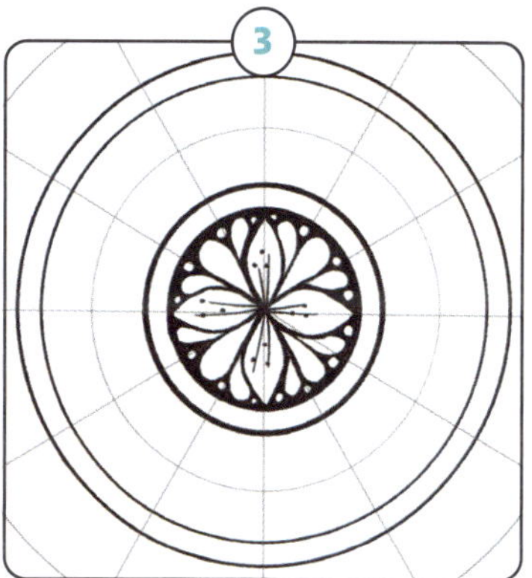

Fill the center. Create a design that fills the center. You can follow the design shown, make up your own, or choose one of the examples from the front of the book!

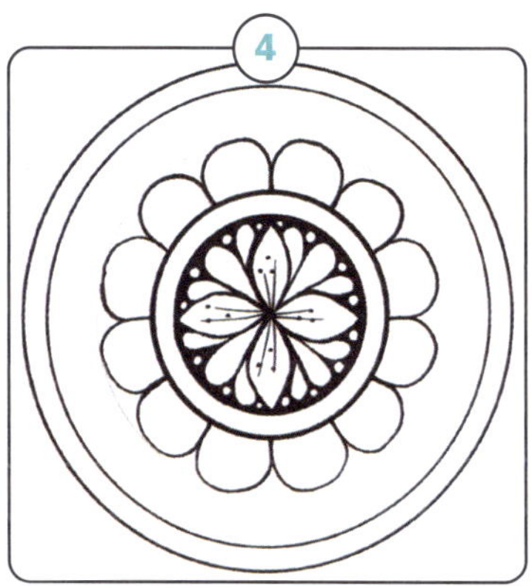

Add domes. Draw a dome between each ray in one entire ring.

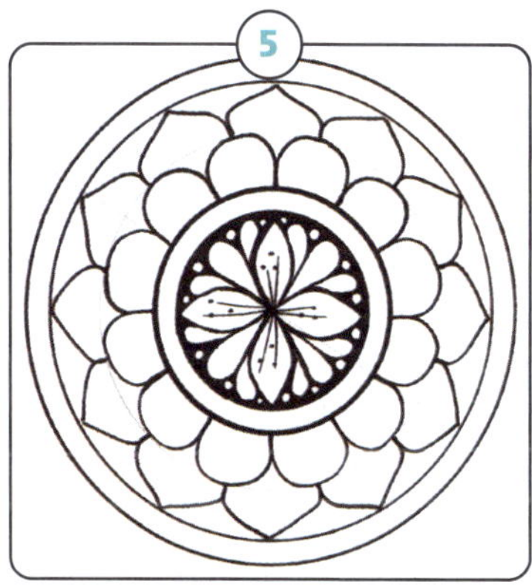

Add pointed leaves. In the next ring, draw a pointed leaf centered on each ray.

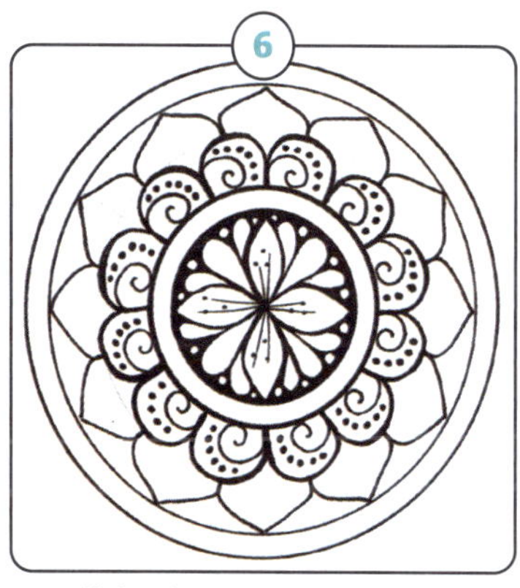

Detail the domes. Add a curling line and a series of dots to each dome.

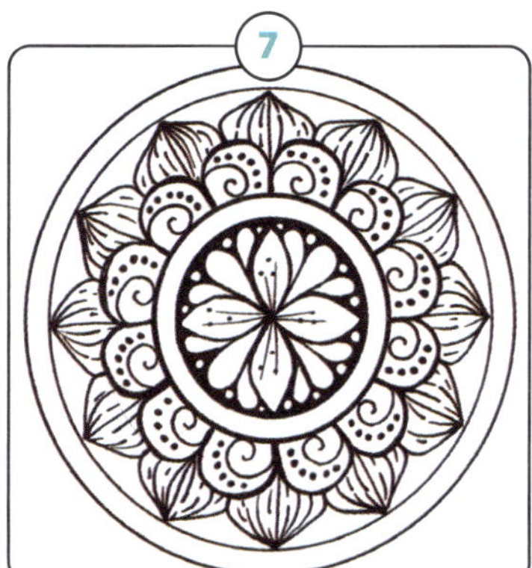

Detail the pointed leaves. Add solid and broken lines to each pointed leaf to give them a textured, rounded effect—imagine an onion.

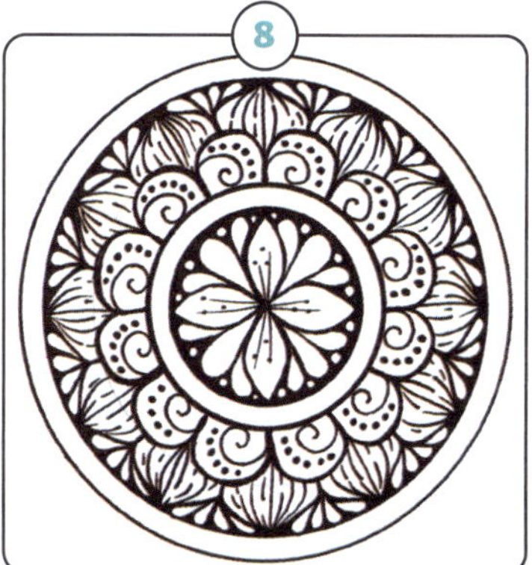

Add teardrops. Draw four teardrops between each pointed leaf, then fill in around them.

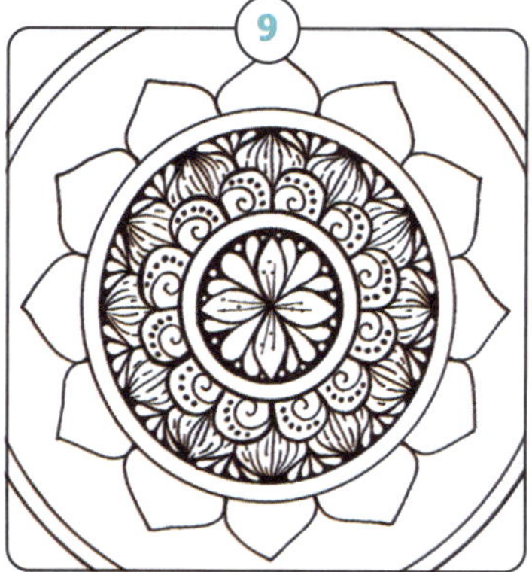

Start a new ring. Draw a pointed leaf centered on each ray in a new ring.

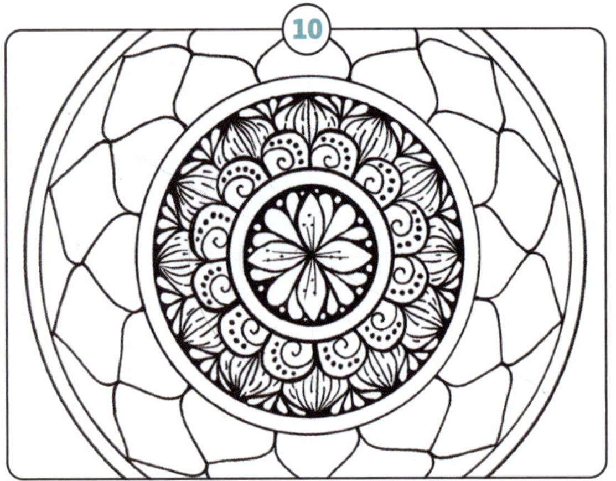

Jump to another ring. In the next ring, draw a pointed leaf between each ray.

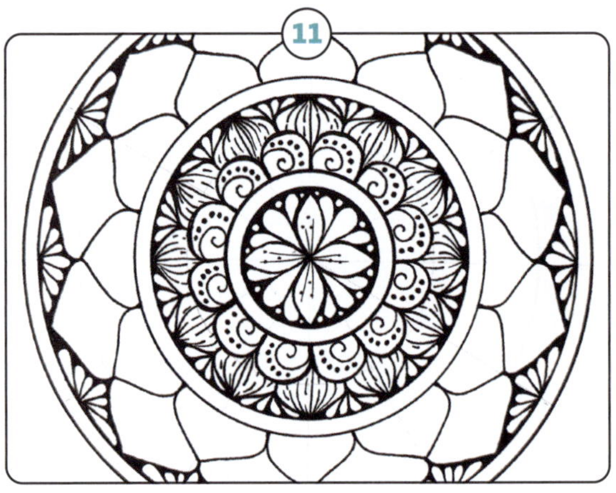

Add teardrops. Draw seven teardrops between each pointed leaf in the last ring you drew, this time emanating the teardrops down from the top. Fill in around them.

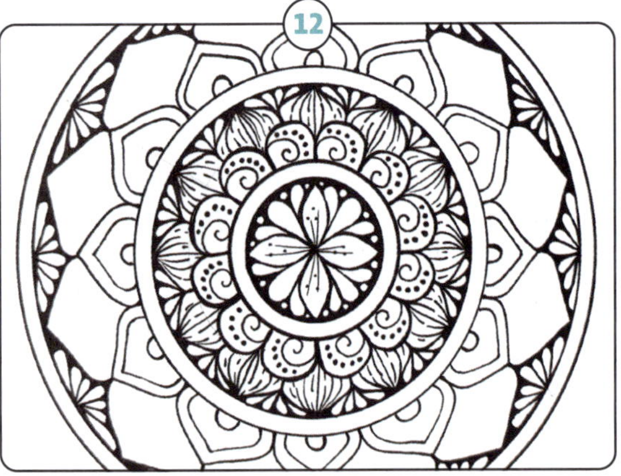

Start detailing the leaves. In the first ring of pointed leaves, add an inset pointed leaf as well as a small dome.

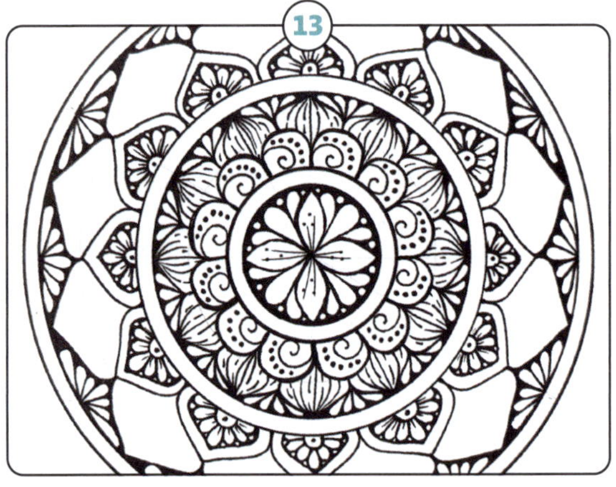

Finish the leaves. Add seven petals with a freehand circle between each petal, then fill in around them. Add a dot to each dome and a delicate detail line to each petal.

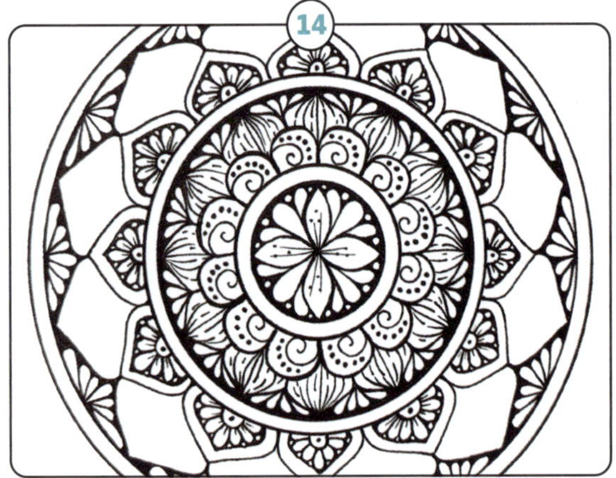

Thicken the middle ring edge. Go back to the middle ring's outer edge and thicken it with your pen to give it more presence.

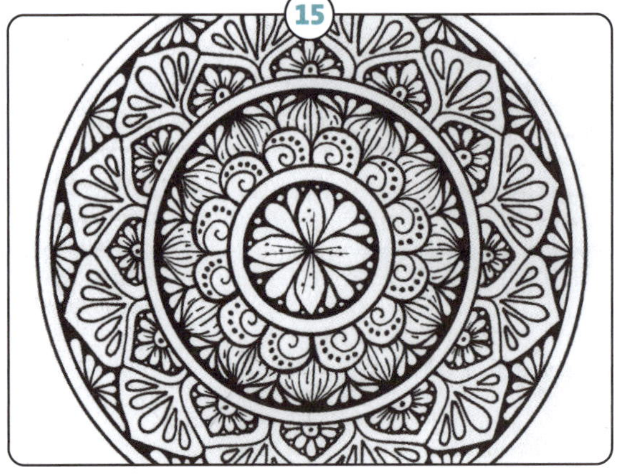

Finish with teardrops. Add five floating teardrops inside the remaining empty pointed leaves.

LET'S CHECK IN

How did it feel to start working on two different rings at once and move back and forth between them?

Were you able to intentionally slow down while drawing this mandala? Did you notice your posture changing, your breathing changing, or other positive changes?

If you've been following along with the book, this is your fifth mandala. Do you feel ready to take on the upcoming independent challenge mandala?

You can, you should, and
if you're brave enough to start, you will.
–Stephen King

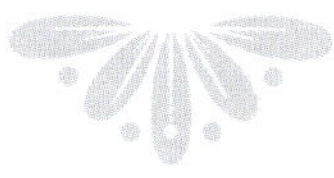

Circles Galore

CHALLENGE YOURSELF

It's time to take the training wheels off! Use what you learned while working on the previous mandalas to build up this design yourself independently, referring to just the few basic steps that are provided as guideposts.

As you draw this mandala, let go of your expectations that everything will be clearly laid out for you, but also let go of your expectation that you will re-create exactly the mandala shown.

52

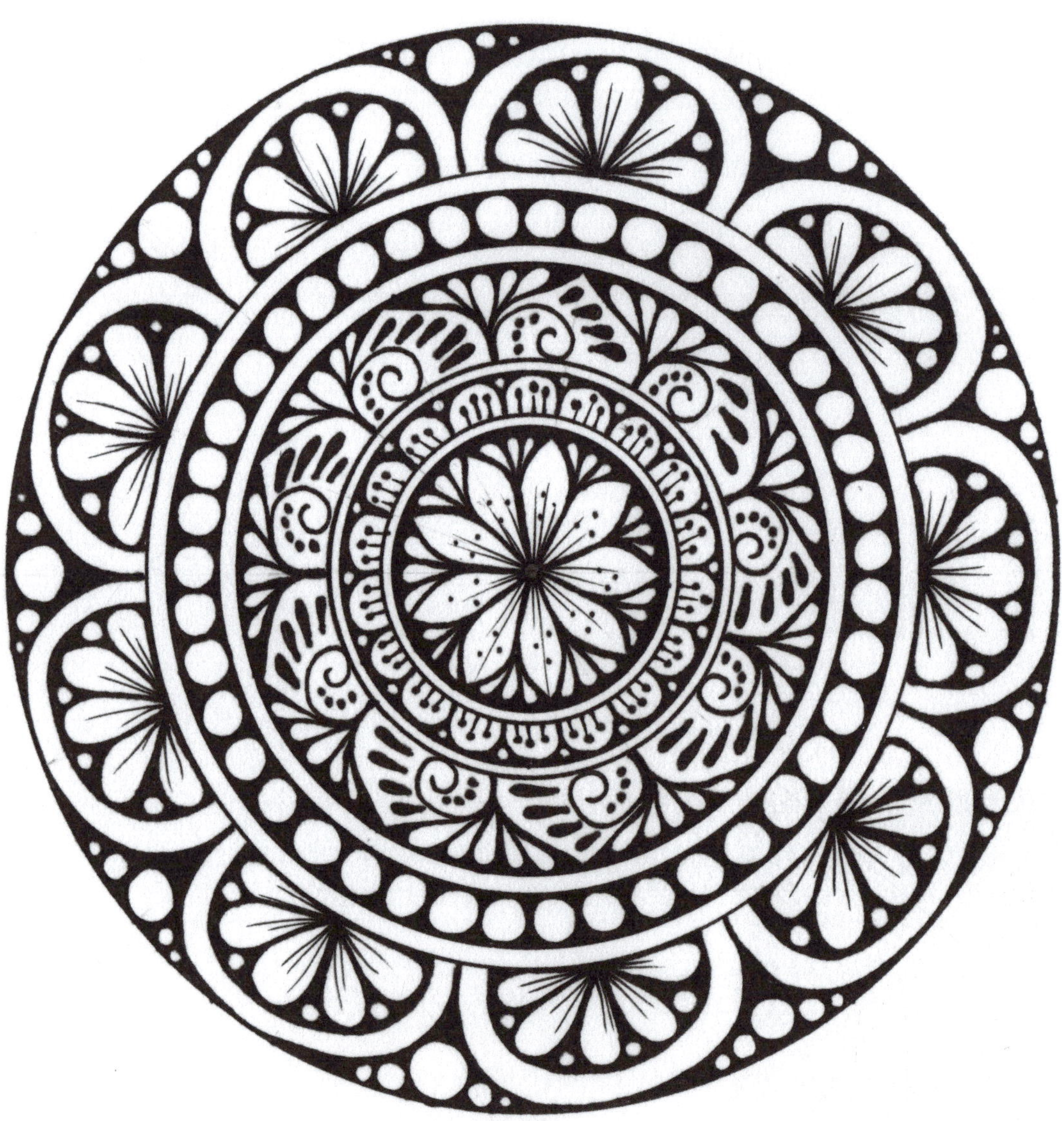

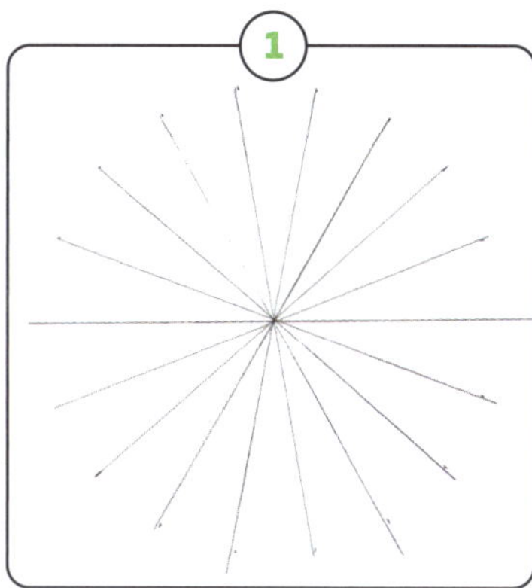

Draw rays. Using pencil, draw a straight horizontal line, then draw a ray every 20° on the top half and bottom half (eight rays total on each half).

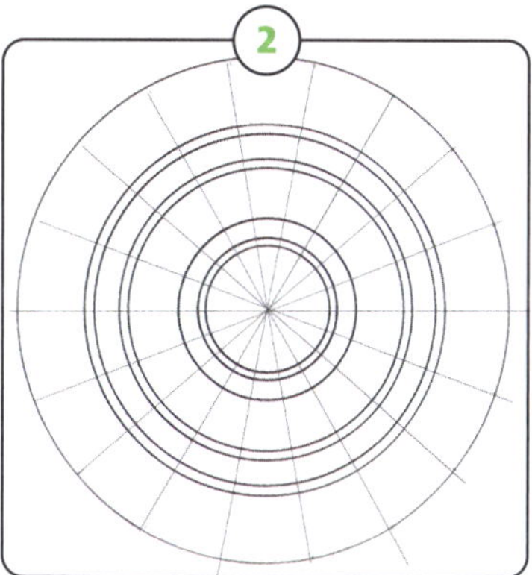

Draw circles. In pen, draw eight circles as shown. For reference, the outermost circle radius is 3⅛" (8 cm); the innermost circle radius is ¾" (2 cm).

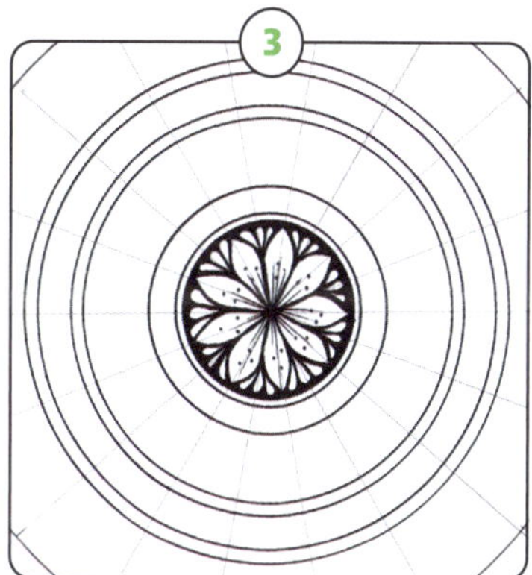

Create a center design. Draw a detailed center design inspired by a flower.

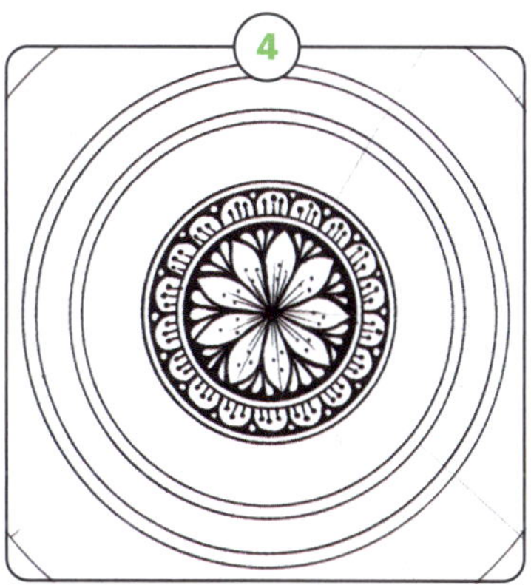

Fill the next ring. Create a design that fills the next ring with elements like domes, tiny freehand circles, and lines capped with dots.

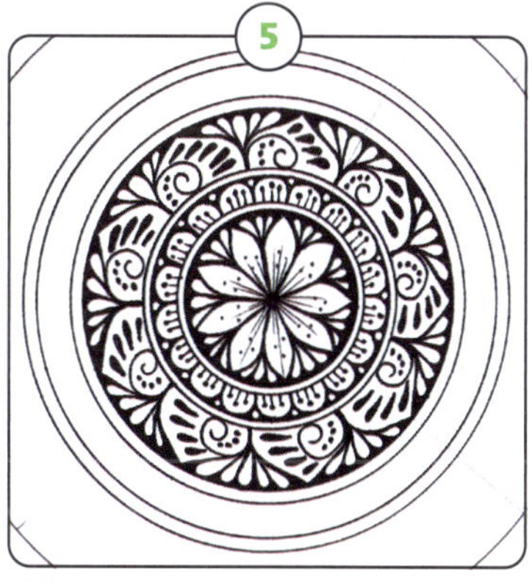

Fill a new ring. Create a design that fills the next ring with elements like pointed leaves, teardrops, curling lines, and dots.

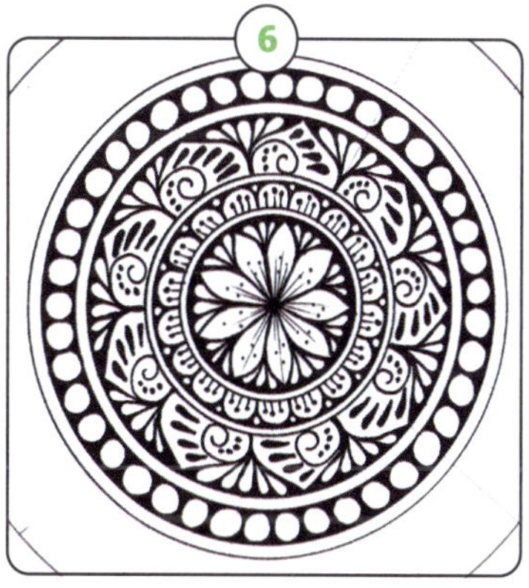

Make a simpler ring. Fill a new ring with a simpler design—in this case, tightly packed circles.

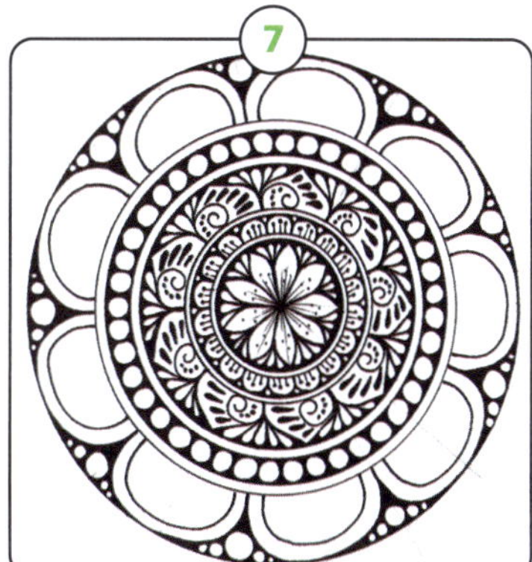

Start the final ring. Draw domes with inset domes as well as freehand circles of various sizes.

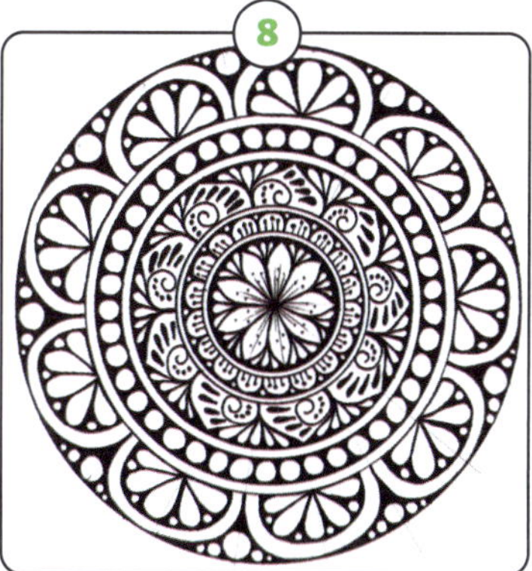

Finish the final ring. Fill the domes with teardrops and more freehand circles.

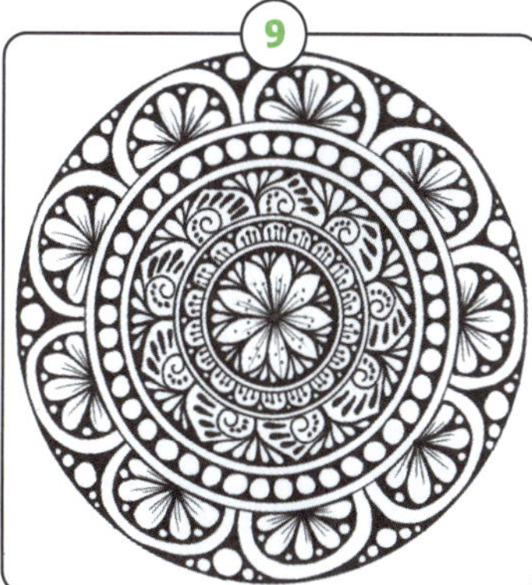

Add final details. Draw delicate lines in the final teardrops, and use a white gel pen to add a white dot to the very center of the mandala.

Repetitive Rings

Welcome to your first mandala made with colored pen instead of black pen! At first this mandala may seem intimidating, but it's actually pretty simple to execute because you have so many rays and circles to work within, blocking out small areas for you to draw shapes in— almost like a coloring page!

As you draw this mandala, focus on the repetitiveness of each different ring; try to get into a smooth groove where each different ring simply flows out of your hand.

MANDALAS

54

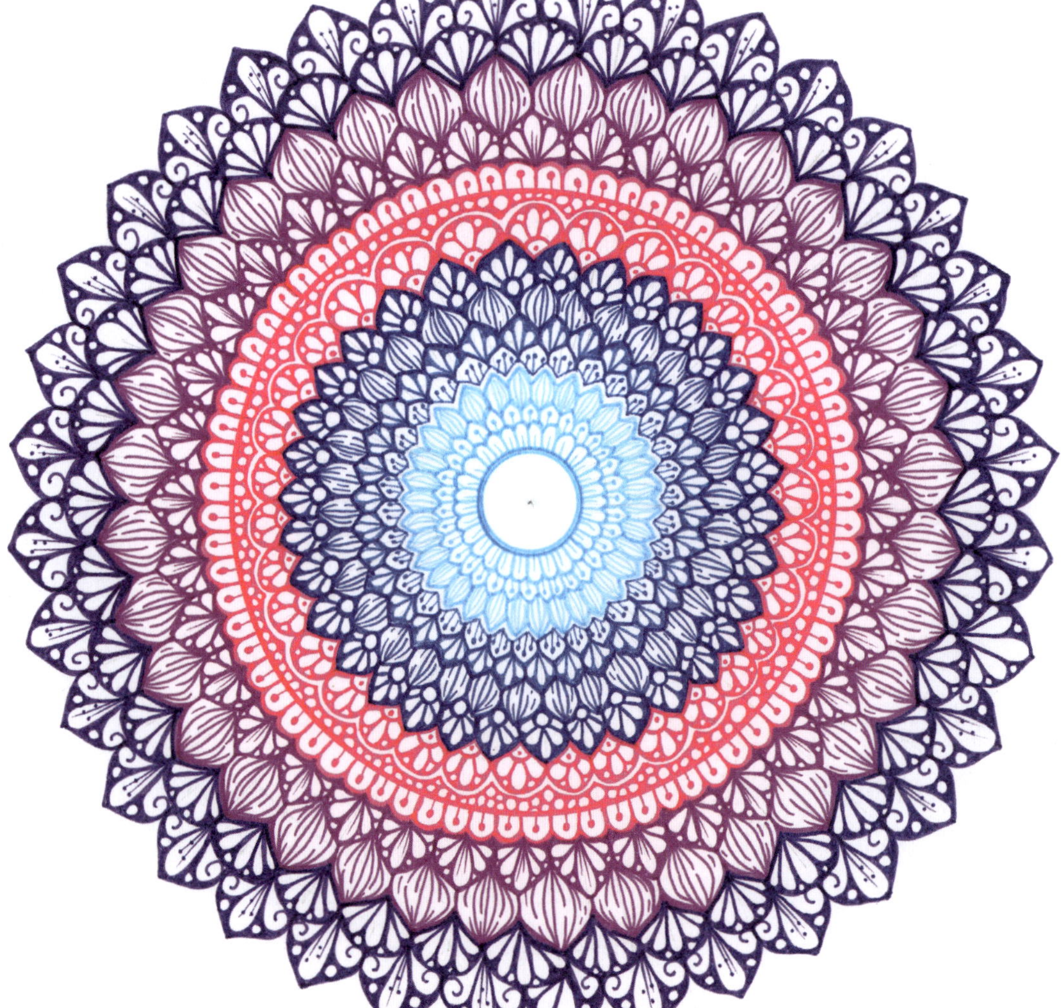

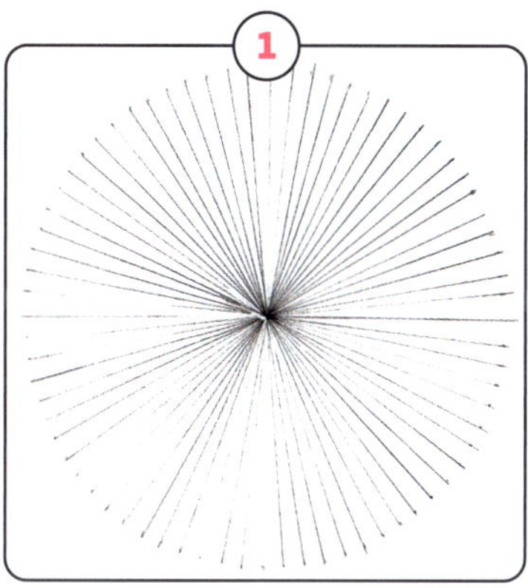

Draw rays. Using pencil, draw a straight horizontal line, then draw a ray every 5° on the top half and bottom half (35 rays total on each half).

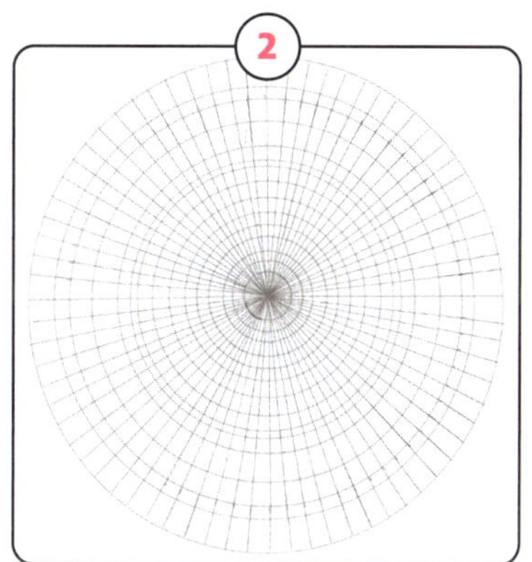

Draw circles. Draw 15 circles as shown. For reference, the outermost circle radius is 3⅝" (9.3 cm); the innermost circle radius is ⅜" (1 cm).

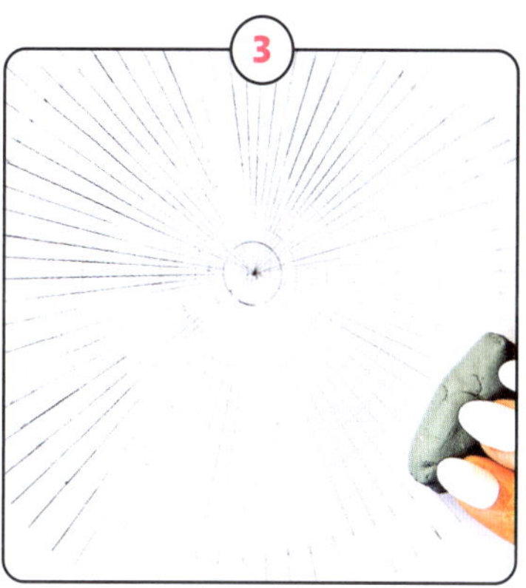

Lighten the circles. If your pencil lines are very dark, use an eraser to lighten them without removing them entirely.

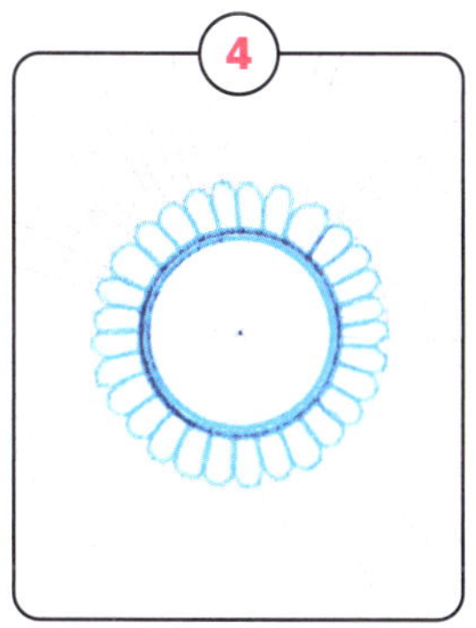

Start with light blue. Trace the center circle in light blue and add another circle right inside it. Then add about 30 petals around the ring.

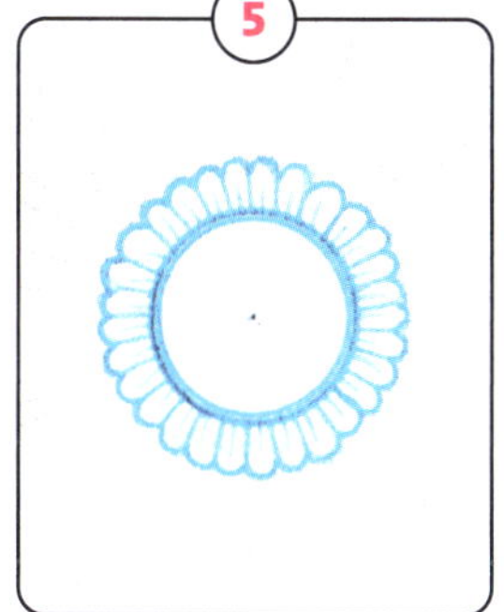

Finish the petals. Add a delicate line inside each petal. Then trace an unbroken line along the tops of the petals.

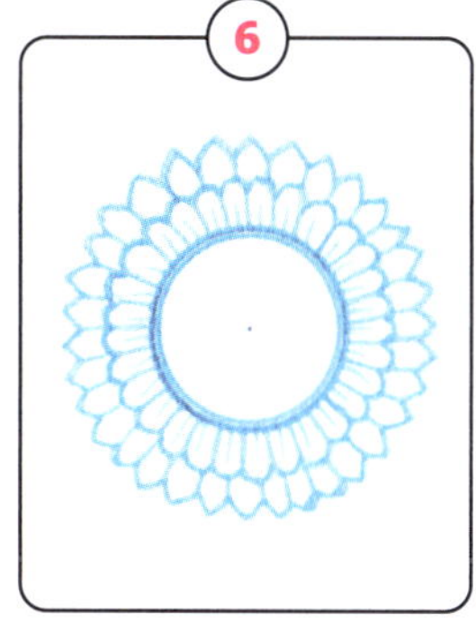

Add pointed leaves. Draw about 33 pointed leaves to fill the next ring.

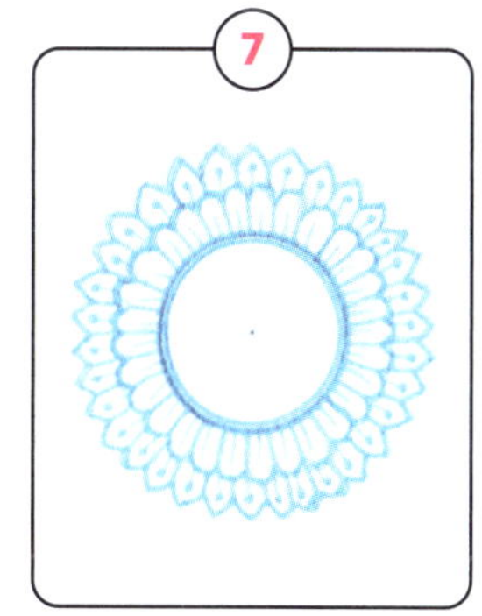

Finish the leaves. Add a line capped with a dot to each pointed leaf.

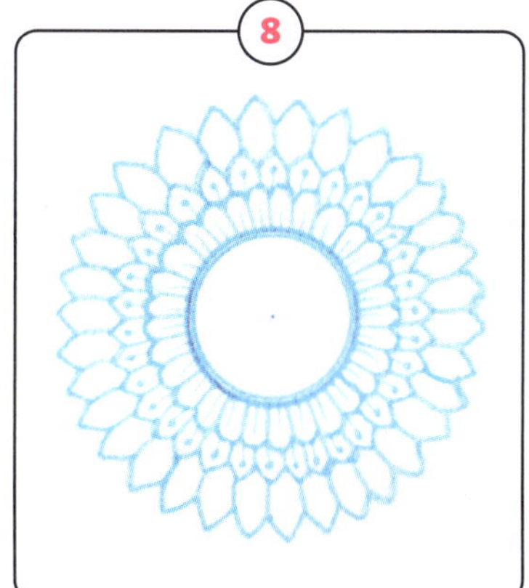

Add more leaves. Draw about 33 pointed leaves to fill the next ring, placing one between each set of adjacent pointed leaves in the previous ring.

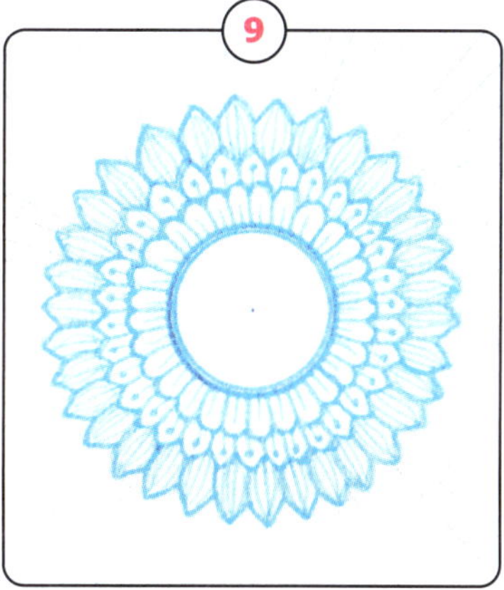

Finish the leaves. Add several delicate detail lines inside each pointed leaf.

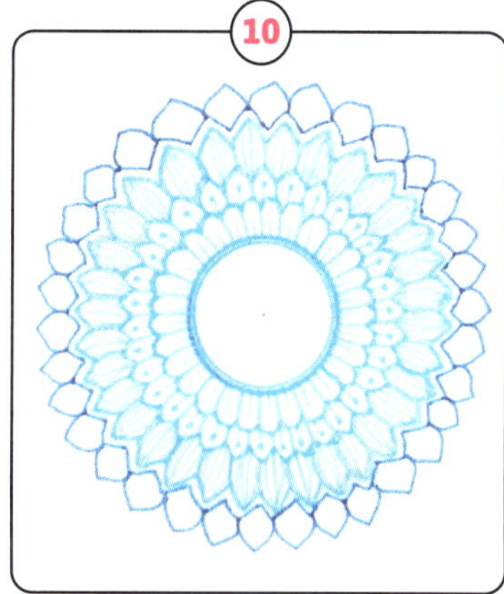

Switch to medium blue. Using medium blue, draw an unbroken zigzag line along the tops of the pointed leaves, then add 33 more pointed leaves to fill the ring.

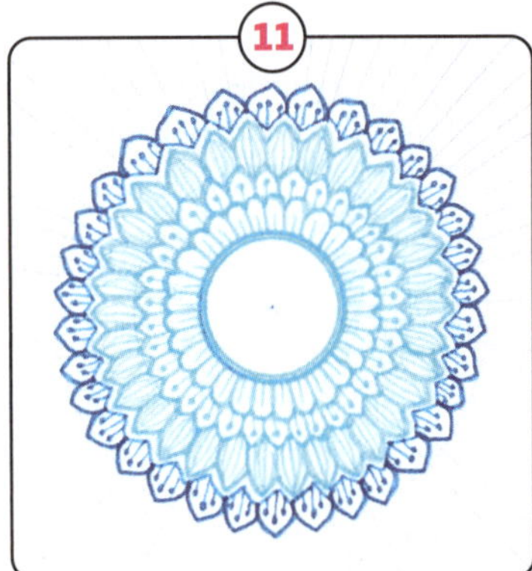

Finish the leaves. Add three lines capped with a dot to each pointed leaf.

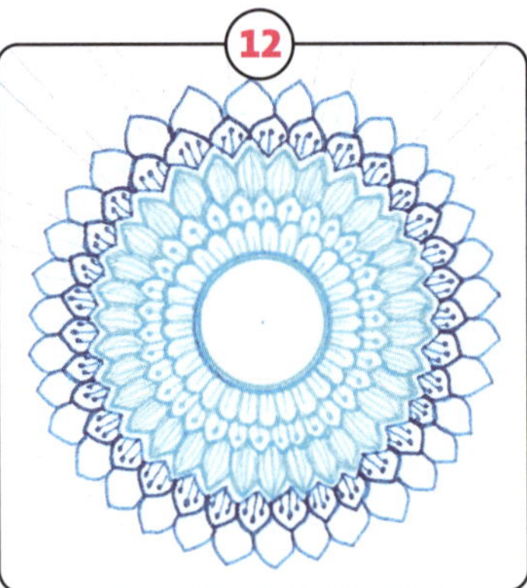

Add more leaves. Draw about 33 pointed leaves to fill the next ring, placing one between each set of adjacent pointed leaves in the previous ring.

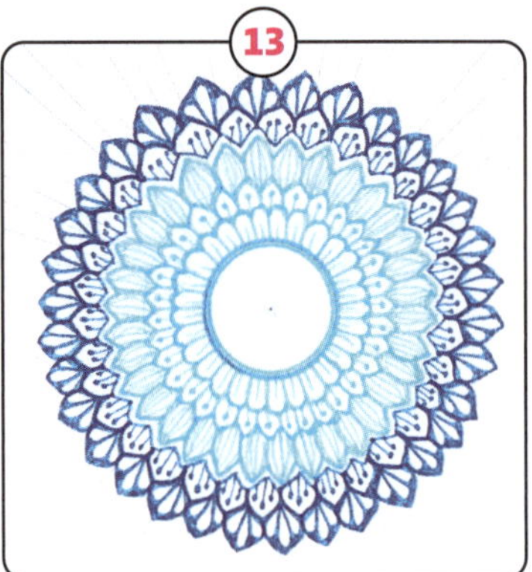

Finish the leaves. Draw three teardrops in each pointed leaf, then fill in around them.

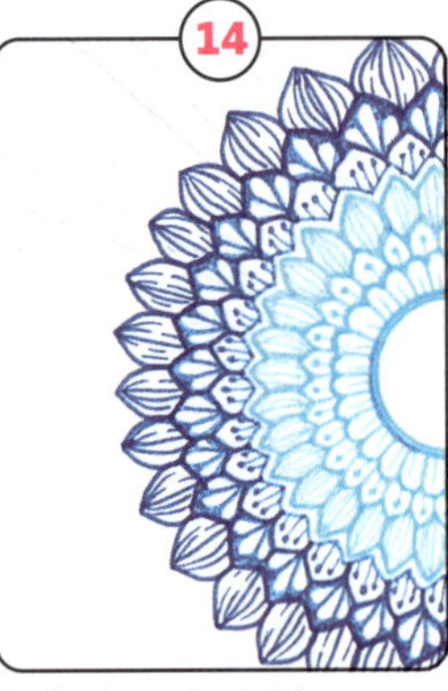

Switch to dark blue. Using dark blue, draw about 33 pointed leaves to fill the next ring. Then add several delicate detail lines inside each one.

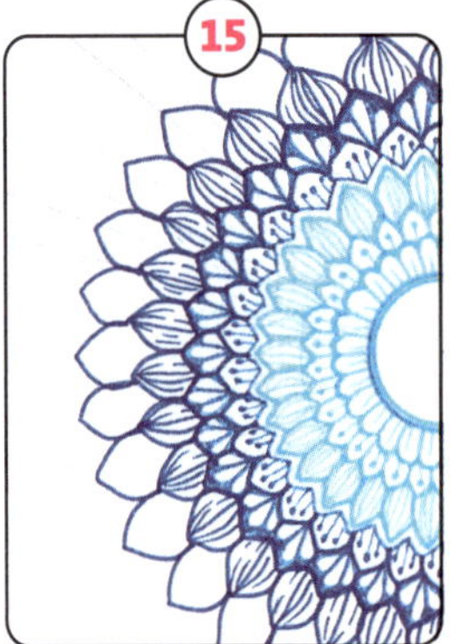

Add more leaves. Draw about 33 pointed leaves to fill the next ring.

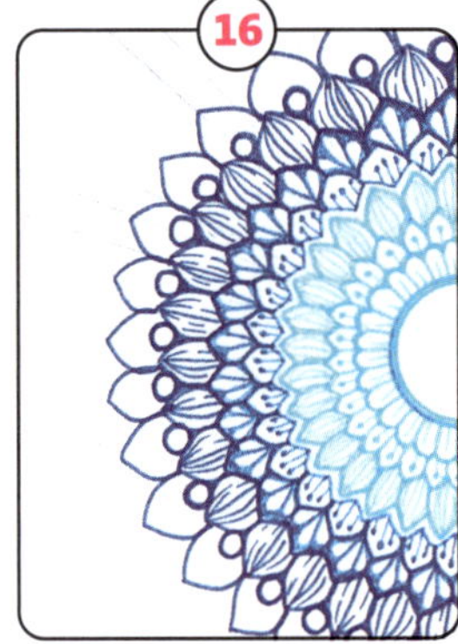

Start building a pattern. Draw a circle nestled in the bottom of each pointed leaf.

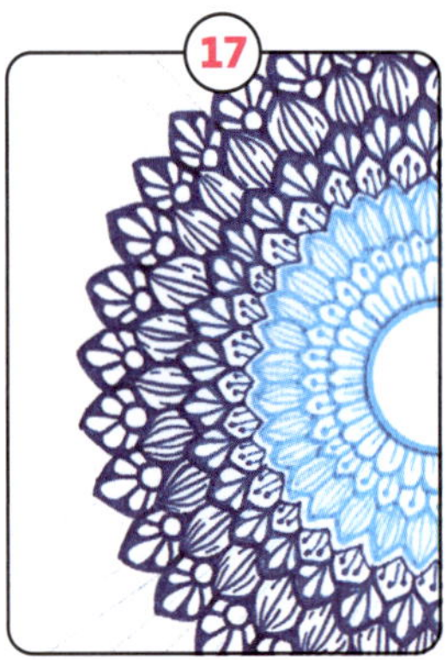

Finish the pattern. Add five teardrops to each pointed leaf, then fill in around them.

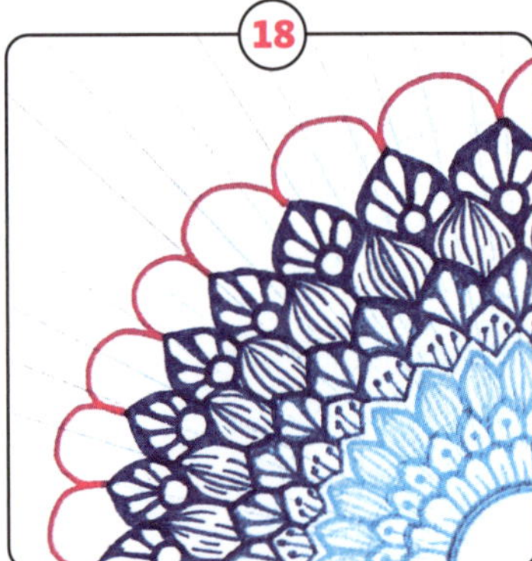

Switch to pink to draw domes. Draw about 33 domes to fill the next ring, placing one between each set of adjacent pointed leaves in the previous ring.

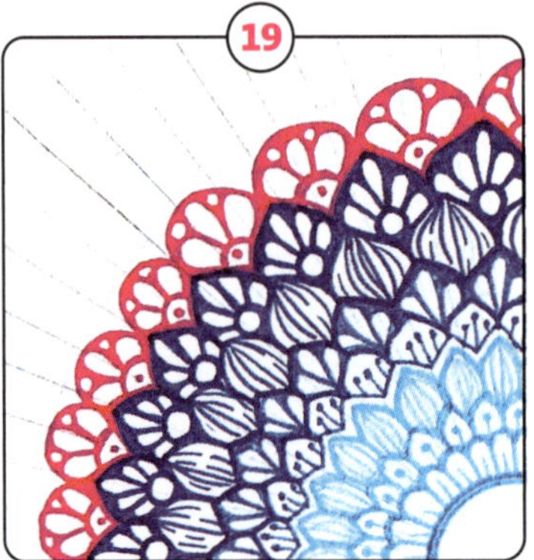

Fill the domes. Draw a semicircle, three teardrops, and two tiny circles inside each dome, then fill in around the tiny circles and add a dot inside each semicircle.

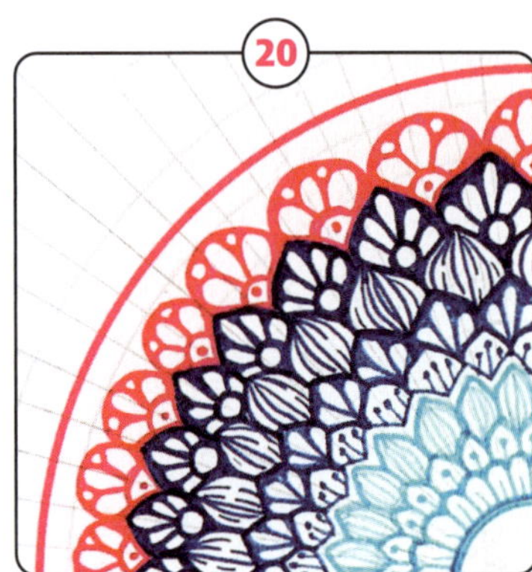

Trace the next circle. Trace the next circle in pink.

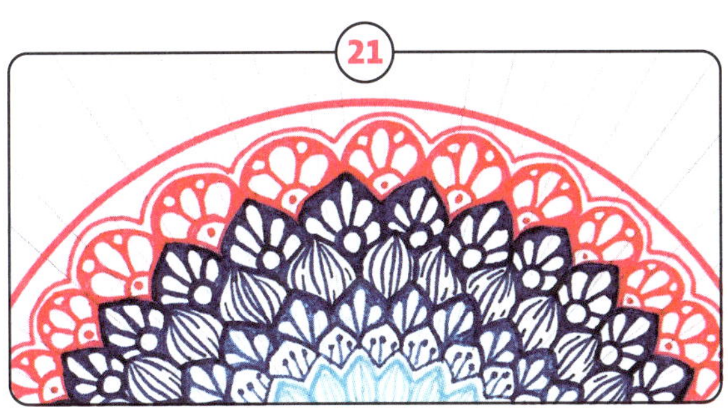

Draw along the domes. Draw an unbroken line along the tops of the domes.

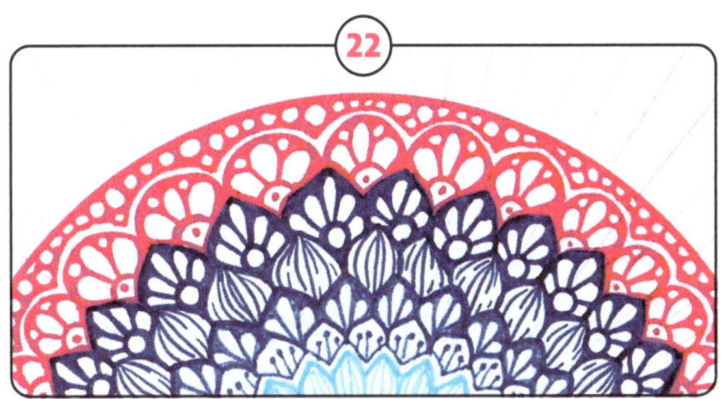

Fill the ring. Fill the ring between the two pink lines with tiny freehand circles, then fill in around them.

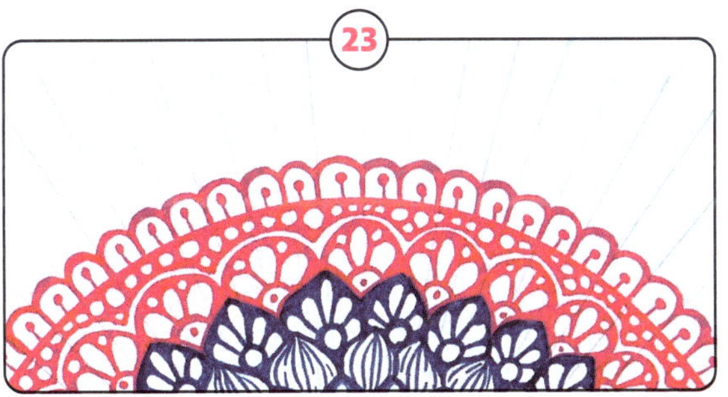

Fill the next ring. Draw a dome between each ray to fill the next ring. Add a line capped with a dot to each dome.

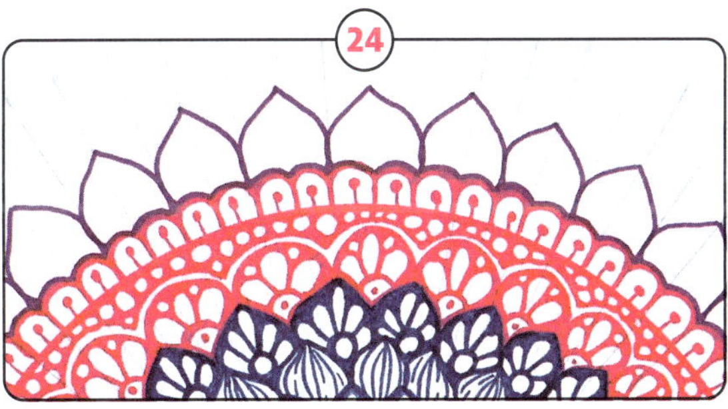

Switch to magenta. Using magenta, draw an unbroken line touching the tops of the domes, then draw pointed leaves centered on alternating rays to fill the next ring.

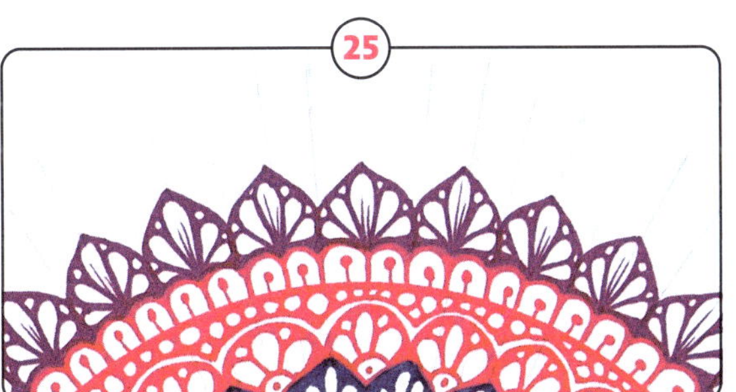

Detail the leaves. Fill each pointed leaf with five teardrops and two tiny freehand circles, then fill in around them. Add delicate lines to each center teardrop.

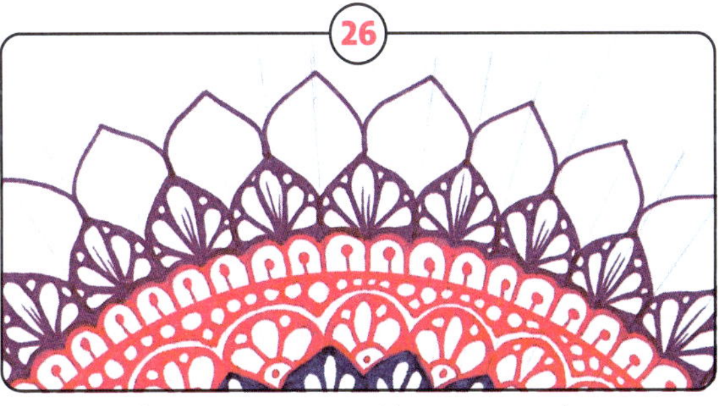

Add more leaves. Draw pointed leaves centered on alternating rays to fill the next ring.

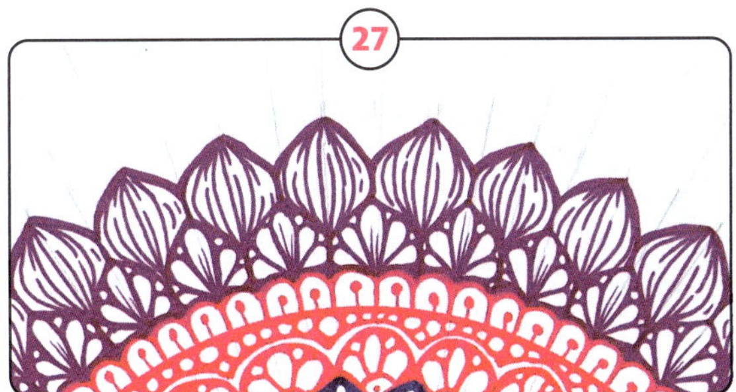

Detail the leaves. Add solid and broken lines to each pointed leaf to give them a textured, rounded effect—imagine an onion.

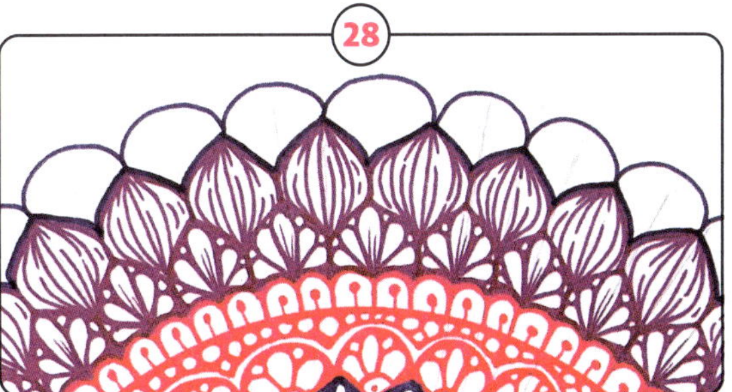

Switch to violet. Using violet, draw an unbroken line touching the tops of the pointed leaves, then draw domes centered on alternating rays to fill the next ring.

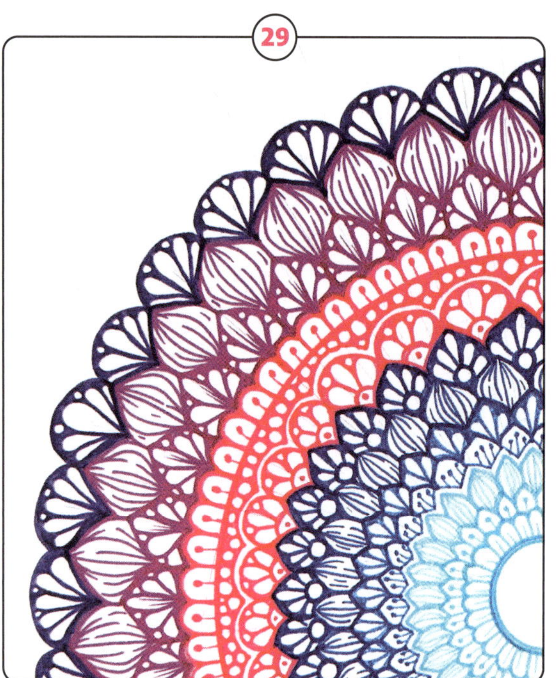

Detail the domes. Fill each dome with five teardrops and two tiny freehand circles, then fill in around them.

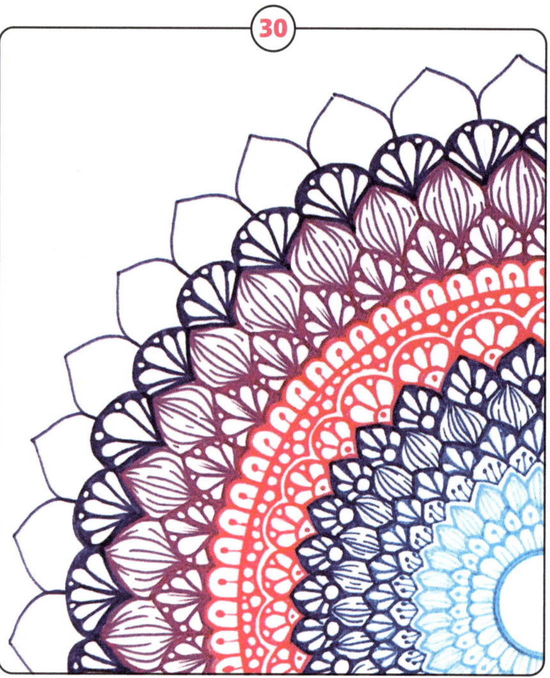

Add more leaves. Draw pointed leaves centered on alternating rays to fill the next ring.

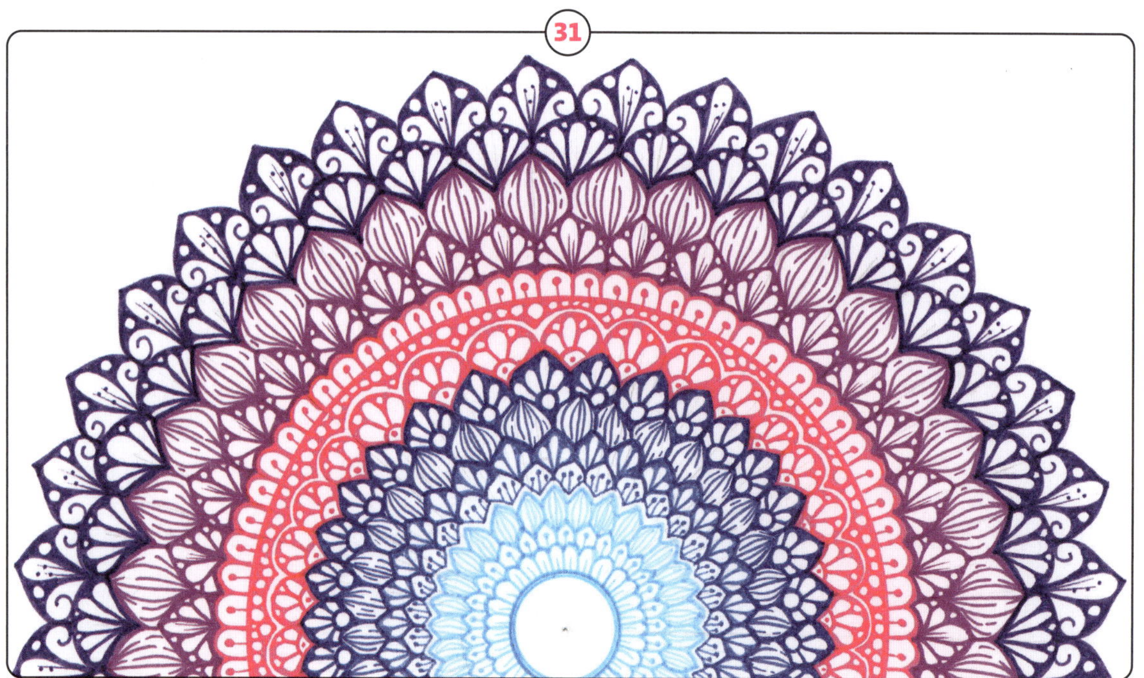

Add a pattern. Inside each leaf, draw a central teardrop, a curling line on each side of it, and two freehand circles, then fill in around them. Add delicate details to the teardrop.

LET'S CHECK IN

How did using color instead of black feel? Was it overwhelming, inspiring, or both?

How does it feel to leave the center empty/unadorned? Do you feel a need to fill it?

What about color speaks to you? Is it the interplay of different colors, specific colors that you love, or something else?

*Color is a power which
directly influences the soul.*
–Wassily Kandinsky

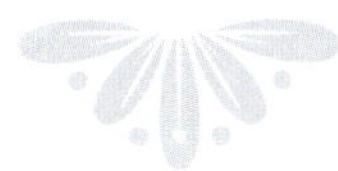

Monochrome Flower

Now let's try using shades of just one color! This mandala is built from quite a few circles and has dense, flourishing details, but it only requires three shades of blue instead of many colors, and it's still pretty easy because you can switch to a new blue whenever you feel like it.

As you draw this mandala, reflect on how the different blues make you feel. Do they all have a similar effect on you? Do you feel an emotional change as the blues change? Do you have a favorite?

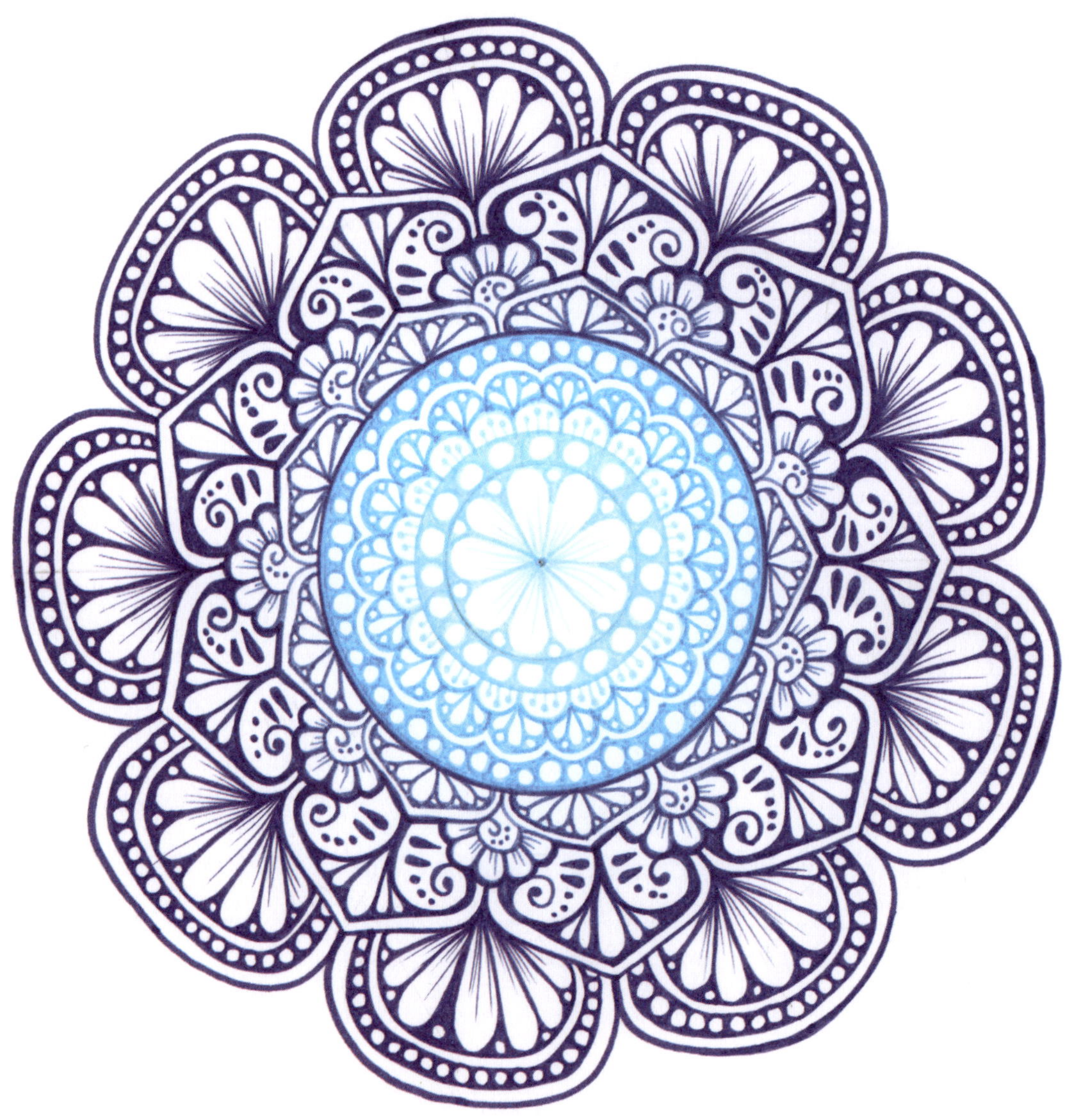

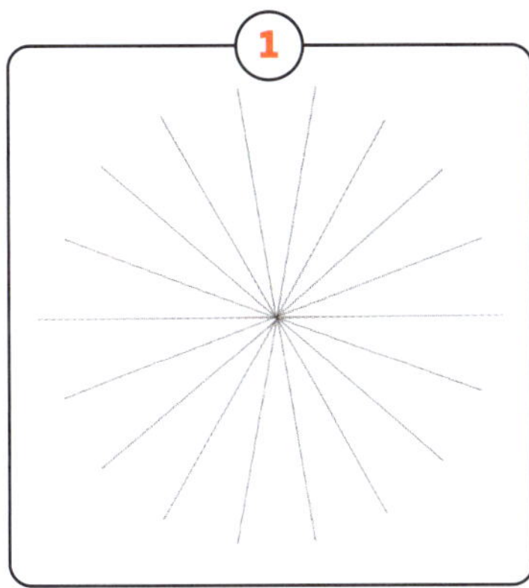

Draw rays. Using pencil, draw a straight horizontal line, then draw a ray every 20° on the top half and bottom half (eight rays total on each half).

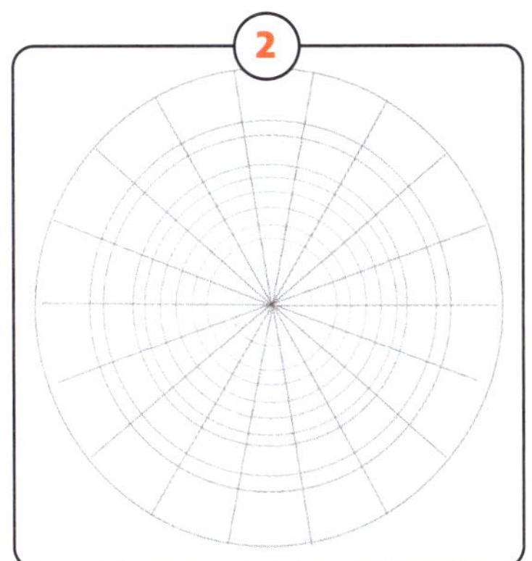

Draw circles. Draw 11 circles as shown. For reference, the outermost circle radius is 3¼" (8.3 cm); the innermost circle radius is ⅝" (1.5 cm).

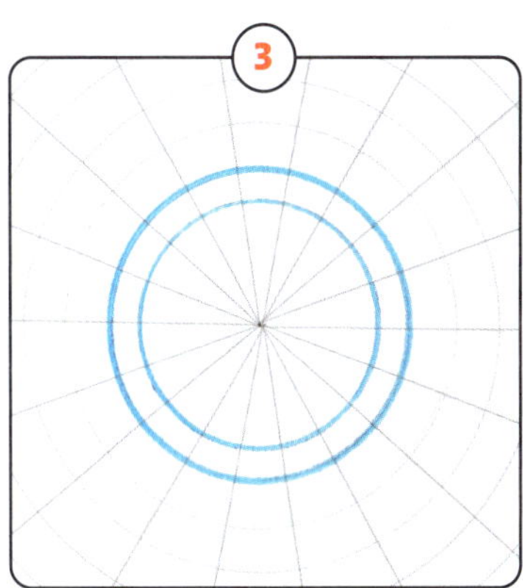

Start with light blue. Trace the first two circles in light blue.

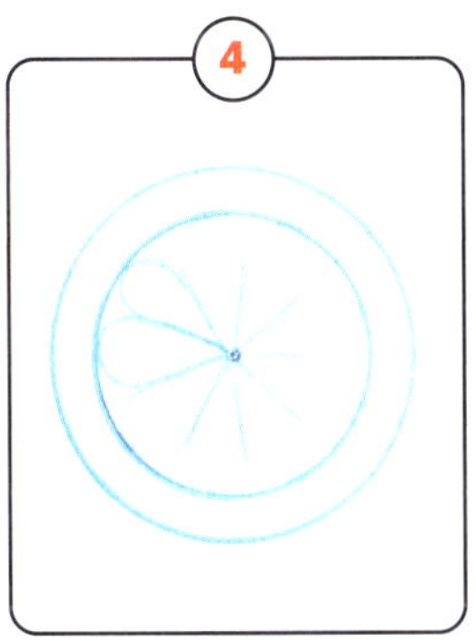

Start the center. In the center, draw teardrops centered on alternating rays.

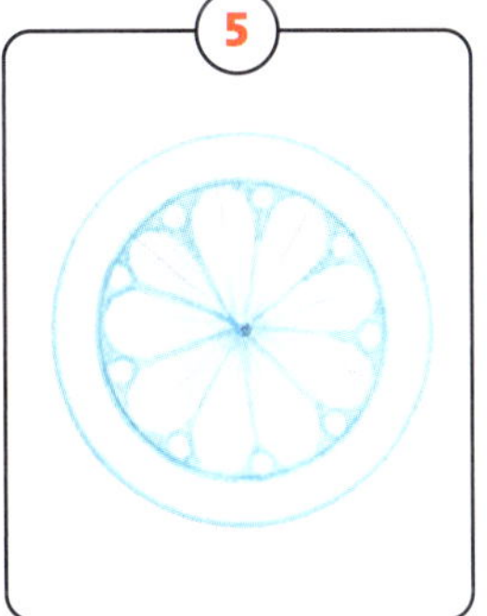

Finish the center. Draw a small circle between each teardrop, then fill in around them. Add delicate detail lines emanating from the very center.

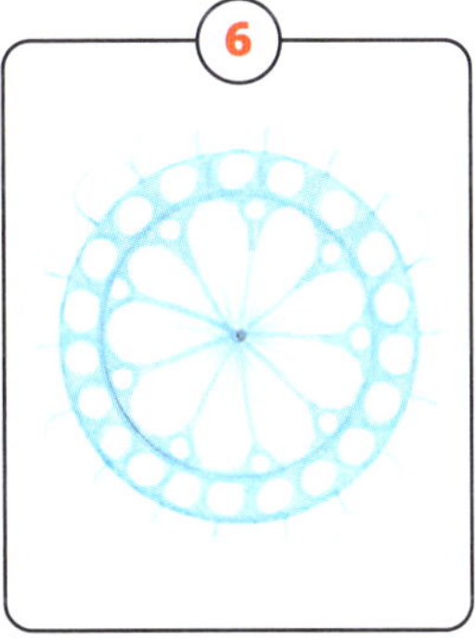

Start the rings. Draw a circle between each ray in the next ring, then fill in around them. Then, in the next ring, draw a dome between each ray.

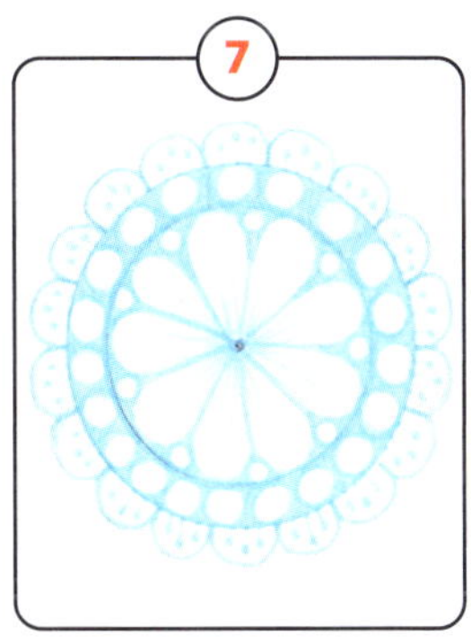

Finish the ring. Add three lines capped with dots inside each dome.

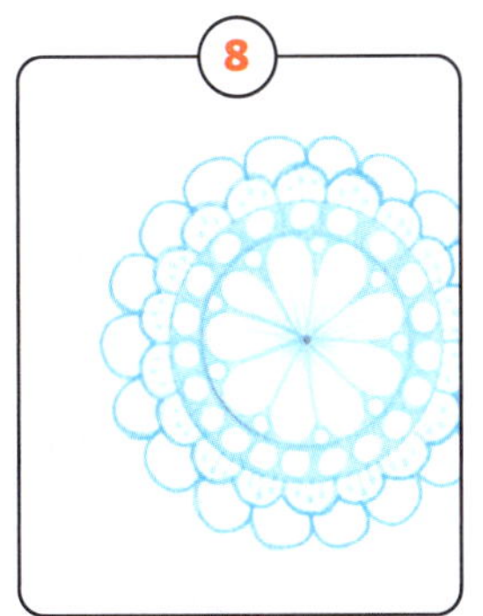

Start the next ring. Draw a dome centered on each ray in the next ring.

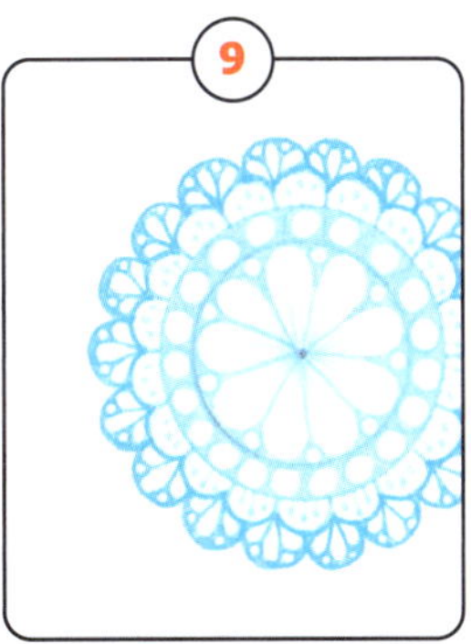

Fill the domes. Add three teardrops and two freehand circles to each dome, then fill in around them.

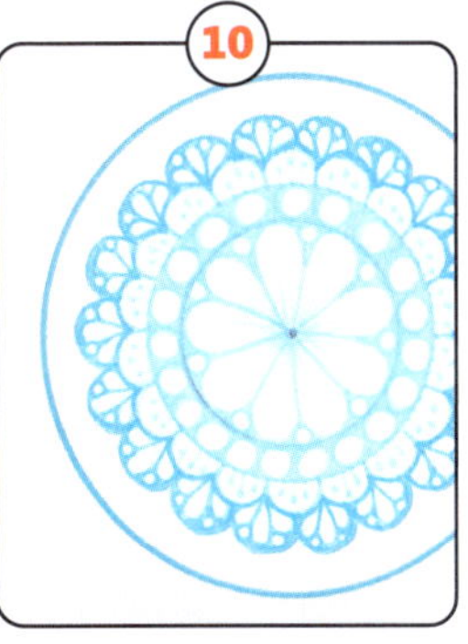

Trace the next circle. Trace the next circle in light blue.

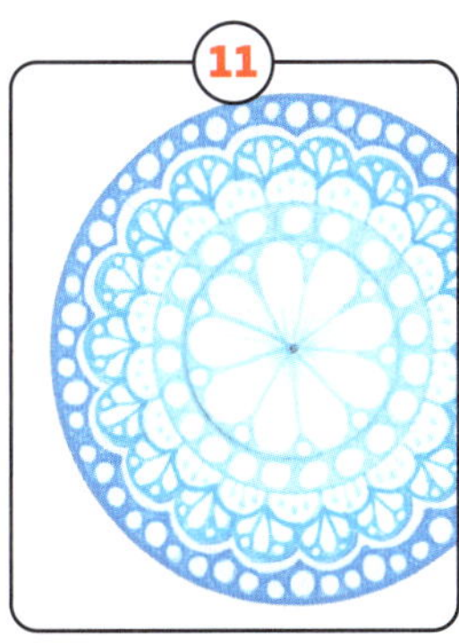

Fill the next ring. Draw an unbroken line along the tops of the domes. Draw large and medium freehand circles within the ring, then fill in around them.

COLORED LINES

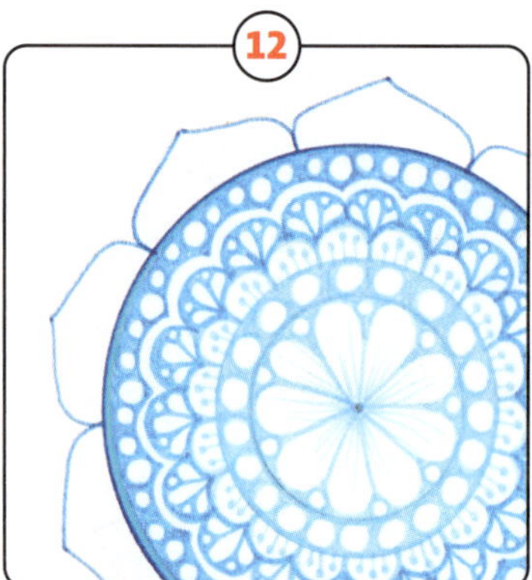

12

Switch to medium blue. Using medium blue, in the next ring, draw pointed leaves centered on alternating rays. Also trace along the edge of the previous circle.

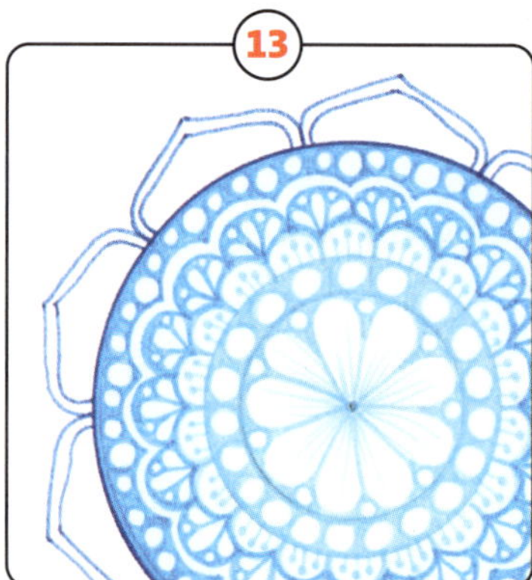

13

Add insets. Inside each pointed leaf, draw a smaller, inset pointed leaf that follows the same contour.

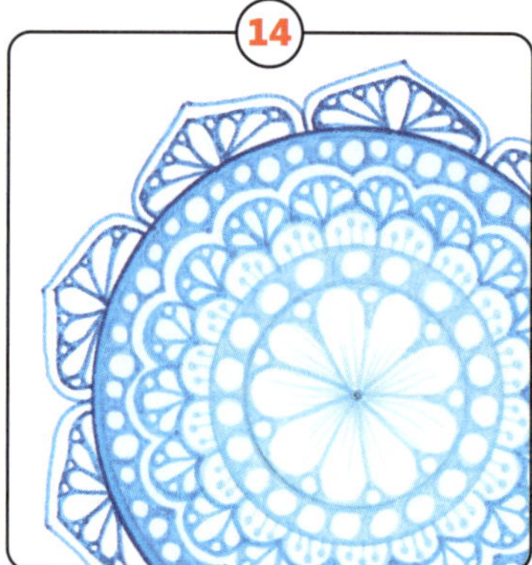

14

Fill the insets. Fill each inset leaf with seven teardrops. Draw a freehand circle between each teardrop, then fill in around them.

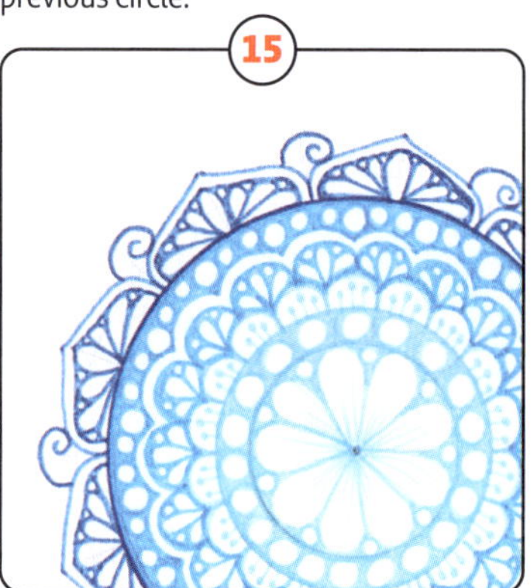

15

Add curling lines. Still within the same ring, draw a curling line between each pointed leaf.

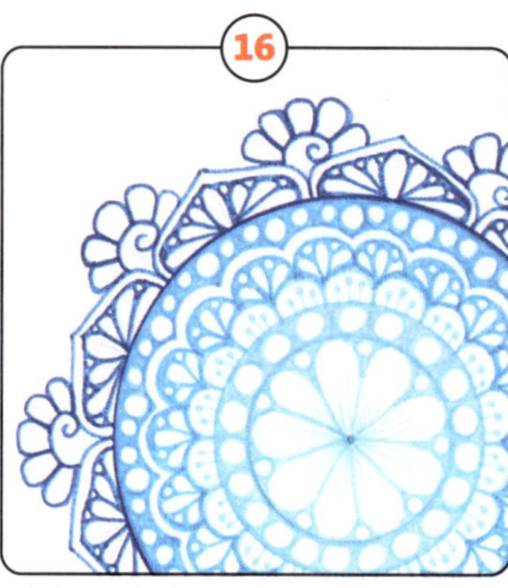

16

Add petals. Draw five petals coming out of each curling line.

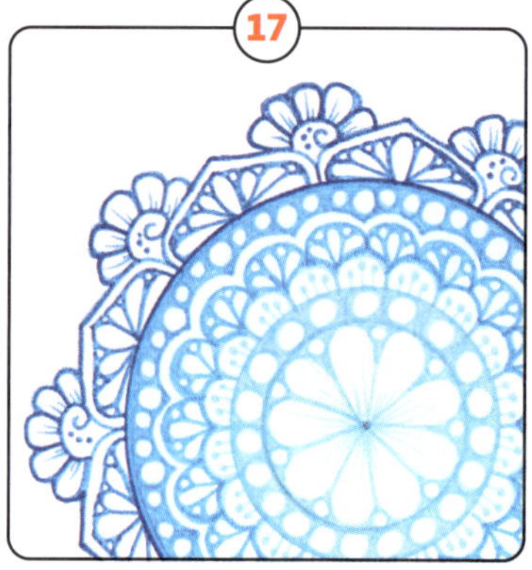

17

Add details. Add three dots inside each curling line and a delicate line or two inside each petal. Also make the outer edges of the petals thicker.

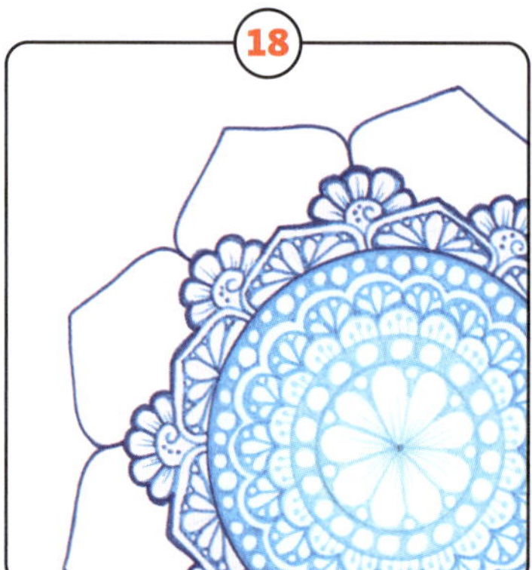

18

Switch to dark blue. Using dark blue, trace along the edge of the entire mandala. Then draw pointed leaves centered on alternating rays that touch the next-to-last circle.

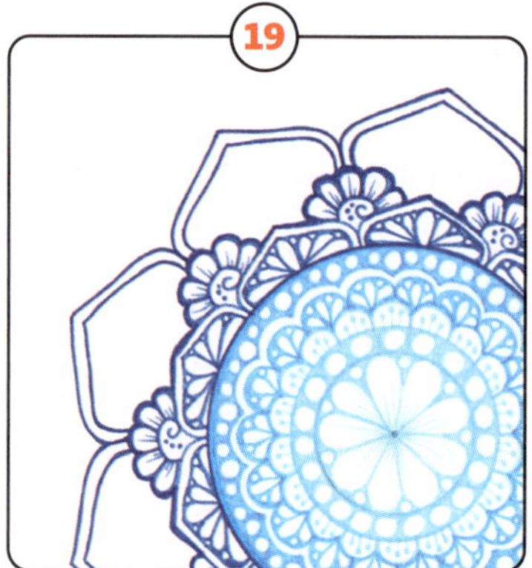

19

Add insets. Inside each pointed leaf, draw a smaller, inset pointed leaf that touches the third-from-last circle.

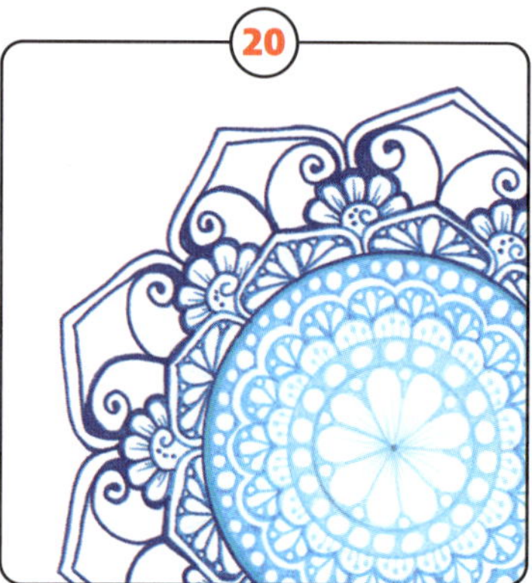

20

Add curling lines. Draw two curling lines inside each inset leaf, then fill in wherever there is empty space trapped between a curling line and medium-blue petals.

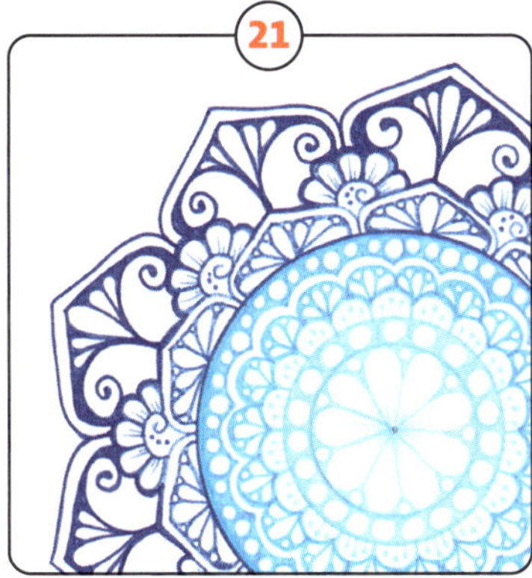

Add teardrops. Add five teardrops between each pair of curling lines, then fill in around them.

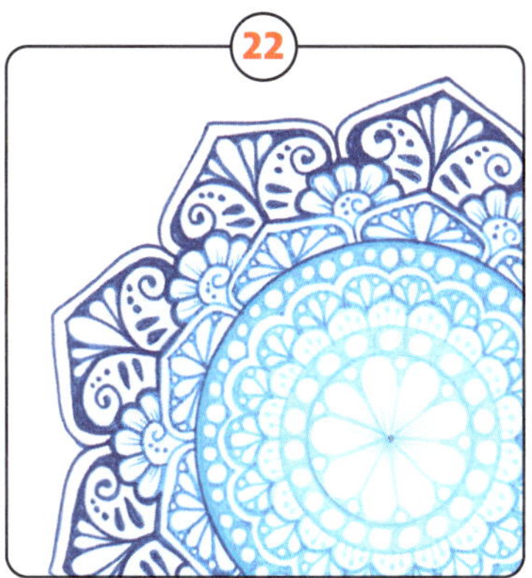

Detail the sections. Add three dots and two filled-in teardrops inside each curling line.

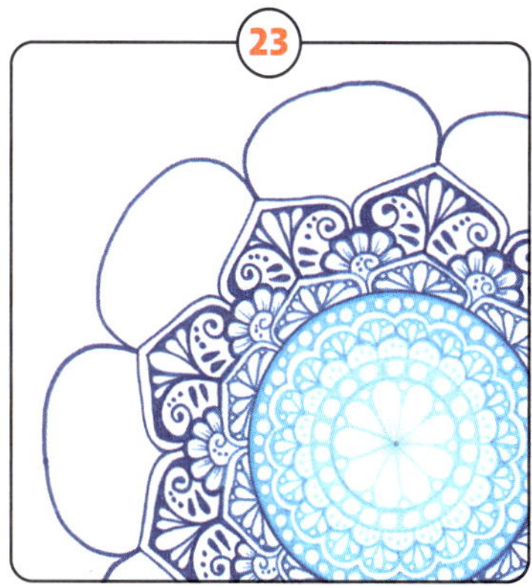

Start the last ring. Draw domes centered on alternating rays in the next ring.

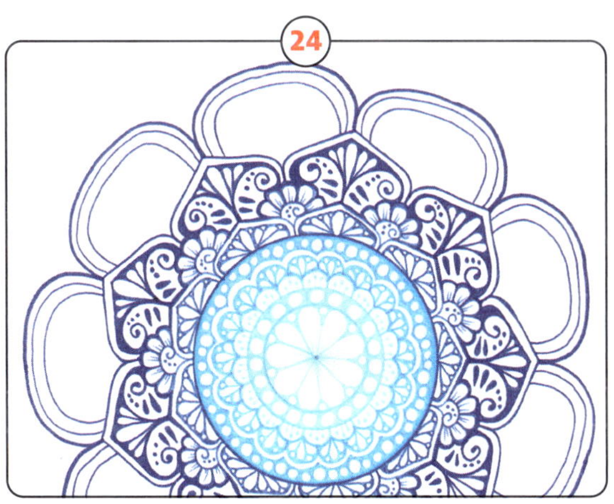

Add insets. Inside each dome, draw two smaller, inset domes.

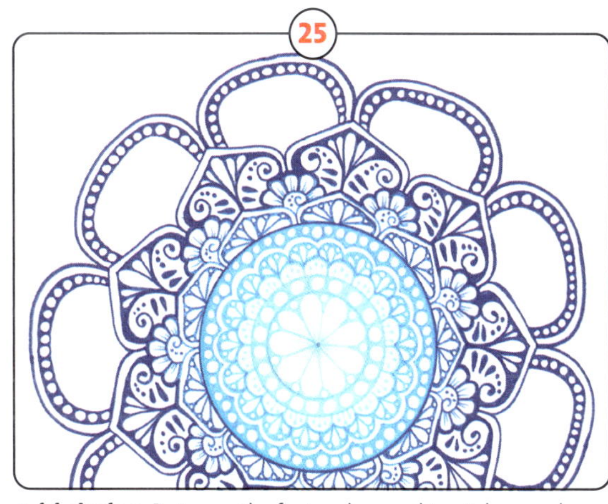

Add circles. Between the first and second inset domes, draw freehand circles, then fill in around them.

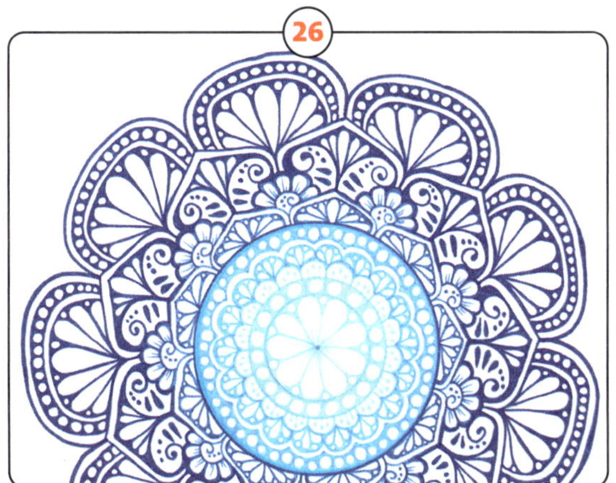

Add designs. Inside each inset dome, add seven teardrops with a tiny circle between each teardrop, then fill in around them.

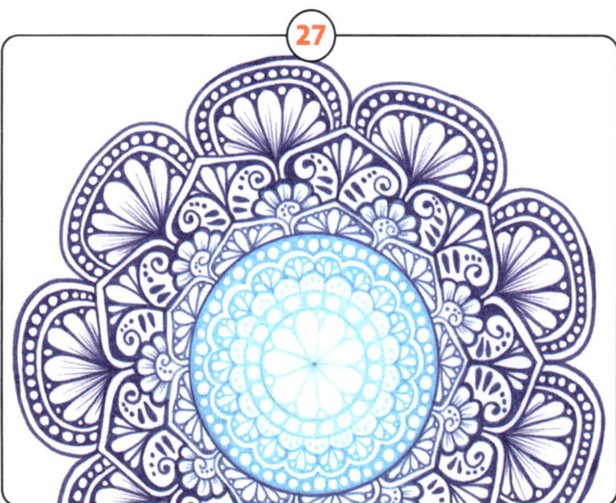

Add final details. Draw delicate detail lines inside the teardrops.

Blooming Gradient

Let's keep increasing the challenge level! For this mandala, unlike the previous two, you will use your colored pens to draw colored circles in advance, effectively preplanning your many color switches. It's a large mandala, but, as with any mandala, it's achievable step by step and ring by ring!

MANDALAS

INTENTION

As you draw this mandala, try to stay centered within the current ring and color that you're working on. Don't worry about the color switches that are coming; don't worry about the more elaborate designs.

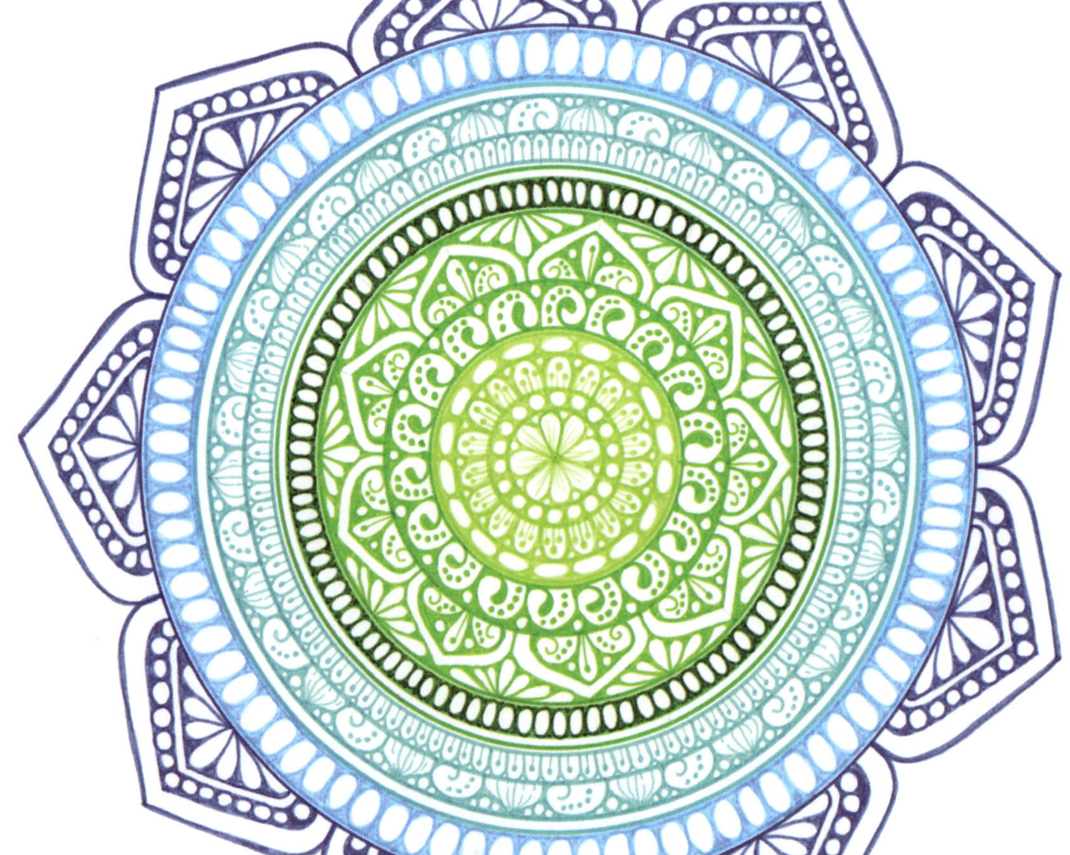

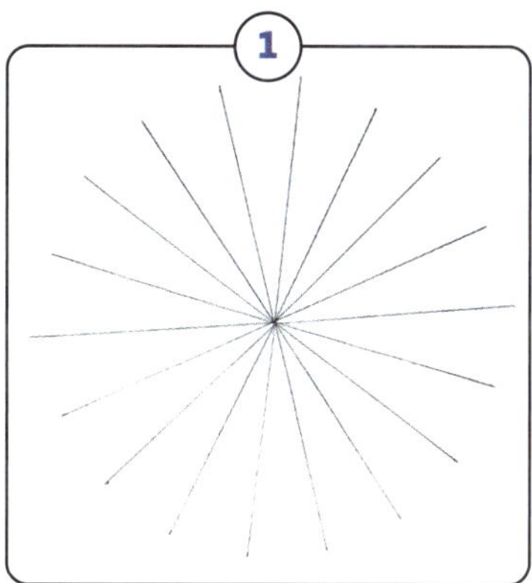

Draw rays. Using pencil, draw a straight horizontal line, then draw a ray every 20° on the top half and bottom half (eight rays total on each half).

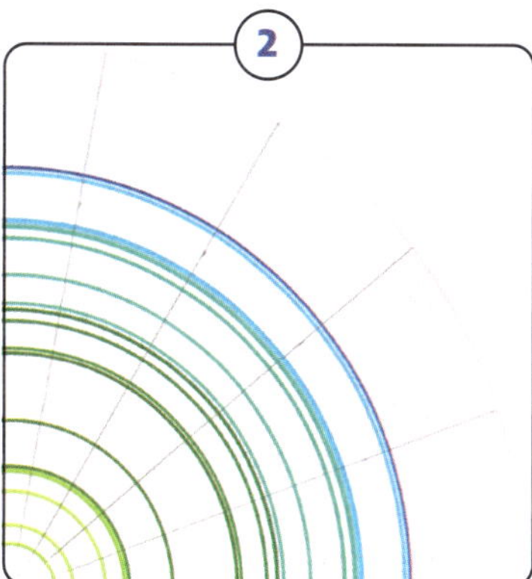

Draw circles. Draw 18 circles as shown in six colors and pencil. For reference, the outermost circle radius is 4¼" (10.6 cm); the innermost circle radius is ⅜" (1 cm).

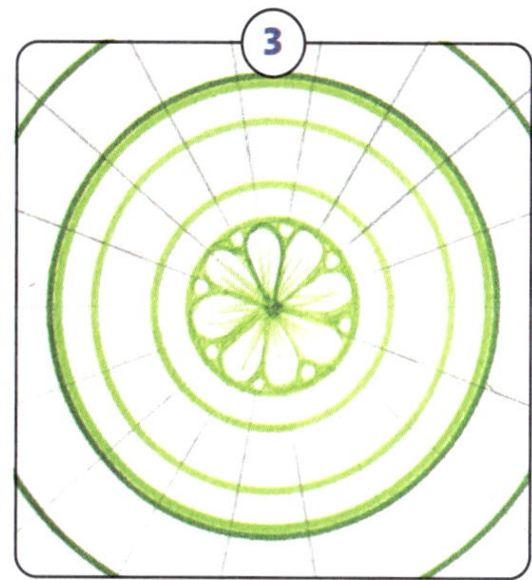

Start with light green. Draw a central design consisting of eight teardrops with a circle between each one. Add delicate detail lines emanating from the very center.

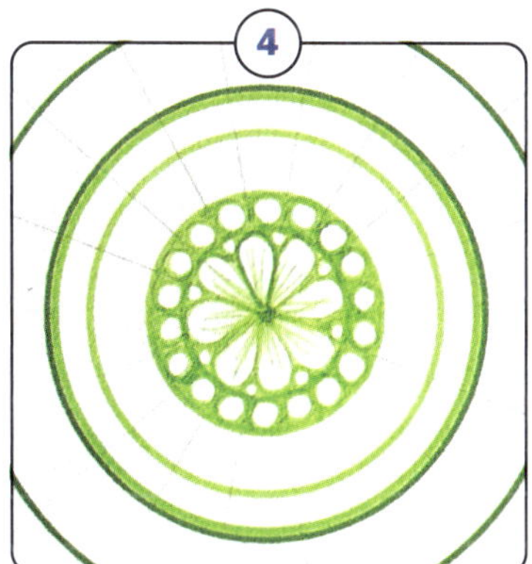

Complete the first ring. Draw a circle between each ray in the first ring, then fill in around them.

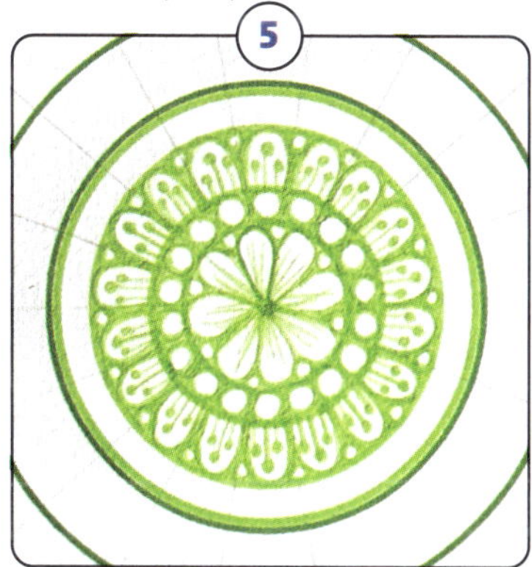

Complete the next ring. Draw a dome between each ray and a circle between each dome, then fill in around them. Add lines capped with dots to the domes.

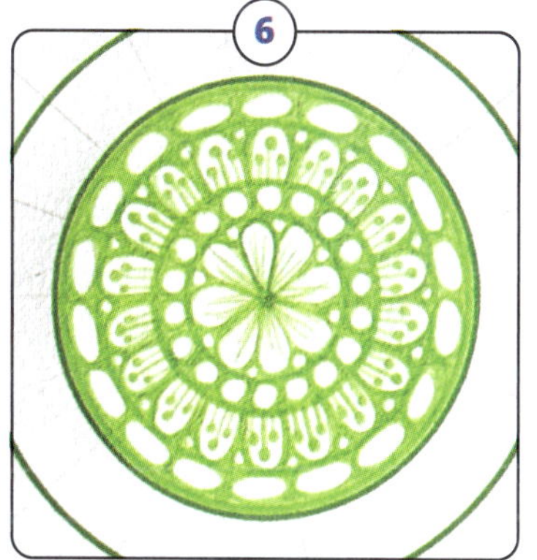

Complete the next ring. Draw a flattened oval between each ray, then fill in around them.

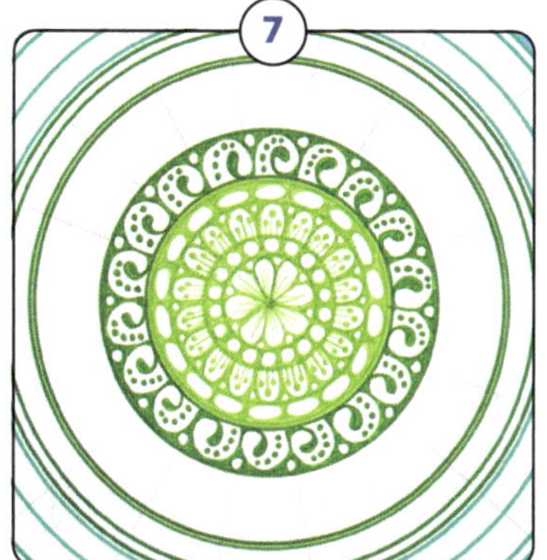

Switch to medium green. Between each ray, draw a rounded, flopped-over shape as shown. Add five dots inside the shape. Draw a circle between each and fill in around them.

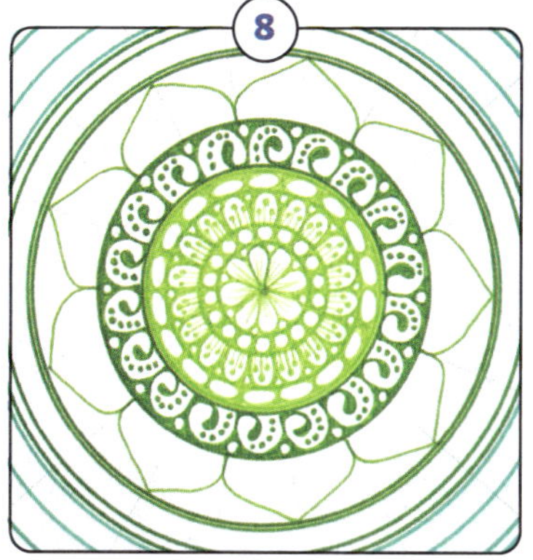

Start the next ring. Add pointed leaves centered on alternating rays in the next ring.

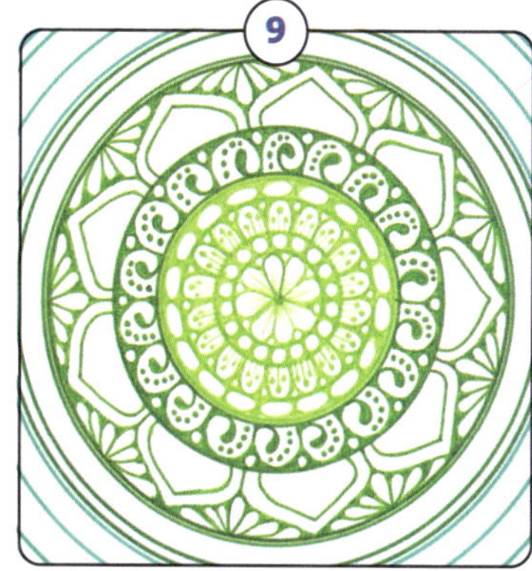

Finish the ring. Add an inset to each leaf. Draw seven teardrops coming down between each leaf, then fill in around them.

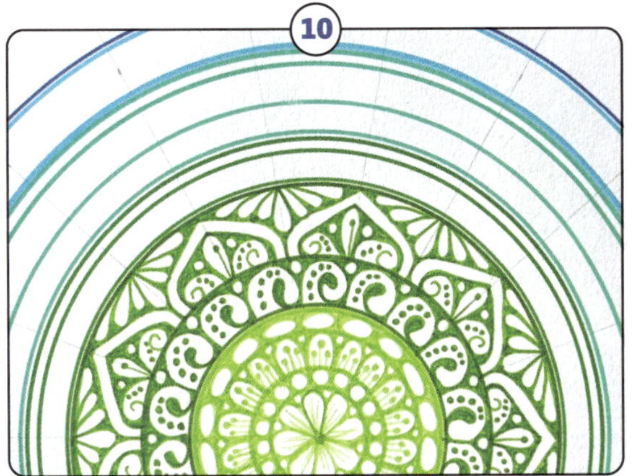

Add filler. Fill each inset pointed leaf with a pattern as shown, consisting of a teardrop, two curling lines, two freehand circles, some dots, and a line capped with a dot.

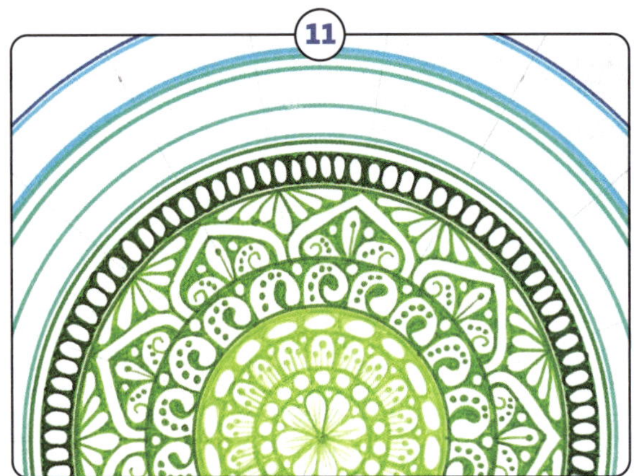

Switch to dark green. In the next ring (between two dark-green circles), draw about five or six tall ovals between each ray, then fill in around them.

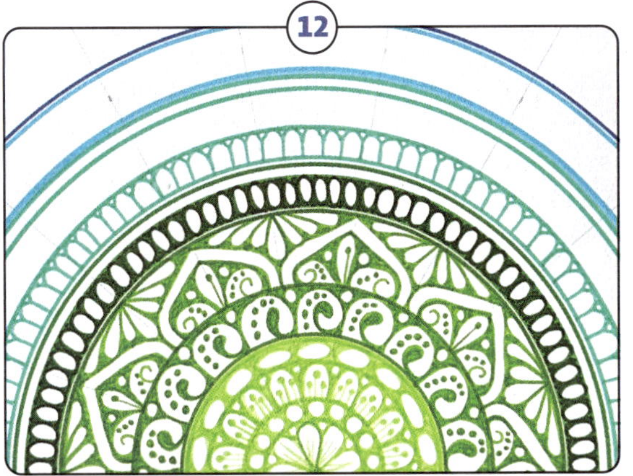

Switch to turquoise. In the next ring (between two turquoise circles), draw about five or six tall domes between each ray.

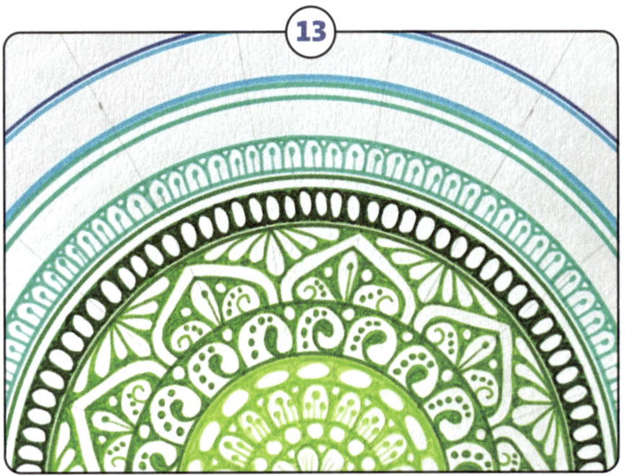

Finish the ring. Add a line capped with a dot to each tall dome.

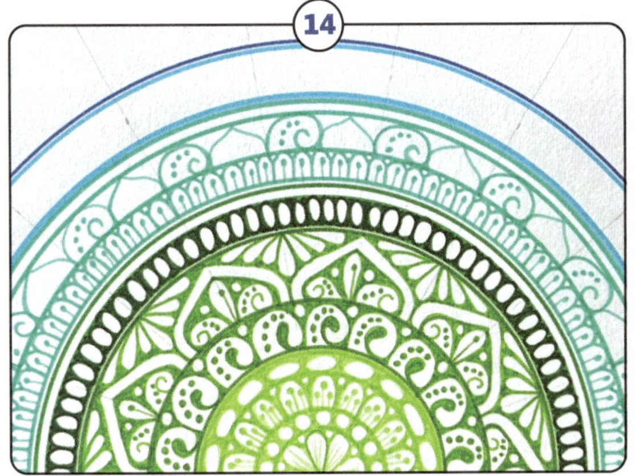

Start the next ring. Between each ray, draw one curling line next to one pointed leaf. Add dots inside the curling lines.

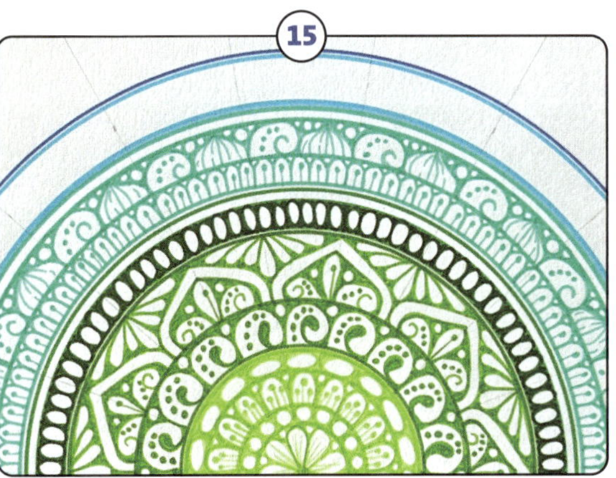

Finish the ring. Add solid and broken lines to the pointed leaves. Draw circles of various sizes between each curling line and pointed leaf, then fill in around them.

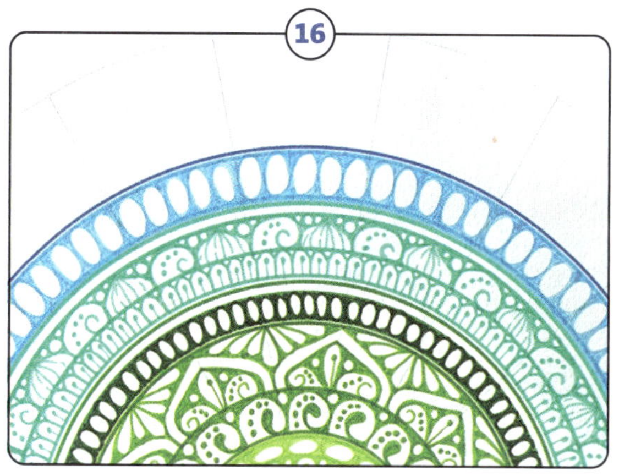

Switch to medium blue. In the next ring (between two medium-blue circles), draw about five tall ovals between each ray, then fill in around them.

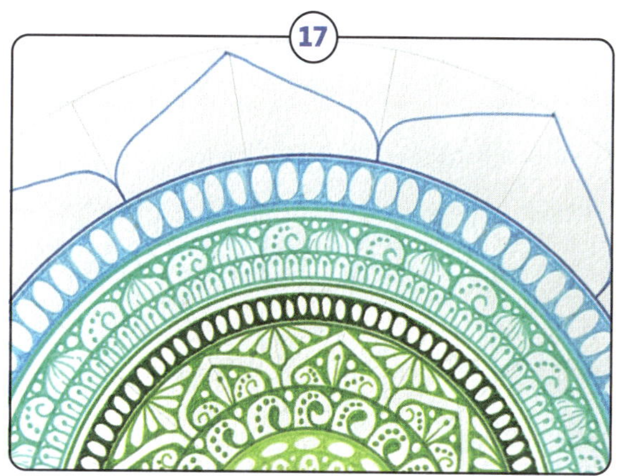

Switch to dark blue. In the final ring (between the dark-blue circle and the pencil circle), draw pointed leaves centered on alternating rays.

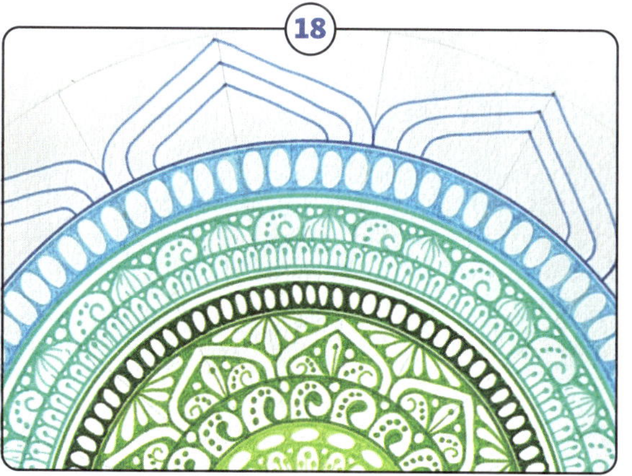

Add insets. Draw two inset pointed leaves inside each existing pointed leaf.

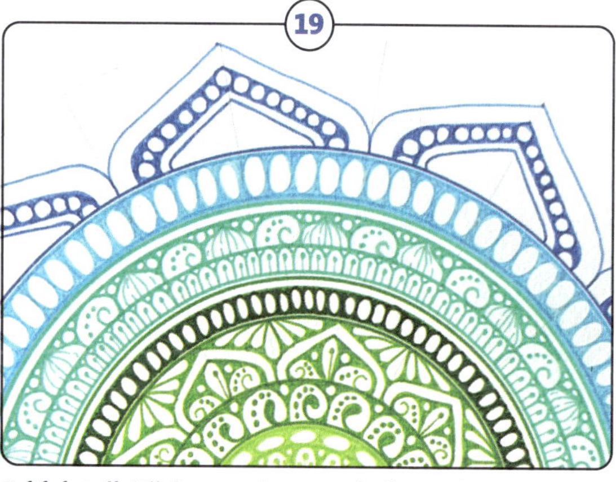

Add detail. Fill the space between the first and second inset leaves with circles, then fill in around them. Add a third inset leaf.

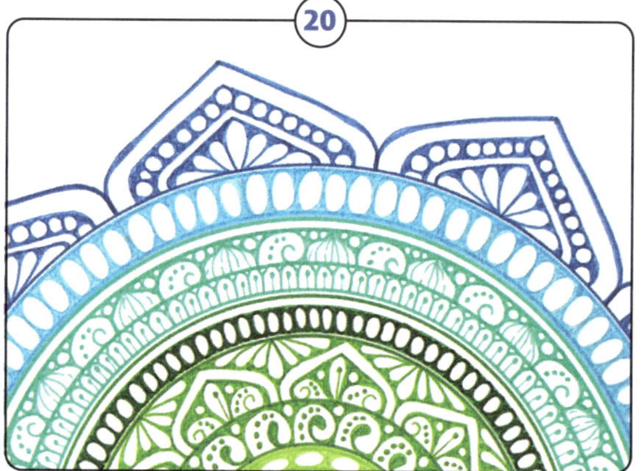

Finish the details. Add seven teardrops inside each smallest inset leaf, then fill in around them.

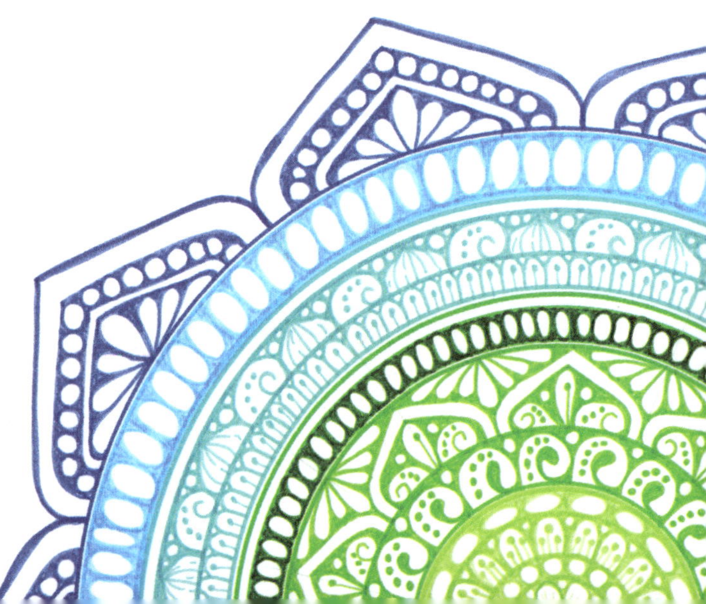

Floral Layers

This is like a more complex version of the previous mandala. As with that one, you will preplan your colors by drawing colored circles but also include some pencil circles. This mandala also includes even more rays than the previous one.

INTENTION

As you draw this mandala, imagine you are laying a mosaic tile by tile. Each tile has a dedicated place and an order in which it is placed. At the end, you have a gorgeous result.

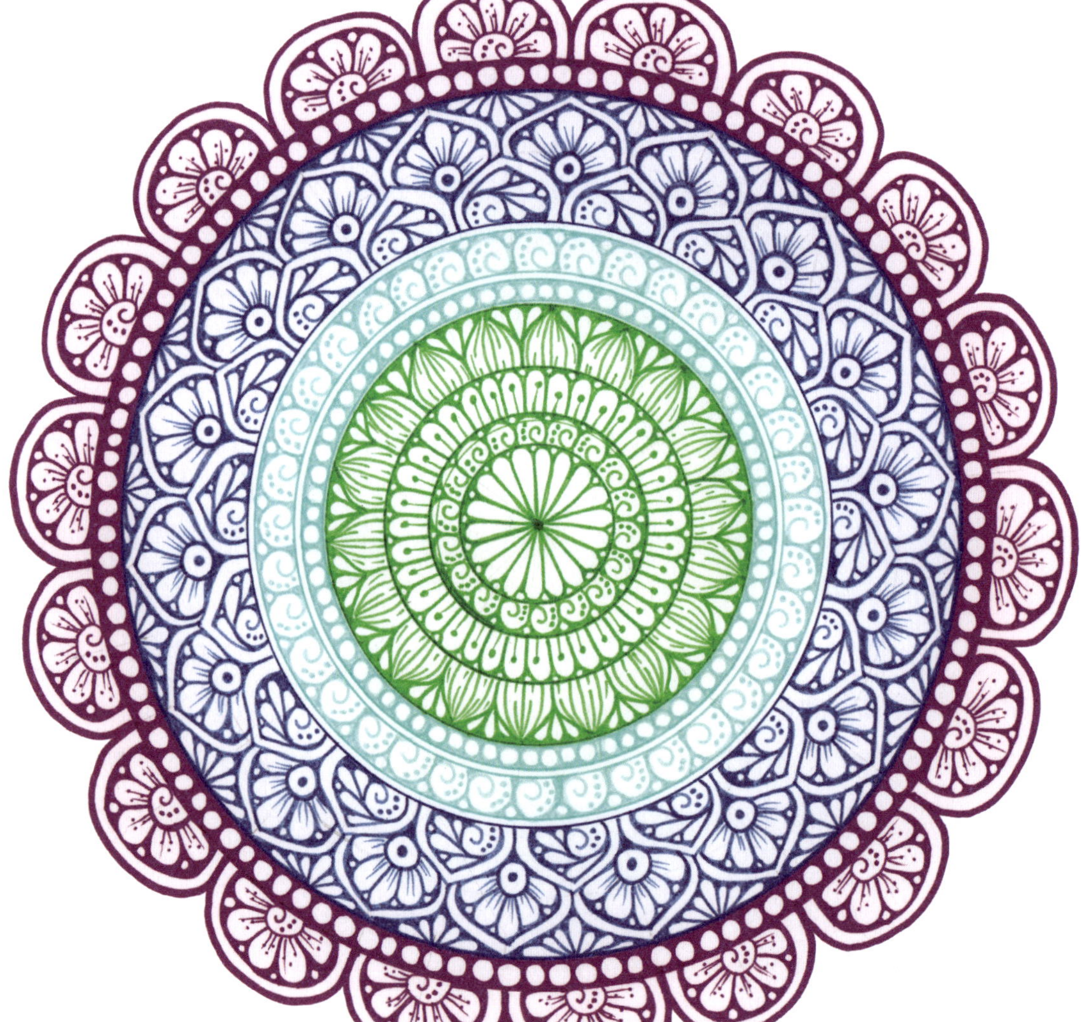

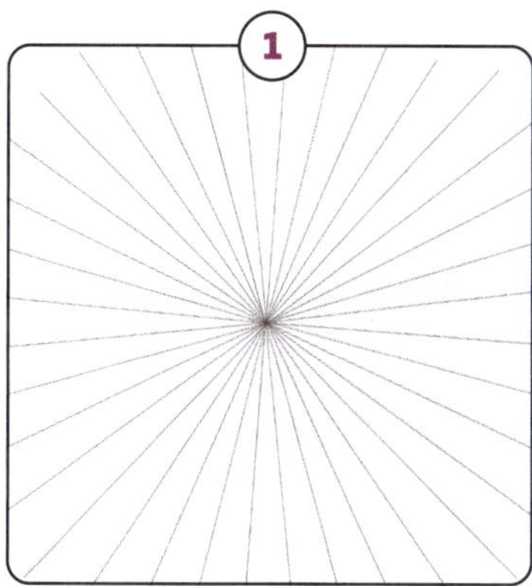

Draw rays. Using pencil, draw a straight horizontal line, then draw a ray every 10° on the top half and bottom half (17 rays total on each half).

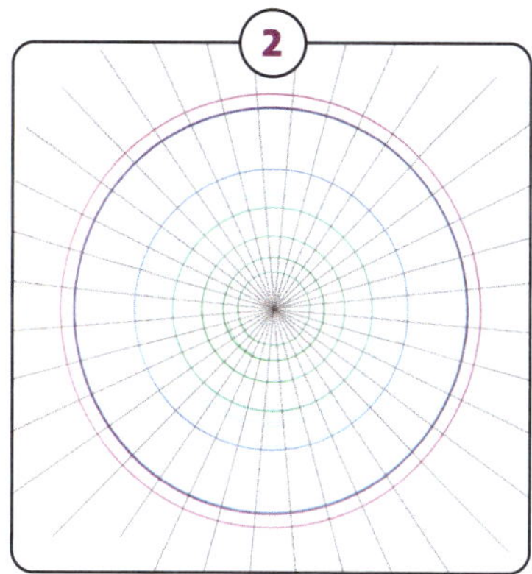

Draw circles. Draw 14 circles as shown in four colors and pencil. For reference, the outermost circle radius is 4" (10 cm); the innermost circle radius is ⅝" (1.5 cm).

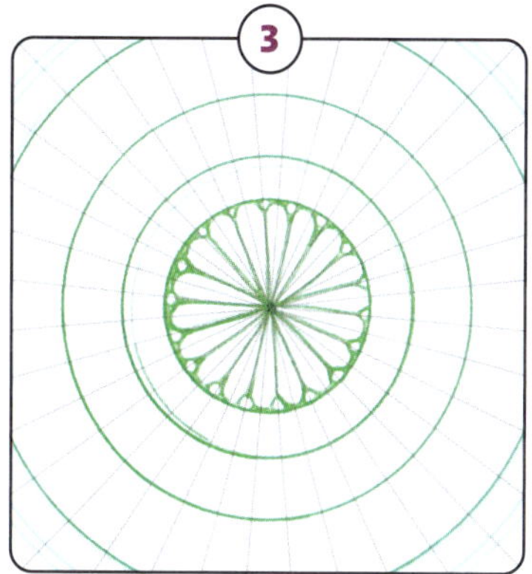

Start with green. In the center, draw teardrops centered on alternating rays. Add a circle between each one, then fill in around.

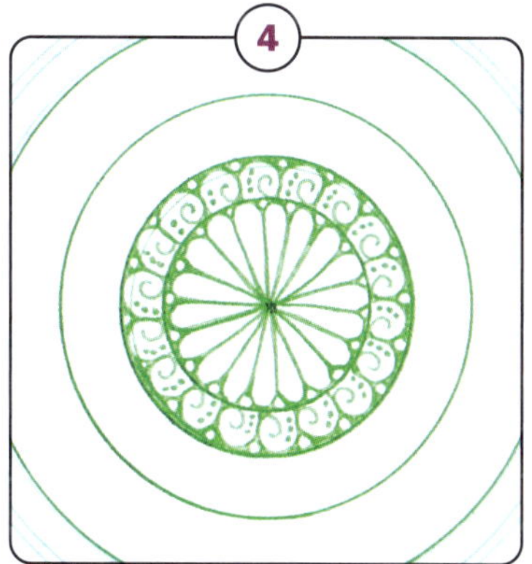

Complete the first ring. Draw curling lines centered on alternating rays. Add a circle between each one, then fill in around. Add three dots to each curling line.

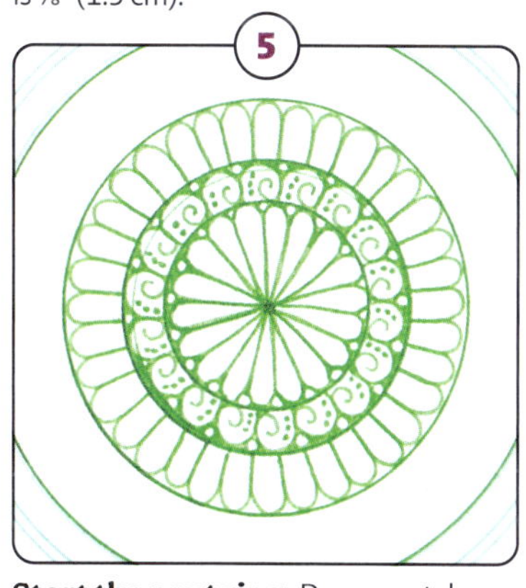

Start the next ring. Draw a petal between each ray.

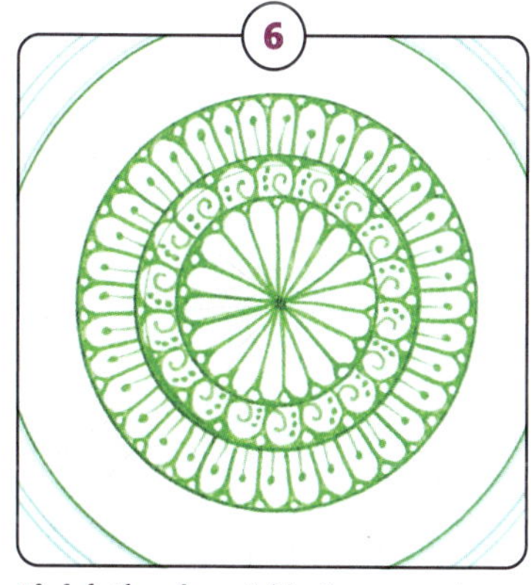

Finish the ring. Add a line capped with a dot to each petal. Draw a circle between each petal, then fill in around them.

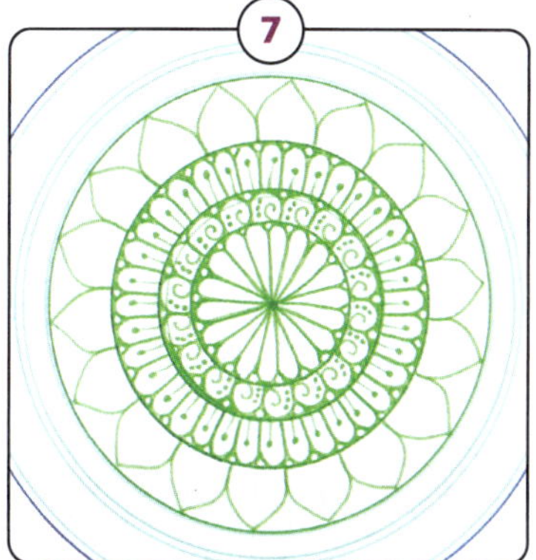

Start the next ring. Draw pointed leaves centered on alternating rays in the next ring.

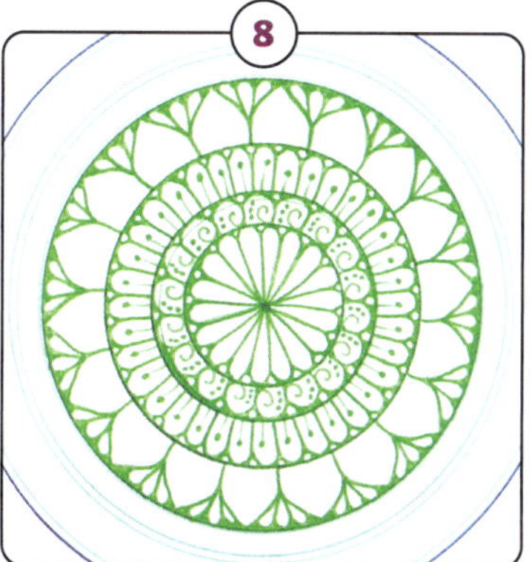

Add teardrops. Draw three teardrops between each pointed leaf, then fill in around them.

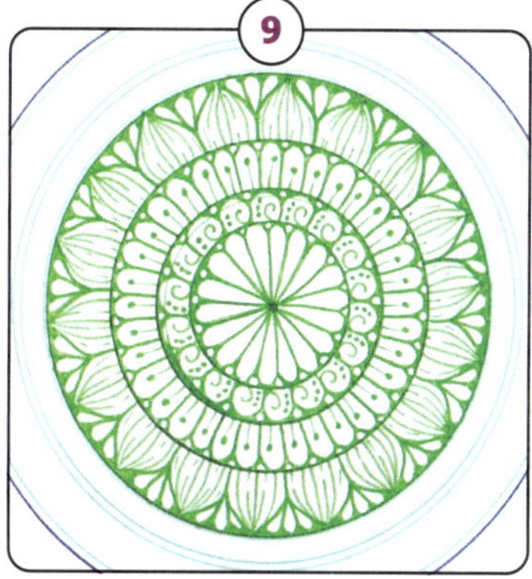

Finish the ring. Add solid and broken lines to the pointed leaves to give them a textured, rounded effect—imagine an onion.

MANDALAS

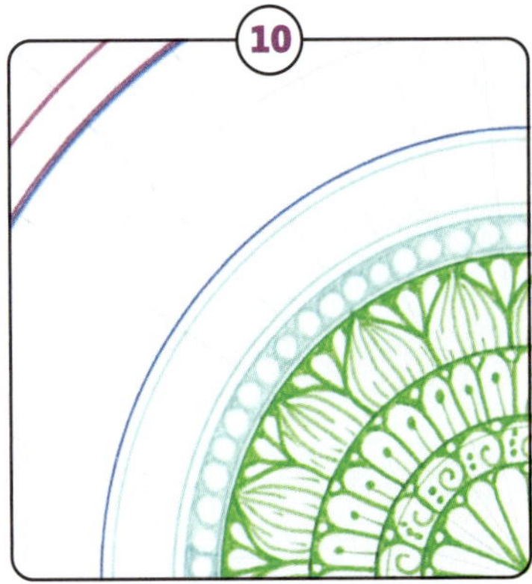

10 Switch to light blue. In the next ring, draw two circles between each ray, then fill in around them.

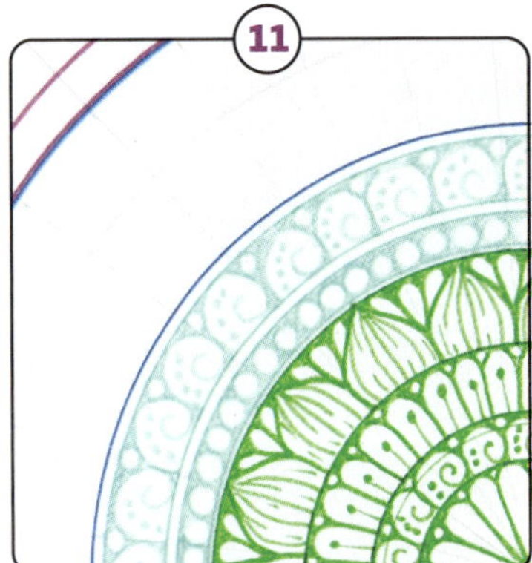

11 Repeat a previous design. In the next ring, repeat the design from step 4, this time drawing one complete design between each ray and adding four dots to each.

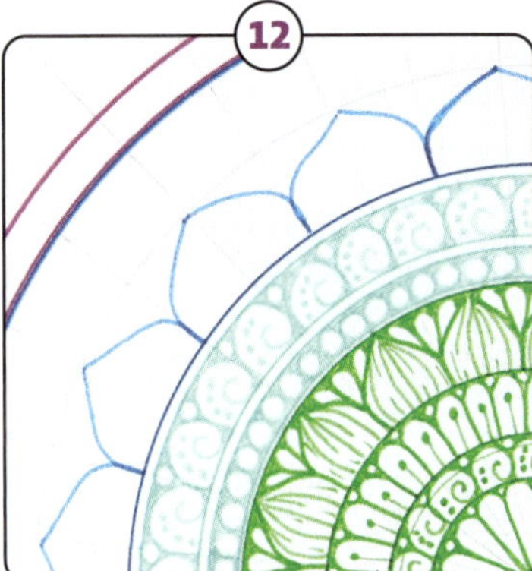

12 Switch to dark blue. Draw pointed leaves centered on alternating rays in the next ring.

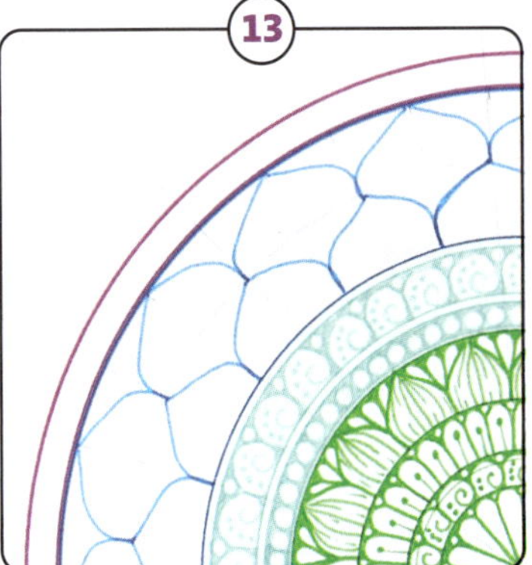

13 Continue to the next ring. In the next ring after that, also draw pointed leaves centered on alternating rays, offset so they fall between the previous ring's leaves.

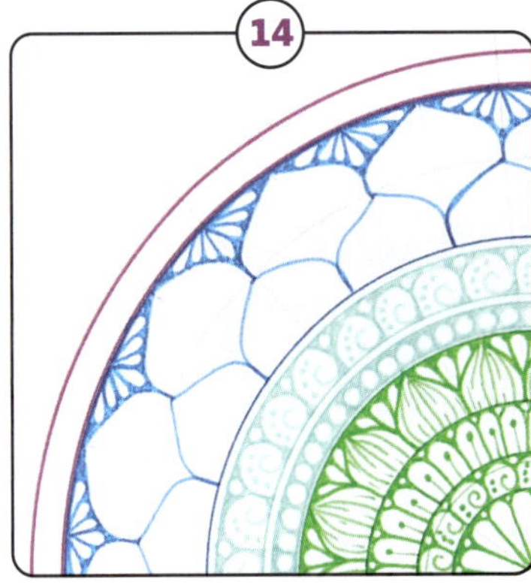

14 Add teardrops. Coming down from the topmost dark-blue circle, draw seven teardrops between each pointed leaf, then fill in around them.

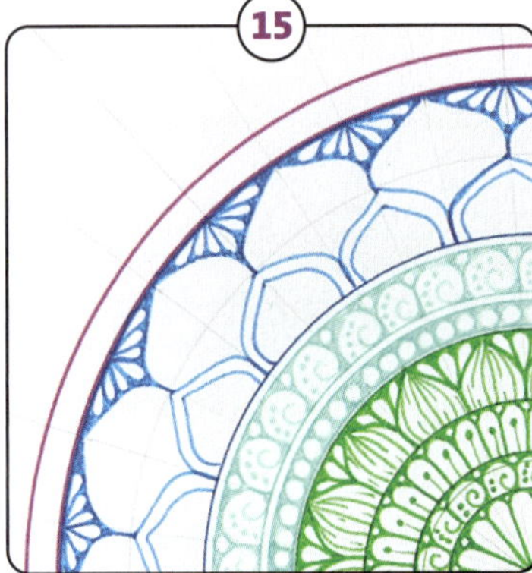

15 Add insets. In the inner ring of pointed leaves, add an inset leaf to each leaf.

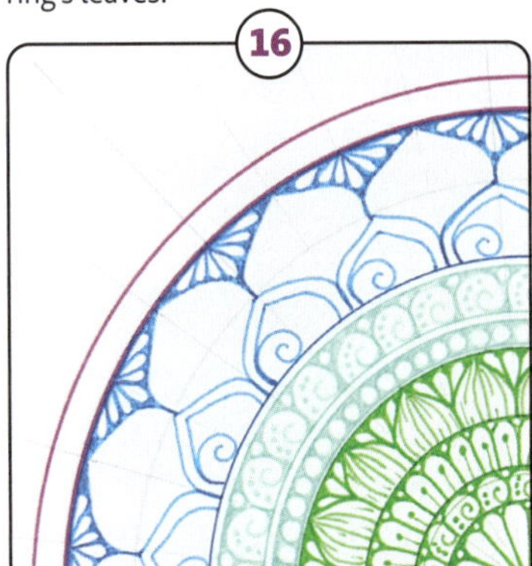

16 Add curling lines. In the same ring, add a curling line to each pointed leaf that takes up half the leaf's width.

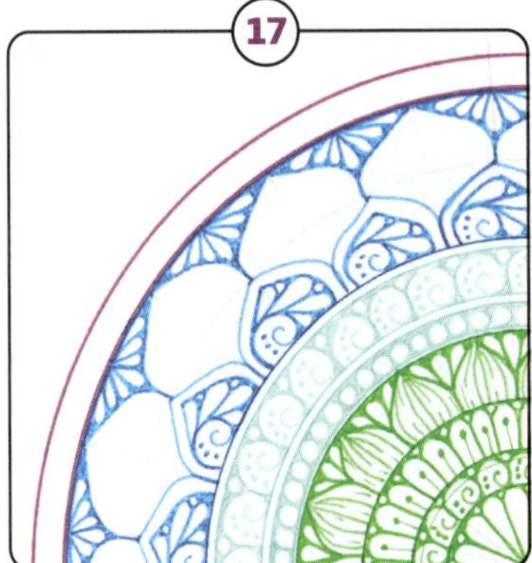

17 Finish these leaves. In the remaining space inside each of these leaves, add four teardrops and two tiny circles, then fill in around them.

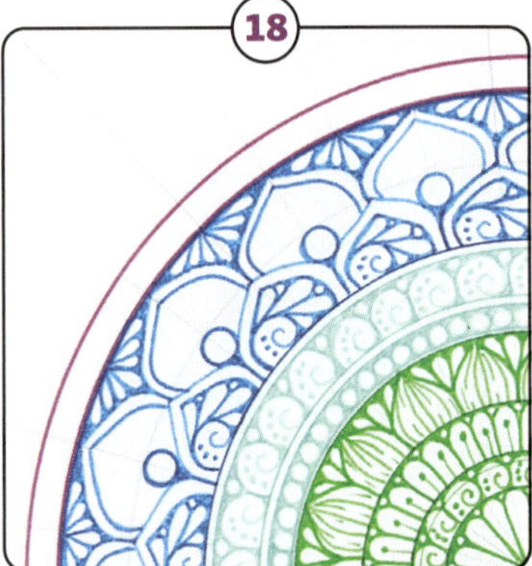

18 Start the large leaves. Nestled between each of the finished pointed leaves (at the bottom center of each unfinished pointed leaf), draw a circle.

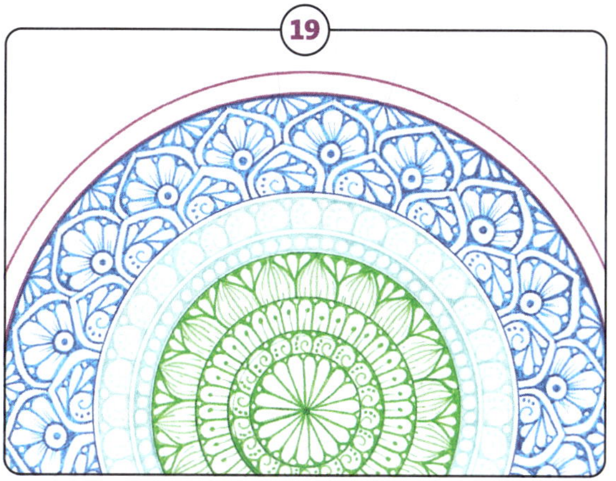

Finish the large leaves. To each large leaf, add a thick dot inside the circle, five petals, and a tiny circle between each petal, then fill in around them.

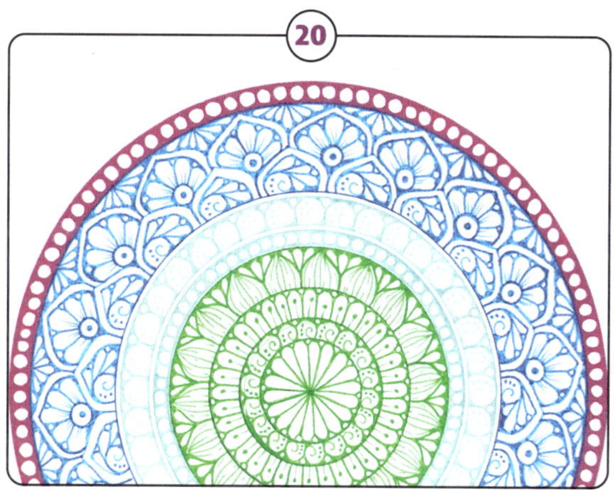

Switch to purple. Draw three circles between each ray in the next ring, then fill in around them.

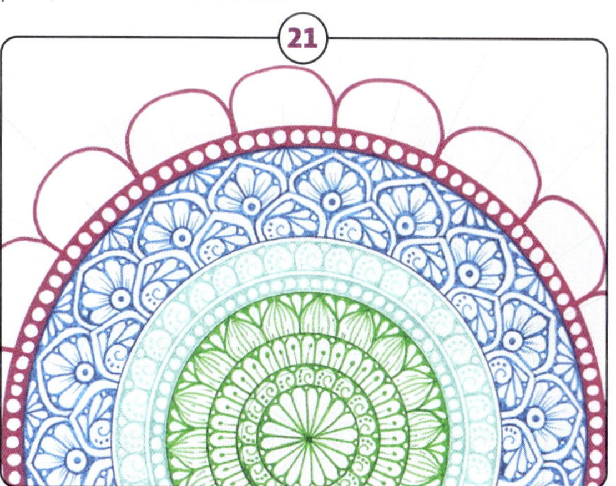

Start the next ring. Draw domes centered on alternating rays in the next ring.

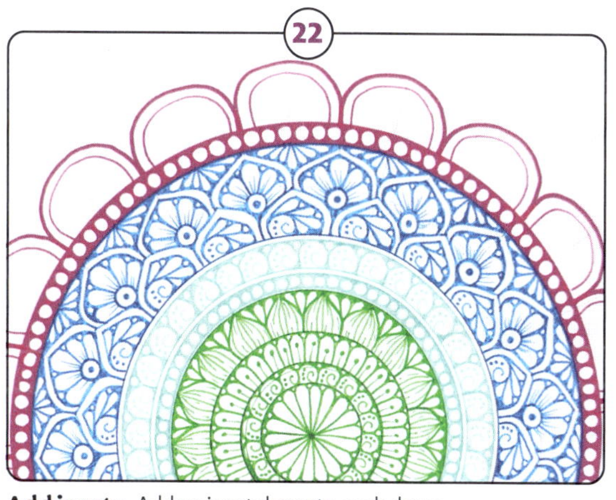

Add insets. Add an inset dome to each dome.

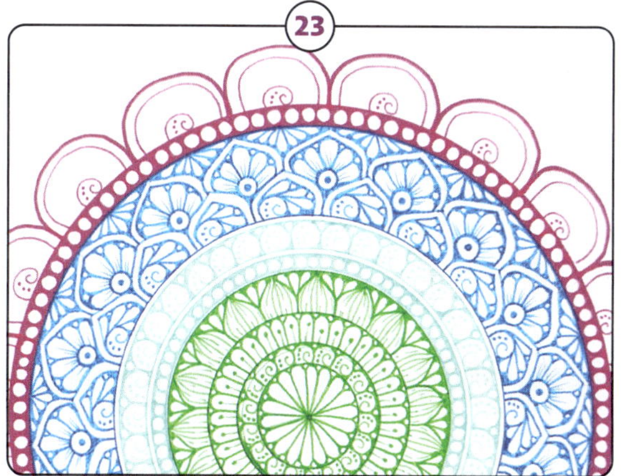

Start a new pattern. Draw a small curling line at the bottom center of each dome. Add three dots inside each one.

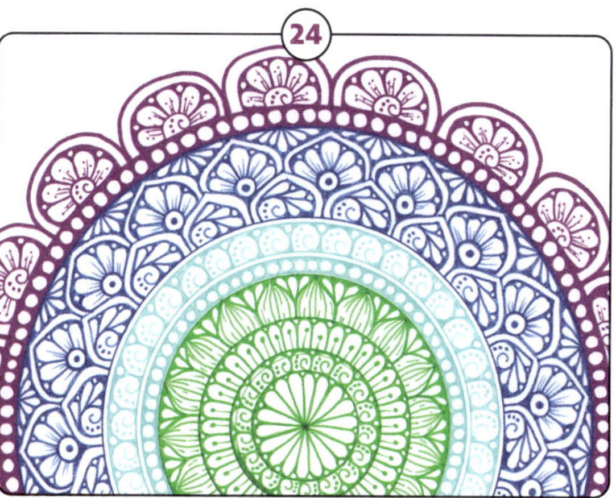

Finish the pattern. Add five petals to each dome, draw a circle between each petal, and fill in around them. Add a few delicate lines and dots inside the petals.

Mirror Flip

Here's an interesting new concept! In this mandala, you'll learn how to create a dual-toned design that's split down the center. When you start, make the delineation between the two halves very clear in pencil. And, as you're drawing, always use your lighter color first in case you accidentally go too far around and into the wrong half!

INTENTION

As you draw this mandala, think about opposites and complements: light and dark, cold and hot, energy and calm.

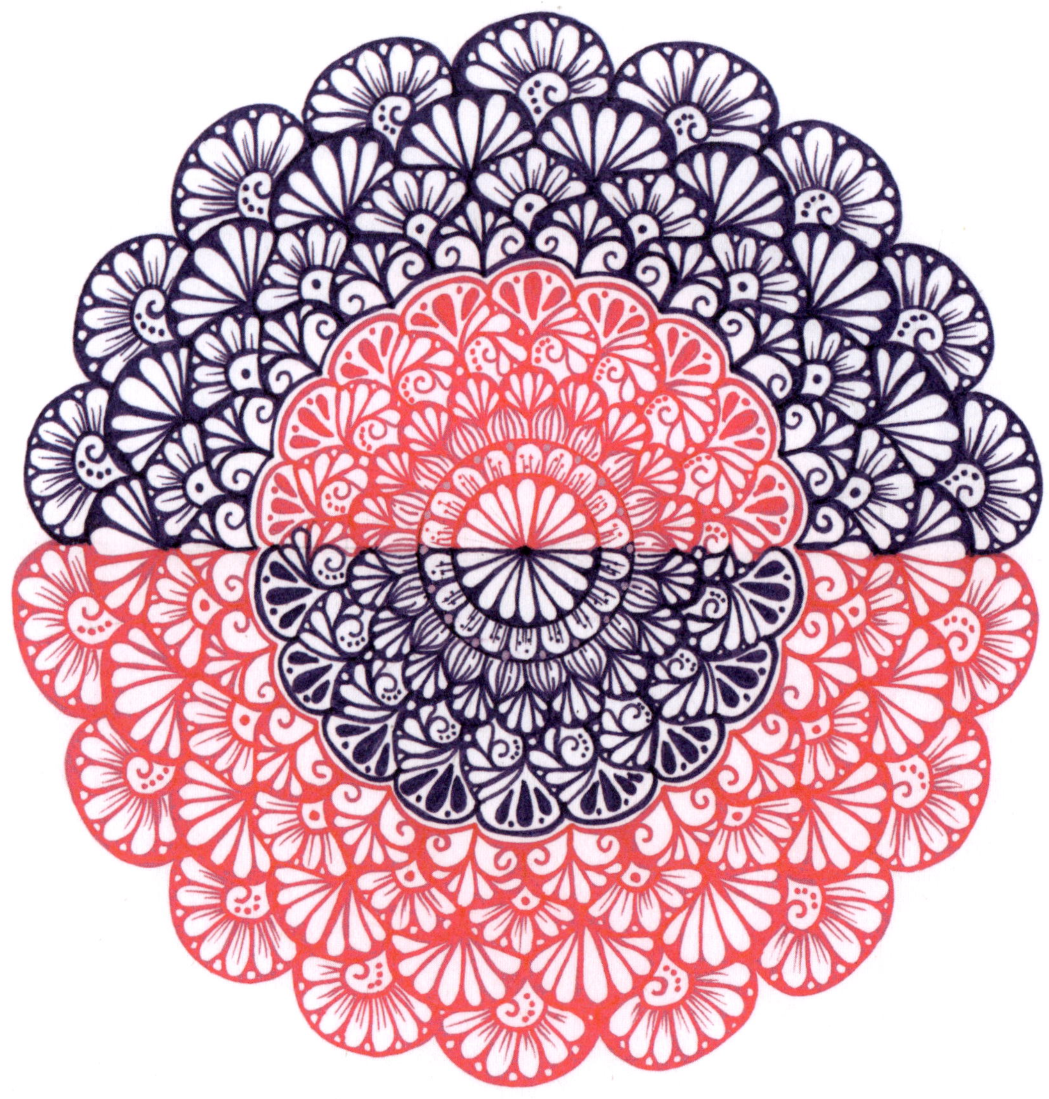

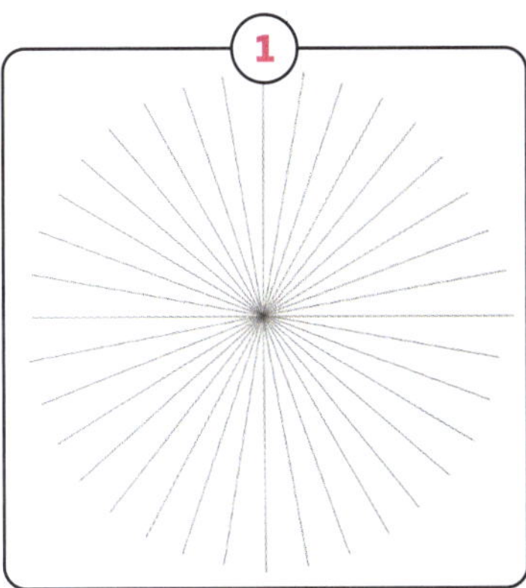

Draw rays. Using pencil, draw a straight horizontal line, then draw a ray every 10° on the top half and bottom half (17 rays total on each half).

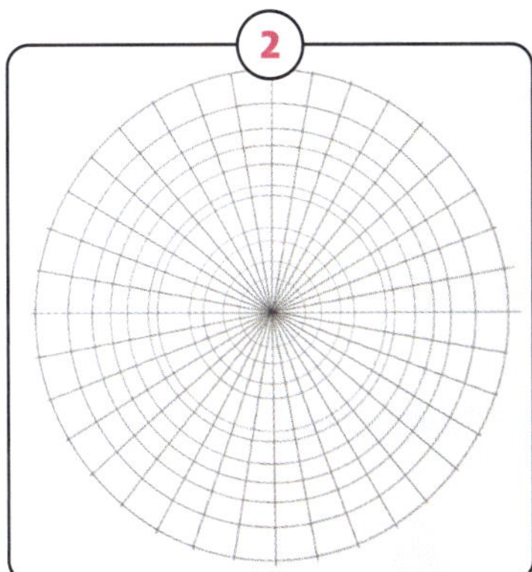

Draw circles. Draw 11 circles as shown. For reference, the outermost circle radius is 3" (7.7 cm); the innermost circle radius is ½" (1.1 cm).

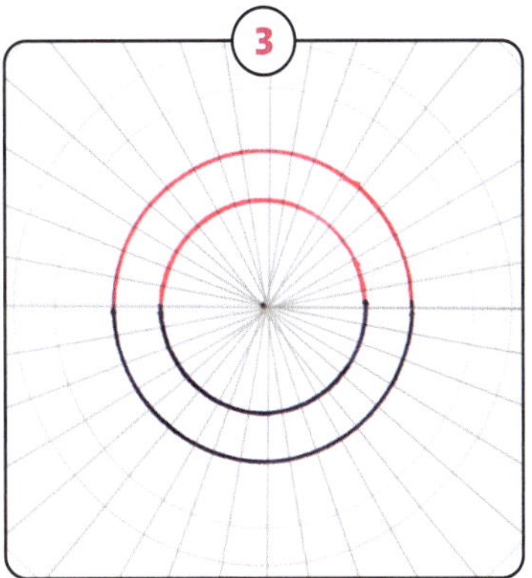

Trace the first two circles. Starting with pink for the top half and purple for the bottom half, trace the first two circles.

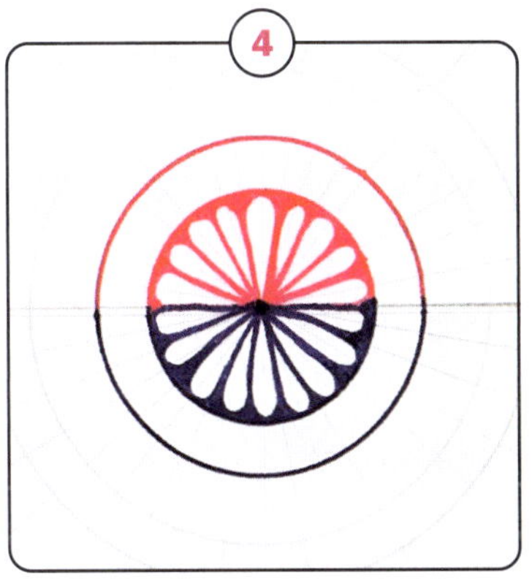

Draw the center. In the center, draw teardrops centered on alternating rays, then fill in around them.

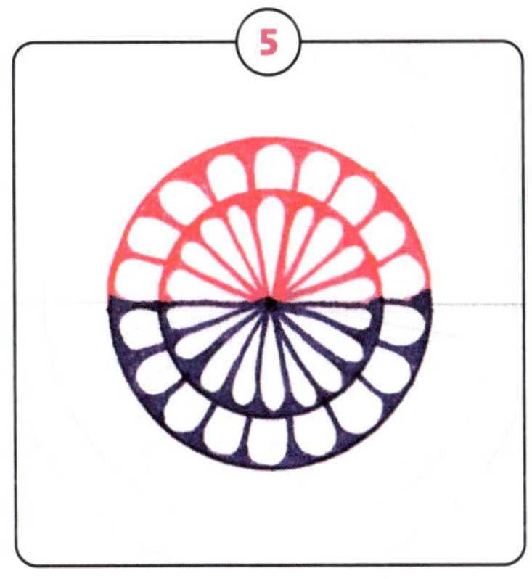

Start the first ring. Draw domes centered on alternating rays (the same rays as the previous teardrops), then fill in around them.

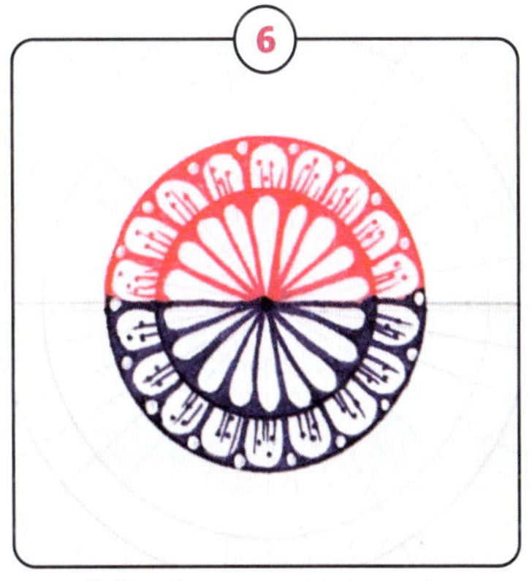

Detail the domes. Add about three lines and three dots to each dome. Go back with a white gel pen to add a dot/circle between each dome.

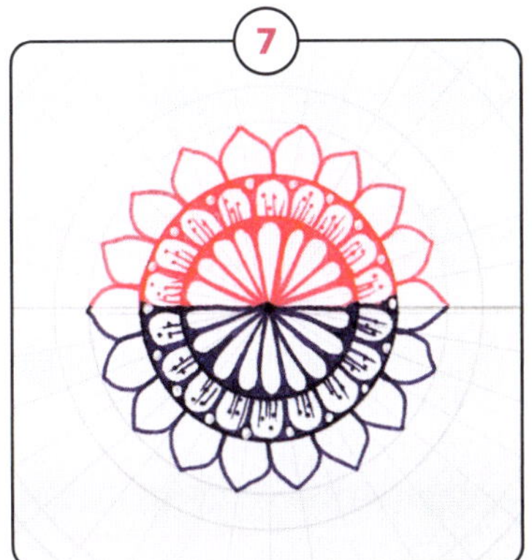

Add pointed leaves. Draw pointed leaves centered on alternating rays in the next ring. Start along the horizontal axis with a leaf that is half pink, half purple.

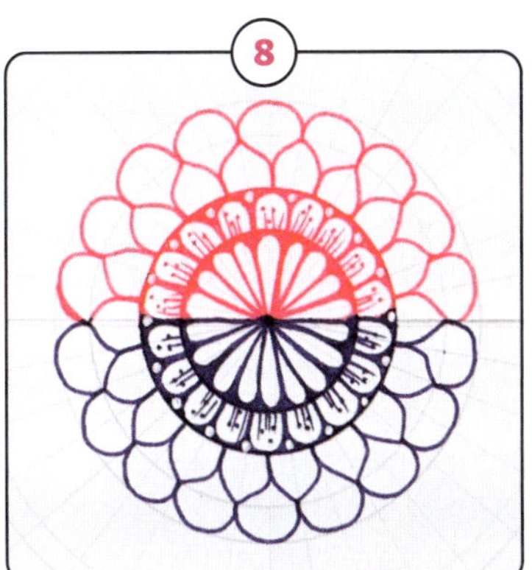

Continue to the next ring. Draw domes centered on alternating rays in the next ring, offset from the previous ring of pointed leaves.

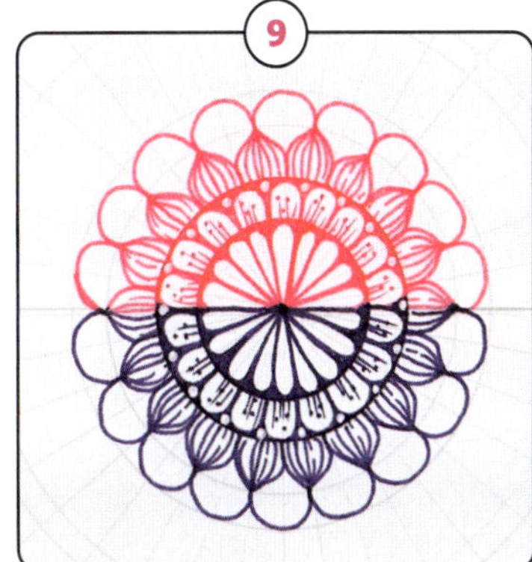

Detail the leaves. Add solid and broken lines to the pointed leaves to give them a textured, rounded effect—imagine an onion.

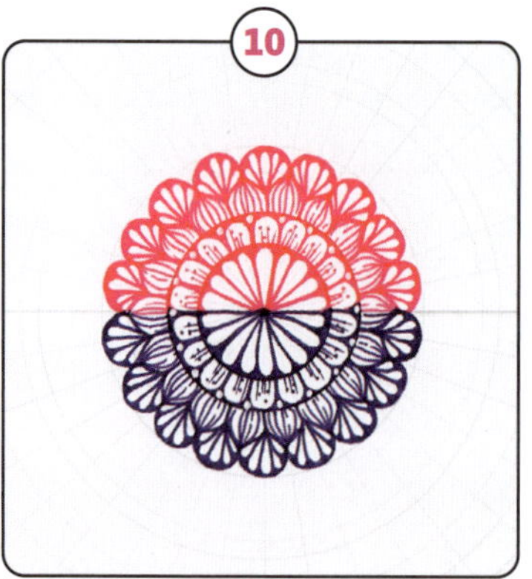

Detail the domes. Draw five teardrops inside each dome, then fill in around them.

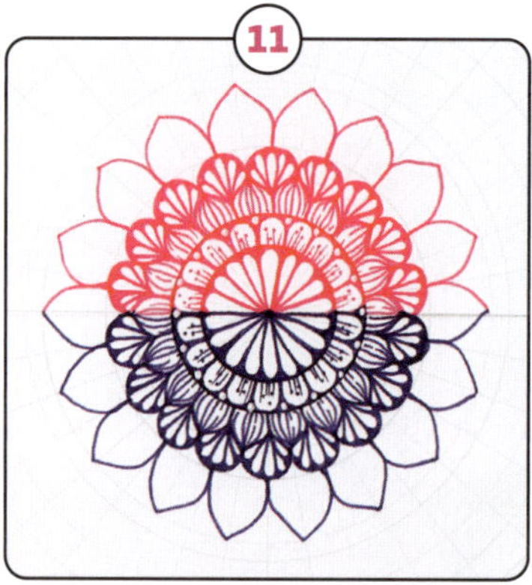

Start a new ring. Draw pointed leaves centered on alternating rays in the next ring. Start along the horizontal axis with a leaf that is half pink, half purple.

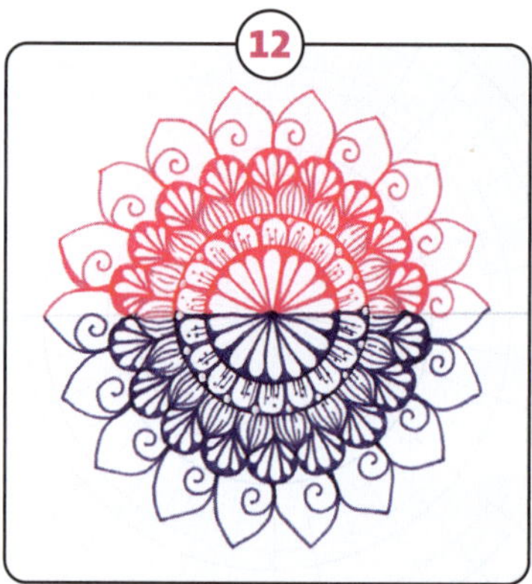

Add curling lines. Draw a curling line in each pointed leaf that is half the width of the leaf.

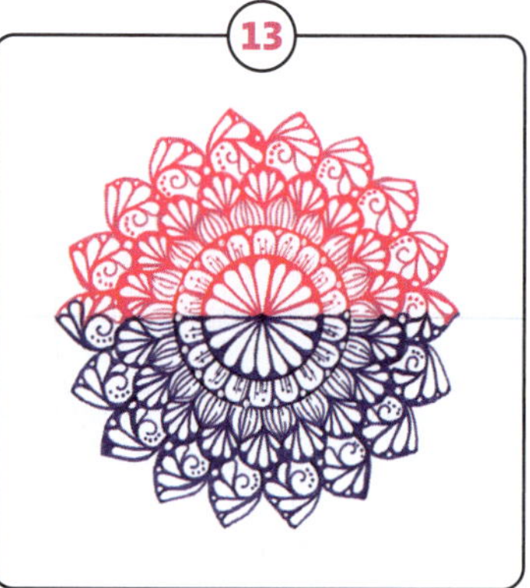

Fill the leaves. Inside each pointed leaf, add four dots underneath the curling line, draw four teardrops, add a circle between each teardrop, and fill in around them.

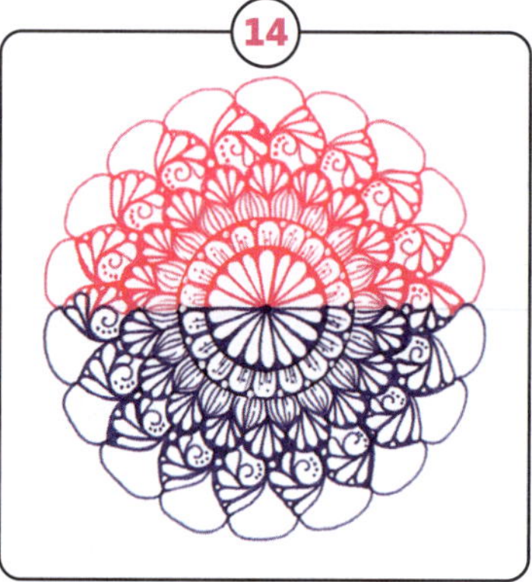

Start the next ring. Draw domes centered on alternating rays in the next ring, offset from the previous ring of pointed leaves.

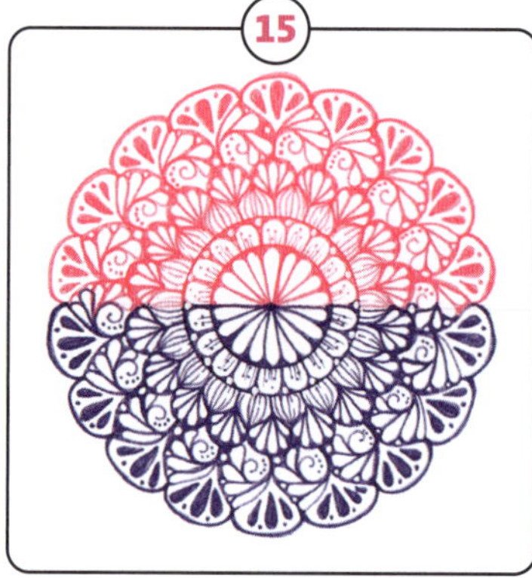

Fill the domes. In each dome, draw three filled-in teardrops and two dots. Thicken the outer edge of each dome with your colored pen.

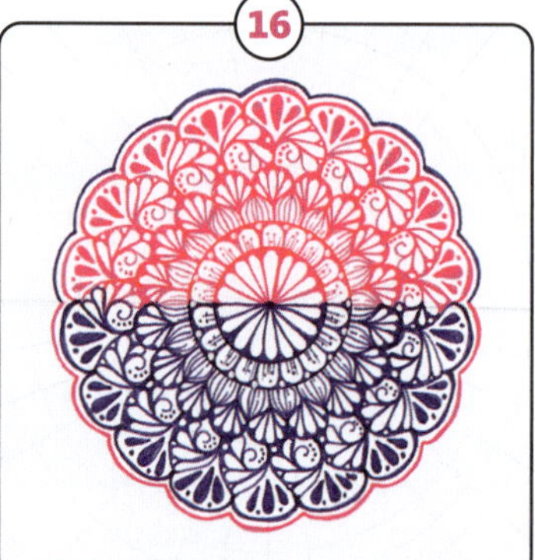

Swap color halves. On the top half of the mandala, draw an unbroken purple line following along the contour of the tops of the domes; do the same in pink on the bottom half.

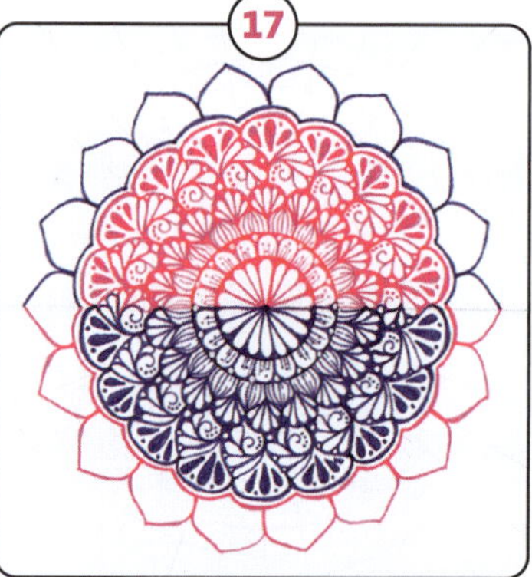

Start a new ring. Draw pointed leaves centered on alternating rays to create the next double-wide ring. Start along the horizontal axis with a leaf that is half purple, half pink.

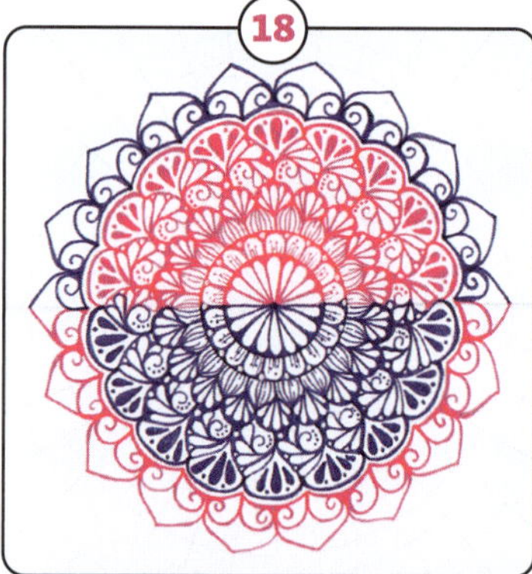

Add curling lines. Draw two curling lines inside each pointed leaf. Make sure the halves match the correct color in each transitional leaf along the horizontal axis.

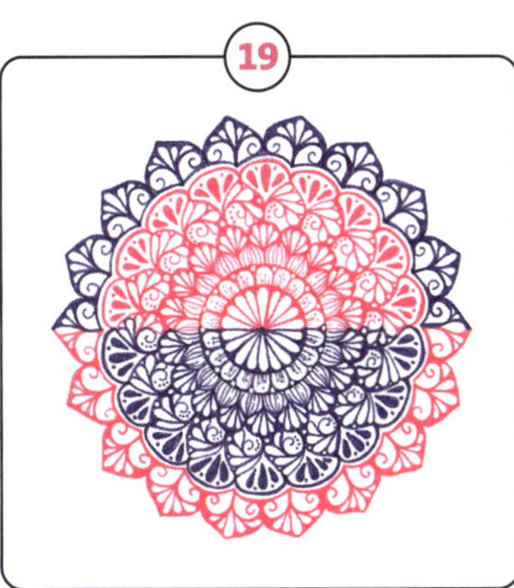

Add teardrops. In each leaf, draw five teardrops, then fill in around them. Make sure the halves are correct along the horizontal axis again.

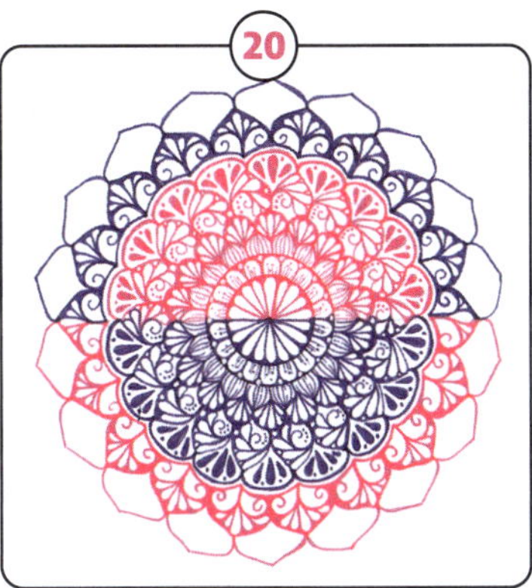

Start a new ring. Draw pointed leaves centered on alternating rays to create the next ring, offset from the previous ring of pointed leaves.

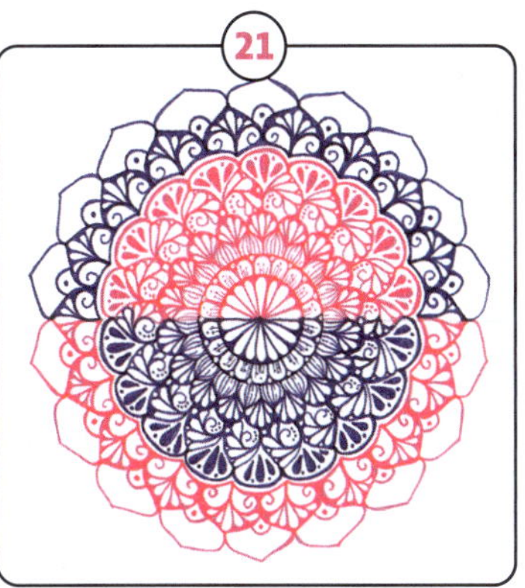

Start a pattern. Nestled between each of the finished pointed leaves (at the bottom center of each unfinished pointed leaf), draw a semicircle with a dot in it.

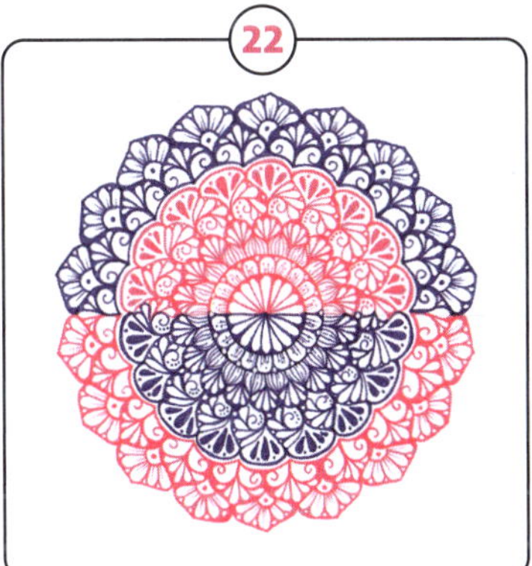

Finish the pattern. To each unfinished leaf, add five petals and a tiny circle between each petal, then fill in around them. Add delicate detail lines to the petals.

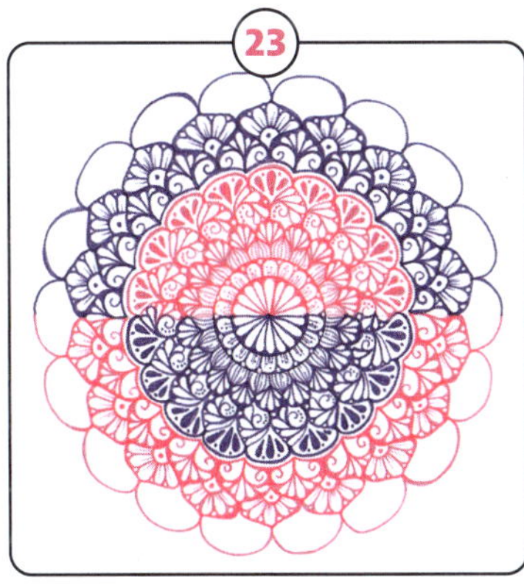

Start a new ring. Draw domes centered on alternating rays to create the next ring. Start along the horizontal axis with a leaf that is half purple, half pink.

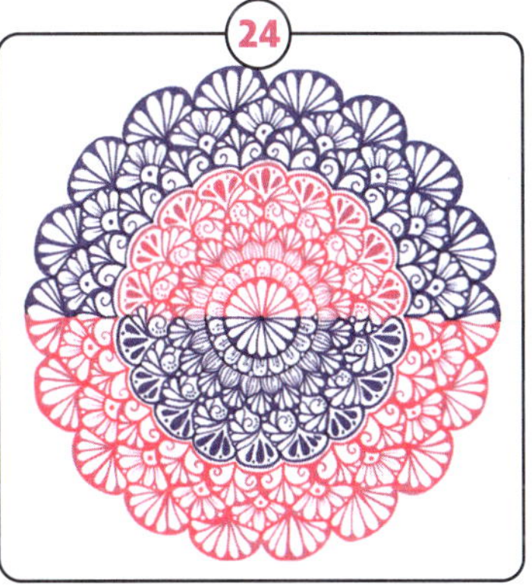

Add teardrops. Inside each dome, draw seven teardrops, then fill in around them. Make sure the colors of the halves are correct along the horizontal axis.

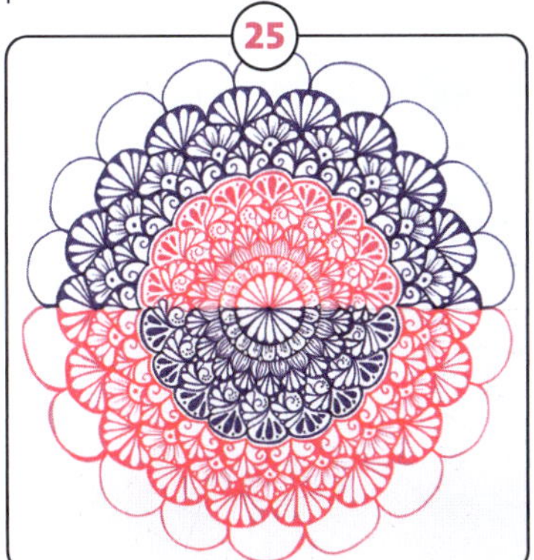

Start the last ring. Draw domes centered on alternating rays to create the next ring, offset from the previous ring of domes.

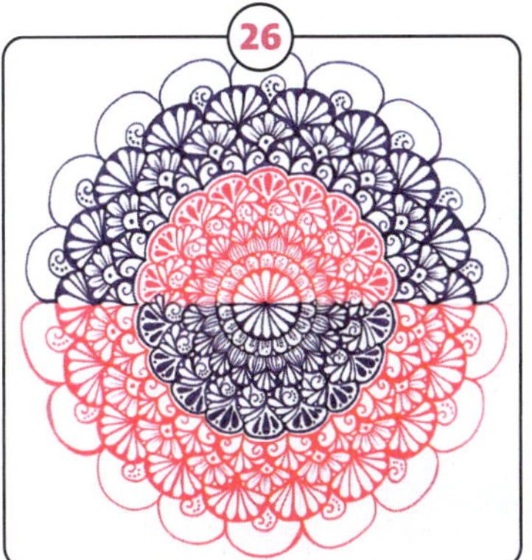

Add curling lines. Nestled between each of dome of the previous ring (at the bottom center of each unfinished dome), draw a curling line with four dots inside it.

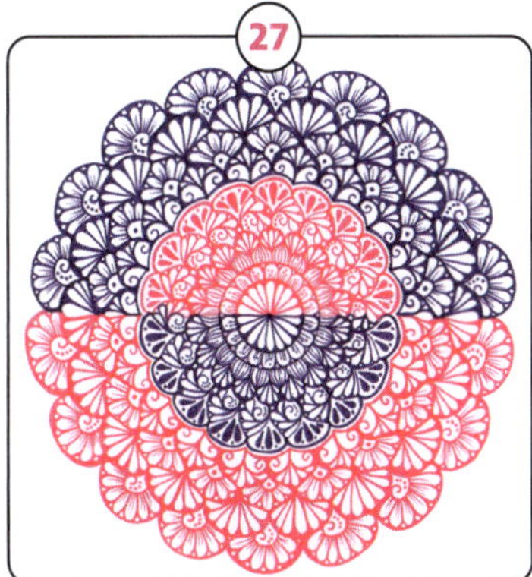

Finish the details. Draw seven petals inside each dome. Add a tiny circle between each petal, then fill in around them. Add delicate detail lines to each petal.

Full-Page Rainbow

This gorgeous nine-color design goes all the way off the edges of the page! Make sure you choose a square piece of paper that isn't too big to create this design. It's definitely an intricate mandala with a higher time investment and ton of rays and circles, but on-the-fly color changes make the process flow easily and calmly.

As you draw this mandala, imagine that you are creating a rainbow color by color that is stretching out from you in all directions into the wider world, lighting up the sky for everyone to enjoy.

MANDALAS

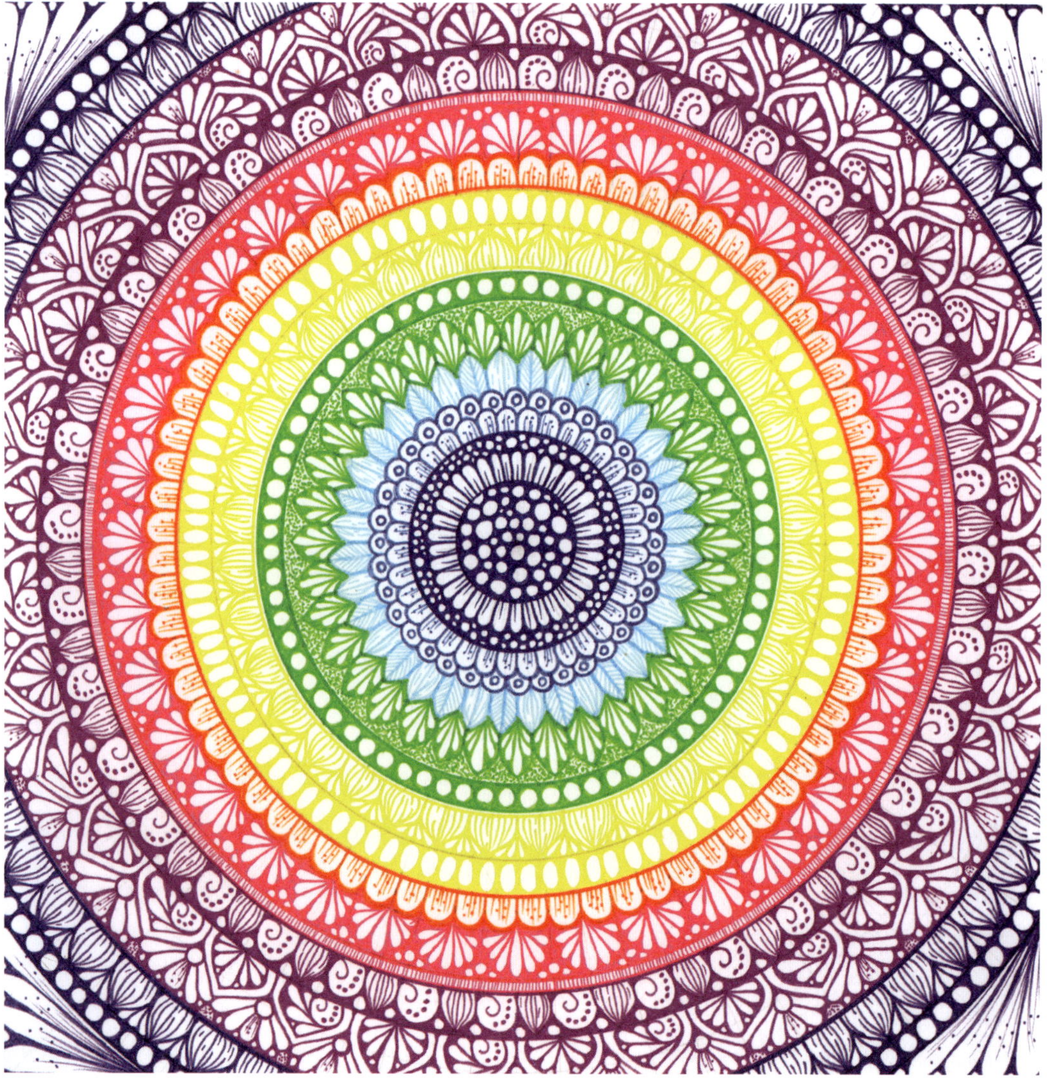

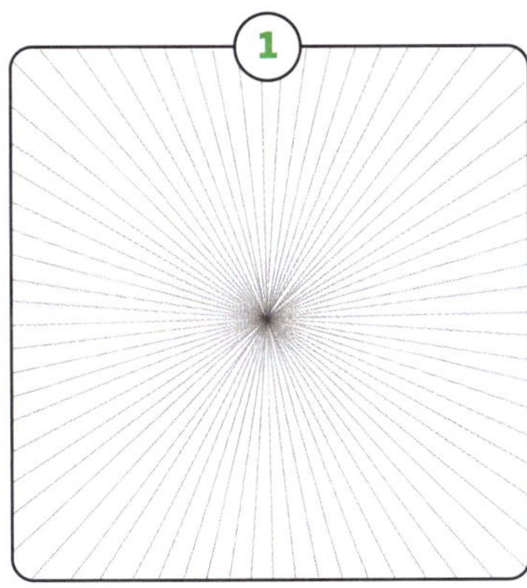

Draw rays. Using pencil, draw a straight horizontal line, then draw a ray every 5° on the top half and bottom half (35 rays total on each half).

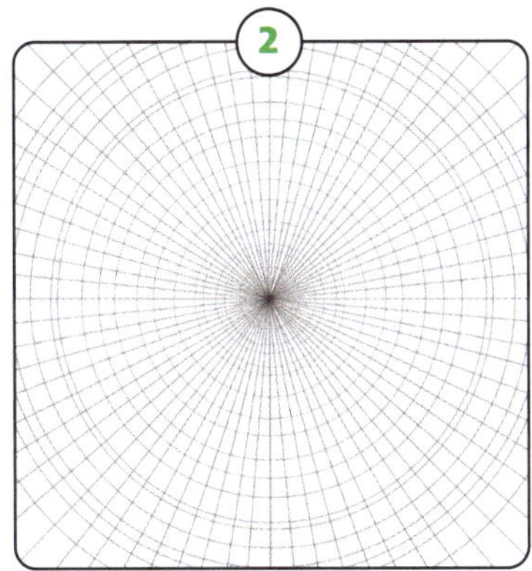

Draw circles. Draw 18 circles as shown. For reference, the outermost circle radius is 5⅛" (13 cm); the innermost circle radius is ½" (1.3 cm).

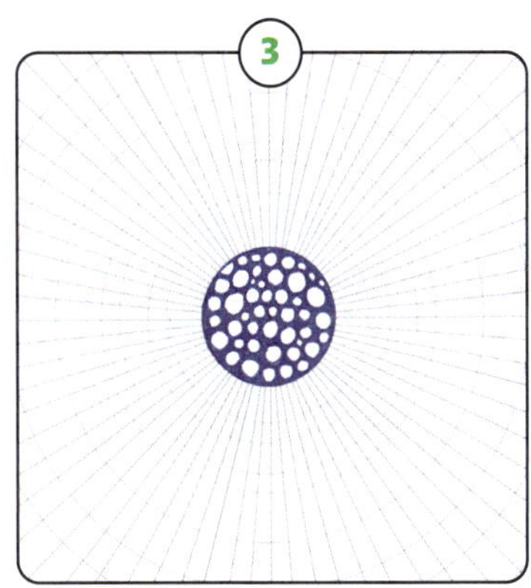

Start with dark blue. Trace the innermost circle in dark blue. Fill it with freehand circles in a variety of sizes, then fill in around them.

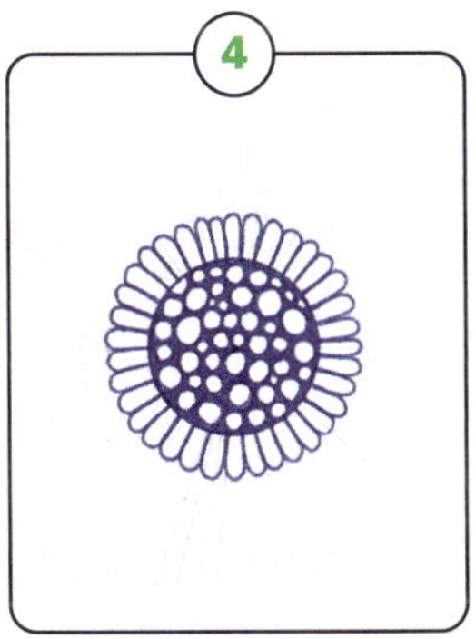

Add petals. Draw petals centered on alternating rays to create the first ring.

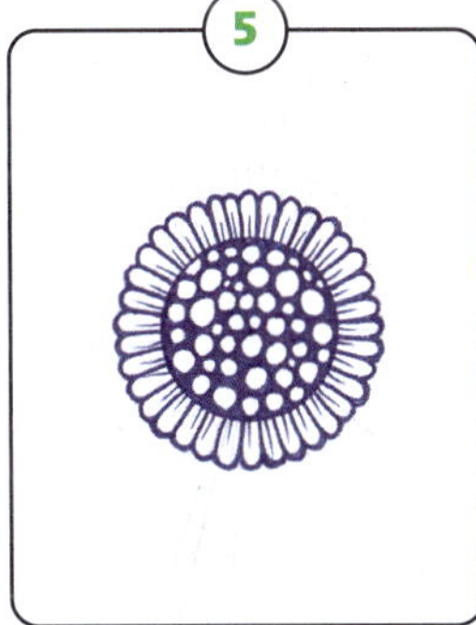

Detail the petals. Draw a delicate detail line inside each petal.

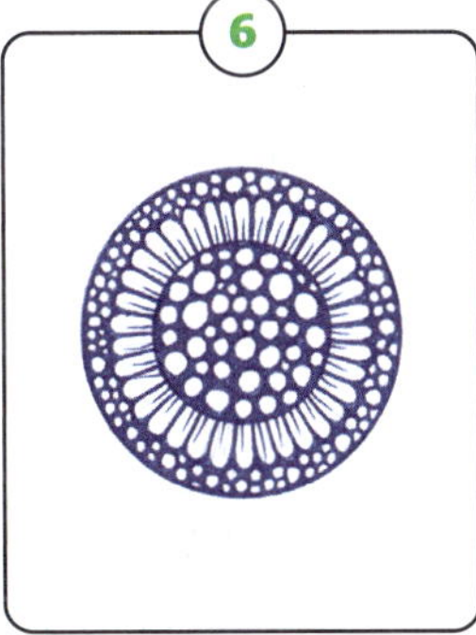

Complete the next ring. Trace the next circle in dark blue. Fill the ring with freehand circles in a variety of small sizes, then fill in around them.

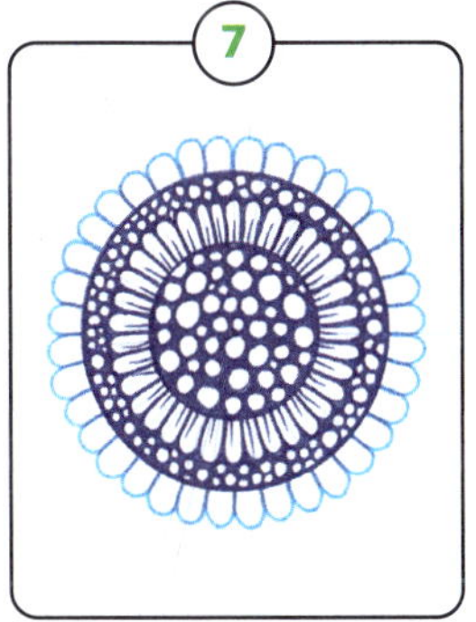

Switch to medium blue. Draw domes centered on alternating rays for the next ring.

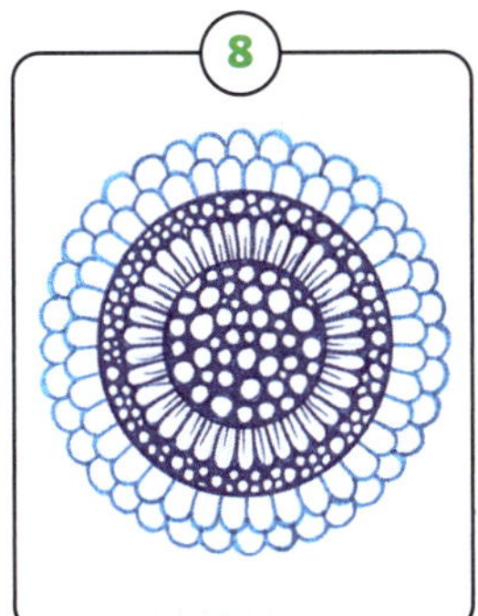

Move on to the following ring. Continuing to the next ring, draw domes centered on alternating rays, offset from the previous ring of domes.

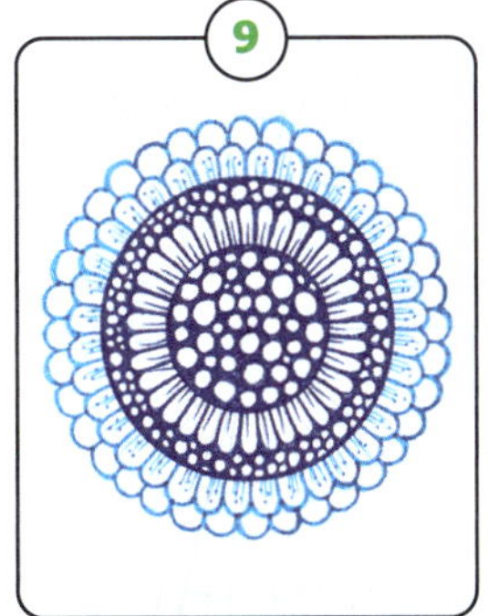

Detail the first set of domes. For the first ring of domes, add a smattering of delicate detail lines and dots inside each dome.

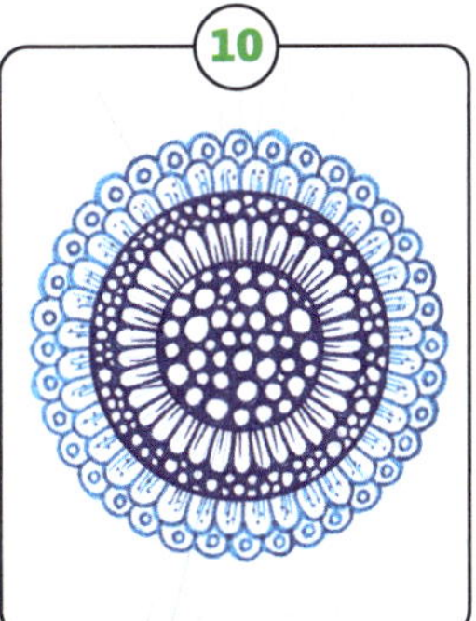

Detail the second set of domes. For the second ring of domes, draw a circle inside each dome.

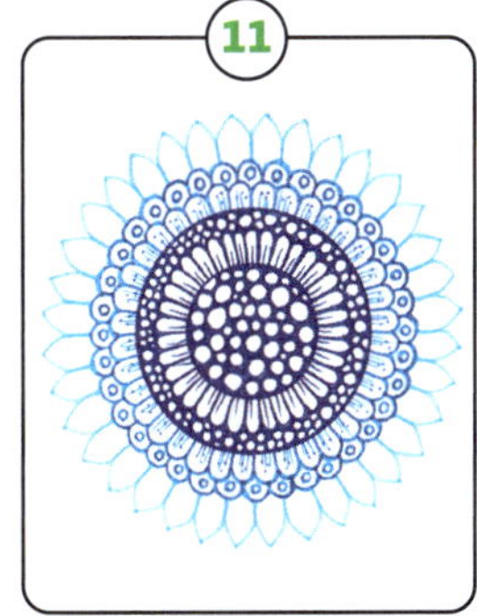

Switch to light blue. Draw pointed leaves centered on alternating rays, offset from the previous ring of domes.

MANDALAS

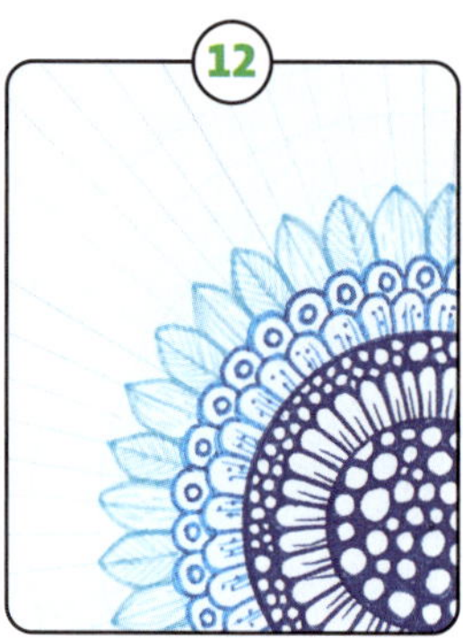

Add details. In some leaves, draw a central spine and veins like a real leaf. In other leaves, add a mix of solid and broken lines to give them a textured, rounded effect.

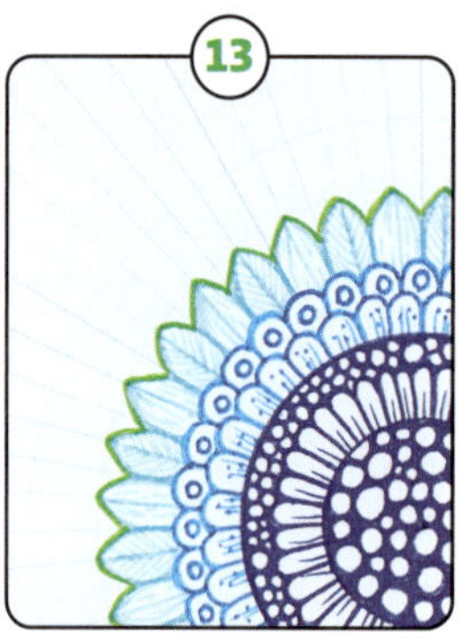

Switch to green. Draw an unbroken zigzag line along the tops of the pointed leaves.

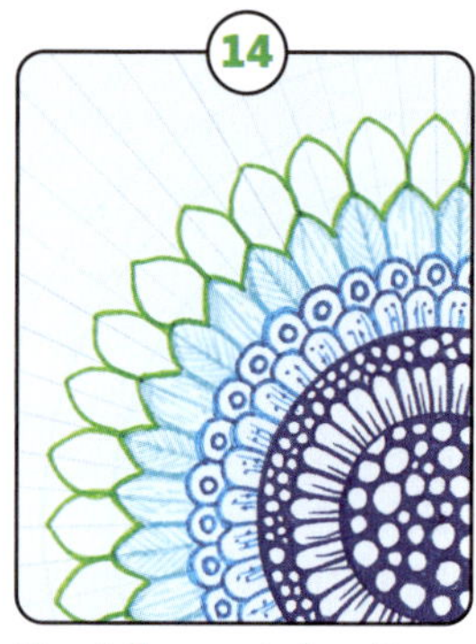

Start the next ring. Draw pointed leaves centered on alternating rays, offset from the previous ring of pointed leaves.

Add teardrops. In each pointed leaf, draw five teardrops, then fill in around them.

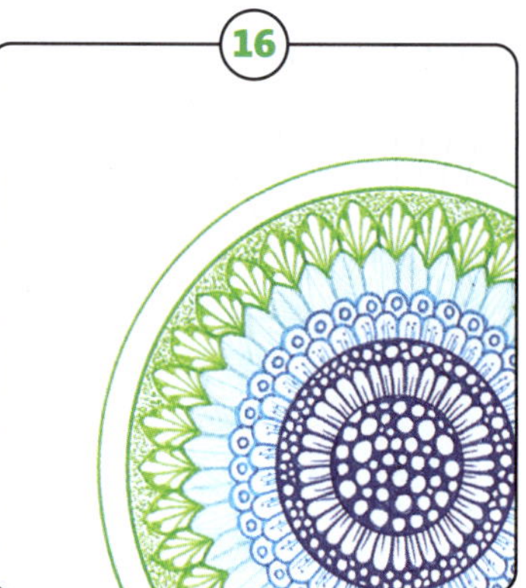

Start the next ring. Trace the next two circles (including the one the last row of leaves touches) in green. Densely stipple the trapped area between the leaves.

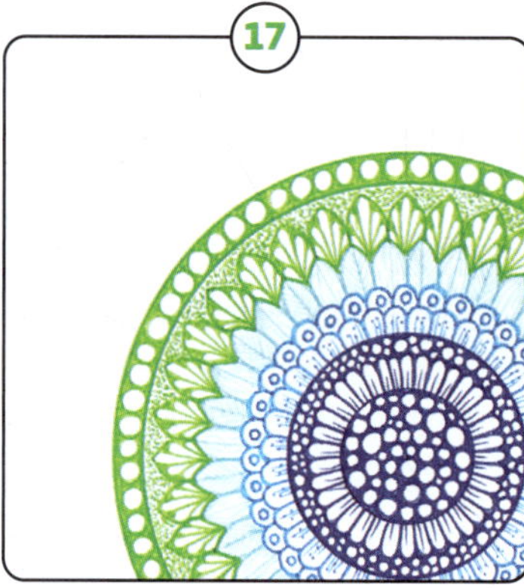

Fill the next ring. Draw a circle between each ray in the next ring, then fill in around them.

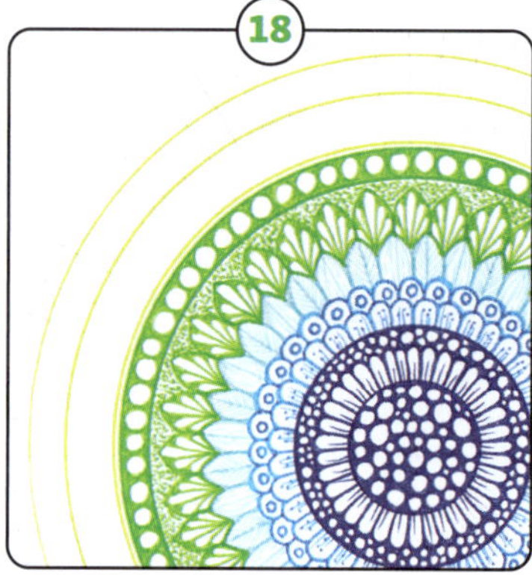

Switch to yellow. Trace the next two circles in yellow and add another yellow circle right next to the last green one.

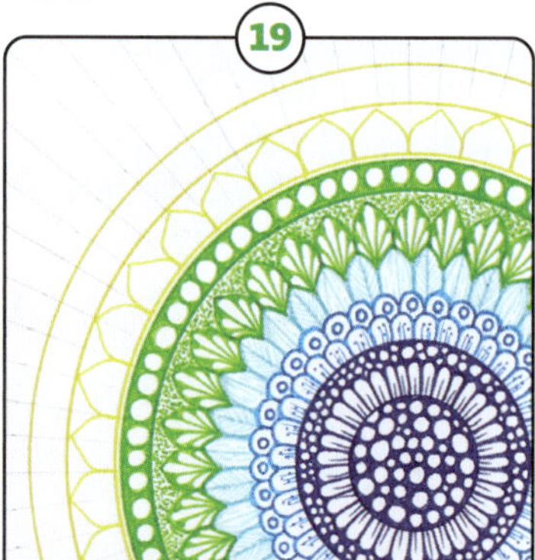

Add pointed leaves. To the first yellow ring, add pointed leaves centered on each ray, offset from the previous green ring of pointed leaves.

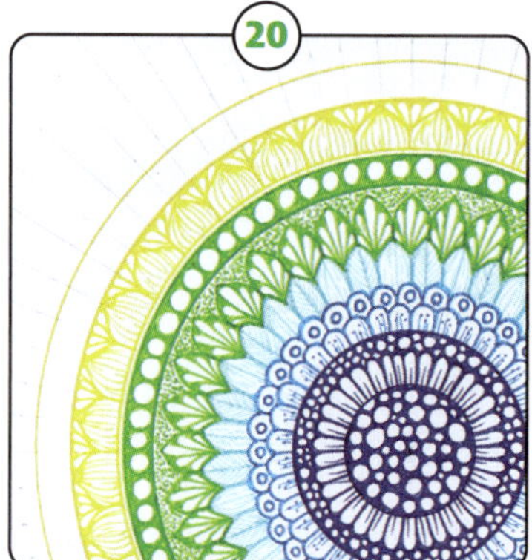

Detail the ring. Add four teardrops between each pointed leaf, then fill in around them. Inside the leaves, add a mix of solid and broken lines.

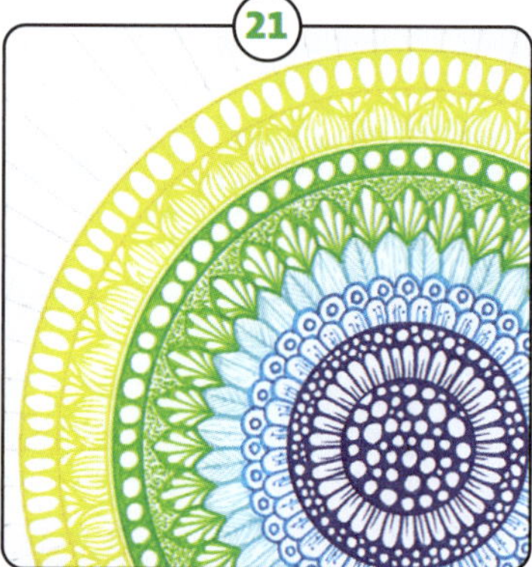

Complete the next ring. Fill the next ring with tall ovals, drawing about one to one and a half ovals between each ray, then fill in around them.

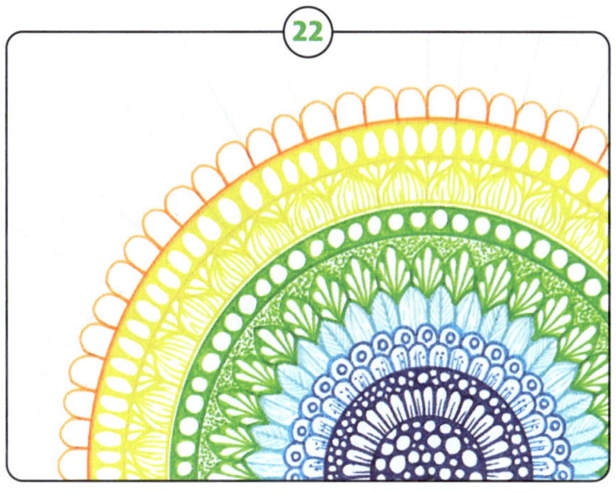

Switch to orange. Trace a fresh orange circle right up against the last yellow circle. Then draw a dome between each ray.

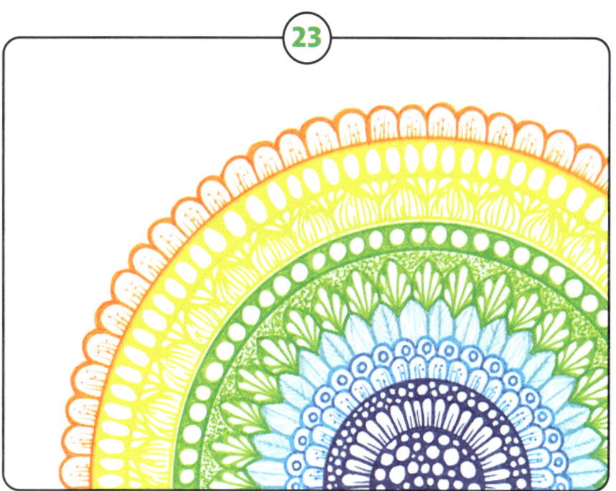

Add details. Draw some delicate lines and dots inside each dome. Thicken the outer border of all the domes.

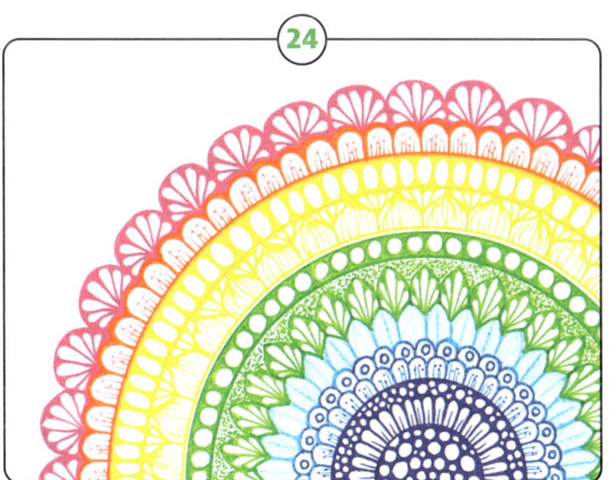

Switch to pink. Draw domes centered on alternating rays in the next ring. Draw seven teardrops in each dome, then fill in around them.

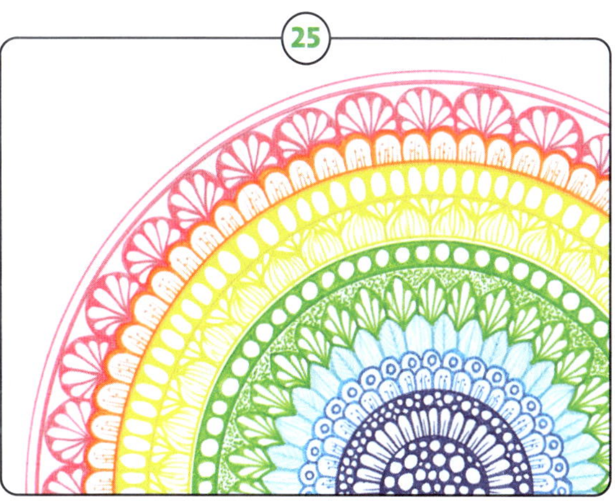

Trace two more circles. Trace the next two circles (including the one the last row of domes touches) in pink.

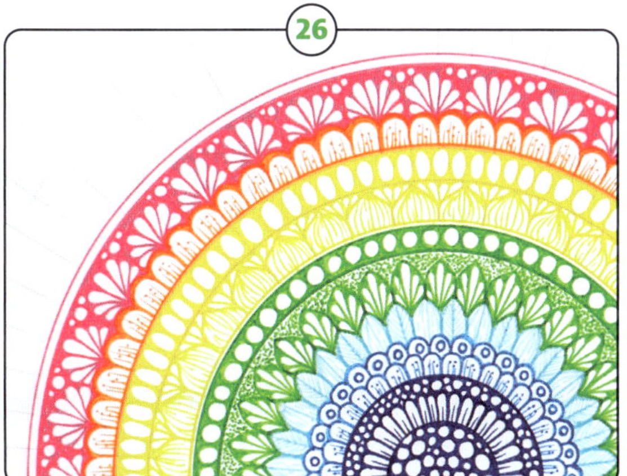

Finish filling the ring. In each trapped area between the inner pink circle and a finished dome, draw three freehand circles, then fill in around them.

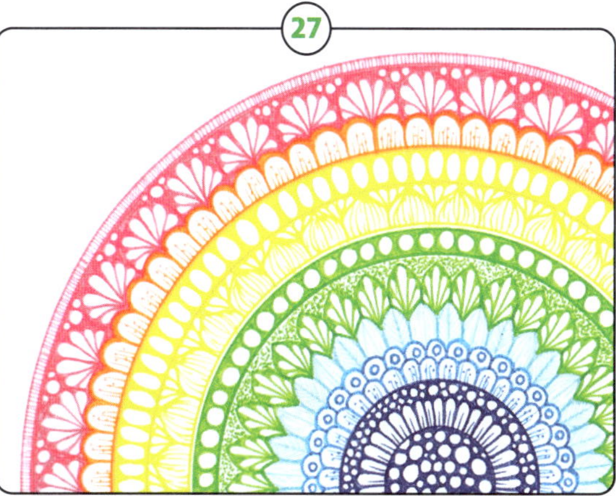

Fill the thin ring. In the very thin pink ring that remains, draw densely packed vertical lines.

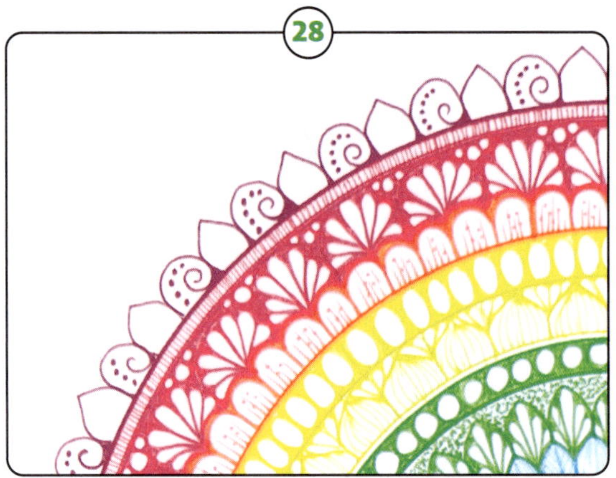

Switch to purple. Trace a circle in purple right next to the last pink circle. Alternate drawing a curling line with dots and a pointed leaf between each ray.

Finish the leaves. In the pointed leaves, add a mix of solid and broken lines to give them a textured, rounded effect—imagine an onion again.

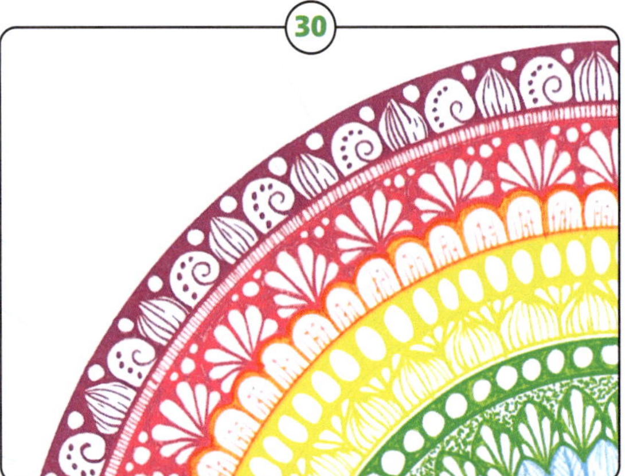

Complete the ring. Trace the circle that touches the leaves and curling lines. Draw a circle between each leaf and curling line, then fill in around them.

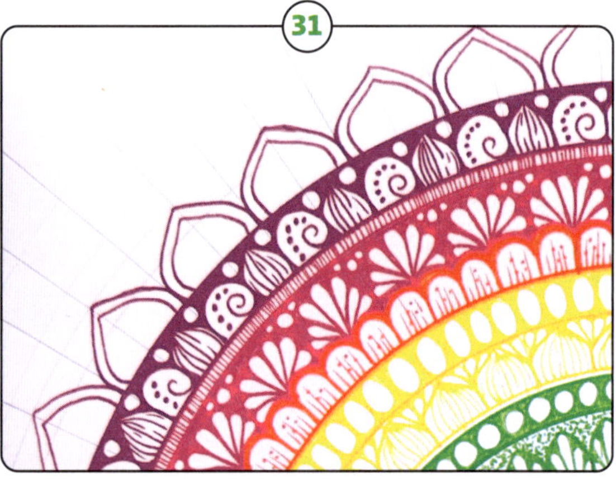

Fill with two patterns. Refer to the photo to fill the inset pointed leaves with one of two different alternating patterns as shown.

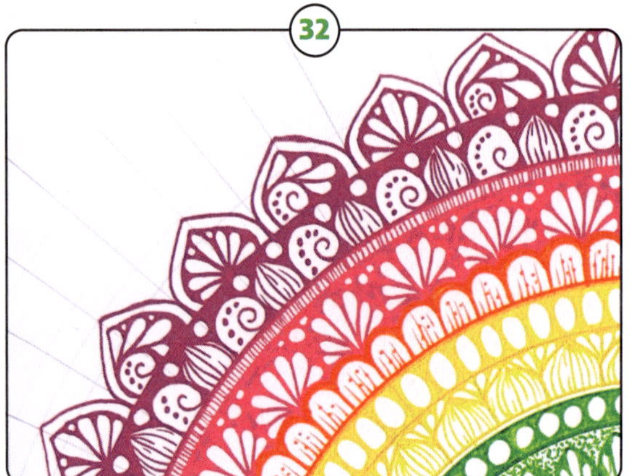

Fill with two patterns. Refer to the photo to fill the inset pointed leaves with one of two different alternating patterns as shown.

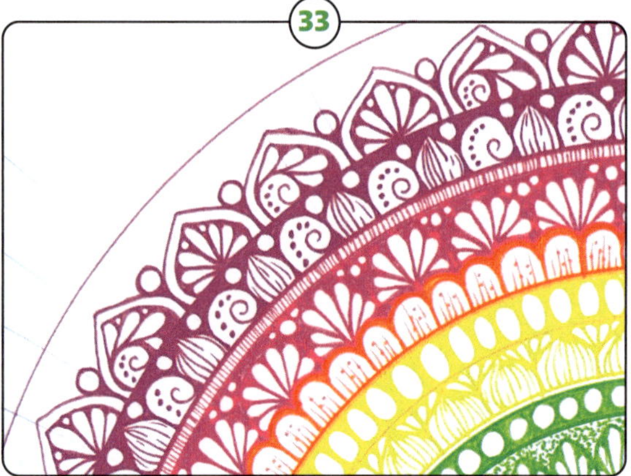

Start the next ring. Nestled between each pointed leaf, draw a small circle. Then trace the next circle.

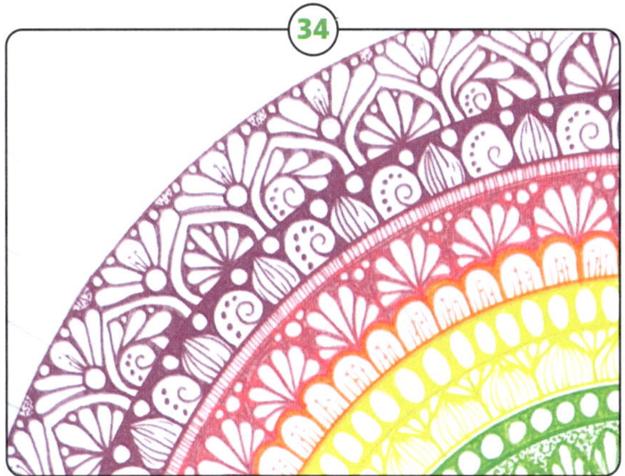

Finish this ring. Refer to the photo to fill the space trapped inside the last traced circle as shown. Note the tiny areas of stippling between each "bloom."

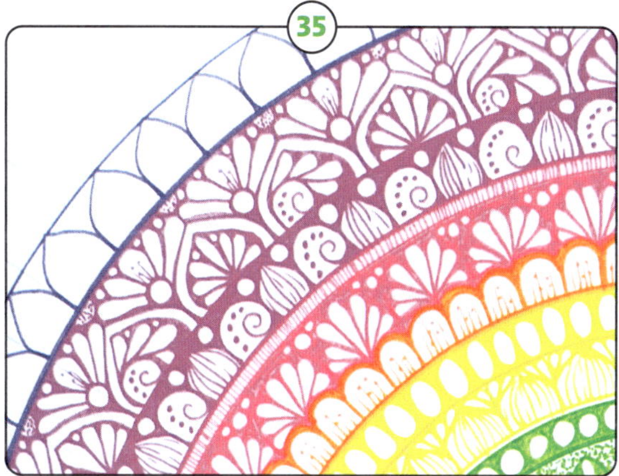

Switch to violet. Trace a fresh violet circle right against the last purple circle, as well as tracing the next circle. Draw a pointed leaf between each ray.

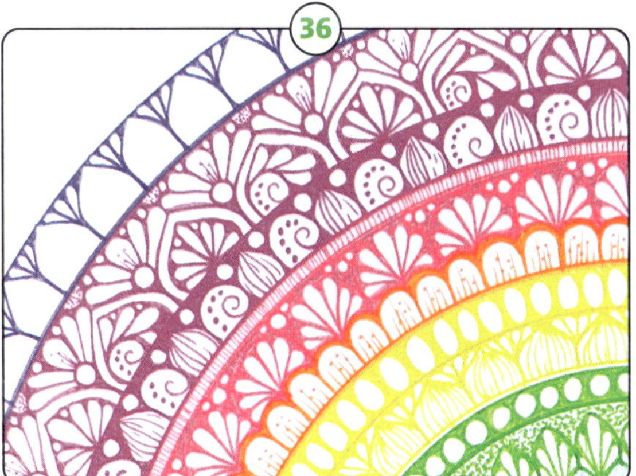

Add teardrops. Draw three teardrops between each pointed leaf, then fill in around them.

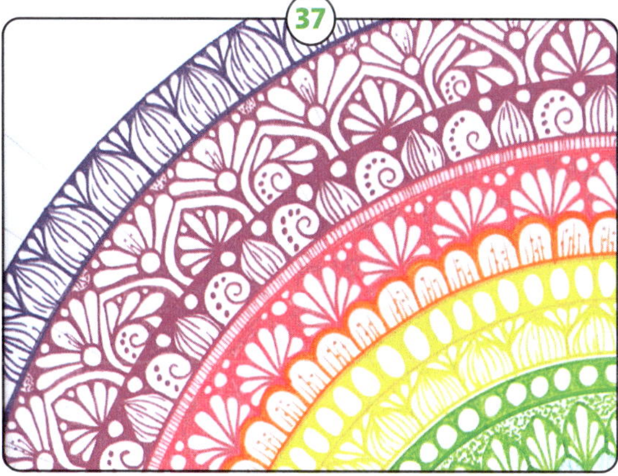

Detail the leaves. In the pointed leaves, add a mix of solid and broken lines to give them a textured, rounded effect— imagine an onion again.

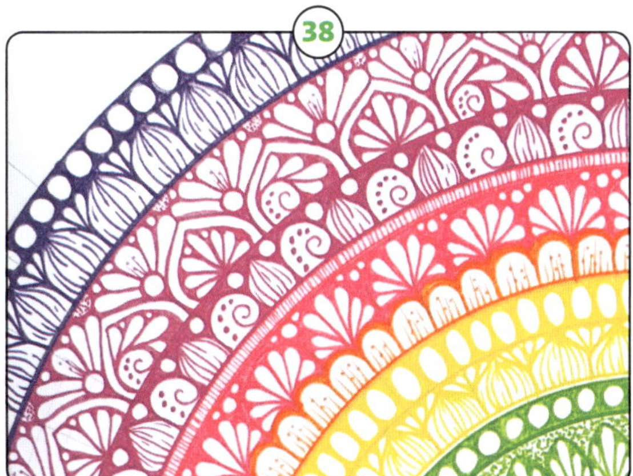

Add an unplanned ring. Add a totally new circle outside the original 18th circle from the start. Fill the resulting ring with circles, then fill in around them.

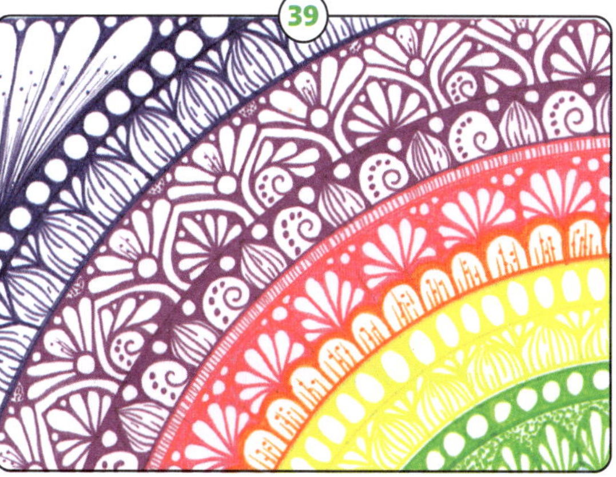

Fill the corners. Refer to the photo to fill each of the four remaining corners of the page with long teardrops, tiny circles, and delicate detail lines and dots.

Autumn Glow

CHALLENGE YOURSELF

This mandala is the most similar to Repetitive Rings because it starts with many pencil rays and circles and has colors that change organically. Use what you learned while working on the previous mandalas to build up this design yourself independently, referring to just the few basic steps that are provided as guideposts.

INTENTION

As you draw this mandala, imagine passing through the months of autumn, starting with the last of the flowers, changing to brightly colored leaves, and ending with calm, brown fields and trees.

MANDALAS

82

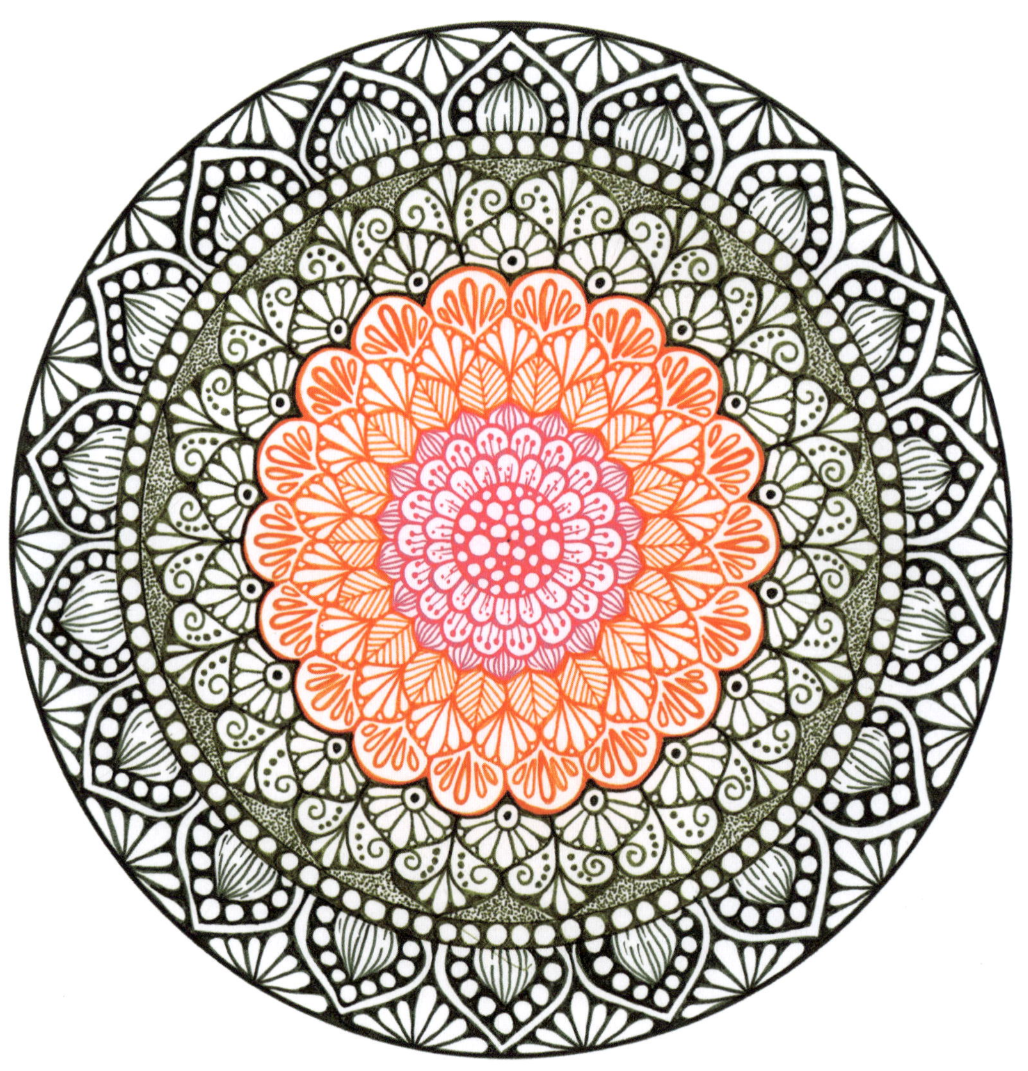

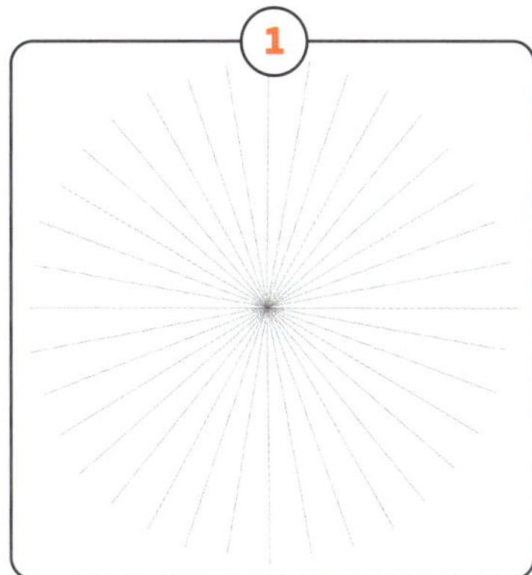

Draw rays. Using pencil, draw a straight horizontal line, then draw a ray every 10° on the top half and bottom half (17 rays total on each half).

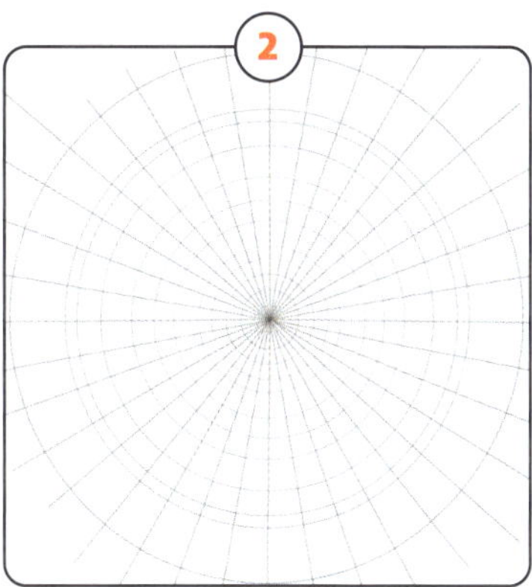

Draw circles. Draw 11 circles as shown. For reference, the outermost circle radius is 4" (10 cm); the innermost circle radius is ½" (1.1 cm).

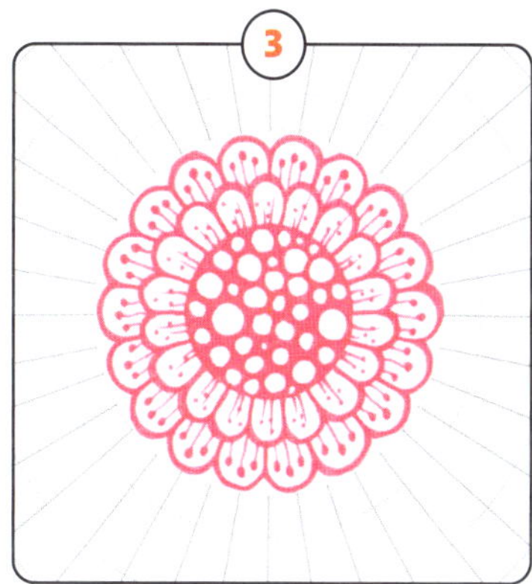

Start with the center. Using the center as well as the first two rings, draw a design inspired by a flower.

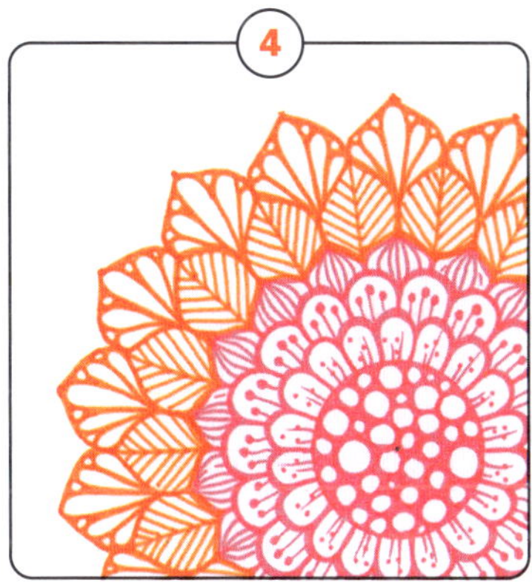

Add rings of pointed leaves. First in pink and then in orange, fill the next three rings with pointed leaves that have different filler designs.

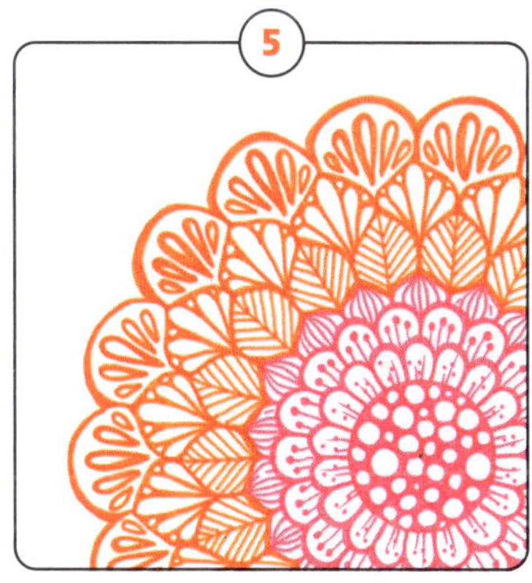

Add a ring of domes. In the next ring, add domes with a floating filler teardrop design.

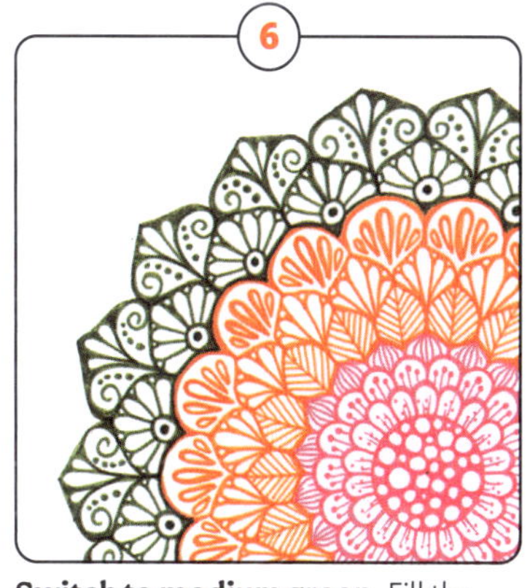

Switch to medium green. Fill the next two rings with pointed leaves that have different filler designs.

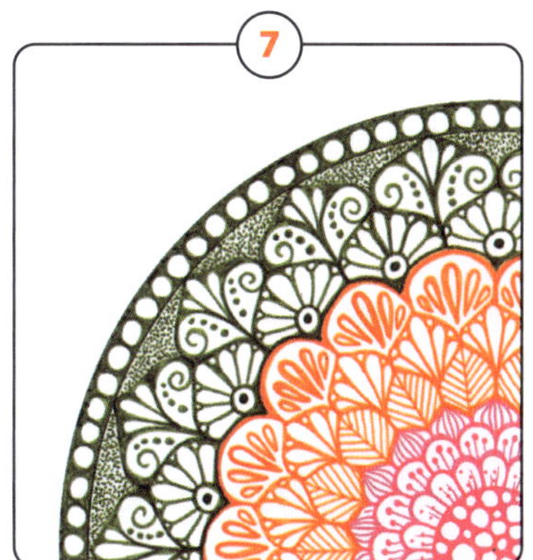

Keep going with medium green. Stipple the spaces between the pointed leaves of the last ring. Fill the next ring with circles, then fill in around them.

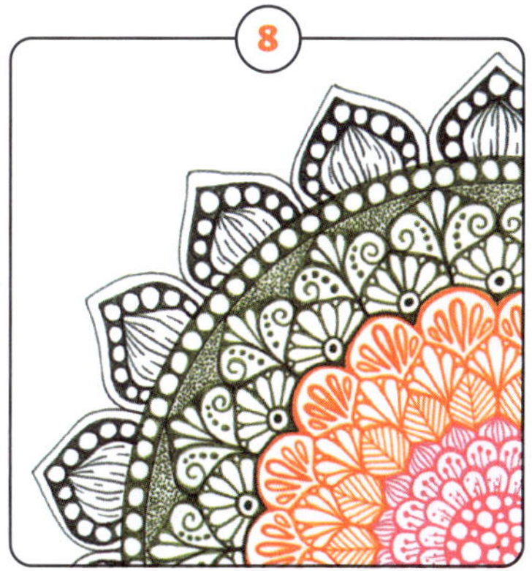

Switch to dark green. Fill the final ring with elaborate pointed leaves as shown.

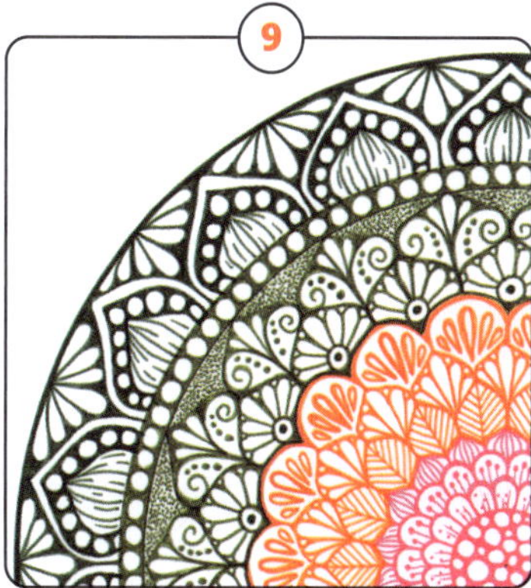

Finish the final ring. Trace the last circle. Add teardrops coming down from it between each pointed leaf, then fill in around them to complete this mandala!

Glowing Gem

Are you ready for your first foray into colored mandalas? For this and every mandala in this section, we will first draw the mandala in black and white, then color it using either markers or colored pencils. If you decide to use markers, I recommend using water-based markers so that the black lines do not get muddied up as you color on top of them—but you can make alcohol markers work too if that's what you have!

As you draw this mandala, think about how the subtle color shifts combine to create the final, "glowing" effect. How can small factors add up to big impacts in your life?

84

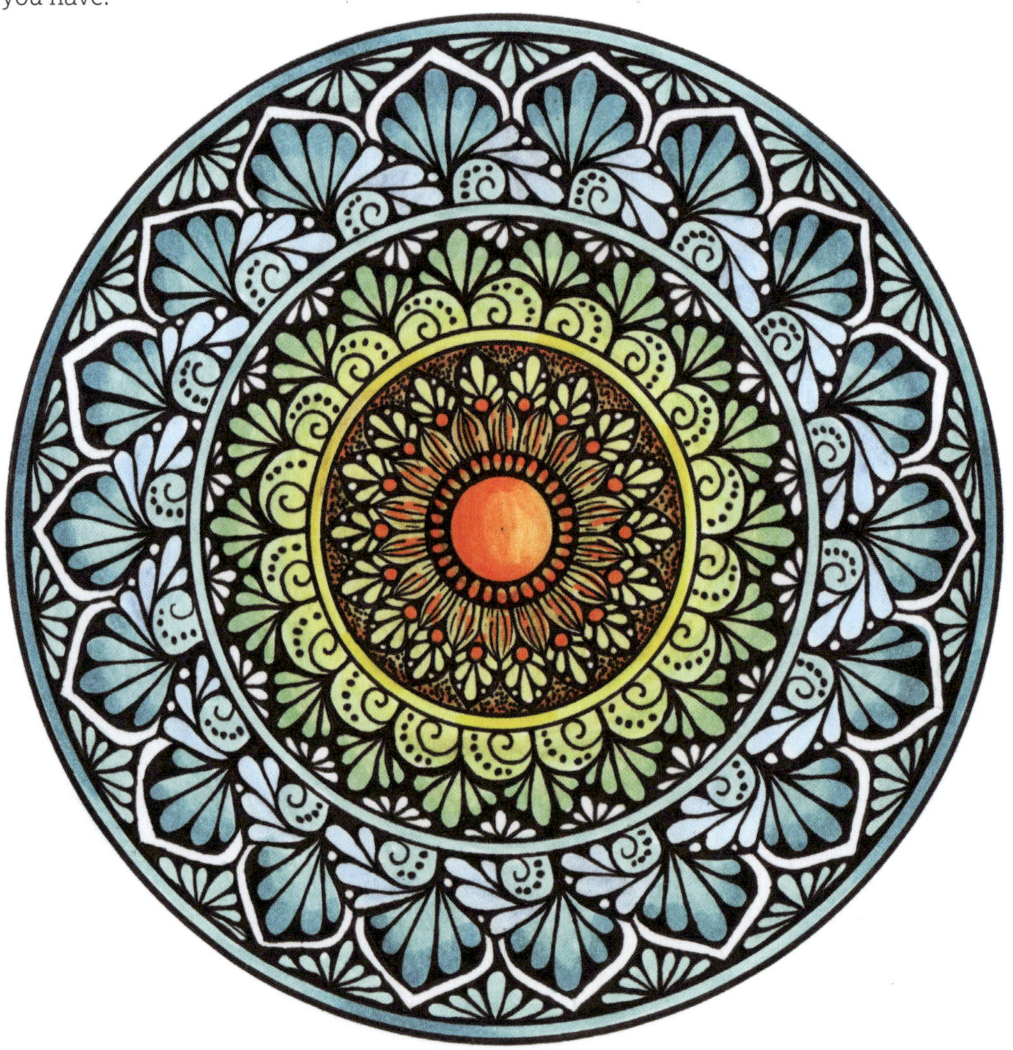

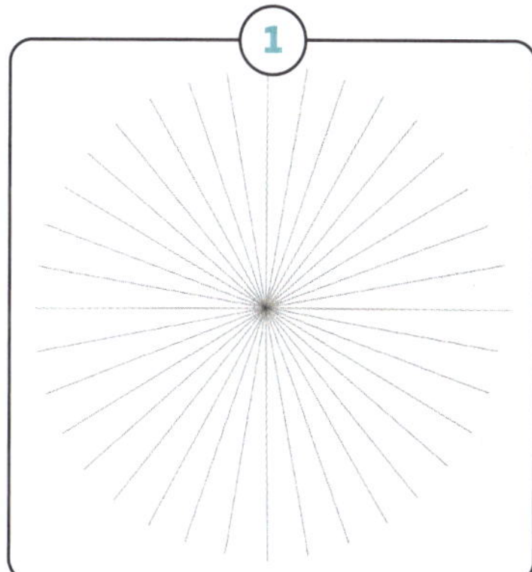

Draw rays. Using pencil, draw a straight horizontal line, then draw a ray every 10° on the top half and bottom half (17 rays total on each half).

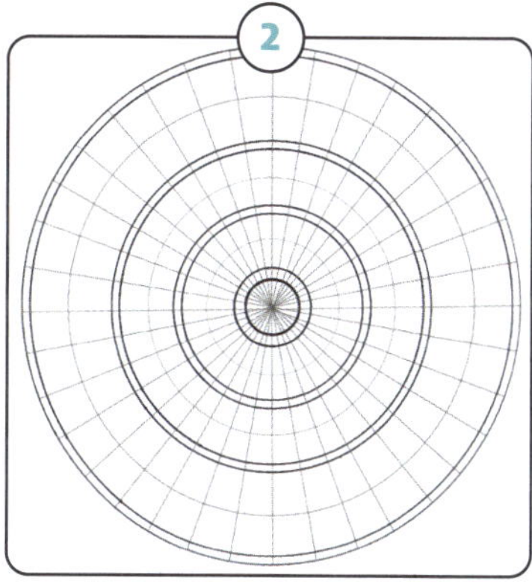

Draw circles. Draw 11 circles as shown in pencil and in pen. For reference, the outermost circle radius is 3⅝" (9 cm); the innermost circle radius is ⅜" (1 cm).

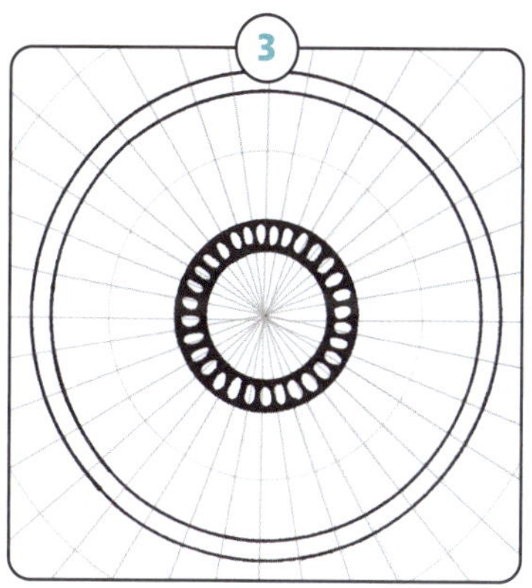

Draw the first ring. Erase the center. Fill the first ring with about 30 tall ovals, then fill in around them.

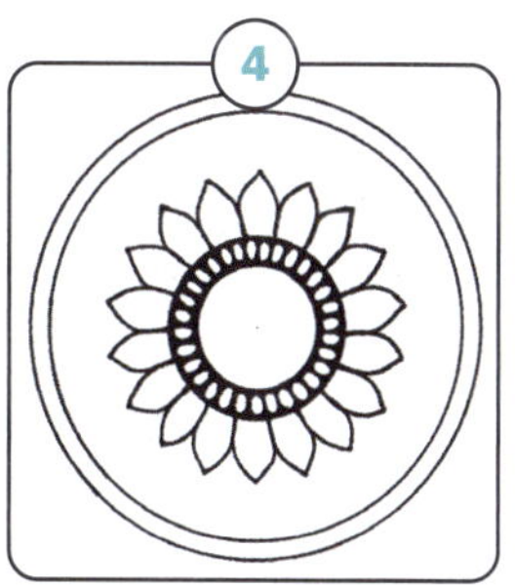

Start the next ring. Draw pointed leaves centered on alternating rays in the next ring.

Detail the leaves. Add solid and broken lines to the pointed leaves to give them a textured, rounded effect—imagine an onion.

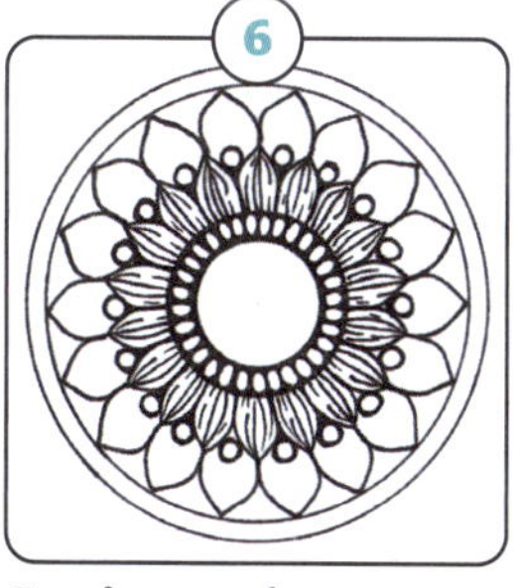

Continue to the next ring. Draw a circle between each pointed leaf, then fill in below it. Repeat step 4, offset from the previous ring of pointed leaves.

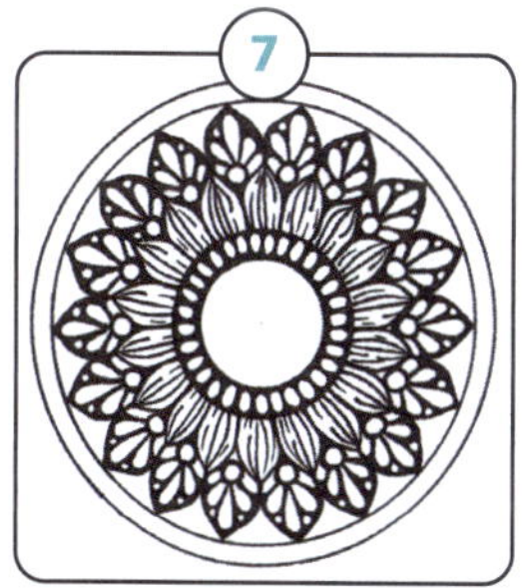

Fill the leaves. Fill each pointed leaf with a pattern of five teardrops and two circles as shown.

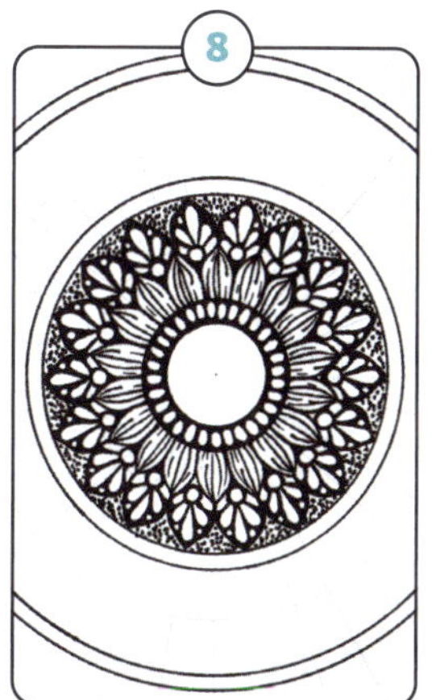

Finish the ring. Add dense stippling in the area between each finished pointed leaf.

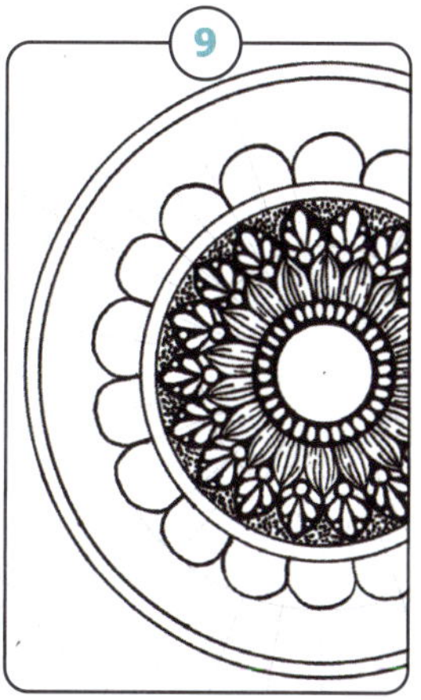

Start a new ring. Draw domes centered on alternating rays in the next wide ring, offset from the previous ring of pointed leaves.

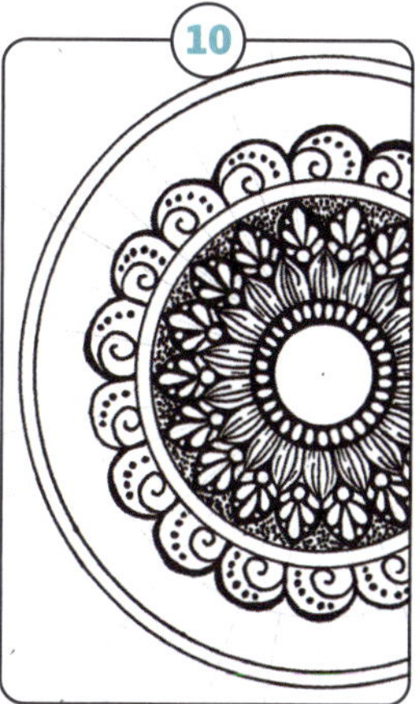

Decorate the domes. Fill each dome with a curling line and five dots. Thicken the outer border of some, but not all, of the domes.

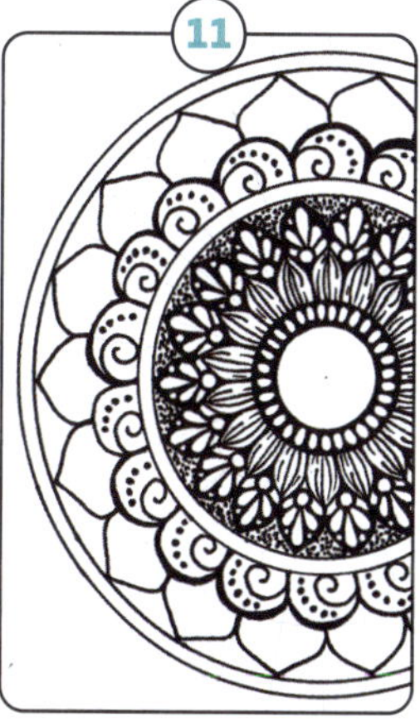

Start a new ring. Draw pointed leaves centered on alternating rays in the next ring, offset from the previous ring of domes.

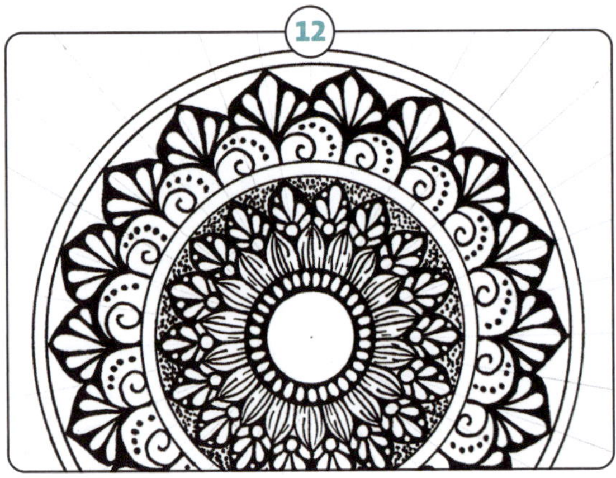

Decorate the leaves. Draw five teardrops in each pointed leaf, then fill in around them.

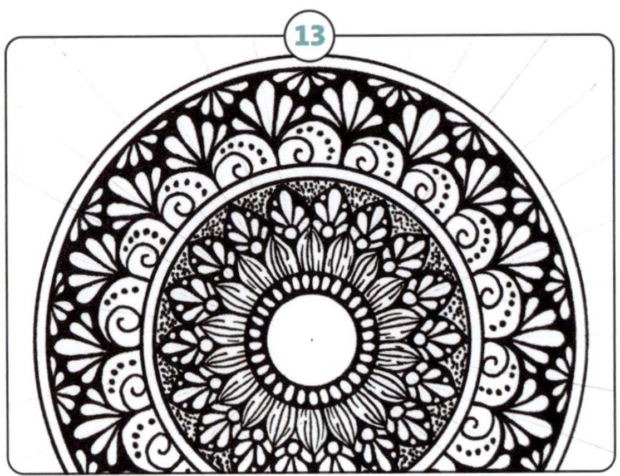

Add more teardrops. Draw five teardrops coming down between each pointed leaf, then fill in around them too, effectively combining the two filled-in areas.

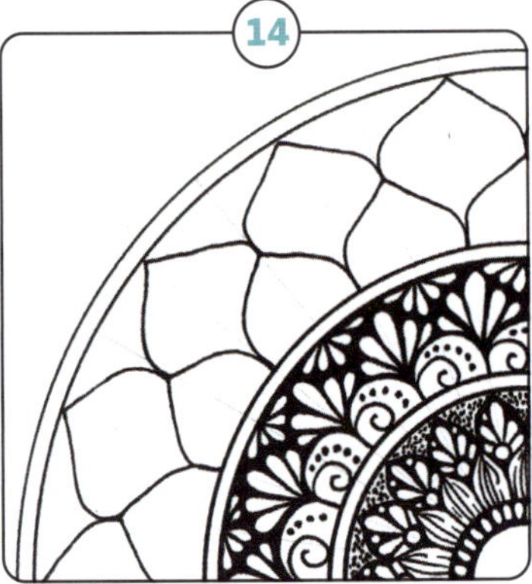

Start two more rings. Draw pointed leaves centered on alternating rays in the next two rings, each offset from the previous ring of pointed leaves.

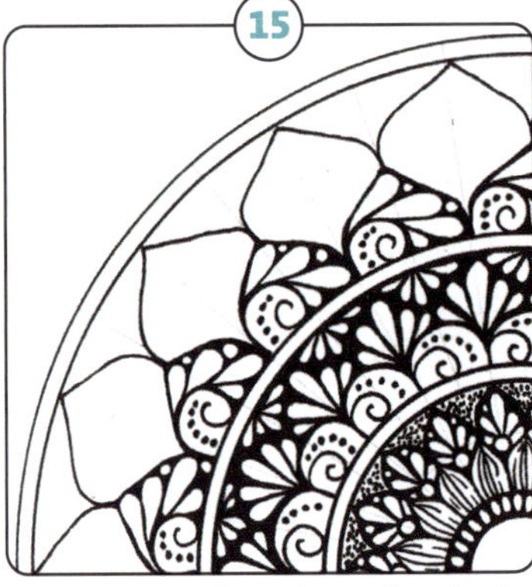

Decorate the first ring. Fill each of the pointed leaves in the first ring with the pattern shown.

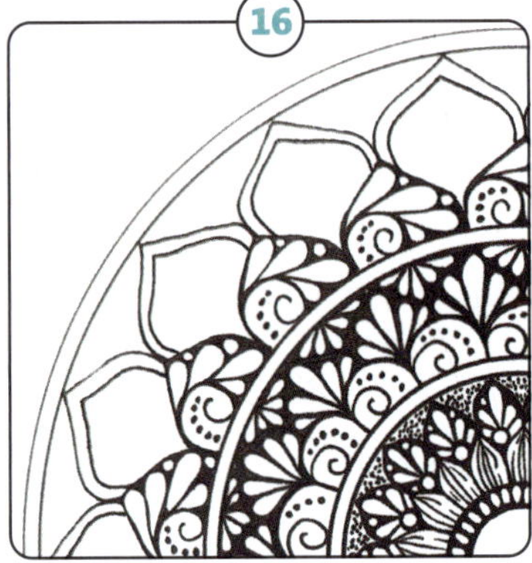

Add insets. Add an inset pointed leaf to each pointed leaf in the unfinished ring.

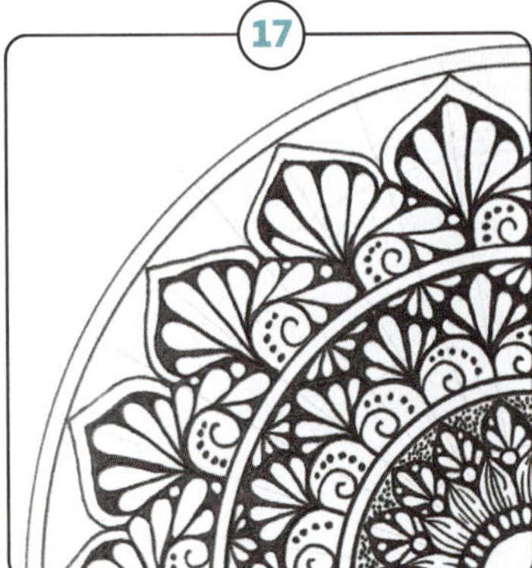

Add teardrops. Draw five teardrops in each unfinished pointed leaf, then fill in around them.

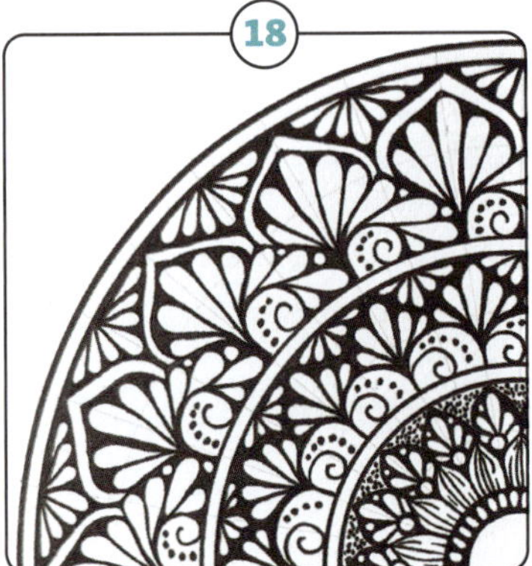

Add more teardrops. Draw seven teardrops coming down between each pointed leaf, then fill in around them. Thicken the final circle.

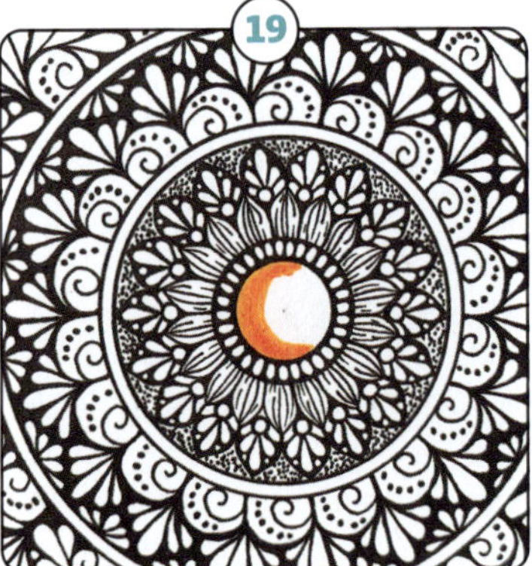

Start the central gem. Color half of the center with orange marker in a crescent moon shape.

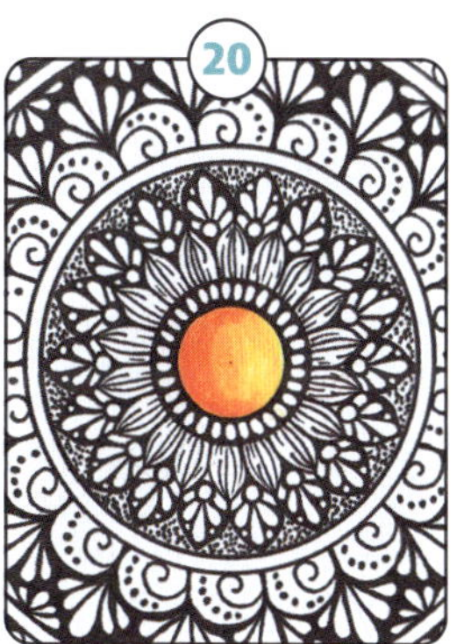

Finish the gem. Switch to yellow to color the rest of the center, blending out from the orange to create a 3D effect. (You could use colored pencil here instead.)

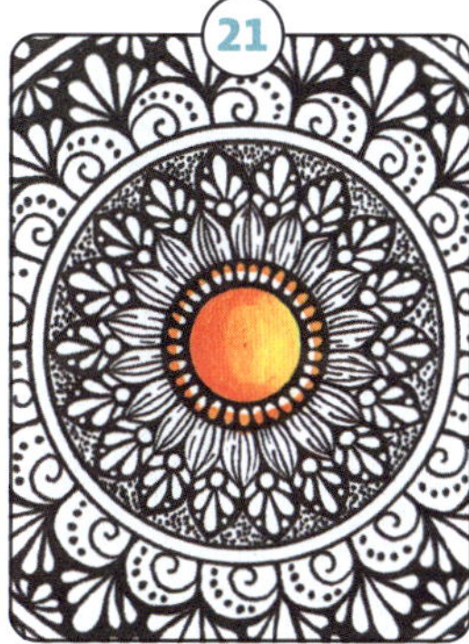

Start the first ring. Switch back to orange to color the outer half of the first ring.

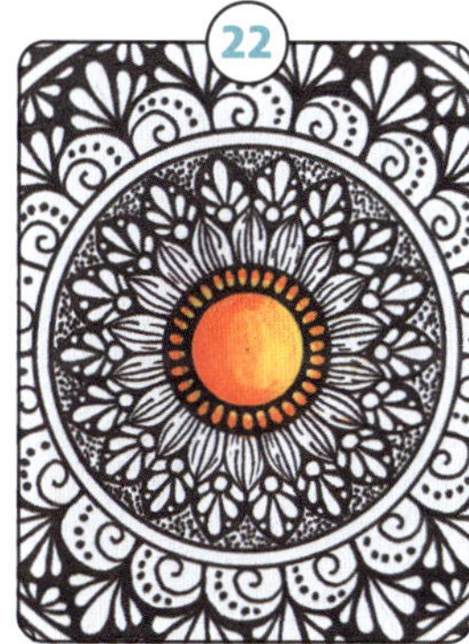

Finish the first ring. Switch back to yellow to color the inner half of the first ring.

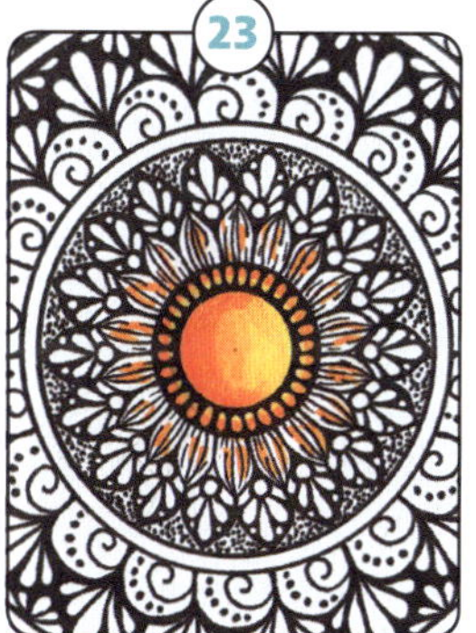

Start the next ring. With orange again, add some random dashes of color within the pointed leaves of the next ring.

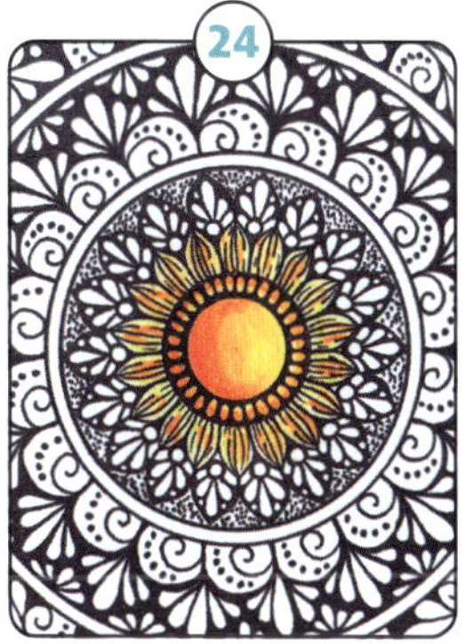

Finish the leaves. Switch to yellow to fill in the rest of the pointed leaves, making sure not to completely blend away the orange.

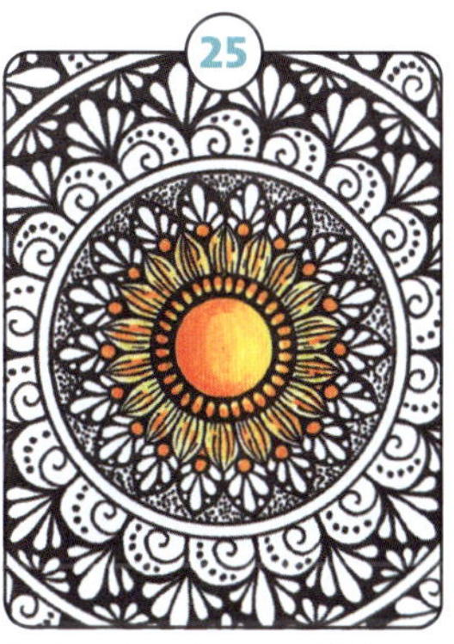

Color the circles. With orange again, color the circles between each pointed leaf.

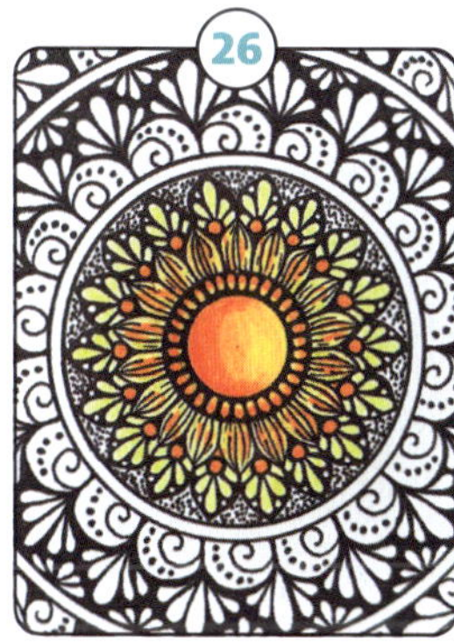

Color the teardrops. Switch back to yellow to color the five teardrops in each pointed leaf in the next ring.

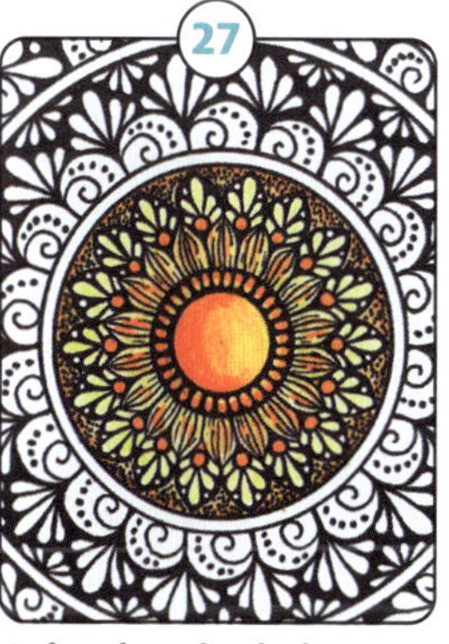

Color the stippled area. With orange, color the outer half of the stippled ring. Then use yellow to color down into the points between the leaves.

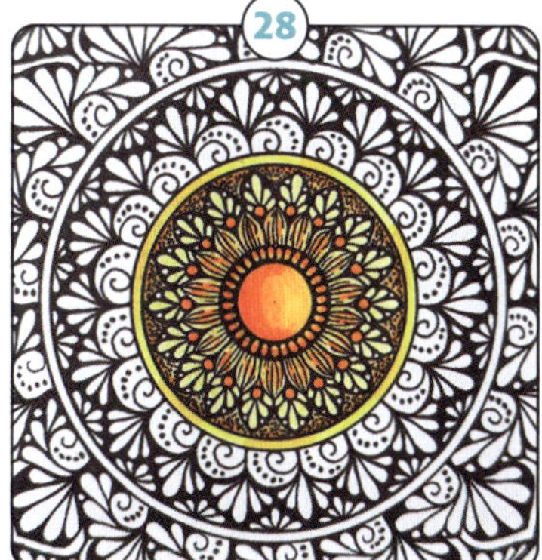

Color the empty ring. Use yellow to fill in the entire empty ring. Then go back in with the same yellow to darken some areas of the ring.

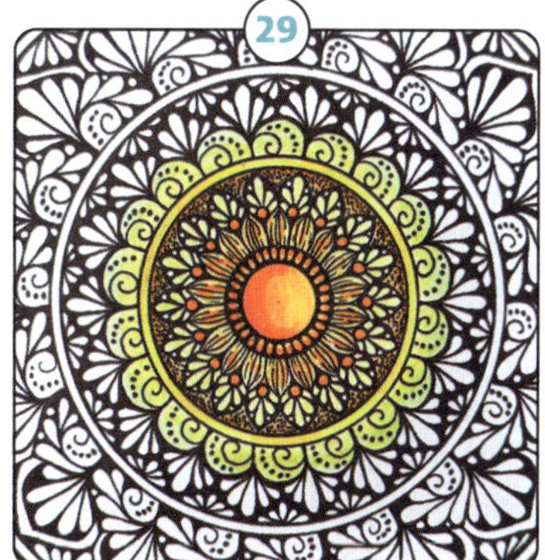

Color the domes. Use yellow to fill the domes of the next ring. Use a greenish yellow along the tops of these domes.

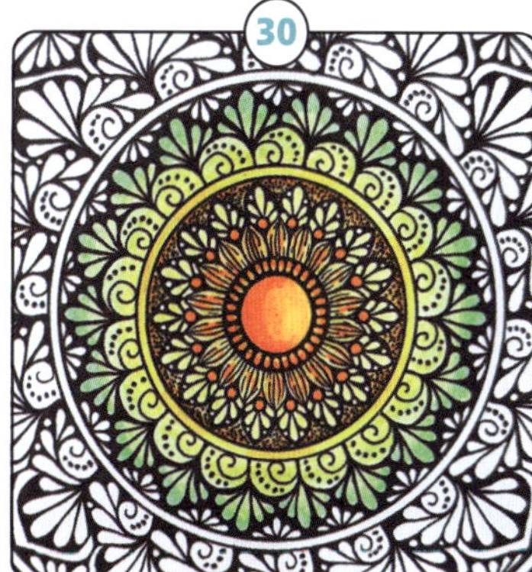

Color the teardrops. Use the greenish yellow from step 29 to color the teardrops of the next ring. Then go in with a green to darken the outer area of the teardrops.

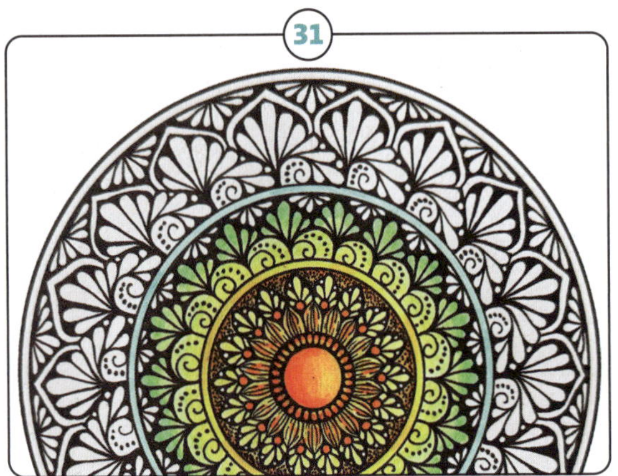

Color the empty ring. Use light blue to fill in the entire empty ring. Then go back in with the same light blue to darken some areas of the ring.

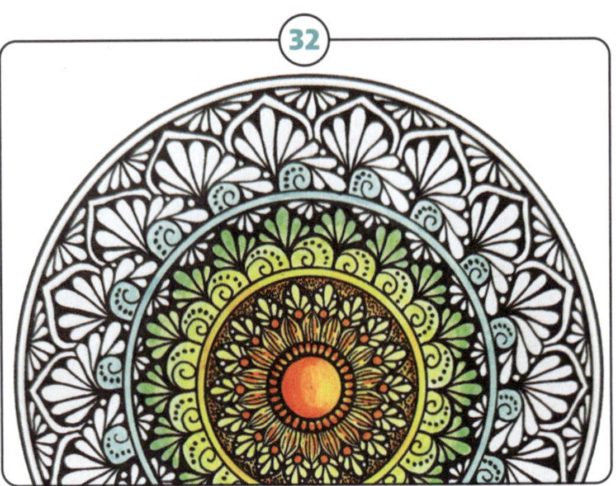

Color the curling lines. Use the same light blue to color the curling line segments of the next ring.

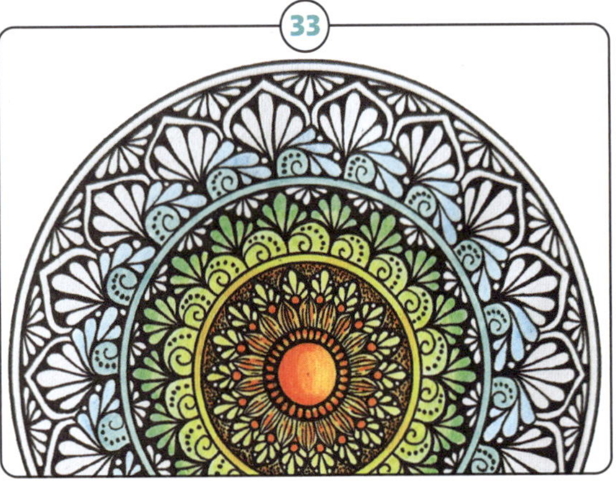

Color some teardrops. Switch to a different light blue to color the four teardrops that emanate from each curling line.

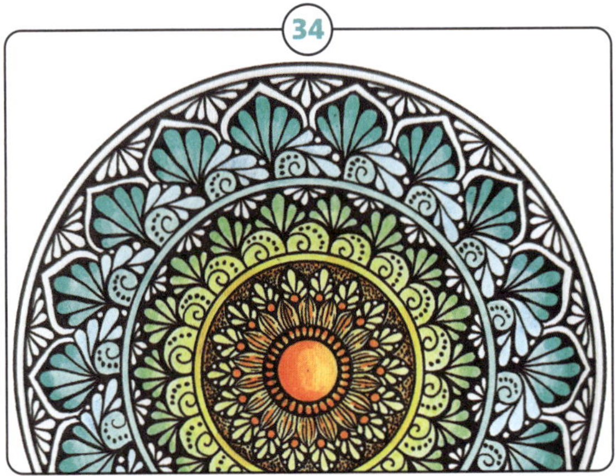

Color the next ring. With aqua (a third blue), color the teardrops of the next ring. Then go back in with the same aqua to darken the outer halves of the teardrops.

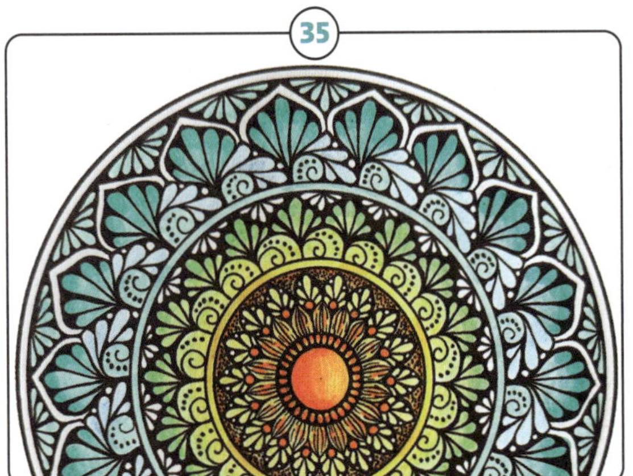

Color the last teardrops. With the same light blue as in step 32 for the curling lines, color the remaining teardrops emanating down from the outermost ring.

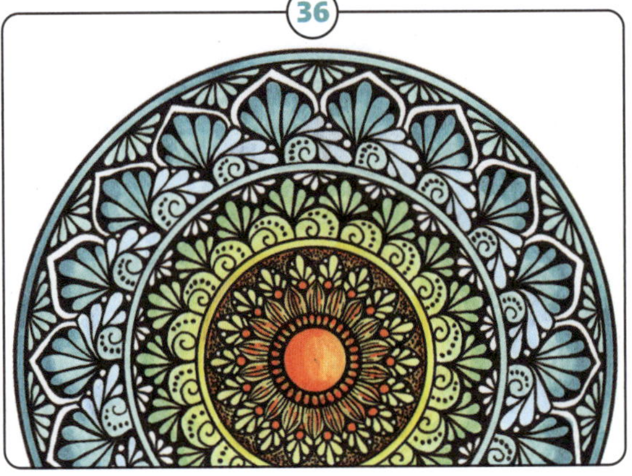

Color the final ring. Use aqua to fill in the entire empty ring. Then go back in with the same aqua to darken some areas of the ring.

LET'S CHECK IN

How did it feel to add color on top of existing black designs? Was it scary, satisfying, or both? Did you worry you'd "ruin" your work?

Are you happy with your final color result? If not, what can you change next time to get a result you like better?

Look at the glowing finished mandala and think about how light and creativity emanate from you. What are some ways you can continue to bring this energy into the world?

Color! What a deep and mysterious language,
the language of dreams.
–Paul Gauguin

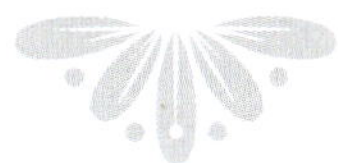

Moody Contrast

This marker-colored mandala is very similar to the previous mandala but includes more colors and has crisp, white borders between the rings as well as many uncolored circles. This means you will have to be more careful about your color placement as you're working.

As you draw this mandala, think about the energies that different colors communicate. How does the bright-yellow center make you feel? How about the deep-violet and blue edges?

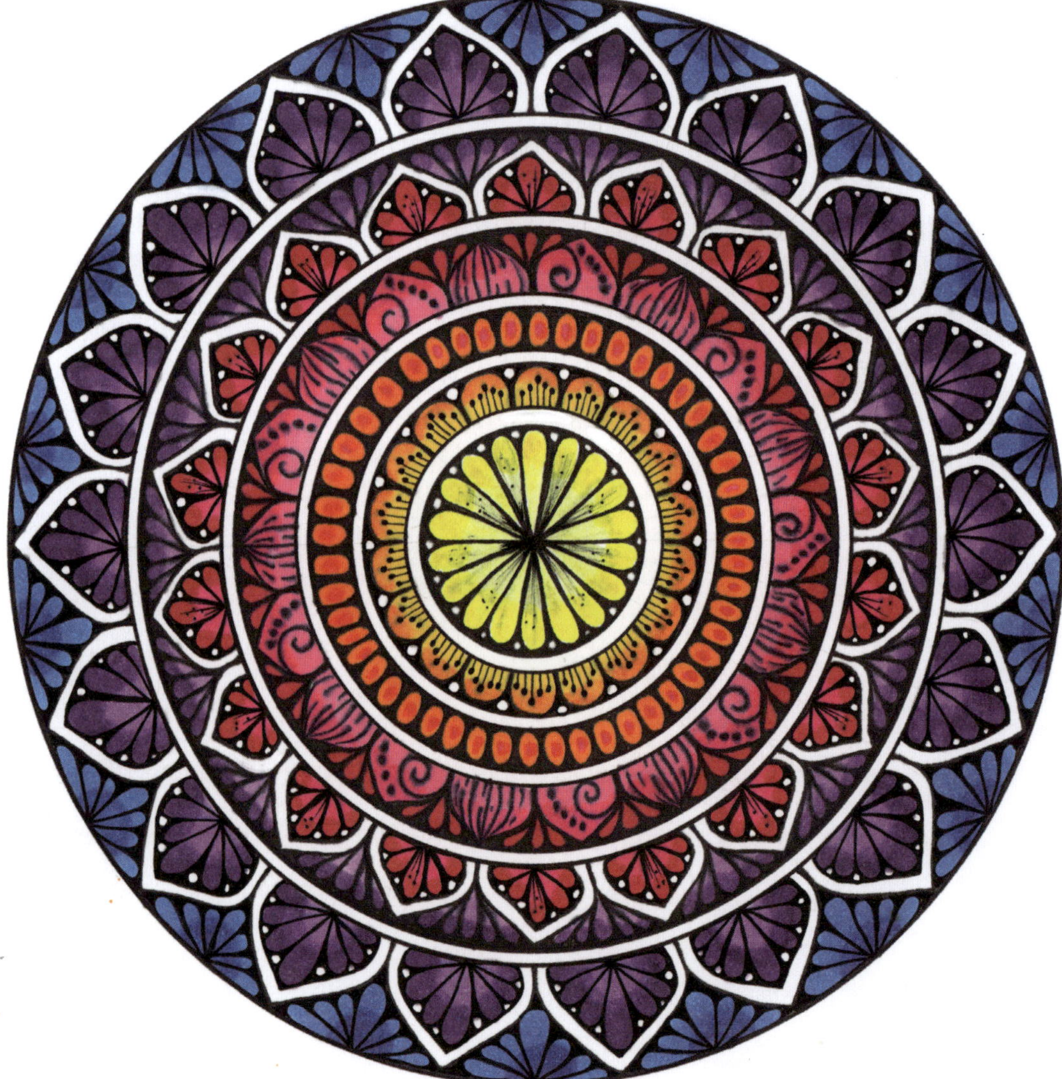

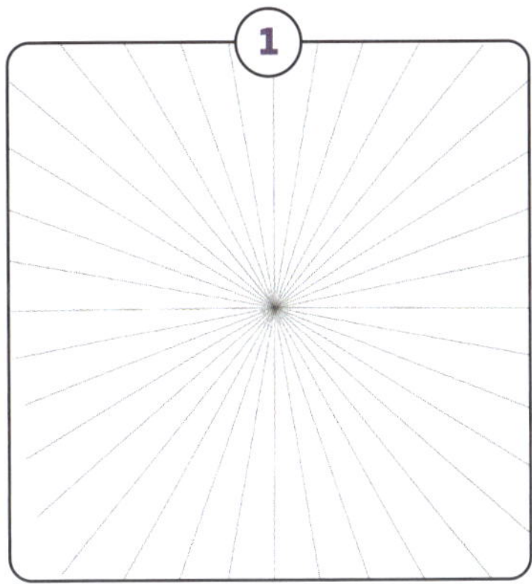

Draw rays. Using pencil, draw a straight horizontal line, then draw a ray every 10° on the top half and bottom half (17 rays total on each half).

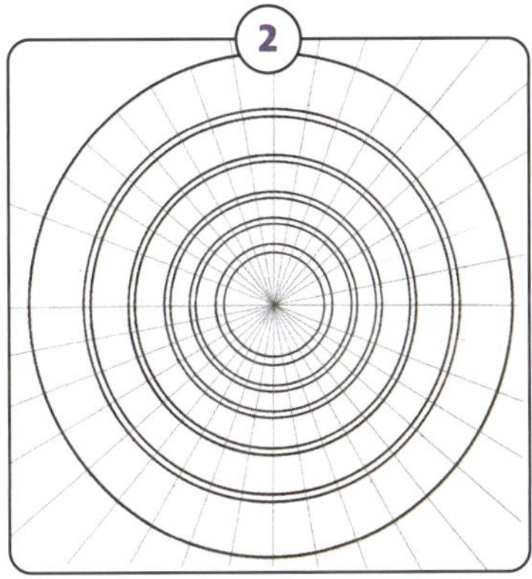

Draw circles. In pen, draw 11 circles as shown. For reference, the outermost circle radius is 3¾" (9.5 cm); the innermost circle radius is ¾" (2 cm).

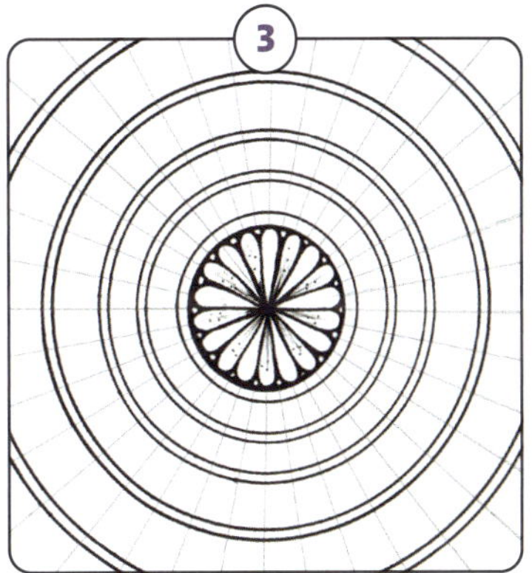

Create the center. Fill the center with a design as shown, drawing teardrops centered on alternating rays.

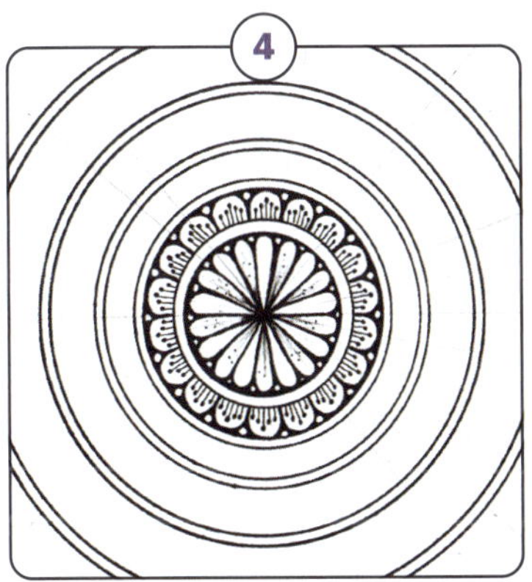

Fill the first ring. Fill the first ring with a dome-based design as shown, drawing domes centered on alternating rays.

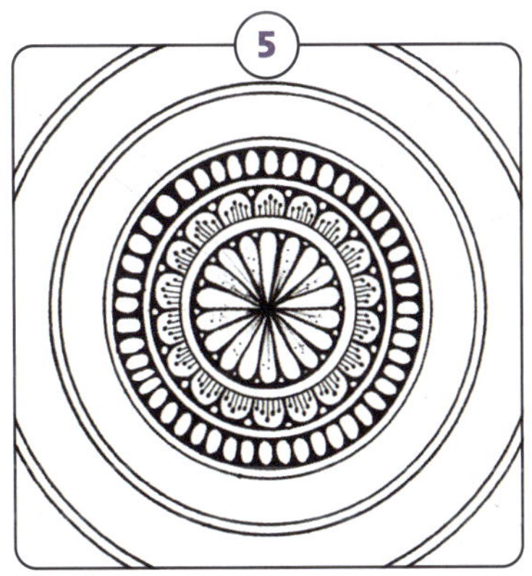

Fill the next ring. Draw one to one and a half ovals between each ray in the next ring, then fill in around them.

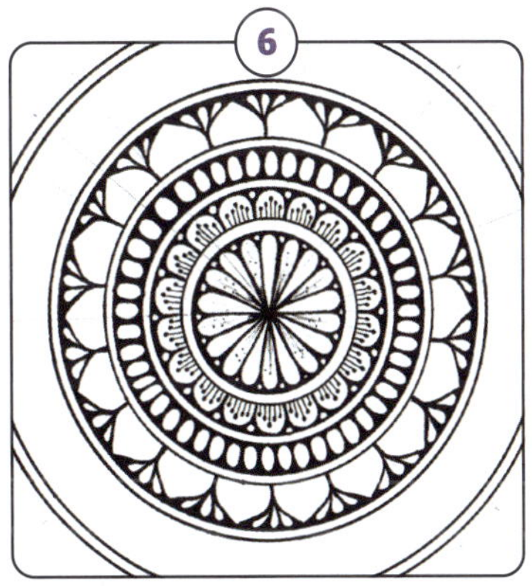

Start a new ring. In the next ring, draw pointed leaves centered on alternating rays. Add three teardrops between each leaf, then fill in around them.

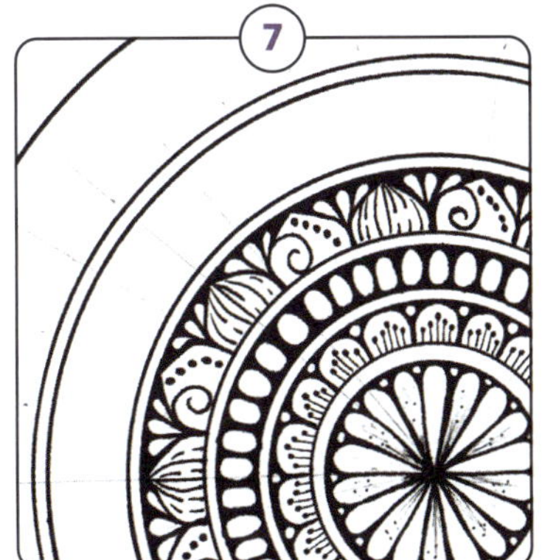

Finish this ring. Fill the pointed leaves with two different alternating patterns as shown.

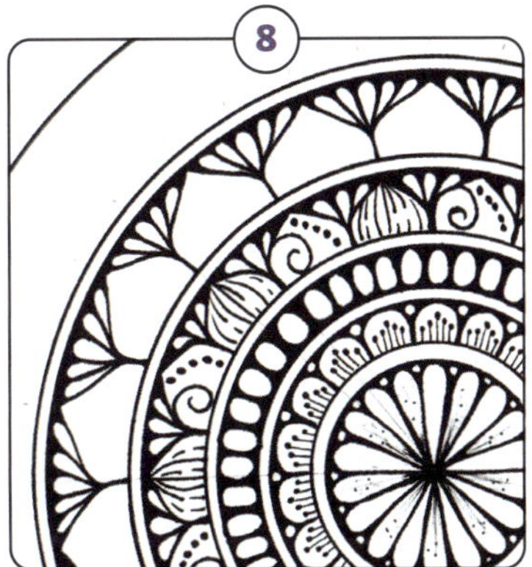

Start a new ring. Repeat step 6, making these pointed leaves offset from the previous ring of pointed leaves and adding five teardrops instead of three.

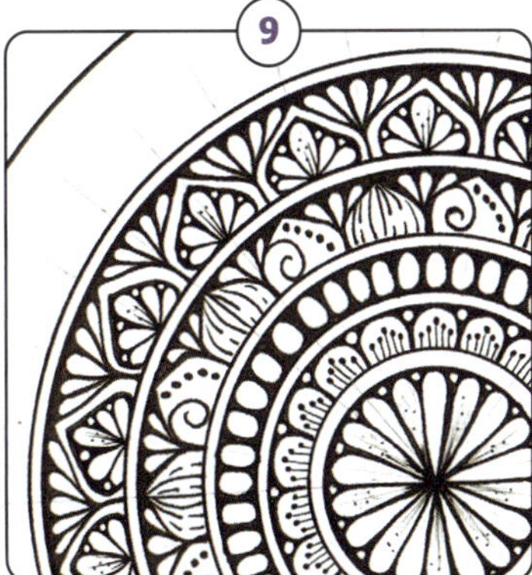

Finish this ring. Add an inset pointed leaf to each pointed leaf, then fill all the insets with the same pattern as shown.

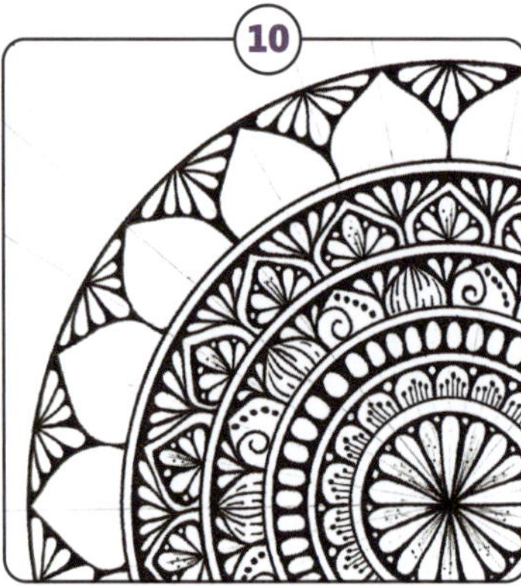

Start the last ring. Repeat step 8, making these pointed leaves offset from the previous ring and adding seven teardrops that emanate down from the outer circle.

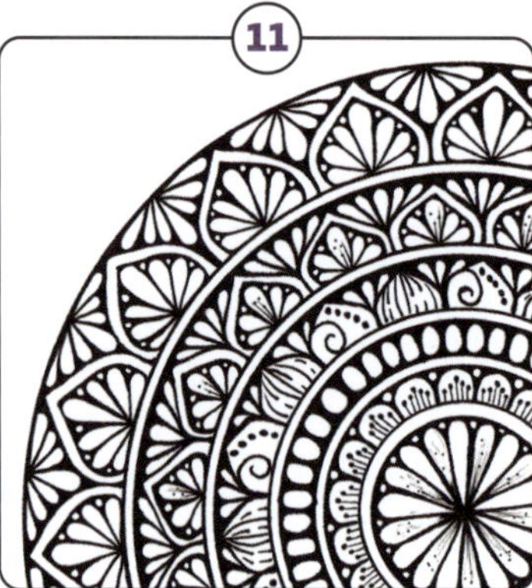

Finish the last ring. Add an inset pointed leaf to each pointed leaf, then fill all the insets with the same pattern as shown.

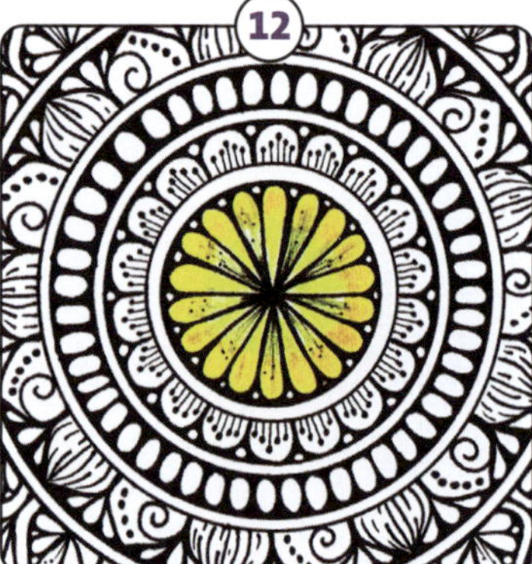

Color the center. Use a medium yellow to color the outer half of the center. Then switch to a light yellow to color the inner half of the center.

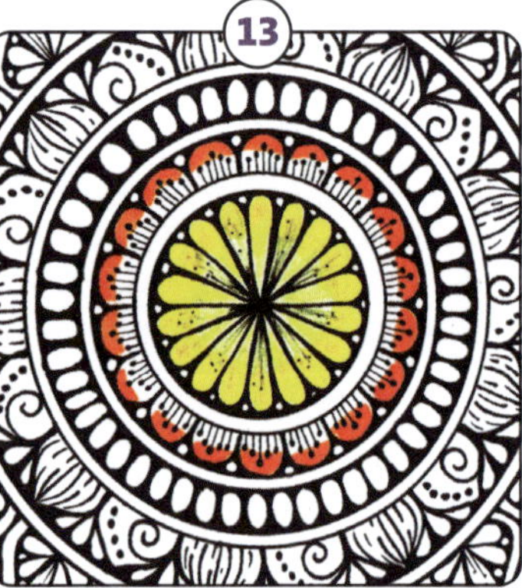

Start the dome ring. Use orange to color the outer halves of the domes in the next ring.

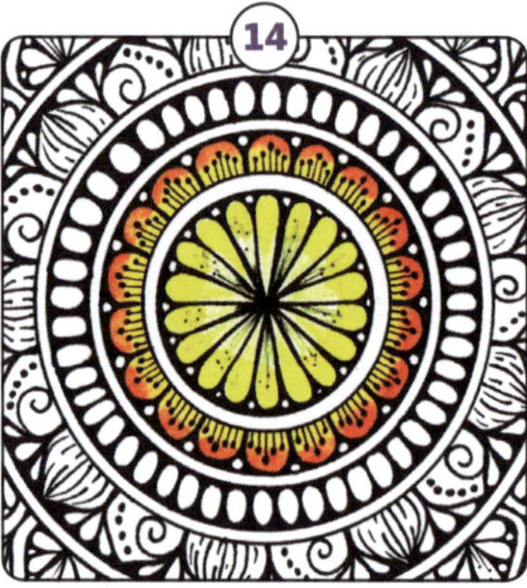

Finish the dome ring. Switch back to the medium yellow to color the inner halves of the domes.

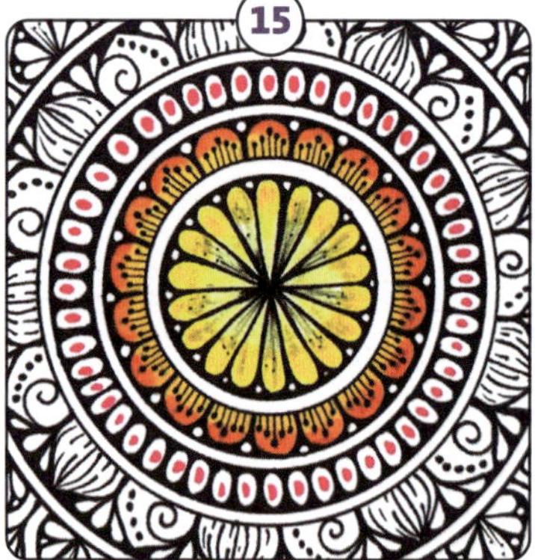

Start the ovals. Use dark pink to add a thick oval dot to each oval in the next ring.

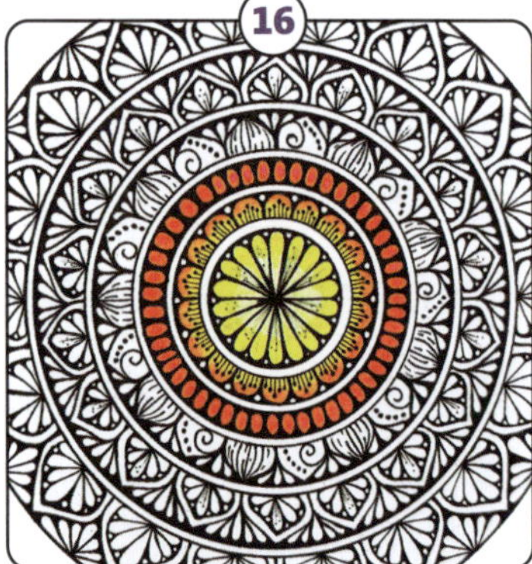

Finish the ovals. Switch back to orange to fill the ovals.

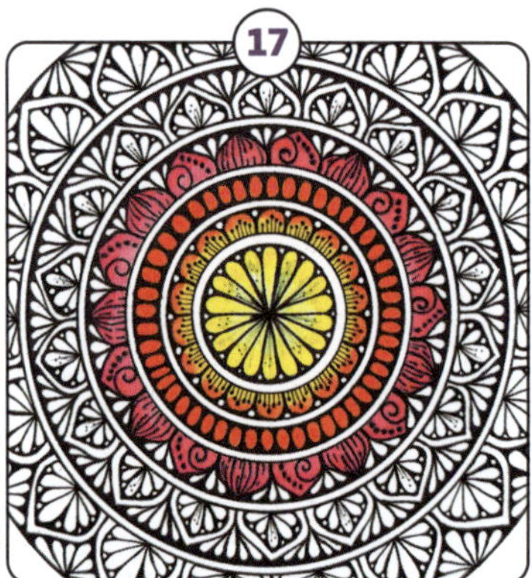

Color the pointed leaves. Use the dark pink to color the outer halves of the pointed leaves in the next ring. Then use a light pink to color the inner halves.

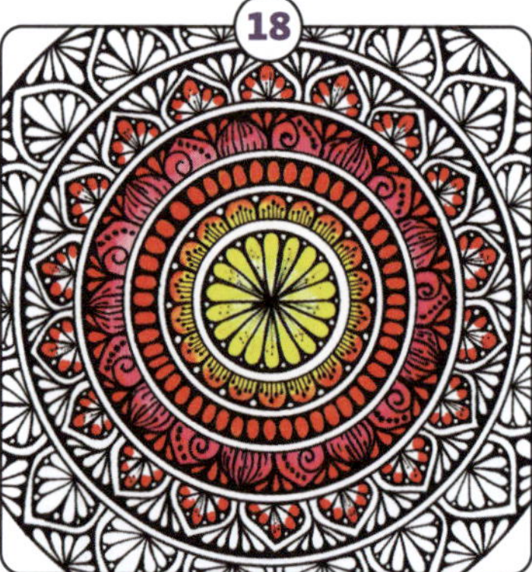

Start the next ring. Use red to color the outer halves of the inset teardrops in the next ring.

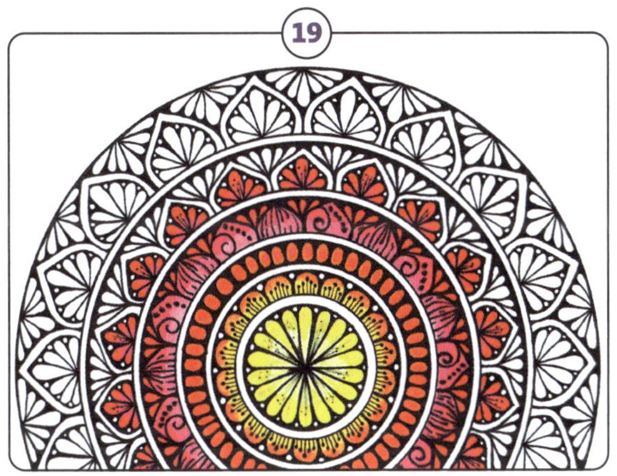

Finish the next ring. Use the dark pink to color the inner halves of the inset teardrops.

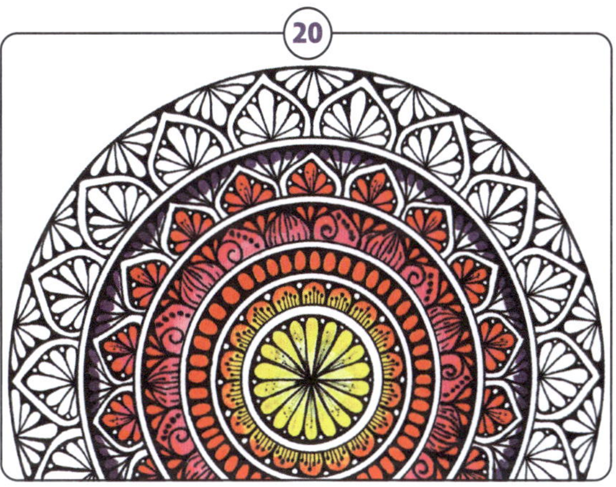

Do the next set of teardrops. Use dark purple to color the outer halves of the teardrops between the leaves in the same ring.

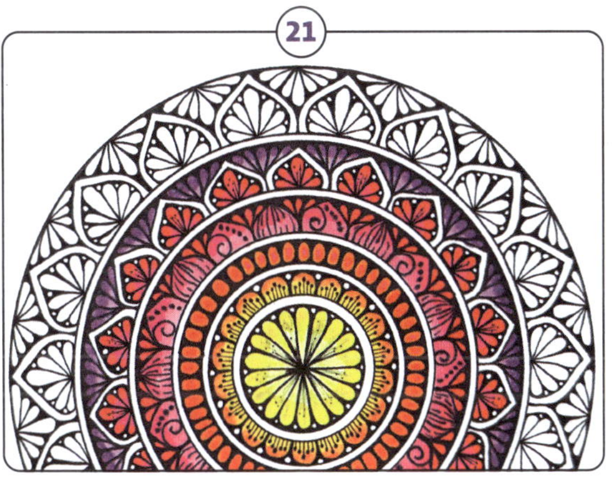

Finish these teardrops. Use light purple to color the inner halves of these teardrops.

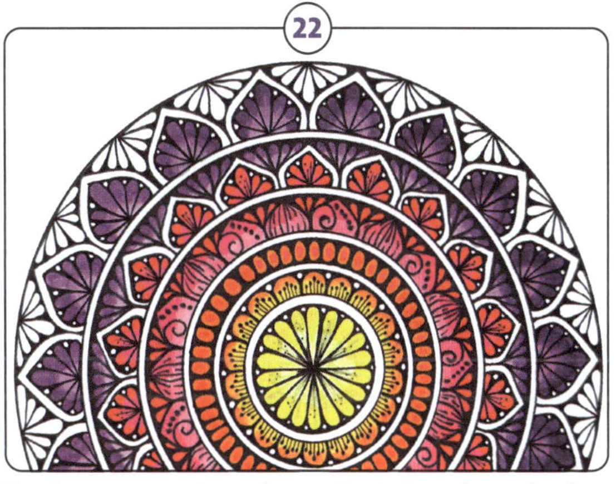

Do the next set of teardrops. Use dark purple to color the outer halves of the inset teardrops in the next ring. Then use light purple to color the inner halves.

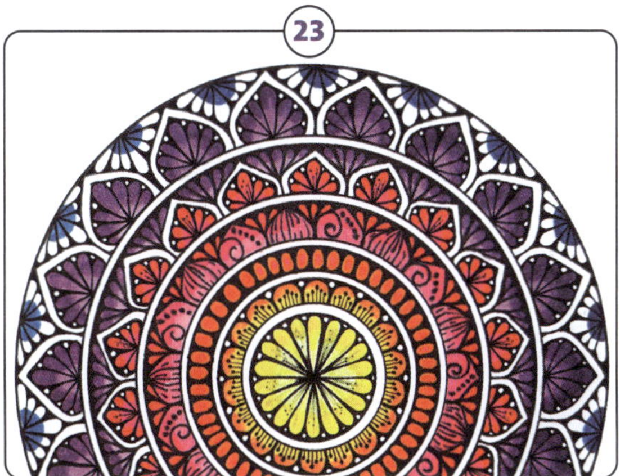

Start the final teardrops. Use dark blue to color a neat semicircle at the top center of each final set of teardrops along the outer edge of the mandala.

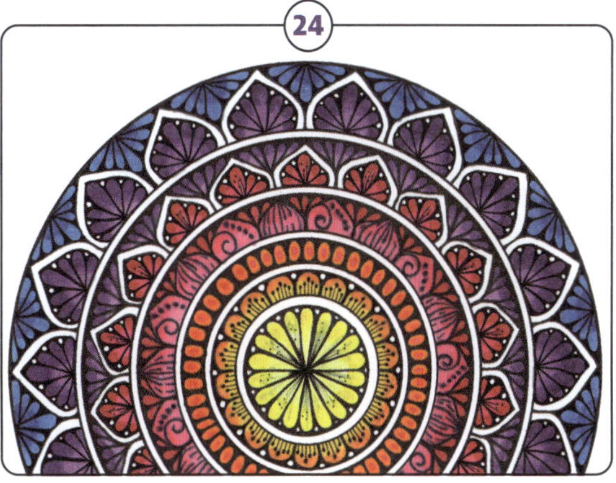

Finish the final teardrops. Use medium blue to color the remaining area of these final teardrops.

Moody Contrast

Ombré Sunrise

This is a fun half mandala that is quite large and has lots of complexity but that comes together surprisingly quickly because it's only a semicircle! It is colored using markers and includes two different tones of most colors to create a smooth ombré effect.

MANDALAS

INTENTION

As you draw this mandala, examine whether you feel like it feels "incomplete" since it is only half of the standard mandala circle. How might you creatively use the space above the mandala?

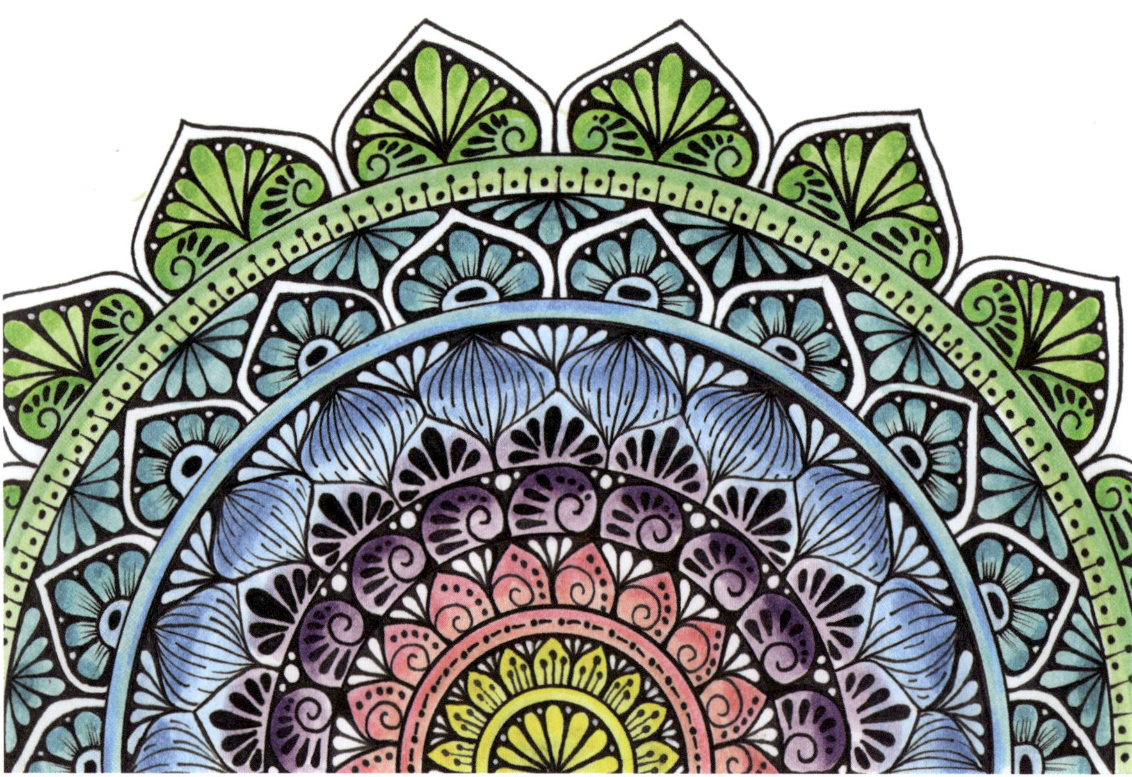

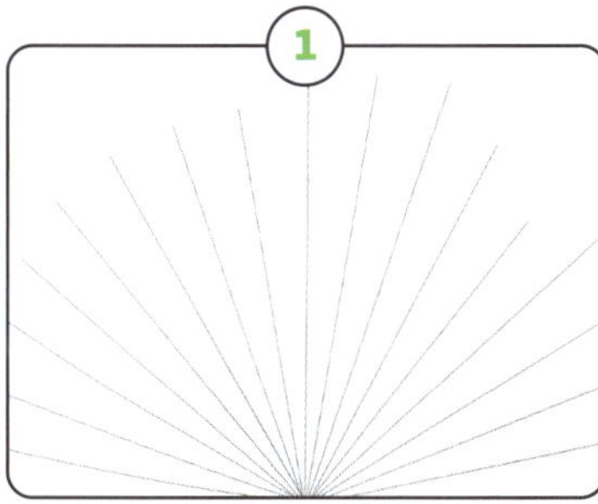

1

Draw rays. Using pencil, draw a ray every 10°, with the bottom of your page serving as the horizontal axis (17 rays total).

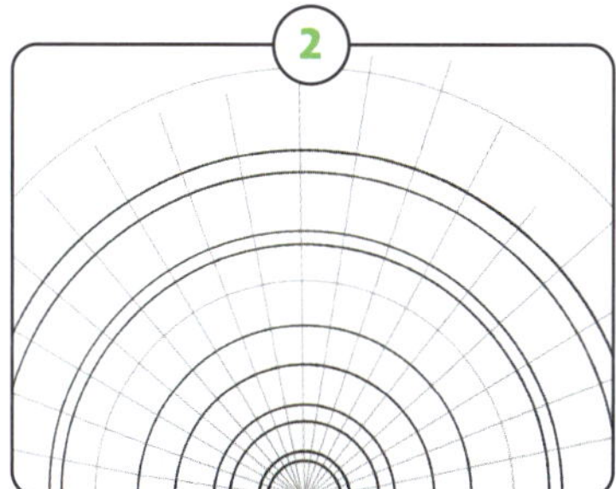

2

Draw circles. Draw 12 circles as shown in pencil and in pen. For reference, the outermost circle radius is 5¾" (14.5 cm); the innermost circle radius is ⅝" (1.5 cm).

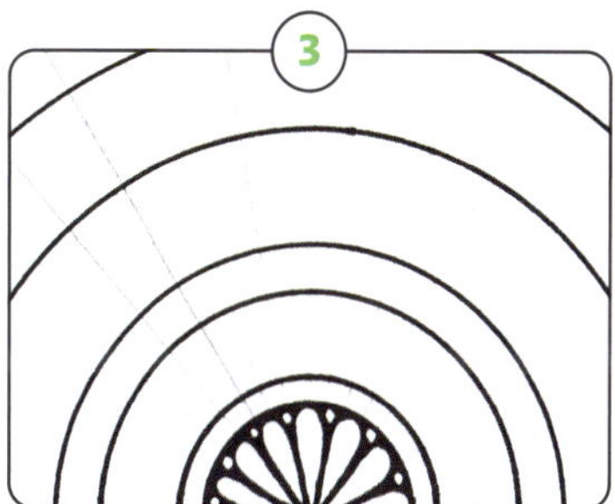

3

Create the center. Draw about seven teardrops to fill the center. Draw a circle between each one, then fill in around them.

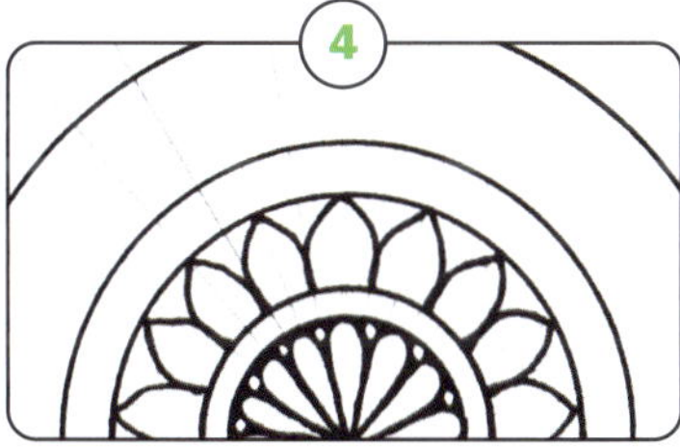

4

Start pointed leaves. Draw pointed leaves centered on alternating rays in the next ring.

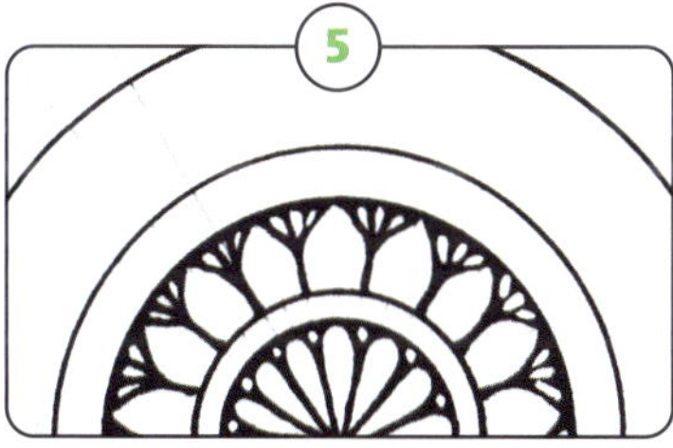

5

Add teardrops in between. Draw three teardrops between each pointed leaf, then fill in around them.

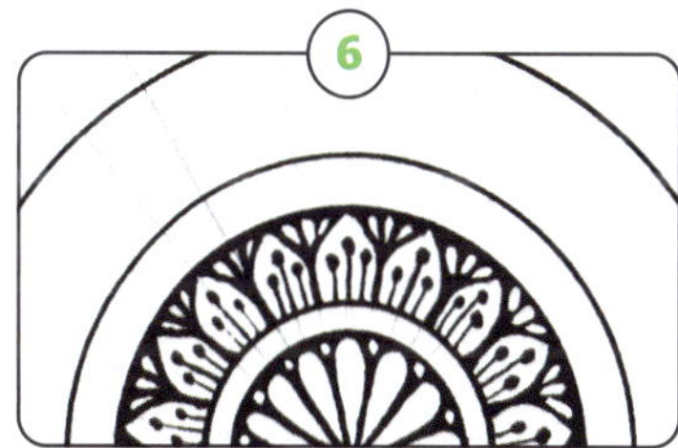

6

Detail the leaves. Add three lines capped with dots to each pointed leaf.

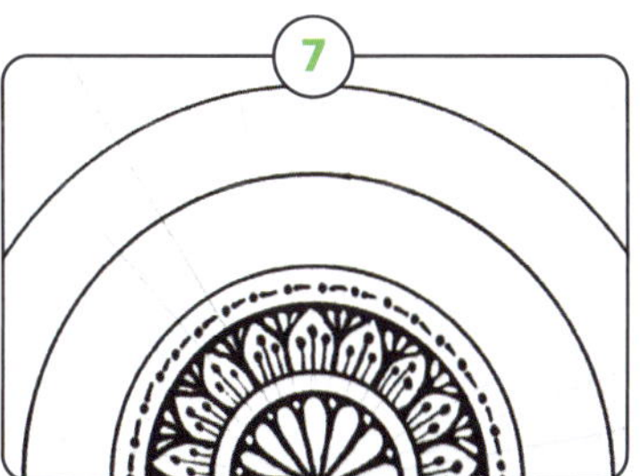

7

Fill the next ring. In the very next ring, add a Morse code–inspired pattern of alternating dots and dashes along the center of the ring.

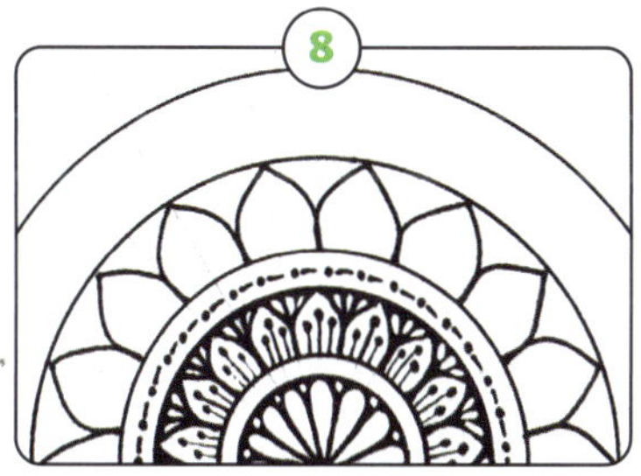

8

Start a new ring. Draw pointed leaves centered on alternating rays in the next ring, offset from the previous ring of pointed leaves.

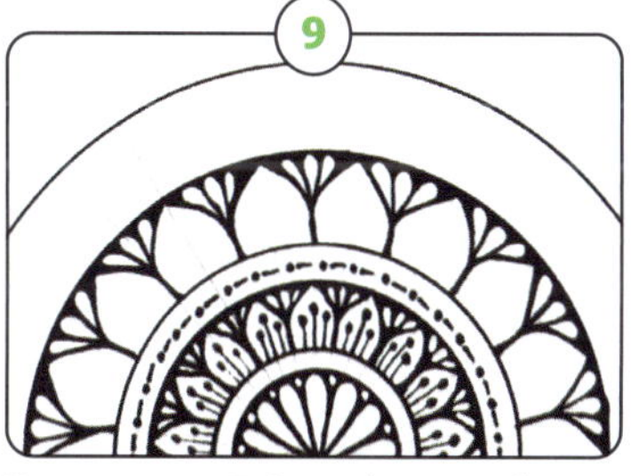

9

Repeat step 5. Draw three teardrops between each pointed leaf, then fill in around them.

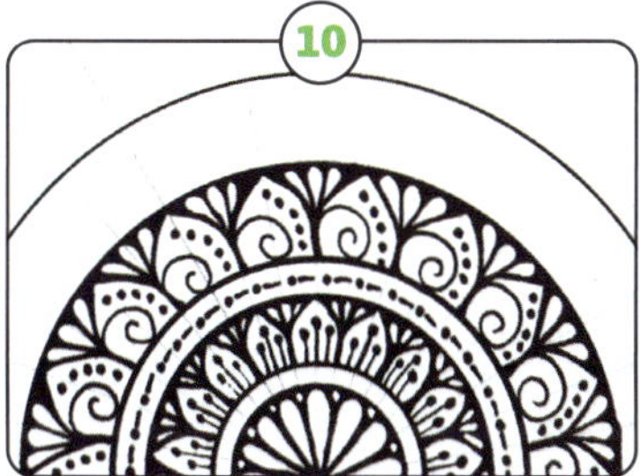

10

Fill the leaves. Fill each leaf with a pattern consisting of a curling line and five dots.

11

Start a new ring. Draw curling lines centered on alternating rays in the next ring, offset from the previous ring of pointed leaves.

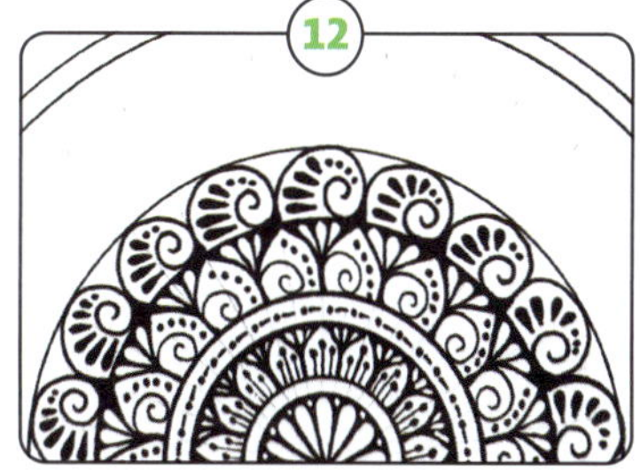

12

Fill the curling lines. Fill each curling line with four filled-in teardrops and two to four dots.

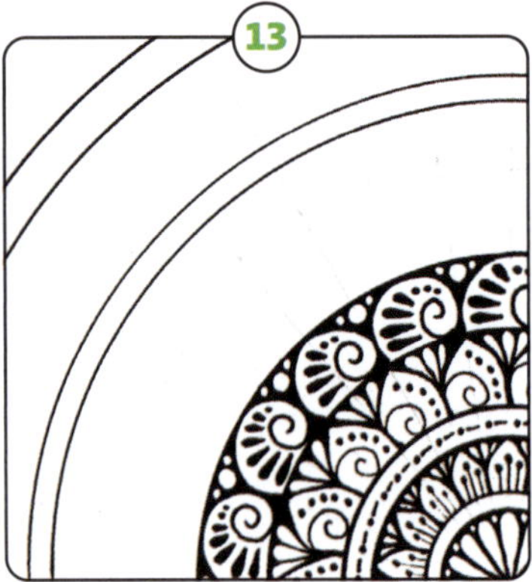

Fill the space between. Between each curling line, draw three freehand circles where one is bigger and two are smaller, then fill in around them.

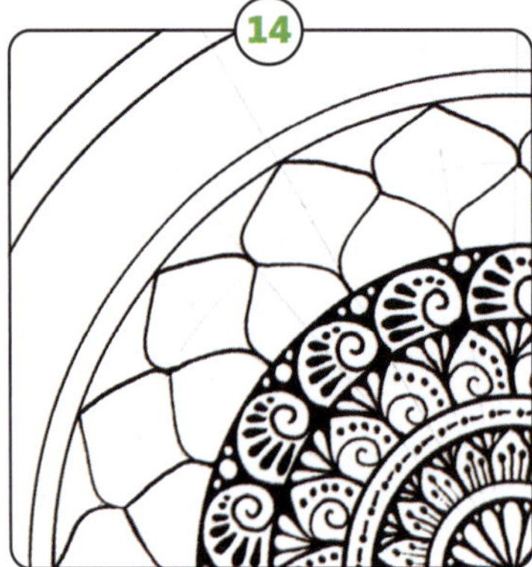

Start the next two rings. Draw pointed leaves centered on alternating rays in the next two rings, with the second ring offset from the first ring.

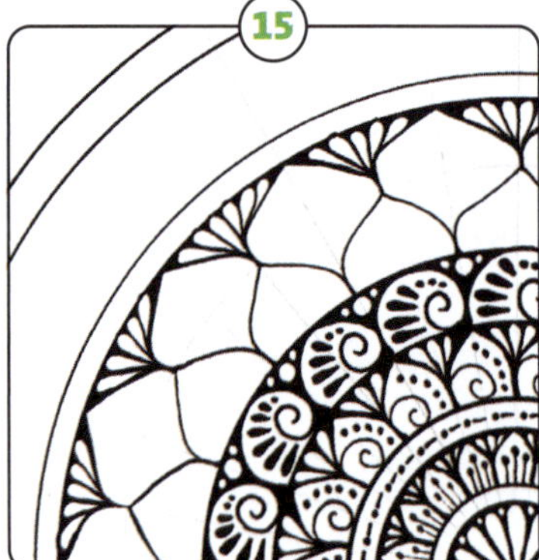

Add teardrops. Draw five or six teardrops between each pointed leaf in the second ring, then fill in around them.

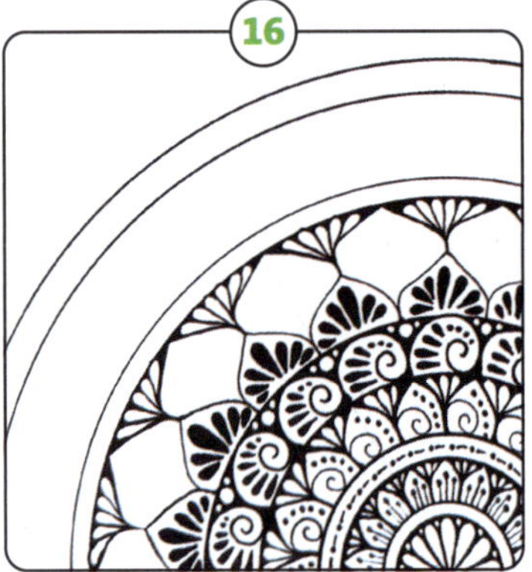

Add more teardrops. Draw six or seven filled-in teardrops inside each pointed leaf in the first ring.

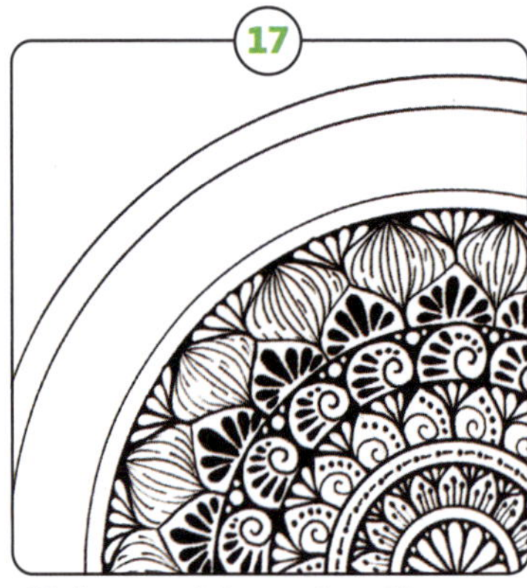

Fill the remaining pointed leaves. Add solid and broken lines to the second ring of pointed leaves to give them a textured, rounded effect—imagine an onion.

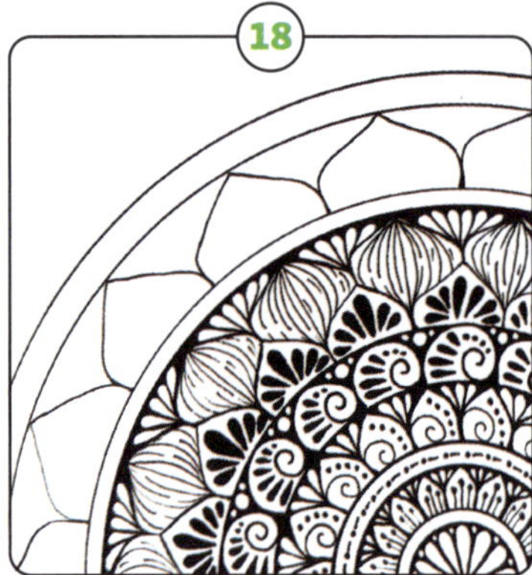

Start a new ring. Draw pointed leaves centered on alternating rays in the next ring.

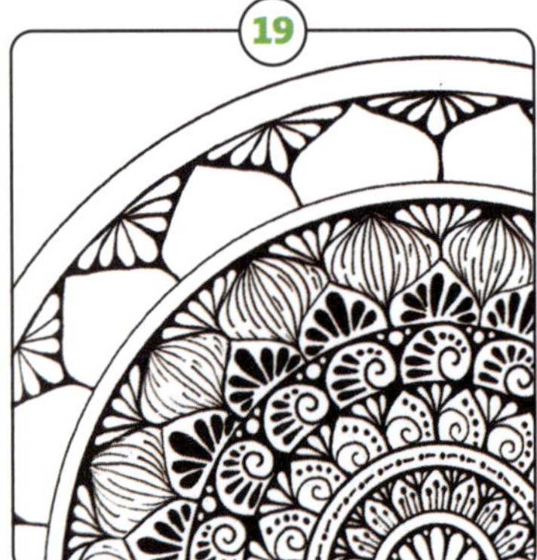

Add teardrops. Draw seven teardrops coming down from the outer edge of the ring between each pointed leaf, then fill in around them.

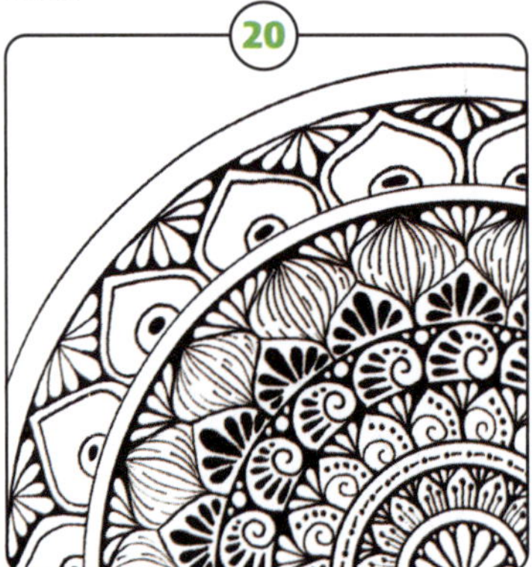

Start detailing the leaves. In each pointed leaf, add an inset leaf, a small semicircle, and a filled-in oval inside the semicircle.

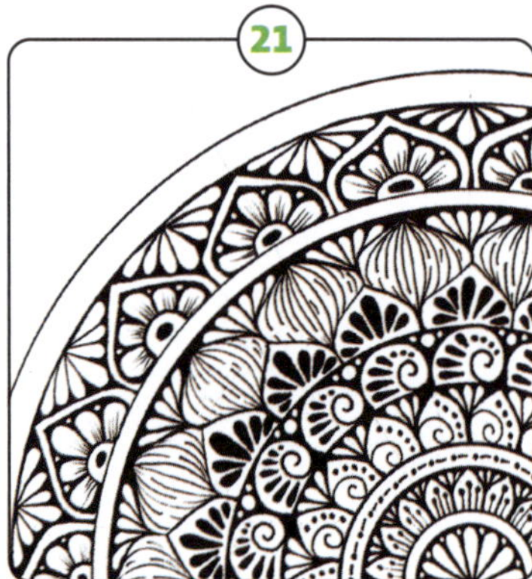

Finish the leaves. Add a detailed petal design to each pointed leaf as shown.

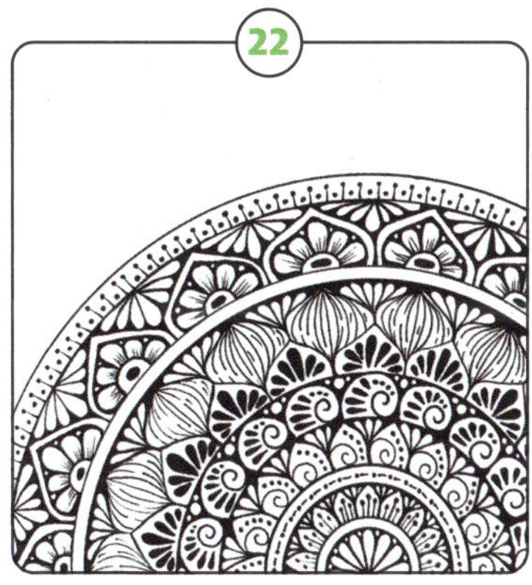

Complete the next ring. In the next small ring, draw a pattern of alternating dots and lines capped with dots.

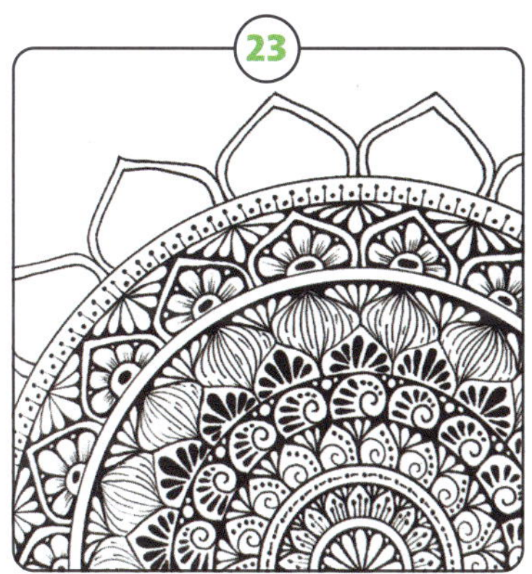

Start the last ring. Draw pointed leaves centered on alternating rays in the last ring. Add an inset pointed leaf to each one.

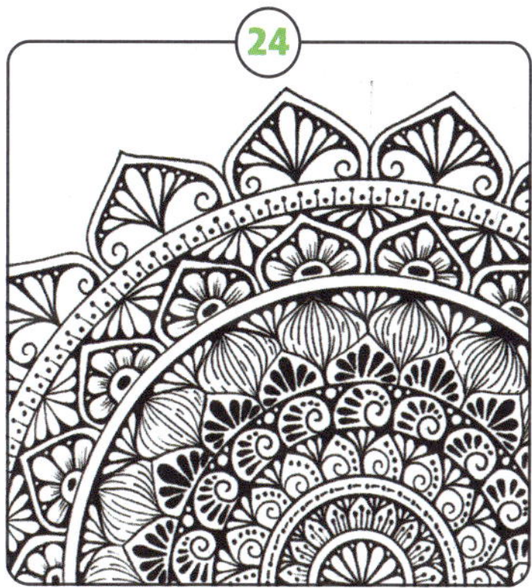

Detail the leaves. Fill each pointed leaf with a detailed pattern as shown.

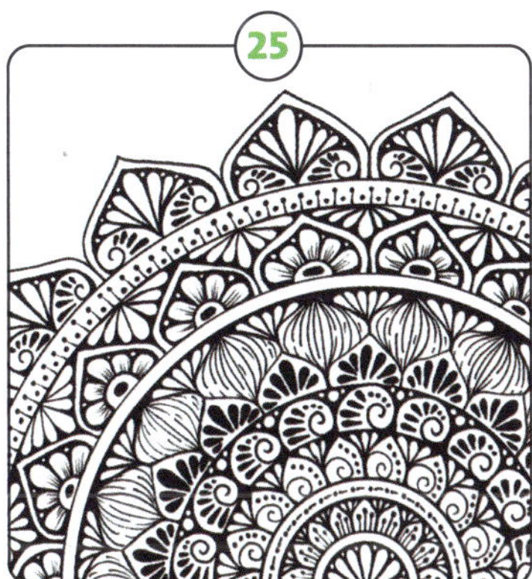

Finish the pattern. Add filled-in teardrops to each pointed leaf to complete the pattern as shown.

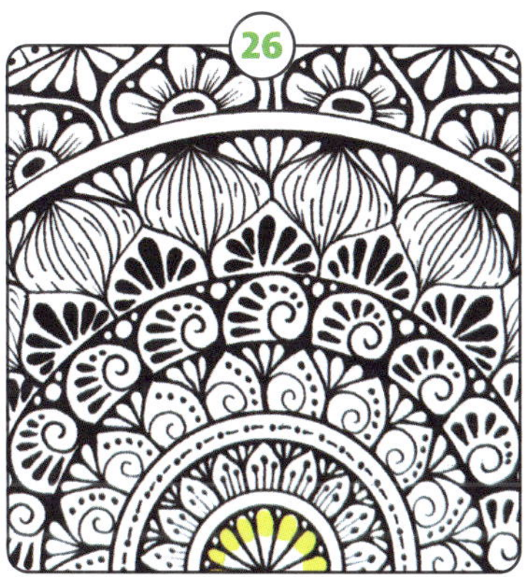

Start coloring the center. Use a medium yellow to color the outer half of the center.

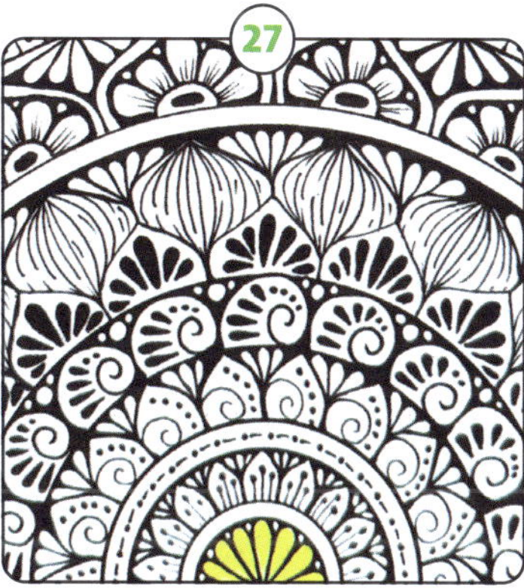

Finish the center. Switch to a light yellow to color the inner half of the center.

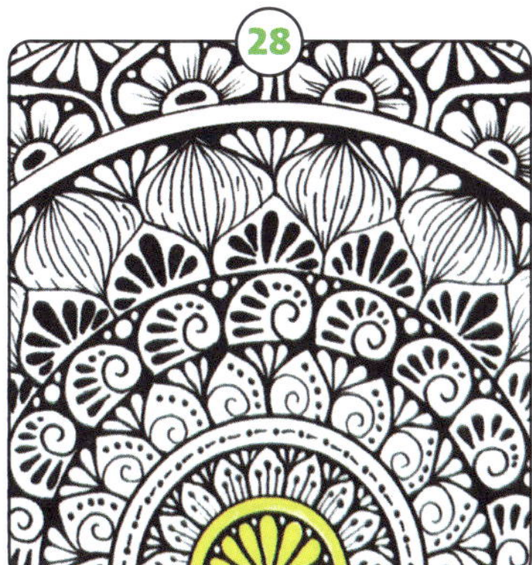

Color the next ring. Repeat steps 26 and 27 to color in the thin next ring.

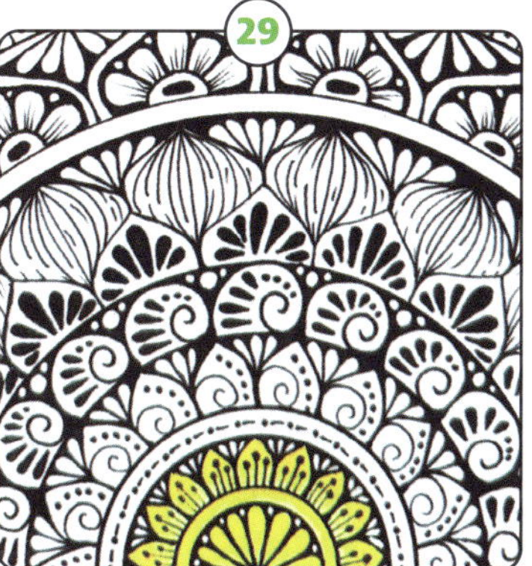

Color the next ring. Repeat steps 26 and 27 to color in the pointed leaves of the next ring.

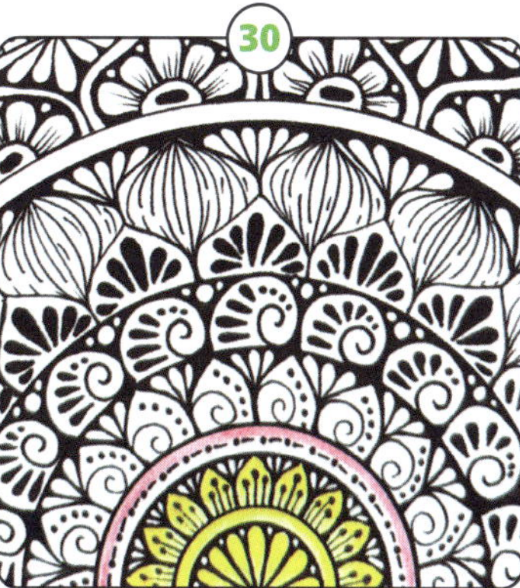

Start the Morse code ring. Use dark pink to color the outer half of the Morse code ring.

Ombré Sunrise

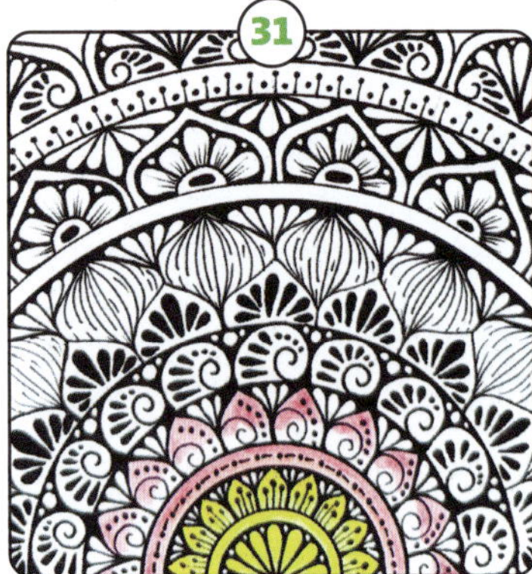

Keep going with pinks. Use light pink to finish the Morse code ring. Then switch back to dark pink to color the outer halves of the pointed leaves of the next ring.

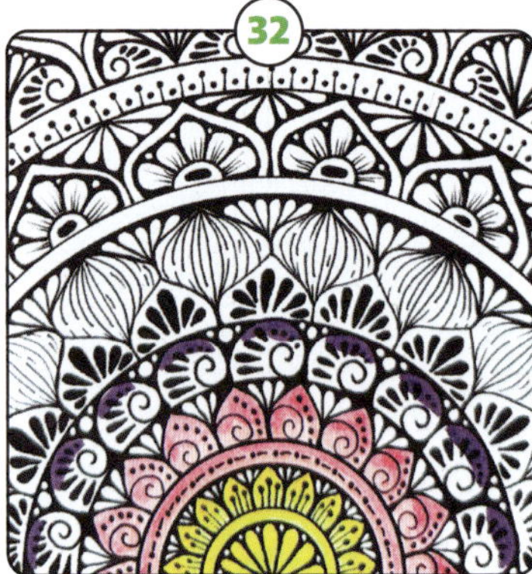

Start the curling-lines ring. Use dark purple to color the outer halves of the curling line segments of the next ring.

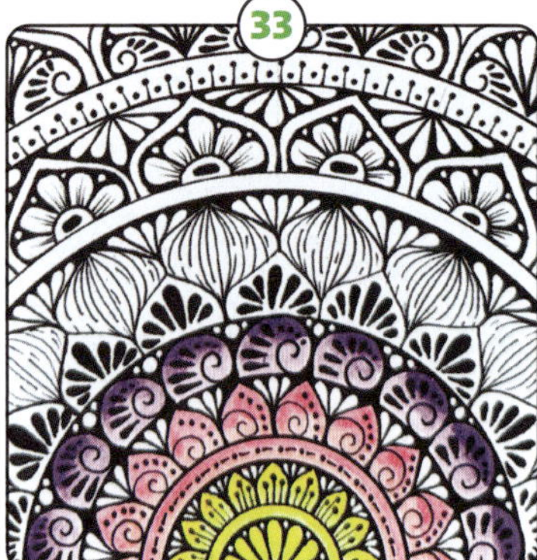

Finish the curling-lines ring. Use light purple to color the inner halves of these curling line segments.

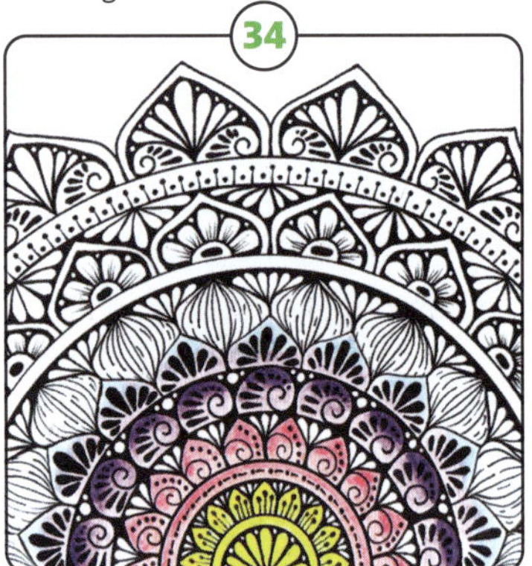

Color the next set of pointed leaves. Use light purple on the inner halves and light blue on the outer halves to color the next ring of pointed leaves.

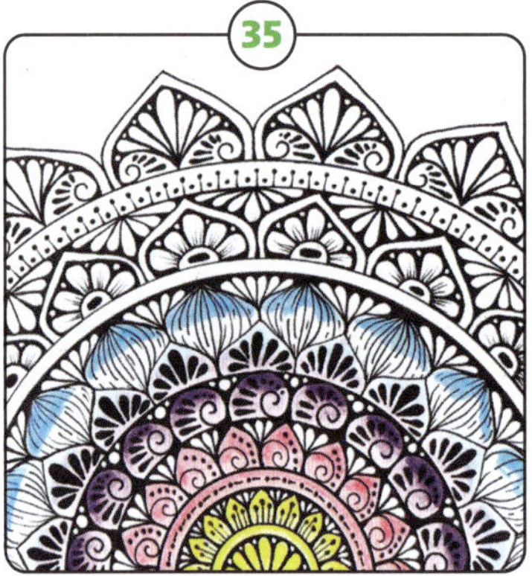

Start coloring the onions. Use medium blue to color the outer halves of the onion segments of the next ring.

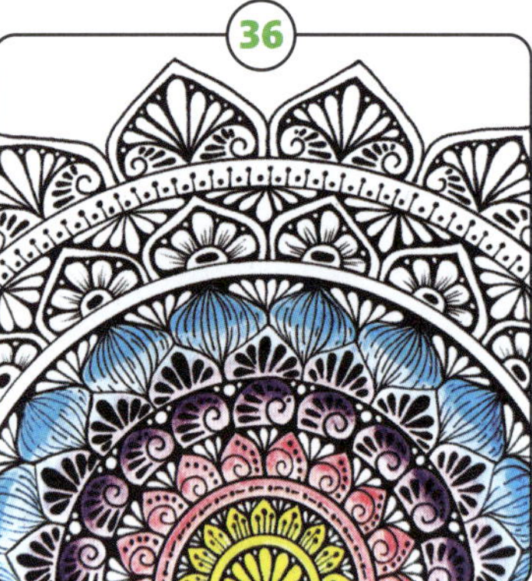

Finish the onions. Switch back to light blue to color the inner halves of the onion segments.

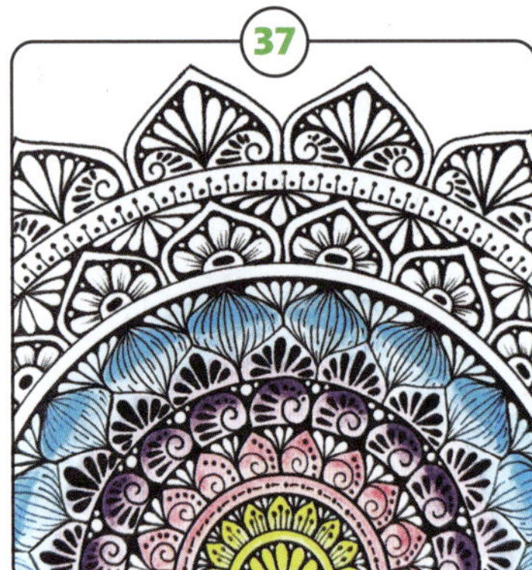

Color the teardrops. Continue with light blue to color the teardrops to complete this ring.

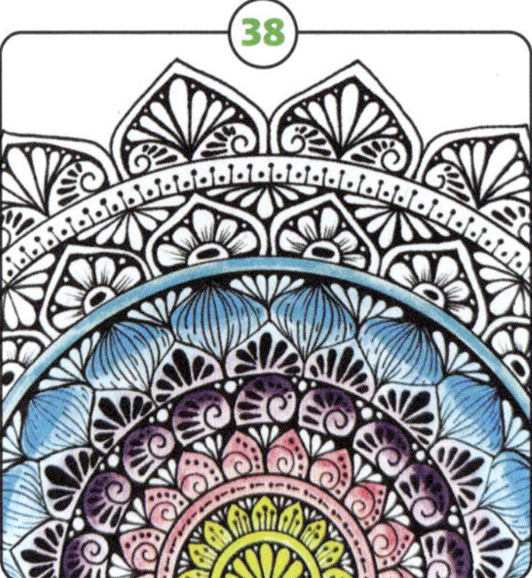

Color the next ring. Fill the next thin ring with a mix of medium blue and light aqua (a new blue).

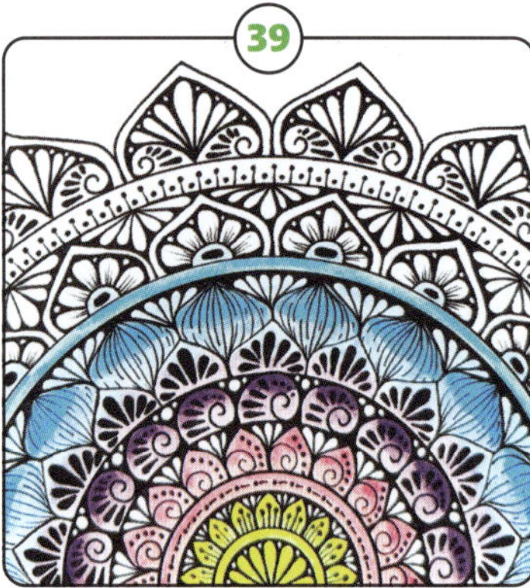

Start the next ring. Use light blue to fill the semicircles inside the next ring.

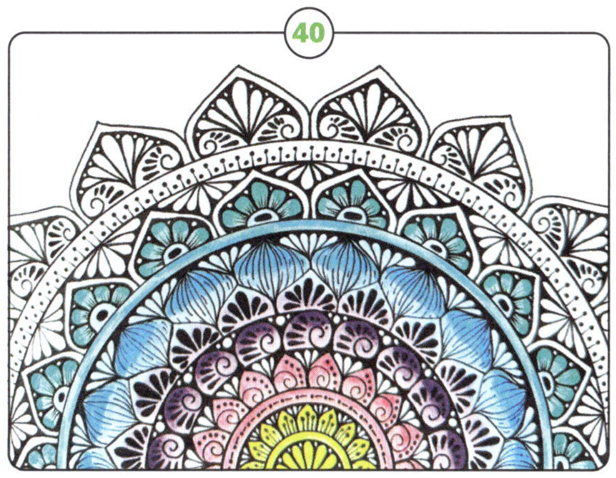

Color the petals. Use light aqua on the inner halves and medium aqua on the outer halves to color the petals in this ring.

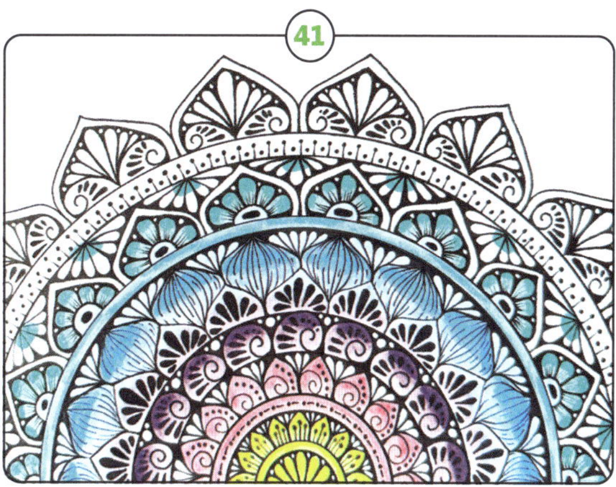

Start the next set of teardrops. Use medium aqua to color a neat semicircle at the top center of each set of teardrops along the outer edge of this ring.

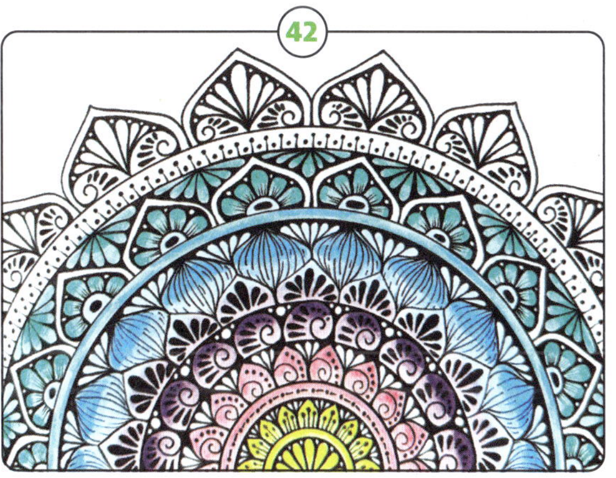

Finish the teardrops. Use light aqua to color the remaining area of these teardrops.

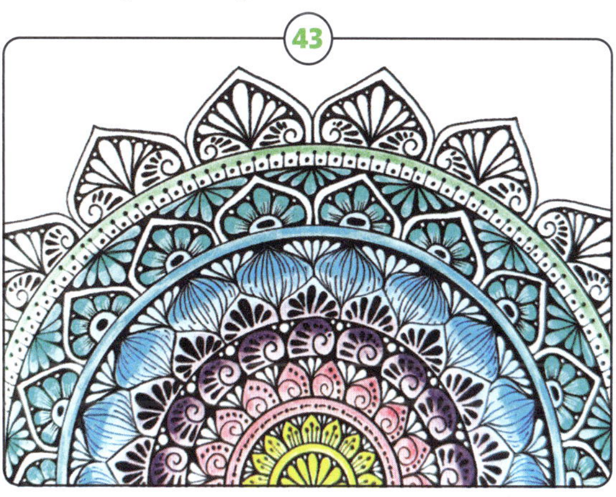

Start the next thin ring. Use medium green to color the outer half of the thin ring that's decorated with lines and dots.

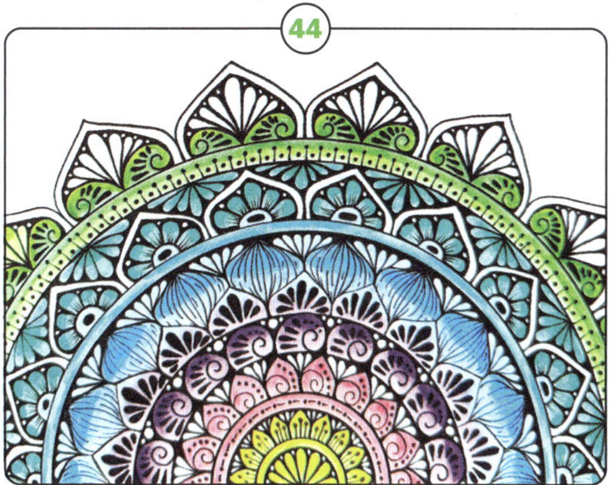

Keep going with greens. Use light green to finish the thin ring. Then use a combo of medium and light green to color the curling line segments of the next ring.

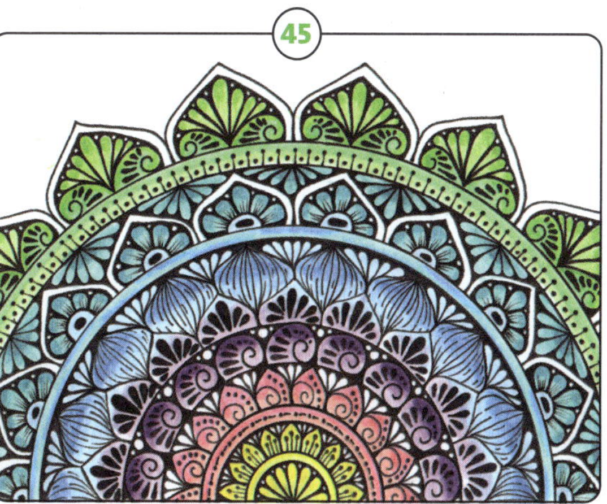

Finish with greens. Use a combo of medium and light green again to color the final teardrops.

Faceted Jewelry

Here's a totally different concept and structure than anything you've seen before! This marker-colored design comprises five different layered mandalas: a unique central mandala surrounded by four identical orbiting mandalas. The result looks almost like a fancy brooch or carving you'd find on a fantasy door.

INTENTION

As you draw this mandala, do your best to really sink into the meditative, repetitive motions of drawing the guideline rays, repeating the same patterns in four of the mandalas, and adding color ring by ring.

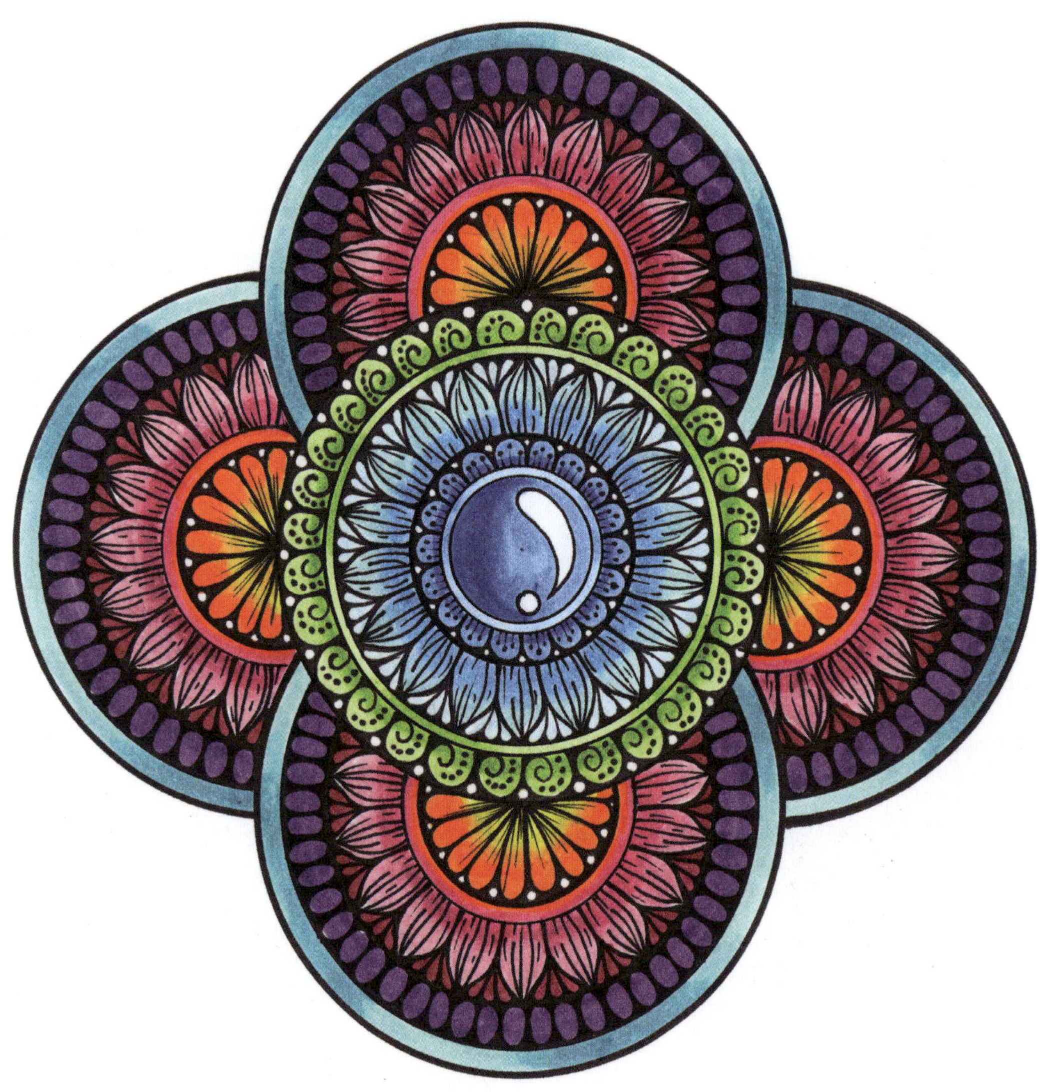

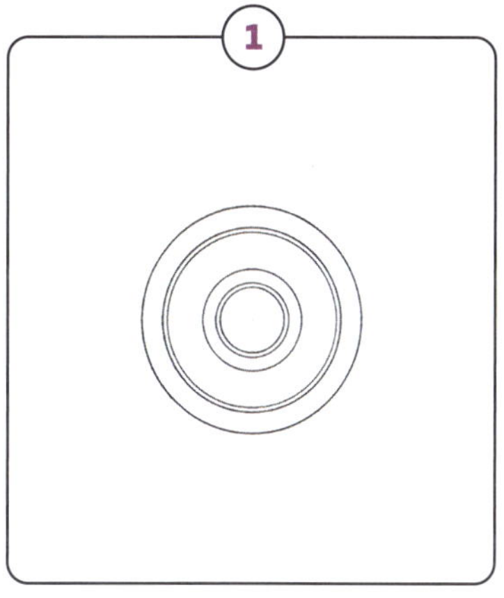

Draw the first set of circles. Draw six circles in pen as shown. For reference, the outermost circle radius is 1¾" (4.5 cm); the innermost circle radius is ½" (1.3 cm).

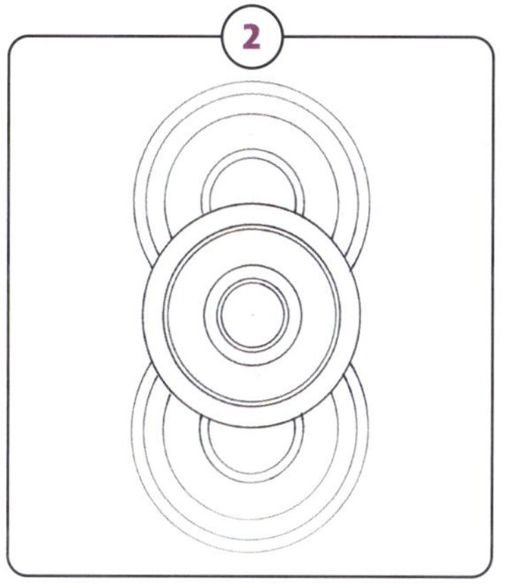

Draw two more sets of circles. Draw five circles as shown, twice. For reference, the outermost circle radius is 1⅞" (4.8 cm); the innermost circle radius is ¾" (1.8 cm).

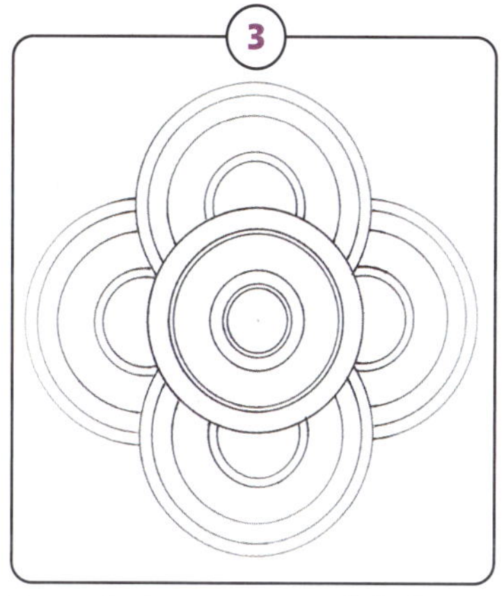

Draw the last two sets of circles. Draw two more sets of circles that are identical to the two you drew in step 2, placed either side of the central circle.

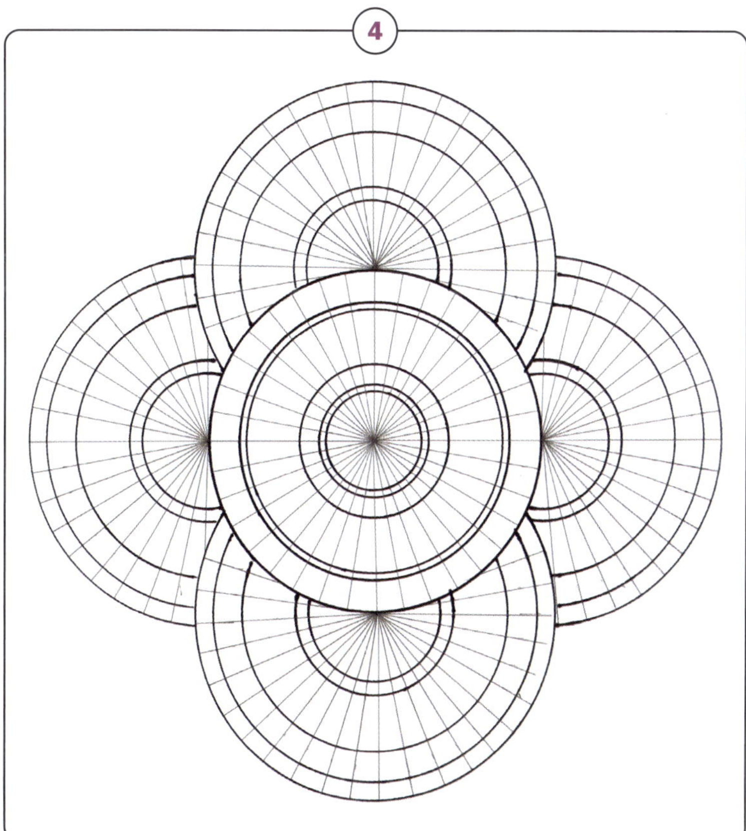

Draw rays. Using pencil, draw a straight horizontal line in each circle set, then draw a ray every 10° on the top half and bottom half (17 rays total on each half).

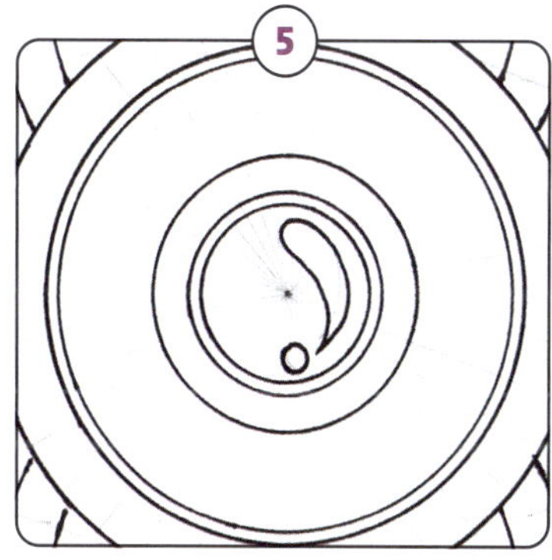

Draw the shine. Draw a small circle and a curving teardrop to represent the central gem's shine. It will look 3D once it is colored!

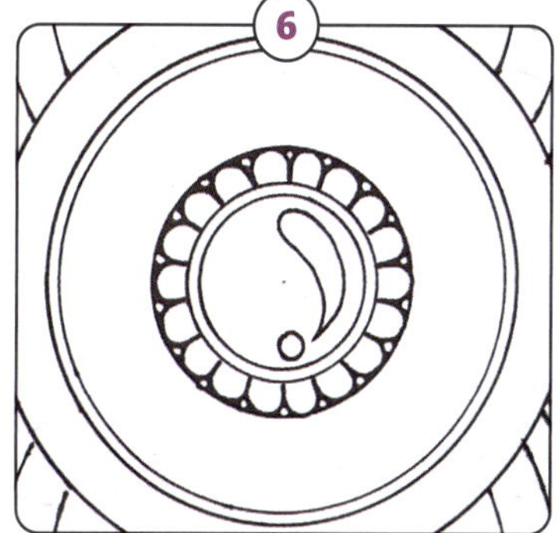

Start the first ring. Draw small domes centered on alternating rays in the first ring. Add a tiny circle between each dome, then fill in around them.

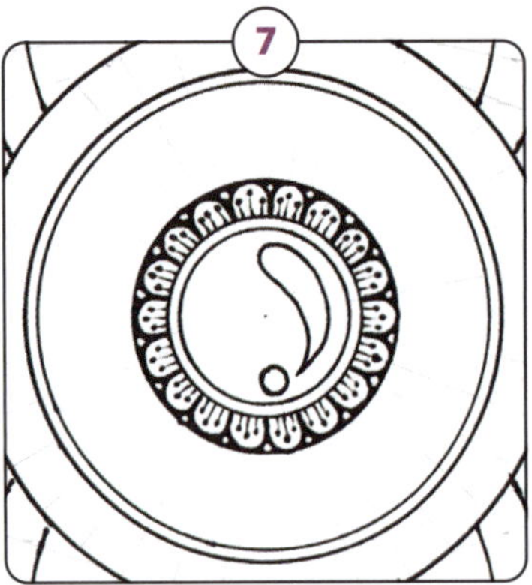

Finish the first ring. Add three lines capped with a dot to each dome.

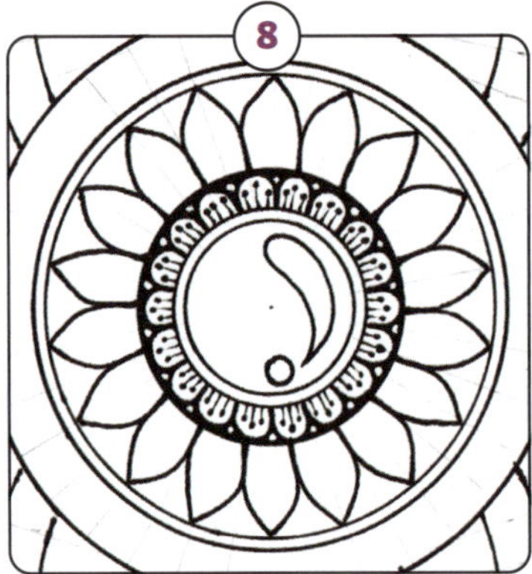

Start the next ring. Draw pointed leaves centered on alternating rays in the next ring, offset from the previous ring of domes.

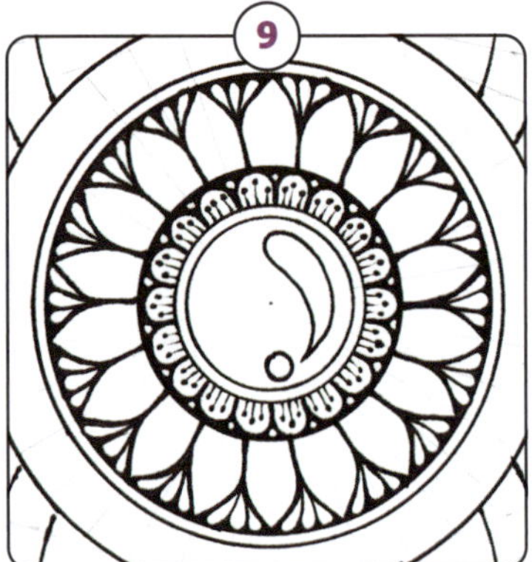

Add teardrops. Add three teardrops between each pointed leaf, then fill in around them.

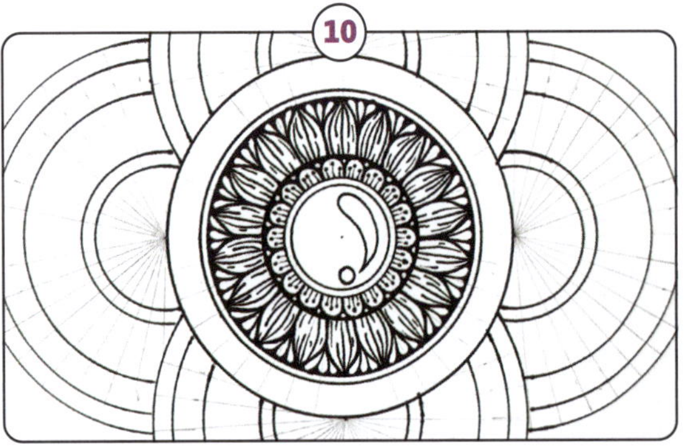

Finish this ring. Add solid and broken lines to the pointed leaves to give them a textured, rounded effect—imagine an onion.

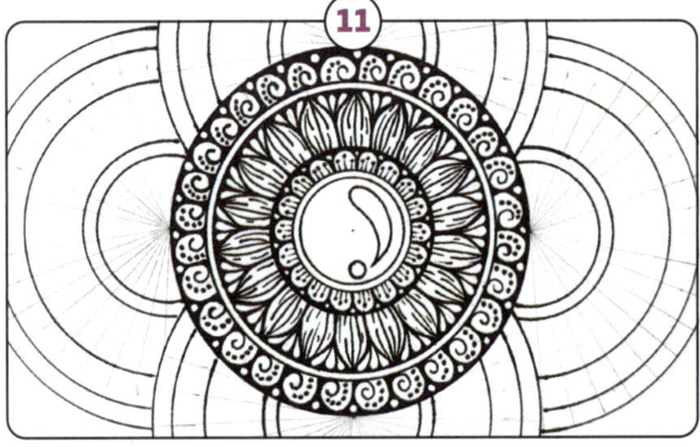

Complete the central mandala. Fill the final ring of this mandala with a pattern consisting of curling lines, dots, and circles as shown.

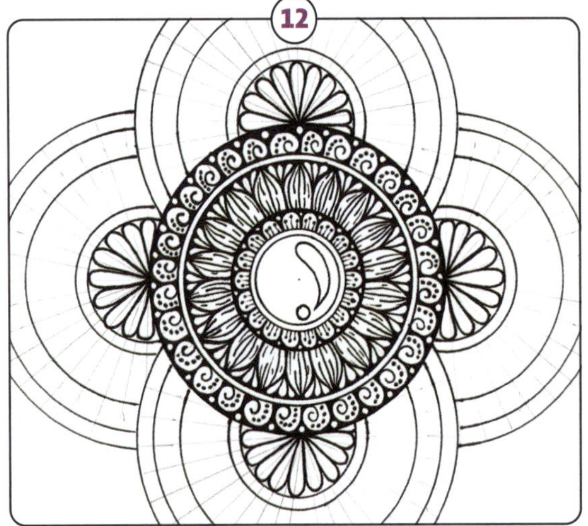

Start the outer mandalas. In the center of each of the other, outer mandalas, draw teardrops centered on alternating rays.

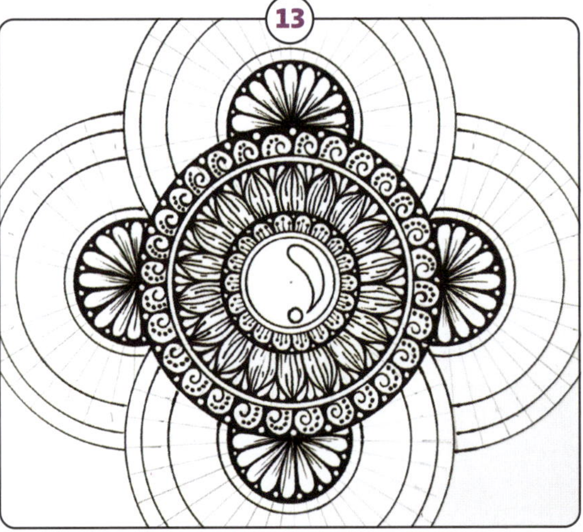

Finish the centers. Draw a freehand circle between each teardrop, then fill in around them. Add some delicate detail lines inside the teardrops.

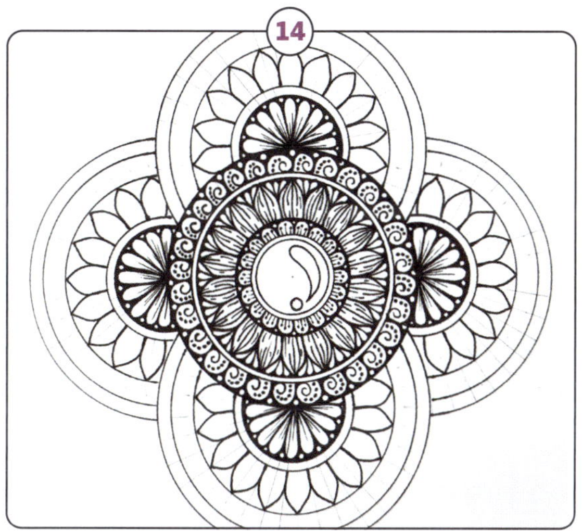

Start the first rings of the outer mandalas. In the first ring of each of the outer mandalas, draw pointed leaves centered on alternating rays.

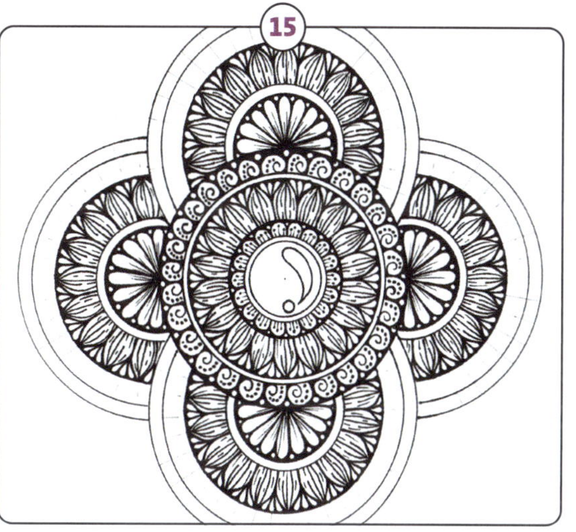

Finish these rings. Repeat steps 9 and 10 to finish these rings in each of the outer mandalas.

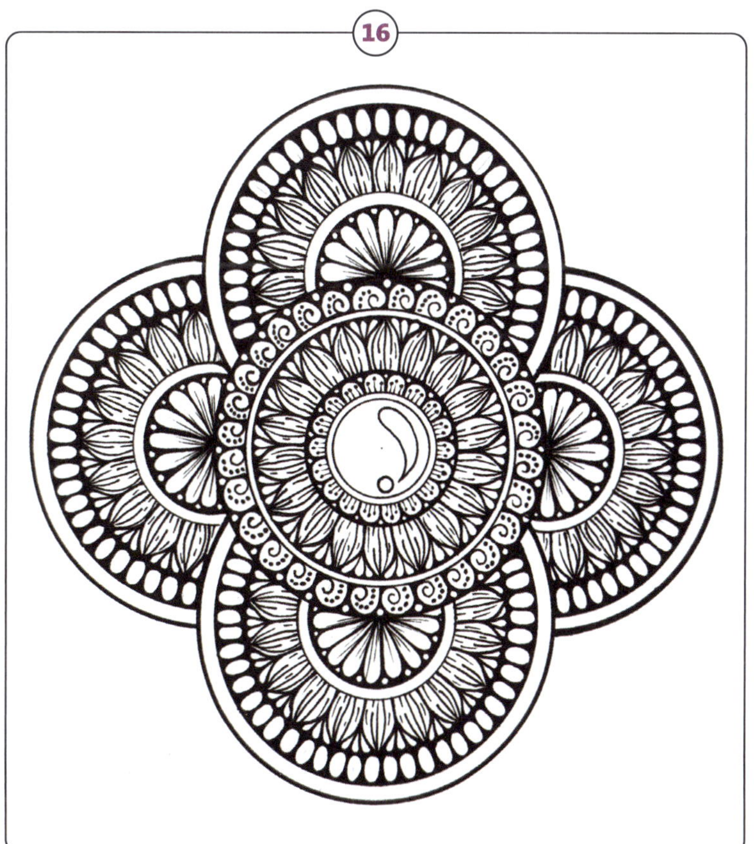

Fill the final rings of the outer mandalas. In the last ring of each of the outer mandalas, draw about 24 to 26 ovals to fill the ring, then fill in around them.

Start coloring the center. Use a dark blue to color a crescent moon section of the center of the inner mandala.

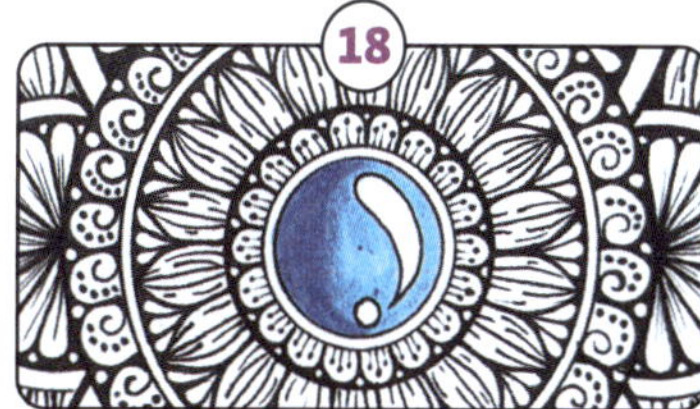

Finish the center. Switch to a medium blue to color the rest of the center, doing your best to blend the two colors and create a 3D effect.

Start the dome ring. Use dark blue to color the inner halves of the domes in the next ring.

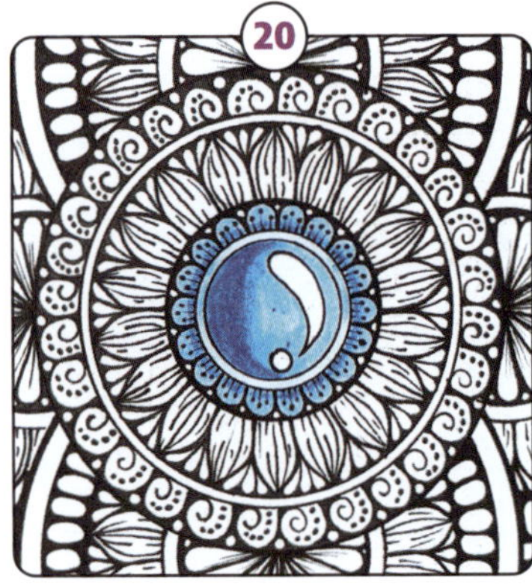

Finish the dome ring. Switch back to medium blue to color the outer halves of the domes.

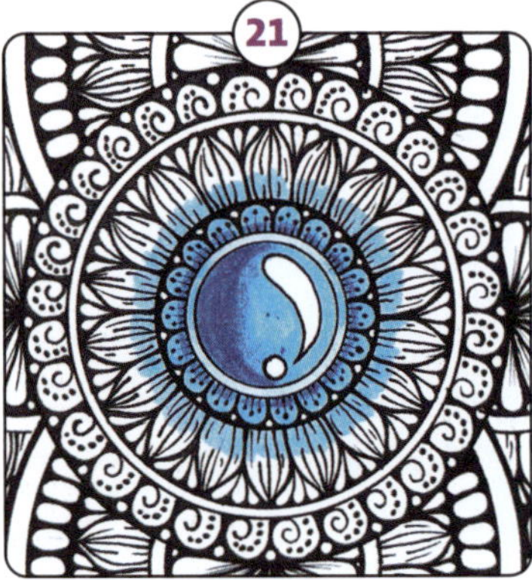

Start the leaf ring. Use medium blue to color the inner halves of the pointed leaves in the next ring.

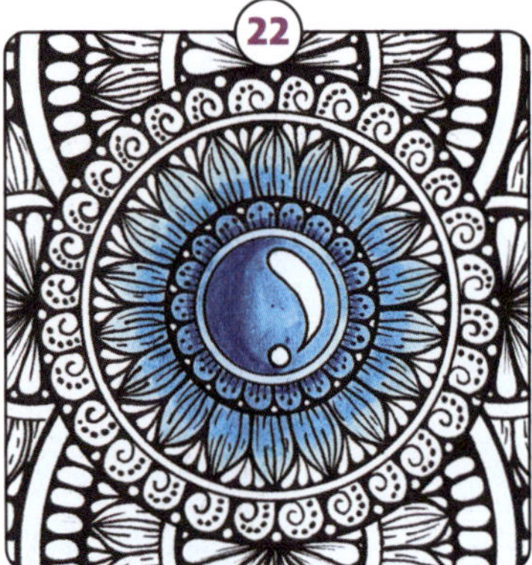

Finish the leaf ring. Switch to light blue to color the outer halves of the pointed leaves.

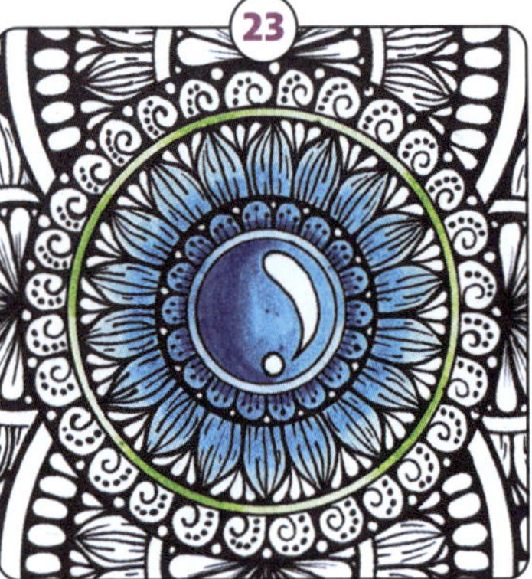

Color the bordering ring. Fill the next thin ring with a mix of medium green and light green.

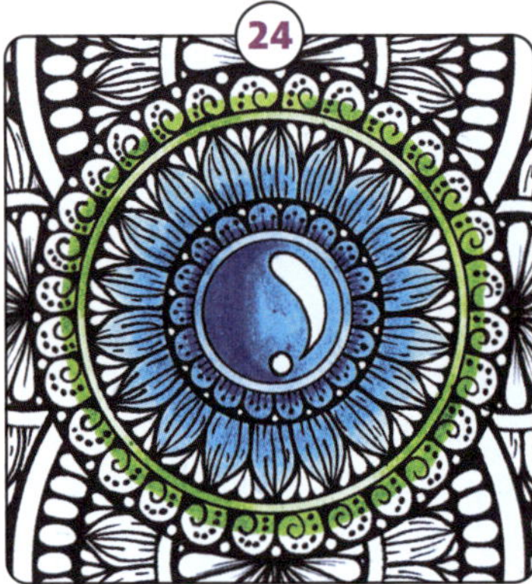

Start the curling-lines ring. Use medium green to color the inner halves of the curling line segments in the next ring.

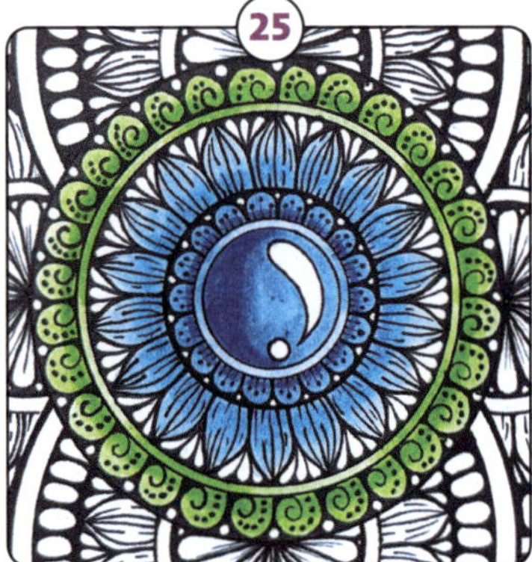

Finish the curling-lines ring. Switch back to light green to color the outer halves of the curling line segments.

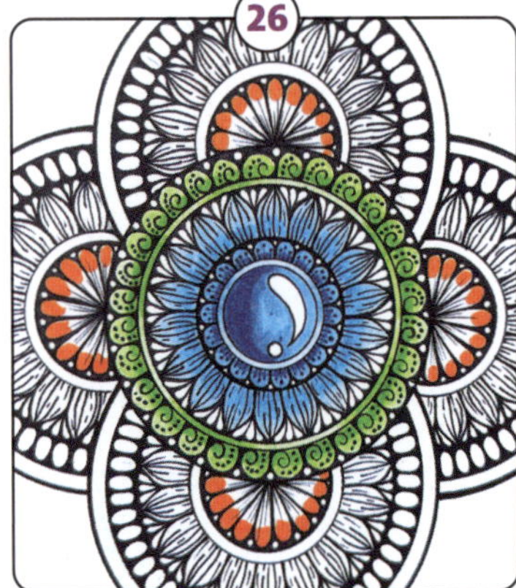

Start the outer mandalas. In the center of each of the outer mandalas, use dark orange to color the outer halves of the teardrops.

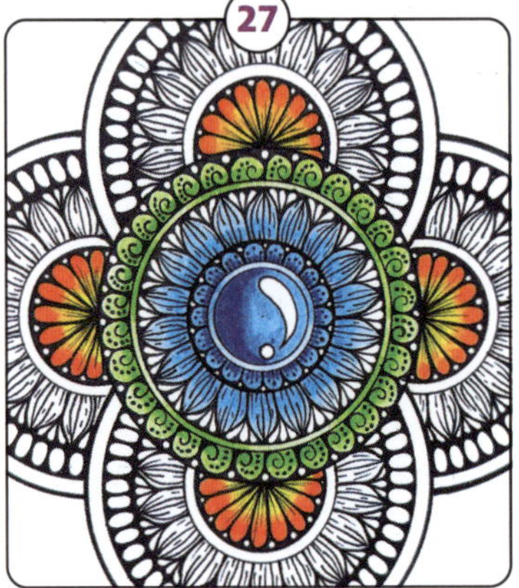

Finish the centers. Use medium orange to color the inner halves of the teardrops.

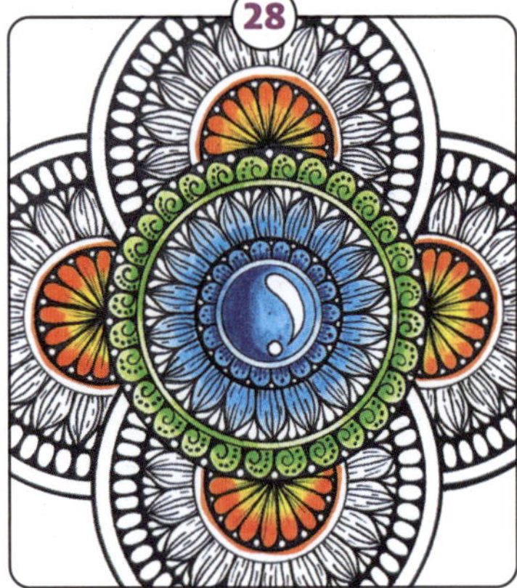

Start the blank rings. Use dark orange to color the inner half of the entire next blank ring in each of the outer mandalas.

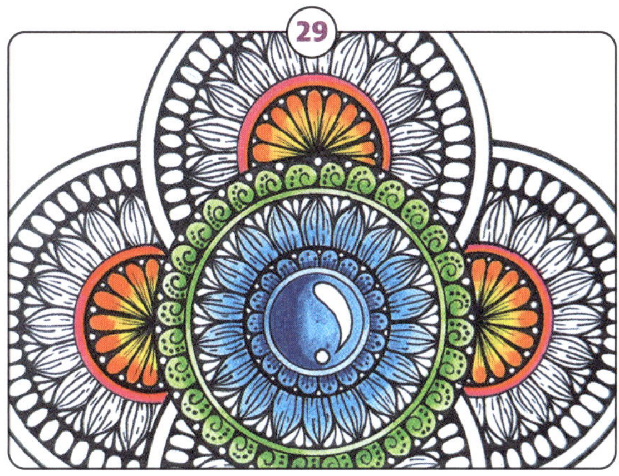

Finish the blank rings. Use dark pink to color the outer half of each of these blank rings.

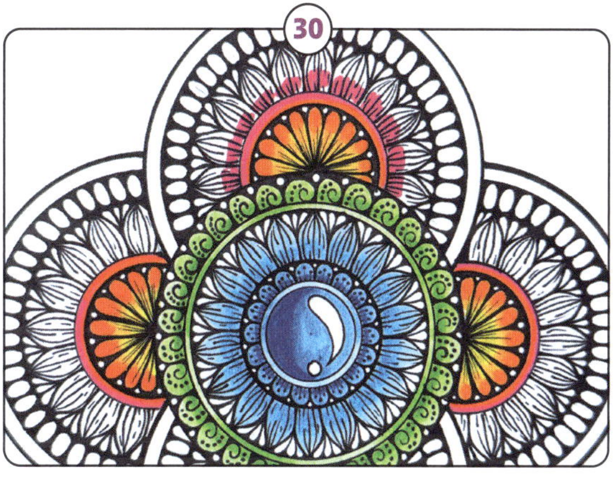

Start the onions ring. Use dark pink to color the inner halves of the pointed leaf "onions" in the next ring in each of the outer mandalas.

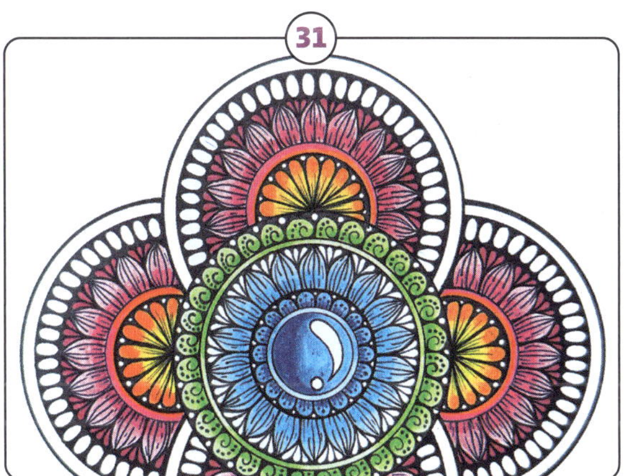

Finish the ring. Use light pink to color the outer halves of these pointed leaf "onions", then fill the teardrops in the same ring with maroon.

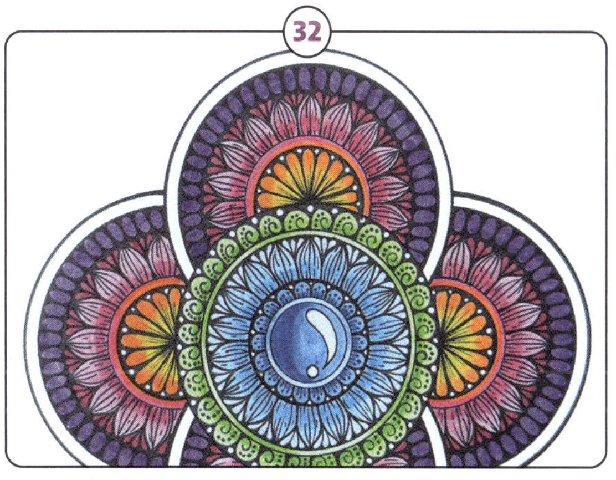

Color the ovals ring. In the next ring in each of the outer mandalas, fill the ovals with purple.

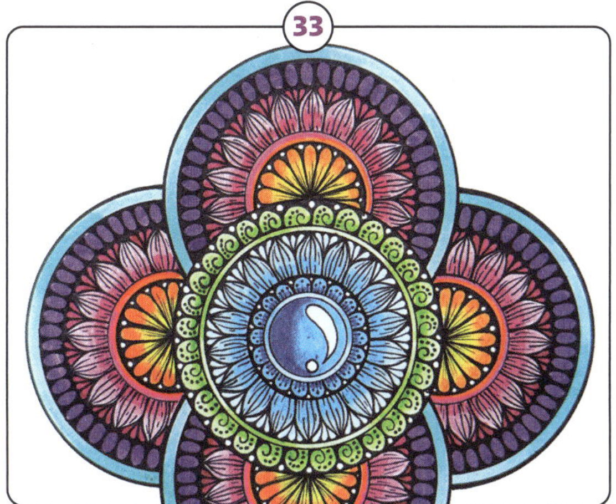

Finish with aquas. Fill the final thin ring of each of the outer mandalas with a mix of medium aqua and light aqua.

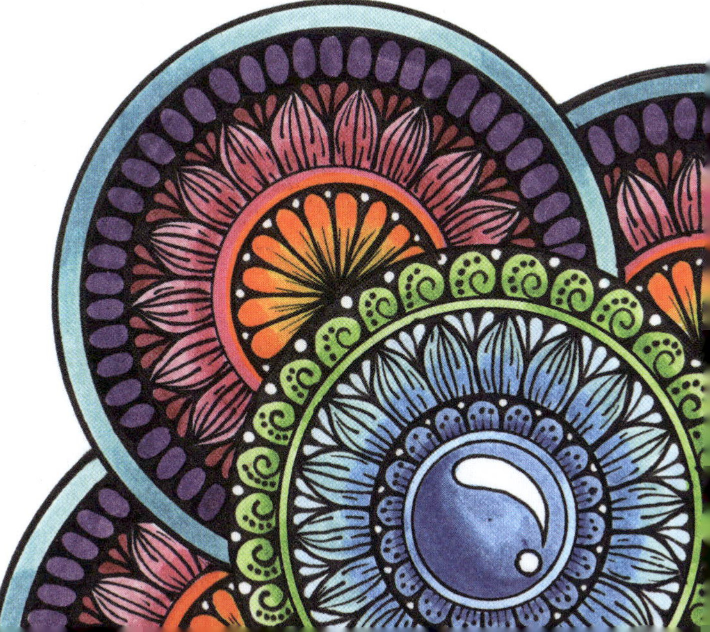

Soothing Blue

CHALLENGE YOURSELF

Are you ready to tackle a colored mandala on your own? Try re-creating—or adapting—this monochromatic blue design. For this mandala, use colored pencil instead of markers. Use what you learned while working on the previous mandalas to build up this design yourself independently, referring to just the few basic steps that are provided as guideposts.

As you draw this mandala, let go of expectations that you must make perfect transitions between the exactly "correct" shades of blue on every ring. Pick and use the blues you feel drawn to in the moment.

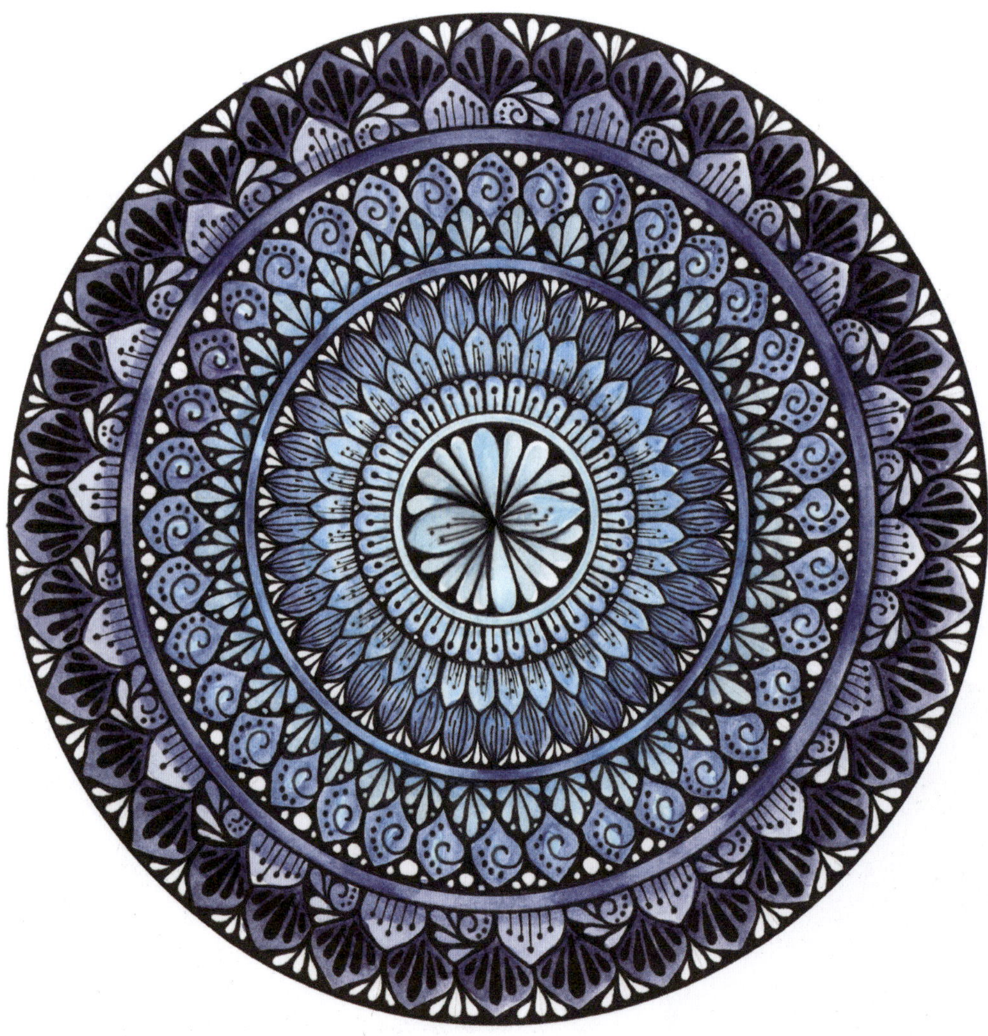

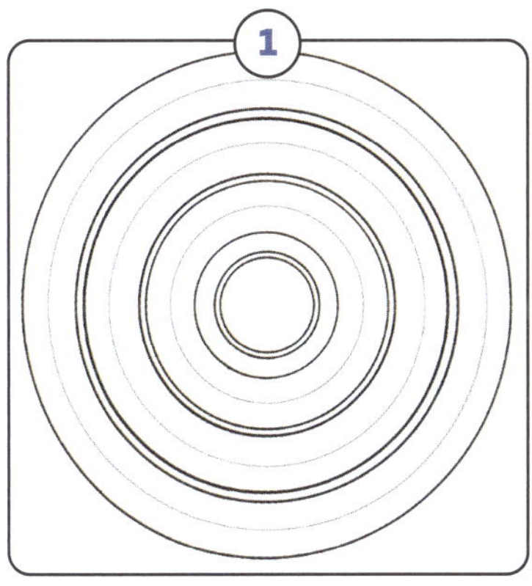

Draw circles. Draw 11 circles as shown in pen and in pencil. For reference, the outermost circle radius is 3⅞" (9.8 cm); the innermost circle radius is ¾" (1.8 cm).

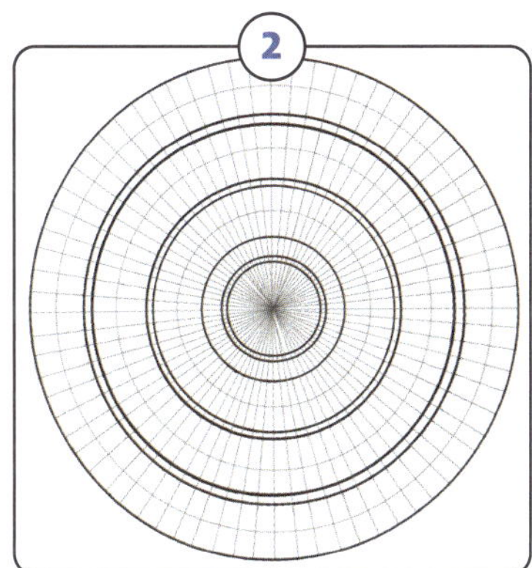

Draw rays. Using pencil, draw a straight horizontal line, then draw a ray every 5° on the top half and bottom half (35 rays total on each half).

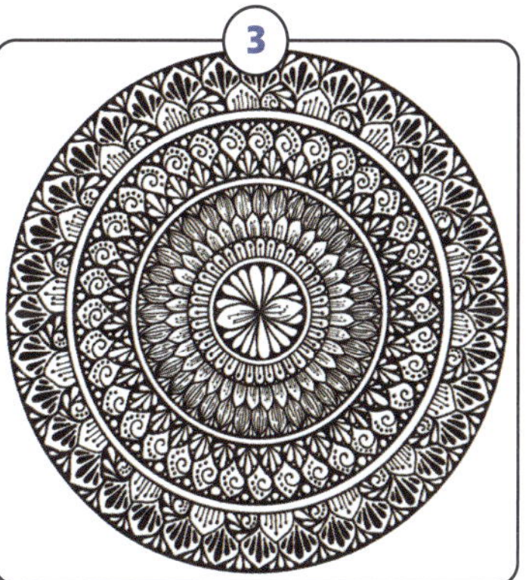

Draw the entire mandala. The training wheels are truly off! Refer to the image of the finished mandala to complete the black designs—or come up with your own!

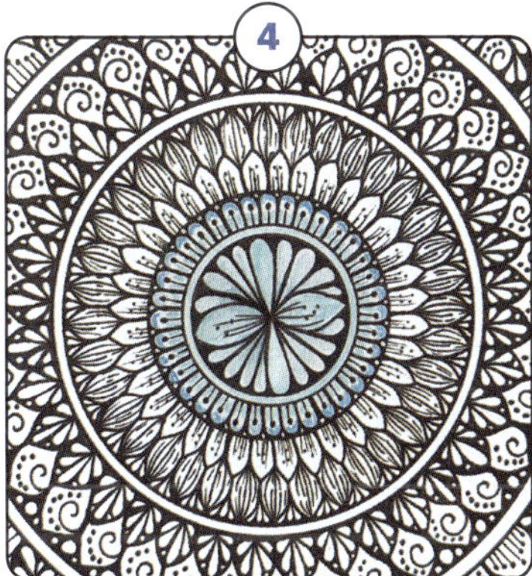

Start in the center. In this mandala, many sections are filled by first partially coloring a shape with two different blues, then blending them together in the middle.

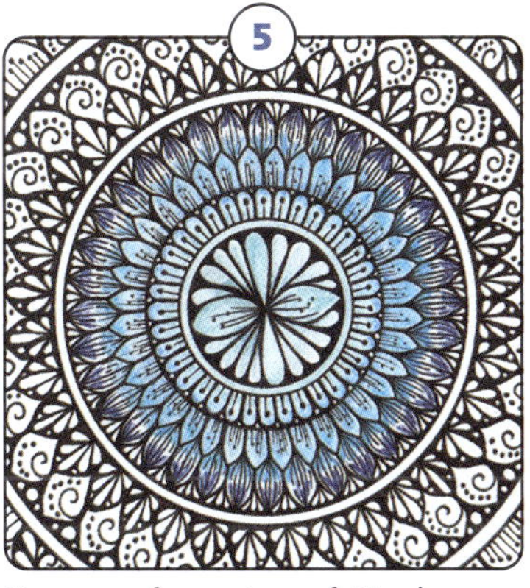

Keep moving outward. Here's another example of two different blues that are blended together in the center.

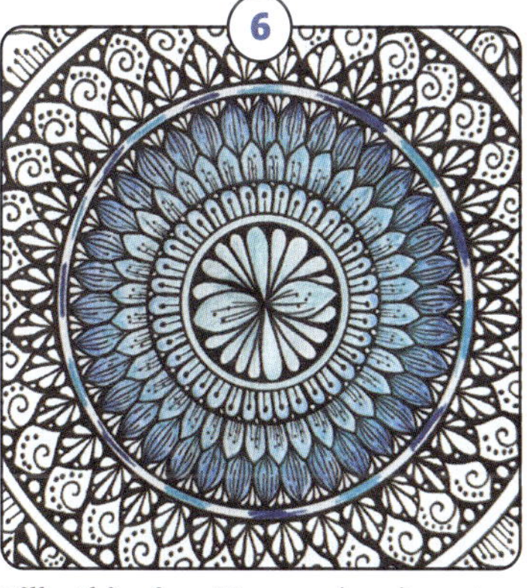

Fill a thin ring. You can also alternate two different blues within a thin ring as shown, then blend them together.

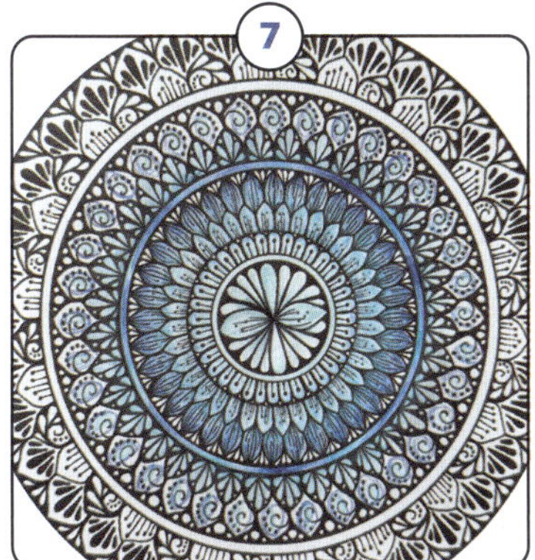

Try a swirl approach. Another way to create a blend is to fill the center of a shape with one blue, swirl a rough circle around it with another blue, then blend together.

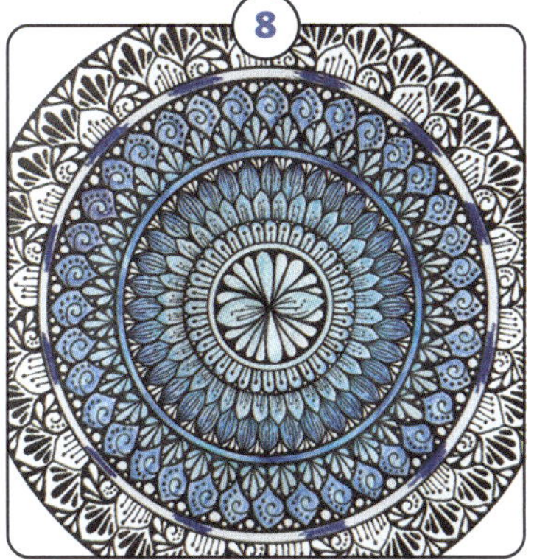

Try just one blue. Another option is to partially fill a ring with one single dark blue, then blend it out into a lighter shade in the empty areas.

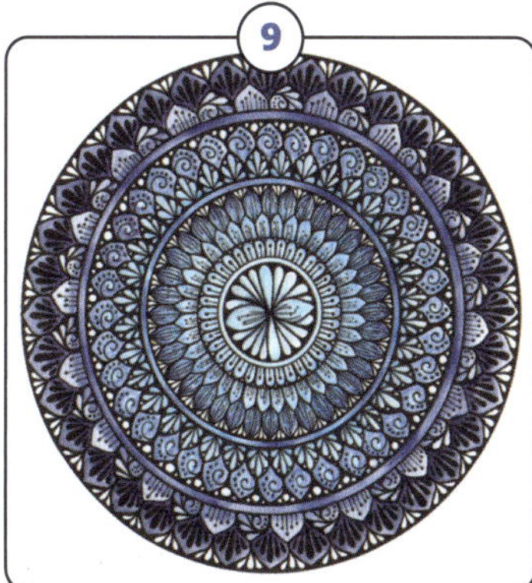

Go from dark to light. Keep working your way outward until you're using a dark navy in the last ring, blending it out from the inside toward the outside.

Simple Sunflower

Up to this point, the mandalas you've learned have been mostly focused on one single circular base, and you've been approaching color in only one specific way in each mandala section. In this section, you'll start breaking away from simple circles to create special shapes, and you'll also combine different coloring techniques in single mandalas. Let's get started with this easy design that combines colored lines and black lines in a special sunflower shape!

INTENTION

As you draw this mandala, imagine a real sunflower blooming in the daylight. Imagine it turning its face to the sun; imagine collecting its seeds and crunching on them joyously.

108

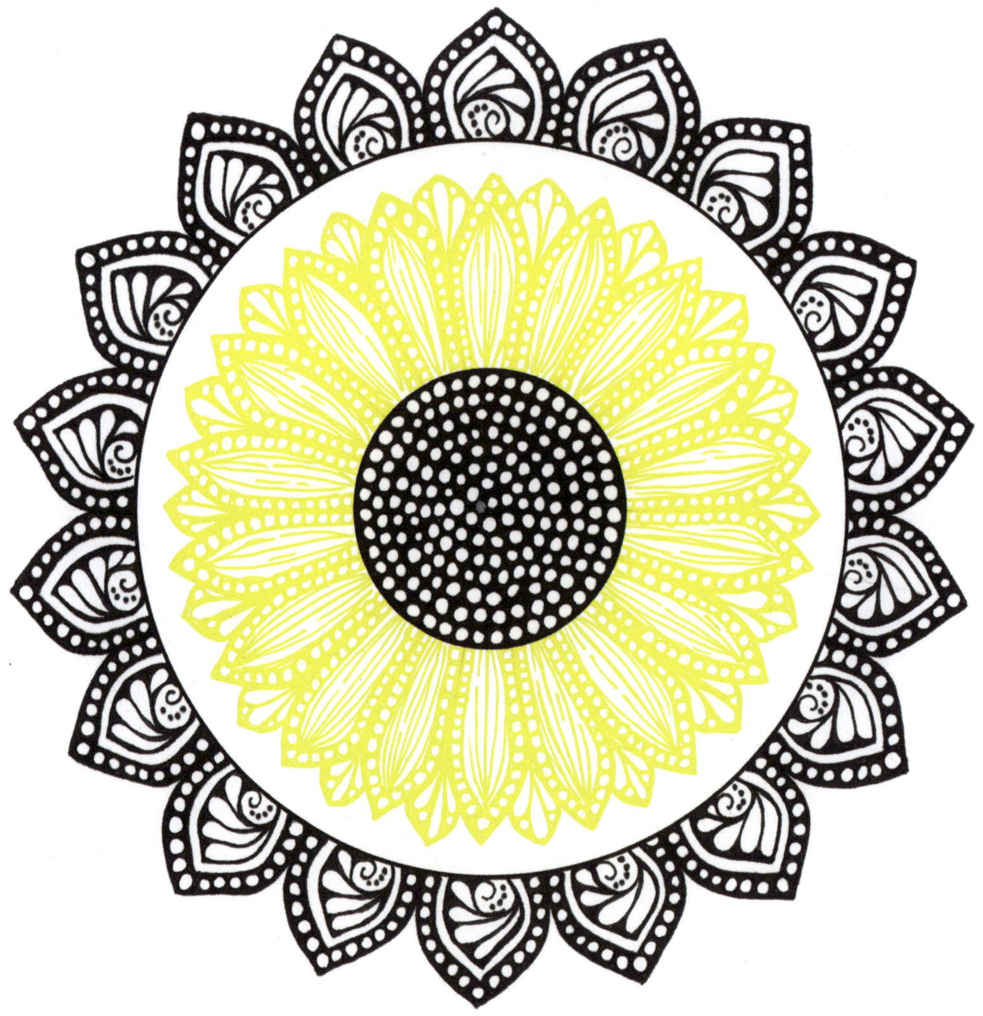

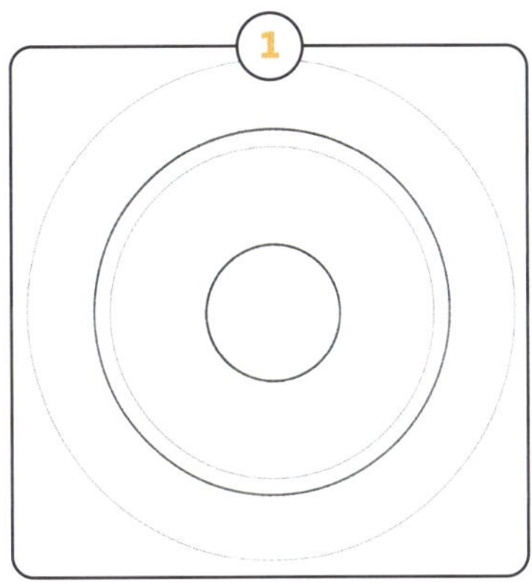

Draw circles. Draw four circles as shown in pencil and in pen. For reference, the outermost circle radius is 3⅞" (9.8 cm); the innermost circle radius is 1⅛" (2.7 cm).

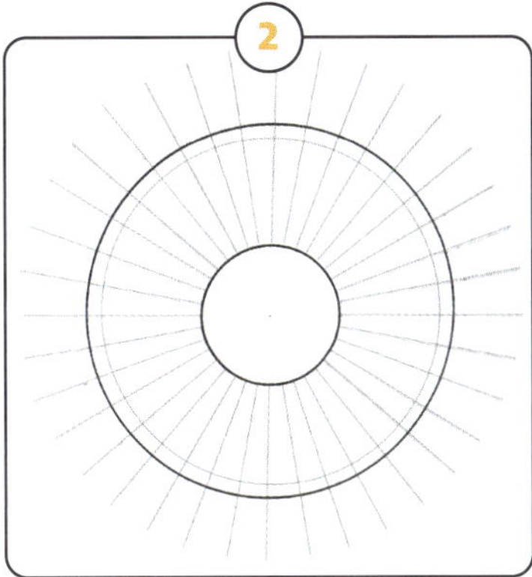

Draw rays. Using pencil, draw a straight horizontal line, then draw a ray every 10° on the top half and bottom half (17 rays total on each half). Erase the very center.

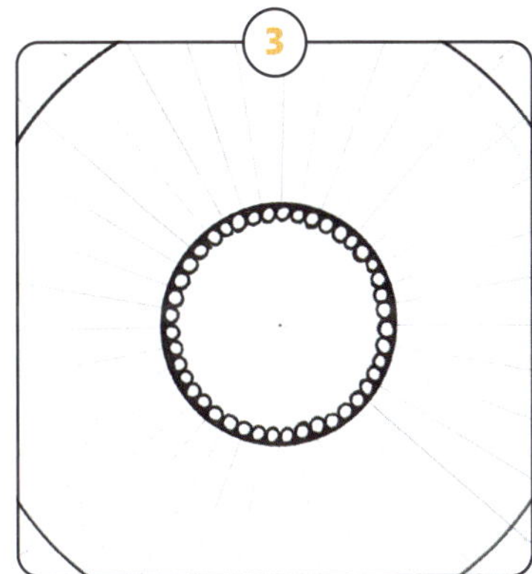

Add an inner ring of circles. Draw a ring of small, touching circles just inside the center circle, then fill in the space trapped between them and the center circle.

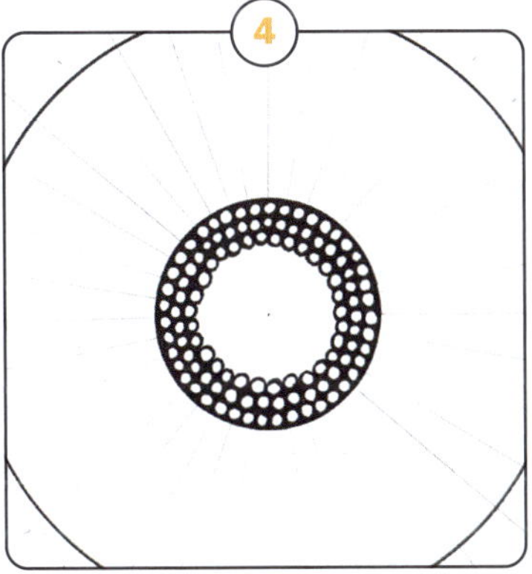

Draw two more rings. Draw another ring of circles just inside the first ring of them, then draw a third inside that. Fill in the space trapped between each of the rings.

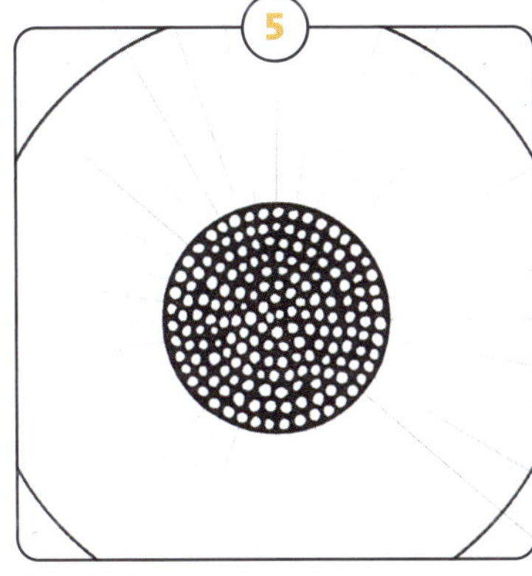

Finish the center. Keep working your way inward like this for about three or four more rings, then break away from the neat rings to finish filling the very center.

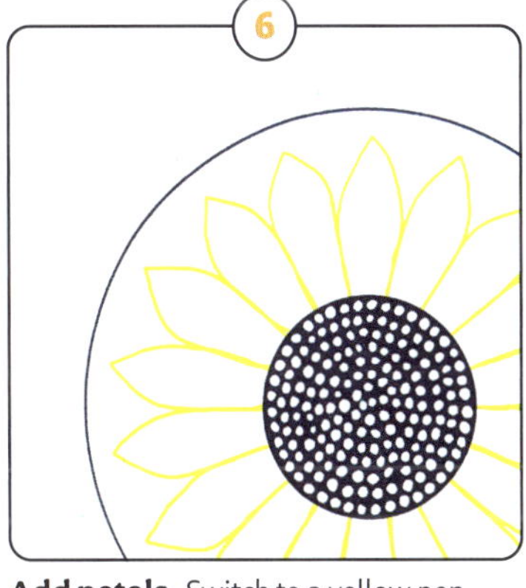

Add petals. Switch to a yellow pen. Draw pointed leaves centered on alternating rays in the first ring. These should be shaped like long petals.

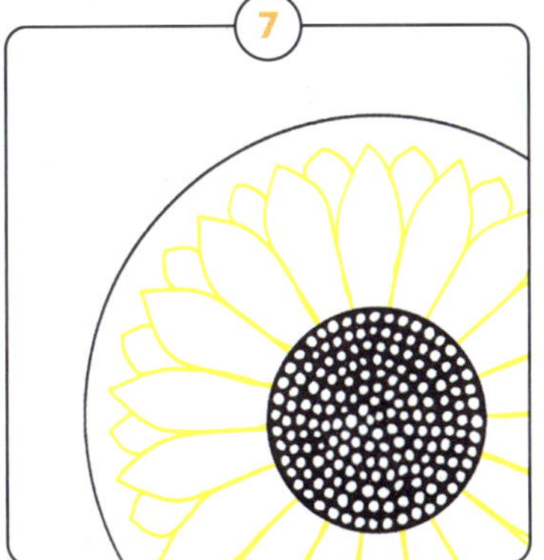

Add background petals. Draw the top of another petal between each existing petal, creating a layered effect.

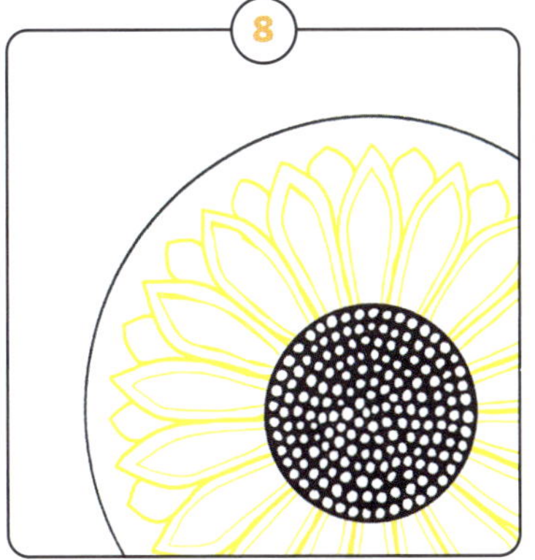

Add insets. Add an inset petal to each full petal.

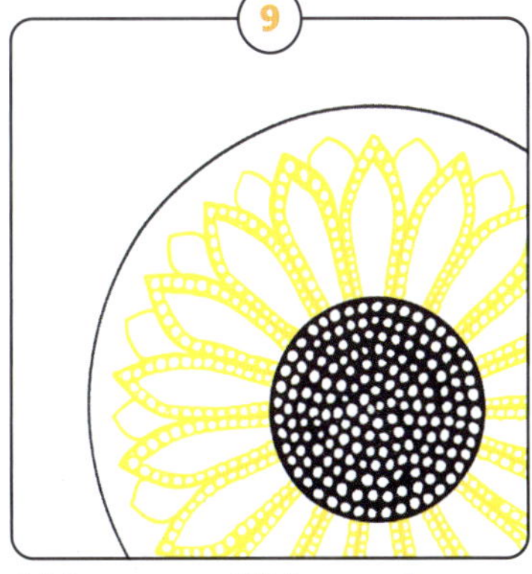

Add a pattern. Fill the space between each full petal and its inset with tightly packed circles, then fill in around them.

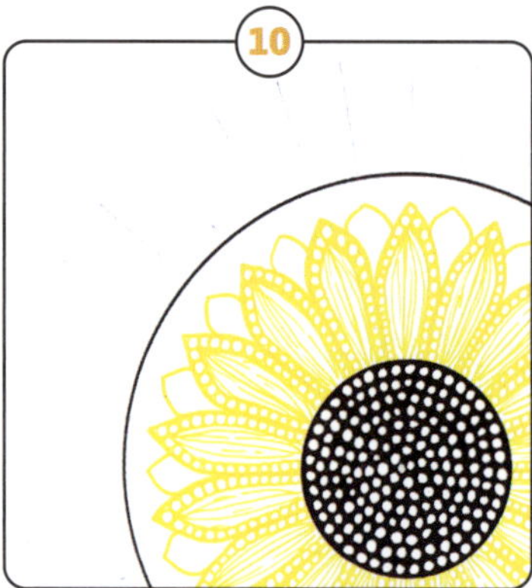

Finish the main petals. Add solid and broken lines to the inset petals to give them a textured, rounded effect—imagine an onion.

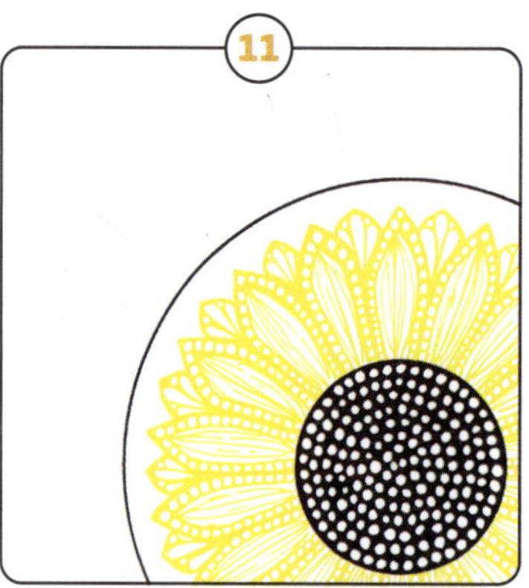

Finish the background petals. Draw three teardrops inside each background petal, draw a tiny freehand circle between each teardrop, then fill in around them.

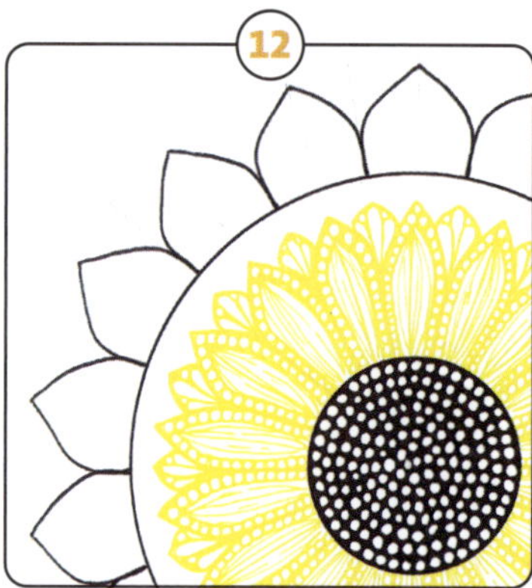

Start the outer ring. Switch back to a black pen. Draw pointed leaves centered on alternating rays in the last ring.

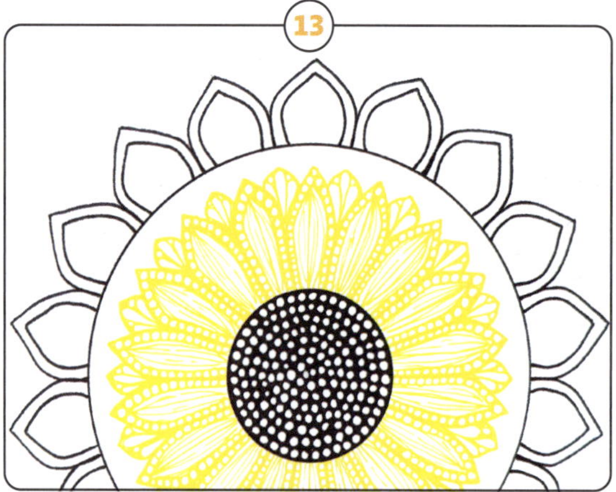

Add insets. Add an inset leaf to each pointed leaf.

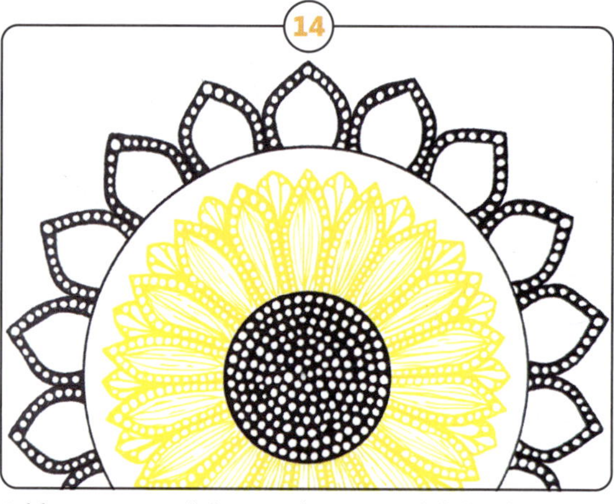

Add a pattern. Fill the space between each full leaf and its inset with tightly packed circles, then fill in around them.

Add more insets. Add another inset leaf to each existing inset pointed leaf.

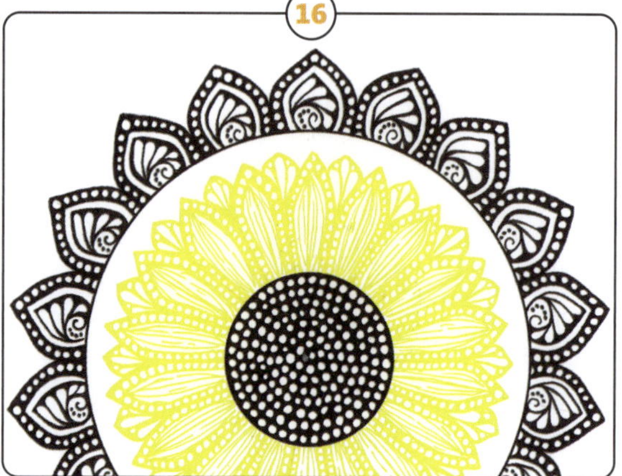

Finish with a pattern. Fill each inset leaf with a pattern of curling lines, dots, and teardrops as shown.

LET'S CHECK IN

Were you able to focus on the intention set at the beginning of this mandala, or did your mind go elsewhere? Have you tried setting your own intention when starting a mandala?

What ideas of your own do you have for drawing mandalas based on specific shapes? Write some down here.

By this point in the book, you've drawn many mandalas in many different styles! What do you keep feeling drawn back to in terms of details, colors, shapes, or intentions?

We are what we repeatedly do.
Excellence, then, is not an act but a habit.
–Will Durant

Rainbow Rising

This lovely mandala is half a normal mandala, half a rainbow! It should be interesting for you to draw familiar mandala designs and shapes inside arches rather than rings. Swatch your chosen eight rainbow colors ahead of time to make sure you'll be happy with your result!

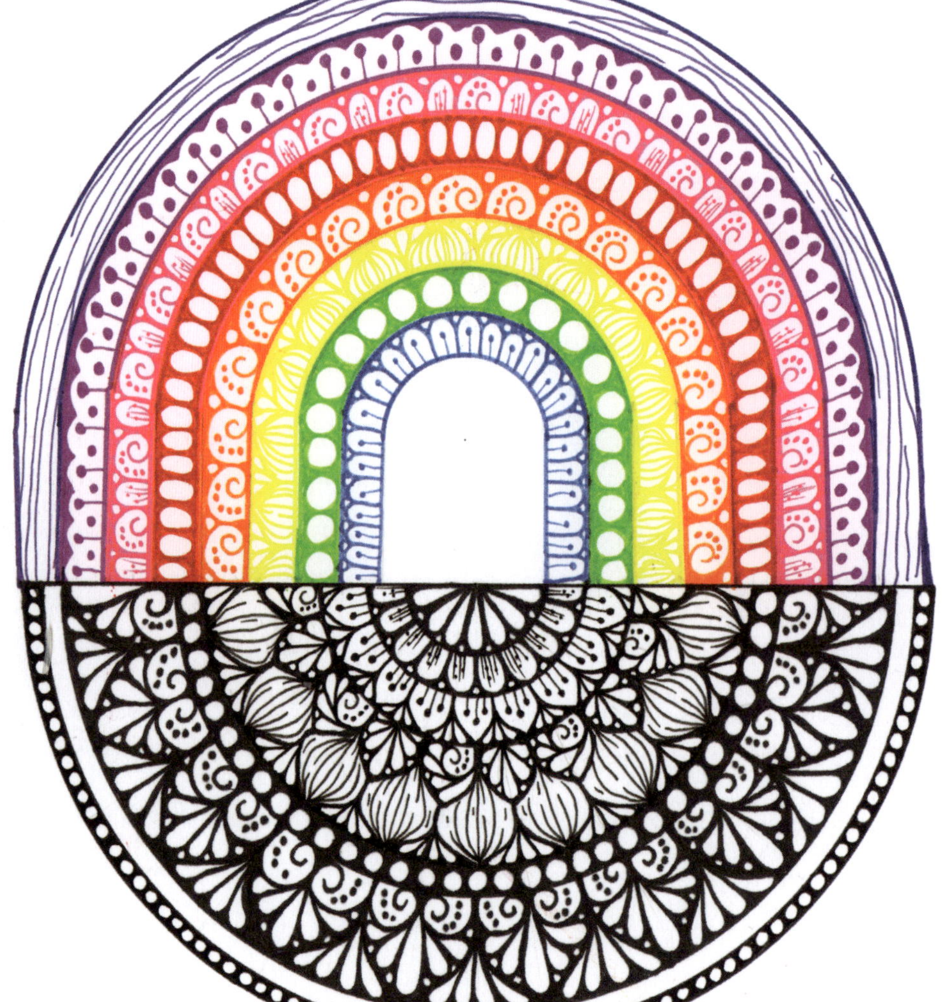

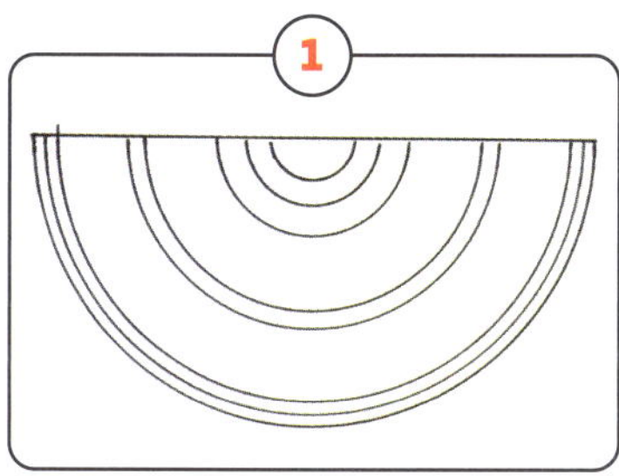

Draw circles. Draw eight half circles as shown. For reference, the outermost circle radius is 3¼" (8.2 cm); the innermost circle radius is ½" (1.3 cm).

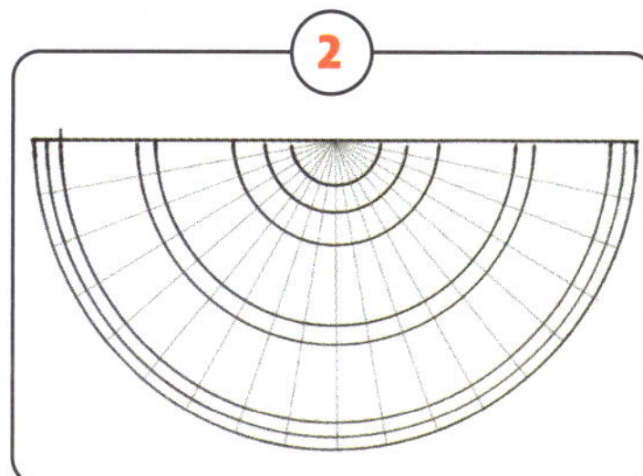

Draw rays. Using pencil, draw a ray every 10° on this half mandala (17 rays total).

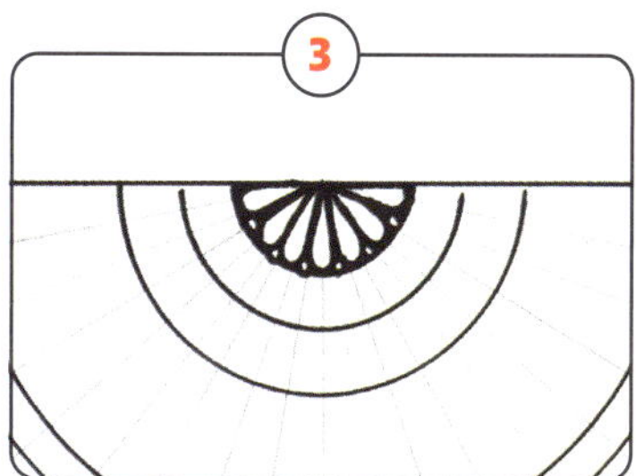

Fill the center. Draw seven teardrops emanating from the center point, add a tiny circle between each teardrop, then fill in around them.

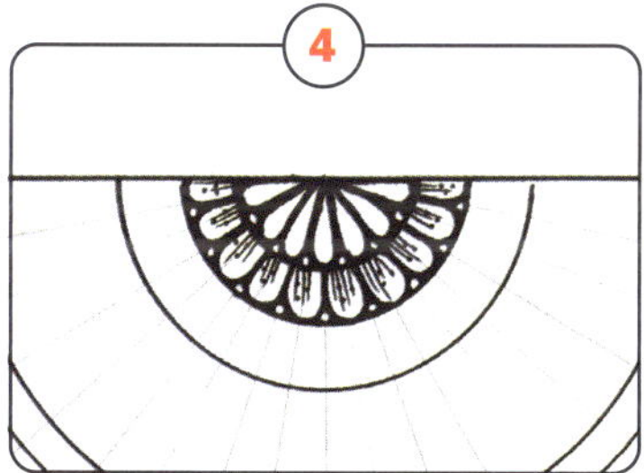

Fill the first ring. Draw domes centered on alternating rays in the first ring. Add a circle between each dome, then fill in around them. Decorate the domes.

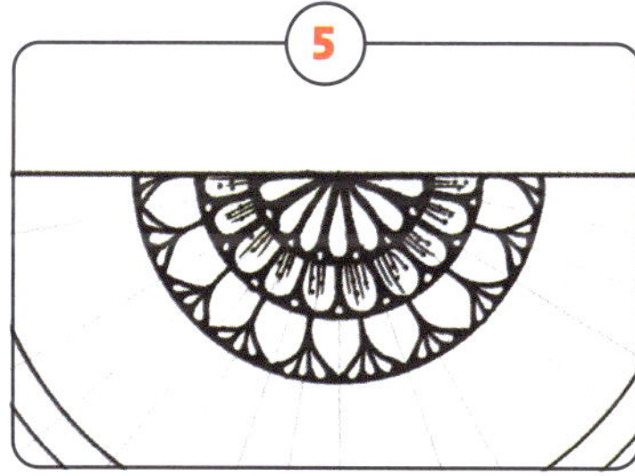

Start the next ring. Draw pointed leaves centered on alternating rays in the next ring, offset from the domes. Add three teardrops between each one.

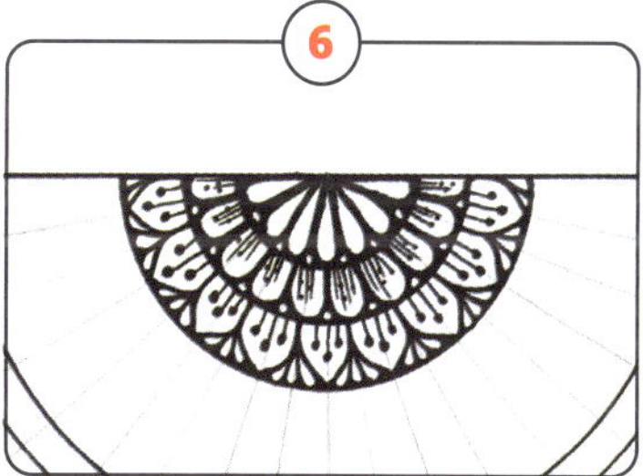

Finish this ring. Add three lines capped with dots to each pointed leaf.

Add a new ring. Use a pencil to add a new circle to the mandala, creating a new ring. Fill the ring with pointed leaves decorated with alternating patterns as shown.

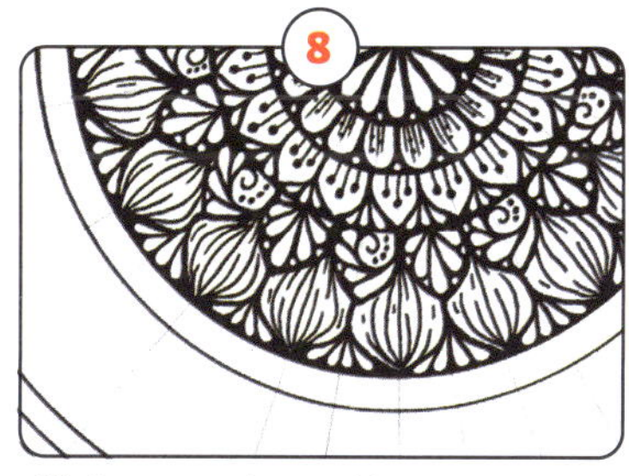

Fill the next ring. Add pointed leaves to the next ring and fill them with the "onion" pattern of broken and unbroken lines. Add four teardrops between each one.

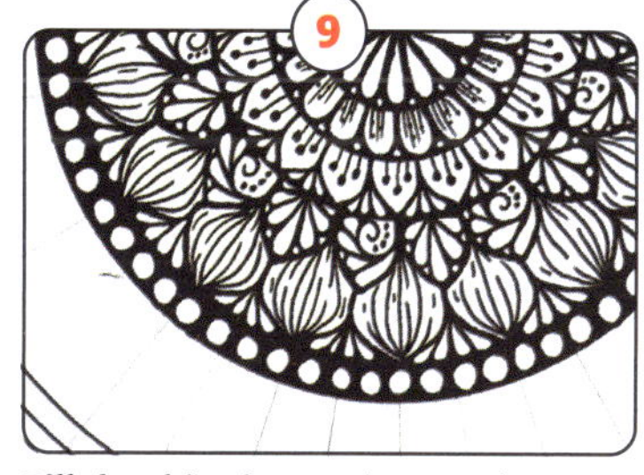

Fill the thin ring. In the next thin ring, draw densely packed circles, then fill in around them.

Start a new ring. Repeat step 5 in the next ring, but with four teardrops between each pointed leaf instead of three.

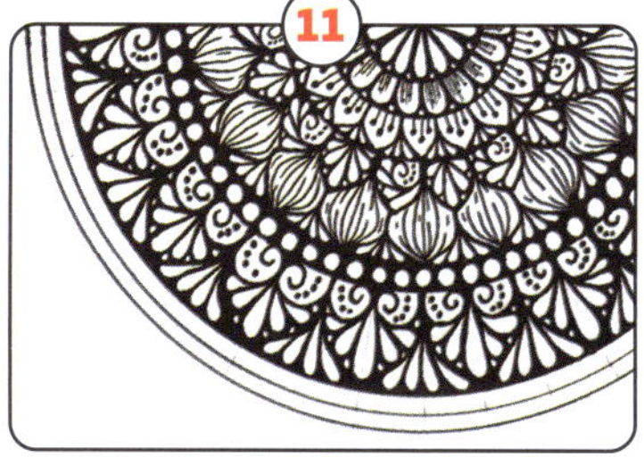

Finish this ring. Fill each pointed leaf with a decorative pattern of curling lines, dots, and teardrops as shown.

Fill the final ring. Repeat step 9 to finish the black section of the mandala.

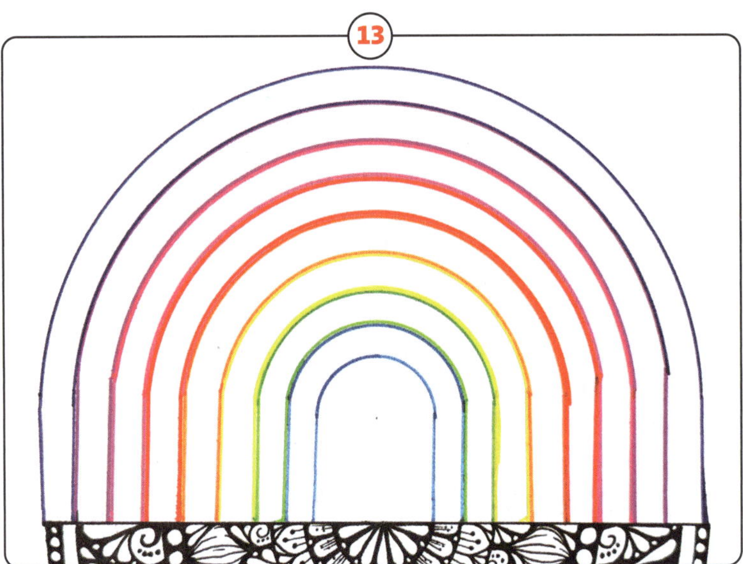

Create the rainbow. The rainbow comprises eight total arches (made from nine half-circle lines). If your half mandala is the exact same size as mine, you can use my measurements for this step; if it's not, you will need to do the math to figure out how wide to make each arch in your mandala. First, use your compass to draw a large half circle whose center is a little ways above the existing half mandala. Connect its ends to the edge of the half mandala. Then repeat eight more times, making each half circle and arch ¼" (0.7 cm) smaller than the previous arch. Finally, color each arch in one of eight rainbow colors—in my case, that's blue, green, yellow, orange, red, pink, purple, and navy.

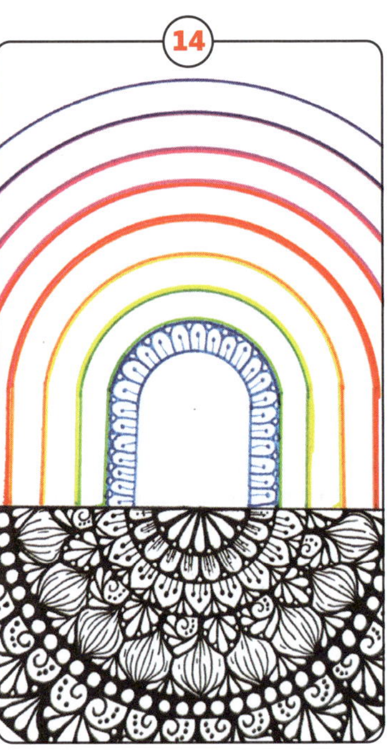

Create the blue arch. Fill the blue arch with domes. Add a line capped with a dot to each dome. Draw a tiny circle between each dome.

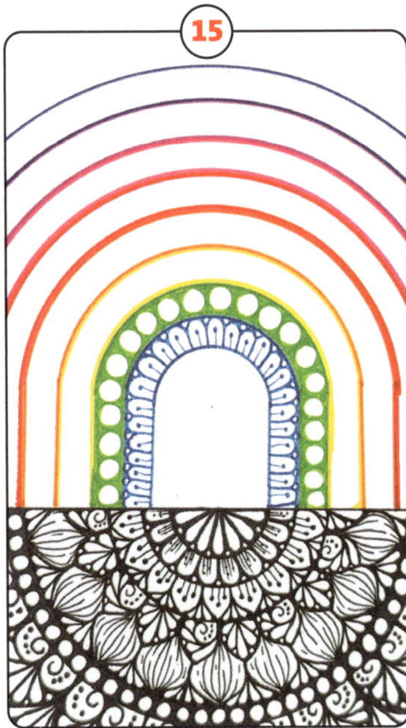

Create the green arch. Draw densely packed circles in the green arch, then fill in around them.

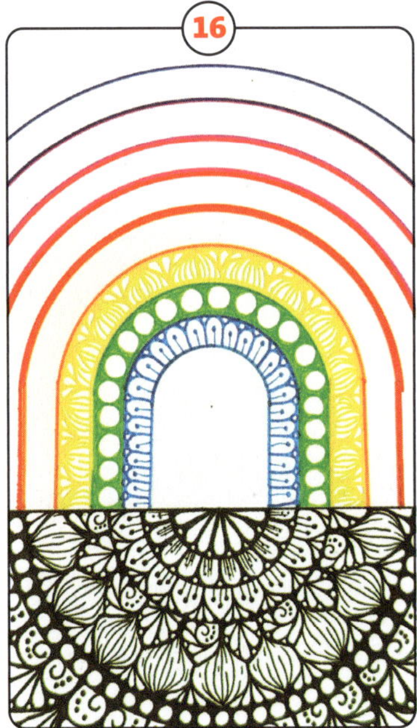

Create the yellow arch. Draw pointed leaves to the next arch and fill them with the "onion" pattern. Add three teardrops between each one.

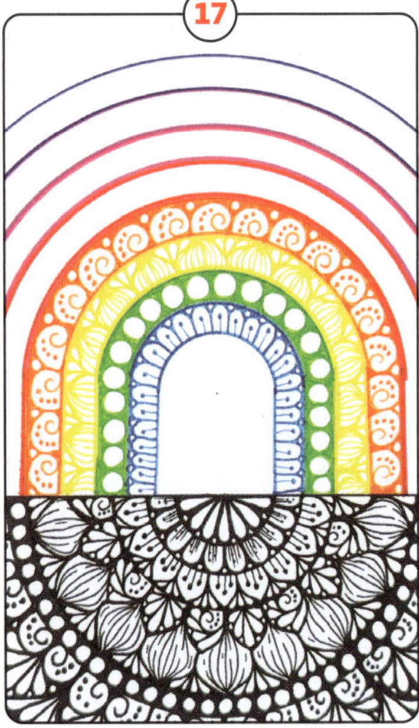

Create the orange arch. Draw curling lines in the next arch. Add four dots inside each one. Draw a circle between each one, then fill in around them.

MANDALAS

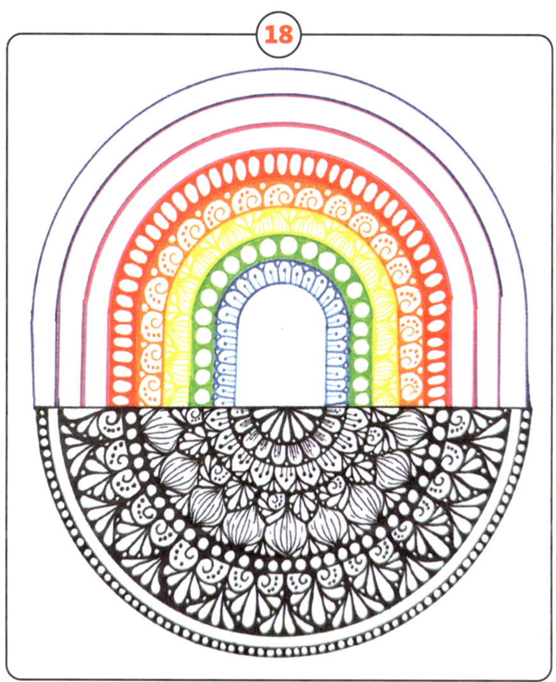

Create the red arch. Draw densely packed tall ovals in the red arch, then fill in around them.

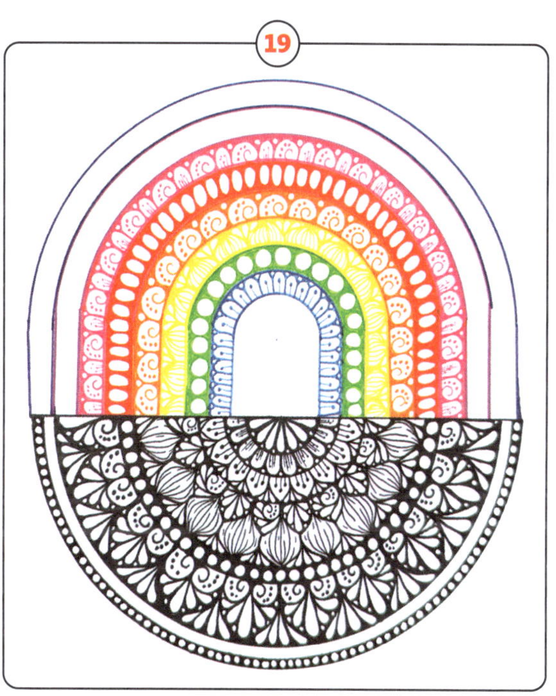

Create the pink arch. Draw alternating domes and curling lines in the next arch. Add patterning to each as shown as well as dots between each, then fill in around them.

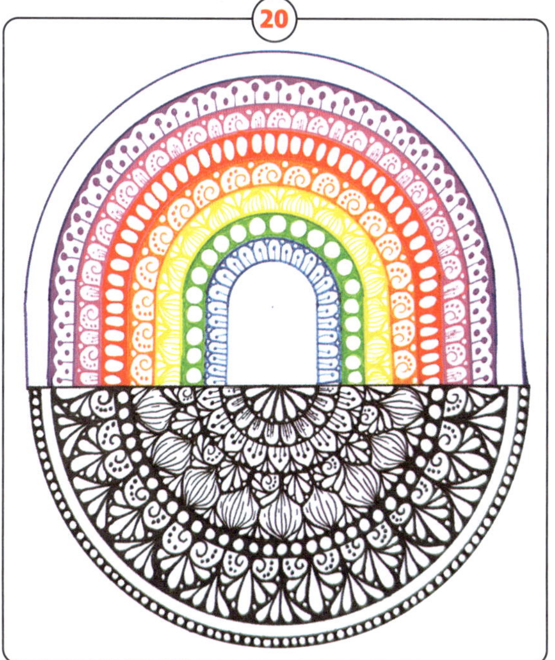

Create the purple arch. Draw alternating dots and lines capped with dots in the next arch. Draw a scalloped line along the top of the design, then fill in above it.

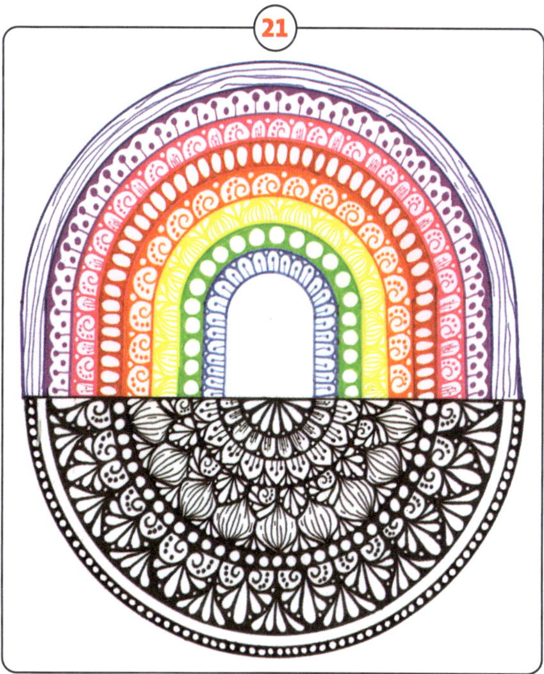

Create the navy arch. Fill the final arch with long, thin, irregular lines to give it a textured, almost wood-grain-like feel.

Colorful Heart

Let's start working inside a carefully constructed, limiting shape. You could freehand this heart design and create your mandala inside it, but it's a good idea to practice drawing precisely measured shapes sometimes. In this case, making a precise heart shape will ensure that your resulting finished piece will have two lobes that are nice, symmetrical matches in terms of the designs you draw inside them. (You'll get the chance to draw inside freehand shapes in the last chapter!) I used marker to color this design.

MANDALAS

116

INTENTION

As you draw this mandala, give your heart an opportunity to feel whatever it's feeling. This could be something good or something difficult—whatever is on your heart in this moment.

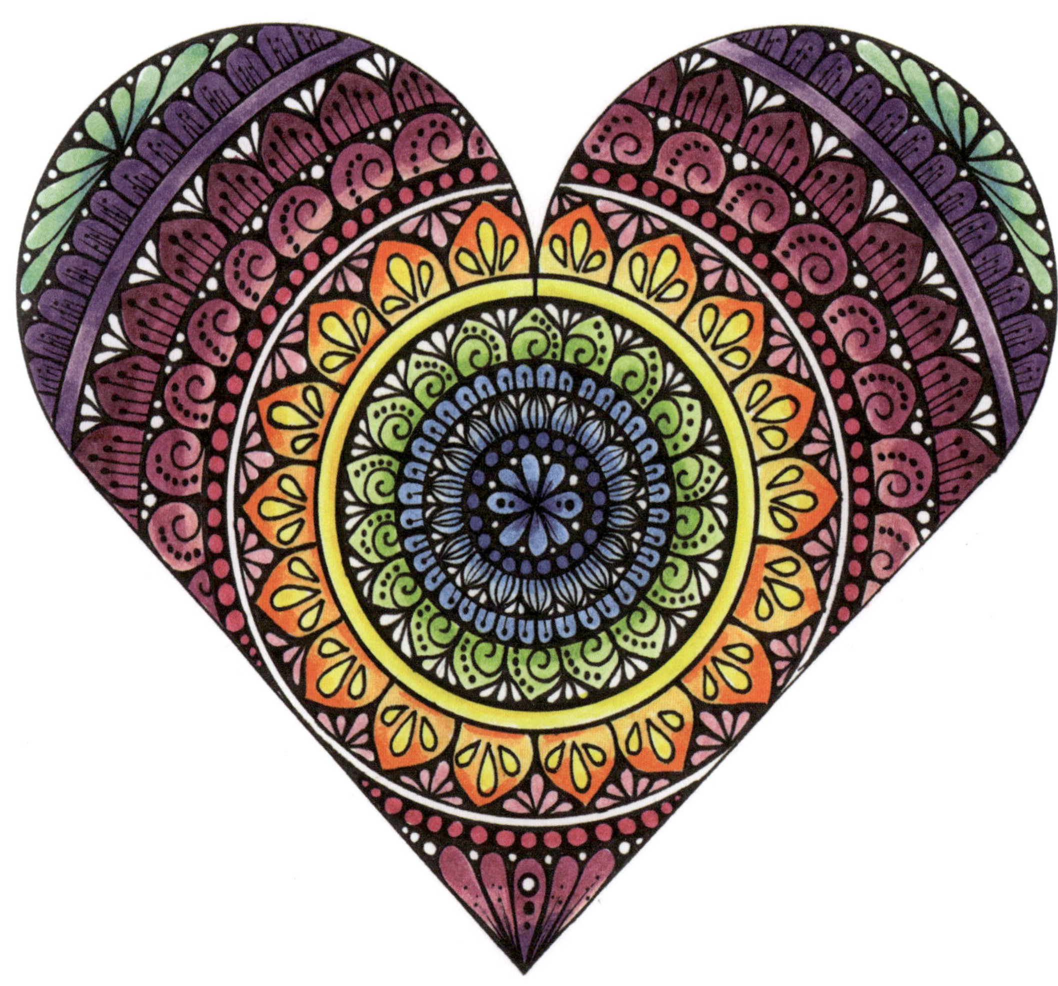

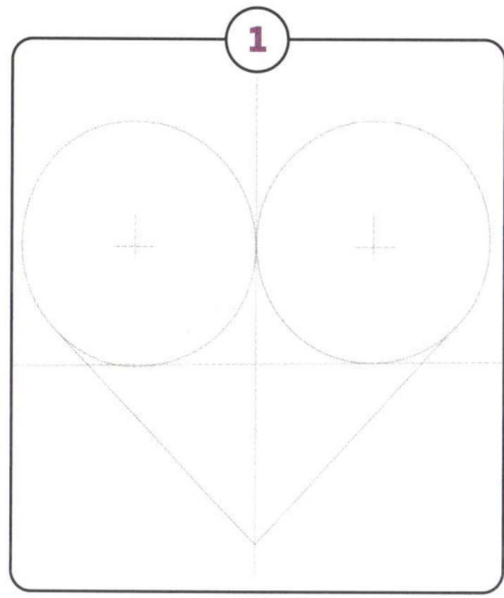

Make the heart. Draw a large plus sign. Draw two circles of 2" (5.1 cm) radius that touch both the x- and y-axes of the plus sign. Add lines to form a point.

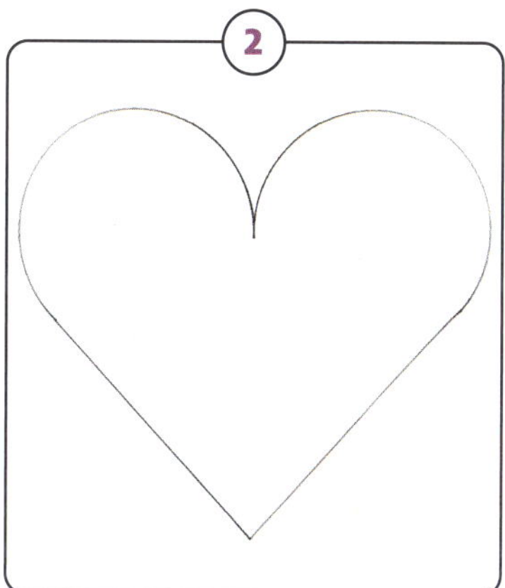

Ink the heart. Once you are happy with your heart shape, use your black pen to trace the final outline of the heart. Erase the rest of the pencil marks.

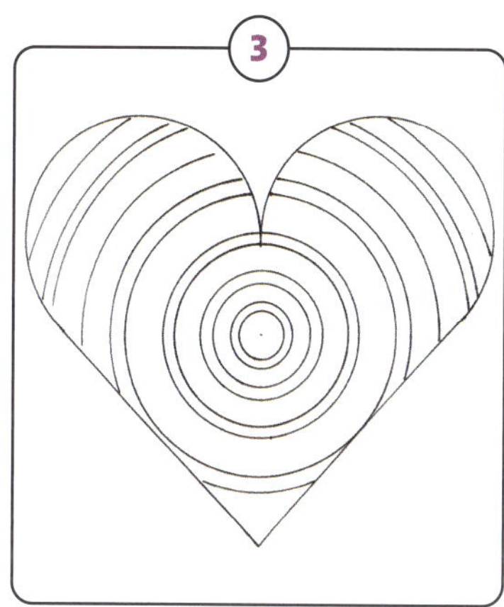

Draw circles. Draw 12 circles as shown. For reference, the outermost circle radius is 4⅛" (10.6 cm); the innermost circle radius is ⅜" (1 cm).

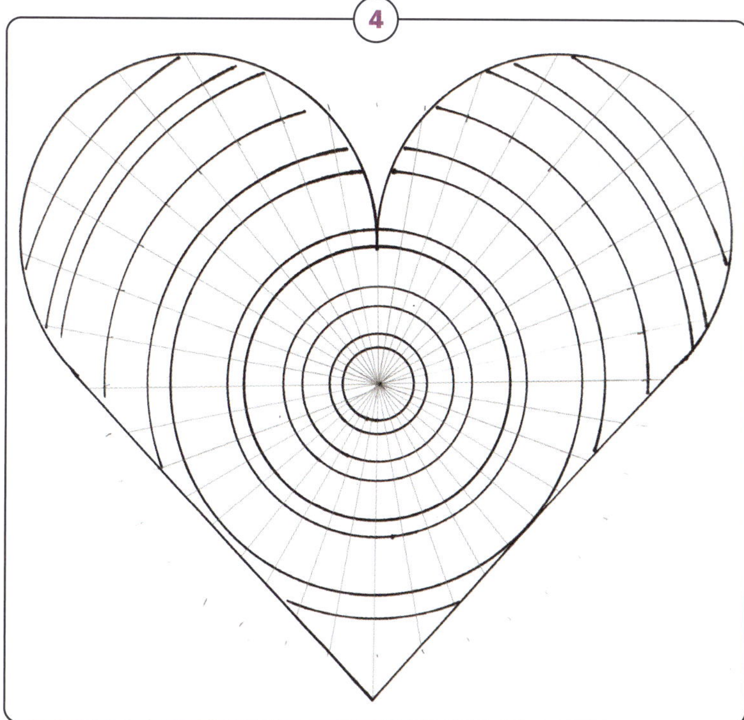

Draw rays. Using pencil, draw a straight horizontal line, then draw a ray every 10° on the top half and bottom half (17 rays total on each half).

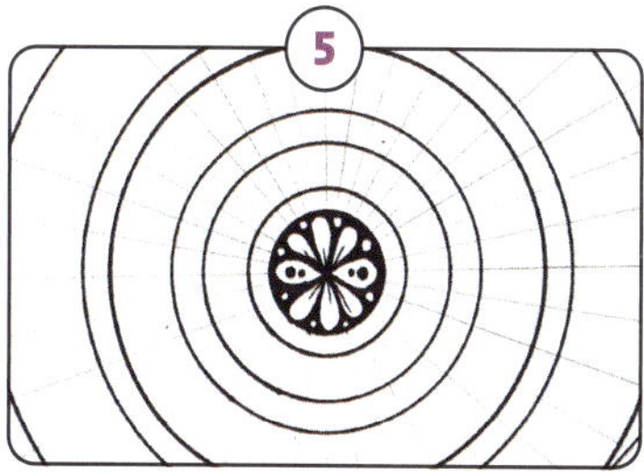

Draw the center. Create a center design as shown.

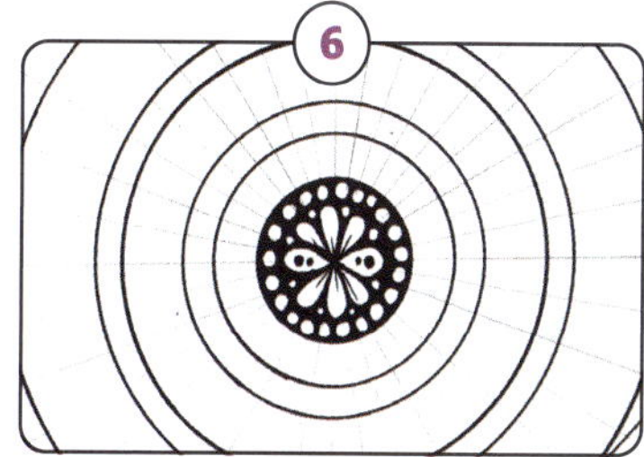

Fill the first ring. Fill the first ring with densely packed circles, then fill in around them.

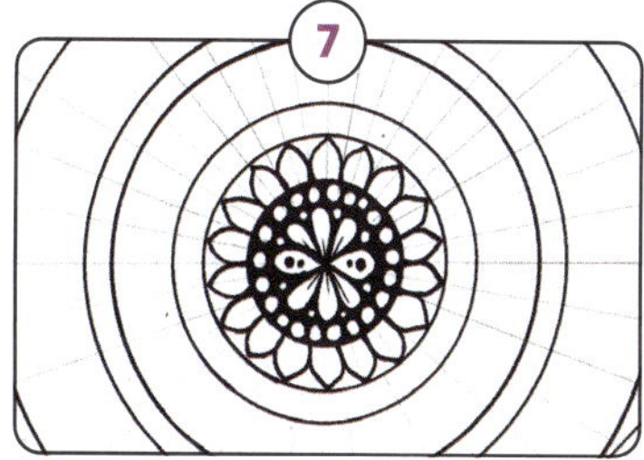

Draw pointed leaves. Draw pointed leaves centered on alternating rays in the next ring.

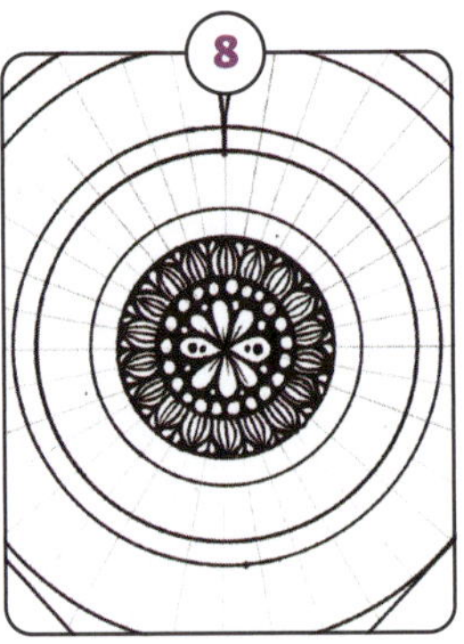

Finish this ring. Add "onion" texture to the pointed leaves. Draw two teardrops between each leaf, then fill in around them.

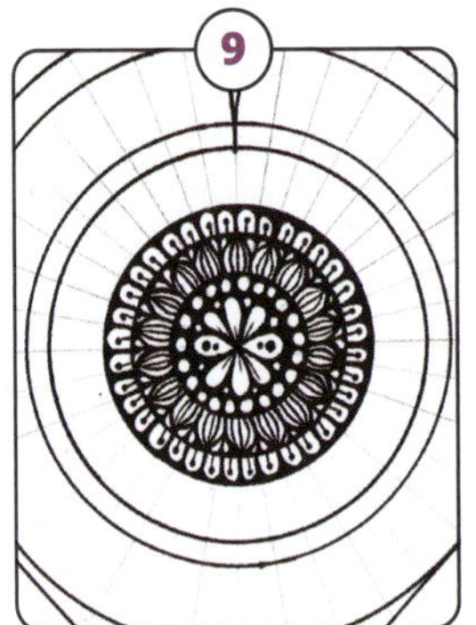

Fill the next ring. Draw small domes in the next ring. To each one, add a line capped with a dot. Fill in above them.

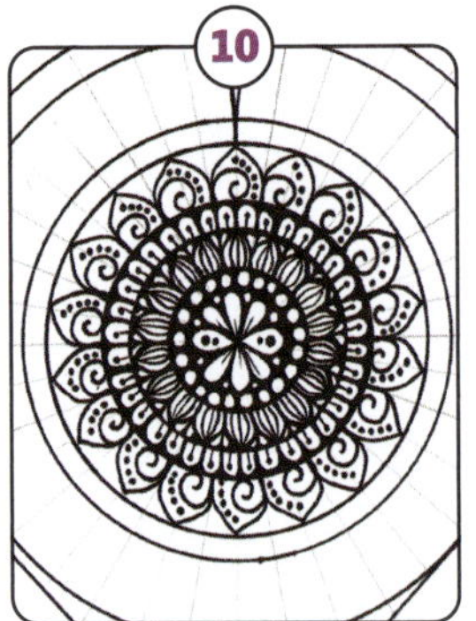

Start the next ring. Draw pointed leaves centered on alternating rays in the next ring. Add a curling line and a series of dots to each one.

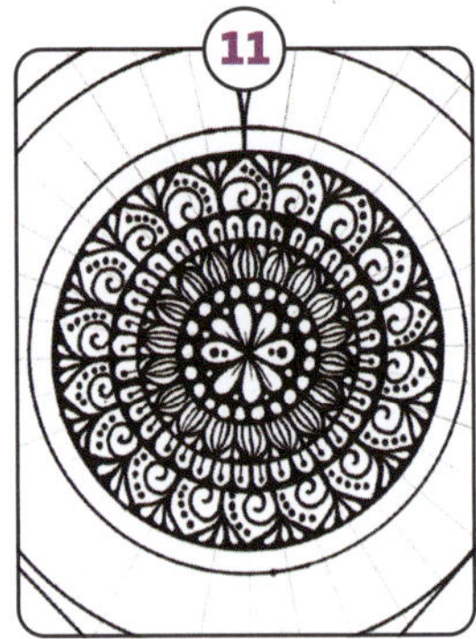

Finish this ring. Draw three teardrops between each leaf, then fill in around them.

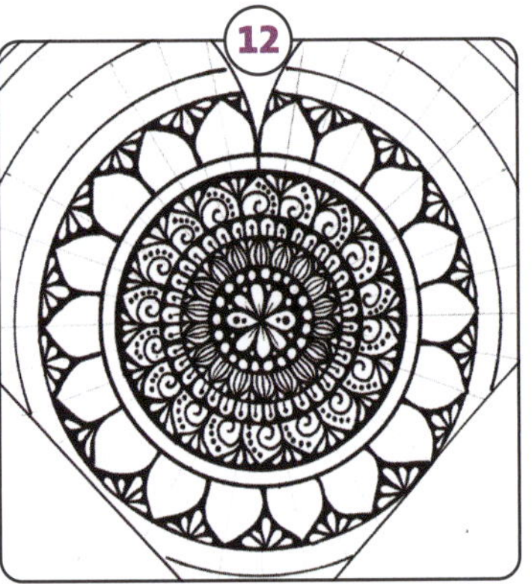

Start the next ring. Repeat step 7, offset from the previous ring. Draw five teardrops between each leaf, then fill in around them.

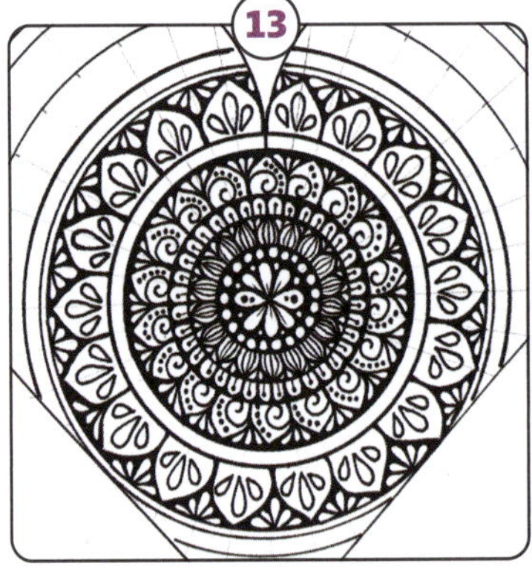

Finish this ring. Draw three teardrops floating within each of the pointed leaves.

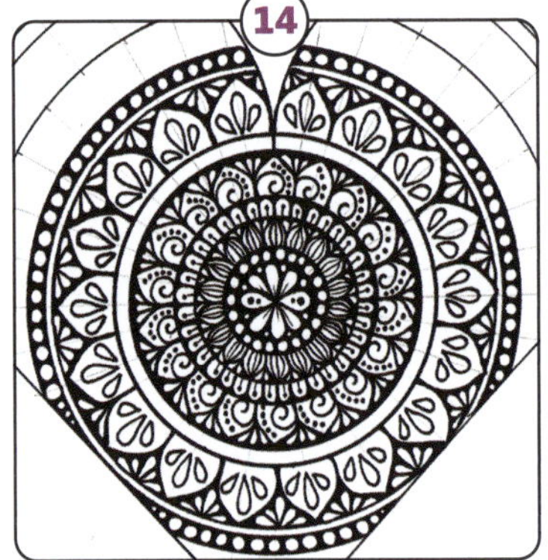

Fill the next ring. Fill the next ring with densely packed circles, then fill in around them.

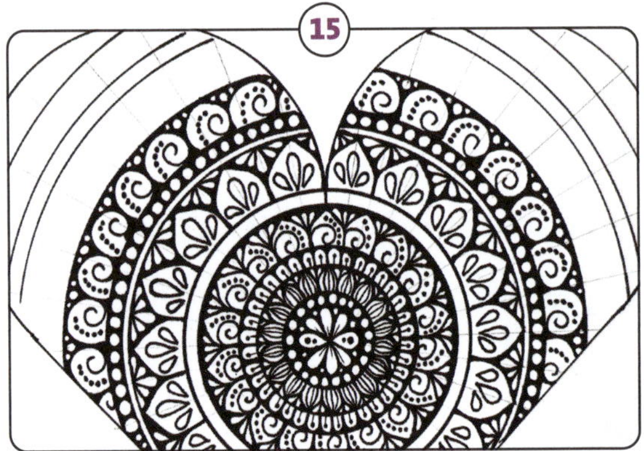

Fill the following ring. In the next ring, draw a pattern as shown, consisting of curled lines, dots, and freehand circles. Do not fill the bottom of the heart!

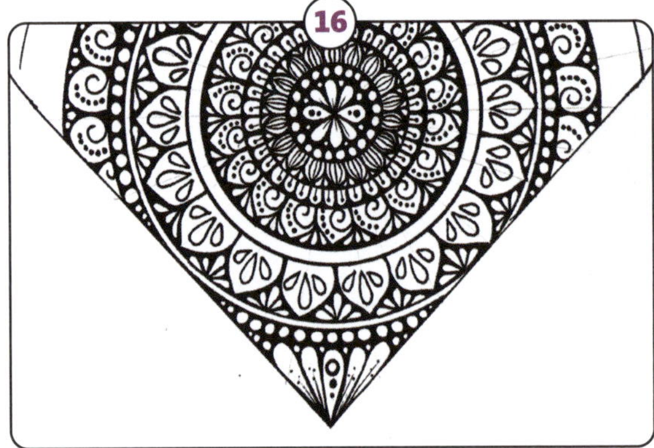

Fill the bottom of the heart. Create a pattern as shown, specifically tailored to filling the bottom point of the heart.

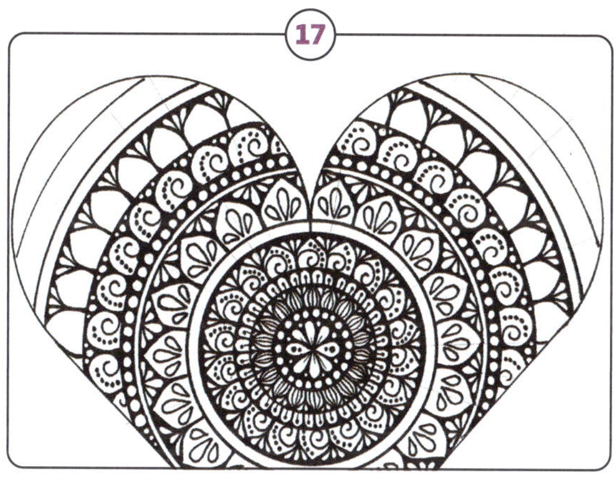

Continue with the rings. Repeat step 7, offset from the previous ring of pointed leaves. Draw three teardrops between each leaf, then fill in around them.

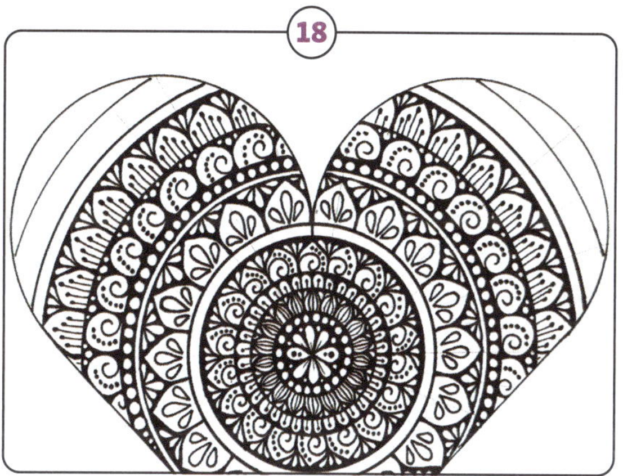

Finish this ring. To each pointed leaf, add fives lines capped with dots.

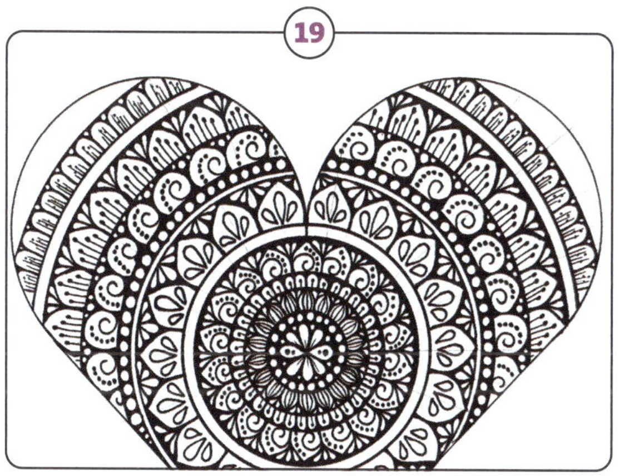

Fill the next ring. Repeat step 9, but with a different pattern in each dome as shown, and with tiny freehand circles between each dome.

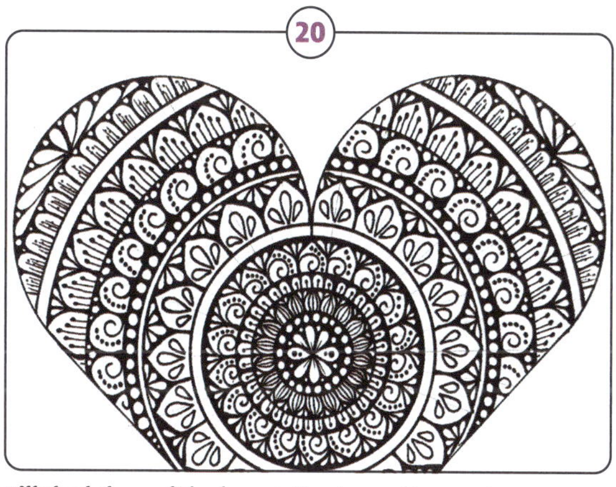

Fill the lobes of the heart. Create a pattern as shown, specifically tailored to filling the remaining space of the two lobes of the heart.

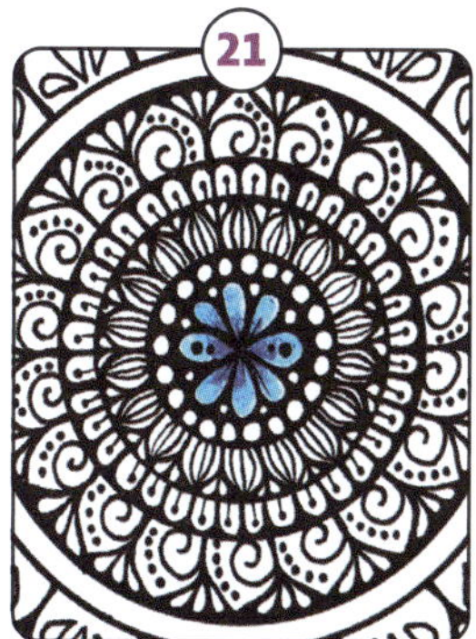

Start coloring. Fill the central design of the heart with a mix of dark blue in the very center and light blue around the edges.

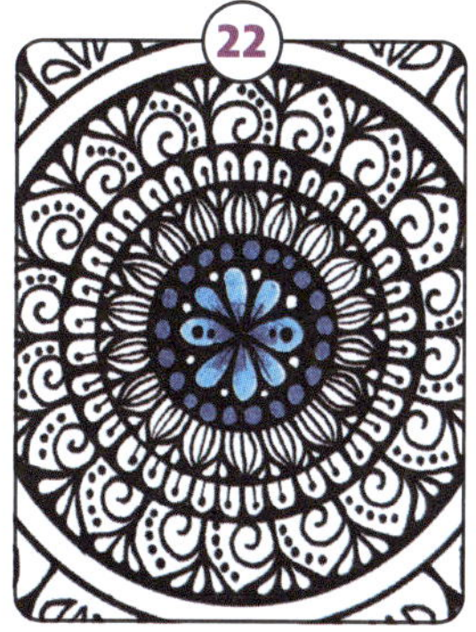

Continue with blue. Fill the ring of circles with dark blue.

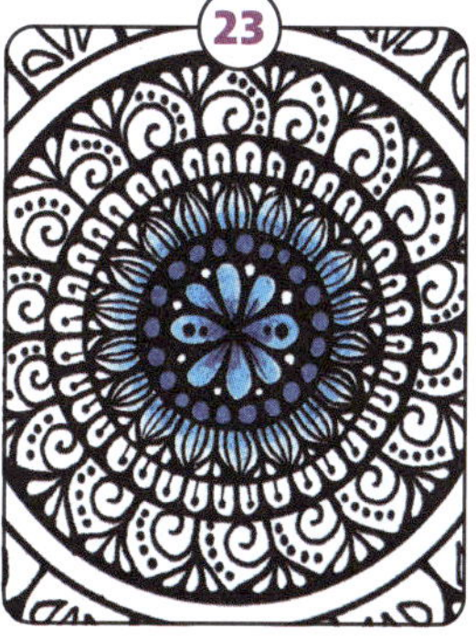

Color the "onions." Fill the "onions" of the next ring with light blue.

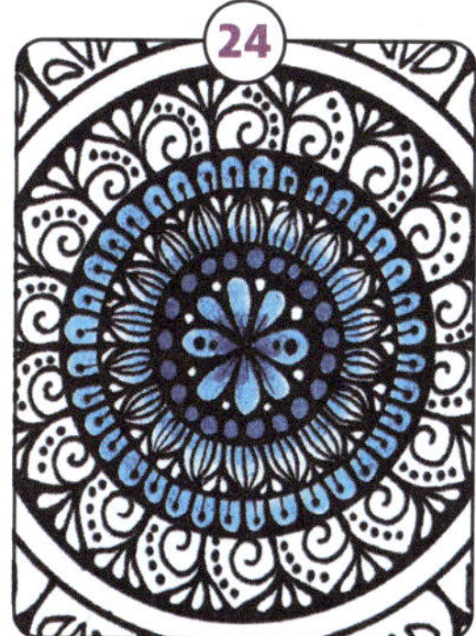

Color the domes. Fill the domes of the next ring with dark or light blue.

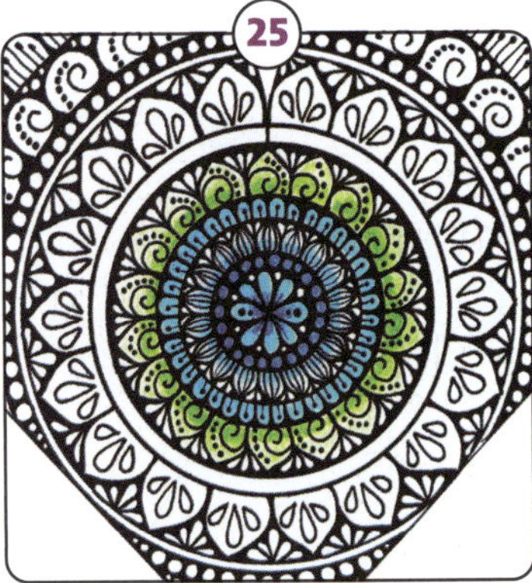

Color the pointed leaves. Fill the pointed leaves of the next ring with a mix of dark and light green, with dark toward the inside and light toward the tips.

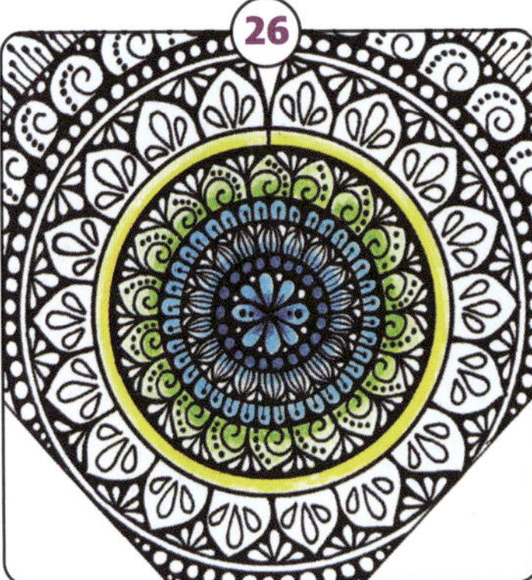

Color the empty ring. Fill the empty ring with dark yellow toward the inside and light yellow toward the outside.

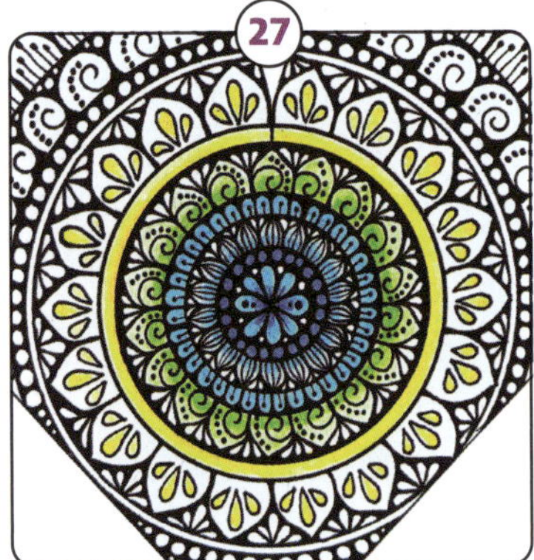

Color the floating teardrops. Fill the floating teardrops of the next ring with light yellow toward the inner pointed tips and dark yellow toward the outward rounded ends.

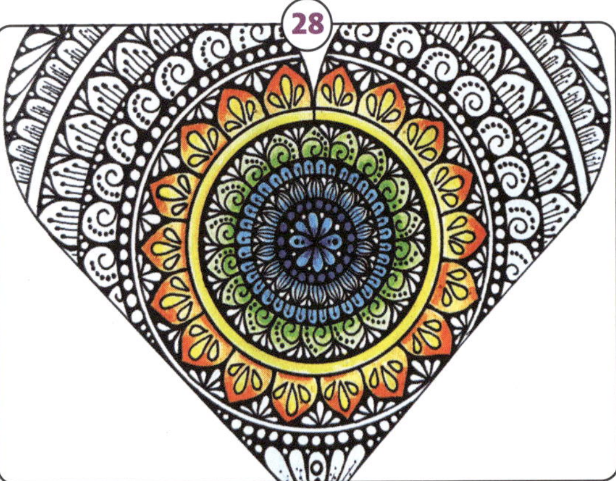

Color the pointed leaves. Fill the pointed leaves of this same ring with a mix of dark and light orange, with dark toward the outside and light toward the inside.

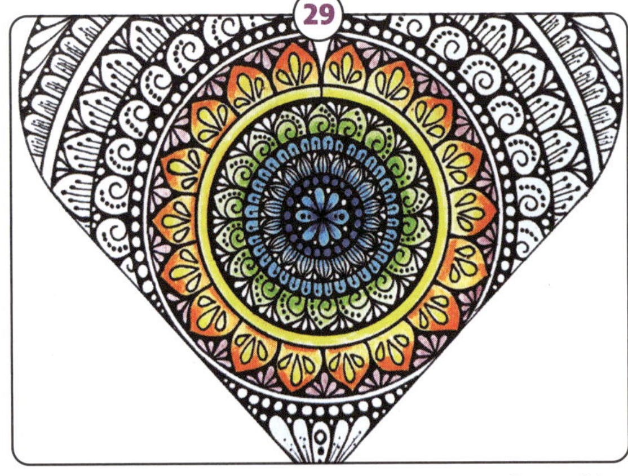

Finish coloring this ring. Fill the remaining teardrops of this same ring with light pink.

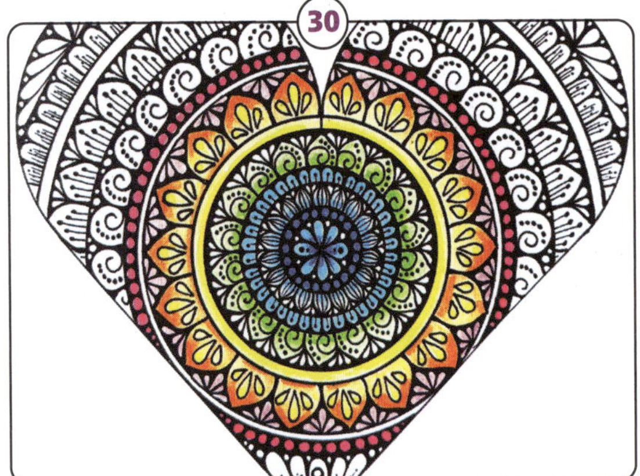

Continue with dark pink. Fill the ring of circles with dark pink.

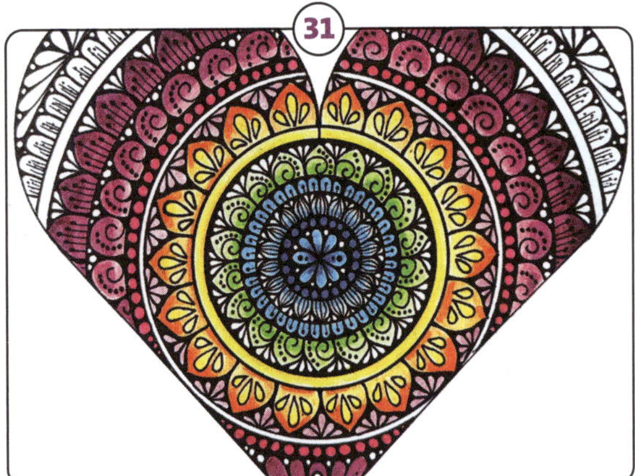

Color the next two rings. Fill the curling lines of the next ring with light pink and medium magenta, then the leaves of the ring after with medium magenta and dark magenta.

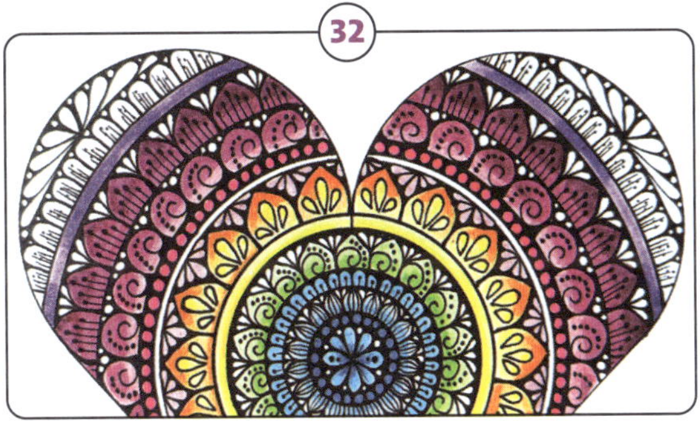

32

Color the empty ring. Fill the empty ring with a mix of light purple and dark purple in alternating swatches.

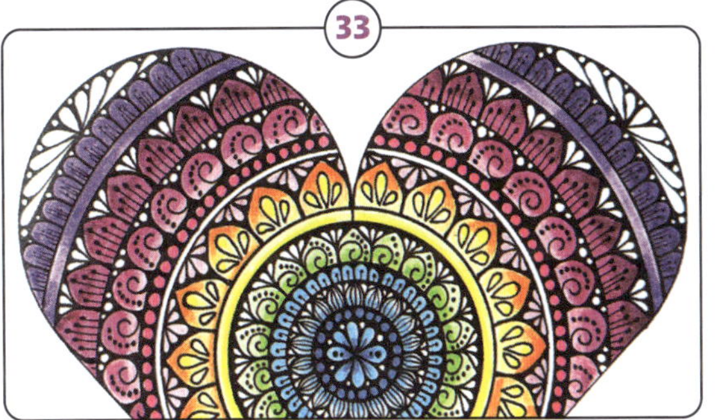

33

Color the domes. Fill the domes of the next ring with dark purple.

34

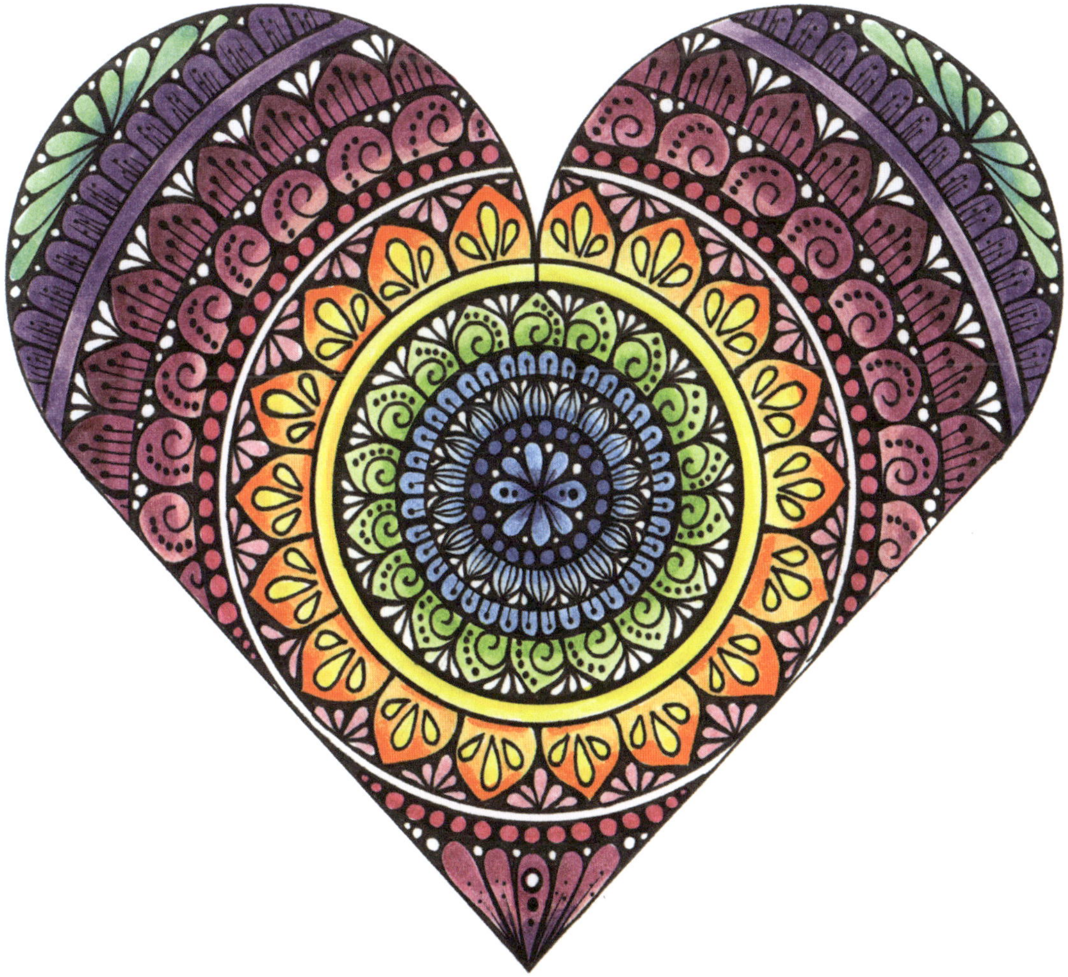

Finish the lobes. Finish the final teardrop designs in each lobe with turquoise toward the inside of each set of teardrops and jade toward the outside.

Intricate Yin-Yang

Here's a chance to tackle a big, detailed, challenging mandala. If you take the time to draw the shape neatly at the start, you shouldn't have any trouble. With just four colors, there are very few color switches to trip you up. Take your time with each ring and design and you will be amazed at what you can create!

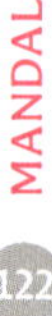

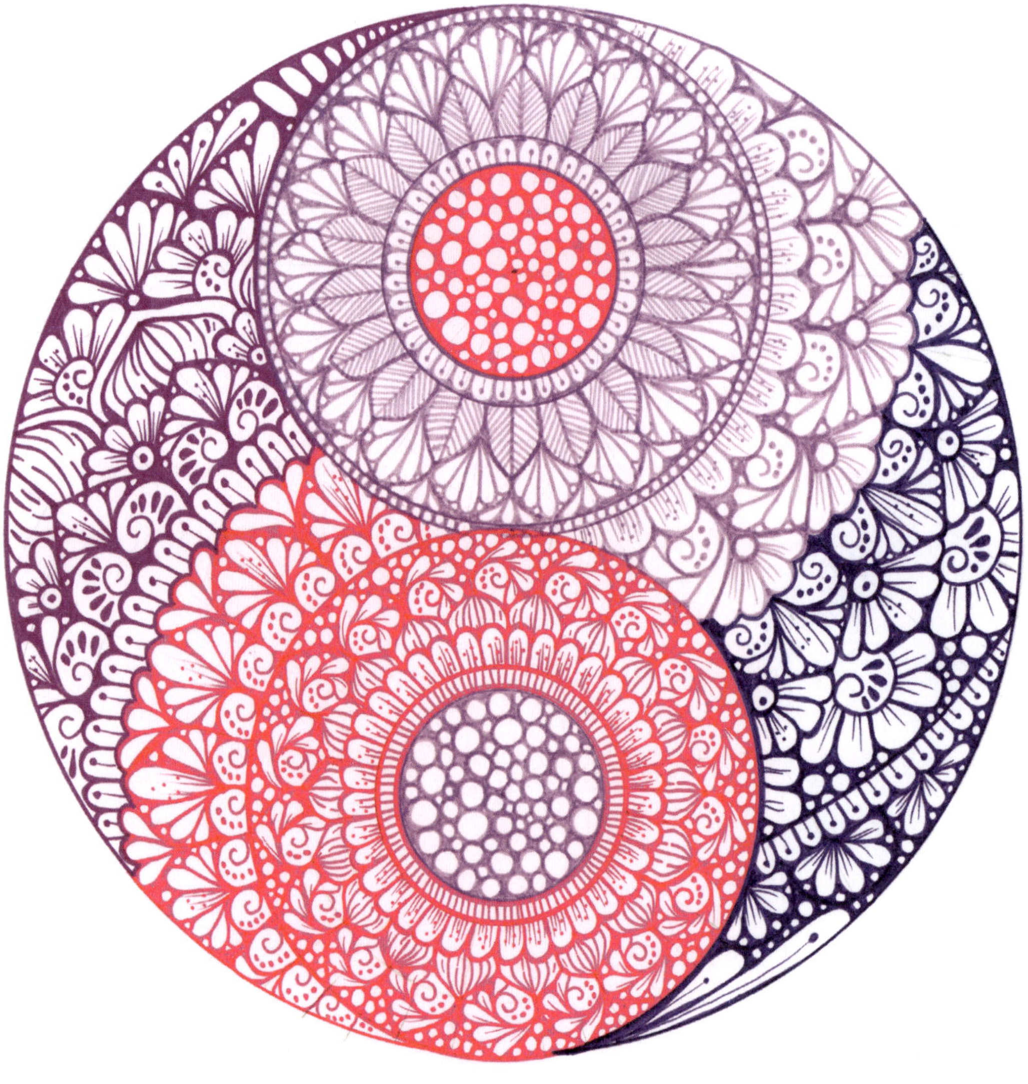

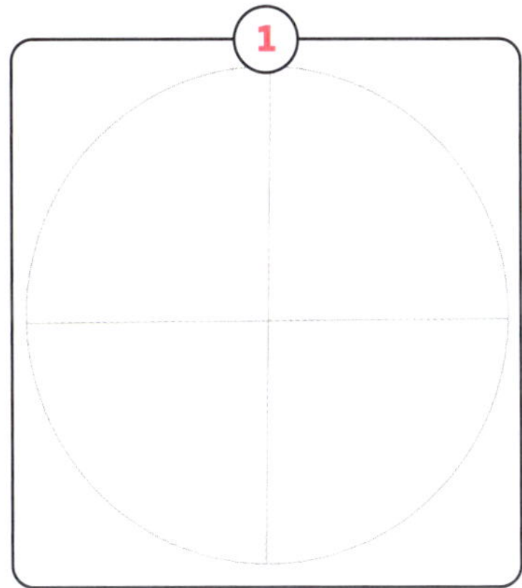

Start with a structure. Draw a circle with a radius of 3⅝" (9 cm). Draw a large plus sign through the center.

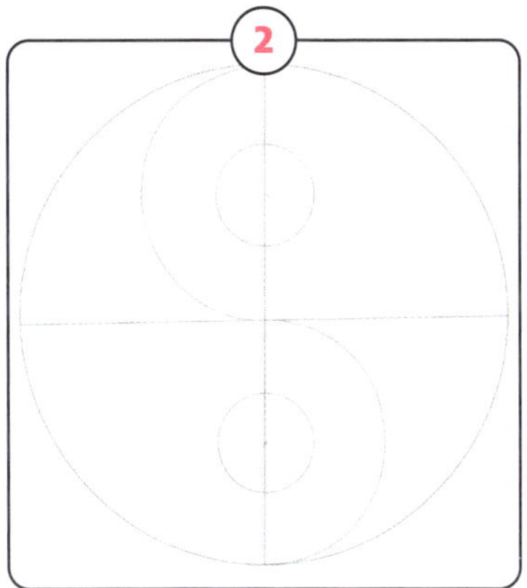

Draw the main circles. Centered on both the top and bottom half, draw two circles with radii of 1⅞" (4.6 cm) and ¾" (1.8 cm).

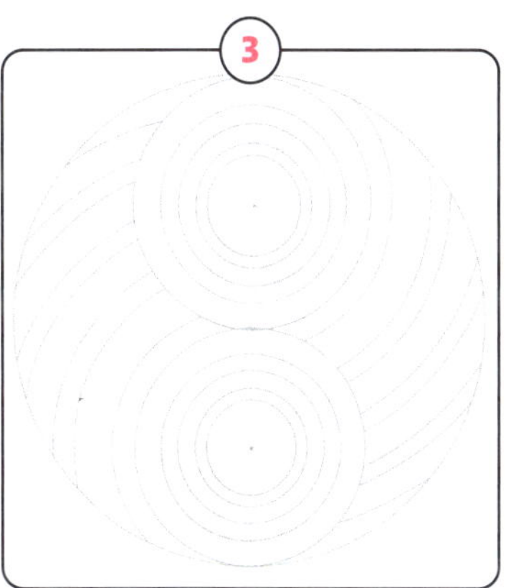

Add circles. Build out a series of 11 more circles on each side of the yin-yang as shown—so, 13 total circles, including those drawn in step 2.

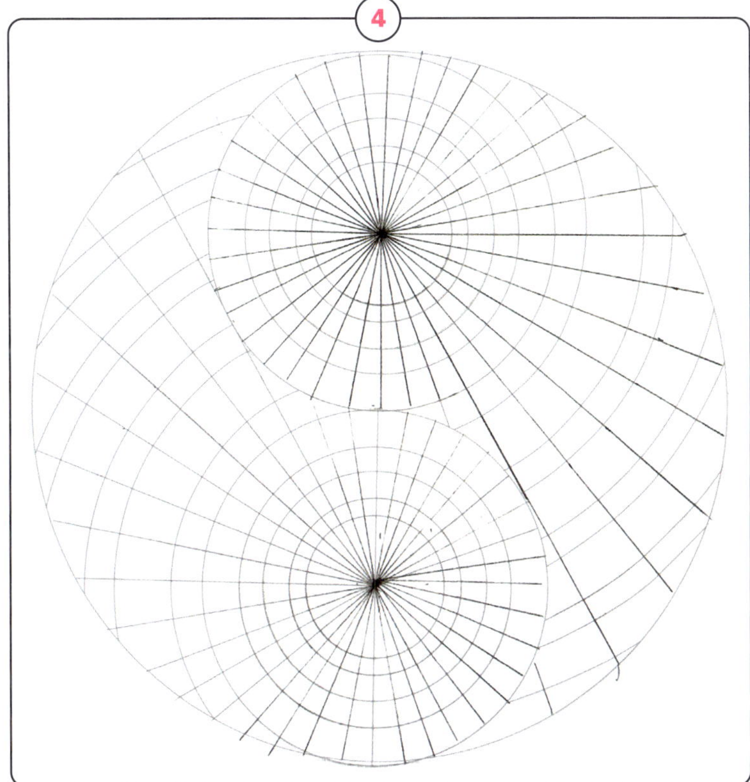

Draw rays. Draw a straight horizontal line through each half's smallest circle, then draw a ray every 10° on the top half and bottom half (17 rays total on each half).

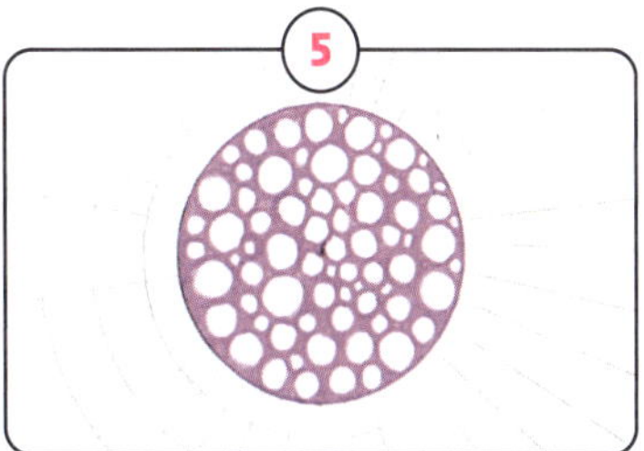

Start with purple. Fill the bottom center with densely packed freehand circles of different sizes, then fill in around them.

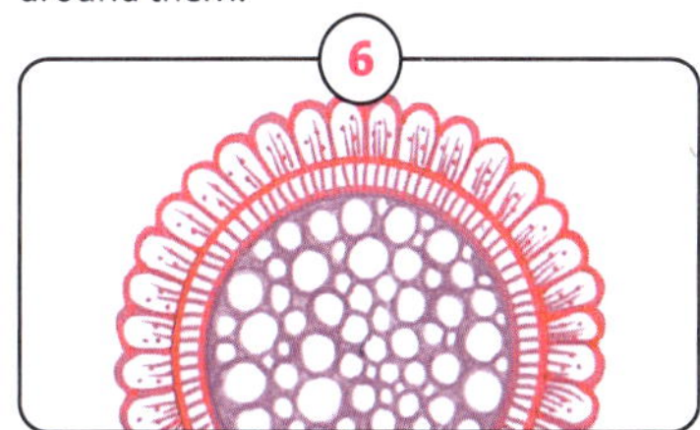

Switch to pink. Fill the next ring with simple lines. Fill the ring after that with domes centered between rays, then add delicate lines and dots inside them.

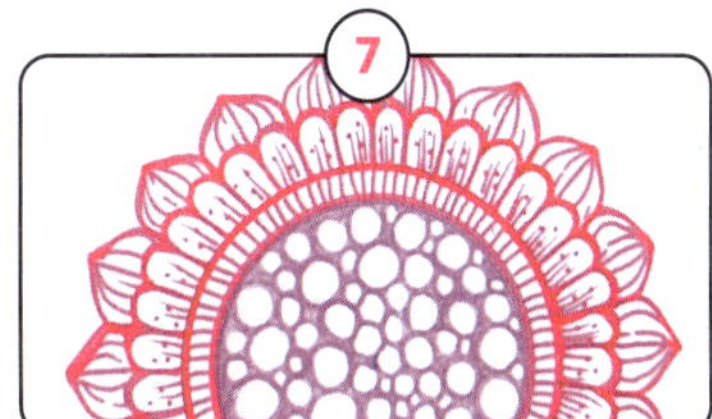

Add pointed leaves. In the next ring, draw pointed leaves centered on alternating rays, then fill them with solid and broken lines to create the "onion" effect.

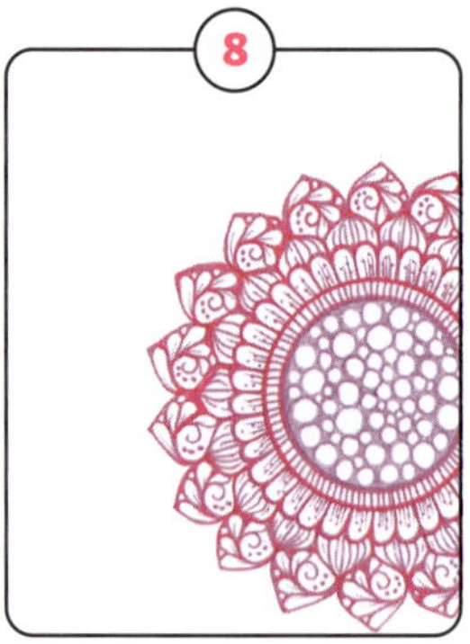

8

Add more pointed leaves. In the next ring, draw pointed leaves centered on alternating rays, offset from the previous ring. Fill them with a pattern as shown.

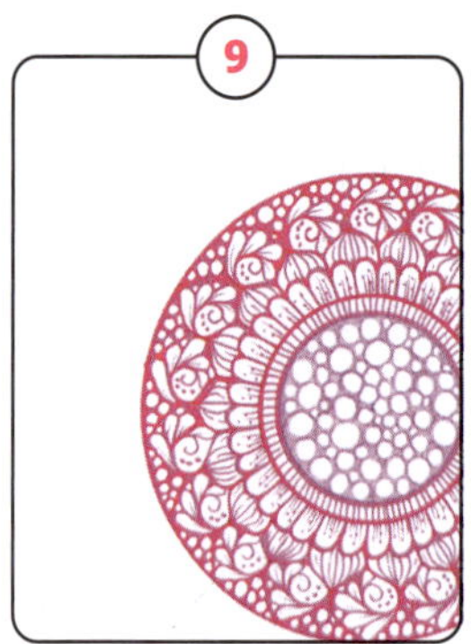

9

Finish this ring. In the same ring, fill the remaining space with densely packed freehand circles of different sizes, then fill in around them.

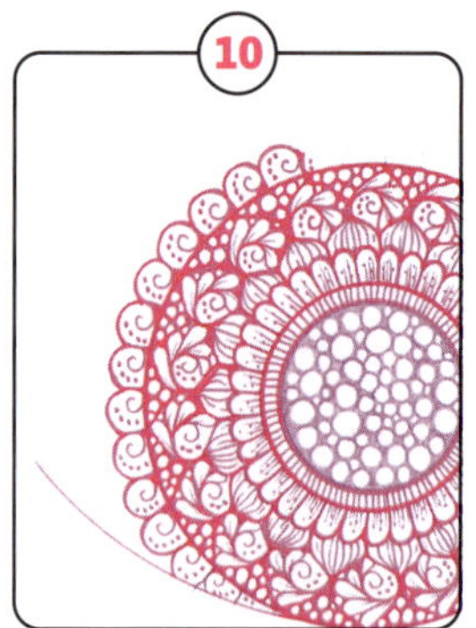

10

Continue on just one side. From now on, work only the left side of the design. In the next ring, draw curling lines centered between rays, then add dots to each one.

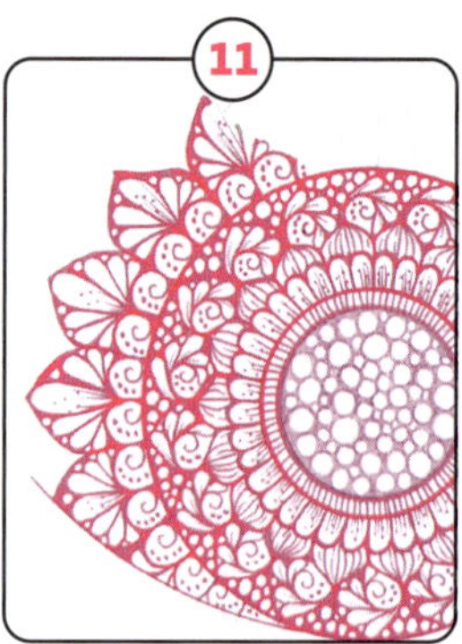

11

Add more pointed leaves. In the next ring, draw pointed leaves centered on alternating rays, offset from the previous ring. Fill them with a pattern as shown.

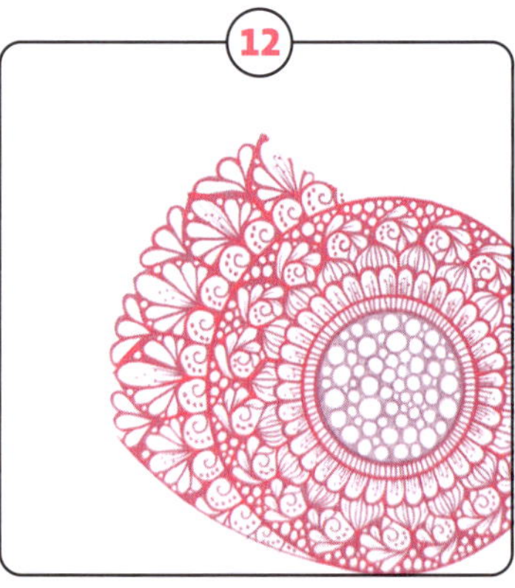

12

Fill out this ring. Draw three teardrops between each of the pointed leaves of this ring.

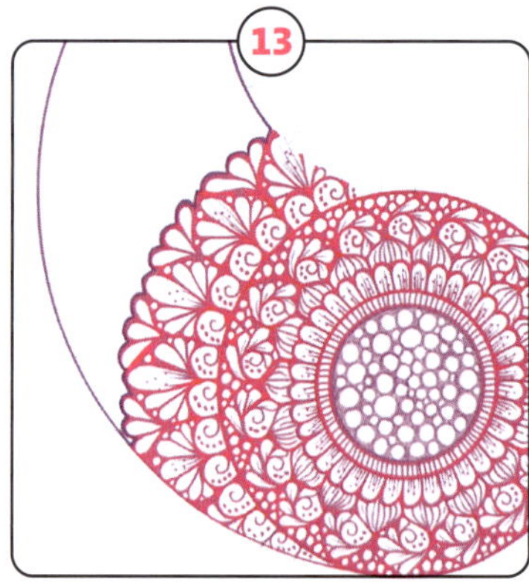

13

Outline in violet. Switch to violet to outline the entire remaining left side of the yin-yang, including following along the top edge of the previously completed ring.

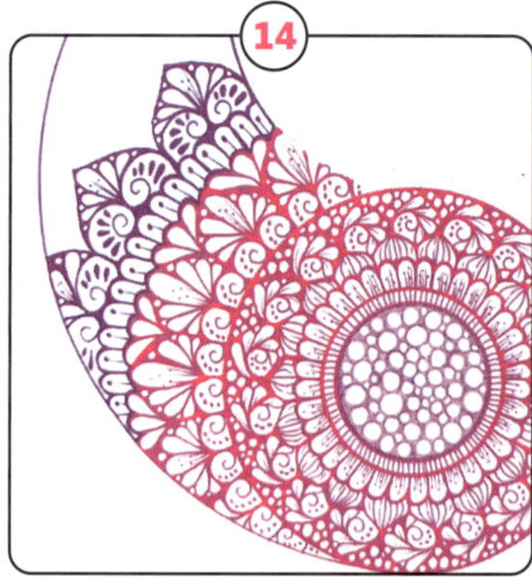

14

Keep drawing in violet. Draw the following rings as shown; the first is made of domes, and the second is made of elaborately patterned pointed leaves.

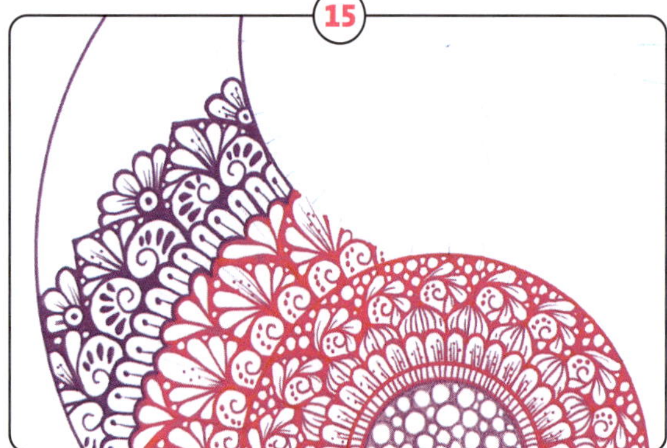

15

Fill next to the pointed leaves. Add the pattern shown between each of the previously completed pointed leaves.

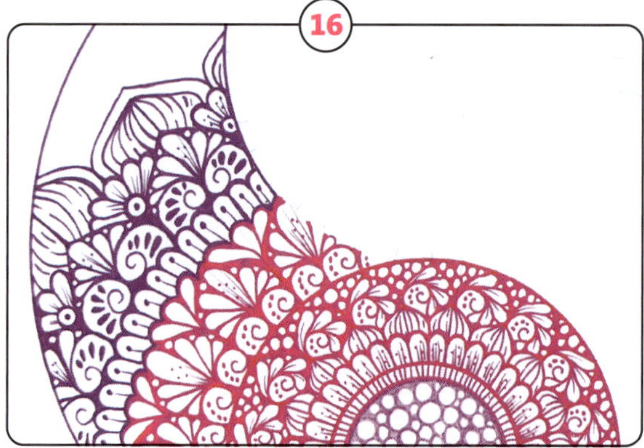

16

Start a fresh ring. In the next ring, draw pointed leaves with inset pointed leaves, then add the "onion" texture to the insets.

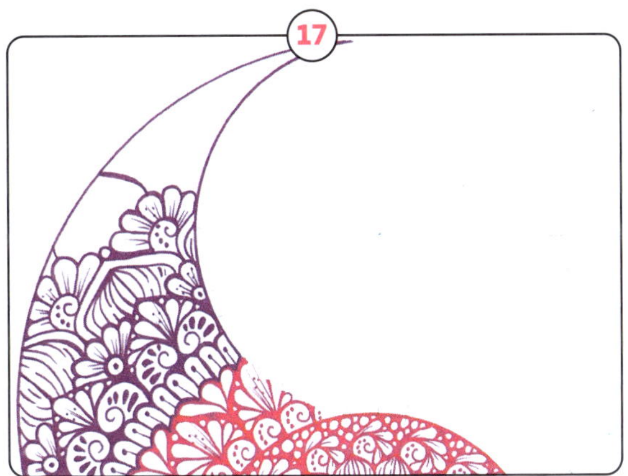

Continue working. Keep going to fill the space between the previous pointed leaves with a daisy design as shown.

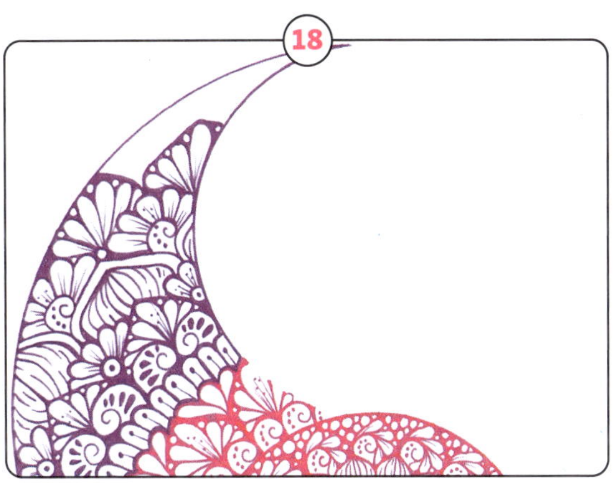

Add more pointed leaves. Space is shrinking! In the next ring, draw pointed leaves with the fill pattern shown.

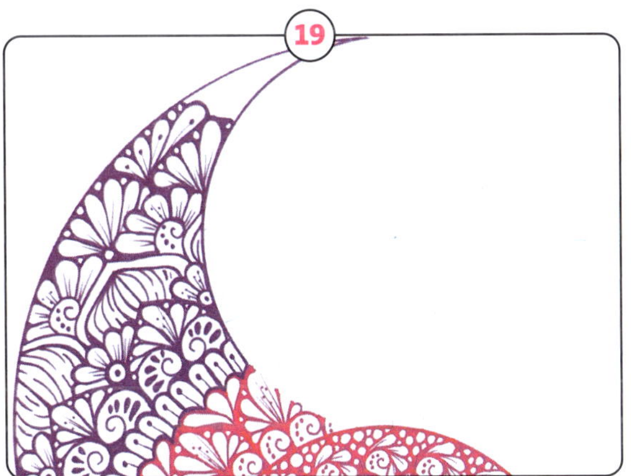

Add a stretched pattern. At this point it's okay to break away from the ring guidelines. Draw a stretched-out teardrop pattern as shown.

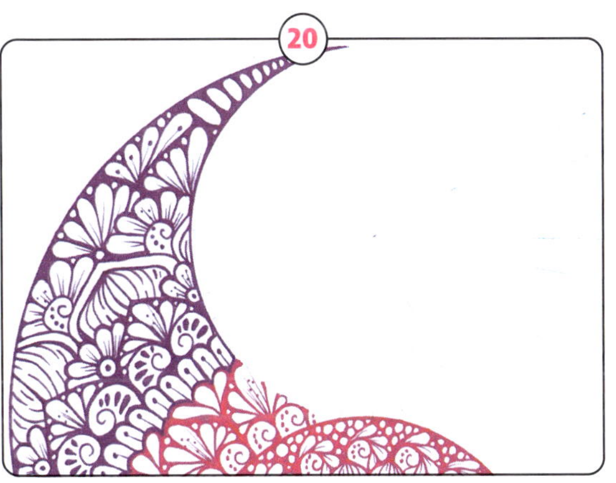

Finish the left side. Fill the remaining space in the left half of the yin-yang with skinny ovals of decreasing size into the point, then fill in around them.

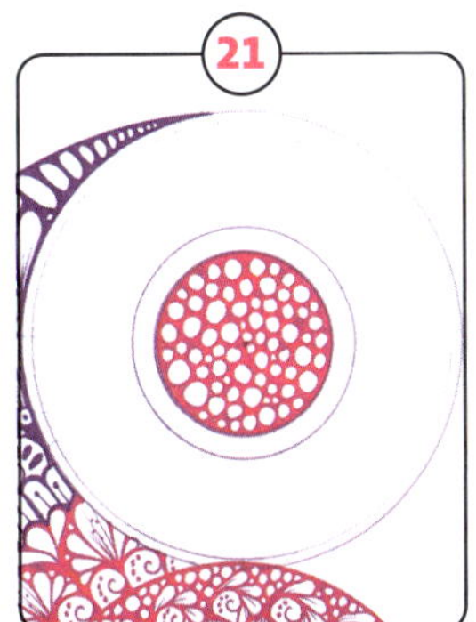

Start the right side. Repeat step 5 for the top-half center, but in pink. Then outline three of the circles in purple as shown.

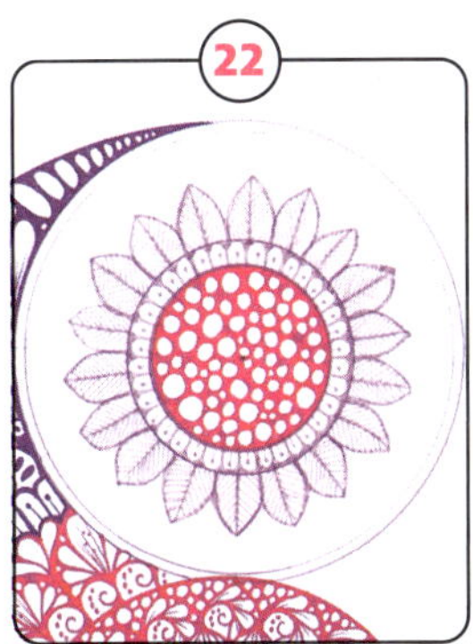

Complete the first two rings. Fill the first ring with a dome pattern as shown, then fill the next two rings with tall pointed leaves with a leaf-vein-pattern fill.

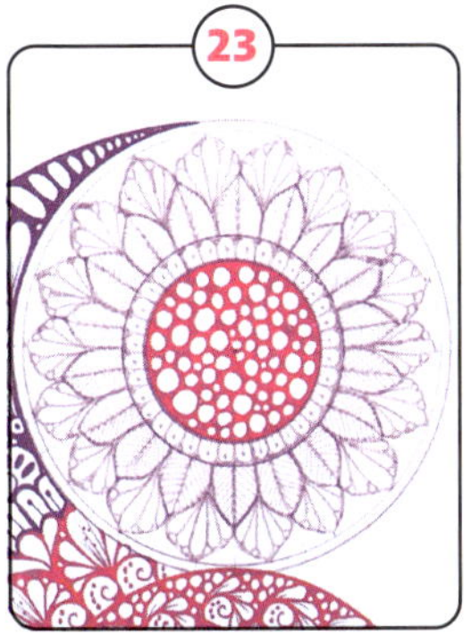

Continue drawing pointed leaves. Fill the next ring with another round of pointed leaves, offset from the previous ring. Fill each with the pattern shown.

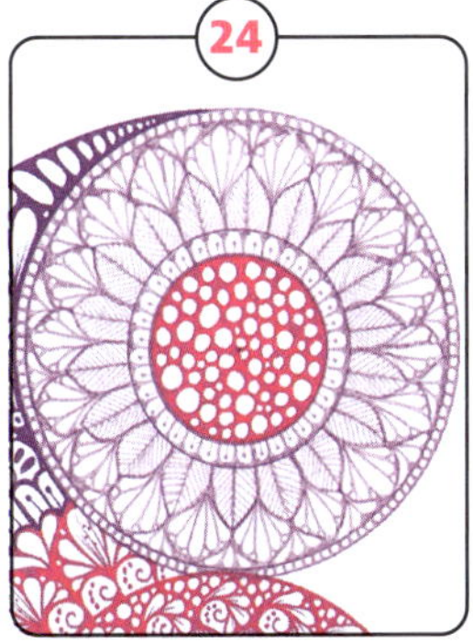

Finish the full circle. Draw three teardrops between each pointed leaf, then fill in around them. Draw densely packed circles in the final ring, then fill in around them.

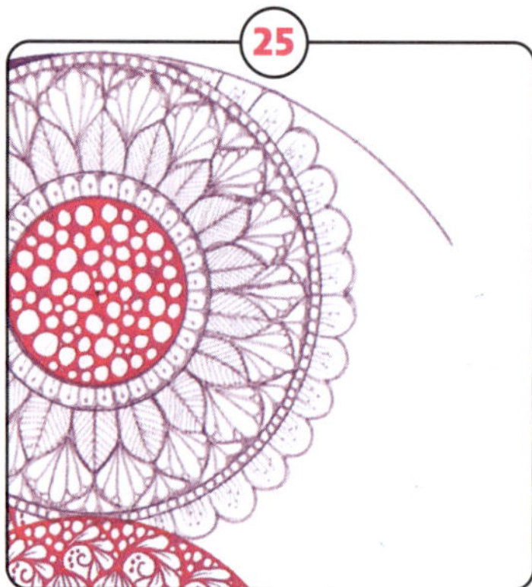

Continue on just one side. From now on, work only the right side of the design. In the next ring, draw domes centered between rays, then add details to them.

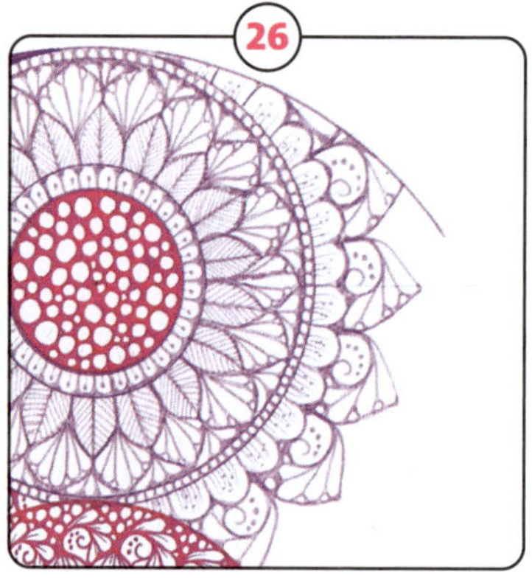

Add pointed leaves. In the next ring, draw pointed leaves centered on alternating rays. Fill them with a pattern as shown.

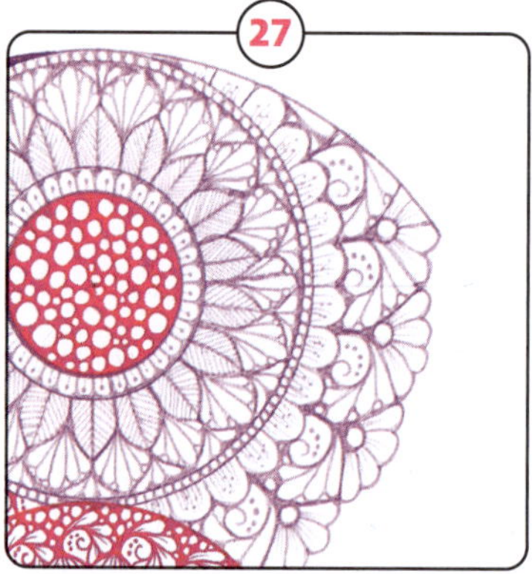

Continue working. Keep going to fill the space between the previous pointed leaves with a daisy design as shown. This daisy design can surpass the existing ring.

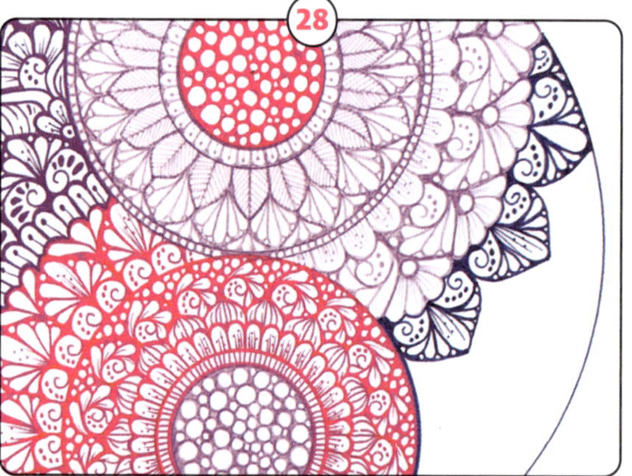

Switch to navy. Switch to navy to repeat step 13 for the right side. Add a fresh set of patterned pointed leaves in the next ring.

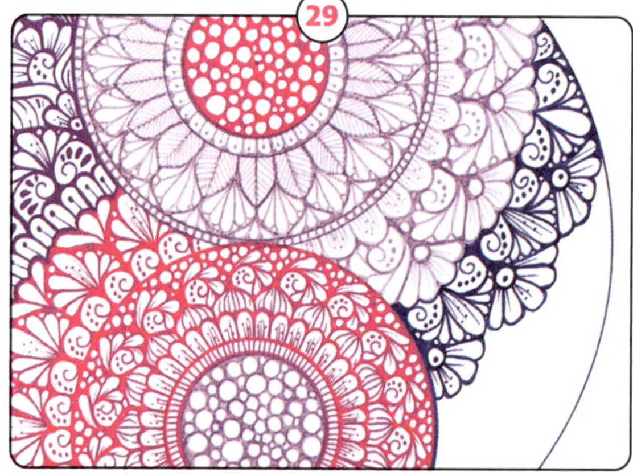

Add more daisies. Fill the space between the previous pointed leaves with a daisy design as shown.

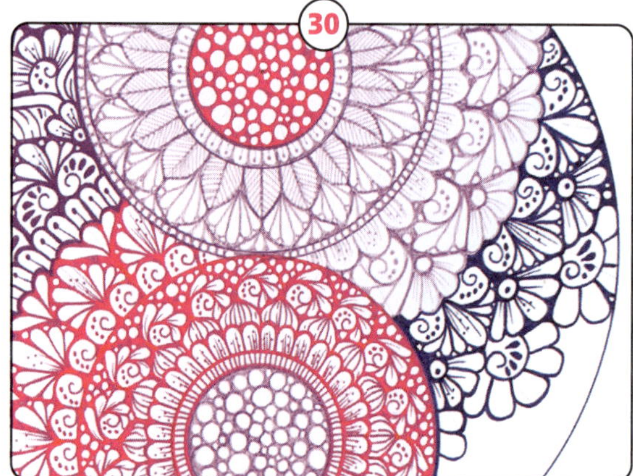

Continue to the next ring. Start a new ring with a floral design as shown.

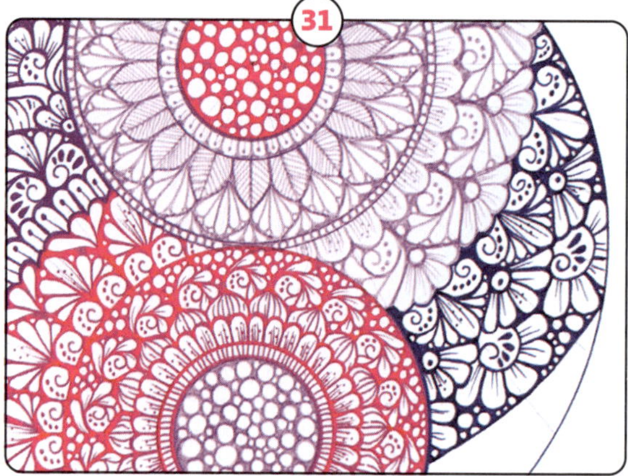

Finish this ring. In the same ring, fill the remaining space with densely packed freehand circles of different sizes, then fill in around them.

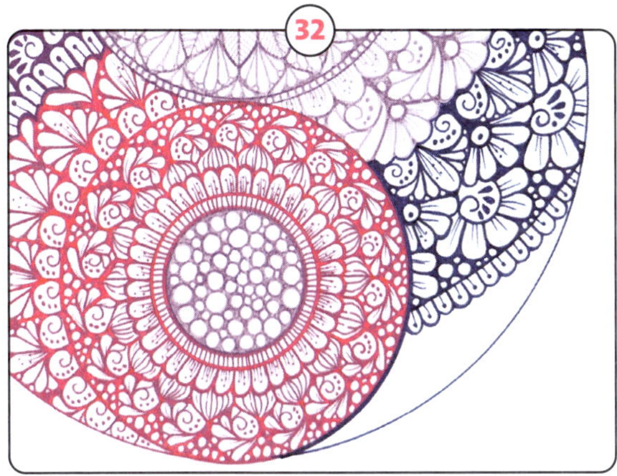

Add a dome ring. In the next ring, draw domes, then draw a line capped with a dot inside each one.

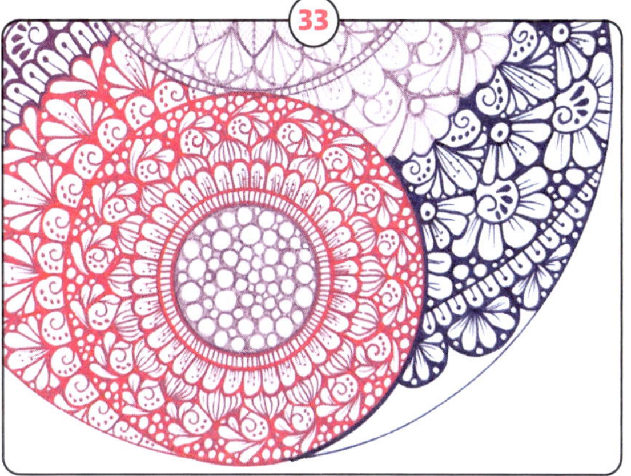

Add a bigger dome ring. In the next ring, draw large domes, then fill each with a pattern as shown.

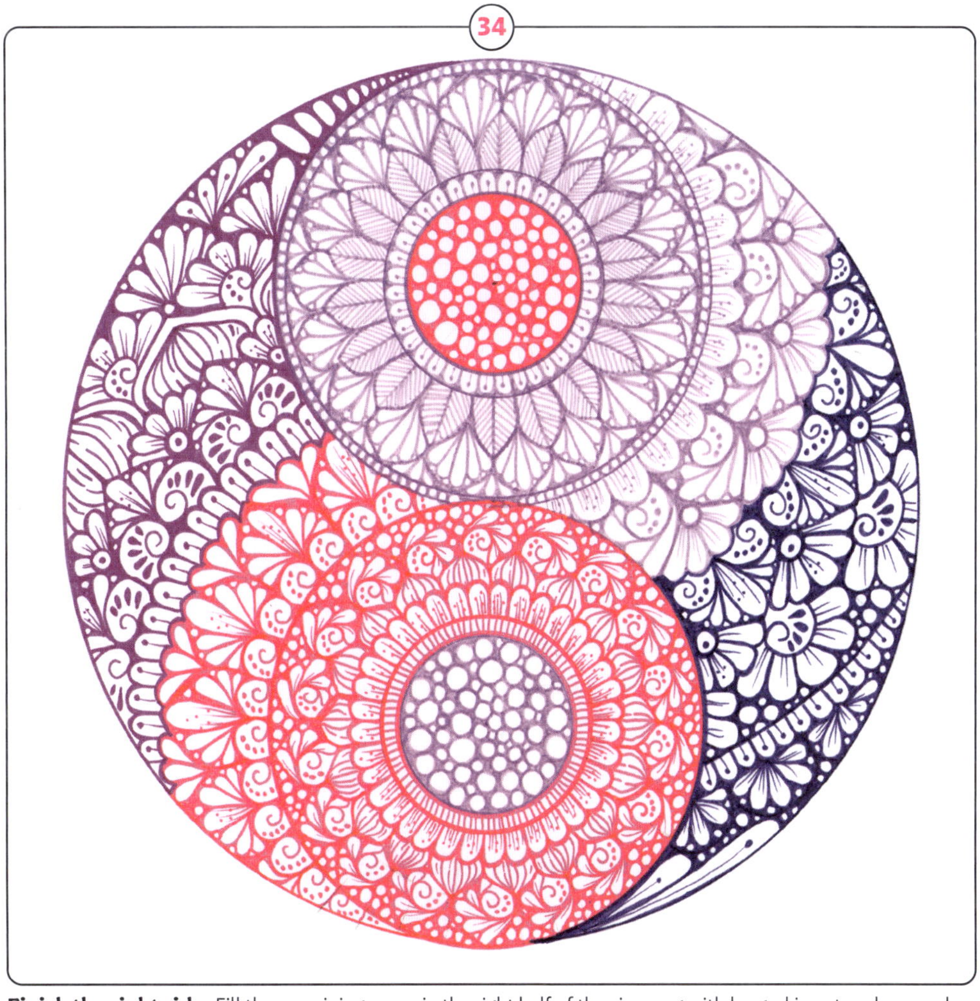

Finish the right side. Fill the remaining space in the right half of the yin-yang with long, skinny teardrops and freehand circles as shown. Fill in around them.

Crescent Moon

CHALLENGE YOURSELF

Here's one last design idea to inspire you! This mandala is similar to Intricate Yin-Yang in its approach, but it uses many more colors. Use what you learned while working on the previous mandalas to build up this design yourself independently, referring to just the few basic steps that are provided as guideposts.

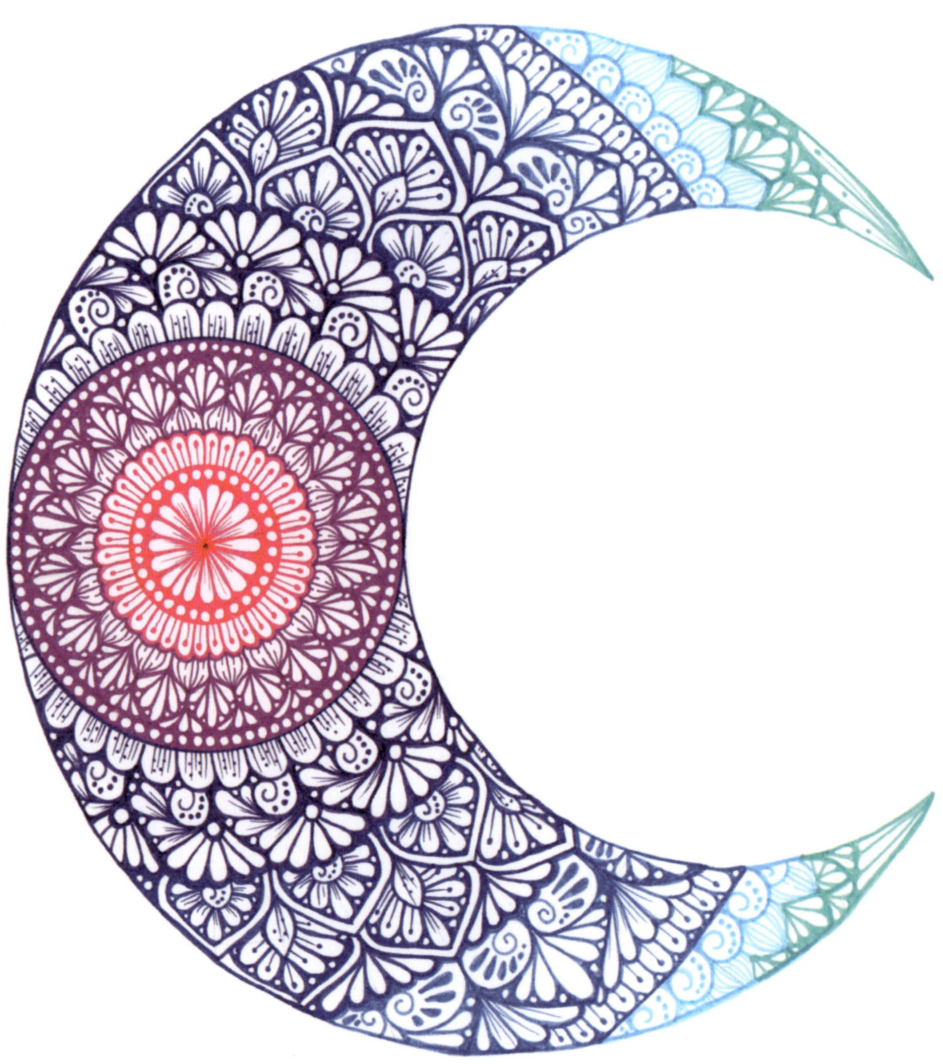

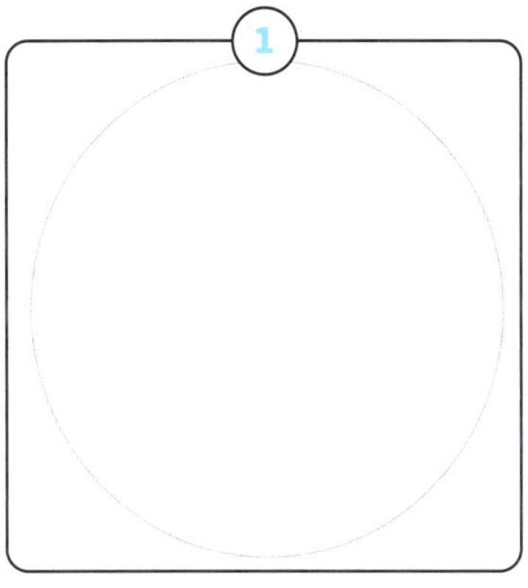

Start with a circle. Draw a circle with a radius of 3⅞" (9.9 cm).

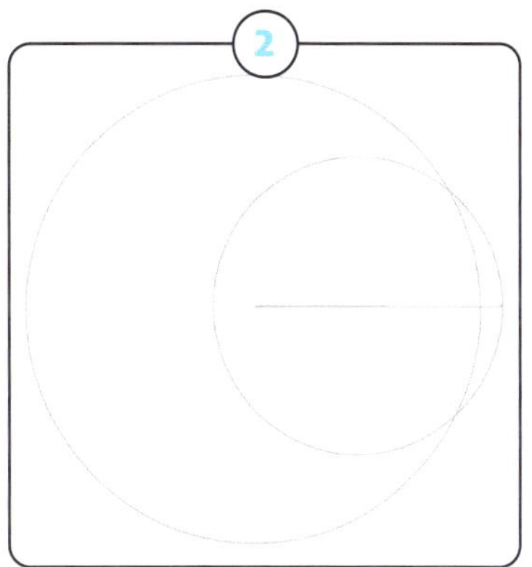

Set up the crescent. Draw a second, smaller circle with a radius of 2½" (6.4 cm) whose rightmost edge is about ⅛" (1 cm) out from the right edge of the big circle.

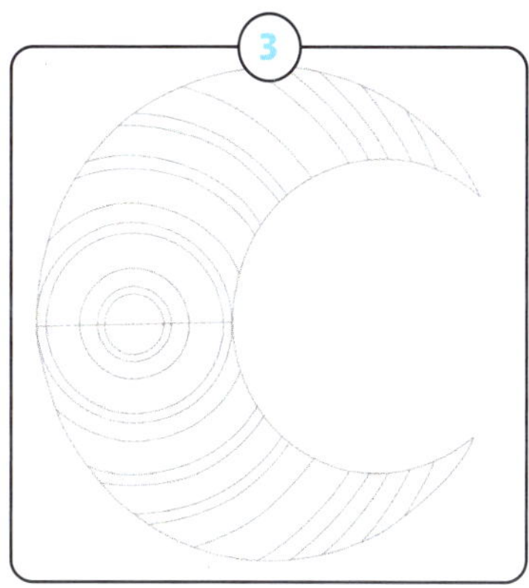

Draw circles. Draw 16 circles as shown. For reference, the outermost circle radius is 5⅜₆" (14 cm); the innermost circle radius is ½" (1.2 cm).

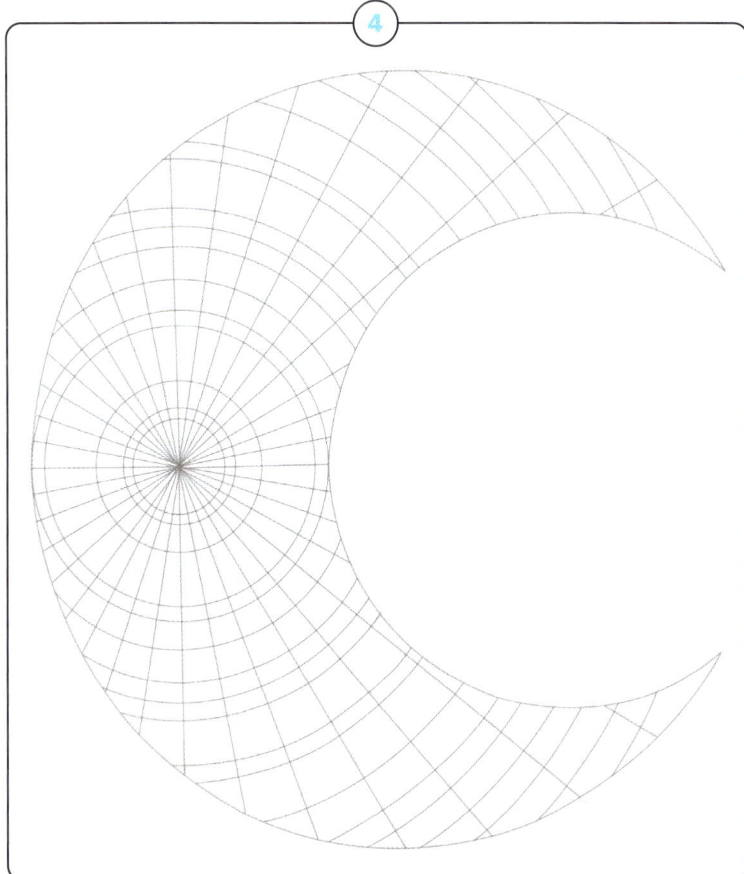

Draw rays. Using pencil, draw a straight horizontal line, then draw a ray every 10° on the top half and bottom half (17 rays total on each half).

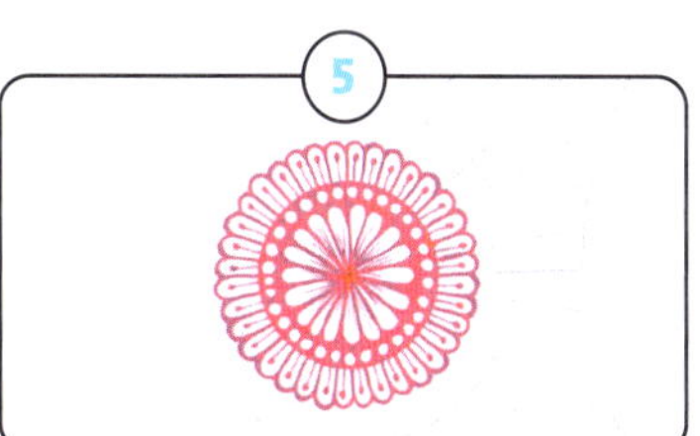

Start drawing in pink. Draw the center and first two rings in pink.

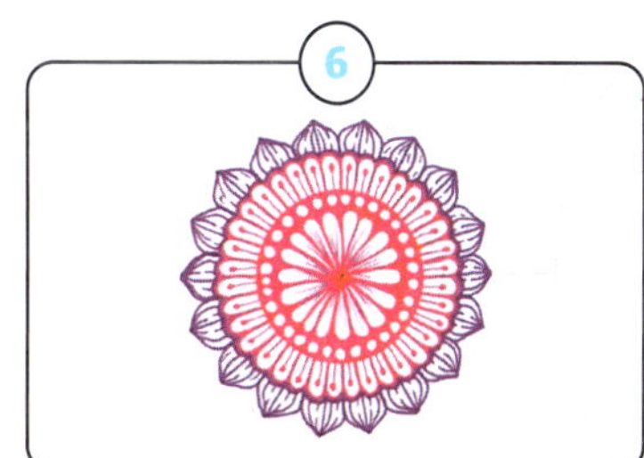

Draw in light purple. Draw a ring of light-purple pointed leaves with the "onion" texture in the next ring.

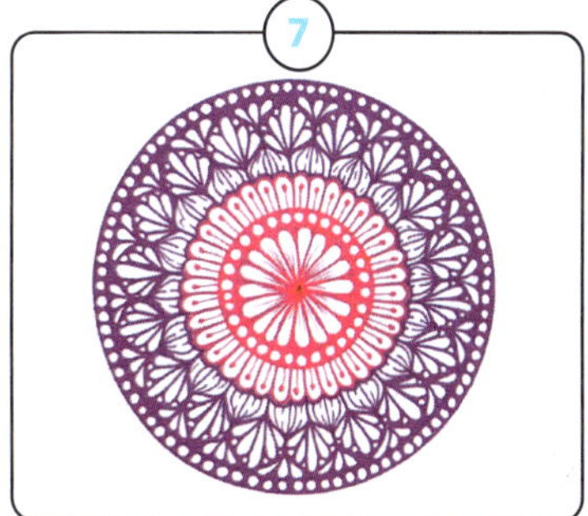

Draw in dark purple. Fill the next two rings with designs in dark purple.

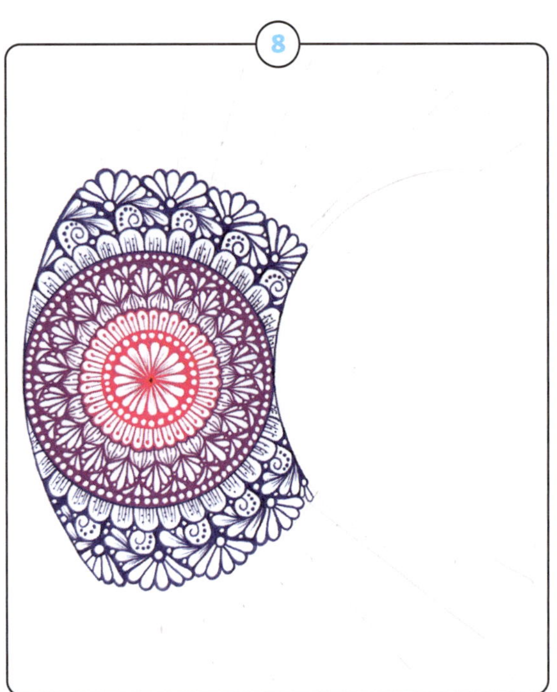

Draw in violet. Fill the next several rings with designs in violet. Note that this is three designs that fill four rings—the last design, the large daisies, fills two rings.

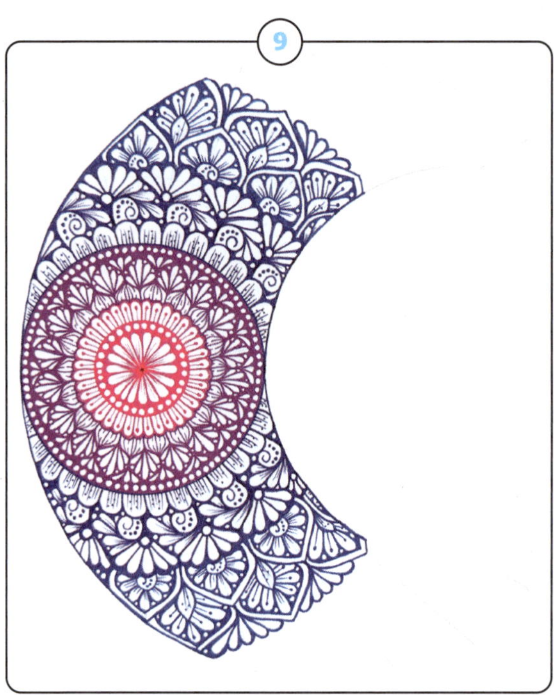

Draw in dark blue. Fill the next several rings with designs in dark blue. Note that this is two pointed-leaf designs that fill three rings total.

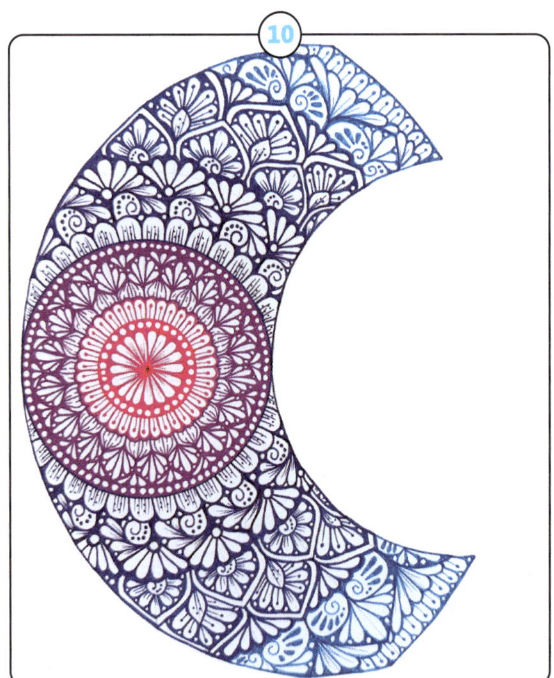

Draw in medium blue. Fill the next three rings with designs in medium blue, combining curling lines, pointed leaves, teardrops, and domes.

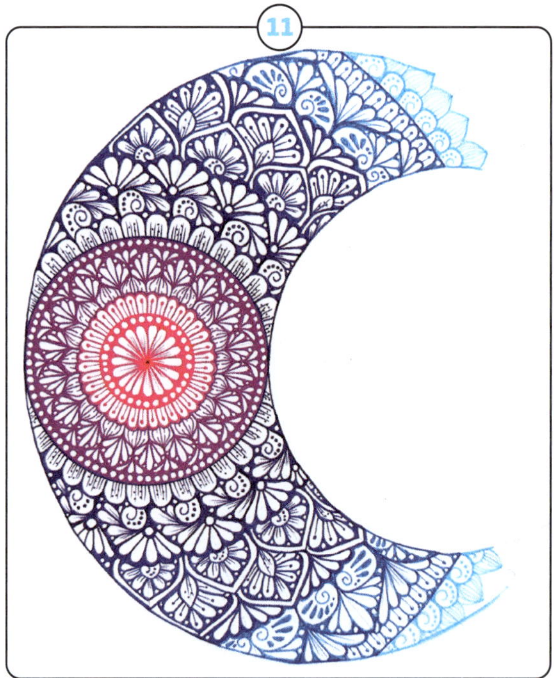

Draw in light blue. Fill the next two rings with designs in light blue—one ring of curling lines, one ring of pointed leaves.

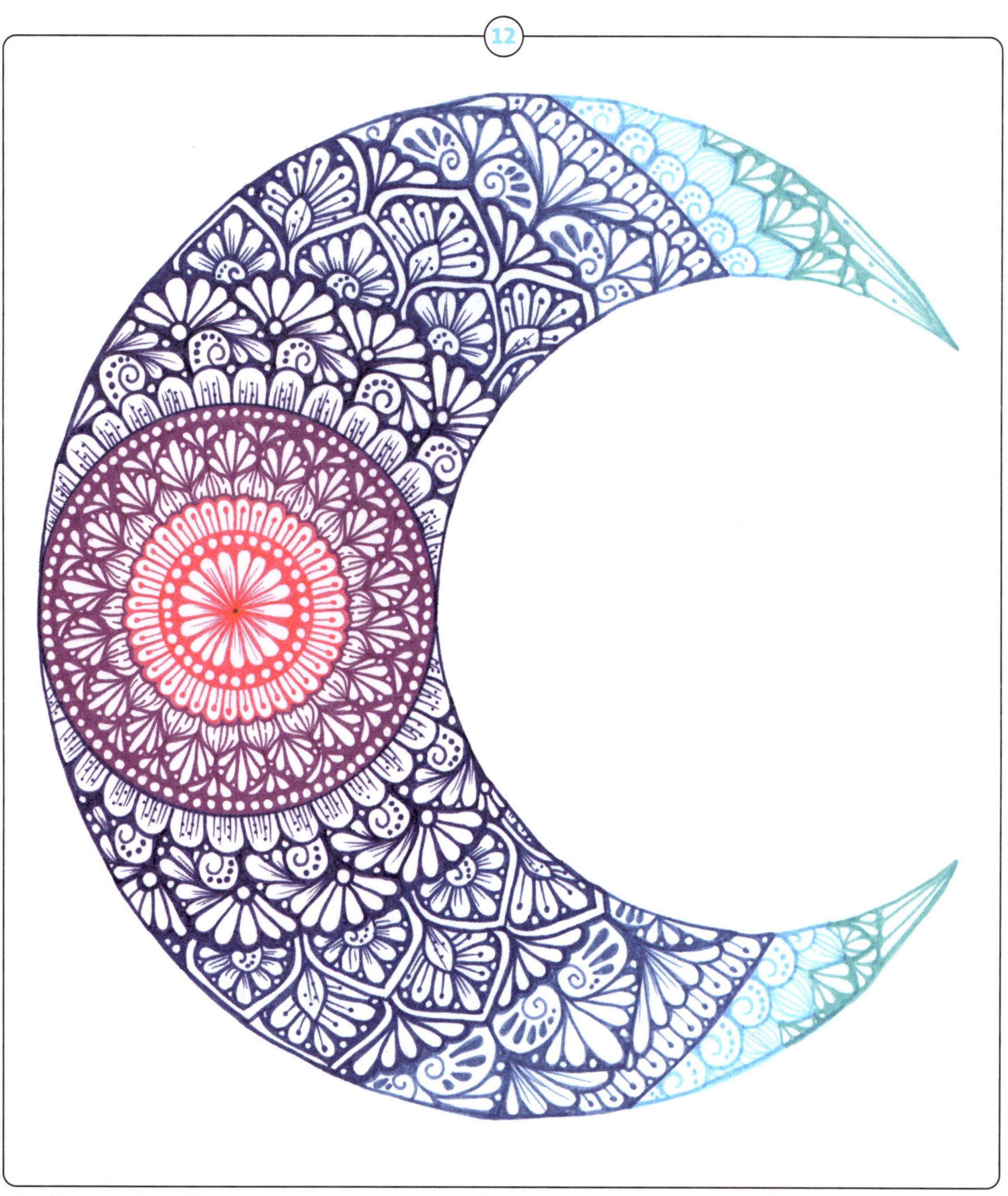

Finish in turquoise. Fill the remaining space with a pattern of pointed leaves, teardrops, and long, skinny teardrops that extend from the crescent points.

Hummingbird

The animal section of this book builds on what you learned in all four previous sections, but especially in the Special Shapes section. For this first animal, the Hummingbird, you'll learn not only how to draw within an animal's shape, but also how to incorporate repetitive designs into specific parts of the animal's shape outside of the standard mandala rings and rays—in this case, in the bird's wings.

As you draw this mandala, imagine a hummingbird flitting from flower to flower, drinking nectar with its long beak. Every time it visits a new flower, it adds a new color to its wings.

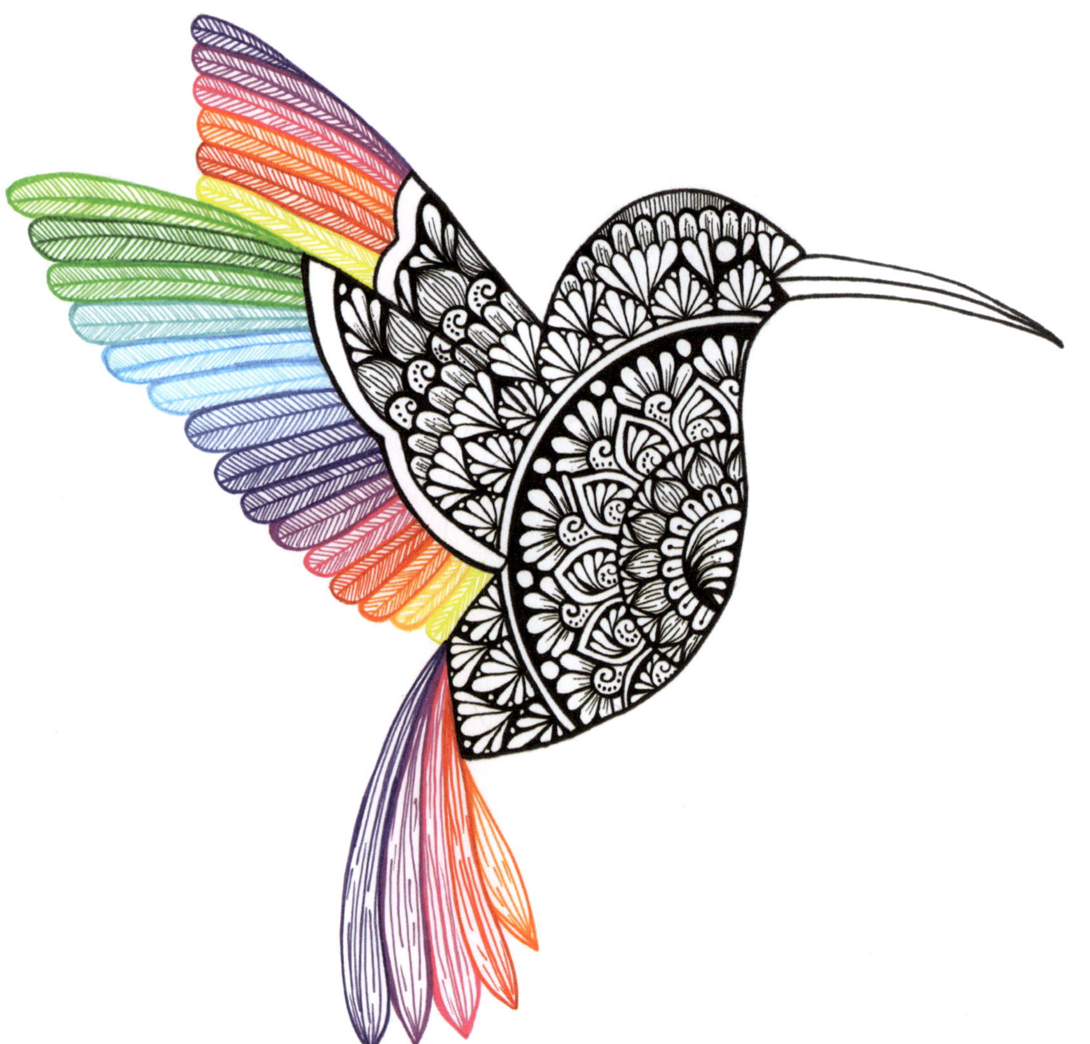

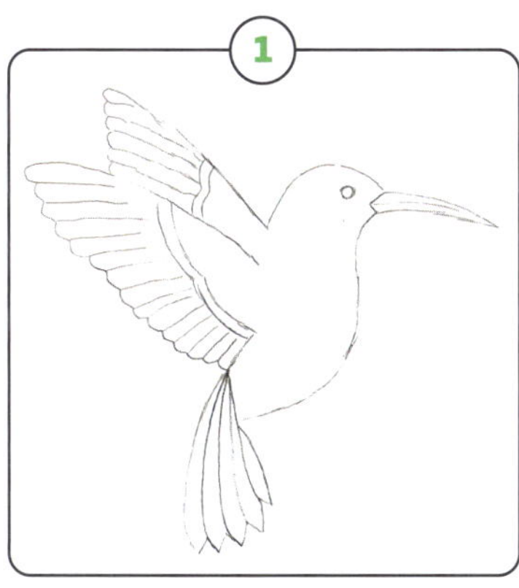

Draw the hummingbird. Draw or trace a hummingbird outline as shown, with five tail feathers, 15 feathers in the full wing, and six in the partial wing.

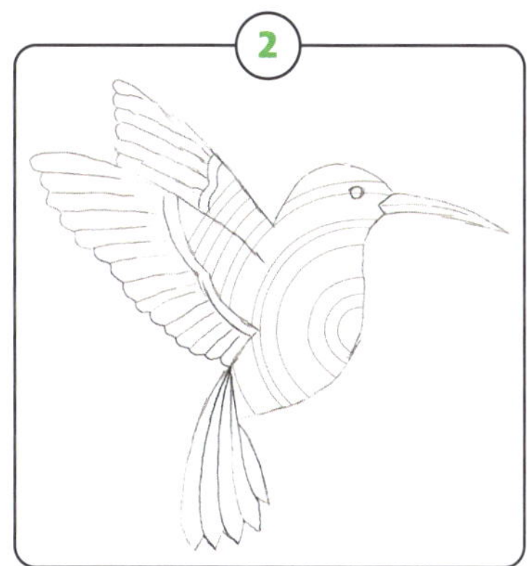

Draw circles. Draw 12 circles as shown. For reference, the outermost circle radius is 3¼" (8.3 cm); the innermost circle radius is ⅜" (1 cm).

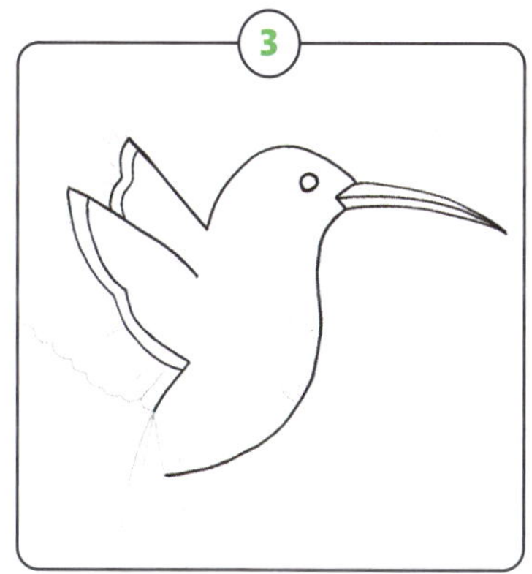

Outline the black section. Use a black pen to outline only the black section of the bird as shown. Don't close off the tail section.

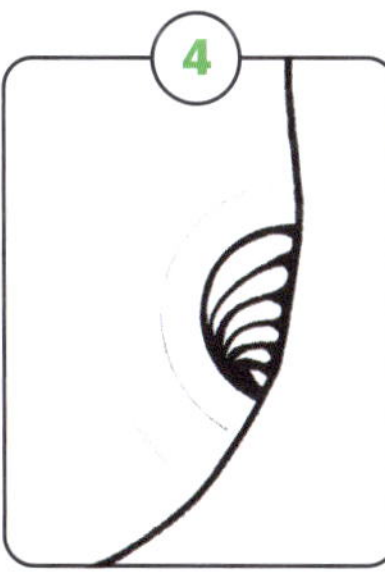

Fill the center. Fill the center of the mandala with six curved teardrops of decreasing size, then fill in around them.

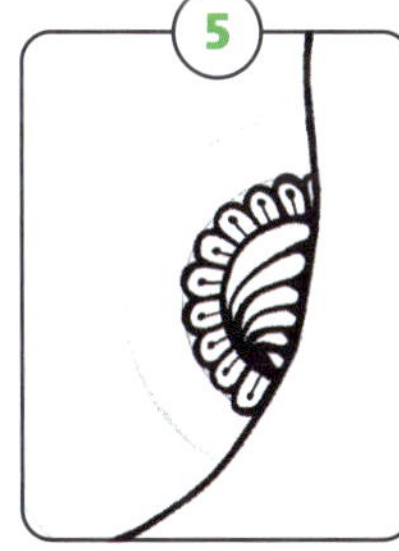

Draw the first ring. Fill the first ring with small domes. Draw a line capped with a dot in each dome.

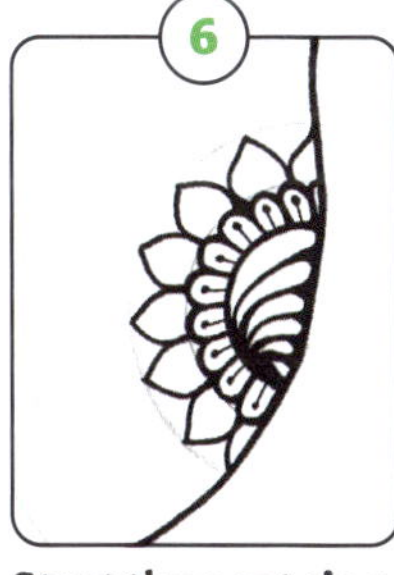

Start the next ring. Draw pointed leaves in the next ring—about six full leaves and two half leaves.

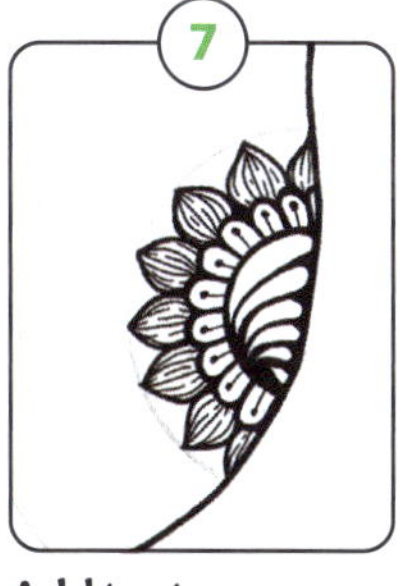

Add texture. Add solid and broken lines to the pointed leaves to give them a textured, rounded effect—imagine an onion.

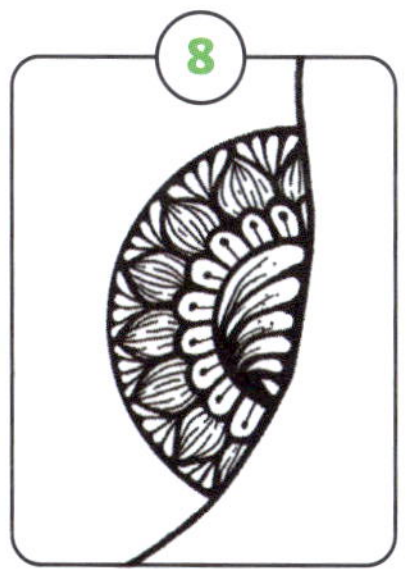

Finish the ring. Draw three or four teardrops between each pointed leaf, then fill in around them.

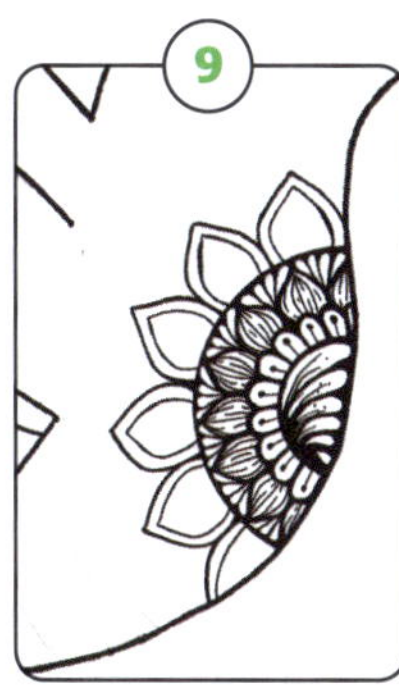

Start the next ring. Draw pointed leaves in the next ring—about five full leaves and one half leaf—then draw an inset leaf in each one.

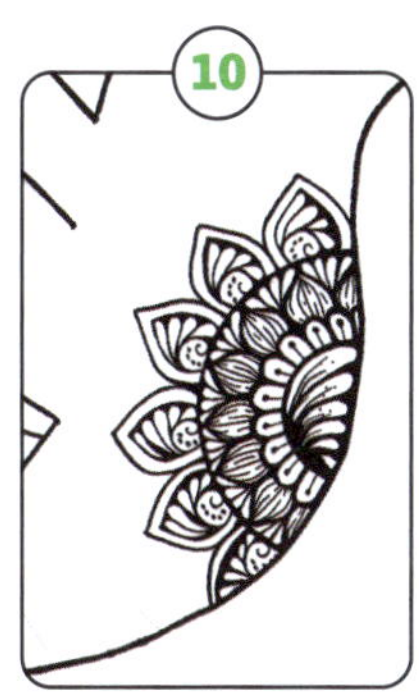

Pattern the leaves. Fill each inset pointed leaf with a detailed pattern as shown.

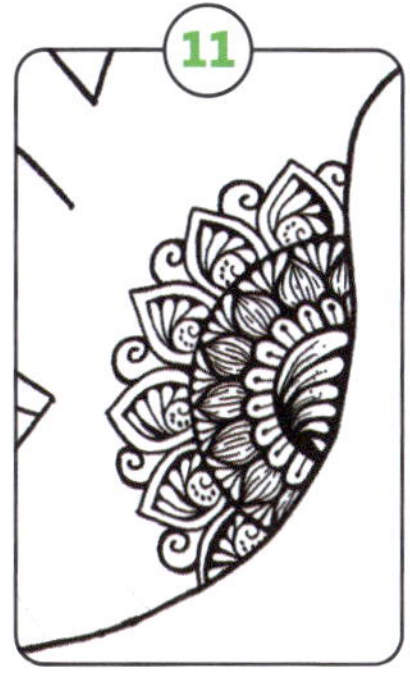

Add curling lines. Add a curling line between each pointed leaf.

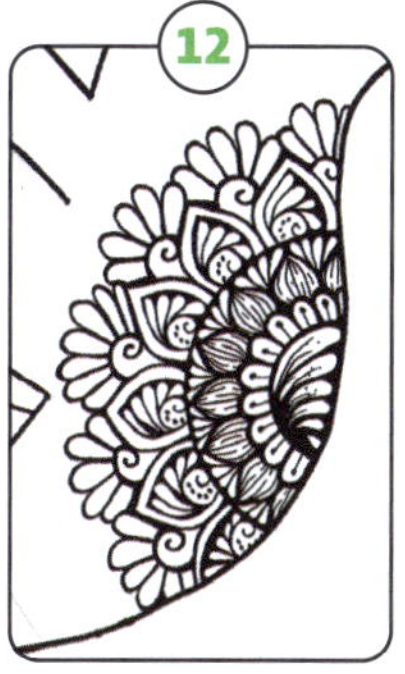

Continue into the next ring. Emanating from each curling line, draw about five petals, creating a daisy effect.

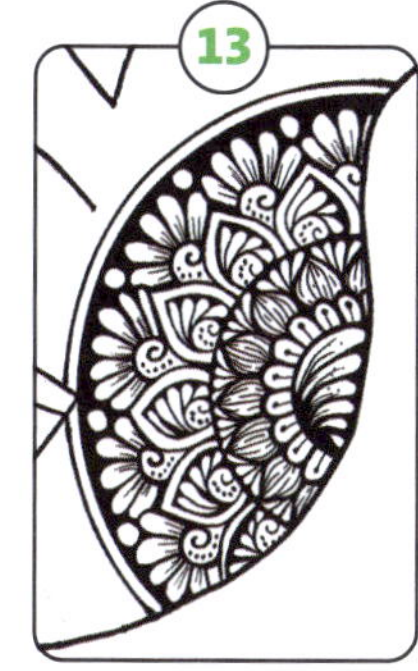

Keep going. Draw a freehand circle between each daisy, add details to each daisy, trace the next ring, and fill in all the trapped space around the daisies and circles.

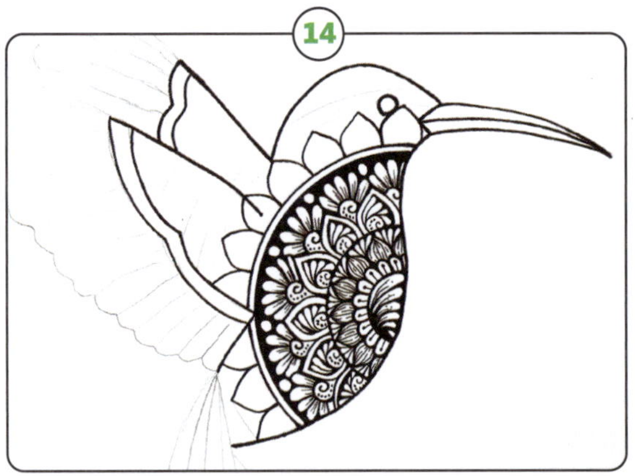

Start the next ring. Draw about 10 pointed leaves in the next ring, imagining how they would line up even when the ring disappears, such as under the wing.

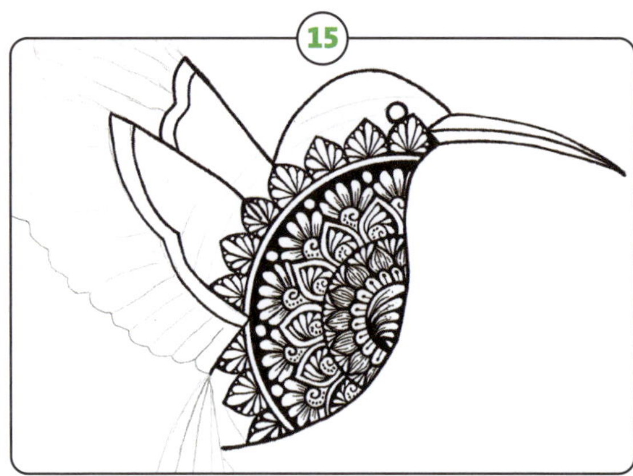

Pattern the leaves. Fill each pointed leaf with a detailed pattern as shown.

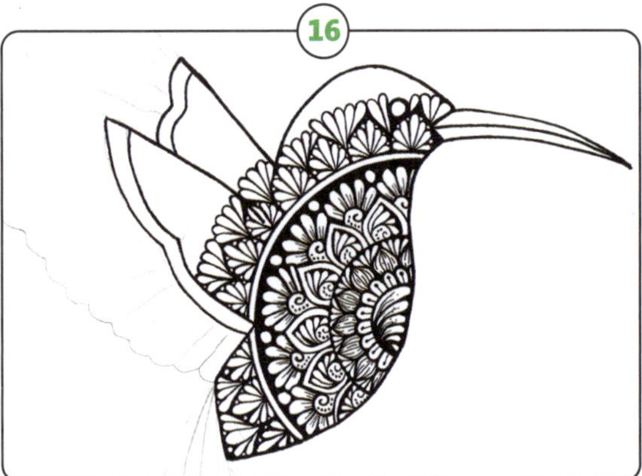

Add teardrops. Between each leaf, draw three to five teardrops that reach all the way into the next ring. Adjust the size and spacing to fill in next to the tail.

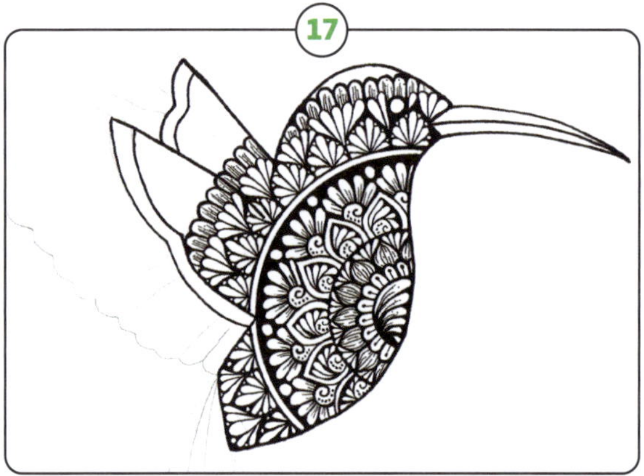

Add domes. Fill the next ring with domes, then add delicate detail lines to each dome. Be careful to work around the bird's eye.

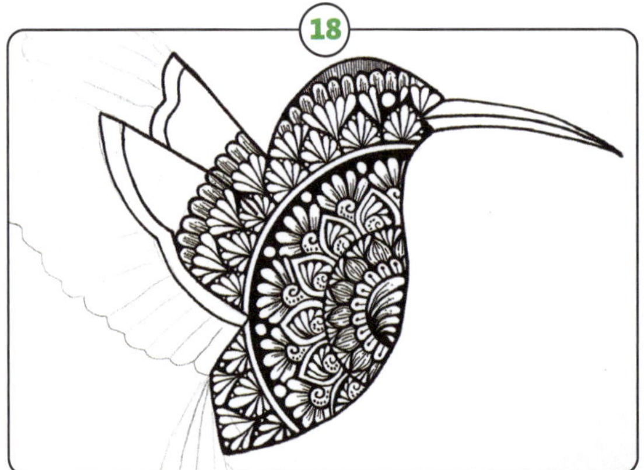

Finish the head. Finish filling the remaining space at the top of the bird's head with simple, densely packed lines.

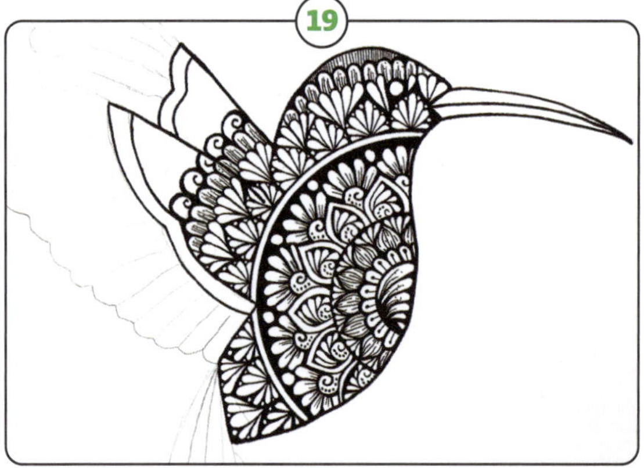

Start the next ring. Draw curling lines in the next ring. Be careful to cut off the curling line where the front wing ends.

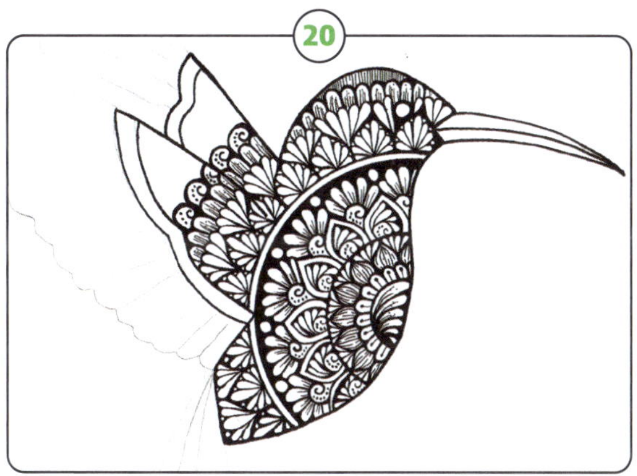

Finish the ring. Add dots to the curling lines, then fill in around them.

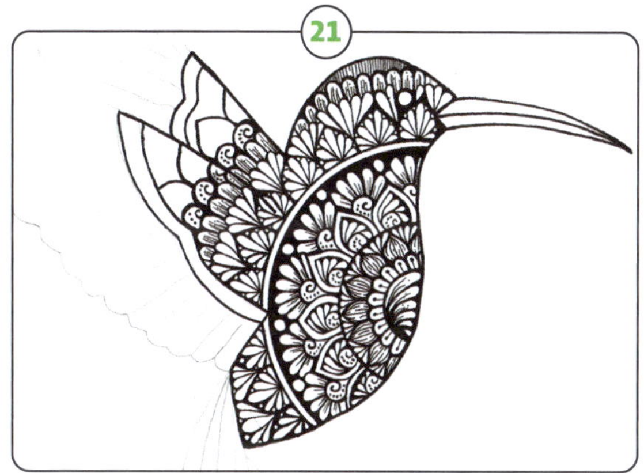

Start the next ring. Draw pointed leaves that extend not only through the next ring, but the next two rings.

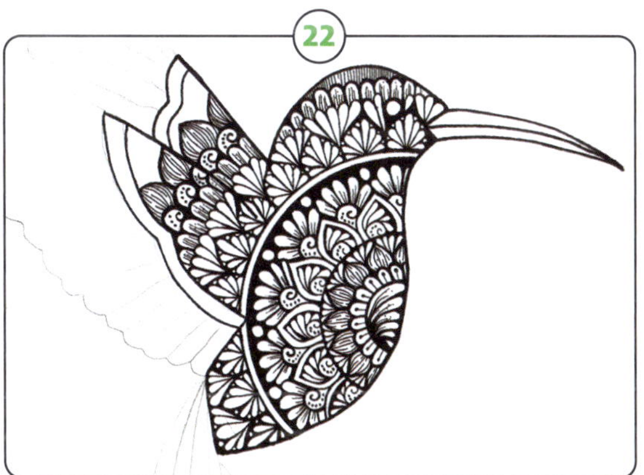

Add texture. Repeat step 7 to add texture to these pointed leaves.

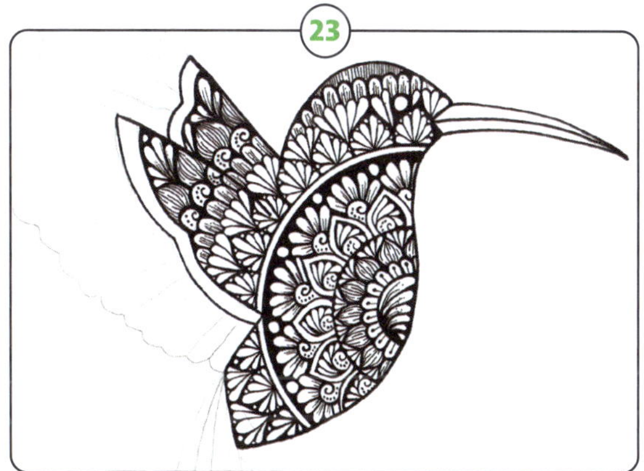

Finish the black. In the remaining space inside each wing, drawn variously shaped teardrops, then fill in around them. Add a couple of delicate detail lines too.

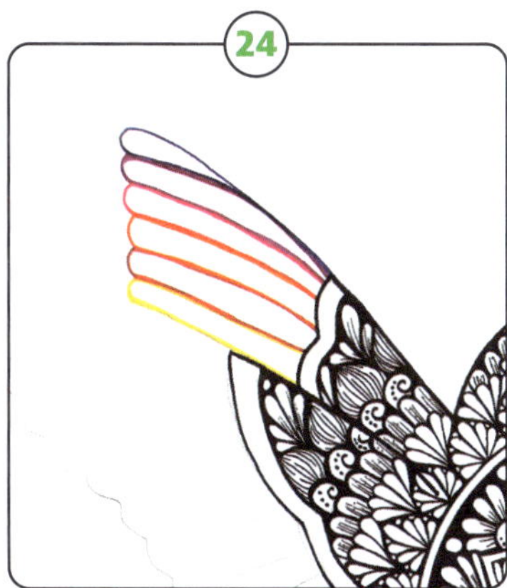

Outline the partial wing. Outline each feather in a different color from top to bottom: violet, purple, pink, orange, red, and bright yellow.

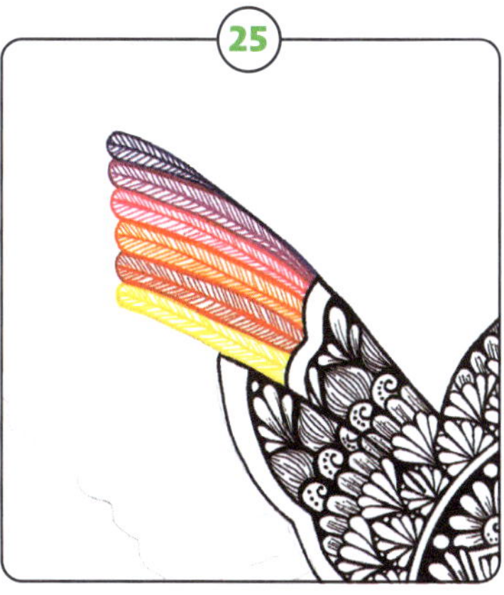

Add feather texture. Fill each feather with a single long, central vein and individual short lines on either side to create a feather effect.

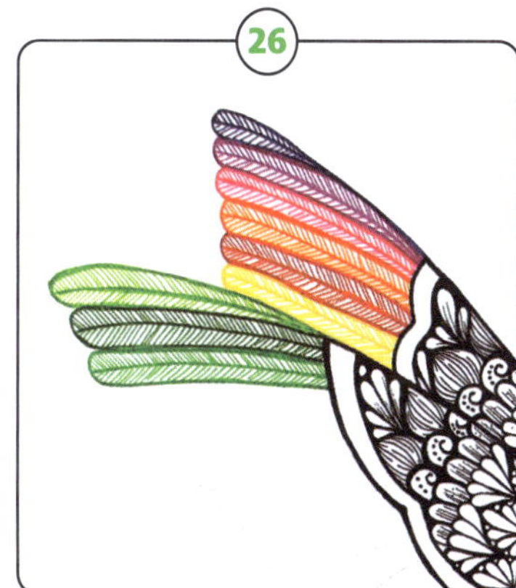

Start the full wing. Work on the full wing, feather by feather, first outlining, then adding detail. Start with bright green, dark green, and medium green.

136

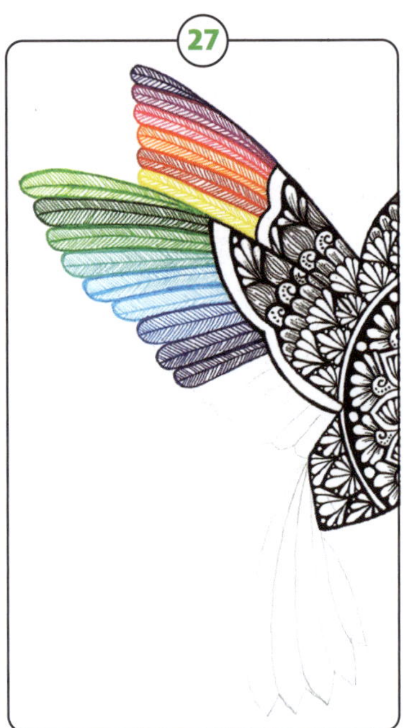

Continue with more colors.
Continue the feathers: blue-green, light blue (for two feathers), medium blue, dark blue, and violet.

Finish the wing. Finish the feathers: purple, pink, red, orange, medium yellow, and bright yellow.

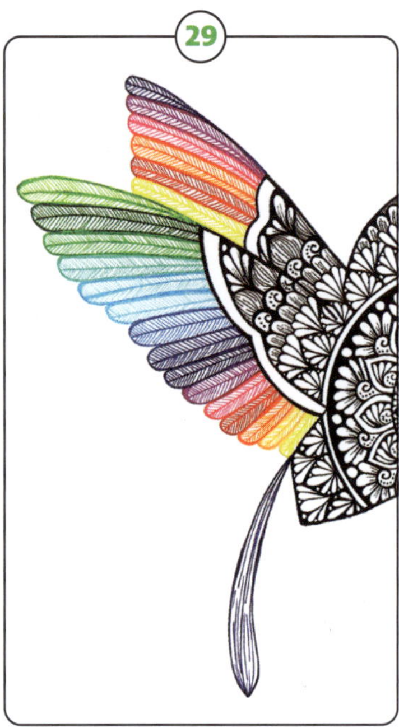

Start the tail. Outline the longest tail feather in violet. Add several long solid and broken lines to it to create a different, elongated texture.

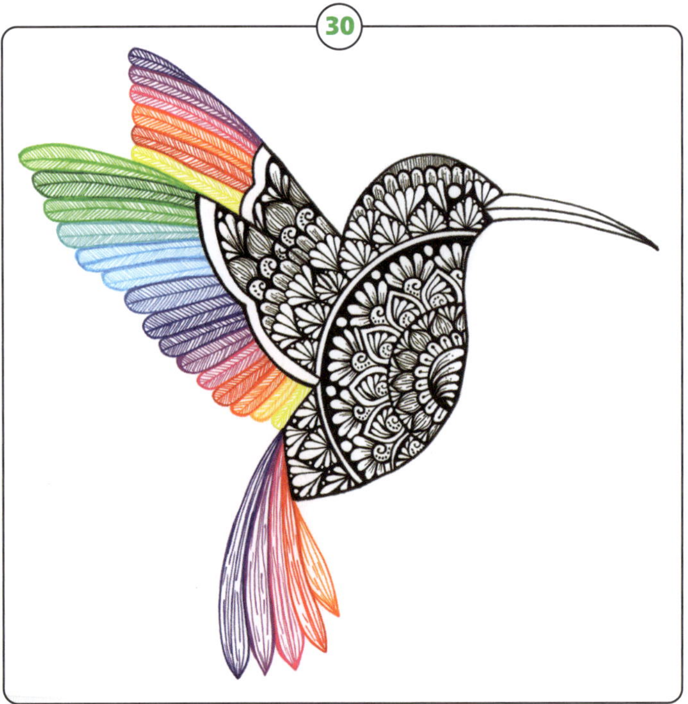

Finish the tail. Repeat this technique for each remaining tail feather in a different color: purple, pink, red, and orange.

LET'S CHECK IN

Did you freehand draw the animal or did you trace it? Why did you choose that approach? Do you feel like you can adapt to drawing within a shape that is not identical to the finished example?

How was the experience of drawing without ray guidelines?
Did it feel liberating, scary, or both?

In what ways does drawing any mandala—this one or a previous one—make you feel more connected to yourself or the world?

Until one has loved an animal,
a part of one's soul remains unawakened.
–Anatole France

Whale

For this animal design, we'll take a step toward realism by creating an animal shape that has minimal but realistic details that won't be too challenging even for a beginner. First, you will draw and detail the whale in a limited set of colors; then you'll add the mandala to the whale using the same colors. The final effect is gorgeous and cohesive.

As you draw this mandala, try to channel the calm and confidence of a whale making its slow way through the ocean, filter feeding, singing to its neighbors.

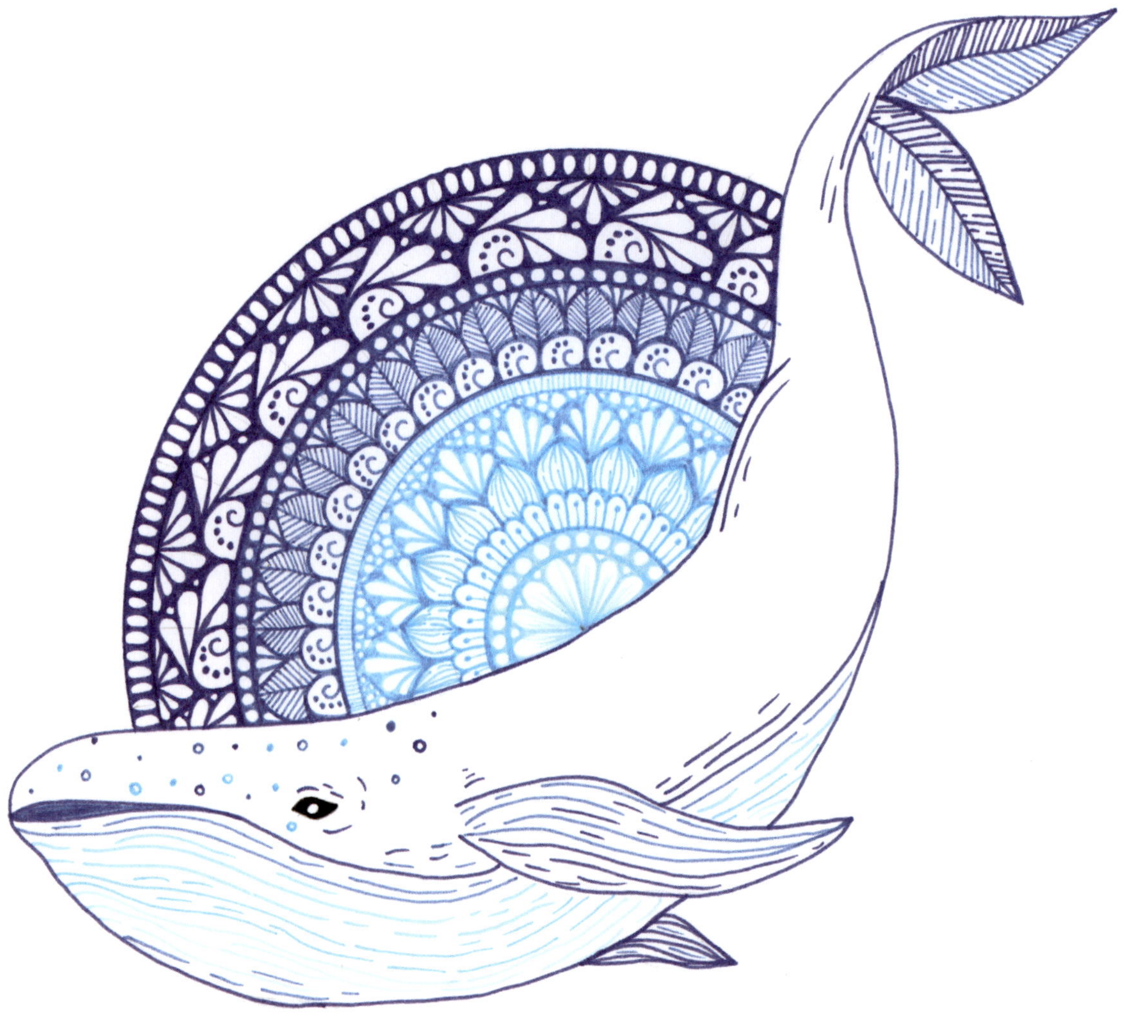

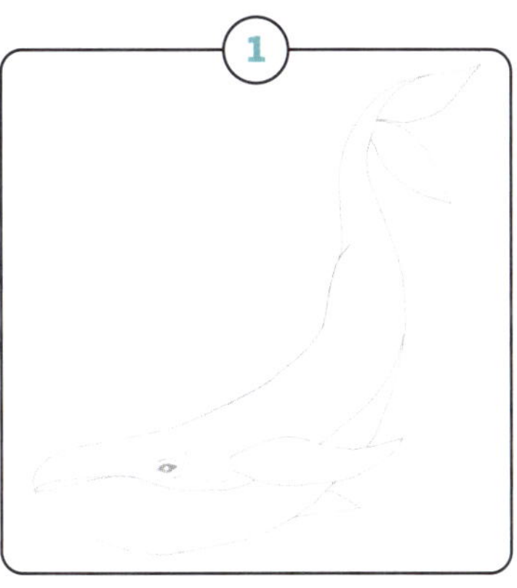

Draw the whale. Draw or trace a whale outline as shown, including its eye, some detail lines around the eye, and an extra line for the mouth.

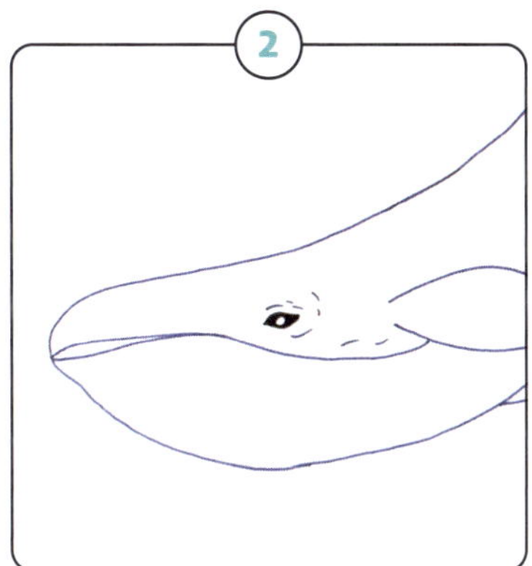

Outline the whale. Use dark blue to outline the entire whale and its details. Also fill in the whale's eye, leaving a white iris.

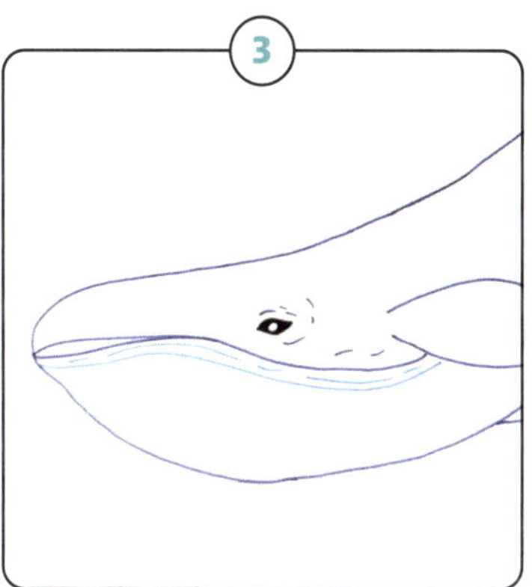

Start adding texture. Switch to medium blue to begin adding texture to the lower half of the body: long broken and unbroken lines that follow the body's contours.

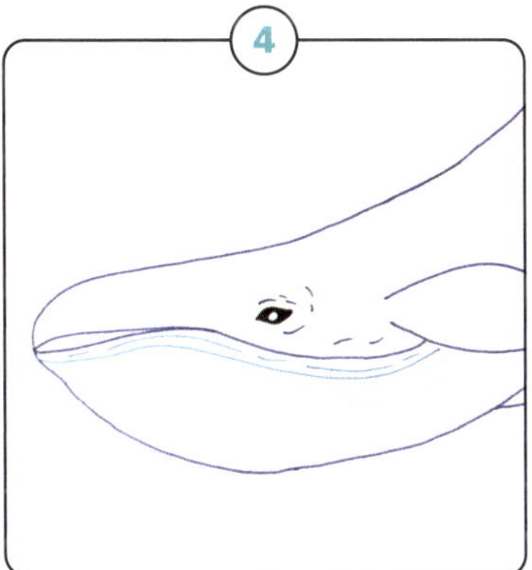

Continue adding texture. Switch to light blue to continue adding this same texture effect.

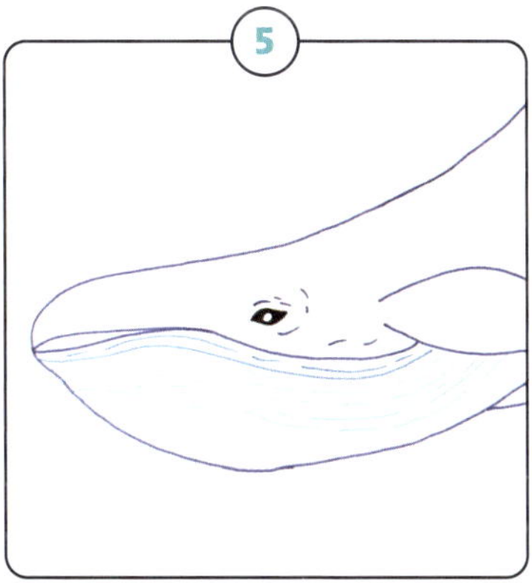

Change colors again. Switch to clear blue to continue adding this same texture effect.

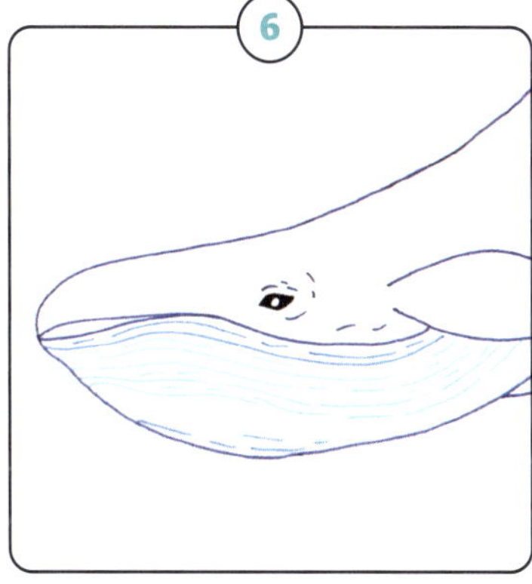

Finish texturing the body. Add a few more strokes of clear blue, then switch back to medium blue to add a few more texture strokes along the very bottom.

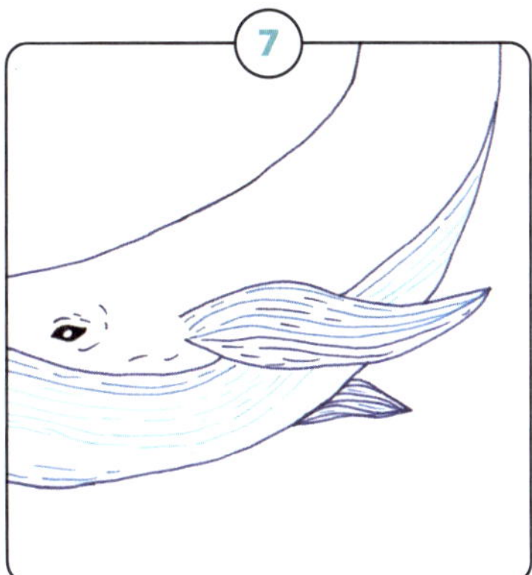

Texture the flippers. Use a mix of dark blue and medium blue to add similar texture to the two flippers.

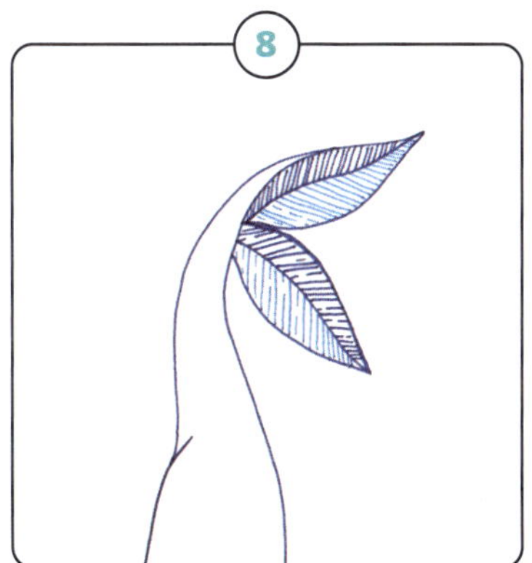

Texture the tail. Draw a dark-blue central vein in each tail half. In both dark blue and medium blue, add long broken and unbroken lines spoking out from the veins.

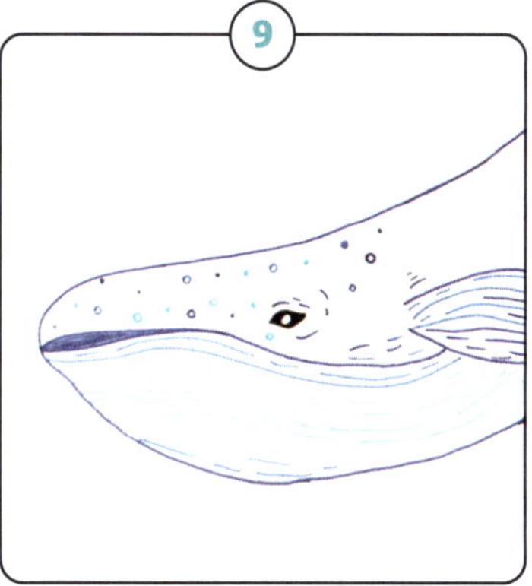

Finish the body. Add a few more texture lines to the body in dark blue. Fill the mouth with medium blue. Add some tiny circles on the face in several blues.

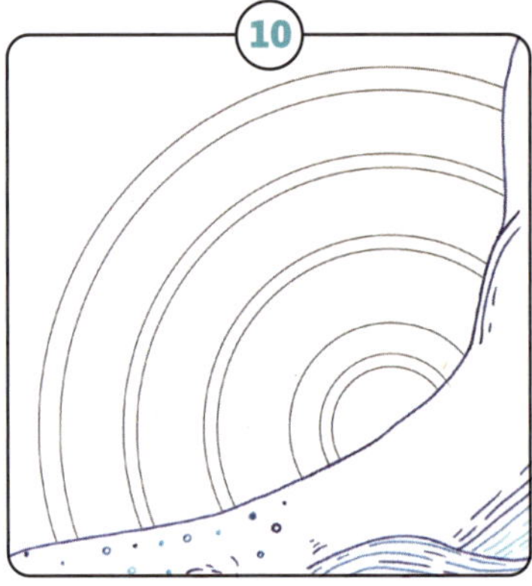

Draw circles. Draw nine circles as shown. For reference, the outermost circle radius is 3⅛" (7.9 cm); the innermost circle radius is ½" (1.3 cm).

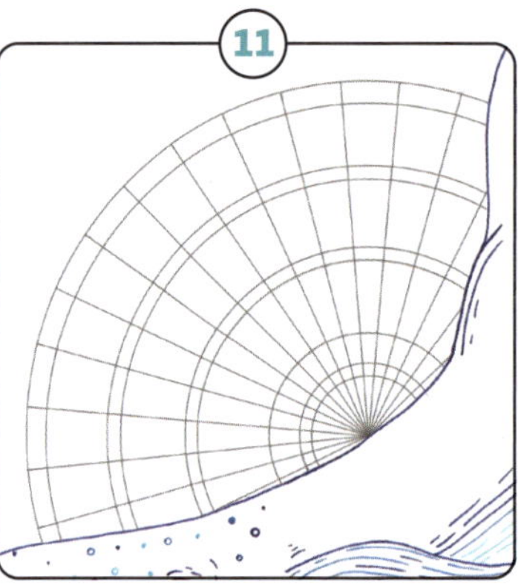

Draw rays. Using pencil, draw a ray every 10° in the available space (about 17 rays total, including ones you can barely see).

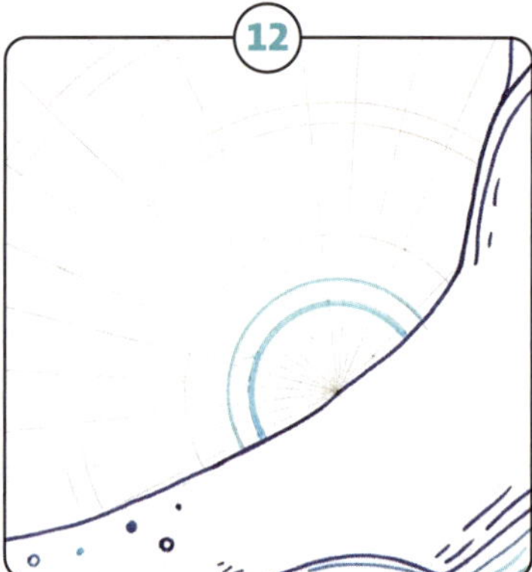

Start with light blue. Trace the first two circles in light blue.

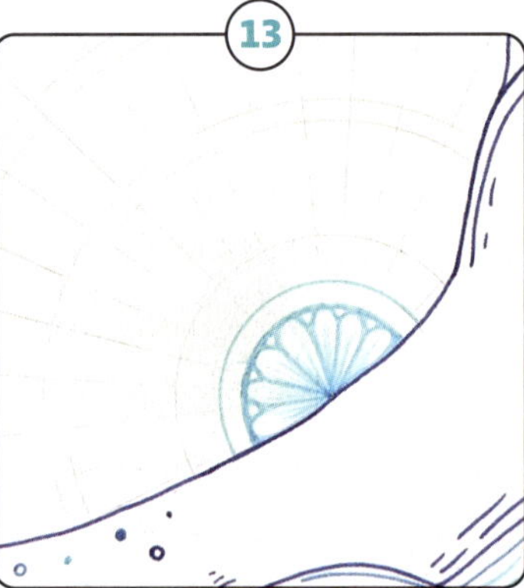

Fill the center. Draw teardrops in the center. Add a circle between each teardrop. Add delicate detail lines to each teardrop.

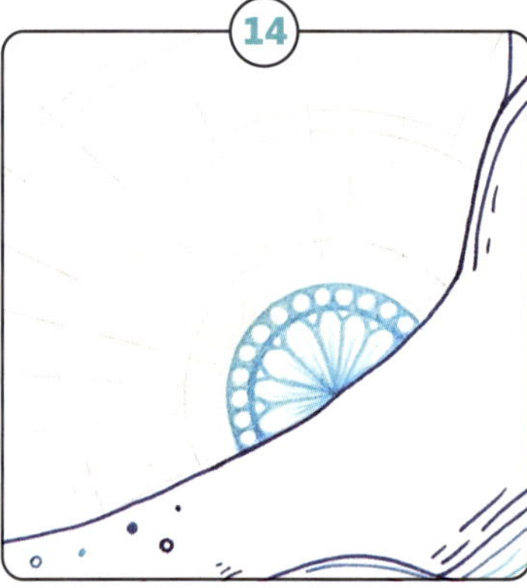

Fill the first ring. In the first ring, draw densely packed circles, then fill in around them.

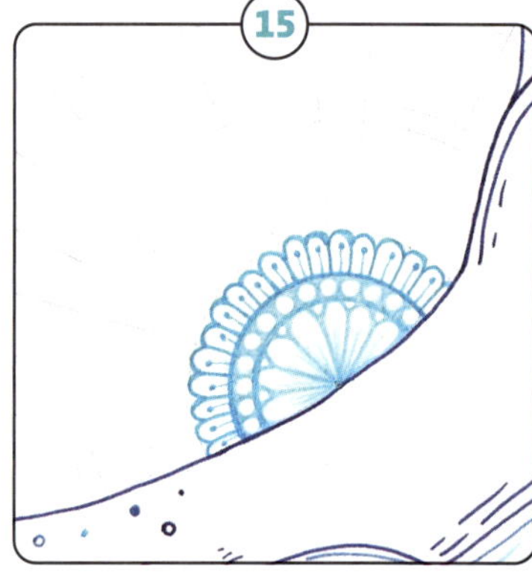

Fill the second ring. In the next ring, draw a dome centered between each ray. Add a line capped with a dot to each dome.

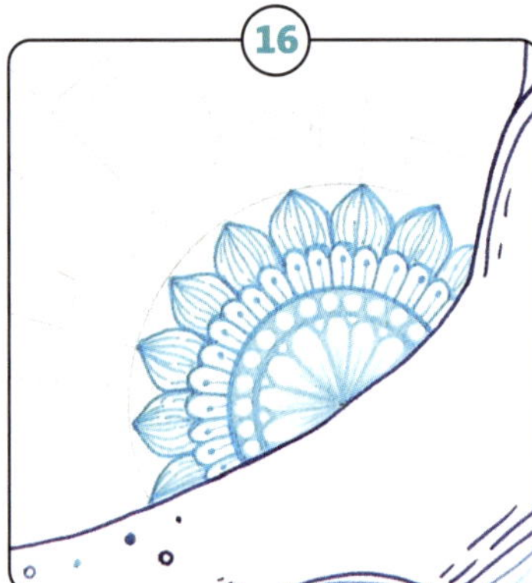

Add a new ring. Add a new ring in pencil. Draw pointed leaves centered on alternating rays in this new ring, then fill them with the "onion" texture.

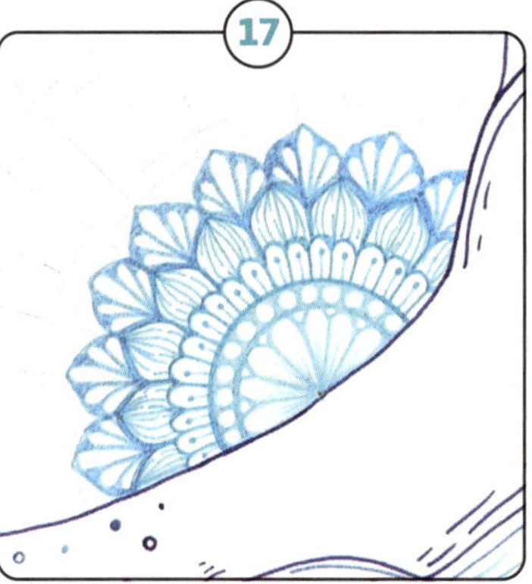

Fill the next ring. Between each pointed leaf, add a new pointed leaf. Draw five teardrops in each one, then fill in around them.

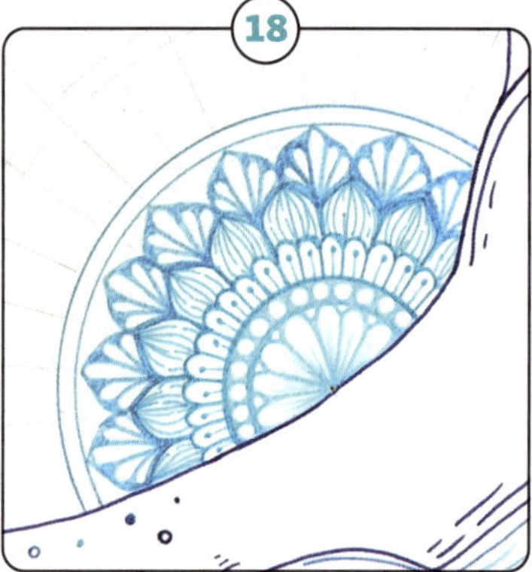

Prep the next section. Trace the next two circles, still using light blue.

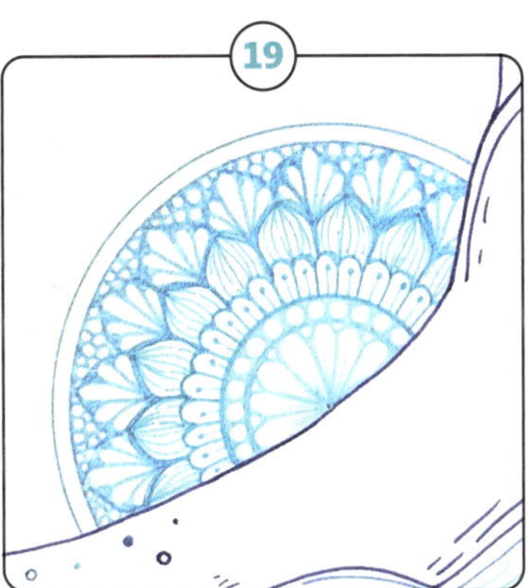

Fill the previous ring. Fill the area trapped below the smaller circle with freehand circles of varying sizes.

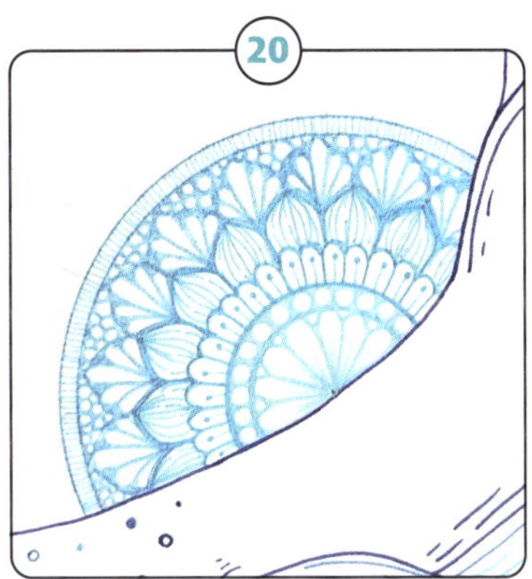

Fill the next ring. Fill the thin ring with densely packed straight lines.

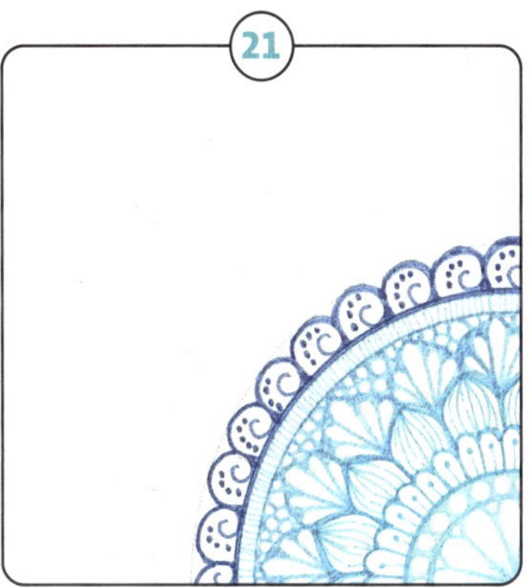

Add a new ring. Add a new ring in pencil. Switch to medium blue. Draw a curling line centered between each ray in this new ring. Decorate them with dots.

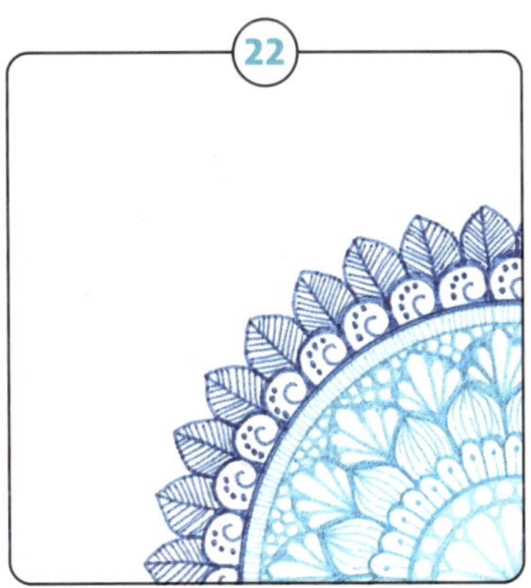

Draw pointed leaves. Draw pointed leaves centered on alternating rays in the next ring. Add a leaf pattern to each one.

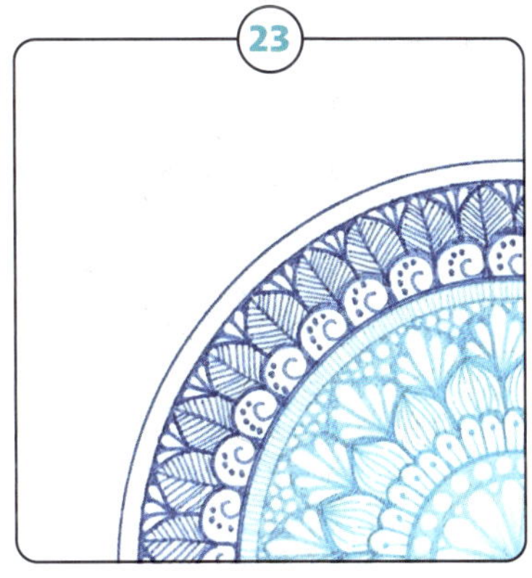

Continue with medium blue. Trace the next two circles. Draw three teardrops between each pointed leaf, then fill in around them.

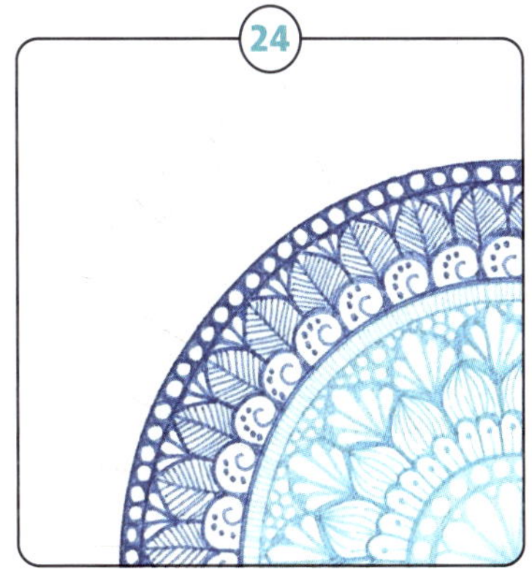

Fill the next ring. Draw densely packed circles in the next thin ring, then fill in around them.

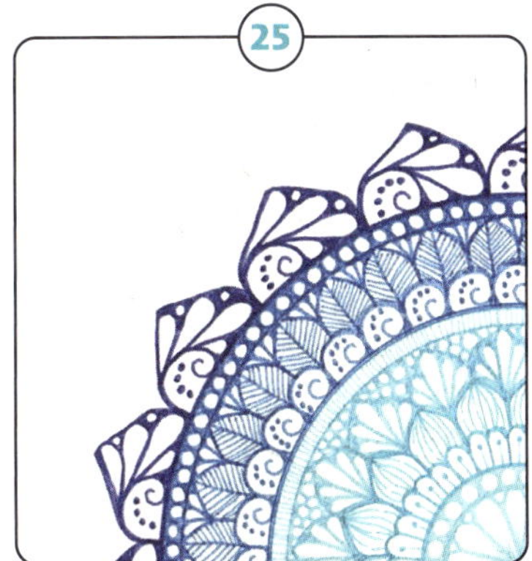

Switch to dark blue. Draw pointed leaves centered on alternating rays in the next ring. Fill each one with a detailed pattern as shown.

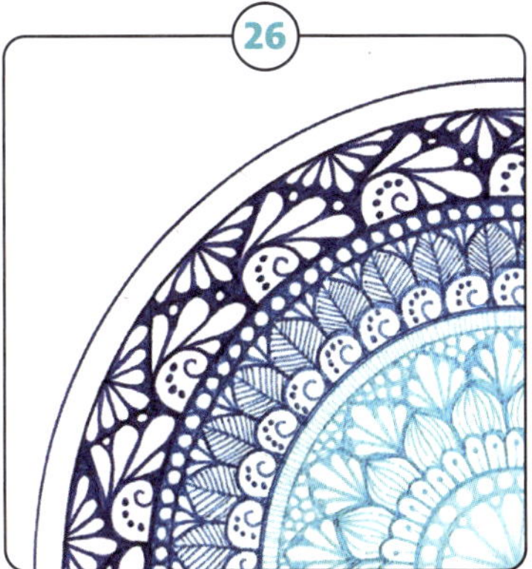

Finish this ring. Trace the last two circles. Draw seven teardrops between each pointed leaf, coming down from the final ring, then fill in around them.

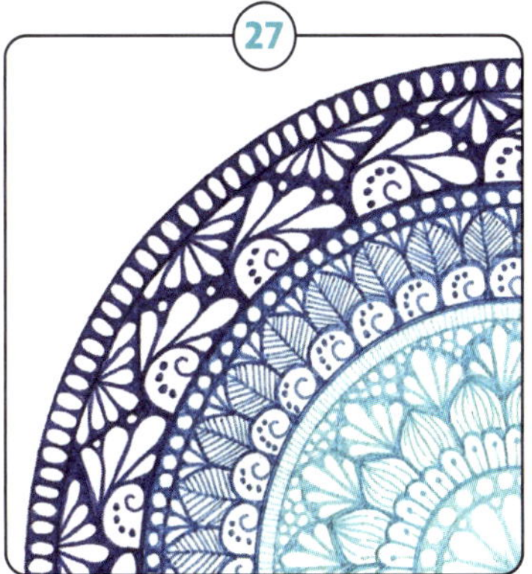

Fill the last ring. Draw densely packed ovals in the last ring, then fill in around them.

Bumblebee

Let's keep upping the complexity. For the Bumblebee, you will now tackle two separate mandala sections—the thorax and the abdomen—as well as give careful consideration to the limbs and draw detailed wings. By selecting all your colors in advance and drawing carefully at the start, you will set yourself up for success.

As you draw this mandala, think about how—whether you like them or not—bees and other insects all contribute to a balanced, complex, and wondrous ecosystem.

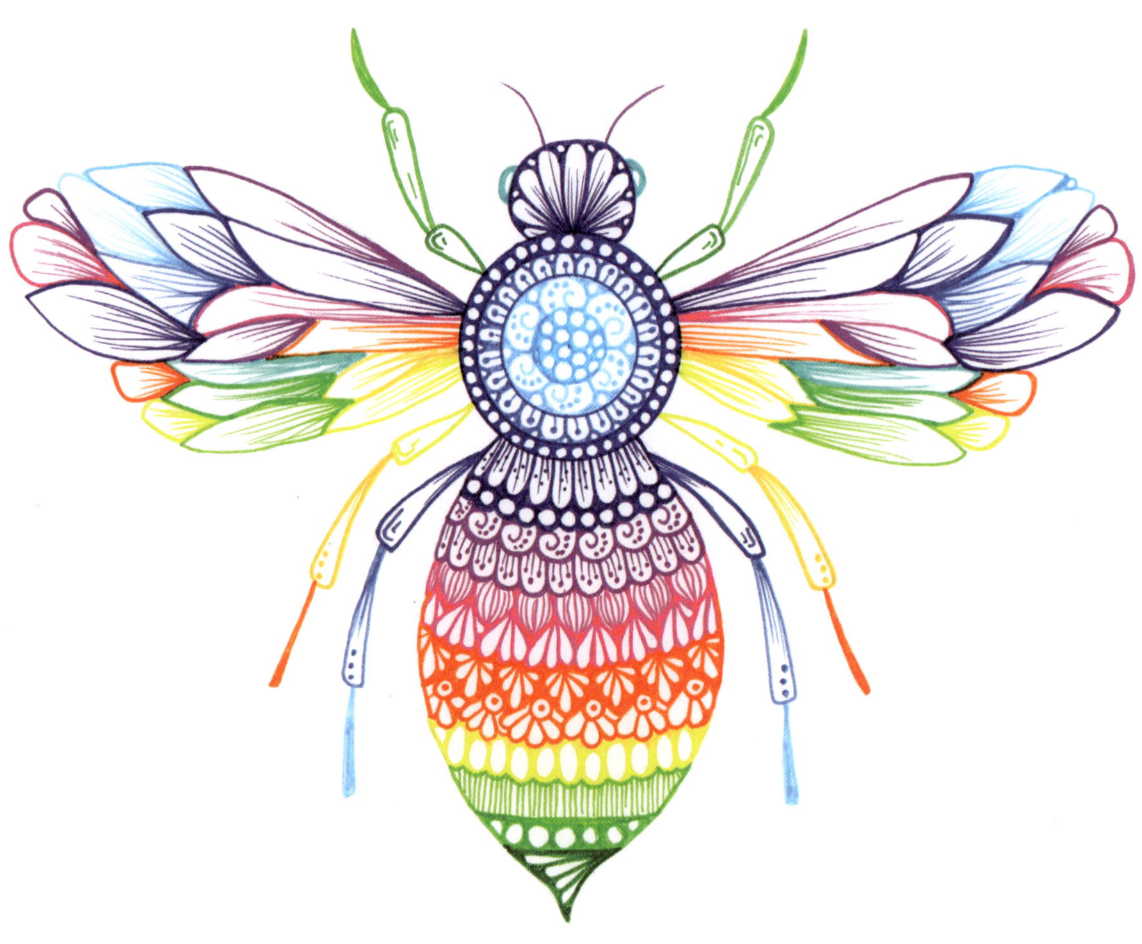

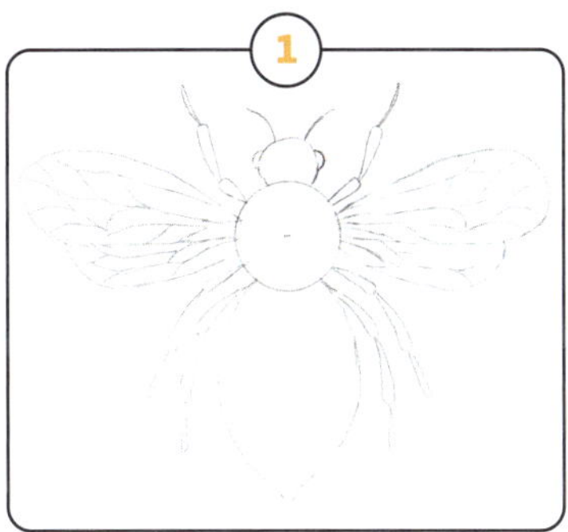

Draw the bee. Draw or trace a bee outline, including three-section legs and about 21 symmetrical segments per wing. The thorax is a circle with a ¾" (1.9 cm) radius.

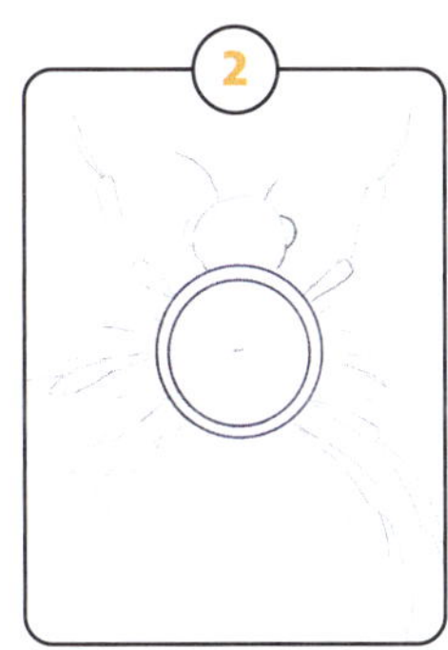

Outline the thorax. Use dark blue to outline the thorax circle. Draw another, smaller blue circle inside it.

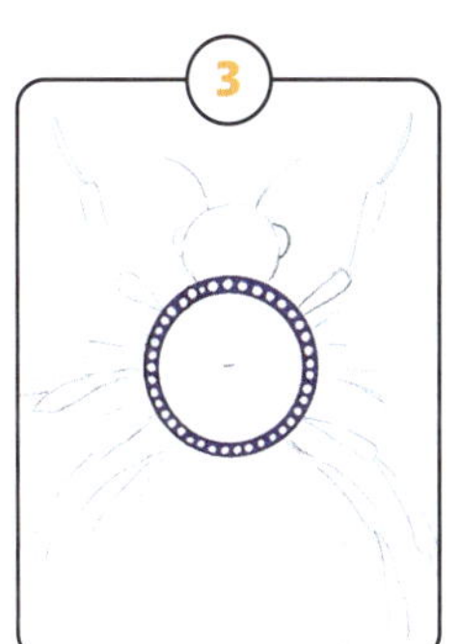

Fill the first ring. Fill this dark-blue ring with densely packed circles, then fill in around them.

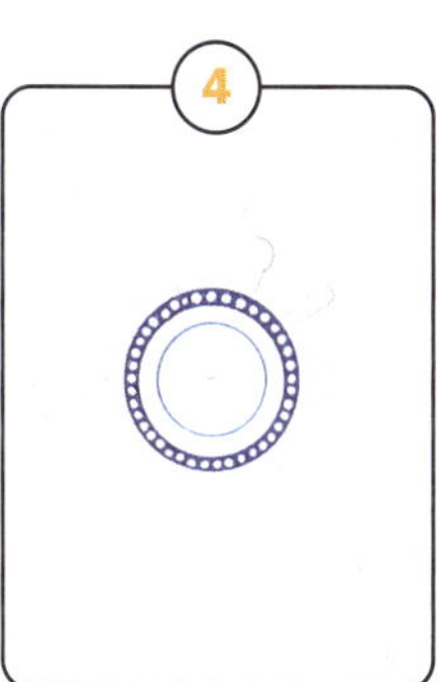

Create the second ring. Switch to medium blue. Draw another, smaller blue circle inside the thorax.

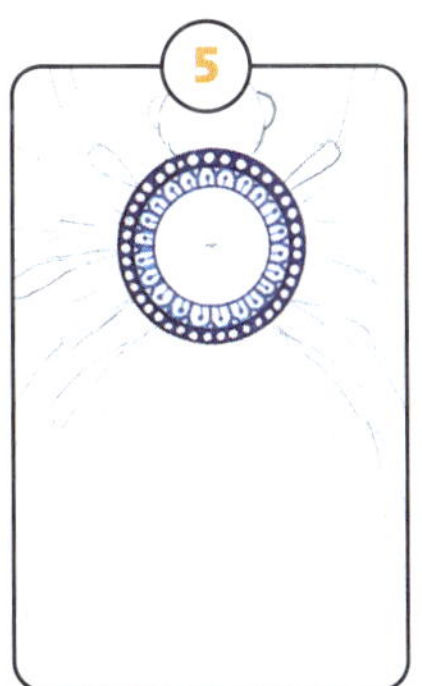

Fill the second ring. Fill this medium-blue ring with domes. Add a line capped with a dot to each dome.

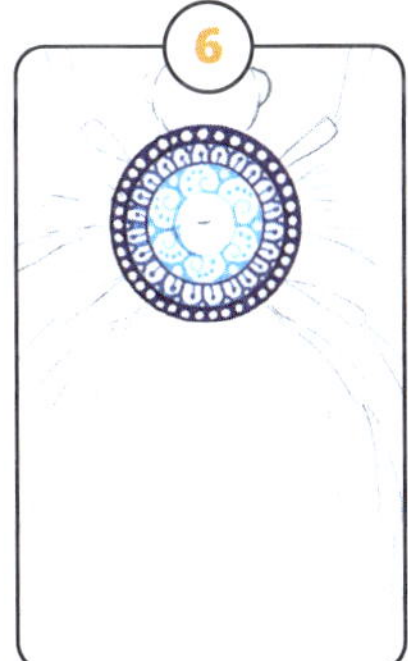

Create a third ring. Switch to light blue. Draw another, smaller blue circle inside the thorax. Fill the resulting ring with the pattern shown.

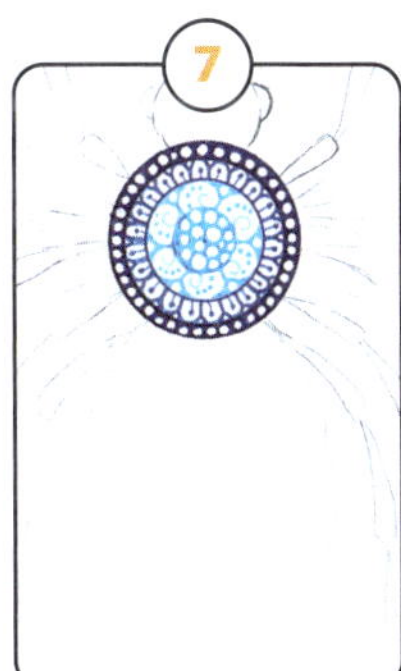

Fill the center. Draw densely packed circles of varying sizes in the center, then fill in around them.

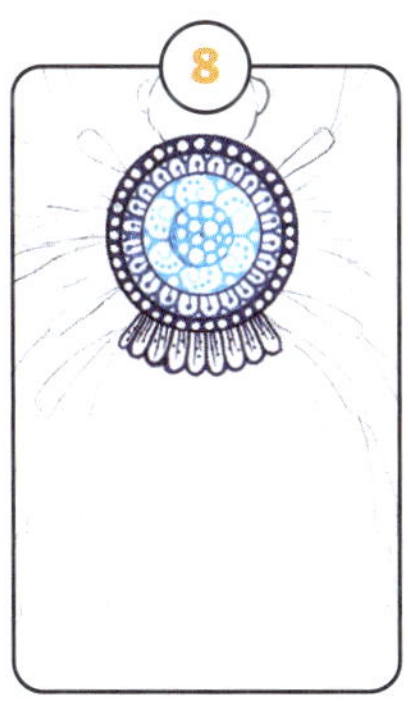

Start the abdomen. Use your compass and a pencil to draw 12 curved lines inside the abdomen. Using violet, fill the first ring with domes. Add details.

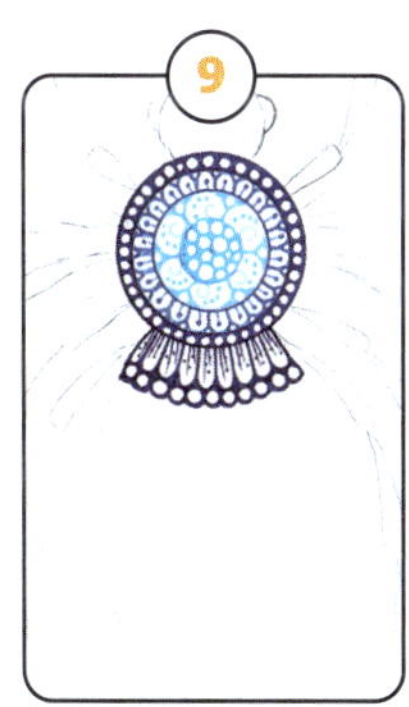

Continue with violet. Still using violet, fill the next ring with circles, then fill in around them.

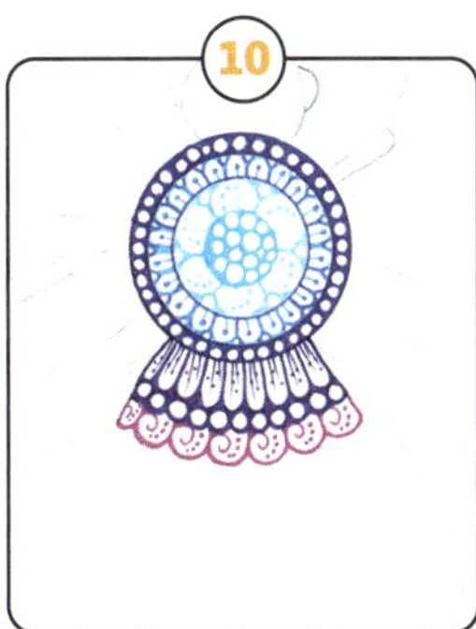

Switch to purple. Fill the next ring with purple curling lines. Add dots to them.

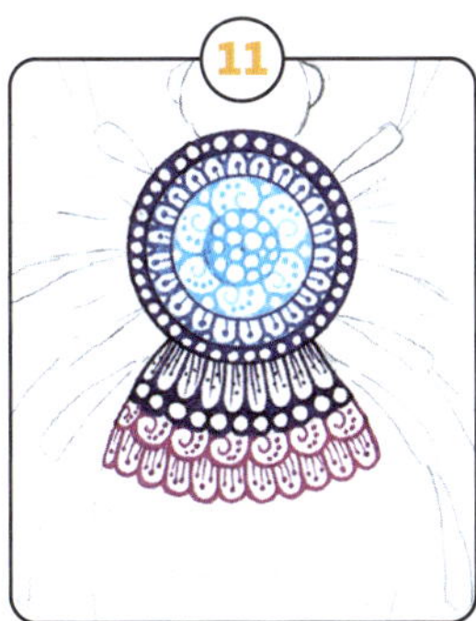

Fill the next ring. Still using purple, ignore the next ring circle and fill up to the following ring circle with domes. Add three lines capped with dots to each dome.

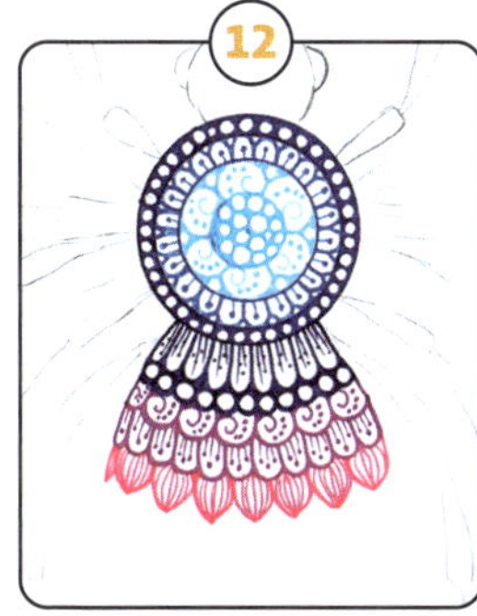

Switch to pink. In the next ring, draw pink pointed leaves. Add the "onion" texture to them.

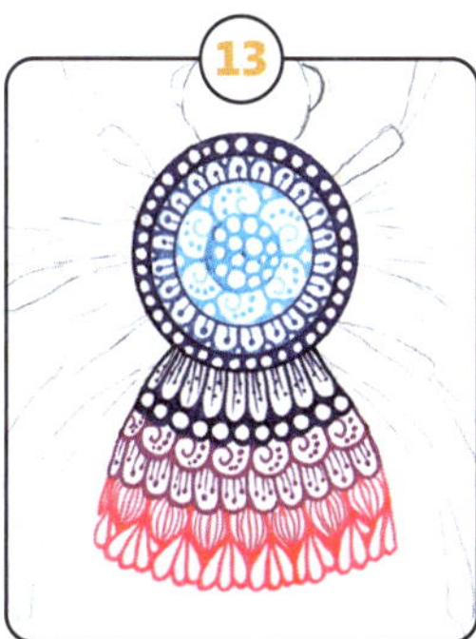

Fill the next ring. Still using pink, draw three teardrops between each pointed leaf to fill the next ring.

Bumblebee

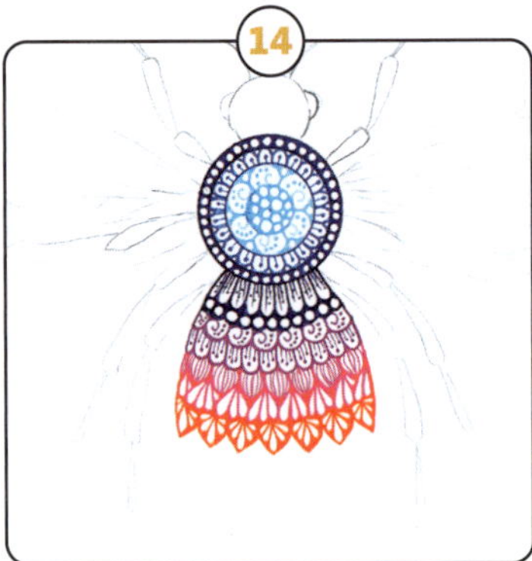

Switch to orange. In the next ring, draw orange pointed leaves. Add the teardrop pattern shown to them.

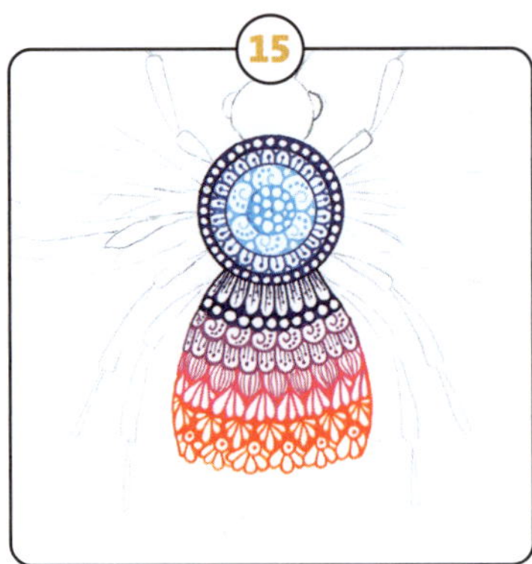

Fill the next ring. Still using orange, draw a daisy pattern as shown between each pointed leaf to fill the next ring.

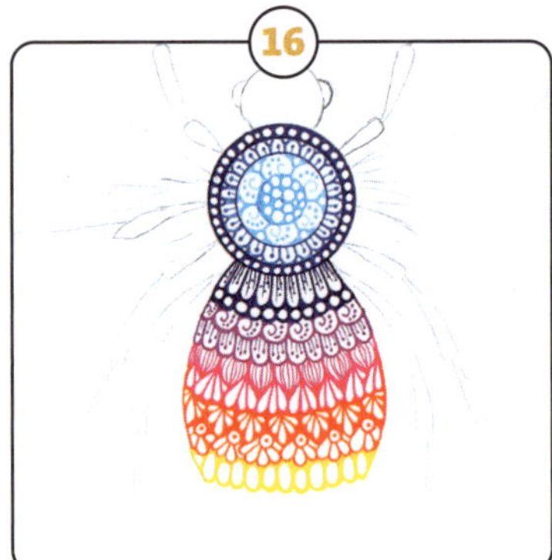

Switch to bright yellow. In the next ring, draw bright-yellow ovals. Give them thick outlines.

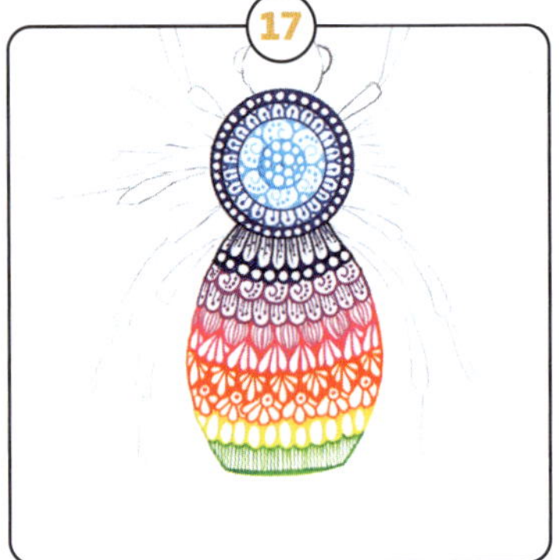

Switch to bright green. Trace both sides of the next ring in bright green, following the contour of the ovals on the upper side. Fill the ring with straight lines.

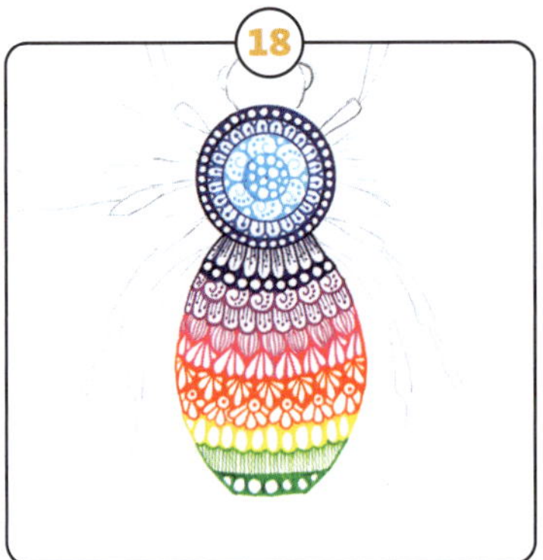

Switch to medium green. In the next ring, draw densely packed circles, then fill in around them.

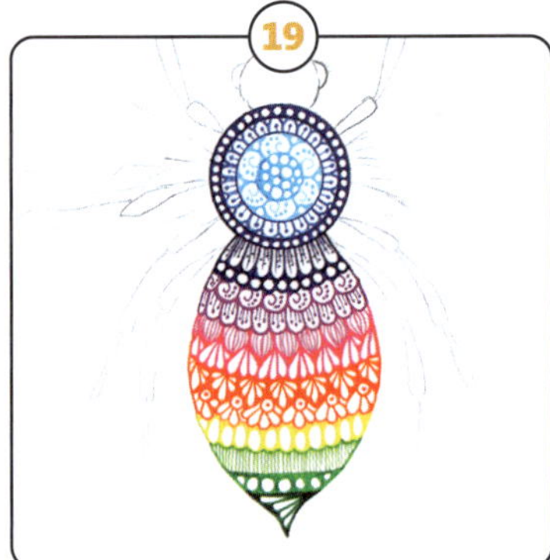

Switch to dark green. In the final segment, draw some elongated teardrops, then fill in around them.

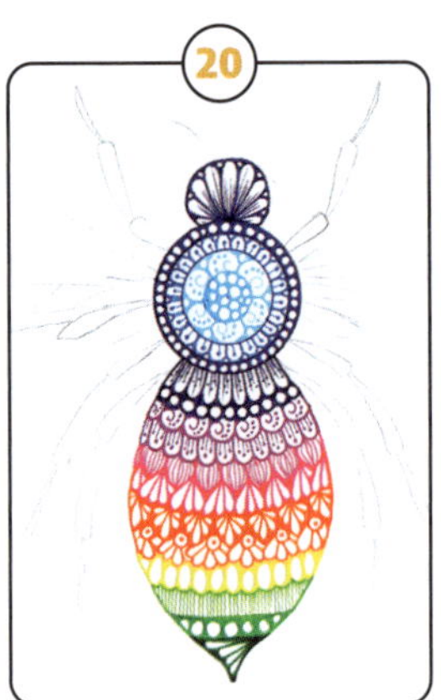

Fill the head. Use violet to create a pattern as shown that fills the bee's head.

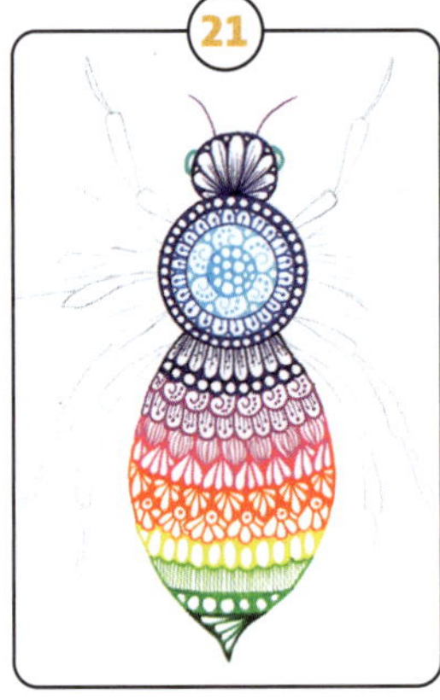

Finish the head. Use violet to trace the antennae. Use turquoise for the eyes.

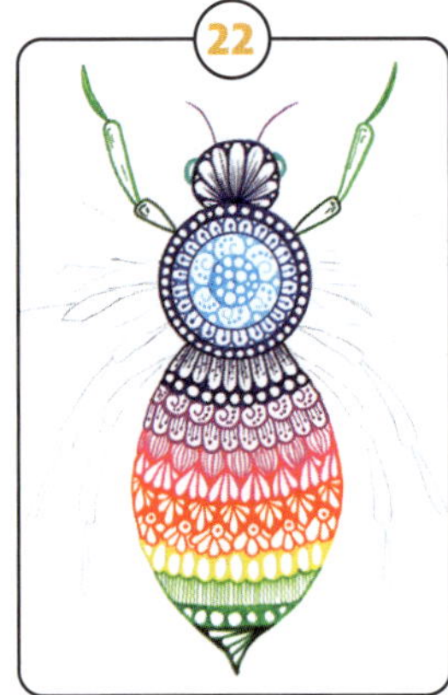

Color the front legs. Use dark green, medium green, and bright green to color the three segments of the front legs. Add a couple of detail lines for texture.

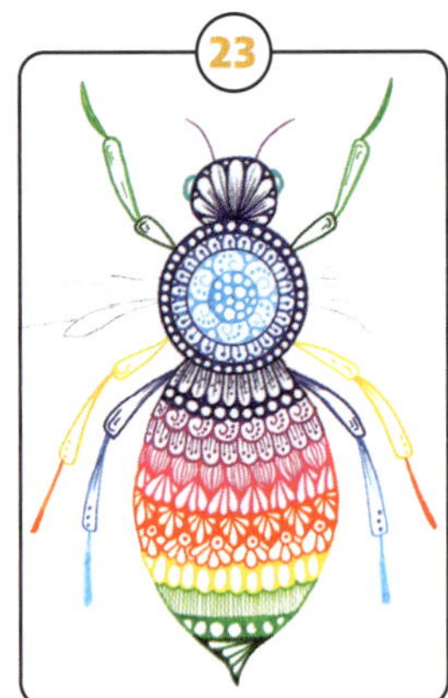

Color the remaining legs. Repeat step 22, using bright yellow, medium yellow, and orange for the middle legs and your three blues for the lower legs.

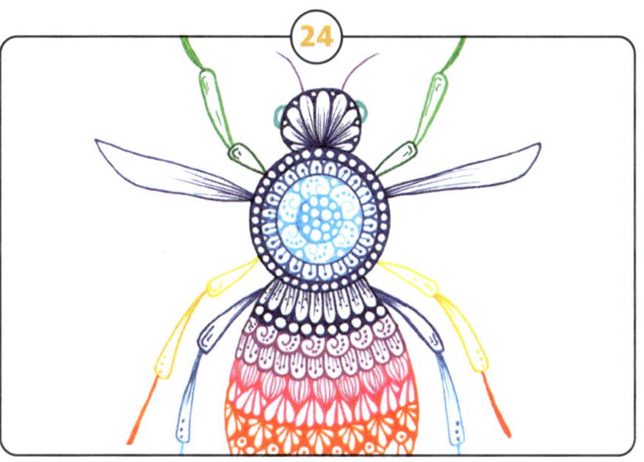

Start the wings. Using violet, trace the outline of one pair of wing segments. Add delicate detail lines emanating from near the body.

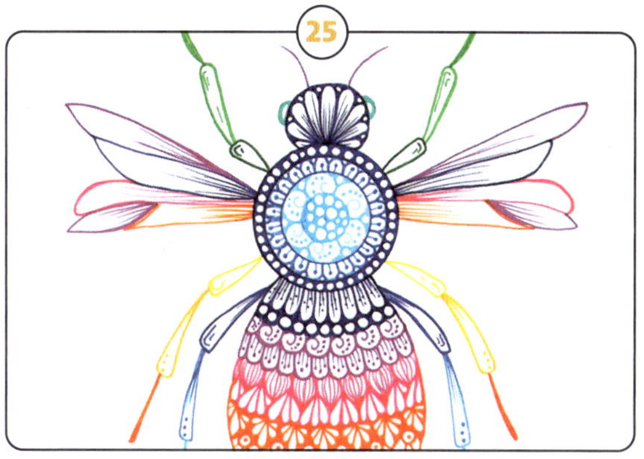

Continue the wings. Add two purple, one pink, and one orange segment to the wings.

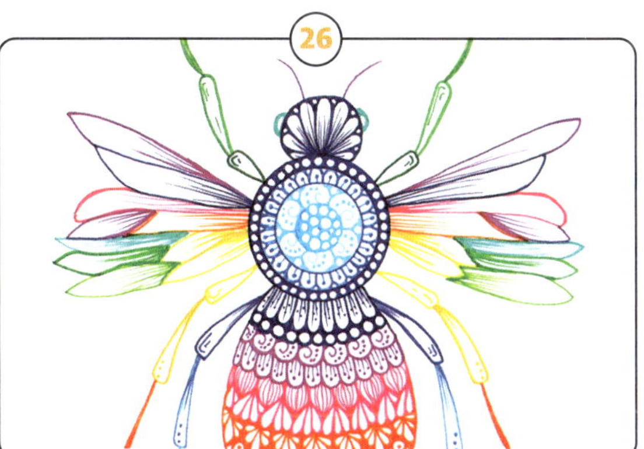

Keep adding to the wings. Add one segment each in bright yellow, medium yellow, bright green, medium green, and turquoise to the wings.

Finish the wings. Add two segments in light blue and one segment each in bright yellow, orange, violet, medium blue, dark blue, pink, and purple.

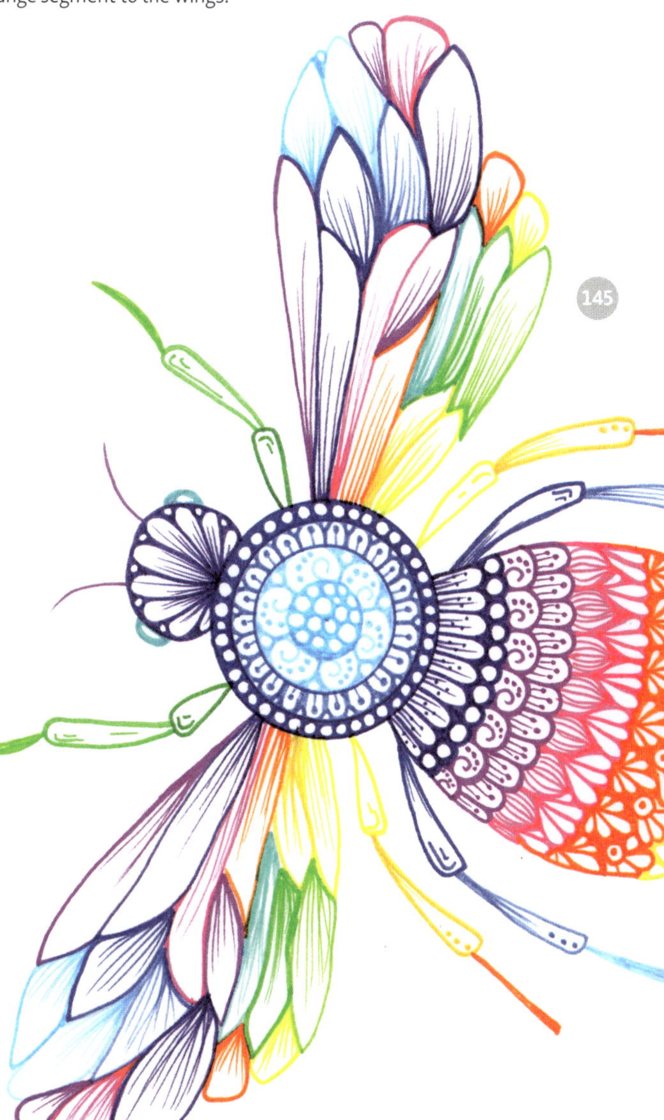

Turtle

At first glance the Turtle may seem simple, with its one central mandala for a shell, but it will teach you something new: how to freehand mandala designs in curvy, irregular spaces. In this case, that's the turtle's feet and head! By this point in the book, you are so practiced at drawing shapes with the help of guiding rays that you should be ready to leave the rays behind and freehand-fill small spaces.

As you draw this mandala, imagine that each ring of designs is adding to the sturdiness of a turtle's shell—its body, its protection, its home.

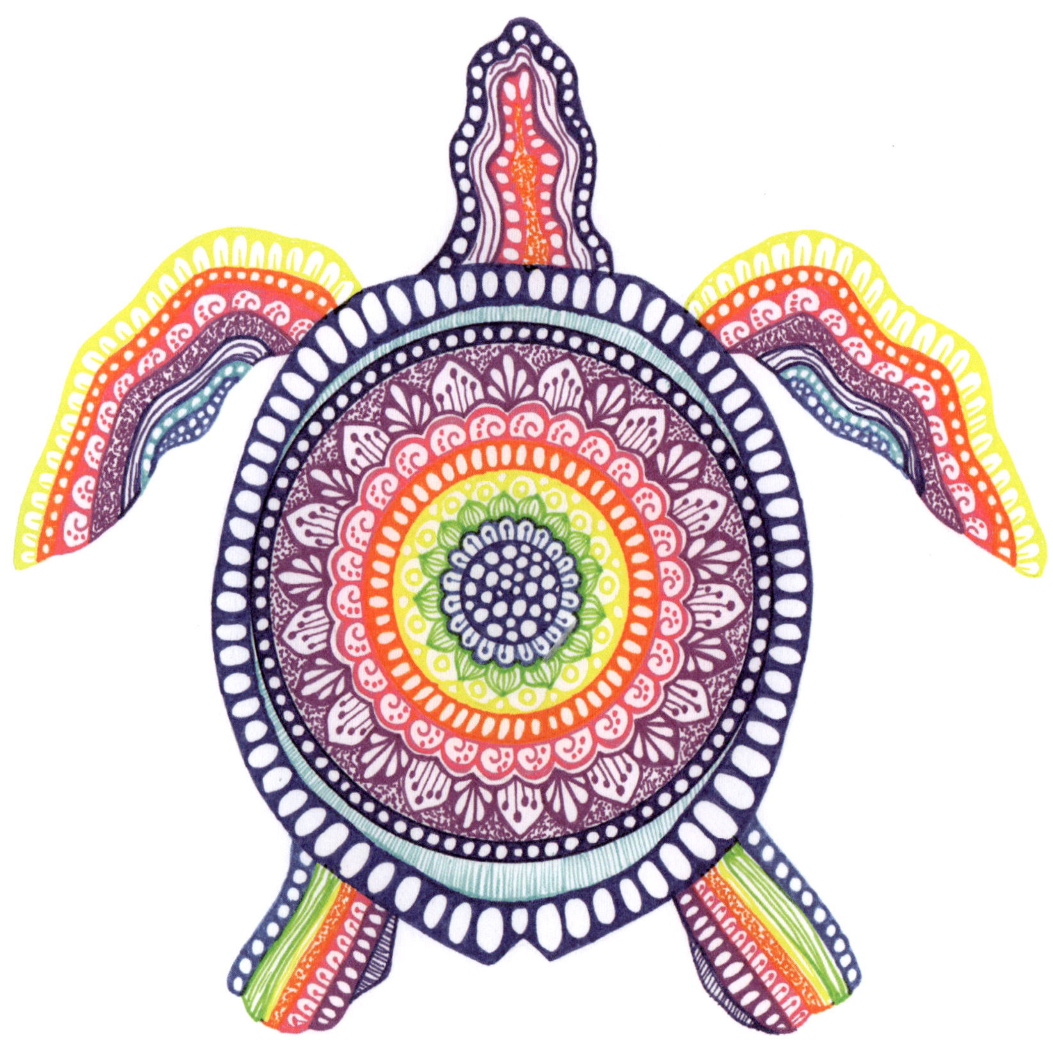

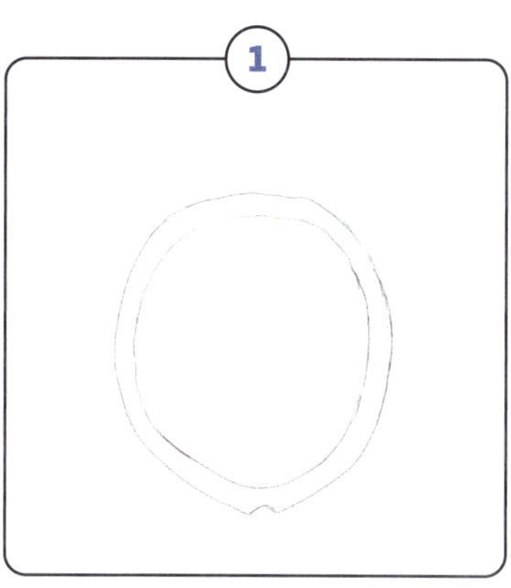

Draw the shell. Draw a not-quite-perfect-circle freehand shell with a notch at the bottom. Add an inset not-quite-perfect circle.

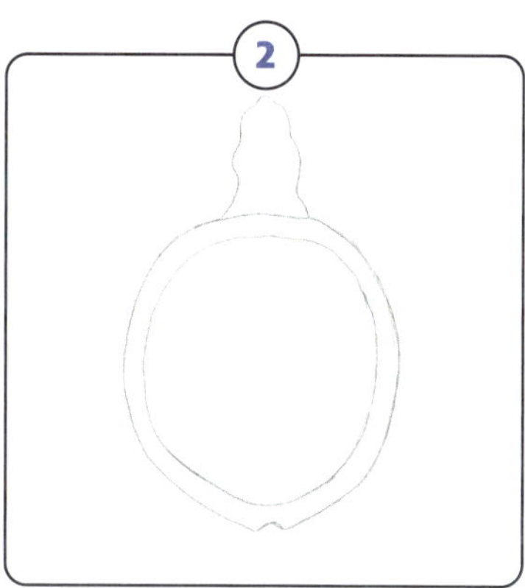

Add the head. At the top of the shell, draw a head shape with several dips and curves.

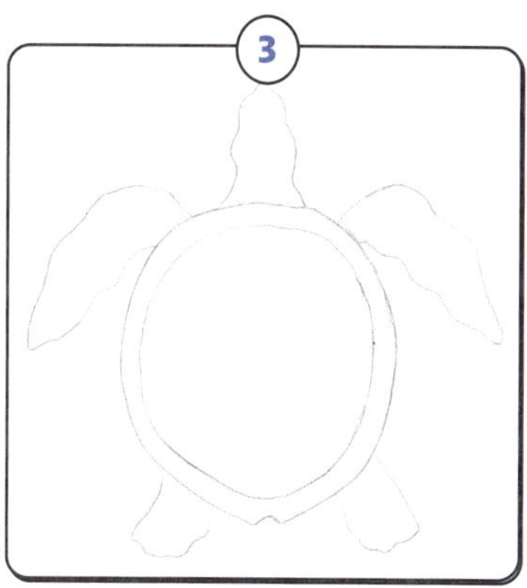

Add the feet. Add two long, wavy-edged front feet and two stumpy, smaller back feet.

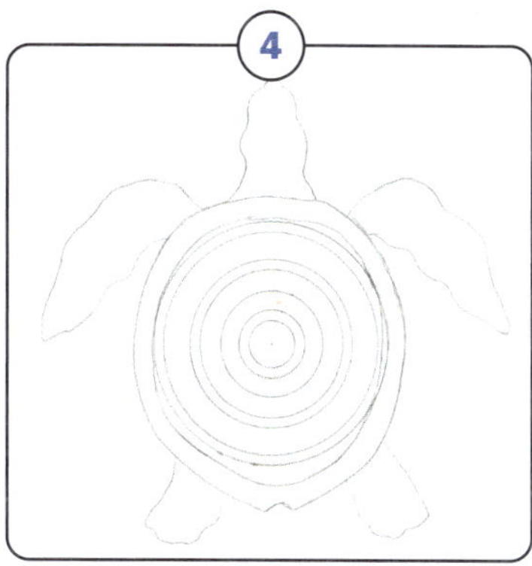

Draw circles. Draw seven circles inside the shell as shown. For reference, the outermost circle radius is 1¾" (4.3 cm); the innermost circle radius is ⁵⁄₁₆" (0.8 cm).

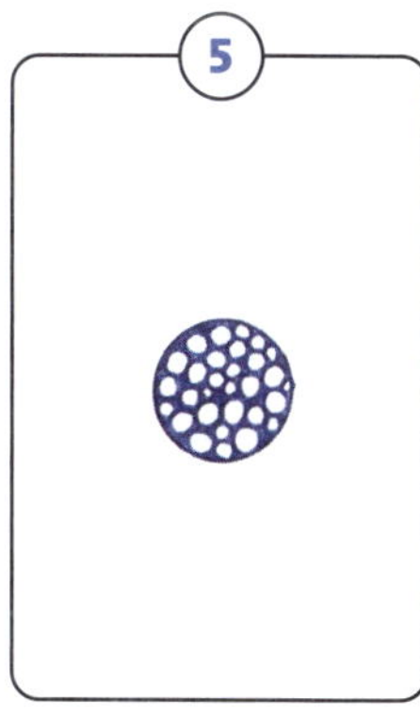

Fill the center. Use dark blue to draw densely packed circles of varying sizes in the center. Fill in around them.

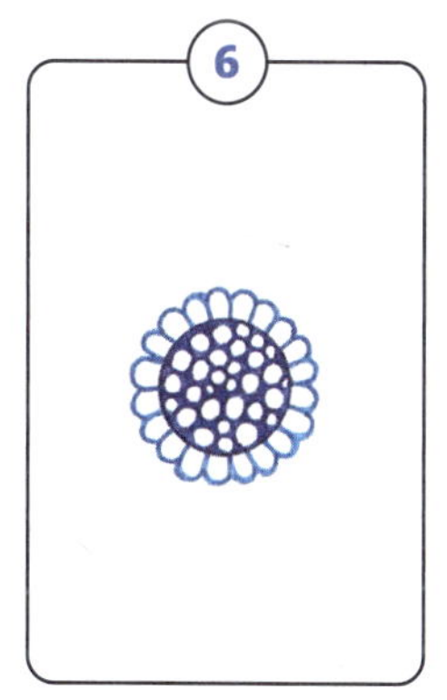

Start the first ring. Switch to medium blue. Fill the first ring with small domes.

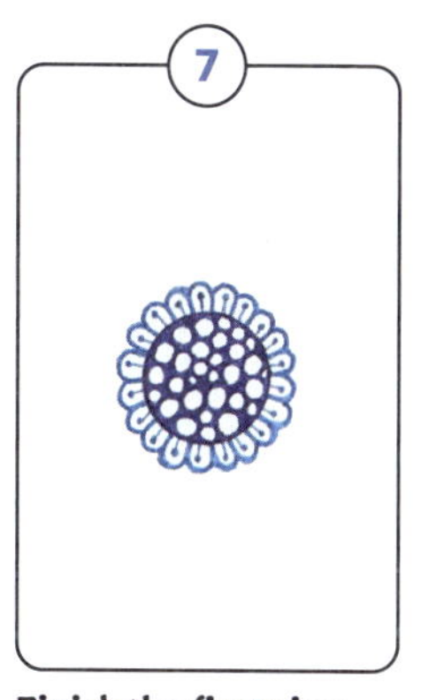

Finish the first ring. Add a line capped with a dot to each dome.

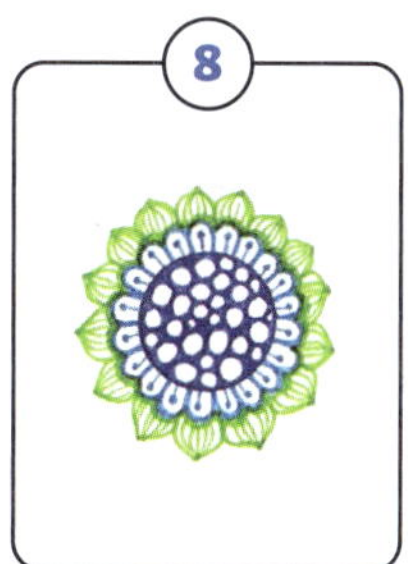

Add a new ring. Use pencil to add a fresh new ring. Switch to green. In this new ring, draw pointed leaves, then fill each one with the "onion" texture.

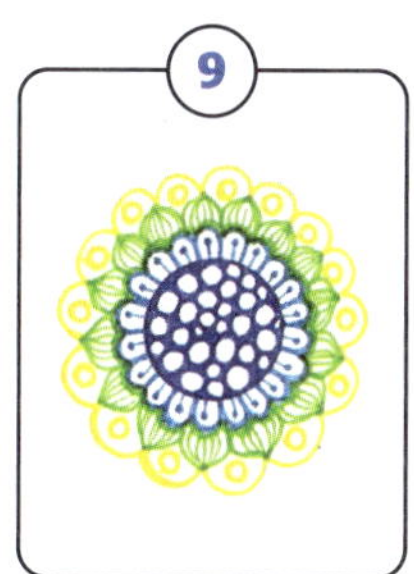

Start the next ring. Switch to yellow. Fill the next ring with domes, placing one dome between each pointed leaf. Add a circle to each dome.

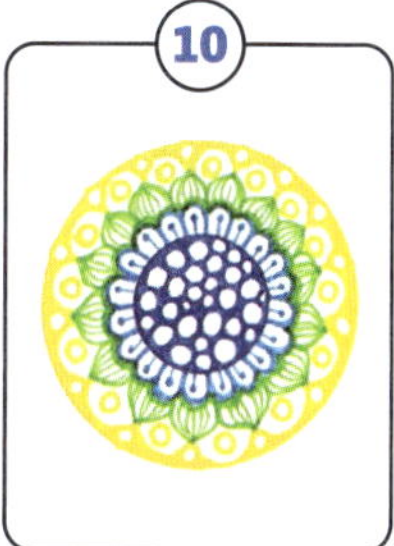

Finish this ring. Draw a tiny circle between each dome, then trace the entire circle right past these circles. Fill the remaining trapped space within the ring.

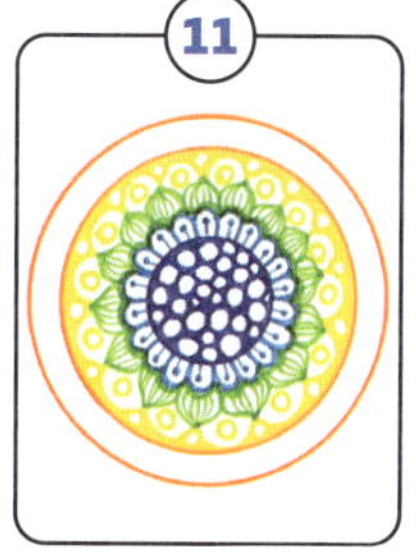

Outline the next ring. Switch to orange. Trace right along the edge of the finished yellow ring, then also trace the next circle.

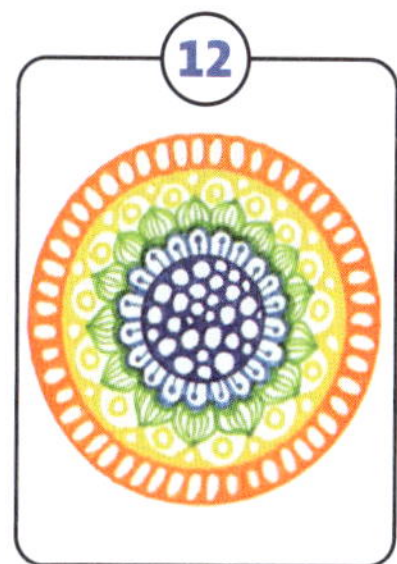

Fill this ring. Draw densely packed ovals in the ring, then fill in around them.

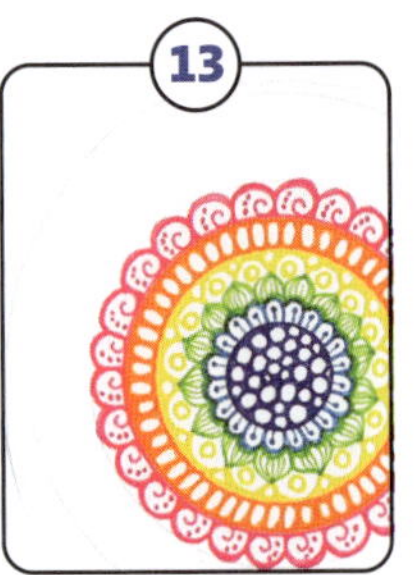

Make a pink ring. Switch to pink. Draw curling lines in the next ring. Add three dots to each. Thicken the outer border of the ring, following the wavy contour.

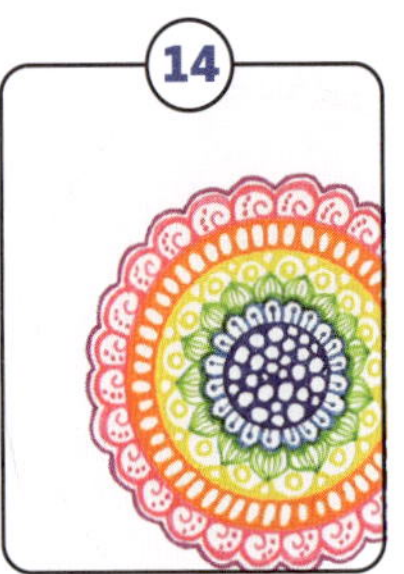

Add a purple outline. Switch to purple. Draw a wavy border that follows the contour of the pink ring, with just a little space between them.

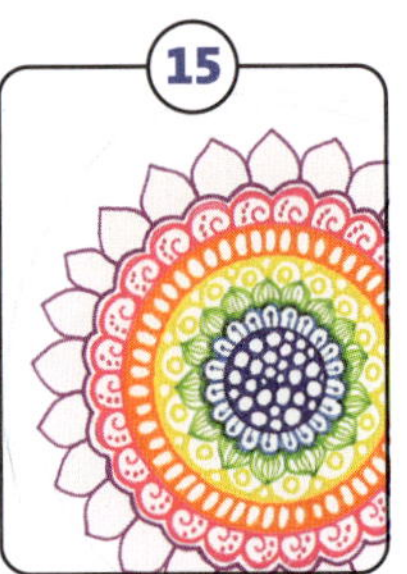

Start the next ring. In the next ring, draw a purple pointed leaf between each pink curling line of the previous ring.

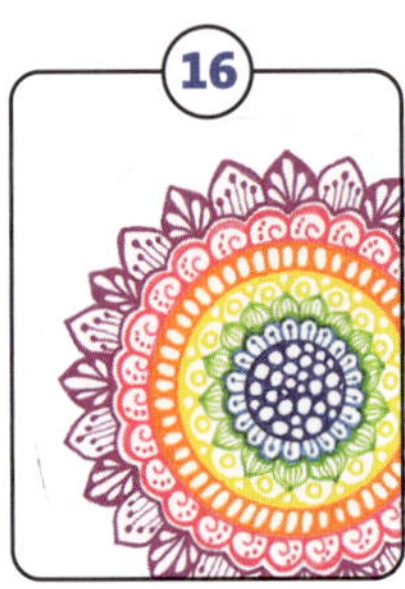

Add patterns to the leaves. Fill each leaf with one of two alternating patterns as shown.

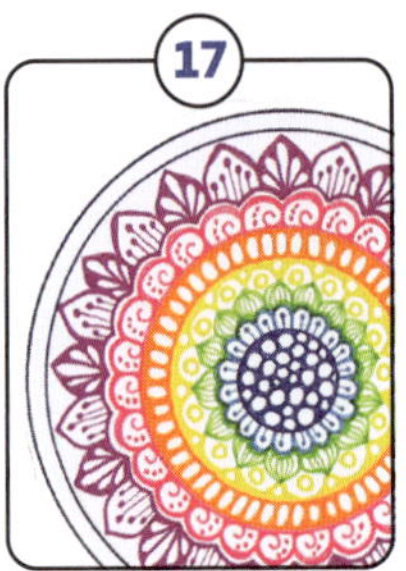

Outline the last ring. Switch to violet to trace the final two circles. Make sure you're tracing the circles, not the irregular inset shell shape you drew in step 1.

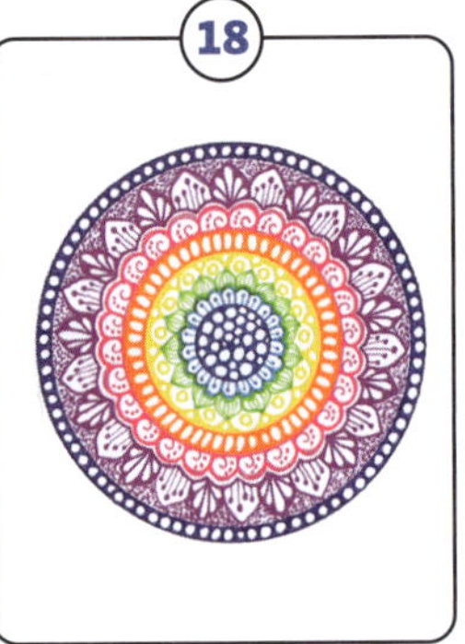

Fill the last ring. Draw circles in this final ring, then fill in around them. Switch back to purple to add stippling in the trapped space within the purple ring.

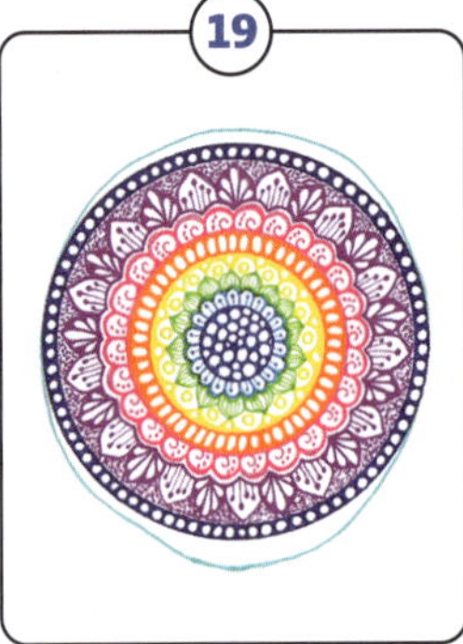

Outline the inset shell. Switch to aqua to trace the irregular inset shell shape you drew in step 1.

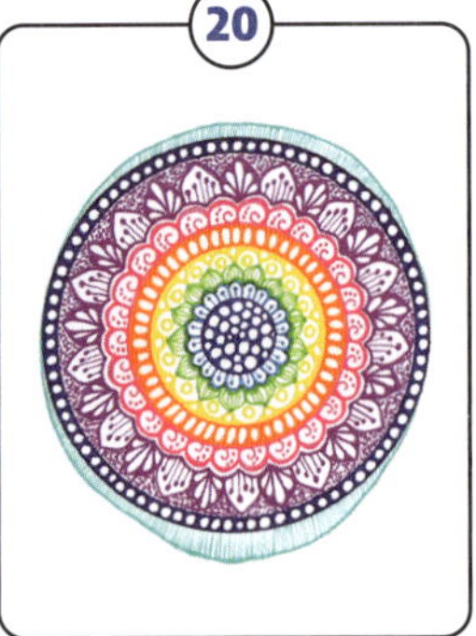

Fill the inset shape. In the spaces trapped between the inset shell and the violet ring, draw densely packed straight lines.

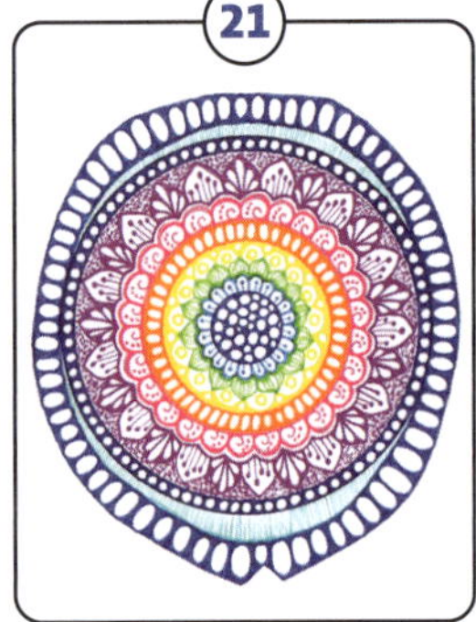

Finish the shell. Switch to dark blue. In the remaining space inside the main shell, draw densely packed ovals, then fill in around them.

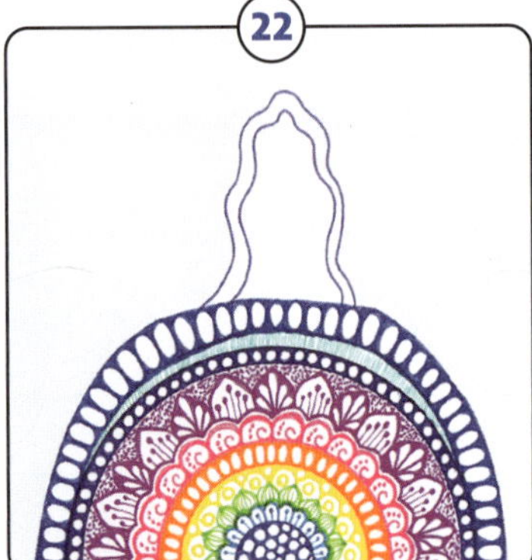

Start the head. Switch to violet. Trace the outline of the head, then draw an inset head outline inside it.

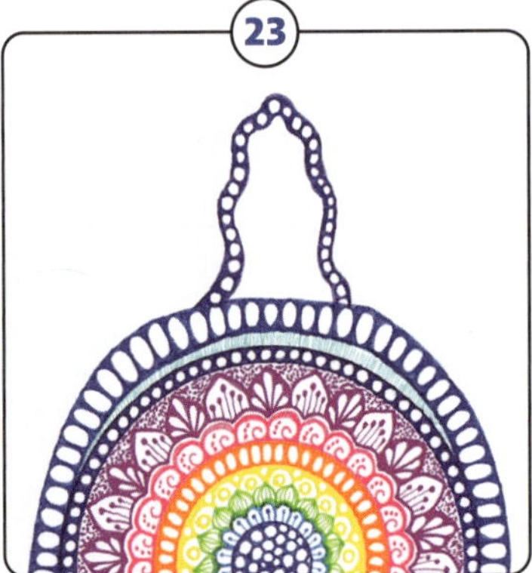

Fill the first section. Draw densely packed circles inside this first section—not really a ring, since it's not circular! Then fill in around them.

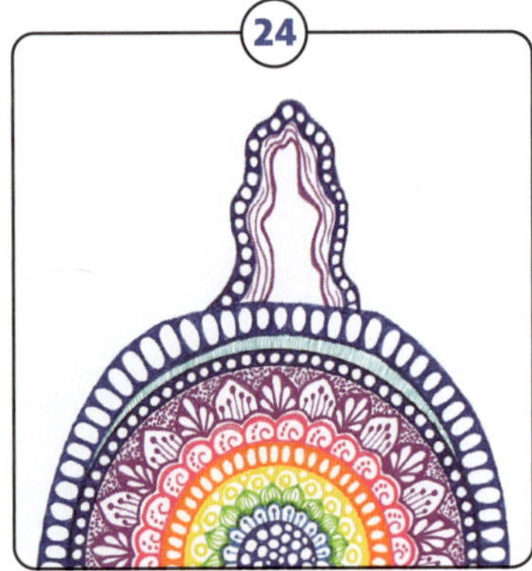

Create a new section. Switch to purple to draw another inset head. Fill this new section with several long broken and unbroken lines.

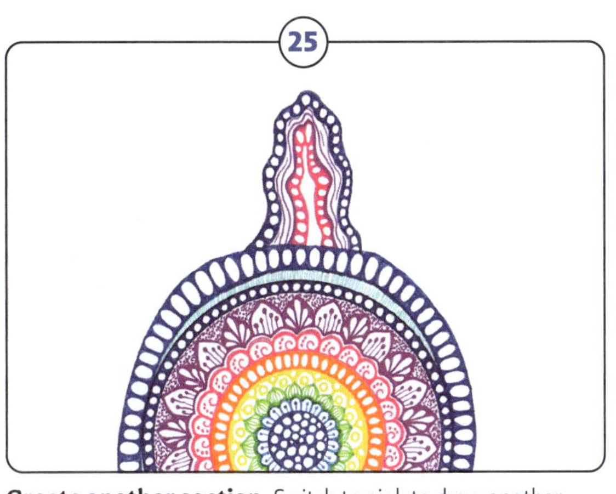

Create another section. Switch to pink to draw another inset head. Fill this new section with densely packed ovals, then fill in around them.

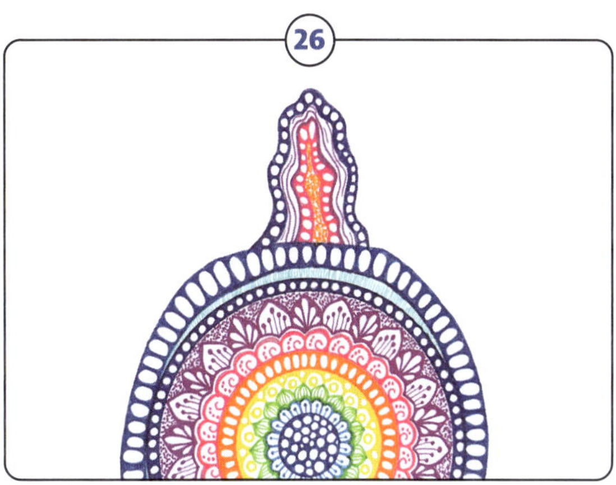

Finish the head. Switch to orange. Fill the remaining center of the head with dense stippling.

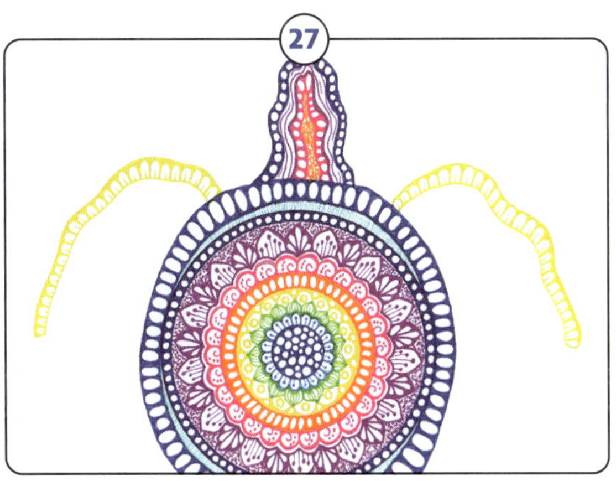

Start the front feet. Switch to yellow. Draw a line that follows the contour of the top of the foot. Fill the section with a dome pattern as shown.

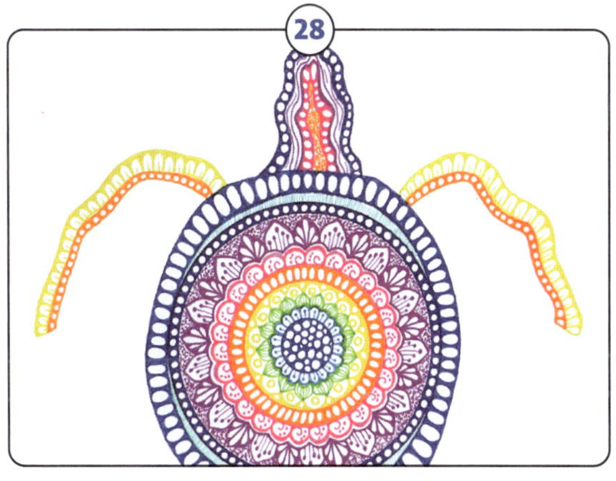

Switch to orange. Draw a new line in orange. Fill the section with densely packed circles, then fill in around them.

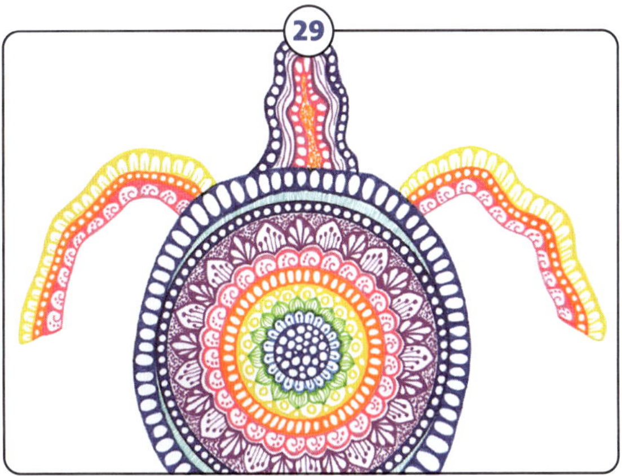

Switch to pink. Draw a new line in pink. Fill the section with curling lines, then fill in around them. Add a few dots inside each curling line.

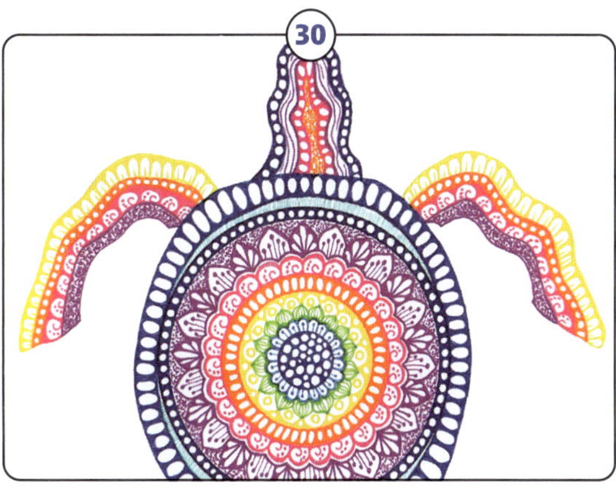

Switch to purple. Draw a new line in purple. Fill the section with dense stippling.

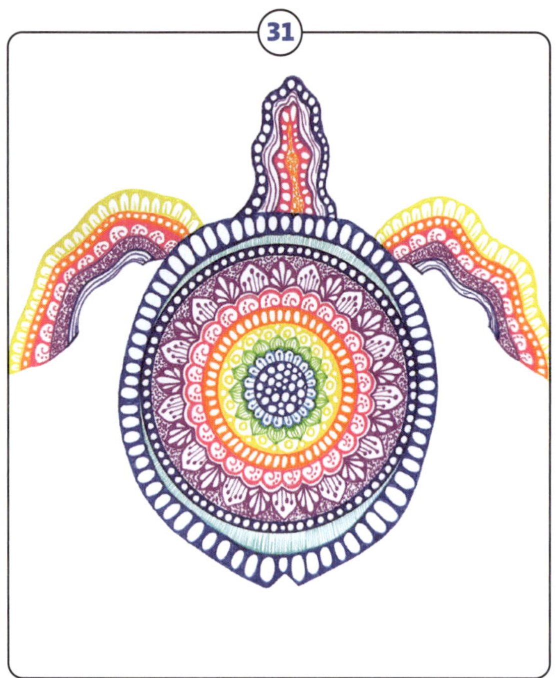

Switch to violet. Draw a new line in violet. Fill the section with several long broken and unbroken lines.

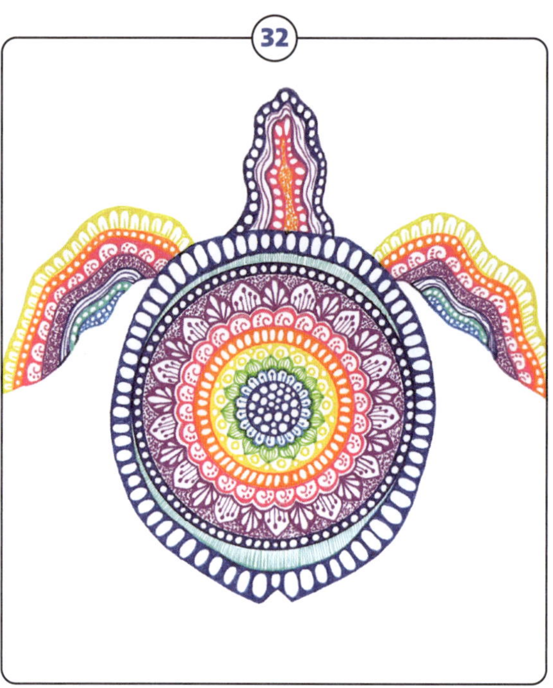

Finish the front feet. Repeat step 28 but with aqua. Then fill the remaining space within the front feet using medium blue to draw circles of varying sizes.

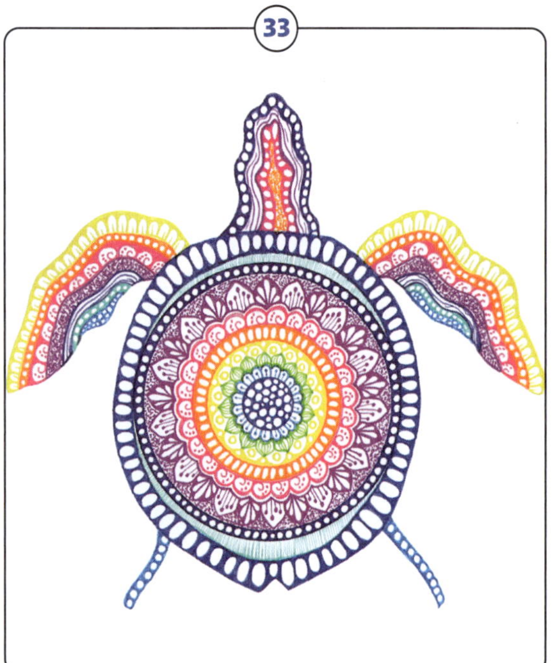

Start the back feet. Still using medium blue, draw a line that follows the contour of the top of the foot. Fill the section with densely packed circles.

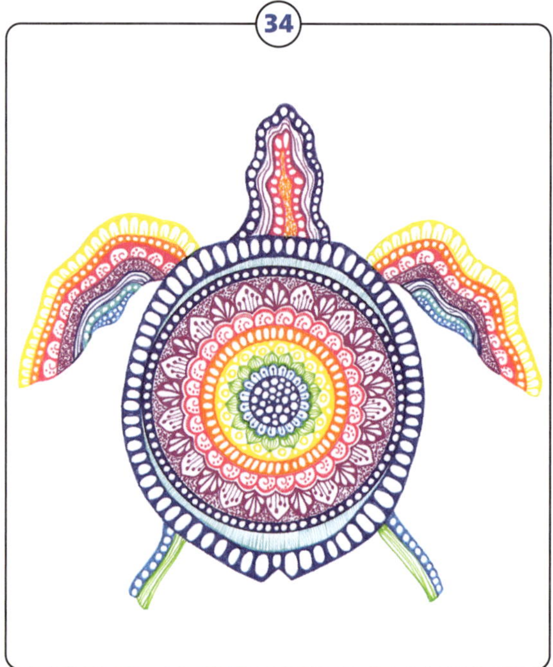

Switch to green. Draw a new line in green. Fill the section with several long broken and unbroken lines.

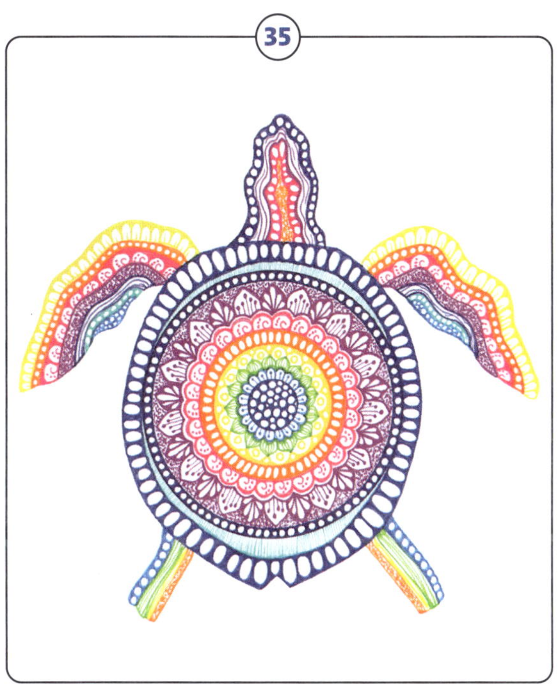

Do two more color sections. Repeat step 34 but with yellow. Then repeat step 30 but with orange.

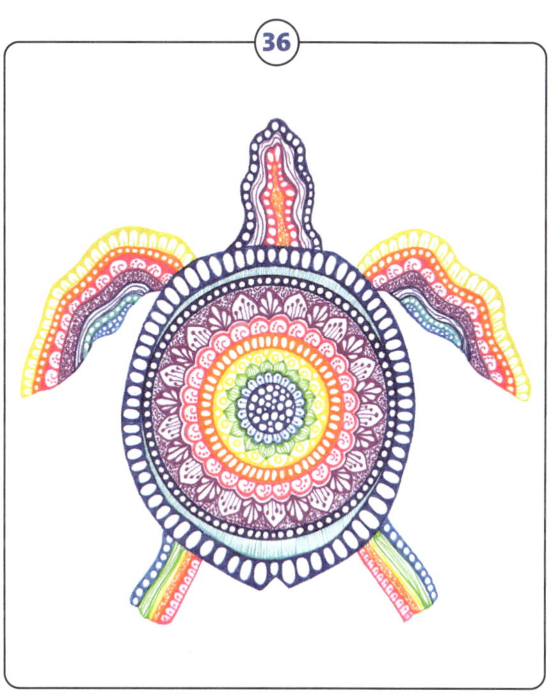

Switch to pink. Draw a new line in pink. Fill the section with a dome pattern as shown.

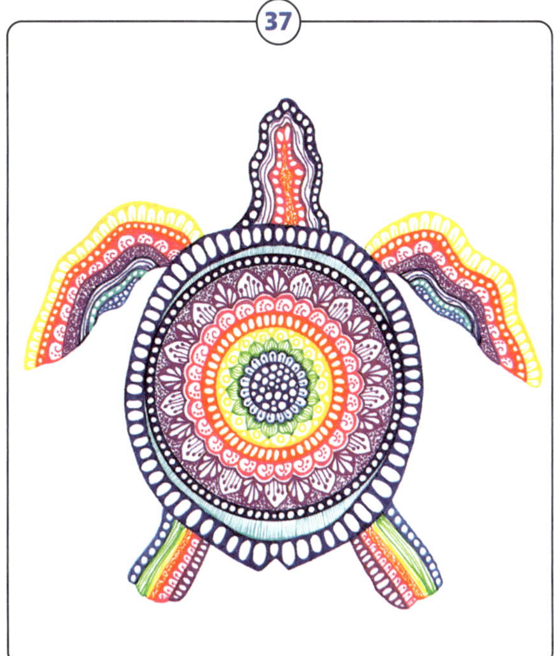

Switch to purple. Draw a new line in purple. Fill the section with densely packed ovals, then fill in around them.

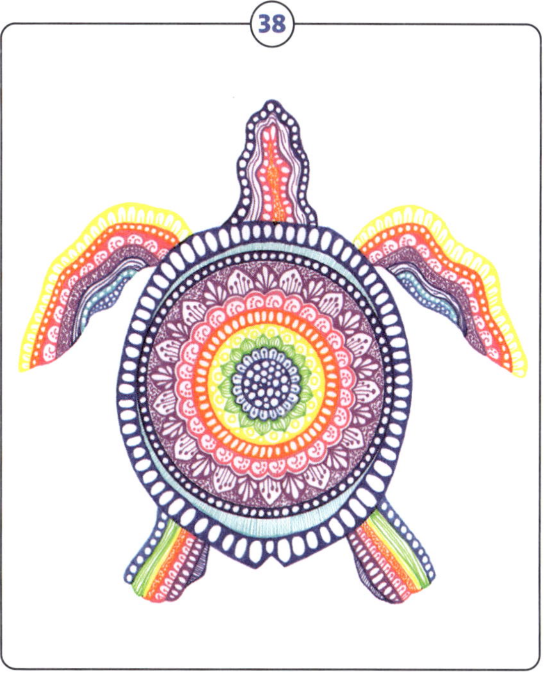

Finish with violet. Trace the remaining space in violet. Fill this last section with straight lines.

Elephant

The Elephant combines a lot of what you've learned up to this point in the Animals section: multiple mandalas, freehand sections without ray guidelines, and a surprising sense of realism. Pick out your colors ahead of time, take care when drawing each section, and you're sure to be delighted by your finished piece.

INTENTION

As you draw this mandala, reflect on your personal relationships to elephants, or other animals that have a history entwined with humans.

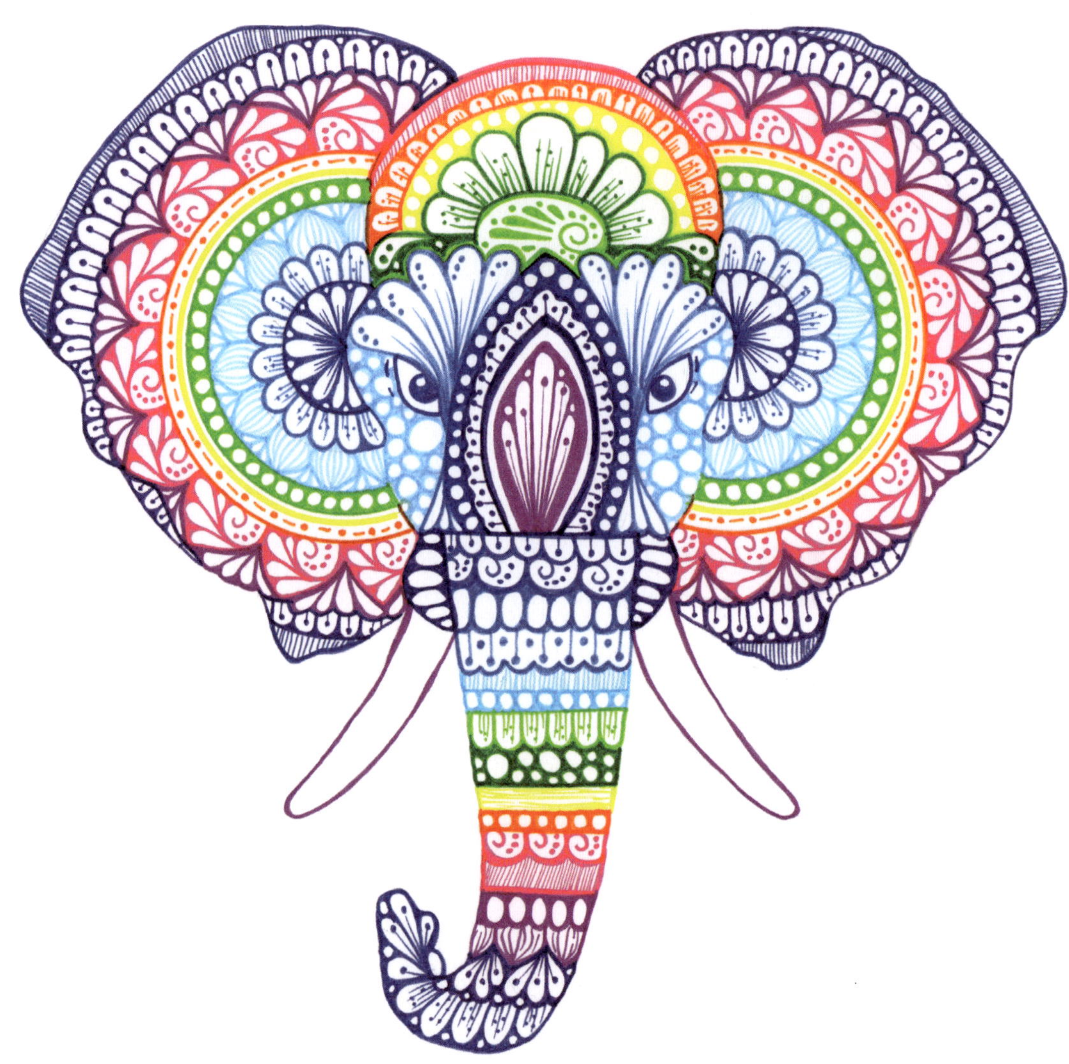

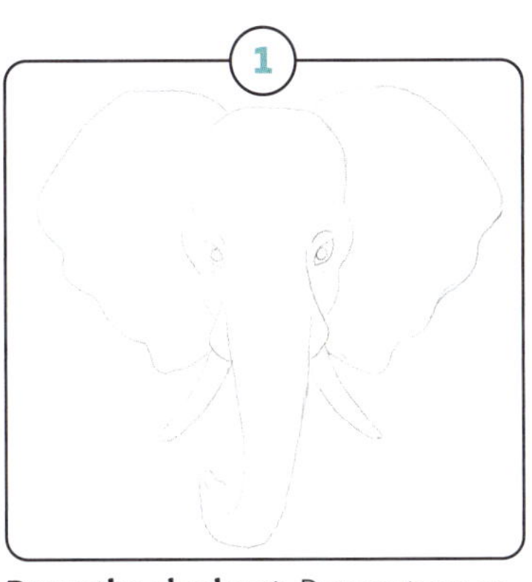

Draw the elephant. Draw or trace an elephant outline, including detailed eyes. Make your drawing as symmetrical as you can.

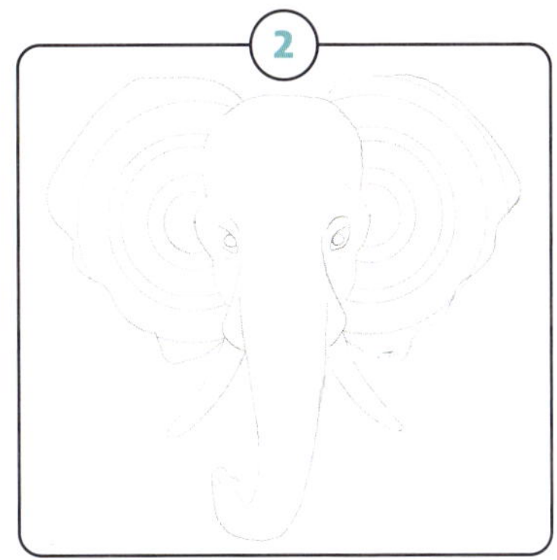

Draw circles. Draw six circles in each ear as shown. For reference, the outermost circle radius is 2¹⁄₁₆" (5.2 cm); the innermost circle radius is ⅞" (1.1 cm).

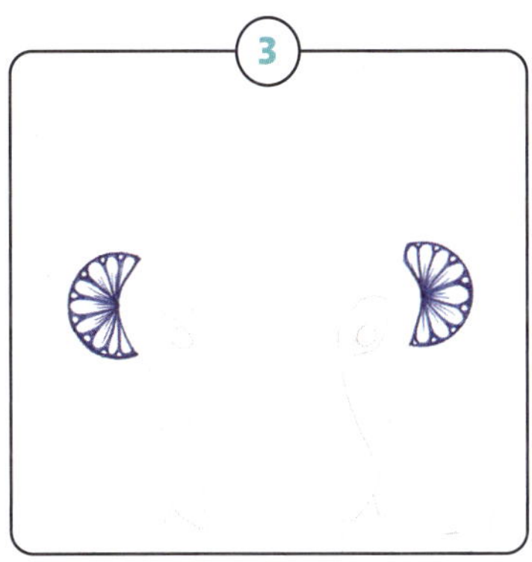

Fill the center. Using dark blue, fill the center with a teardrop pattern as shown.

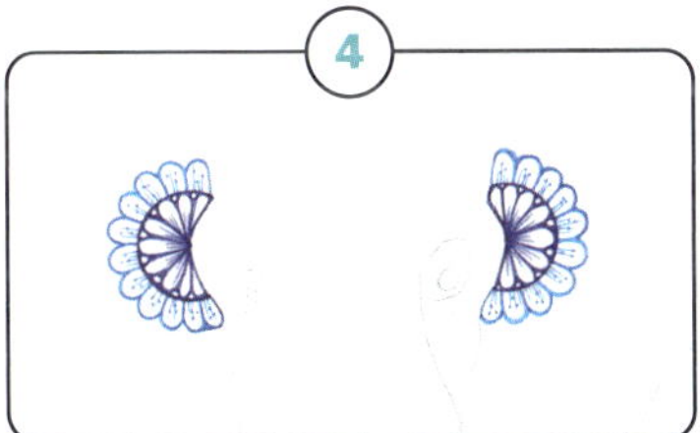

Complete the first ring. Switch to medium blue. Draw domes in the next ring. Add a few delicate lines and dots to each dome.

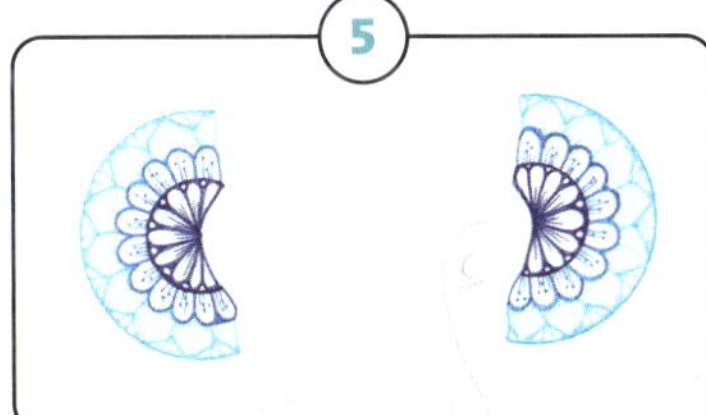

Add a new ring. Use a pencil to add a new circle to the mandala, creating a new ring. Switch to light blue. Fill the new ring with pointed leaves and teardrops as shown.

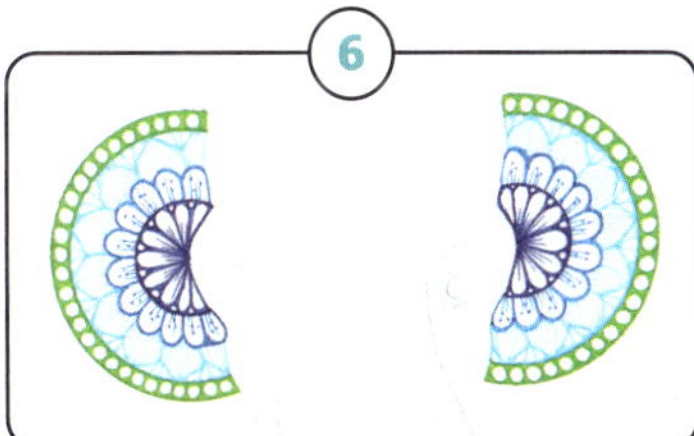

Fill the next ring. Switch to bright green. Draw densely packed circles in the next ring, then fill in around them.

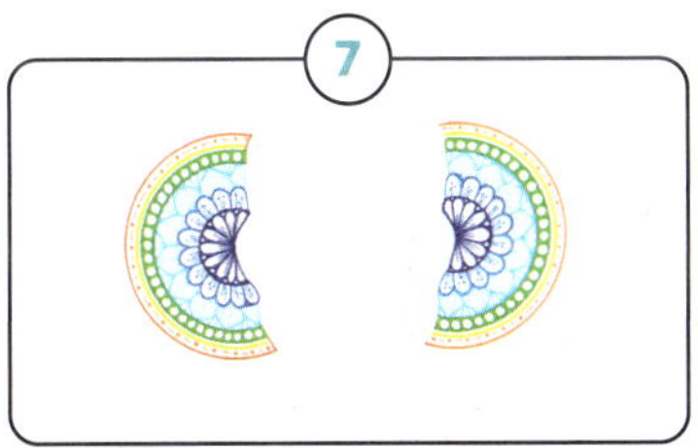

Use two colors in the next ring. Trace the next circle with orange. Inside this ring, draw alternating dashes and dots in orange. Then add a thick yellow line.

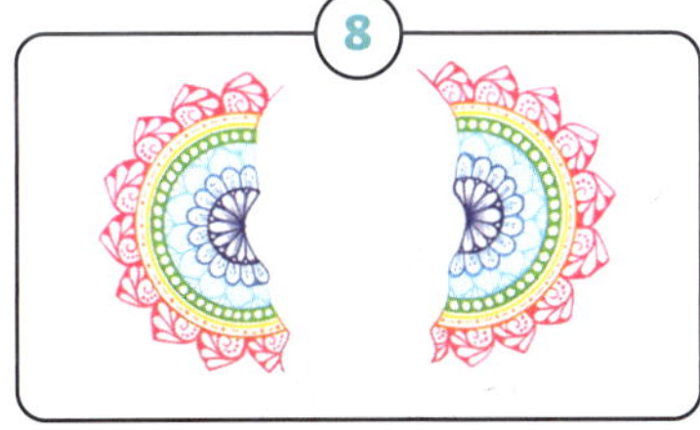

Start the next ring. Switch to pink. Draw pointed leaves in the next ring. Fill each one with a pattern as shown.

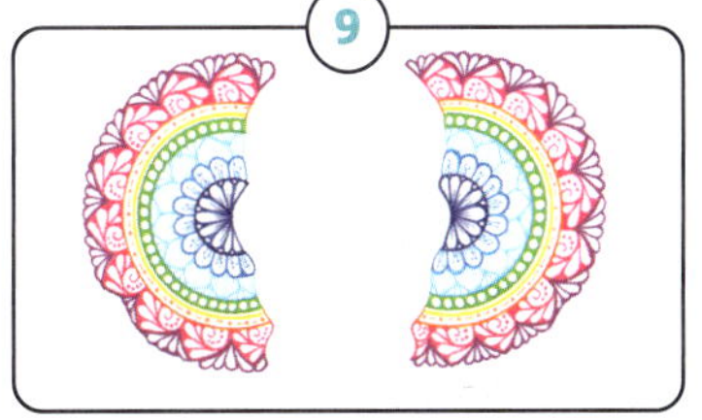

Finish this ring. Switch to purple. Draw four teardrops between each pointed leaf.

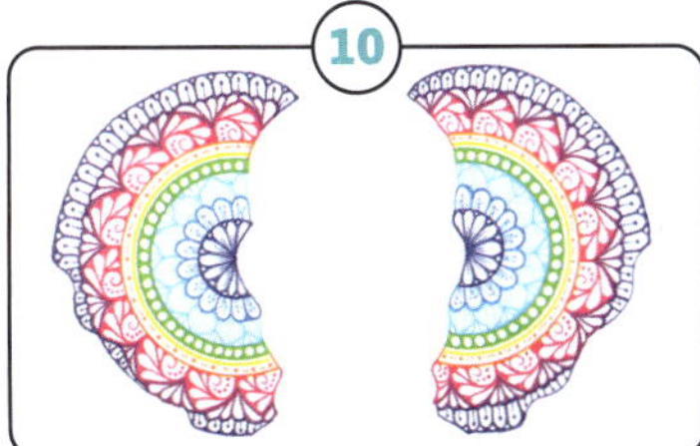

Complete another ring. Switch to violet. Fill the next ring with domes. Add a line capped with a dot to each dome. Draw a tiny circle between each dome.

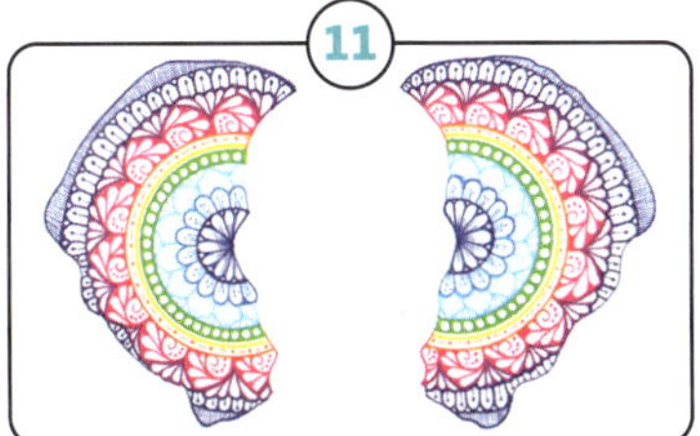

Finish the ears. Switch to dark blue. Trace the edges of the remaining spaces at the top and bottom of the ear. Fill the spaces with straight lines.

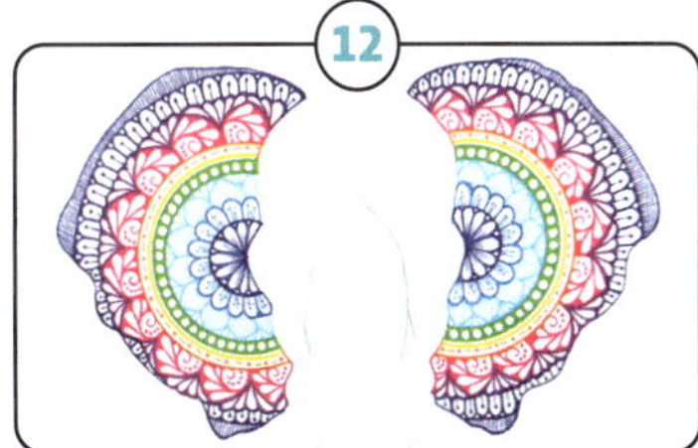

Start the head. Using a pencil, draw a straight line across the elephant's face, above the tusks, then a single large, pointed leaf between the elephant's eyes.

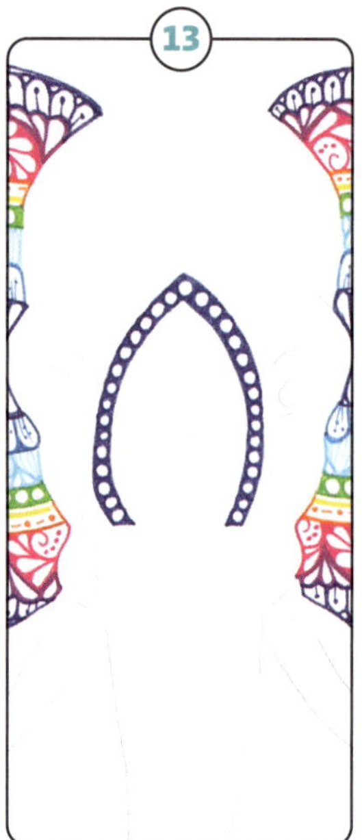

Start adding color. Outline the large leaf in dark blue. Draw an inset leaf inside it. Fill the section with densely packed circles, then fill in around them.

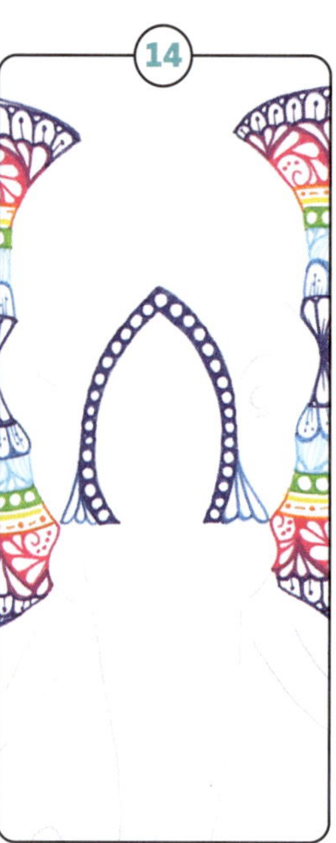

Close off the face. Switch to medium blue. Draw three teardrops on either side of the base of the large leaf, closing off the line between the tusks/trunk and face.

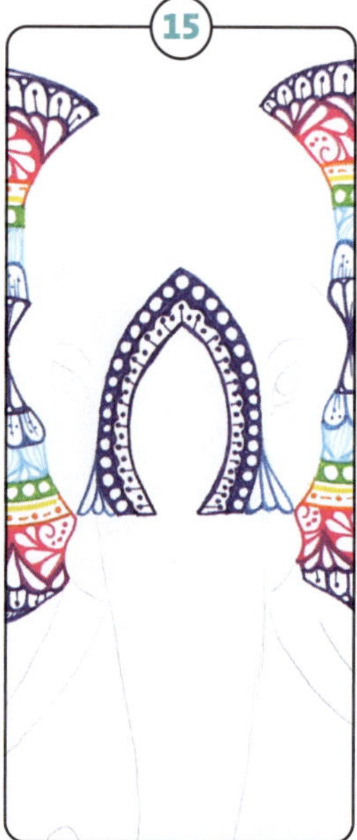

Add a new section to the leaf. Switch to violet. Draw another inset leaf. Fill the section with alternating dots and lines capped with dots.

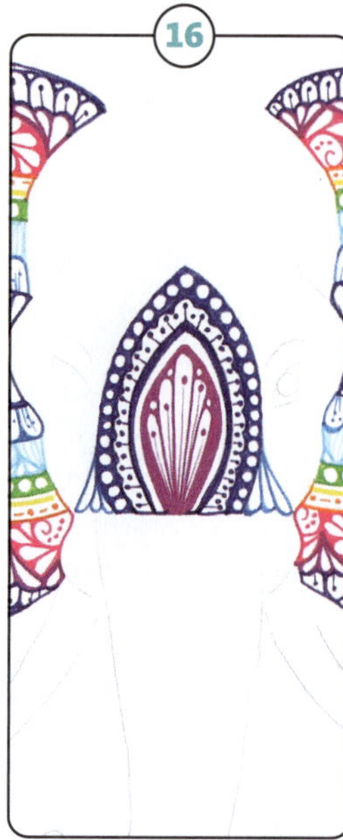

Finish the leaf. Switch to purple. Draw a central emblem inside the large leaf as shown.

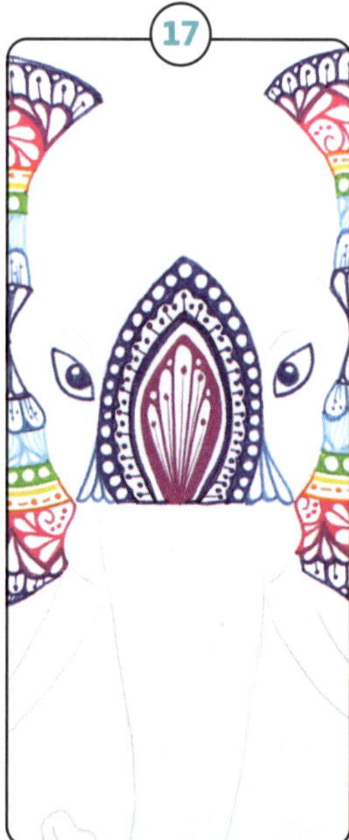

Color the eyes. Switch to dark blue. Trace and fill in the eyes.

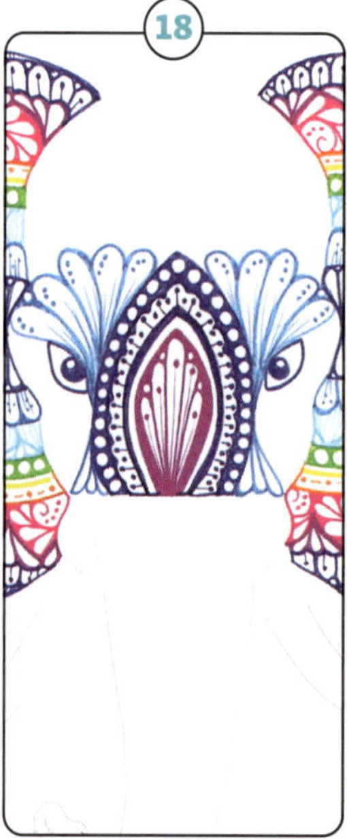

Detail the browbones. Switch to medium blue. Fill both browbones above the eyes with a teardrop design as shown.

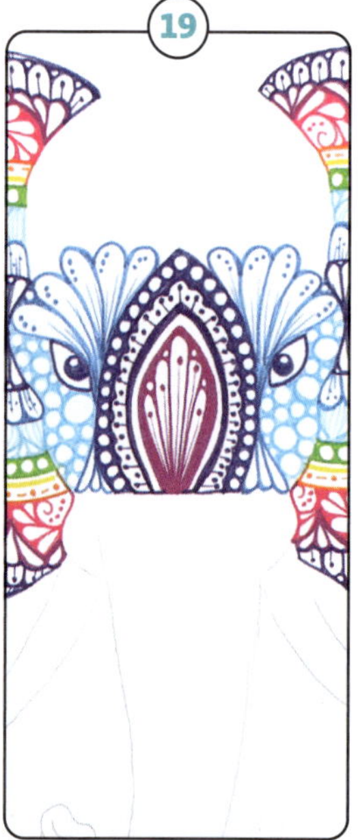

Finish the lower face. Switch to light blue. Draw circles of varying sizes in the remaining space around the eyes, then fill in around them.

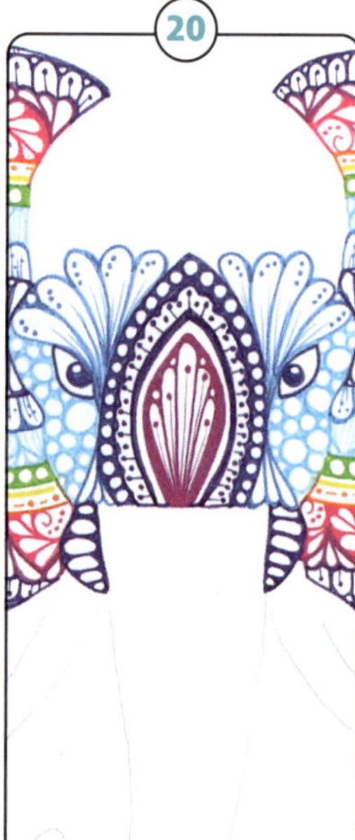

Color above the tusks. Switch to violet. Fill the small section above each tusk on either side of the trunk with ovals, then fill in around them.

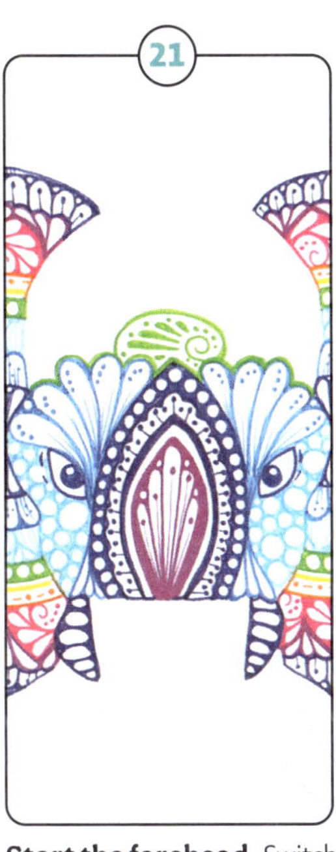

Start the forehead. Switch to bright green. Outline the wavy edge of the teardrops above the eyes, then draw an elaborate curling-line design above that.

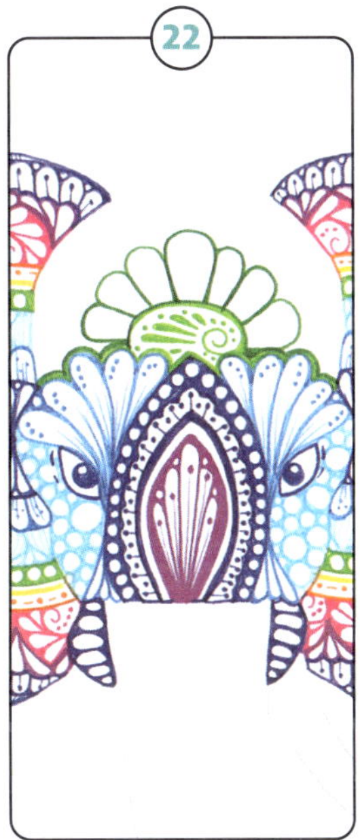

Add petals. Switch to dark green. Outline the entire edge of what you just drew. Draw seven large petals sticking out from the curling-line design.

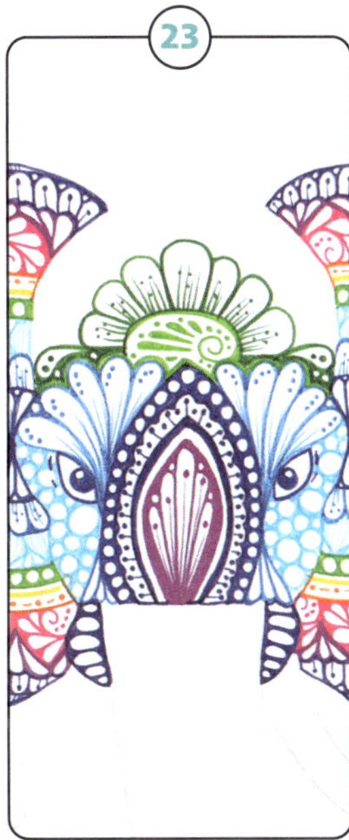

Add details. Detail the petals as shown. Add a small teardrop and a couple of tiny circles on each side of the forehead, then fill in below them.

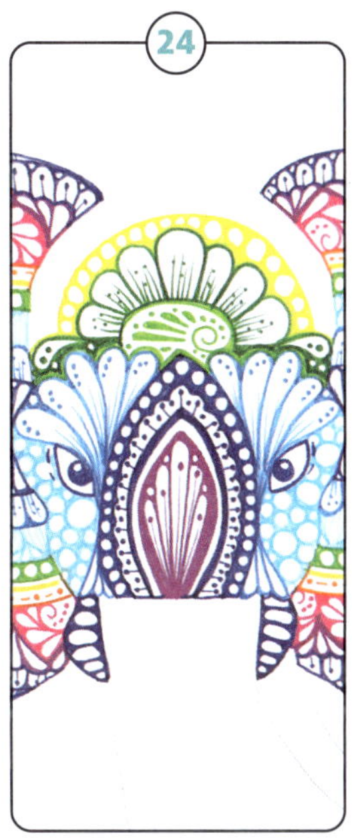

Add a new section. Switch to yellow. Draw an arched line above the dark-green section, fill it with densely packed circles, then fill in around them.

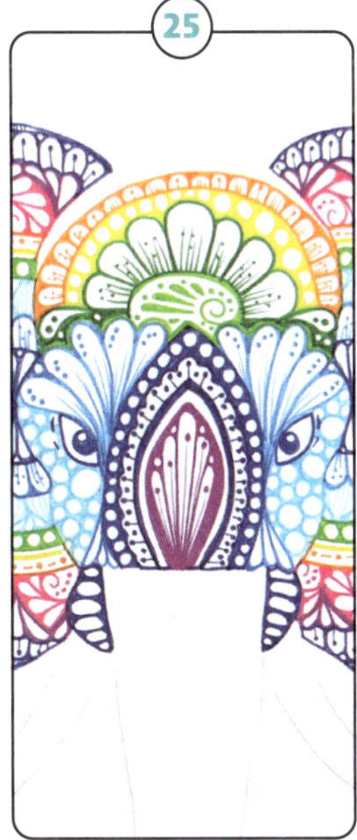

Add another section. Switch to orange. Draw another arched line above the yellow section, then fill it with a dome pattern as shown.

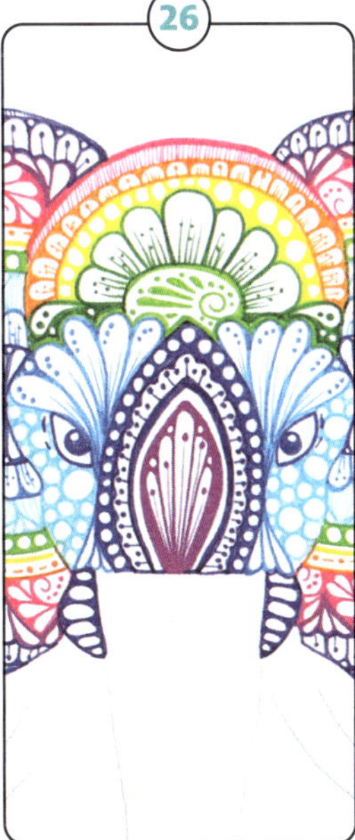

Finish the forehead. Switch to pink. Trace the entire outline of the remaining area of the head. Fill this section with straight lines.

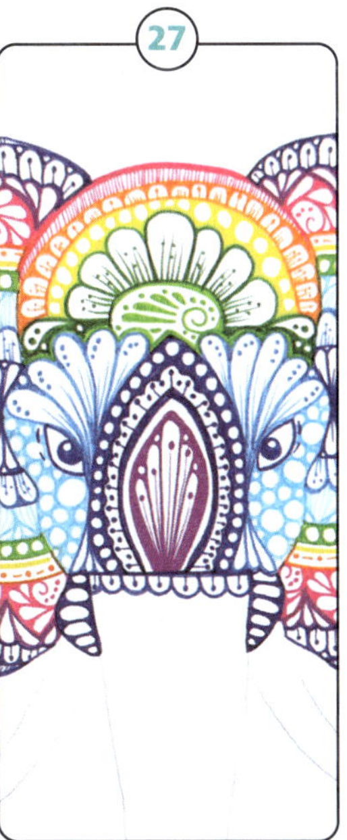

Start the trunk. Switch to dark blue. At the top of the trunk, draw a row of domes. Add a line capped with a dot to each dome.

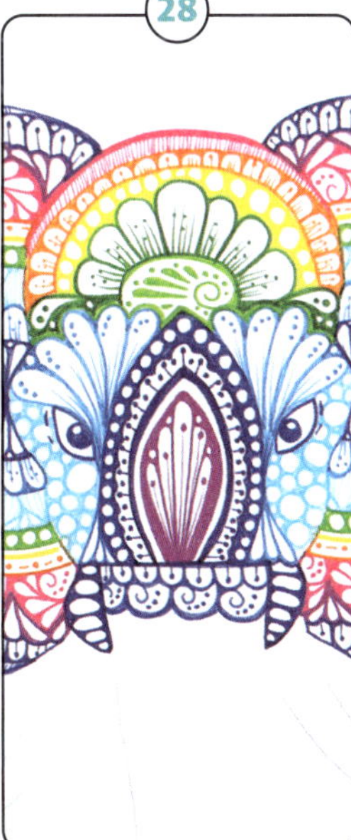

Continue with dark blue. Add a row of curling lines. Add dots inside each curling line.

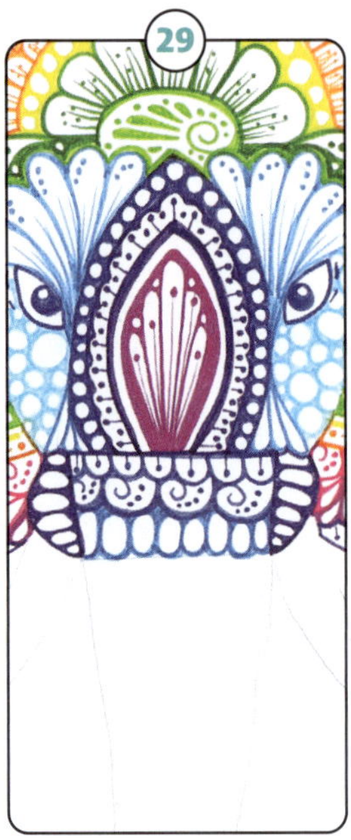

Add guidelines. Use pencil to draw 12 straight guidelines across the remaining trunk. Switch to medium blue. Fill the next row with ovals.

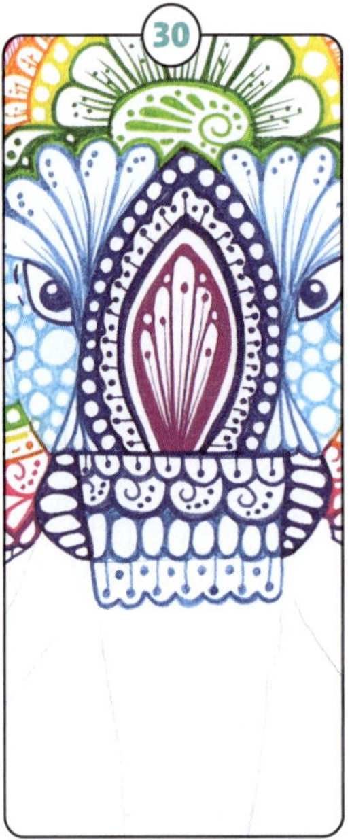

Add a new row. Still using medium blue, add a row of alternating dots and lines capped with dots. Draw a wavy border below it along the pencil guideline.

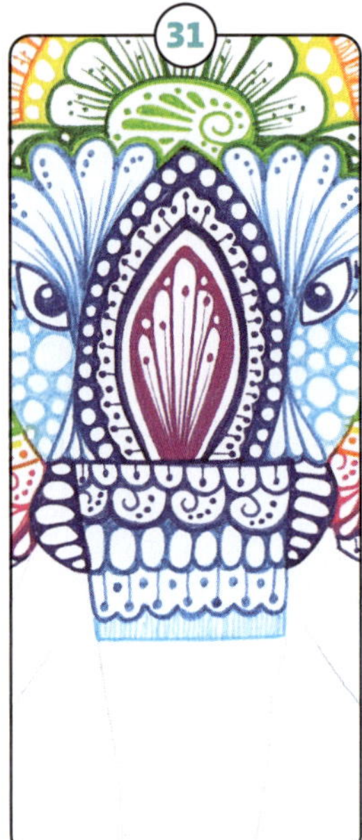

Switch to light blue. Trace the next pencil guideline. Fill the section with straight lines.

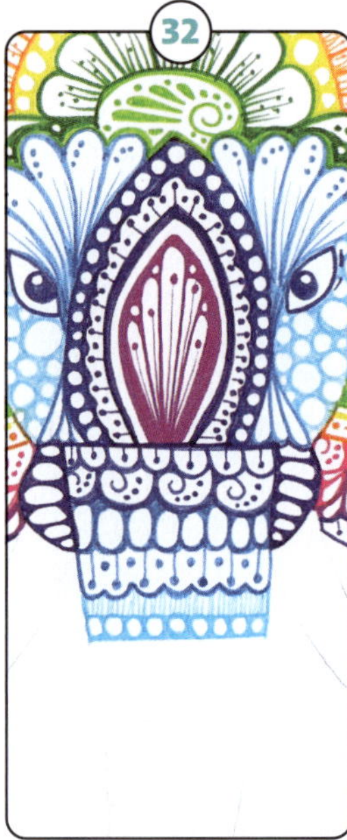

Add a new row. Still using light blue, trace the next pencil guideline. Fill the section with circles, then fill in around them.

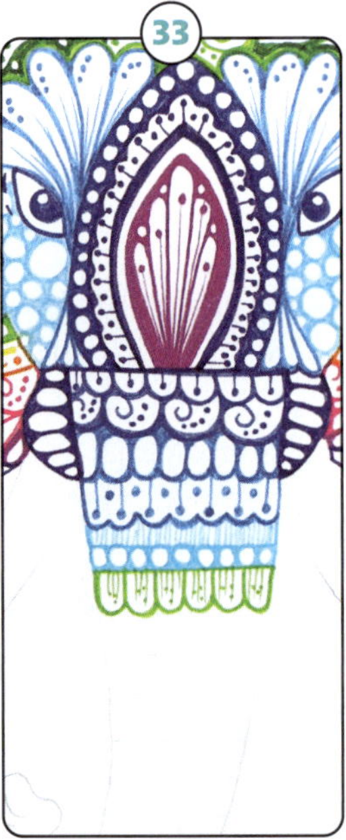

Switch to bright green. Fill the next row with domes. Add delicate detail lines and dots to each dome.

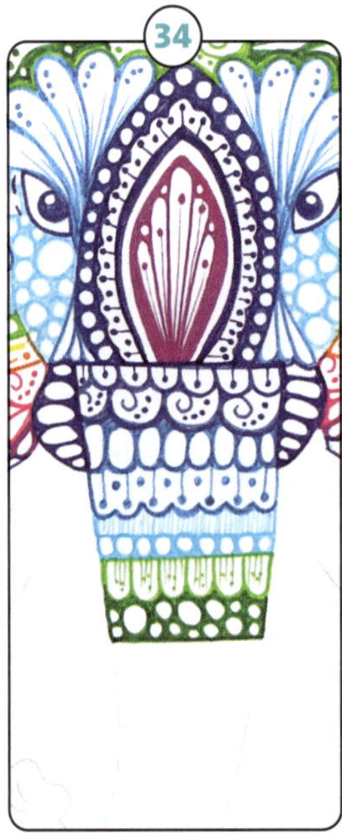

Switch to dark green. Trace the next pencil guideline. Fill the section with circles of varying sizes, then fill in around them.

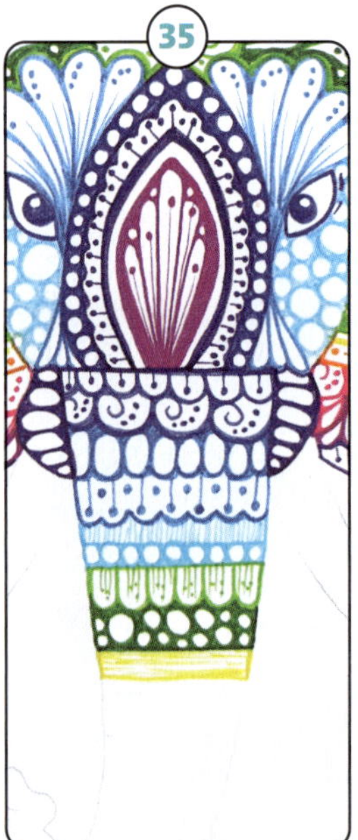

Switch to yellow. Trace the next pencil guideline. Fill the section with long, horizontal lines.

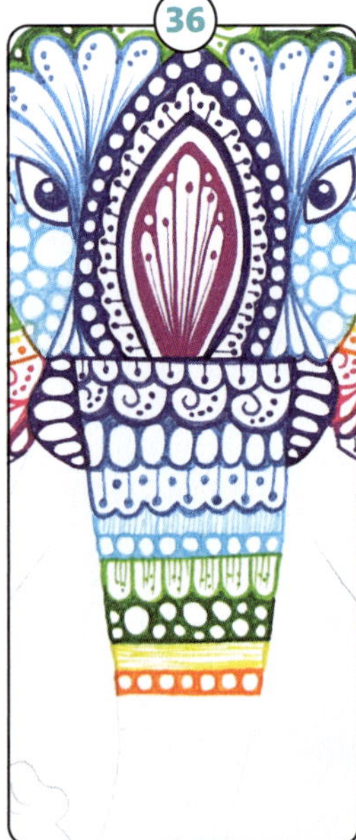

Switch to orange. Trace the next pencil guideline. Fill the section with circles, then fill in around them.

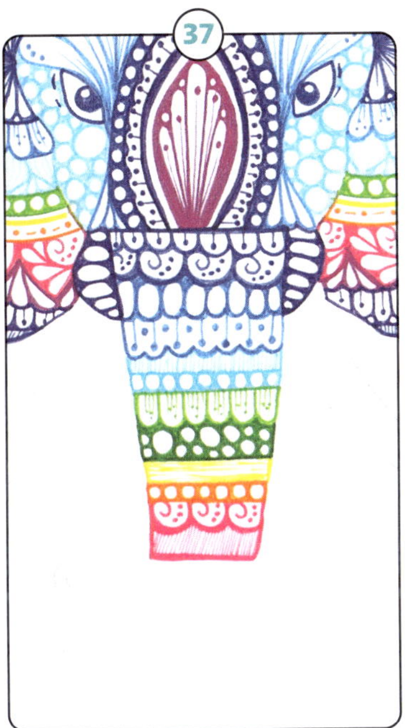

Switch to pink. Draw curling lines in the next section. Add dots to them. Then, still using pink, trace the next pencil guideline. Fill the new section with straight lines.

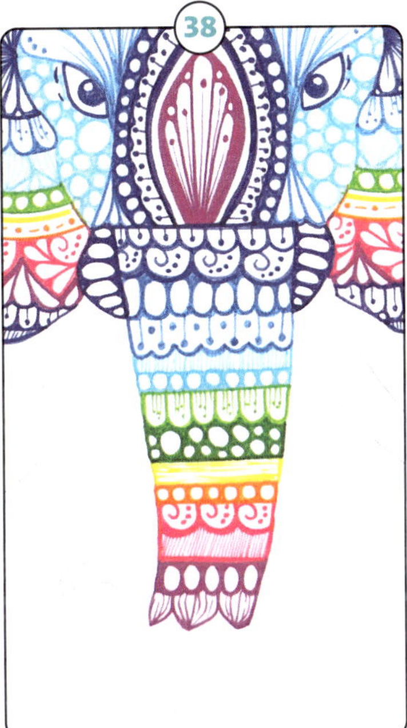

Switch to purple. Draw ovals in the next section. Then, still using purple, fill the section after that with pointed leaves. Fill the leaves with "onion" texture.

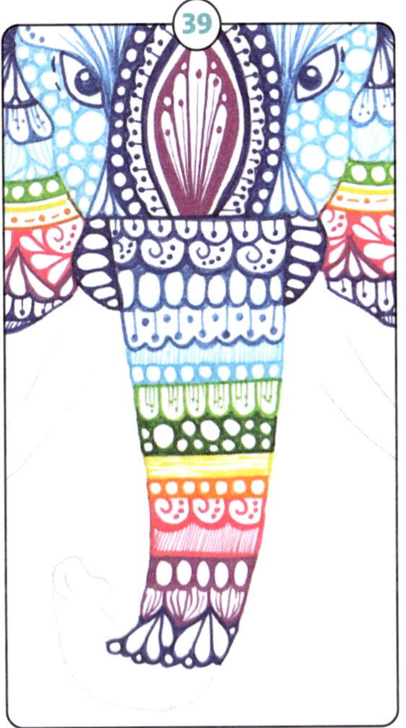

Switch to violet. Draw teardrops that extend past the next pencil guideline all the way to the last pencil guideline. Add a couple of tiny circles along their edges.

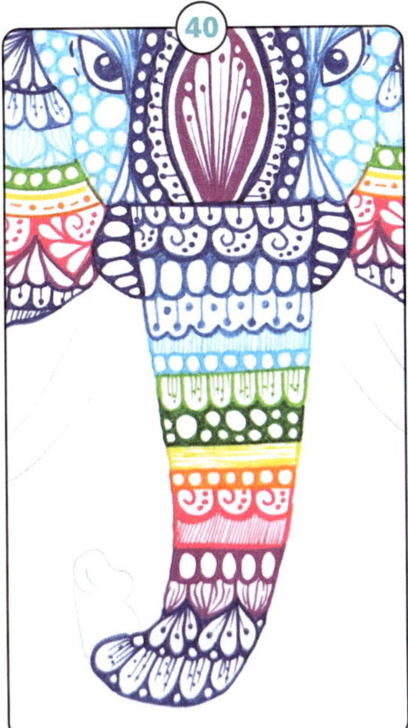

Switch to dark blue. Fill the bottom of the trunk—but not the tip—with domes. Add details as shown.

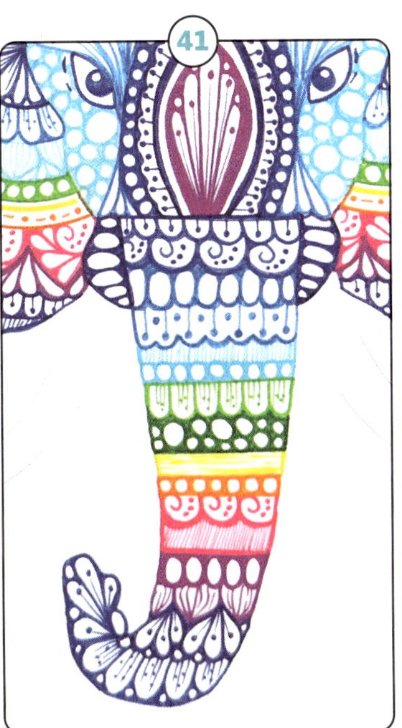

Fill the remaining space. Still using dark blue, fill the tip of the trunk with a teardrop pattern as shown.

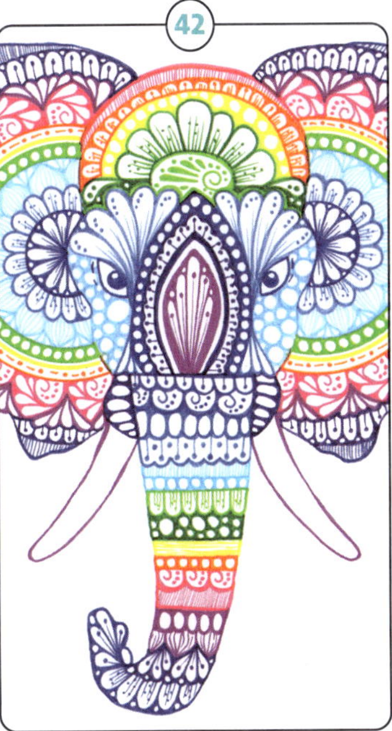

Finish the tusks. Use purple to trace the two tusks.

Owl

For the final full step-by-step animal in this section, let's return to what you learned about coloring in your mandalas in the third section. This Owl consists of only one mandala in the traditional sense, emanating down from the top of the head, but each ring's design can be surprisingly complex. Use your ray guidelines to keep yourself on track, and enjoy the coloring part of the process! I used alcohol markers to color this design.

As you draw this mandala, imagine each ring of designs is a soft layer of downy feathers that compose the owl's plumage. At the end, the owl is fully fledged and ready to soar through the night.

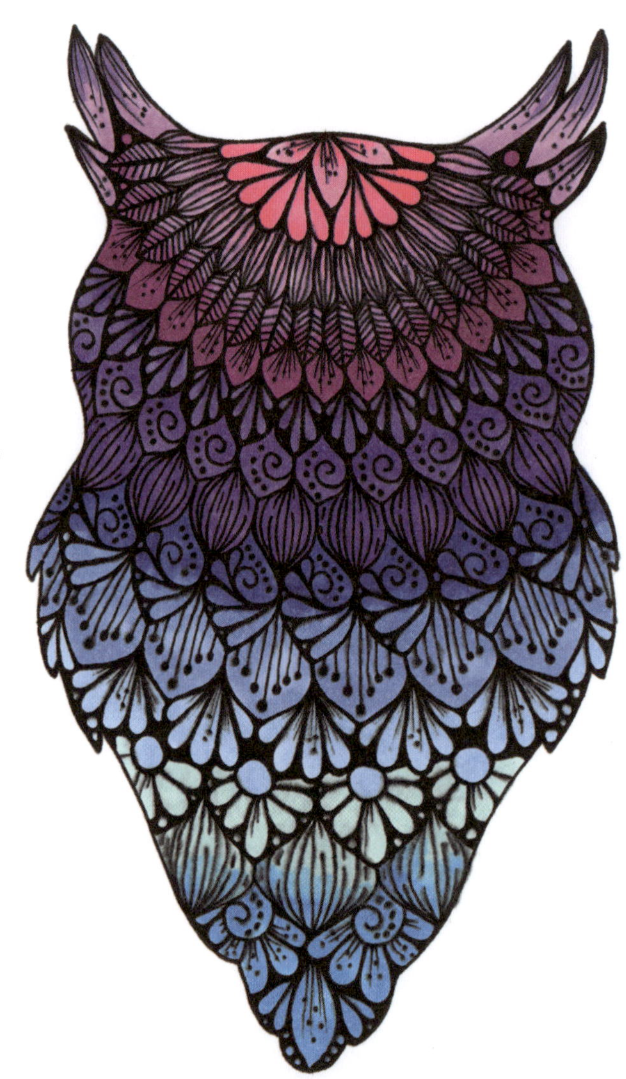

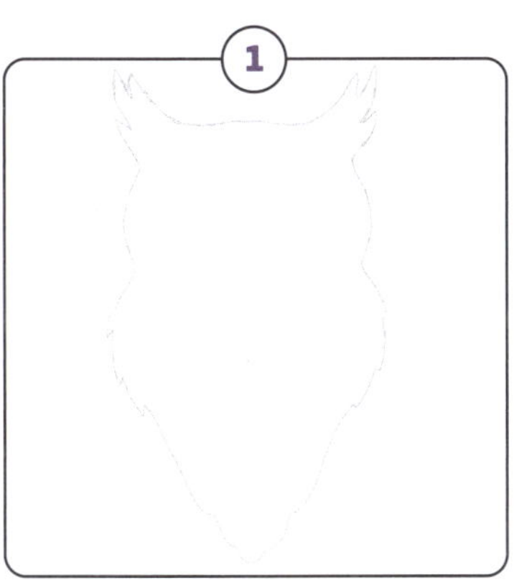

Draw the owl. Draw or trace an owl outline, including some feathery contours. Make your drawing as symmetrical as you can.

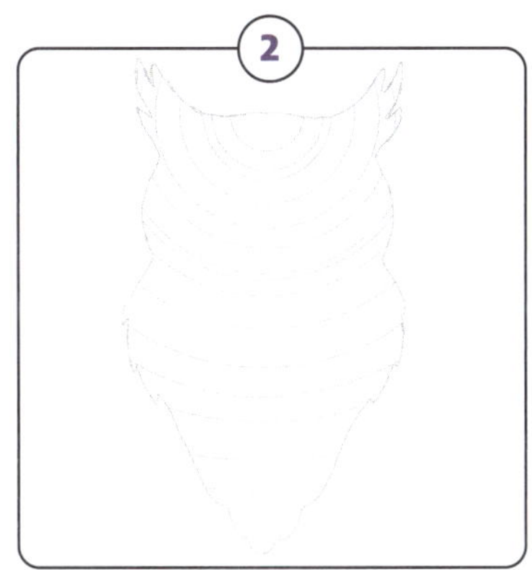

Draw circles. Draw 15 circles as shown. For reference, the outermost circle radius is 6⅜" (16 cm); the innermost circle radius is ⅝" (1.5 cm).

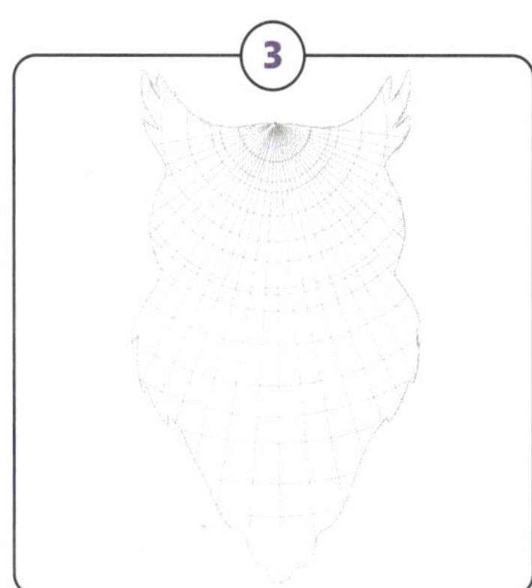

Draw rays. Still using pencil, draw a straight vertical line from the top of the owl's head, then draw a ray every 5° on the left half and right half (17 rays total on each half).

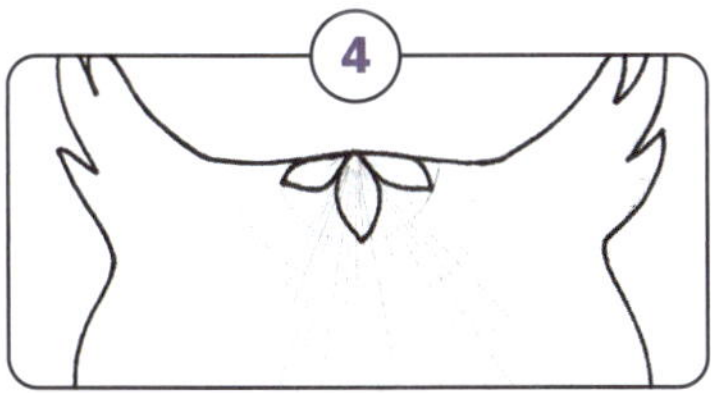

Start with black. Trace the owl's entire outline. Draw three pointed ovals in the center, at the top of the head.

Draw the first ring. Draw five teardrops between each pointed oval and one along the top on either side. These should all extend to fill the first ring.

Draw a new ring. Ignoring the next pencil ring line, draw skinny pointed leaves centered on alternating rays that extend all the way to the following ring line.

Detail the leaves. Fill these long pointed leaves with long but unbroken lines, similar to the onion texture used in the rest of the book.

Start the next ring. In the next ring, draw a pointed leaf between each pointed leaf of the previous ring.

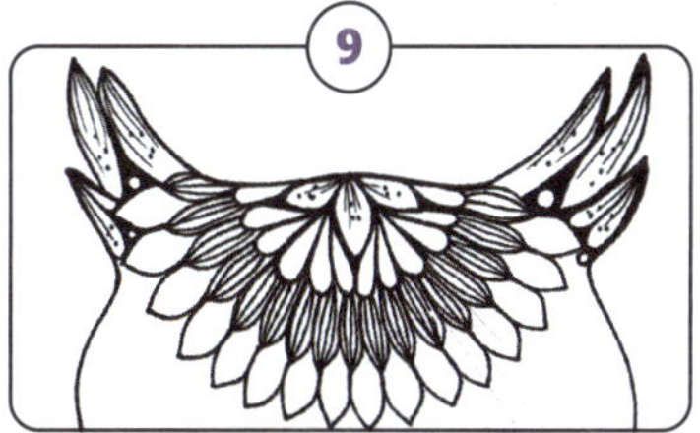

Detail the ears. Fill the three-pointed ears with a detailed pattern as shown.

Finish the previous ring. Return to the half-finished ring. Add a central vein to each leaf, then small veins branching out from that, creating a feather effect.

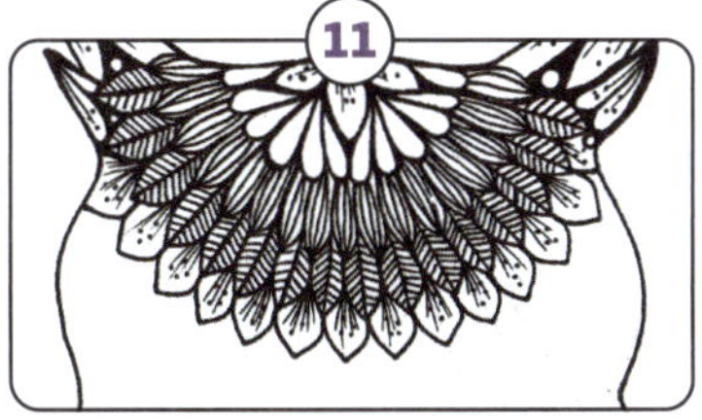

Draw the next ring. In the next ring, draw a pointed leaf between each pointed leaf of the previous ring. Add delicate detail lines and dots to each leaf.

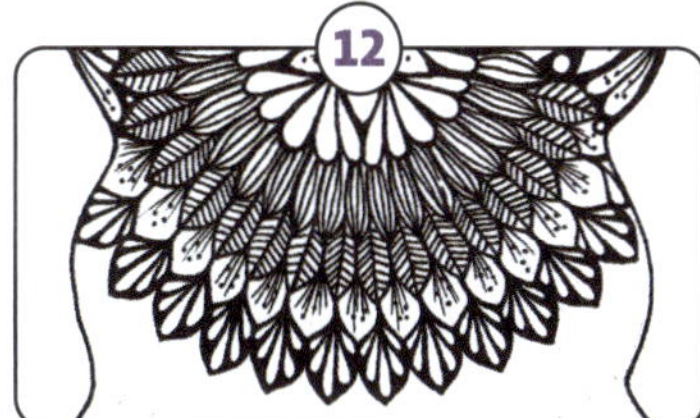

Draw the next ring. In the next ring, draw a pointed leaf between each pointed leaf of the previous ring. Add five teardrops to each leaf, then fill in around them.

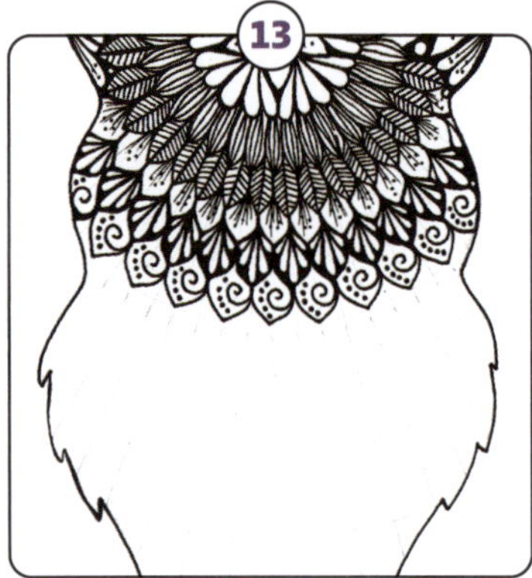

Draw another ring. Ignoring the next two pencil ring lines, draw another ring of pointed leaves. Add a pattern to each one as shown.

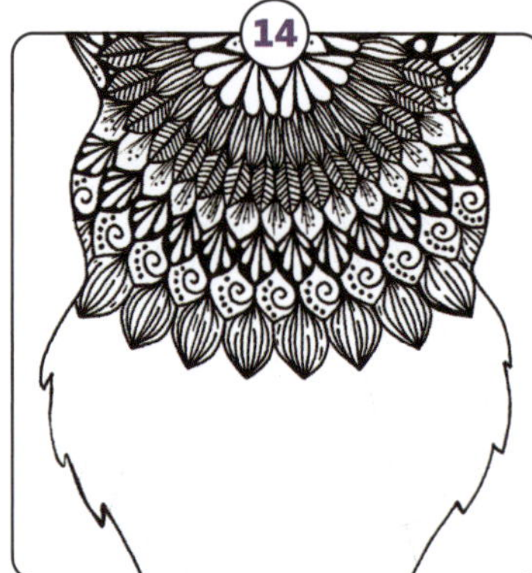

Keep going with more pointed leaves. In the next ring, draw a pointed leaf between each pointed leaf of the previous ring. Add the "onion" texture to each leaf.

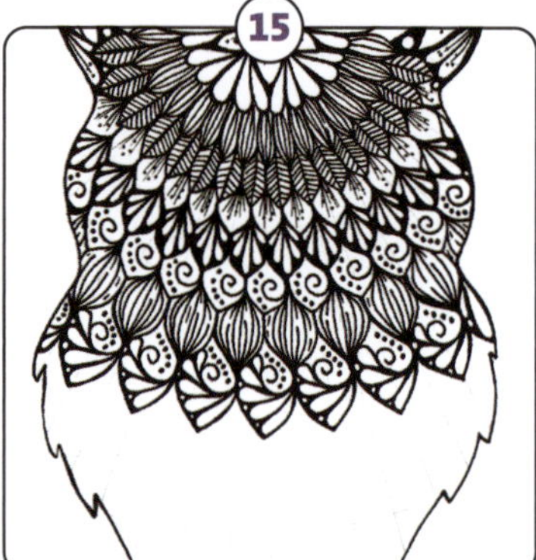

Do another ring. In the next ring, draw a pointed leaf between each pointed leaf of the previous ring. Add a detailed pattern to each one as shown.

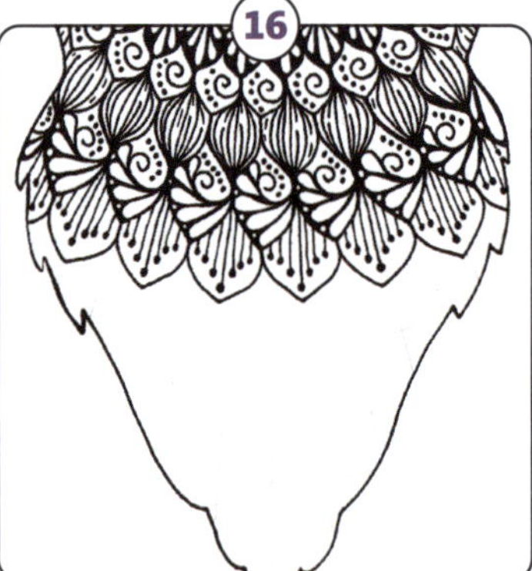

Keep working downward. In the next ring, draw a pointed leaf between each pointed leaf of the previous ring. Add seven lines capped with dots to each leaf.

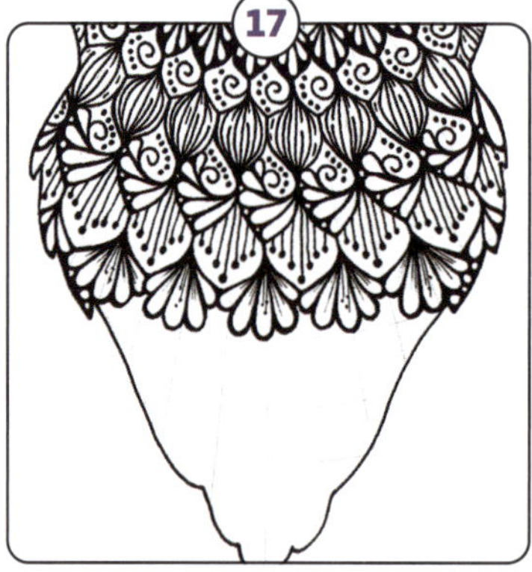

Switch to teardrops. In the next ring, add about five teardrops between each pointed leaf of the previous ring—fewer on the sides. Add details and filler as shown.

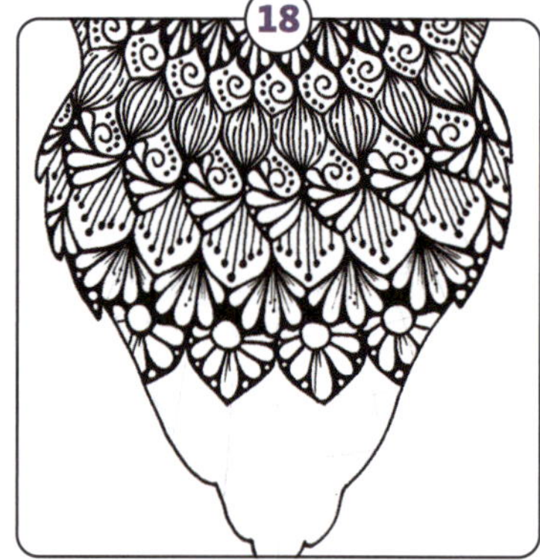

Go back to more pointed leaves. In the next ring, draw a pointed leaf between each set of teardrops of the previous ring. Add a pattern to each as shown.

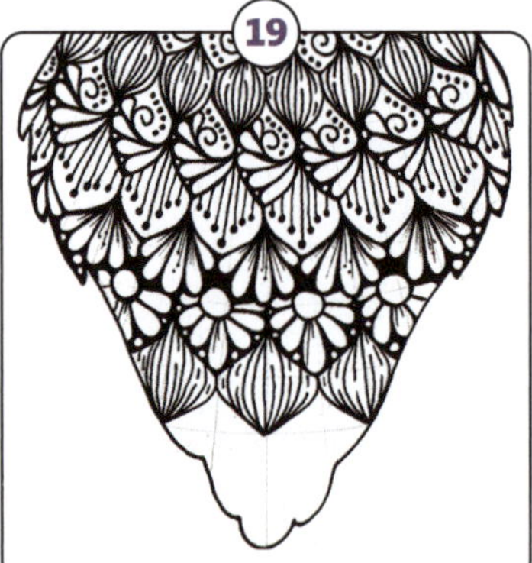

Do another ring. In the next ring, draw a pointed leaf between each pointed leaf of the previous ring. Add the "onion" texture to each. You're down to three leaves!

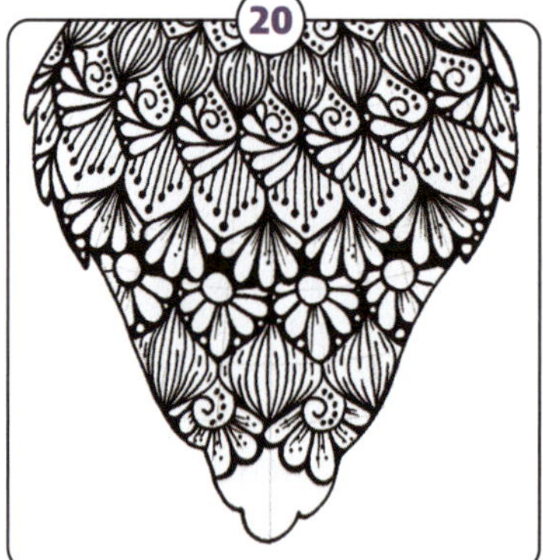

Do one more ring. In about half of the remaining space, draw an elaborate daisylike design, one between each leaf of the previous ring.

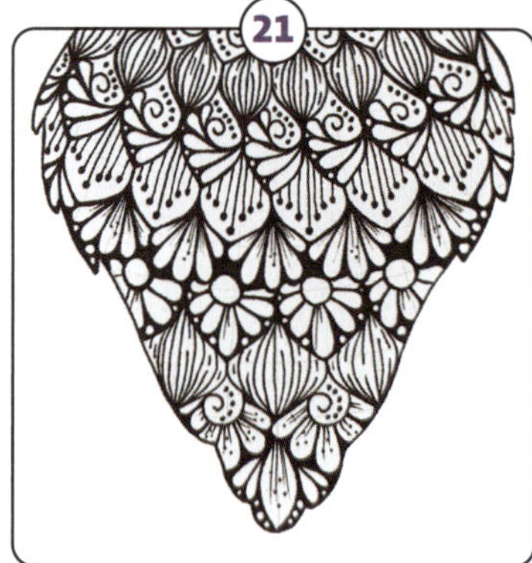

Fill the remaining space. Fill the rest of the body with a teardrop pattern as shown.

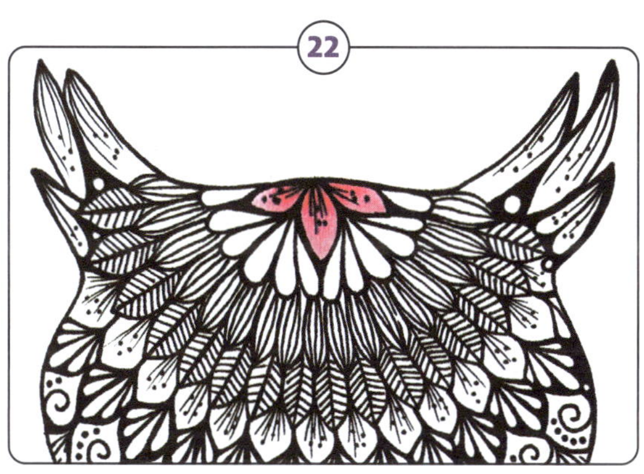

Get coloring! I used alcohol markers to color this owl. Color the very top center of the center design with medium pink, then use light pink to finish filling in the center design.

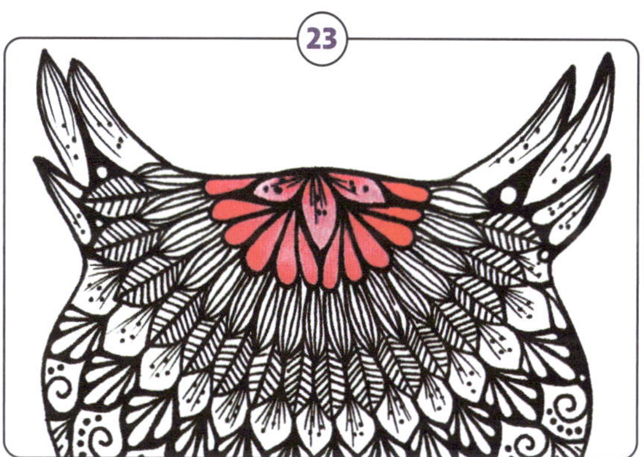

Continue with two pinks. Color the ring of teardrops with medium pink and dark pink.

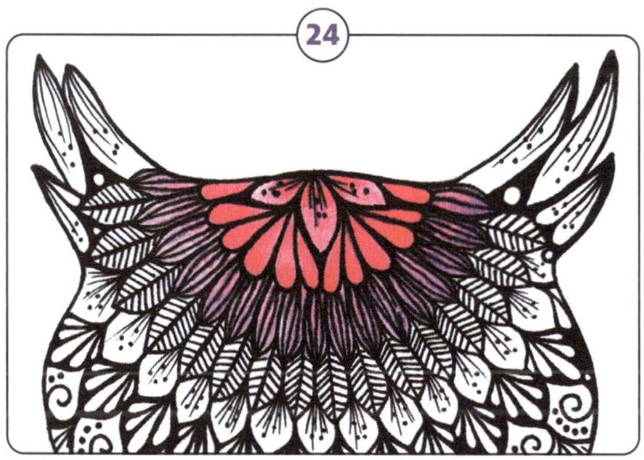

Mix pink and purple. Color the next ring of pointed leaves with medium pink and light purple.

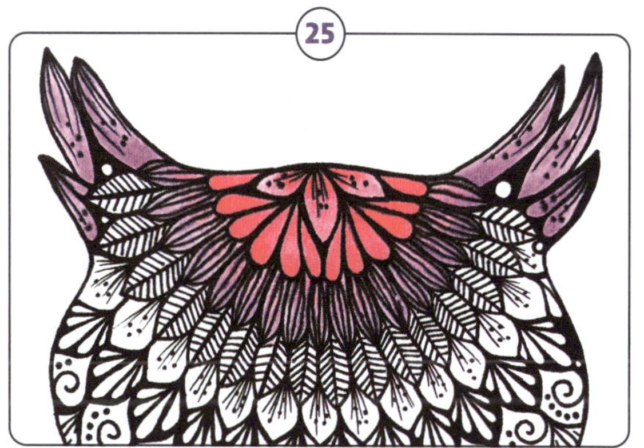

Color the ears. Fill the ears with light purple.

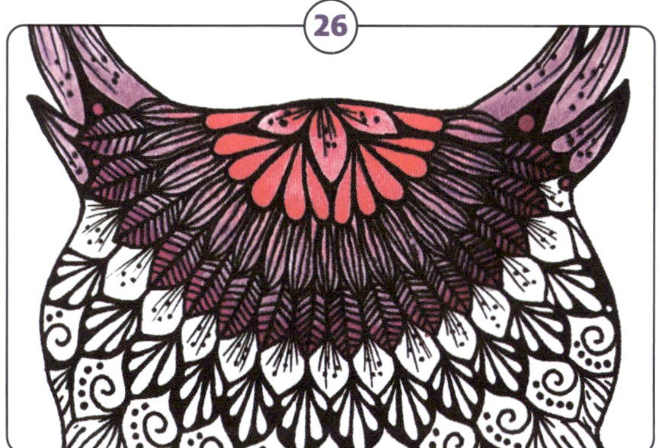

Mix two purples. Color the next ring of "feathers" with light purple and red-purple.

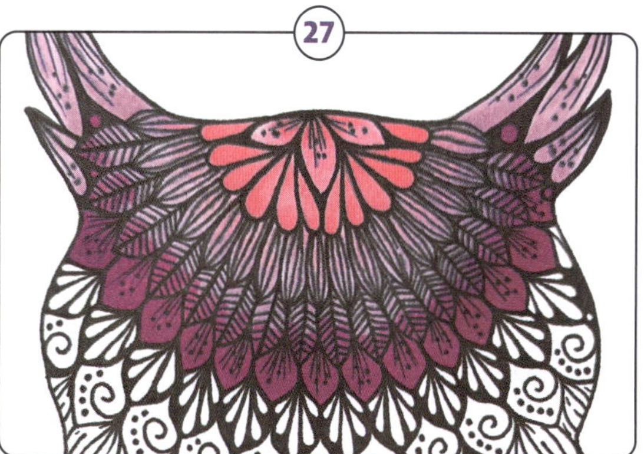

Color the next ring. Color the next ring of pointed leaves with red-purple.

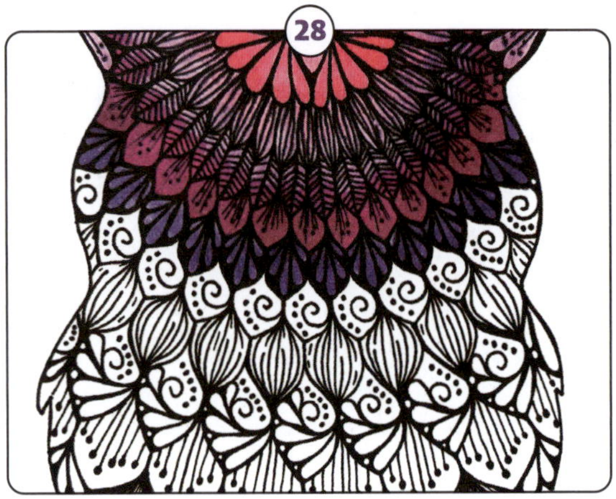

Color the next ring. Color the next ring of pointed leaves with medium purple.

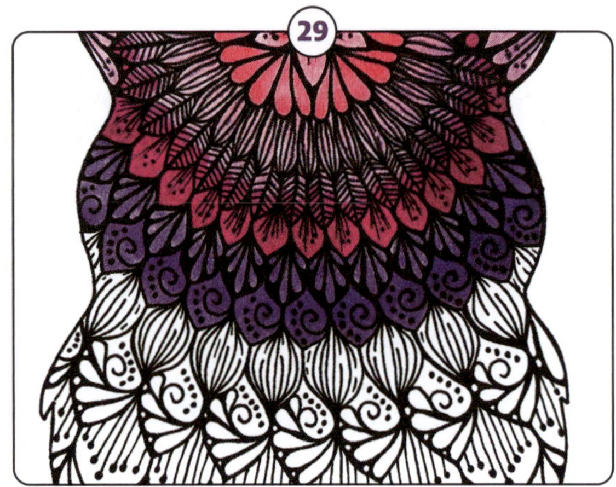

Mix two purples. Color the next ring of pointed leaves with medium purple and dark purple.

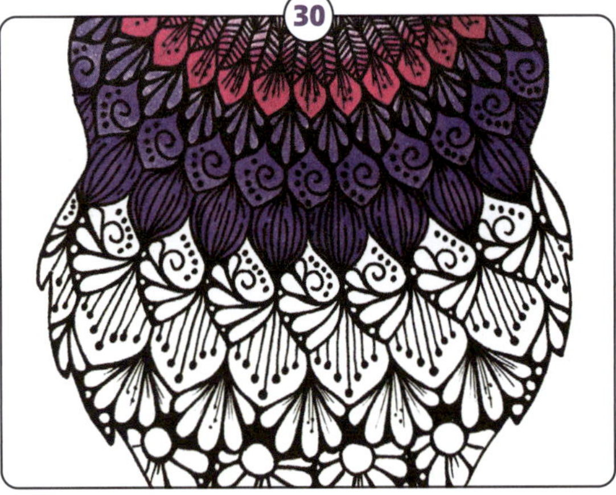

Color the next ring. Color the next ring of pointed leaves with dark purple.

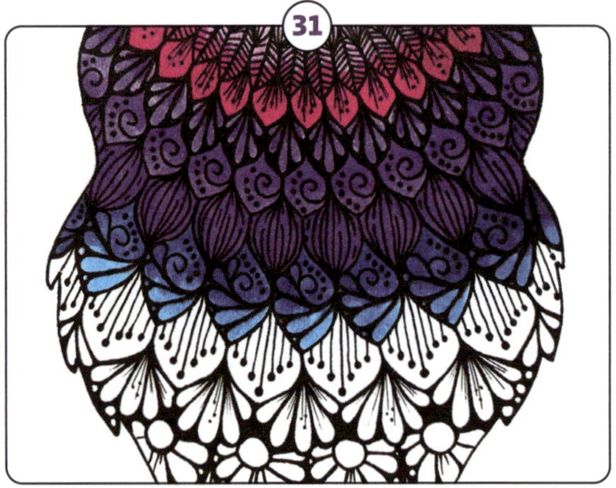

Mix two blues. Color the next ring of pointed leaves with dark blue and medium blue.

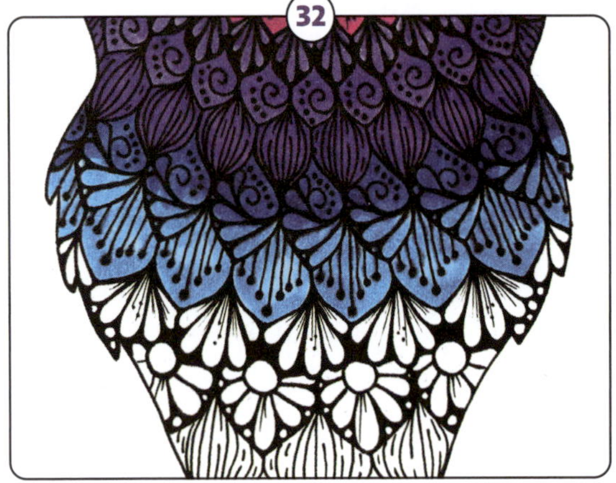

Color the next ring. Color the next ring of pointed leaves with medium blue.

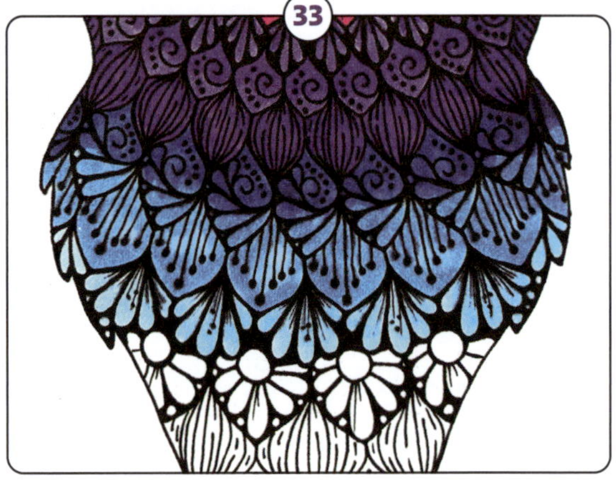

Change to a new blue. Color the next ring of teardrops with light blue.

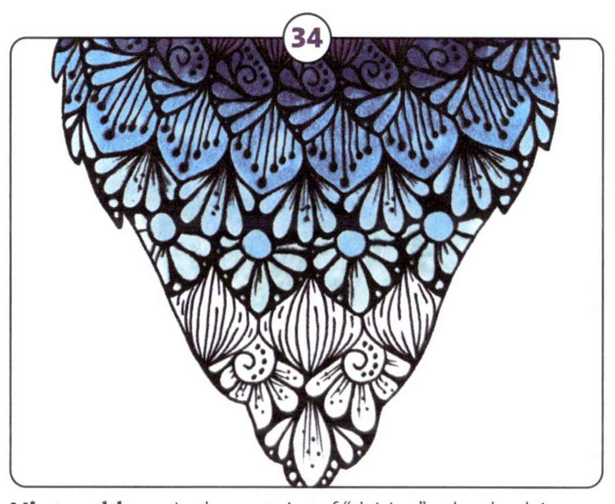

Mix two blues. In the next ring of "daisies," color the daisy centers with light blue and the daisy petals with pale aqua.

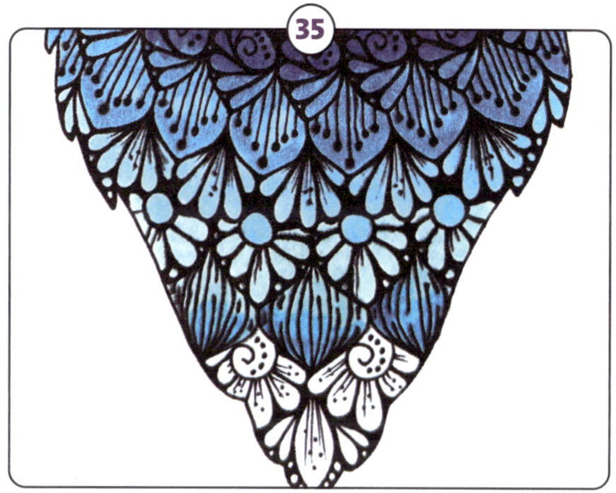

Color the next ring. Color the next ring of pointed leaves with pale aqua and turquoise.

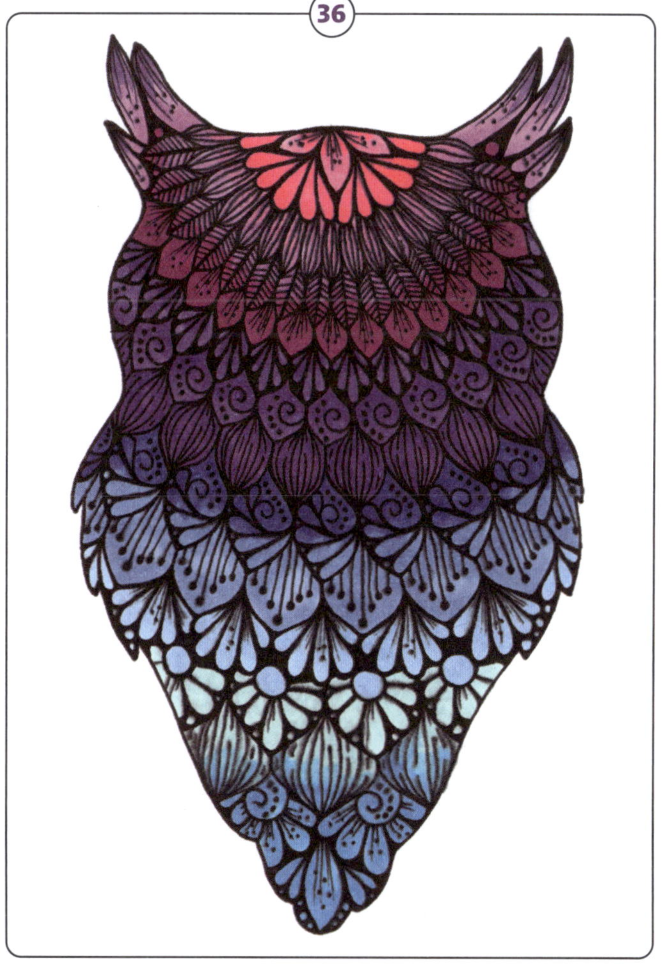

Color the rest of the body. Color the remaining sections with turquoise.

Butterfly

CHALLENGE YOURSELF

You've reached the last mandala in the book and are ready to spread your wings! This mandala is most similar to the Bumblebee. Use what you learned while working on the previous mandalas to build up this design yourself independently, referring to just the few basic steps that are provided as guideposts.

INTENTION

As you draw this mandala, think of yourself as an artist who has been developing slowly but steadily in a chrysalis and who is about to break free, spread their wings, and take flight.

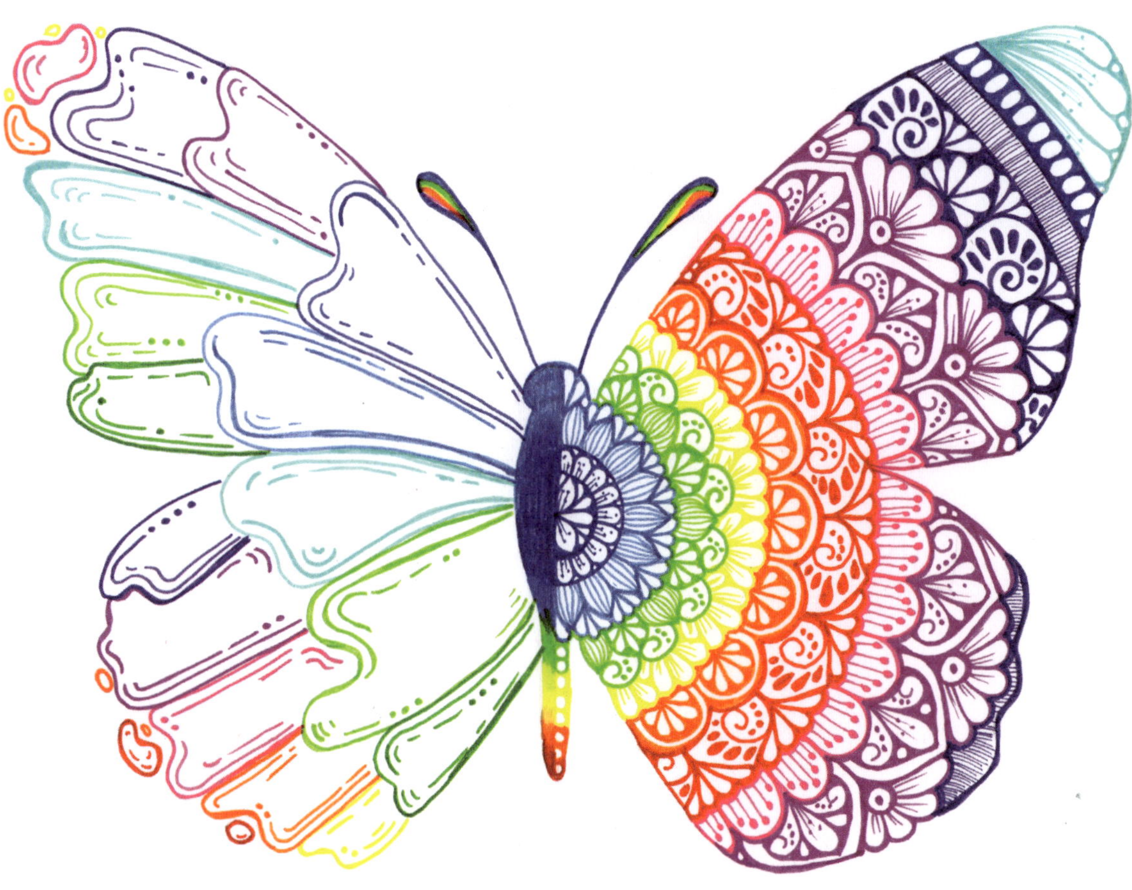

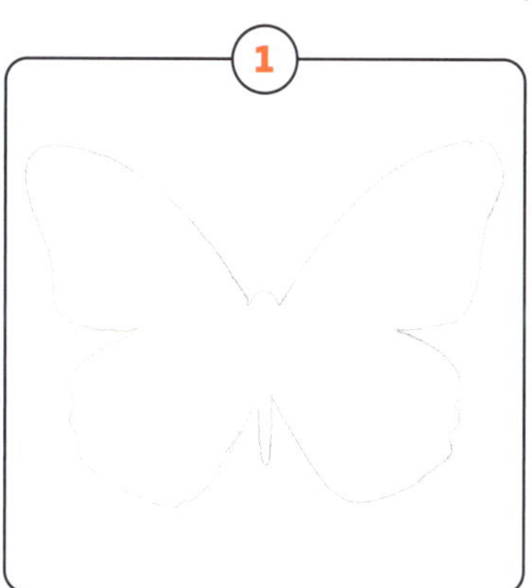

Draw the butterfly. Draw or trace a butterfly outline. Make your drawing as symmetrical as you can.

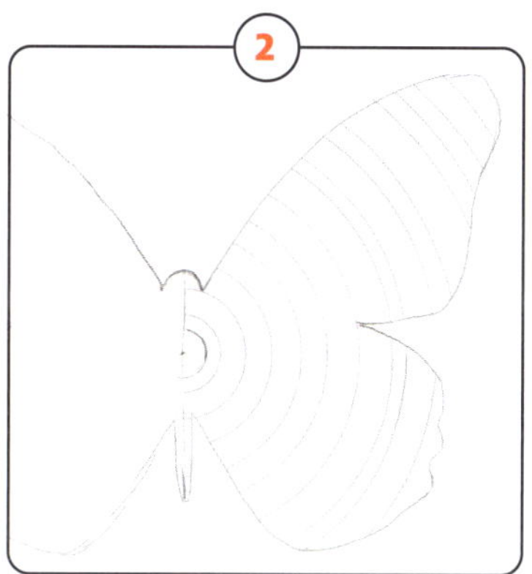

Draw circles. Draw 15 circles as shown in one wing only. For reference, the outermost circle radius is 4⅝" (11.7 cm); the innermost circle radius is ¼" (0.7 cm).

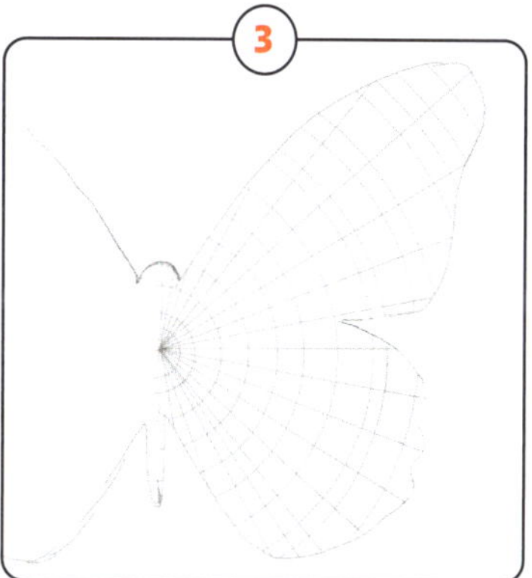

Draw rays. Still using pencil, draw a ray every 10° on the circle wing (17 rays total).

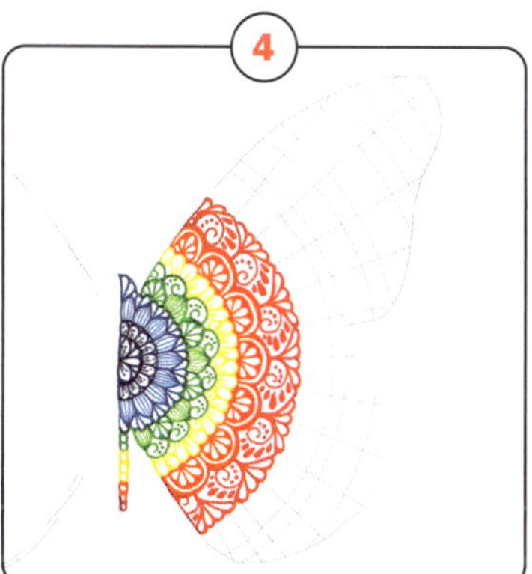

Start drawing. Start filling the mandala from the body outward as shown. The color sequence so far is dark blue, medium blue, bright green, yellow, orange, and red.

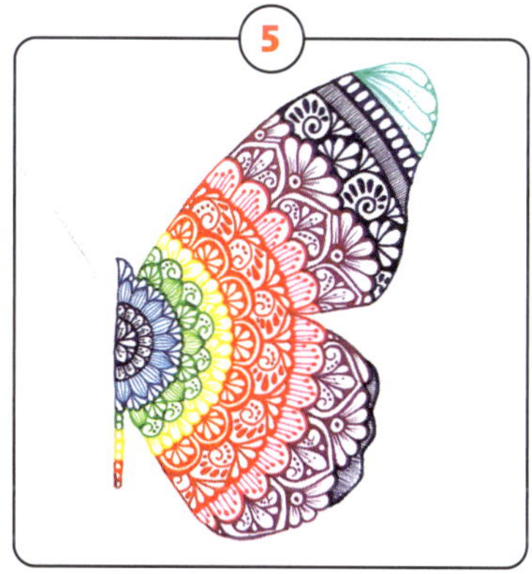

Finish the right wing. Continue until you've filled the wing. The rest of the color sequence shown is pink, purple, violet, dark blue again, and aqua.

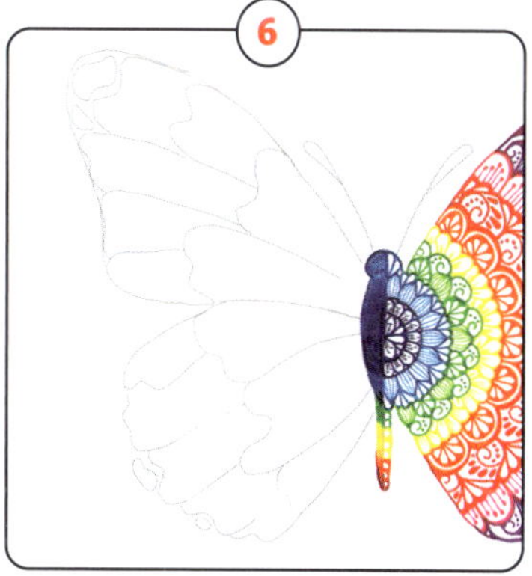

Finish the body. Fill the left half of the body with a rainbow of the first six colors. Using pencil, divide the left wing into 15 main sections and four tiny floating sections.

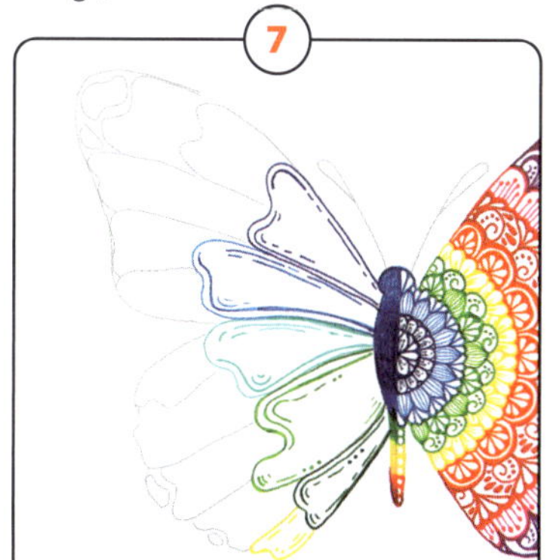

Start the left wing. Outline one segment at a time and add details to each. The colors used so far are dark blue, medium blue, aqua, bright green, dark green, and yellow.

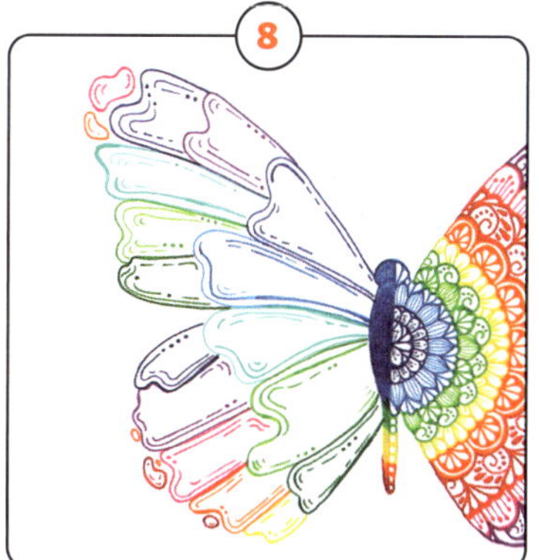

Finish the left wing. Use all your remaining colors to complete the right wing, including reusing dark blue, aqua, and the two greens.

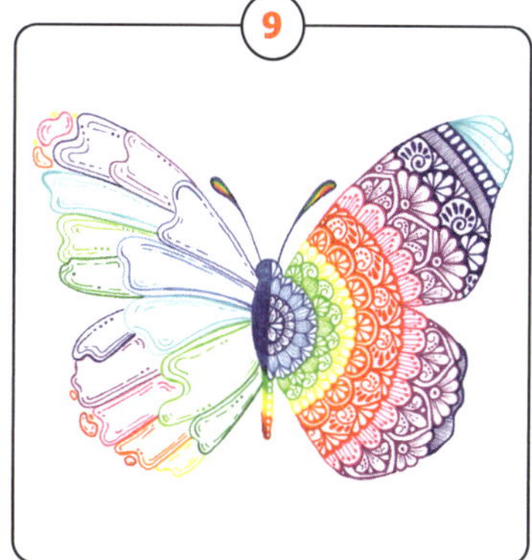

Add antennae. Using dark blue, outline two antennae with open tips. Fill each tip with a tiny rainbow of five to seven colors.

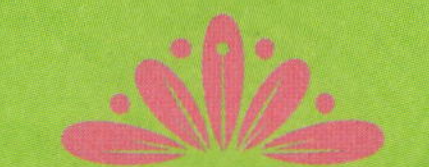

PRACTICE TEMPLATES

This section contains eight templates for you to use however you'd like. Included are the seven animal outlines and the yin-yang. These are the trickiest design outlines to draw freehand, so I'm including them in the book to give you a leg up. You can draw in them right inside the book, or you can photocopy them onto a fresh sheet of paper. I recommend photocopying them so that you can use markers without worrying about the color bleeding through to the back of the page. Have fun creating something unique!

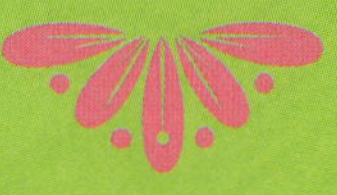

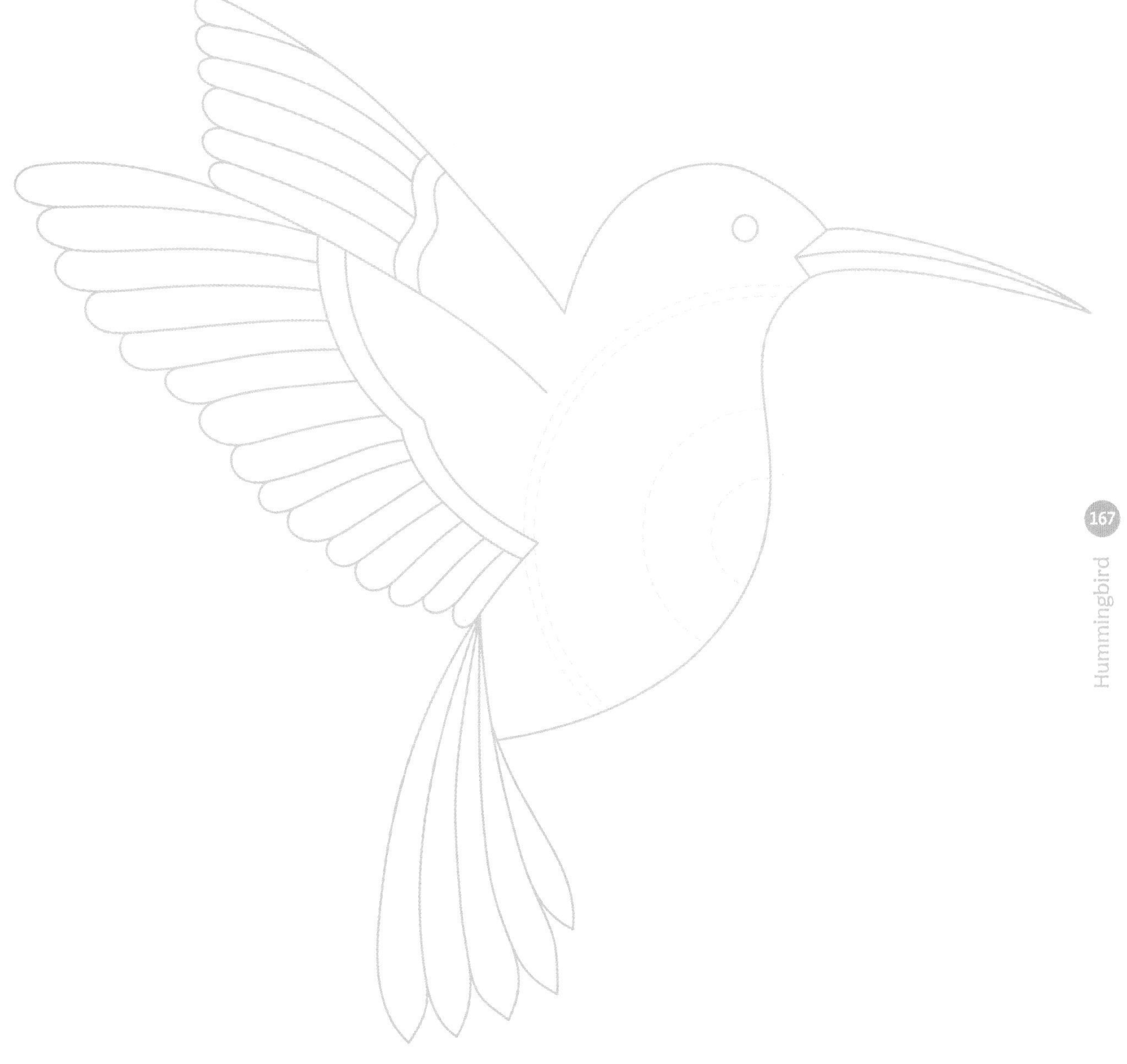

This template is smaller than I originally drew the design, so if you use this template, use your own measurements to draw your circles, not the measurements I provided in the step text. The dashed circles shown in the template can be used as a partial guide.

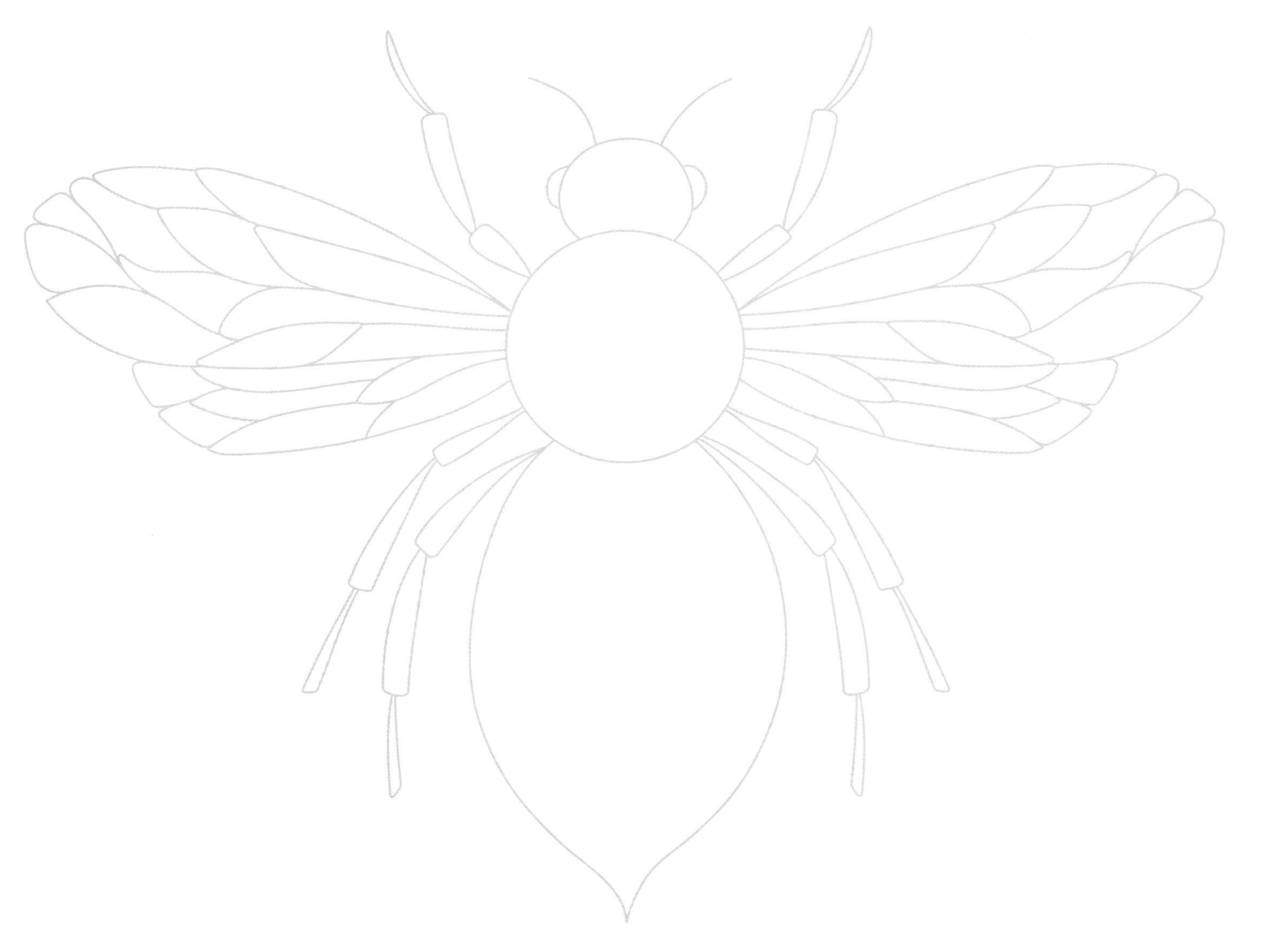

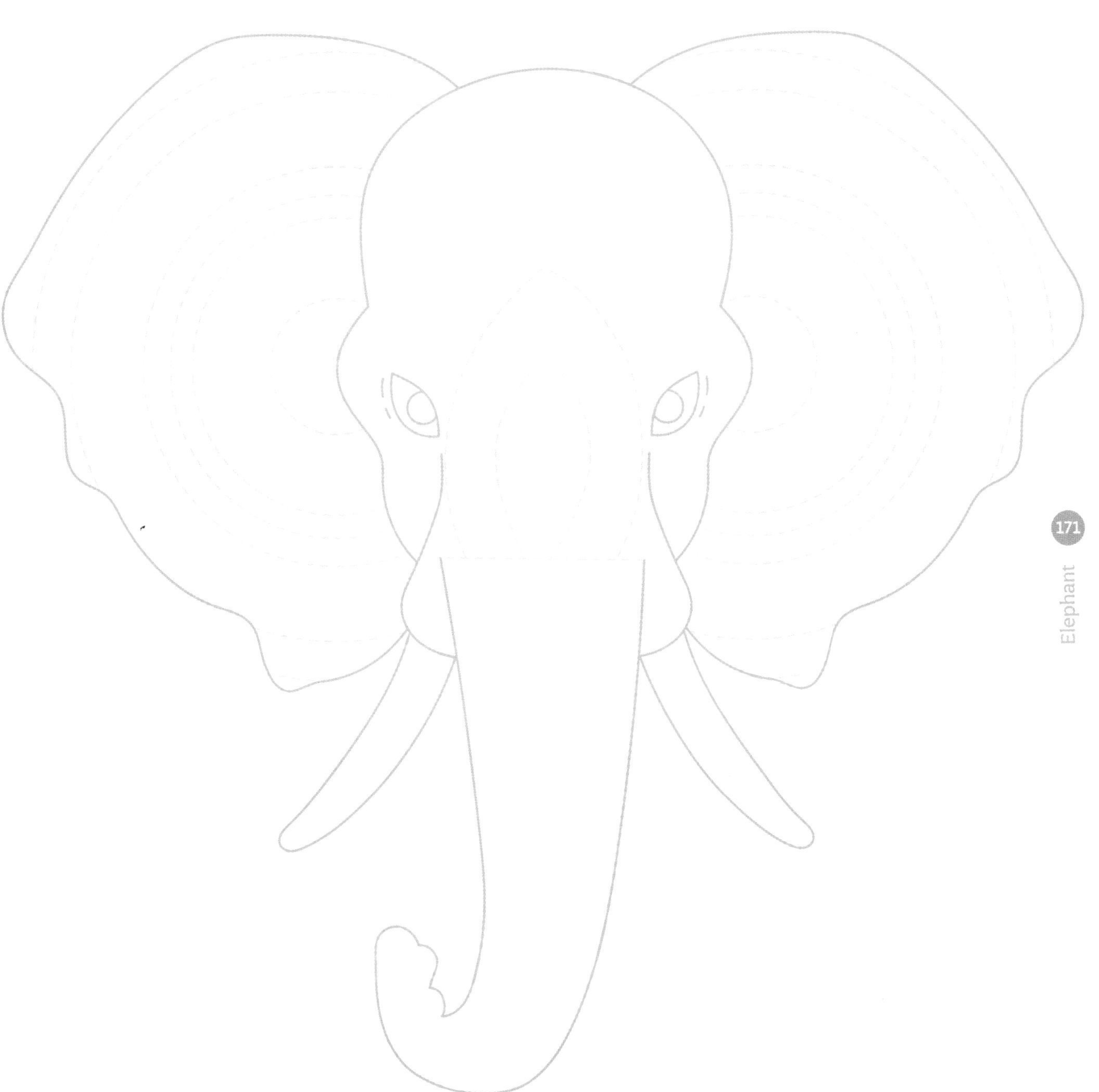

Elephant

Owl

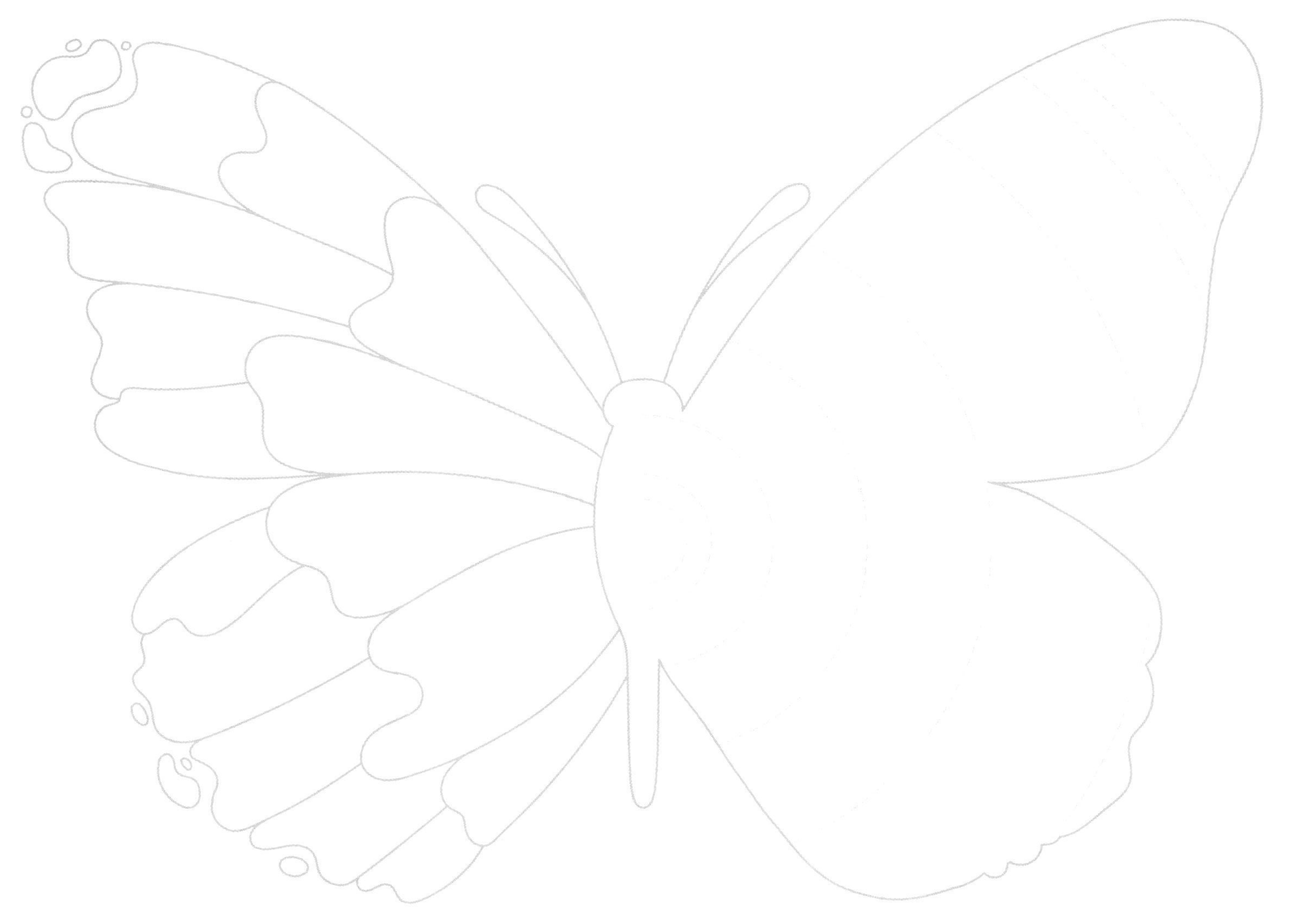

Index

Note: Page numbers in *italics* indicate specific mandalas to draw. Page numbers in (parentheses) indicate templates.

BETTER DAY BOOKS®

HAPPY • CREATIVE • CURATED

Business is personal at Better Day Books. We were founded on the belief that all people are creative and that making things by hand is inherently good for us. It's important to us that you know how much we appreciate your support. The book you are holding in your hands was crafted with the artistic passion of the author and brought to life by a team of wildly enthusiastic creatives who believed it could inspire you. If it did, please drop us a line and let us know about it. Connect with us on Instagram, post a photo of your art, and let us know what other creative pursuits you are interested in learning about. It all matters to us. You're kind of a big deal.

it's a good day to have a better day!®

www.betterdaybooks.com

better_day_books

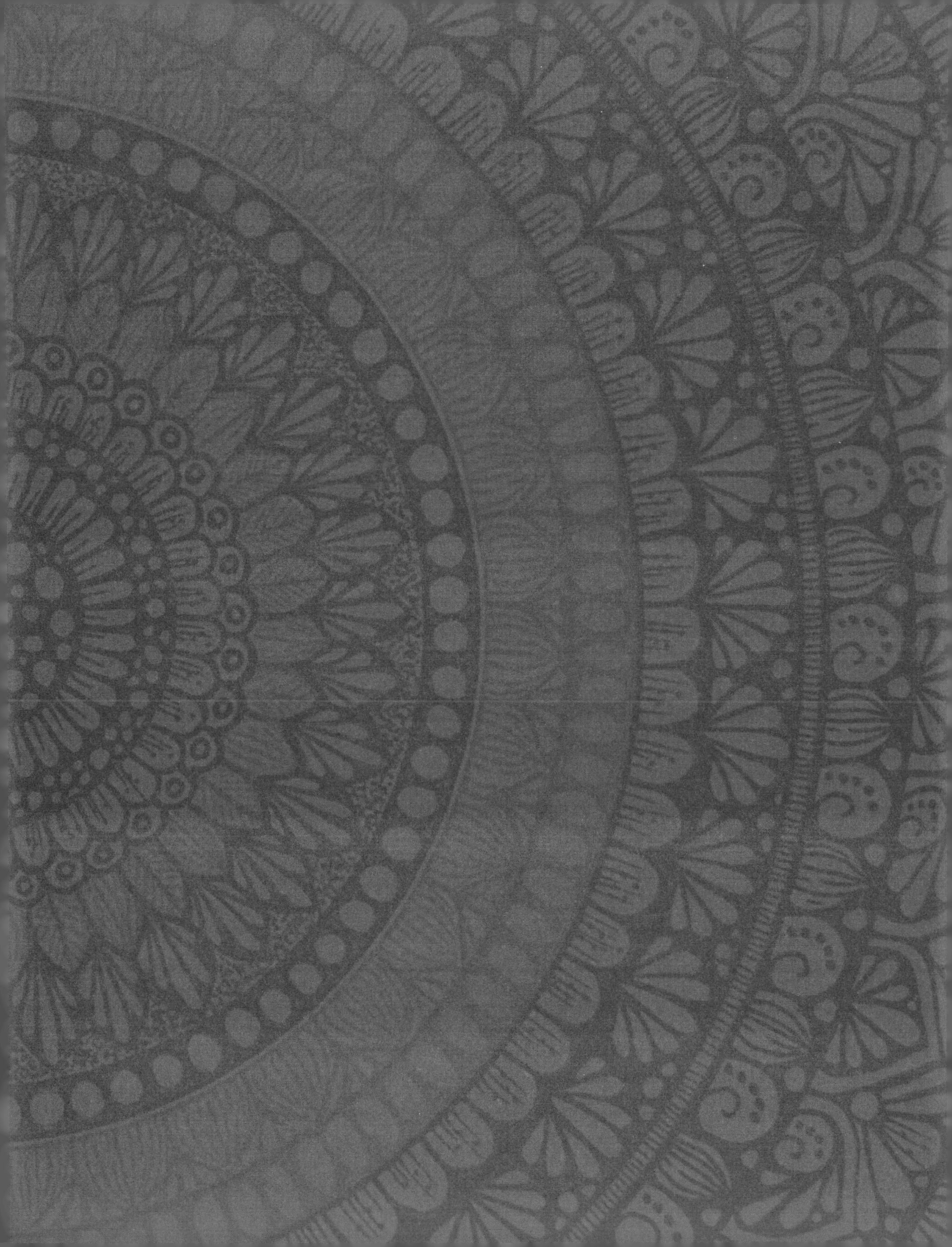

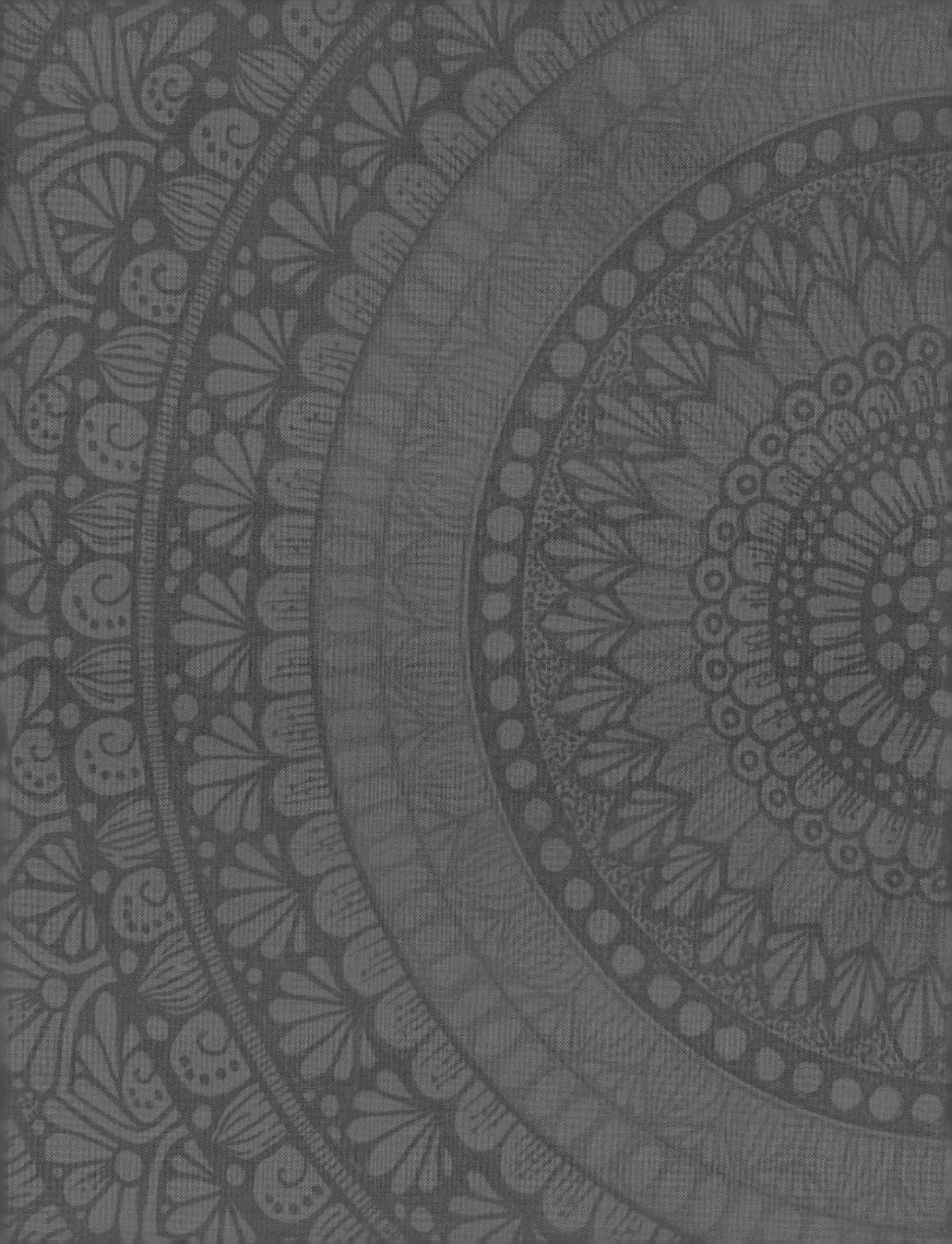